The Linux

The Linux Process Manager

The internals of scheduling, interrupts and signals

John O'Gorman
University of Limerick, Limerick, Republic of Ireland

WILEY

Copyright © 2003 John Wiley & Sons, Ltd, The Atrium, Southern Gate
Chichester, West Sussex, PO19 8SQ, England

Phone (+44) 1243 779777

E-mail (for orders and customer service enquiries): cs-books@wiley.co.uk
Visit our Home Page on www.wiley.co.uk or www.wiley.com

This publication is designed to provide accurate and authoritative information in regard to the subject matter
covered. It is sold on the understanding that the Publisher is not engaged in rendering professional services. If
professional advice or other expert assistance is required, the services of a competent professional should be
sought.

Other Wiley Editorial Offices

John Wiley & Sons, Inc. 111 River Street, Hoboken, NJ 07030, USA

Jossey-Bass, 989 Market Street, San Francisco, CA 94103-1741, USA

Wiley-VCH Verlag GmbH, Pappellaee 3, D-69469 Weinheim, Germany

John Wiley & Sons Australia, Ltd, 33 Park Road, Milton, Queensland, 4064, Australia

John Wiley & Sons (Asia) Pte Ltd, 2 Clementi Loop #02-01, Jin Xing Distripark, Singapore 129809

John Wiley & Sons Canada Ltd, 22 Worcester Road, Etobicoke, Ontario, Canada, M9W 1L1

Wiley also publishes its books in a variety of electronic formats. Some content that appears
in print may not be available in electronic books.

The Linux kernel source code reproduced in this book is covered by the GNU General Public Licence

Library of Congress Cataloguing-in-Publication Data

O'Gorman, John, 1945-
  The Linux process manager : the internals of scheduling, interrupts and signals / John O'Gorman.
     p. cm.
  ISBN 0-470-84771-9 (Paper : alk. paper)
  1. Linux.   2. Operating systems (Computers)   I. Title.

QA76.76.063034354 2003
005.4'469 — dc21

British Library Cataloguing in Publication Data

A catalogue record for this book is available from the British Library

ISBN 0 470 84771 9

Typeset in 10½/12½pt Sabon by Keytec Typesetting, Bridport, Dorset
Printed and bound in Great Britain by Biddles Ltd., Guildford and Kings Lynn
This book is printed on acid-free paper responsibly manufactured from sustainable forestry,
for which at least two trees are planted for each one used for paper production.

Contents

The Linux Process Manager. The Internals of Scheduling, Interrupts and Signals   John O'Gorman
© 2003 John Wiley & Sons, Ltd   ISBN: 0 470 84771 9

Preface

Linux is growing in popularity. Because it is open source, more and more people are looking into the internals. There are a number of books that undertake to explain the internals of the Linux kernel, but none of them is really satisfactory. The reason for this is that they all attempt to do too much. They set out to give an overview of the whole of the kernel and consequently are unable to go into detail on any part of it. This book deals with only a subset of the kernel code, loosely described as the process manager. It would roughly correspond to the architecture-independent code in the /kernel directory and the machine-specific code in the /arch/i386/kernel directories, as well as their associated header files. It is based on version 2.4.18.

When it comes to architecture-dependent code, it deals only with the i386 or PC version. The main reason for this is size. Even with this restriction, the book is still quite sizeable. Another reason is that most Linux users use PCs – the interest in other versions would be quite small.

Because it deals only with a subset of the code, it can afford to go into it in much greater detail than any other commentary currently available. First of all, given the self-imposed limitation of dealing only with the process manager, it is complete. Every function, every macro, every data structure used by the process manager is dealt with and its role in the overall picture explained. But it also goes into more detail in the sense that it is a line-by-line explanation of this subset of the Linux source code.

It is intended as a reference book. Although unlikely to be used as a textbook, I could see it being specified as background reading in an advanced course on operating systems. There is a logical progression through the chapters and within each chapter. Yet it is doubtful if many people would read it from beginning to end. It is far more likely to be a book that one turns to when information is needed on some specific aspect of Linux. The format used is to take one function at a time, give the code for it, explain what it is doing, and show where it fits into the overall picture.

Like any medium-to-large sized piece of software, an operating system has an internal structure that is technically categorised as a graph. This is sometimes dismissed as 'spaghetti code'. When attempting to describe such a complex structure in an essentially linear medium such as a book, it is necessary to flatten it out. I have chosen to order the material in a way I think makes it most intelligible to the reader.

Although dealing with any particular function in isolation, to retain the sense of just

---

The Linux Process Manager. The Internals of Scheduling, Interrupts and Signals   John O'Gorman
© 2003 John Wiley & Sons, Ltd   ISBN: 0 470 84771 9

where it fits into the overall structure, much use is made of cross-references. It is hoped that this will add to the reader's confidence in the completeness of the book. Even if you are not going to look it up right away, the fact that a reference is provided for each of the subroutines being called gives assurance that the explanation will be there if you do want to cross-check it in the future.

The Linux source code is optimised for efficiency, and in places this can make it very convoluted. No attempt is made to straighten out the code, to make it read better. After all, the raw Linux code is what readers want to understand, and they expect this book to help them in that. So every effort is concentrated in making the *explanation* of the code as clear as possible.

At the lower levels, there is a significant amount of inline assembler code used in the Linux kernel. The AT&T syntax used for this is quite abstruse, even for a reader familiar with the standard Intel i386 assembler syntax. There is no skimping on the explanation here. When such code is encountered, it is explained line by line, instruction by instruction.

John O'Gorman

Editor's Note

Shortly after this book was completed we received the sad news that John O'Gorman had passed away. We would like to thank his colleagues at the University of Limerick for helping us to complete this project and to extend our thoughts to his friends and family.

In Memoriam

I have known John since 1984, when he enrolled on the Graduate Diploma in Computing Course. John had taught himself a lot about computing and programming, while he was teaching in Newbridge College, had implemented several administrative applications for the College, and had already published some articles on COMAL, which was then regarded as the best programming language for Secondary School students. Having completed the course he started research leading to a Master's degree, which he completed, and wrote up, within a year, when the regulations at the time specified two years.

His work involved constructing an interpreter for a proprietary language designed for developing and delivering Computer Aided Learning material, which generated Intermediate (what we would now call Byte) Code. John's research was essentially an exercise in systematic reverse engineering, and demonstrated that it was relatively easy to develop alternative interpreters, which could deliver the same lessons on other hardware, such as PCs.

After lecturing on Computer Science in Maynooth he started research for his Doctorate on Systematic Decompilation Techniques, which he completed in 1991. This was based on the thesis that a non-optimizing code generator for Context Free Languages should probably produce code which itself constituted a sentence of another Context Free Language, which should then be describable by means of a Context Free Grammar, which John called a Decompilation Grammar. The purpose of Decompilation was to discover this grammar, and therefore the code-generation practices of the particular compiler. This latter grammar could be used to regenerate source code semantically equivalent to the original source code.

This kind of research was meat and drink to John. He was interested in what was actually the case rather than what should be the case. Possibly because of his training in philosophy, he distrusted grand theories, and like the great political thinker, Edmund Burke, he gloried in the richness of the specific details of each situation. This meant that he carried out some very sophisticated experiments to check the actual structure of software artifacts rather than work from a preconceived theoretically satisfying structure.

He was not interested in fashions in research although many of the areas in which he supervised research students subsequently became very fashionable. Yet because of the quality of his teaching, he found it very easy to induce students to undertake postgraduate research, despite the (then) substantial rewards available in industry.

John carried out research to satisfy his own personal curiosity, and published very little of his work. Indeed, to the best of my knowledge he never attended a technical conference outside of Ireland.

This may have been because John led a double life, as a member of the Dominican Order, of Preachers, as a member of the Academic Community, and fully lived each life, but kept each life tightly compartmentalized from the other, which must have involved considerable discipline in how he managed his time.

John combined his research and teaching interests by writing and publishing several

The Linux Process Manager. The Internals of Scheduling, Interrupts and Signals   John O'Gorman
© 2003 John Wiley & Sons, Ltd   ISBN: 0 470 84771 9

undergraduate textbooks on operating systems. This book represents the last few years of John's life reading and analysing the source code of the Linux operating system. It again reflects his passionate interest in how things actually work rather than how they should work.

Tony Cahill
University of Limerick
Republic of Ireland

Background and overview

Background

The book assumes that the reader has some previous knowledge of operating system structure and terminology. For anyone needing such a background I can recommend my book *Operating Systems* (O'Gorman, 2000), which is a short readable introduction to the topic. *Operating Systems with Linux* (O'Gorman, 2001) is much more detailed, with all examples in it taken from Linux, including areas not covered in this book, such as the memory and input–output managers. The book also presumes a minimum knowledge of C and of computer organisation, particularly the Intel i386 architecture.

One omission that may bother some readers is that it does not cover the implementation of any of the system services. The sheer size of the project forced this decision, and maybe the system services are not the worst choice if something has to be left out. Many of them are covered reasonably well in existing books on Linux kernel internals.

Every effort has been made to ensure that the index is as complete as possible. As well as the usual topic entries, each function, macro and data structure discussed is also referenced there. It is envisaged that this index will be the first port of call for many users of the book.

Overview of contents

The introduction lives up to its name. It zooms in from operating systems, through Linux, to introduce the Linux process manager. It introduces the GCC compiler as well as giving the absolute 'minimum necessary' on initialisation of the process manager.

Linux represents processes by means of a data structure called a `task_struct`. This is at the heart of the whole process manager, indeed the whole operating system. It is quite a sizeable structure and takes a whole chapter to describe properly. This gives an indication of the level of detail of the book.

As there are many of these structures in existence at the same time, their organisation and manipulation is the subject matter of Chapter 3.

The Linux Process Manager. The Internals of Scheduling, Interrupts and Signals   John O'Gorman
© 2003 John Wiley & Sons, Ltd   ISBN: 0 470 84771 9

One fundamental aspect of process management is the ability to put a process to sleep and arrange for it to be woken and run again when some specific event occurs. This, of course, is implemented by manipulating the data structures that represent these processes. The various facilities that the process manager makes available for this are described in Chapter 4, on wait queues.

Moving data structures on and off queues and linked lists as discussed in the previous chapter introduced the vexed question of mutual exclusion. It must be possible to guarantee that such manipulations are atomic and uninterruptible. Linux has a whole range of mechanisms available for this purpose. Those that rely on busy waiting are introduced in Chapter 5, whereas mechanisms that put waiting processes to sleep, such as semaphores, are covered in Chapter 6.

If the `task_struct` is the most important data structure for the process manager, the most fundamental function must be the scheduler. With the background provided in the previous six chapters, this scheduler can now be introduced, and dissected, in Chapter 7.

These first seven chapters between them describe the process manager in a steady state. Two further aspects must be added to this to get the overall picture. Chapter 8 deals with the rather joyful side: the creation of new processes. But sadly, processes have to terminate sometime. Chapter 9 explains all that is involved in this, including the sending of death notices to their parents, how they become zombies for a while and, finally, how all trace of them is removed from the system.

The next seven chapters form a unit, which might be subtitled 'Interrupting Linux'. There are a whole range of agents outside the running process that may interrupt it at unpredictable times, and the process manager must be able to handle these interruptions. The need for seven chapters to cover this is due mainly to the complexity of the interrupt hardware on the i386 architecture.

Chapter 10 introduces the topic of interrupts and exceptions and gives an overview of how the process manager handles them. How control transfers from user mode to the kernel is examined in detail, including system call entry.

There are a number of interrupts generated by the i386 processor itself, in response to various conditions encountered in the program it is executing. These are collectively known as exceptions, and the handlers for them are the subject matter of Chapter 11.

The other main source of interrupts is hardware devices attached to the computer. Handlers for these are device-specific and are not covered in this book, but the process manager must provide some generic code for hardware interrupts, and Chapter 12 describes that.

More recent models of the i386 architecture include an advanced programmable interrupt controller (APIC) as part of the CPU (central processing unit) chip. This routes interrupts from external devices to the processor core. The interrupt manager has to interface with this controller, and the various functions provided for that are described in Chapter 13.

On a multiprocessor system, the routing of interrupts between different CPUs is handled by yet another specialist chip, the input–output APIC. Chapter 14 describes how Linux interfaces with this controller.

The hardware timer interrupt is the heartbeat of the whole operating system and, of course, all the handler code for that interrupt is supplied by Linux. This is described in detail in Chapter 15.

All operating systems divide the handling of interrupts into two levels. There is urgent processing that must be done immediately, and there is less urgent processing that can be delayed slightly. In Linux, the latter processing is known collectively as a software interrupt and is the subject matter of Chapter 16.

The signal mechanism is a venerable part of Unix. It takes three chapters to describe all of the code in the Linux kernel that deals with signals. Chapter 17 introduces the data structures involved, including the alternate stack for handling signals. The functions used to post signals to a process are introduced in Chapter 18, as well as the kernel's role in delivering these signals to the process. The signal handler itself is user-level code, and so to actually run it the kernel must temporarily drop into user mode and then return to kernel mode when it finishes. The description of the mechanics of this takes up the whole of Chapter 19.

The remainder of the book deals with a number of miscellaneous topics that come under the heading of the process manager. Certainly, the code discussed here is in the /kernel directory.

Linux, like other flavours of Unix, is moving from the all-or-nothing privilege-and-protection scheme provided by the superuser mechanism to a more discriminated system of capabilities. This is still rather rudimentary, but the elements of it are described in the short Chapter 20.

A nice feature of Linux is its ability to execute binary programs that were compiled to run under other operating systems on an i386. It recognises executables as having different personalities and emulates the execution domains in which they expect to run. Chapter 21 deals with this aspect of the kernel.

Another long-standing feature of Unix is the ability of one process to trace the execution of another. This is typically used by a debugger. Chapter 22 examines the facilities provided by the kernel to allow this level of interprocess communication.

The BSD version of Unix introduced the process accounting file, and Linux also provides this. Chapter 23 examines when and how records are written to this file.

In order to provide backward compatibility with 16-bit programs written for the 8086, modern 32-bit Intel processors have a special mode of executing in which they emulate an 8086 processor. This is known as vm86 mode. The software provided by the kernel for running in vm86 mode is described in full in Chapter 24.

References

O'Gorman J, 2000 *Operating Systems* (Palgrave, London).
O'Gorman J, 2001 *Operating Systems with Linux* (Palgrave, London).

1

Introduction

An operating system is a large – very large – piece of software, typically consisting of hundreds of thousands of lines of source code. It is questionable if any one person can understand all the ramifications of such a large construct, so we apply a divide-and-conquer approach. This involves breaking it down into smaller pieces and attempting to understand one piece at a time.

It is generally accepted that in order to write a large software system with any hope of success, there must be some overall design structure. This design structure can also be used when trying to understand and explain the system after it is built. Some designers suggest a very rigid layered structure in which modules in one layer only ever interface with the layers immediately above or below them. In reality, it is difficult if not impossible to construct systems in this way, so most tend to end up without such clearcut distinctions. Linux is no exception.

Another possible approach is to divide the operating system up on the basis of functionality. This means identifying the basic functions of an operating system and separating out the code that implements each of these functions. A very course-grained division would be to divide it into a number of different managers. These would include the process manager, memory manager, input–output (I/O) manager, file manager, and network manager. This latter approach fits in well with the structure of Linux. In fact, the source code tree has top-level directories entitled `kernel`, `mm`, `drivers`, `fs`, and `net`. So there is at least a suggestion that we are on the right track when taking this approach to breaking up the operating system for ease of handling. Figure 1.1 shows how the process manager fits into the overall architecture of a Linux system.

C library		Pthreads library	
System services			
Process manager	Memory manager	Input–output manager	
		Filesystems	Network

Figure 1.1 Outline architecture of a Linux system

The Linux Process Manager. The Internals of Scheduling, Interrupts and Signals   John O'Gorman
© 2003 John Wiley & Sons, Ltd   ISBN: 0 470 84771 9

1.1 Overview of the process manager

A **process** is the unit of work in a computer system. As a first cut, a process can be described as 'a program in action'. When the instructions that make up a program are actually being carried out, there is a process.

The process manager is the part of the operating system that is responsible for handling processes, and there is quite a lot involved in that, as can be seen from the size of the book, or from the brief resumé given here.

It must keep track of which processes actually exist in the system. There is a significant amount of information that needs to be recorded about each process or job: not only obvious, if trivial, items such as its name and owner but also such matters as the areas of memory that have been allocated to it, the files and other I/O streams it has open and the state of the process at any given time.

Sometimes a process is running; other times it is ready and able to run but is waiting its turn in a queue; other times again, it is not in a position to run. This can be because it is waiting for some resources it needs, such as data from a disk drive. The process manager has to record the fact that it is waiting, and exactly what it is waiting for. Then when the resource becomes available, it knows which of the many processes to wake up.

Recording this information is obviously very important; but we are still only talking about passive data structures. The active part of the process manager is called the scheduler. This is the code that shares the central processing unit (CPU) among the many contending processes, deciding when to take a CPU from a process, and which process to give it to next.

The concept of an interrupt is fundamental to any modern computer system. Numerous events occur at unpredictable times within the running system, which need to be handled immediately. The CPU suspends whatever it is doing, switches control to a block of code specially tailored to deal with the specific event, and then returns seamlessly to take up whatever it was doing beforehand. The whole procedure is known as interrupt handling and is the responsibility of the process manager.

Interrupts originate from many sources, and the most important of these is the timer interrupt, the heartbeat of the whole system. Closely allied to this is the timing of other events and maintaining the time of day.

As well as its own internal work, the process manager also provides services to user processes, on request. Foremost among these is the facility to create new processes and to terminate them when no longer required by the user. Other services allow processes to communicate among themselves, such as signals, or System V IPC.

When more than one process is running on the one machine there is a need to control process access to the various resources available. Requests for some services may be legitimate from one process but not from another. There is also a need to record what resources any particular process has used. All of this falls on the process manager.

Within the Unix world, quite a number of different flavours have evolved over the years. Linux attempts to cover as many of these as possible. The process manager attempts to support processes executing programs that were compiled on one of a range of other Unix systems. Specific to i386 Linux is the ability to run programs written for earlier 16-bit processors.

A final service, typically required by a debugger, is the ability for one process to control another completely, maybe executing it one instruction at a time, and allowing the program variables to be inspected between each instruction. This is known as **tracing** a process.

1.1.1 Operating system processes

The operating system itself is one large job, and it would seem reasonable for it to be a process in its own right. In fact, an operating system is frequently designed as a set of cooperating processes. For example, each of the managers identified above might be a process in its own right. This means that the process manager we are considering here could be a process itself and be managed by itself. Although this sounds confusing, it can work in practice.

With some operating systems, each source of asynchronous events is given a process of its own. Such an asynchronous event is anything that can happen independently of the running program, and so at unpredictable times. This generally results in a process being dedicated to each hardware device.

For example, there would be a process created for the network device, which would spend most of its time inactive, asleep. But when a message arrives over the network, this operating system process is there waiting to respond. It is woken up (by an interrupt), deals with the network device, passes the message on to the appropriate user process, and goes to sleep again. The user process cannot be expected to do this. It cannot know in advance when a message is going to arrive, and it cannot just sit there waiting for a message – it has to get on with its own processing.

Unix, and hence Linux, has traditionally taken a different approach from the one outlined above. It has very few system processes. Most of the code in the Unix kernel is executed as part of the current user's process, or in the context of the user's process. But while executing kernel code the process has extra privileges – it has access to any internal data structures it requires in the operating system, and it can execute privileged instructions on the CPU.

All modern CPUs operate in at least two different modes. In one of these, called user mode, the CPU can execute only a subset of its instructions – the more common ones, such as add, subtract, load and store. In the other mode, called kernel mode, the CPU can execute all of its instructions, including extra privileged instructions. These typically access special registers that control protection on the machine. Normally, the machine runs in user mode. When it wants to do something special, it has to change into kernel mode.

Obviously, this changing between modes is very dependent on the underlying hardware, but, in general, there is a special machine instruction provided that both changes the CPU to privileged mode and transfers control to a fixed location. Any user process can call this instruction, but it cannot decide where it goes after that. It cannot execute its own instructions with extra privilege; as it is forced to jump to a fixed location, it can execute only those instructions that the designer has placed at that location. In this way, a user process can be allowed strictly controlled access to the kernel of the operating system

1.1.2 Multiprocessors

Although the vast majority of computers still have only one CPU, there is a trend towards machines with two or more CPUs. This is particularly so with servers of all sorts.

Such a situation obviously complicates things for the process manager. It is no longer simply a matter of sharing the one CPU among the contending processes. Now a (small) number of CPUs have to be shared among a (typically large) number of processes. Assumptions that were valid about mutual exclusion on kernel data when dealing with a uniprocessor are no longer valid in the multiprocessor case. The process manager has to be explicitly involved in taking out and releasing locks on various parts of the kernel.

Two different approaches are possible when designing an operating system for a multiprocessor computer. One CPU could be dedicated to running the operating system, leaving the others for user processes. This is known as asymmetric multiprocessing. It is a nice clean design, but in most cases it would probably result in the CPU dedicated to the operating system being idle for some or much of the time.

Another possibility is to treat all CPUs equally, so that when operating system code needs to execute, it uses whichever CPU is available. This is known as symmetric multiprocessing (SMP). It improves overall utilisation of the CPUs, although it does result in some cache inefficiency if the operating system is continually migrating from one CPU to another.

For a system such as Unix, where operating system code does not run in a process of its own but in the context of the calling process, the choice is fairly heavily weighted in favour of SMP, so it is no surprise that this is the way multiprocessors are handled in Linux. But even after settling for the SMP strategy, there are two ways of implementing it. It would be possible to produce a generic kernel, which would handle both the uniprocessor and multiprocessor cases. Decisions on which code branches to execute are then taken at runtime.

This decision could also be taken at compile time, and in fact that is how it is done with Linux. So, effectively two different kernels can be produced. The SMP version is larger, but it has the ability to control a multiprocessor computer. The uniprocessor version omits all of the SMP code, so it is smaller. In line with our stated aim of completeness, this book will consider not just the uniprocessor code but all the SMP code as well.

1.1.3 Threads

Sometimes a process is running on the processor; at other times it is idle, for one reason or another. The overhead involved in moving from running to idle can be considerable. It happens frequently that a process begins running and almost immediately stops again to wait for some input to become available. The operating system has to save the whole state of the machine, as it was at the moment when the process stopped running. There is a similar overhead involved when a process begins running again. All the saved state has to be restored and the machine set up exactly as it was when the process last ran. And this overhead is on the increase, as the number and size of CPU registers grows and as operating systems become more complex, so requiring ever more state to be remembered.

This has led to a distinction being made between the unit of resource allocation and the unit of execution. Traditionally, these have been the same. One process involved one path of execution through one program, using one block of allocated resources, especially memory. Now the trend is to have one unit of resource allocation, one executable program, with many paths of execution through it at the same time. The terminology that is evolving tends to refer to the old system as a heavyweight processes. The new styles are called lightweight processes, or threads. But there is no consistency. A thread has access to all the resources assigned to the process. It can be defined as one sequential flow of control within a program. A process begins life with a single thread, but it can then go on to create further threads of control within itself.

Now that one process can have many threads of control, if one thread is blocked, another can execute. It is not necessary to save and restore the full state of the machine for this, as it is using the same memory, program, files, devices – it is just jumping to another location in the program code. But each thread must maintain some state information of its own, for example the program counter, stack pointer, and general purpose registers. This is so that when it regains control, it may continue from the point it was at before it lost control.

Sometimes a thread package is implemented as a set of library routines, running entirely at the user level. This saves on the overhead of involving the kernel each time control changes from one thread to another. The kernel gives control of the CPU to a process. The program that process is executing calls library functions that divide up the time among a number of threads.

This approach has the serious drawback that if one thread calls a system service such as read(), and it has to wait for a key to be pressed, the kernel will block the whole process and give the CPU to another process. The kernel just does not know about threads. It might be viewed as a cheap way to implement threads on top of an existing system.

The other possibility is for threads to be implemented in the kernel itself, which then handles all the switching between threads. This provides all the benefits of multi-threading. Obviously, if threads are to be provided by the operating system, the responsibility for this will fall on the process manager, but it implies such a radical rewrite of the process manager and other parts of the kernel as well that it is normally implemented only in new operating systems.

Linux has a unique way of providing threads within the kernel. It really creates a new process, but it specifies that the original process and new process are to share the same memory, program, and open files. So it is essentially a thread in its parent process. Each such thread has its own ID number.

There is very little extra code in the process manager to deal with threads. Certainly, there is no suggestion of a thread manager, but the concept of a thread group is introduced. This means that all the processes that represent a group of threads sharing the same code and data are linked together on a list, which is headed from their parent process.

1.2 The GCC compiler

The Linux kernel is written to be compiled by the GCC compiler. There are a number of features of this compiler that impinge on how the code is written. Such features come up frequently throughout the book, so rather than repeating them each time they are gathered together here in the introduction.

1.2.1 C language features

The first group involves features of the C language, how it is parsed by the GCC compiler, and the structure of the assembly language code produced.

1.2.1.1 FASTCALL

By default, the GCC compiler passes parameters to functions by generating code to push them on the stack before calling the function, and popping them afterwards. This default can be overridden by specifying that the parameters are to be passed in registers. The FASTCALL macro is defined in `<linux/kernel.h>` as:

```
44      #define FASTCALL(x) x __attribute__((regparm(3)))
```

This means that the function `x()` has the `regparm(3)` attribute: that is, the compiler will pass it a maximum of three integer parameters in the EAX, EDX, and ECX registers, instead of on the stack, and the function itself will be compiled so as to expect them there. Although this has the drawback that the number and size of the parameters are limited, it does have the advantage of being more efficient. The called function does not have to load its parameters into registers from the stack – they are there already. It is particularly efficient when the function is called from an assembly language routine, that already has the parameters in the appropriate registers. The FASTCALL macro is specific to the i386.

1.2.1.2   Suggest branch directions for compiler

If a compiler can know in advance which branch of an `if` statement is more likely to be taken, then when laying out the code it can give a tiny margin of advantage to one rather than the other. The macros `likely()` and `unlikely()` have been provided to facilitate this (see Figure 1.2, from `<linux/compiler.h>`). An example of its use would be instead of writing `if (x == y)`, to write `if (likely(x == y))`.

```
9     #if __GNUC__ == 2 && __GNUC_MINOR__ < 96
10    #define __builtin_expect(x, expected_value) (x)
11    #endif
12
13    #define likely(x)        __builtin_expect((x),1)
14    #define unlikely(x)      __builtin_expect((x),0)
```

Figure 1.2   Suggest branch direction for compiler

9–11   since version 2.96 of GCC, there is a built-in function called `__builtin_expect()`. This is not available for earlier compilers, so this macro substitutes a dummy for it.

13–14   these lines pass the appropriate second parameter to `__builtin_expect()`. In the `likely()` case this is TRUE; for `unlikely()` it is FALSE. In all cases x is a boolean expression.

1.2.1.3   do { . . . } while(0)

Macros are widely used in the Linux kernel code. Although some are only 'one-liners', others are fairly lengthy and may include their own `if` statements within them.

Remember, macros can be inserted anywhere in C code, even inside an `if . . else` statement. In that case, the `if` in the macro, and the `if . . else` in the main code can confuse the compiler, leading to syntax errors, or incorrect nesting of `if . . else` constructs.

To solve this problem, the definition of many macros is wrapped by a `do { . . . } while(0)` construct. As it stands, it is saying 'do this once', which is just what is required.

Also, the compiler will see this and will not generate any looping code. So why is it there at all?

The do { . . . } while(0) construct is a way of instructing the compiler that the macro is one block of code and is to be treated as such, no matter where it is inserted in the main code.

1.2.2 Assembly language features

There is a small amount of assembly language code included in the kernel, and some generic features of that things that are not specific to operating systems are described here.

1.2.2.1 Aligning code and data

For efficiency of access to main memory, and to cache, it is frequently desirable to have machine code aligned on even boundaries. A number of macros are provided for this (see Figure 1.3) from < linux/l inkage.h > .

```
40    #if defined(__i386__) && defined(CONFIG_X86_ALIGNMENT_16)
41    #define __ALIGN .align 16,0x90
42    #define __ALIGN_STR ".align 16,0x90"
43    #else
44    #define __ALIGN .align 4,0x90
45    #define __ALIGN_STR ".align 4,0x90"
46    #endif

53    #define ALIGN __ALIGN
54    #define ALIGN_STR __ALIGN_STR
```

Figure 1.3   Alignment macros

40–42   this is the version used for 16-byte alignment, when optimizing use of the cache.

41   this tells the assembler to align the next machine instruction on a 16-byte boundary and to fill any padding bytes with 0x90, the NOP instruction.

42   this is the string version of the same macro, for use with inline assembler (see subsection 1.2.2.3).

44–45   these are the 4-byte versions of the macros, used when optimising access to main memory.

53–54   in both cases, ALIGN is an alias for __ALIGN, and ALIGN_STR is an alias for __ALIGN_STR.

1.2.2.2 Visibility

When mixing C code with assembler, it is a common requirement that C identifiers should be visible to the assembler and also that the C code be able to jump to specific routines within the assembler. The macros shown in Figure 1.4, from <linux/linkage.h>, facilitate this.

```
21   #define SYMBOL_NAME(X) X
22
23   #define SYMBOL_NAME_LABEL(X) X##:
56   #define ENTRY(name)                    \
57       .globl SYMBOL_NAME(name);          \
58       ALIGN;                             \
59       SYMBOL_NAME_LABEL(name)
```

Figure 1.4   Macros for mixing C and assembler code

21   this macro is used in assembler code to make the C identifier X visible to the assembler.

23   this macro converts the C identifier X into a label in assembler code. Note the colon (:) at the end of the line.

56–59   this macro sets up a label name: in assembly code, that can be called from C code.

57   declare name as a global symbol.

59   use the macro from line 23 to create a label in the assembly code.

1.2.2.3   Inline assembler

A very small part of Linux is written in pure assembly language code; the most obvious example for the process manager is the file arch/i386/kernel/entry.S, dealt with in Chapter 10. However, frequently in the middle of a unit of C code there is a requirement to carry out some operation that can only be done in assembler. The most common example is to read or write a specific hardware register. For this, inline assembler is used. This is done using the asm() built-in function.

The parameter to this function is a string representing the assembler mnemonic, in AT&T syntax. A very simple example would be asm("nop"). For more complex situations, it is passed a concatenation of strings, each representing one or more assembler instructions, interspersed with formatting instructions such as \t and \n.

It is also possible to pass instructions to the compiler about the location of each of the operands used in the assembly code. Each one is described by an operand constraint string, followed by the C expression representing that operand. A colon separates the assembler template from the first output operand, and another separates the last output operand from the first input operand. An operand constraint string specifies whether the operand is read, or write, or both. It also specifies the location of the operand (e.g. in a register, or in memory).

Some machine instructions have side-effects, altering specific registers or memory in an unspecified way. The compiler can be warned of this by information placed after a third colon.

The GCC compiler reads and interprets only whatever comes after the first colon. It uses this information to generate assembler code that puts the operands in the correct registers beforehand, and it heeds warnings about not caching memory values in registers across the group of assembler instructions in the template. The actual assembler template itself it passes on directly to the gas assembler. Any errors in that string will only be picked up at that stage.

Each time such a portion of inline assembly code is encountered in the book, it is described in some detail. The outline given here will only become fully clear when read again in such a context.

1.3 Initialising the process manager

The material in the remainder of this chapter is difficult to place. Although it logically belongs here at the beginning, it is dealing with the initialisation of data structures and subsystems that have not yet been encountered, so it is most likely to be read in conjunction with later parts of the book, when checking how particular structures got their original values.

When a CPU is powered up, it starts with defined values in all of its registers, including the program counter, so it always looks for its first instruction at a predefined location in memory. A system designer will arrange that some instructions be available in a ROM at that location.

The startup instructions in ROM will generally test the hardware, possibly including identifying peripherals. It then tries to read the boot sector of whichever disk drive is configured as the boot device. Typically, this boot block will contain only sufficient code to identify where exactly on the disk the operating system is located.

The 'gory details' of how Linux is booted are very architecture-dependent. They are certainly not the subject matter of this book. In general, there would be machine-specific code involved in the first stages of booting any operating system. This is sometimes known as the basic input–output system (BIOS). Then there would be architecture-specific Linux code, which initialises the hardware, including memory. Eventually, this transfers control to the architecture-independent routine `start_kernel()` in `init/main.c`.

1.3.1 Starting the kernel

Even the `start_kernel()` function is not really our concern here. It is relevant, however, because it calls a number of other functions that are responsible for starting different parts of the process manager.

Figure 1.5 extracted from `init/main.c`, shows the relevant lines. Each of these functions is discussed further on in the book, as indicated in the comments.

```
551  lock_kernel();
556  trap_init();
557  init_IRQ();
558  sched_init()
559  softirq_init();
596  fork_init();
620  rest_init();
```

Figure 1.5   Starting the process manager

551   this function, to be described in Section 5.5, takes out a lock on the whole kernel while all of this initialisation is going on. It will be released at line 533 of `rest_init()` (see Section 1.3.3).

556   this function sets up the table of interrupt handlers (see Section 10.2.2).

557   the default handlers for the hardware interrupts are set up by this function (see Section 12.5.1).

558   this function is described in Section 1.3.2. It is somewhat misnamed, as the only thing it has to do with scheduling is to initialise a hash table for process structures, but it also initialises the timer subsystem, as well as doing some work for the memory manager.

559   this function sets up the software interrupt mechanism (see Section 16.1.2).

596   this function (see Section 8.1.2), calculates and records the maximum number of processes allowed in the system at any one time, based on the amount of memory available.

620   this function (see Section 1.3.3) does some miscellaneous initialisation. It creates the `init` process and then metamorphoses into the idle process.

1.3.2 Scheduler initialisation

One of the functions discussed in Section 1.3.1 was `sched_init()`, as shown in Figure 1.6, from `kernel/sched.c`. It is called from `main.c`, line 536, and it initialises scheduling.

```
1304 void __init sched_init(void)
1305 {

1310        int cpu =smp_processor_id();
1311        int nr;
1312
1313        init_task.processor = cpu;
1314
1315        for(nr = 0; nr < PIDHASH_SZ; nr++)
1316               pidhash[nr] = NULL;
1317
1318        init_timervecs();
1319
1320        init_bh(TIMER_BH, timer_bh);
1321        init_bh(TQUEUE_BH, tqueue_bh);
1322        init_bh(IMMEDIATE_BH, immediate_bh);

1327        atomic_inc(&init_mm.mm_count);
1328        enter_lazy_tlb(&init_mm, current, cpu);
1329 }
```

Figure 1.6   Function to initialize the scheduler

1310   this finds the ID of the current processor, in this case the boot processor. The `smp_processor_id()`macro is architecture-specific (see Section 7.2.1.4).

1313   this puts the ID value into the `processor` field of the `task_struct` for `init_task`. This structure has already been statically set up by the compiler (see Section 3.3.2).

1315–1316 the hash table, as described in Section 3.2, is initialised to NULL values.

1318 the `init_timervecs()` function, which sets up the internal timer subsystem, will be described in Section 15.3.1.3.

1320–1322 finally, the bottom halves of the interrupt handlers are set up. Most operating systems divide the processing of an interrupt into two parts. There is some urgent work that must be done immediately, and often there is less urgent work that can be done at a later time. For example, when a network card interrupts, it is essential to get the data off the card and into memory as soon as possible. This is so that the card is ready to receive the next message coming over the network. Once this has been done, the operating system can deliver the message to the appropriate user in its own time. To handle this situation, Linux uses 'bottom halves' (see Section 16.3 for full details). The `init_bh()` function is architecture-specific (see Section 16.3.1.3).

1327–1328 these two lines relate to the memory management fields of `init_task` and are not relevant in the context of this book

1.3.3 Starting `init` and the idle process

The remainder of the initialisation has been broken out into a separate function, `rest_init()`, for memory-management reasons, which need not concern us (see Figure 1.7, from `init/main.c`).

```
530  static void rest_init(void)
531  {
532          kernel_thread(init, NULL,
                                  CLONE_FS | CLONE_FILES | CLONE_SIGNAL);
533          unlock_kernel();
534          current->need_resched = 1;
535          cpu_idle();
536  }
```

Figure 1.7 Setting up `init` and the idle process

532 this architecture-specific function is described in Section 8.5. It creates a new thread and arranges for it to run the `init()` function. This starts the background processes running, including login processes on each connected terminal. The original process continues at the next line.

533 the startup process had exclusive control of the kernel up to this point; it now relinquishes that control (see Section 5.5 for the function).

534 by setting this flag in the `task_struct`, a process signals to the scheduler that it is willing to give up the CPU.

535 this function, described in Section 3.4.1, goes into an infinite loop. The process executing the initialisation code (process 0) thus becomes the idle process, but, because it has set its `need_resched` flag at line 534, the scheduler can preempt it at any stage.

2

Representing processes in Linux

The operating system needs to keep track of processes. As with all software systems, it uses data structures to represent the different objects it is dealing with. For each process that it is currently managing, the operating system maintains a data structure known as a **process descriptor** or a **process control block**. In Linux this is a struct task_struct, defined in <linux/sched.h>. One task_struct is allocated per process. It contains all the data needed to control the process, whether it is running or not. The operating system guarantees to keep this information in memory at all times. This is probably the single most important data structure in the Linux kernel, so it will be examined in some detail in this chapter. There is a sense in which it is a sort of table of contents for the remainder of the book.

Many of the fields in this task_struct are concerned with process management, and so each will be dealt with in its own place in the appropriate chapter; their purpose will become clearer when we later examine what use the kernel makes of them. Other fields do not fall within the scope of this book. Those dealing with memory management or input–output would be obvious examples. Because this is the only place where they will be considered, they are covered in a little more detail.

The fields are certainly not arranged in logical order – they seem to have just grown up where they are. The comments in the source file break this large structure up into a number of more manageable sections, and the same divisions will be followed here.

2.1 Important fields hard coded at the beginning

Figure 2.1 shows the first few fields in the task_struct. These are accessed from assembler routines, such as those in arch/i386/kernel/entry.S, by offset, not by name. This means that no matter what else changes, they must always be at the same relative position at the beginning of the structure.

The Linux Process Manager. The Internals of Scheduling, Interrupts and Signals   John O'Gorman
© 2003 John Wiley & Sons, Ltd   ISBN: 0 470 84771 9

```
281   struct task_struct {

285       volatile long              state;
286       unsigned long              flags;
287       int  sigpending;
288       mm_segment_t               addr_limit;

292       struct exec_domain         *exec_domain;
293       volatile long              need_resched;
294       unsigned long              ptrace;
295
296       int                        lock_depth;
```

Figure 2.1 Hard-coded fields in the `task_struct`

2.1.1 Line 285: `state`

Note first of all that `state` is declared `volatile`. This is a warning to the compiler that its value may be changed asynchronously (e.g. an interrupt handler may change a process from waiting to runable), so the optimiser is not to remove any seemingly redundant statements that reference this variable.

Any particular process can be in one of several states, defined as shown in Figure 2.2, from `<linux/sched.h>`. A positive value means that the process is not running, for some reason.

```
86    #define TASK_RUNNING            0
87    #define TASK_INTERRUPTIBLE      1
88    #define TASK_UNINTERRUPTIBLE    2
89    #define TASK_ZOMBIE             4
90    #define TASK_STOPPED            8
```

Figure 2.2 Possible values for the `state` field

86   TASK_RUNNING is applied to both the currently running process or any processes that are ready to run. Such processes are maintained on a linked list called the **runqueue** (see Section 4.8).

87   when in the TASK_INTERRUPTIBLE state, the process is sleeping. It is maintained on a linked list called a **wait queue** (see Chapter 4), but it can be woken by a **signal**. Signals are covered in Chapters 17–19.

88   in the TASK_UNINTERRUPTIBLE state, the process is also sleeping on a wait queue, but it is waiting for some event that is likely to occur very soon, so any signals will be held until it is woken.

89   the TASK_ZOMBIE state refers to a process that has terminated but that has not been fully removed from the system as yet. Such a process is known as a **zombie** in Unix terminology. Each process in Unix has a parent process; the one that created it. When a process terminates, it can pass back information to its parent, usually signifying the reason why it terminated, whether this was normal or abnormal. Such information is stored in the `exit_code` field of the task_struct, which will be seen in Section 2.3. So, the task_struct of this process continues to exist, after the process has terminated, until the parent collects the status information, using the wait() system service. After that, all trace of the process disappears. Chapter 9 deals with process termination.

90   sometimes the process manager stops a process completely. This is not termination, it is, rather, halting it for an indeterminate time. The two common occasions on which this occurs are when a process loses contact with its controlling terminal; or when its execution is being traced by another process (a debugger), and it is stopped after executing each instruction, so that its state can be examined. Stopping and starting processes is done by means of signals, which will be examined in Chapters 17–19. When a process has been stopped like this, then its state is TASK_STOPPED.

Note that changing the state of a process, and moving it from one queue to another, are not necessarily atomic operations.

2.1.2   Line 286: flags

This is a bit field, recording various items of interest about the status of the process. Individual bits in this field denote different milestones in the lifecycle of a process. These bits are defined as shown in Figure 2.3, from <linux/sched.h>. They are not mutually exclusive; more than one can be set at the same time.

```
418   #define PF_ALIGNWARN      0x00000001
419
420   #define PF_STARTING       0x00000002
421   #define PF_EXITING        0x00000004
422   #define PF_FORKNOEXEC     0x00000040
423   #define PF_SUPERPRIV      0x00000100
424   #define PF_DUMPCORE       0x00000200
425   #define PF_SIGNALED       0x00000400
426   #define PF_MEMALLOC       0x00000800
427   #define PF_MEMDIE         0x00001000
428   #define PF_FREE_PAGES     0x00002000
429   #define PF_NOIO           0x00004000
430
431   #define PF_USEDFPU        0x00100000
```

Figure 2.3   Values for the flags field

418   alignment warning messages should be printed. No example of its use has been found anywhere in the code.

420   the process is being created, and so should be left alone until it is fully started. Again, no place has been found in the code where it is actually used, certainly not by fork(), where it might be expected.

421   the process is being shut down, and should also be left alone. This bit is set by the code that implements exit() (see Section 9.1). It is checked by different parts of the I/O manager.

422   the process has never called `exec()`, so it is still running the same program as its parent. This bit is set by the code that implements `fork()` (see Section 8.3.2) and is cleared by functions that implement `exec()`. It only ever seems to be tested when doing BSD style accounting (see Section 23.3.2).

423   the process has used superuser privileges. Note it is not necessarily indicating that the process has superuser privileges now; only that it requested them at some stage. It is set by functions that give such privilege, such as `capable()`, as well as the older style `suser()` and `fsuser()`, (see Chapter 20). It is used by BSD accounting. This bit is cleared when a new process is created.

424   this bit indicates that if the process terminates abnormally, it is to produce a core image on disk. It is set by functions that implement `exec()`.

425   the process has been terminated by the arrival of a signal (see Section 18.4.4).

426–428 these bits are set and tested by various routines within the memory manager. They will not be considered any further here.

429   when this bit is set, the process does not generate any further I/O. As this is the province of the I/O manager, it will not be considered further in this book.

431   this bit is cleared when a new process is created (see Section 8.3.2), and is afterwards manipulated only by architecture-specific code. It signifies that the task used the hardware floating point unit (FPU) during the current time-slice.

Line 287: `sigpending`

This field is a flag that is set when a signal has been posted to the process. Its significance will be examined in detail in Section 18.3.

Line 288: `addr_limit`

This field specifies the maximum size of an address space, for user and kernel threads. As can be seen from the comment in the code, a kernel thread can have a full 4 GB, whereas a user thread can take only a maximum of 3 GB. The definition of `mm_segment_t` is architecture-specific but would generally be a scalar such as an `unsigned long`. It will not be considered further.

Line 292: `exec_domain`

Linux can run programs compiled for different versions of UNIX. This pointer is to a `struct exec_domain`, which identifies the particular UNIX execution domain associated with the process. Note that it is a pointer; the information is not maintained on a process-by-process basis, rather on a systemwide basis. There is a linked list of these set up at boot time, and all processes point to a particular entry on the list. There is no use count, for even when no process is pointing to a particular entry, it still remains in existence, as Linux is still able to support it. Execution domains are dealt with in detail in Chapter 21.

Line 293: `need_resched`

This flag is set to 1 to inform the scheduler that this process is willing to yield the CPU. Its use will be examined in detail when dealing with the scheduler, in Chapter 7.

Line 294: `ptrace`

This is a flag field used only when a process is being traced. The possible values are shown in Figure 2.4, from `<linux/sched.h>`.

```
436  #define    PT_PTRACED          0x00000001
437  #define    PT_TRACESYS         0x00000002
438  #define    PT_DTRACE           0x00000004
439  #define    PT_TRACESYSGOOD     0x00000008
440  #define    PT_TRACE_CAP        0x00000010
```

Figure 2.4 Values for the `ptrace` field

436 this bit is set if the `ptrace()` system service has been called by another process, to trace this process.

437 this process is being traced by another process, but it is only to be interrupted at each system call.

438 this bit notes that the TRAP flag is set in EFLAGS, meaning that the process is to be interrupted after each machine instruction. A process may do this itself, even if not being traced by another.

439 this bit allows a tracing parent to tell whether a child has stopped (in system service code) because of a system call, or because of a SIGTRAP signal, initiated by hardware (see Section 22.5).

440 this bit indicates that tracing can continue even across the `exec()` of a set UID (unique identifier) program. Such a program runs with different privileges from those of the owner of the process.

Process tracing will be dealt with in detail in chapter 22.

2.1.3 Line 296: `lock_depth`

When Linux is running on a uniprocessor, once the current process enters the kernel to execute a system service it cannot be preempted until it leaves the kernel again. This design feature guarantees it mutual exclusion on all the kernel data structures. However, on a multiprocessor machine it is possible for processes executing on two or more CPUs to be active in the kernel at the same time. So, it became necessary to introduce a mutual exclusion lock on the kernel. Because it is possible for a process to recursively acquire this lock, the `lock_depth` field is incremented each time the lock is acquired, and decremented when it is released. So, it is possible to avoid the situation where a process leaves the kernel, still holding the lock. The implementation of this lock is architecture-dependent and will be dealt with in Section 5.5. Note that this field is not the kernel lock itself; it is only an indication of how many times this process has recursively acquired the kernel lock (if at all).

2.2 Scheduling fields

Figure 2.5 shows a group of fields in the `task_struct`, which are used by the scheduler. Grouping them like this is an attempt to keep all fields that are needed for one of the innermost loops in the scheduler (`goodness()`; see Section 7.4.2) in a single cache line of 32 bytes. The `struct list_head` (line 321) consists of two 32-bit pointer fields, and only the first one, the `next` field, fits in the cache line. But that is the only one needed, as reading this list is always done from the beginning forwards. Not all of the scheduling information is included here – other fields will be encountered later on.

```
303  long                    counter;
304  long                    nice;
305  unsigned long           policy;
306  struct mm_struct        *mm;
307  int                     processor;

316  unsigned long           cpus_runnable, cpus_allowed;

321  struct list_head        run_list;
322  unsigned long           sleep_time;
323
324  struct task_struct      *next_task, *prev_task;
325  struct mm_struct        *active_mm;
326  struct list_head        local_pages;
327  unsigned int            allocation_order, nr_local_pages;
```

Figure 2.5   Fields in the `task_struct` used by the scheduler

Line 303: `counter`

The time left (in clock interrupts or ticks) from the quantum for this process is maintained in `counter`. Various functions modify it. It is decremented on each clock tick while the process is running. When it gets to 0, then the `need_resched` flag for this process is set. It is checked when a process wakes up; if it is greater than that of the current process, then the `need_resched` field of the current process is set to 1. All of this is considered in great detail in Chapter 7, on scheduling.

Line 304: `nice`

A process can request that its priority be changed, while it is running. This field contains the requested value.

Line 305: `policy`

The `policy` field determines the scheduling policy associated with this process. It can have the values shown in Figure 2.6, from `<linux/sched.h>`.

```
115  #define SCHED_OTHER          0
116  #define SCHED_FIFO           1
117  #define SCHED_RR             2

123  #define SCHED_YIELD          0x10
```

Figure 2.6 Possible values for the `policy` field

115 this denotes the default time-sharing policy.

116 this is first in, first out; such a process has no quantum. It runs until it blocks or is preempted.

117 this is a round robin; it runs until it blocks, is preempted, or uses up its quantum.

123 a process may decide to give up the CPU for one pass over the runqueue by the scheduler. In that case, every other process on the runqueue would be given an opportunity to run, before this one runs again. An example would be a real-time process, no matter how high its priority, yielding to an interactive process.

How these flags are used by the scheduler will be discussed in Chapter 7.

Line 306: mm

This is a pointer to the data structures used by the memory manager. Figure 2.7 shows the `mm_struct`, from `<linux/sched.h>`. Most of these fields are not relevant to the process manager, but it does operate on this structure when creating (`fork()`) and deleting (`exit()`) processes. The following brief description of the fields in `mm_struct` assumes some knowledge of how a memory manager works. It is included here for completeness.

```
204  struct mm_struct{
205      struct vm_area_struct      *mmap;
206      rb_root_t                  mm_rb;
207      struct vm_area_struct      *mmap_cache;
208      pgd_t                      * pgd;
209      atomic_t                   mm_users;
210      atomic_t                   mm_count;
211      int                        map_count;
212      struct rw_semaphore        mmap_sem;
213      spinlock_t                 page_table_lock;
214
215      struct list_head           mmlist;

220      unsigned long              start_code, end_code,
                                    start_data, end_data;
221      unsigned long              start_brk, brk, start_stack;
222      unsigned long              arg_start, arg_end, env_start,
                                                       env_end;

223      unsigned long              rss, total_vm, locked_vm;
```

```
224        unsigned long              def_flags;
225        unsigned long              cpu_vm_mask;
226        unsigned long              swap_address;
227
228        unsigned                   dumpable:1;

231        mm_context_t               context;
232  };
```

Figure 2.7   Memory management control information

205   this is a header for a linked list of structures representing the regions in the address space of the process.

206   the structures representing the regions in a process are also arranged in a tree, for speed of lookup. This field is the root of that tree.

207   this is a pointer to the most recently accessed region.

208   this is a pointer to the physical page table.

209   this is a reference count of the number of different user space threads sharing this memory map.

210   the mm_count field contains the total number of kernel thread references to this structure. All user space threads count as a single reference.

211   the number of regions in the memory map is in map_count. This is the number of entries in the list headed from mmap.

212   to protect the whole linked list headed from mmap, there is a semaphore mmap_sem.

213   the spinlock page_table_lock is used to guarantee mutual exclusion on the physical page table pointed to by pgd.

215   all the mm_struct in the system are linked together, through this field.

220   the virtual addresses of the beginning and end of the code segment are in start_code and end_code, respectively. Likewise start_data and end_data are, respectively, the virtual addresses of the beginning and end of the initialised data segment.

221   the address of the beginning of the heap is in start_brk. The address of the highest memory allocated dynamically is in brk. The start of the stack is in start_stack.

222   the address of the beginning and end of the area containing the command line arguments passed to the current program are in arg_start and arg_end, respectively. Likewise env_start and env_end contain, respectively, the address of the beginning and end of the area containing the environment.

223   the number of pages actually resident in memory is in rss. The total amount of virtual memory in bytes is in total_vm, and locked_vm contains the bytes of virtual memory which are locked in.

224 the `vm_area_struct` representing each region has a flags field. Unless otherwise specified, any new region created in this particular mapping will have its flags set to the default values specified in `def_flags`.

225 the `cpu_vm_mask` is used only on multiprocessors. Two or more CPUs may have cached copies of the same data. The hardware has to guarantee that all copies are consistent. This is typically done by invalidating cached values. When one CPU writes to cached data, all the other processor caches are informed, by means of an interprocessor interrupt (IPI), and they mark their values as invalid. But such an IPI can arrive in the middle of a context switch, and could be applied to the wrong data. The `cpu_vm_mask` field is a bit used to indicate just when the memory context has changed.

226 the swap device for this memory map is identified by `swap_address`. It is an index into the table of swap device descriptors.

228 the `dumpable` bit indicates whether or not a core file should be written to disk if the process terminates abnormally.

231 some of the CPUs on which Linux is implemented have sophisticated caches that can actually distinguish between the same virtual address in two different address spaces. This results in great savings in cache flushes, but it needs some way of identifying different address spaces. The `context` field holds the address space number assigned to this process. This field is cleared to 0 by `fork()`. Otherwise, its manipulation is totally architecture-dependent. It is not relevant to the i386.

The `mm_struct` will not be considered further in this book.

Line 307: `processor`

When a process is allocated a CPU, the ID number of the CPU is recorded in the `processor` field. A value of 0 here means that this process is not currently assigned a CPU. This field is manipulated by the scheduler, and will be considered in Chapter 7.

Line 316: `cpus_runnable`

This field is all 1s if the process is not running on any CPU. If it is running on a CPU, then the bit corresponding to that CPU is set.

Line 316: `cpus_allowed`

In multiprocessor mode, Linux tries to arrange that processes are scheduled onto CPUs on which they have recently run. This makes better use of caches. This field is a bitmap, specifying the CPUs onto which this process can be scheduled. Its use will be discussed when dealing with the scheduler, in Section 7.4.1.

Line 321: `run_list`

This holds the `task_struct` on the runqueue. It merely contains backwards and forwards pointers.

Line 322: `sleep_time`

This field contains the time at which the process was removed from the runqueue, or put to sleep. Yet another field relevant to the scheduler, it will be discussed in Section 4.8.3.

Line 3.24: `next_task, prev_task`

These are the backward and forward pointers that hold the whole linked list of `task_struct` structures together. Note that both of these are direct pointers, pointing to the appropriate `task_struct`. The list is headed by `init_task`, (see Section 3.3.1).

Line 325: `active_mm`

This field normally has the same value as mm. But for a kernel thread that does not have an address space of its own (its mm field is NULL) this field points to the `mm_struct` representing the address space it is actively using. When the scheduler context switches in a kernel thread, it sets its `active_mm` field to the mm field of the process it is just switching out. It is used to minimise flushing of the translation lookaside buffer, (see Section 7.3.5).

Line 326: `local_pages`

This heads a linked list of `struct page` representing all page frames allocated to this process.

Line 327: `allocation_order`

Specifies the order to be used by the memory manager when allocating page frames.

Line 327: `nr_local_pages`

This is the number of pages on the list headed from `local_pages`.

2.3 General process information

The next block of information in the `task_struct`, loosely gathered together under the heading of general process state information, is shown in Figure 2.8.

```
330  struct linux_binfmt        *binfmt;
331  int                        exit_code, exit_signal;
332  int                        pdeath_signal;
333
334  unsigned long              personality;
335  int                        did_exec:1;
336  pid_t                      pid;
337  pid_t                      pgrp;
338  pid_t                      tty_old_pgrp;
339  pid_t                      session;
```

```
340  pid_t                         tgid;
341
342  int                           leader;

348  struct task_struct            *p_opptr, *p_pptr, *p_cptr,
                                              *p_ysptr, *p_osptr;
349  struct list_head              thread_group;

352  struct task_struct            *pidhash_next;
353  struct task_struct            **pidhash_pprev;
354
355  wait_queue_head_t             *wait_chldexit;
356  struct completion             *vfork_done;
357  unsigned long                 rt_priority;
358  unsigned long                 it_real_value, it_prof_value,
                                              it_virt_value;
359  unsigned long                 it_real_incr, it_prof_incr,
                                              it_virt_incr;
360  struct timer_list             real_timer;
361  struct tms                    times;
362  unsigned long                 start_time;
363  long                          per_cpu_utime[NR_CPUS],
                                      per_cpu_stime[NR_CPUS];
```

Figure 2.8   Process state information in `task_struct`

Line 330: `binfmt`

Linux can run programs compiled into various executable formats, such as `a.out` and ELF. The `struct linux_binfmt` contains a set of pointers to functions for loading and manipulating the specific binary format in which the program being executed is encoded. There are functions to load the executable, to load a shared library, and to write a core file.

Once again, this is a pointer field, as the information resides in a systemwide list. This list is set up at boot time, with one entry for each supported format, as follows.

- a.out: mainly only there for backward compatibility;

- ELF: widely used both for executables and for shared for libraries; Linux's natural format;

- EM86: runs Intel binaries on an Alpha, as if they were native Alpha binaries; this seems to imply either interpretation, or on-the-fly translation;

- Java: executes Java `.class` files by automatically running the Java interpreter;

- Misc: works mainly from the magic number, and can be configured to recognise new magics;

- Script: shell or other interpreted scripts, such as Perl or Python.

Binary formats are really the concern of the file manager and will not be dealt with any further here.

Line 331: `exit_code`

The information to be returned to the parent when this process terminates is in `exit_code`. This field is discussed in Section 9.1, when dealing with process termination.

Line 331: `exit_signal`

If the process was terminated by a signal, then the `exit_signal` field contains the number of that signal.

Line 332: `pdeath_signal`

The signal to be sent to this process when any of its children die is defined in `pdeath_signal`. It is sent by the function `forget_original_parent()` (see Section 9.2.2).

Line 334: `personality`

A Linux process can execute programs that were compiled for different versions of Unix. The version corresponding to the current program is recorded in `personality`. Normally, this is PER_LINUX (0). See Chapter 21 for a full discussion of personalities, including the different possibilities.

Line 335: `did_exec`

The `did_exec` bit indicates whether this process has ever done an `exec()` since it was created, or whether it is still running the same program as its parent. It is cleared to 0 by `fork()`, and set to 1 by `exec()`.

Line 336: `pid`

Each process is given its own unique process identification (`pid`) number when it is created. This number is maintained in the `pid` field. The allocation of `pid` numbers is dealt with in Section 8.3.3.

Line 337: `pgrp`

The kernel provides a facility for grouping a number of processes together. The number of the group of which a process is a member is maintained in `pgrp`. Process groups have particular significance in the area of signals (see Chapter 18).

Line 338: `tty_old_pgrp`

Process groups themselves can be gathered together into a session (see the next field). The process group that is currently controlling the terminal is known as the foreground process group. When a process in that group relinquishes the terminal, the `tty_old_pgrp` field of the session leader (see line 342) is used to store the process group ID that was associated with that terminal.

Line 339: `session`

Process groups can be gathered together into sessions. The number of the session of which this process is a member is in the `session` field. When a user logs on, the logon process becomes both a session leader, and a group leader. The session ID and group ID are both set the same as the process ID. Child processes are created in the same session and group as their parent.

Line 340: `tgid`

The thread group ID. If a new process is created to implement a new thread in an existing process, then this field contains the `pid` of its creator. Otherwise, when a new process is created by `fork()`, this field contains the unique `pid` of the new process (see Section 8.2.5).

Line 342: `leader`

The leader field is a boolean value indicating whether the process is a session leader or not.

Line 348: `p_opptr`, `p_pptr`, `p_cptr`, `p_ysptr`, `p_osptr`

There are a number of pointers to the structures representing other processes that are related to this one. The process that actually created this one (its original parent) is pointed to by `p_opptr`. The process that is currently its parent is pointed to by `p_pptr`. These are normally the same. However, while a process is being traced, the `p_pptr` field points to the tracing process (see Section 22.1). The `p_opptr` field allows this temporary change to be reversed, when tracing has terminated. Its most recently created child process is pointed to by `p_cptr`. The next (surviving) process created by its original parent is pointed to by `p_ysptr`, and `p_osptr` points to the previous sibling. These fields are manipulated by `fork()` and `exit()`, and will be considered in greater detail in Chapters 8 and 9.

Line 349: `thread_group`

The `thread_group` field is relevant only if this process has created any threads. In such a case, the `list_head` structure heads a linked list of `task_struct` structures representing all of the threads in the same process.

Lines 352–353: `pidhash_next`, `pidhash_pprev`

As well as being on a linear list, each `task_struct` is also on a hash chain, threaded through `pidhash_next` and `pidhash_pprev`. Note that `pidhash_pprev` is an indirect pointer, pointing to the `pidhash_next` field in the previous entry. This is dealt with in detail in Section 3.2.

Line 355: `wait_chldexit`

When a process is waiting for a particular child to terminate, as specified by the `wait4()` system service, it waits on a `struct wait_queue` pointed to from the `wait_chldexit` field. This is part of the implementation of `wait()` (see Section 9.3).

Line 356: `vfork_done`

This is a pointer to a `struct completion` (see Section 8.2) used internally by the implementation of `fork()` (see Section 8.2). The fact that this is a pointer, not the `completion` structure itself, implies that it is shared with some other process.

Line 357: `rt_priority`

The `rt_priority` field defines the fixed priority assigned to the process, if it is using either SCHED_FIFO or SCHED_RR scheduling. For an interactive process, this field is 0 (see Section 7.4.2, on scheduling).

Line 358: `it_real_value`, `it_prof_value`, `it_virt_value`

These three fields contain the time in ticks until one of the timers will be triggered. Time is always measured in ticks, which is 10 milliseconds on a PC. See Chapter 15, on time and timers, for this and the following fields.

Line 359: `it_real_incr`, `it_prof_incr`, `it_virt_incr`

The three `incr` fields contain values to which the timers are reinitialised after they have run out.

Line 360: `real_timer`

The `real_timer` field is used to implement the real-time interval timer.

Line 361: `times`

The `struct tms` contains the time the process has spent in user mode, and its time in kernel (system) mode, and the cumulative values of both of these for all its child processes.

Line 362: `start_time`

The time when the process was created is kept in `start_time`.

Line 362: `per_cpu_utime[NR_CPUS]`, `per_cpu_stime[NR_CPUS]`

Cumulative totals for the user and system time that this process has run on each CPU are maintained in `per_cpu_utime[]` and `per_cpu_stime[]`, respectively. They are initialised when the process is created (see Section 8.2.3) and updated by the timer interrupt (see Section 15.1.3.2). NR_CPUS is defined as 1 for a uniprocessor system, up to a theoretical maximum of 32 for multiprocessor.

2.4 Memory management performance information

Figure 2.9 shows the area of the `task_struct` that maintains information about the performance of the memory manager.

```
365  unsigned long      min_flt, maj_flt, nswap, cmin_flt, cmaj_flt, cnswap;
366  int                swappable:1;
```

Figure 2.9   Memory management performance information in the `task_struct`

2.4.1 Line 365: `min_flt`, `maj_flt`, `nswap`, `cmin_flt`, `cmaj_flt`, `cnswap`

The number of memory traps handled without loading a page is kept in `min_flt`; the number of memory traps that required a page fault is next in `maj_flt`. The number of pages belonging to this process that are actually in swap space is kept in `nswap`. The cumulative values of these variables for this process and all of its deceased children are kept in `cmin_flt`, `cmaj_flt`, and `cnswap`, respectively.

Although they are mainly the responsibility of the memory manager, and so outside the scope of this book, the values in these fields may be written to an accounting file (see Section 23.3.2).

Line 366: `swappable`

This bit indicates whether the process can be swapped out or not. Its main use is to prevent the system from swapping out a process that is being forked, before it is fully created (see Section 8.2.2).

2.5 Credentials and limits

Each process has various credentials associated with it that determine what access and resources the operating system will allow it (see Figure 2.10).

```
368  uid_t                    uid,euid,suid,fsuid;
369  gid_t                    gid,egid,sgid,fsgid;
370  int                      ngroups;
371  gid_t                    groups[NGROUPS];
372  kernel_cap_t             cap_effective,cap_inheritable,
                                               cap_permitted;
373  int                      keep_capabilities:1;
374  struct user_struct       *user;
375
376  struct rlimit            rlim[RLIM_NLIMITS];
377  unsigned short           used_math;
378  char                     comm[16];
```

Figure 2.10   Process credentials and limits

Line 368: `uid`, `euid`, `suid`, `fsuid`

These are the user identifiers associated with the process. The operating system uses these IDs to determine whether or not to grant a process access to specific system resources. The real user ID (uid), that is the ID of the user that created the process, is in `uid`. The effective uid (euid) is in `euid`; effective IDs can be acquired temporarily.

The saved uid is `suid`, and the uid used for file access is in `fsuid`. When a program is run, its effective `uid` is saved to its `suid`. In this way it can temporarily revert to its true ID, and then back to the effective one.

Line 369: `gid`, `egid`, `sgid`, `fsgid`

There are corresponding group identifiers associated with the process that identify the primary group to which the owner belongs.

Line 370: ngroups

A process may be associated with other groups besides its primary group. The `ngroups` field specifies how many such groups there are.

Line 371: `groups[NGROUPS]`

The group identifiers themselves are maintained in the array `groups[]`. The `gid_t` is an `int` rather than `unsigned`, as −1 (NOGROUP) is used for empty entries.

This and the nine fields discussed in Sections 2.51–2.5.3 are widely used throughout the kernel.

Line 372: `cap_effective`, `cap_inheritable`, `cap_permitted`

Each process is allocated certain capabilities, which are encoded in a 32-bit bitmap. This is an attempt to get around the all-or-nothing situation with root access. Capabilities can be acquired temporarily, if required. The effective set represents what the process is currently allowed to do. This is the set that is checked. The permitted set specifies those capabilities it may acquire. The inheritable set determines those capabilities a process will have after an exec().

Line 373: keep_capabilities

This bit determines whether capabilities are to be inherited across an exec() or not. Capabilities will be dealt with in detail in Chapter 20.

Line 374: user

Currently the struct user_struct is used only to track how many processes a user has, but it has the potential to track memory usage, files, and so on. Some day it will be a fully-fledged user tracking system. Note that it is a pointer – the one struct is shared by all processes belonging to the same user.

All these structures are maintained in a cache, which is described in detail in Section 8.4.

Line 376: rlim[RLIM_NLIMITS]

The struct rlimit, shown in Figure 2.11, from <linux/resource.h>, tracks resource limits assigned to each process.

```
40    struct rlimit
41        unsigned long              rlim_cur;
42        unsigned long              rlim_max;
43    };
```

Figure 2.11   Structure representing resource limits

41   the current usage limit for the resource.

42   the maximum value to which the resource limit can be extended, using the setrlimit() system service.

There is one entry in the rlim[] array for each resource that is limit controlled. These resources are shown in Figure 2.12, from <asm-i386/resource.h>, and are defined as follows:

```
8     #define RLIMIT_CPU               0
9     #define RLIMIT_FSIZE             1
10    #define RLIMIT_DATA              2
11    #define RLIMIT_STACK             3
12    #define RLIMIT_CORE              4
13    #define RLIMIT_RSS               5
14    #define RLIMIT_NPROC             6
15    #define RLIMIT_NOFILE            7
16    #define RLIMIT_MEMLOCK           8
17    #define RLIMIT_AS                9
```

```
18      #define RLIMIT_LOCKS           10
19
20      #define RLIM_NLIMITS           11
```

Figure 2.12   Resources subject to limit control

8   the total CPU time allowed to the process, in milliseconds;. it is used to prevent a runaway process from dominating the machine;

9   the maximum allowed size to which any one file may grow;

10   the maximum size to which the data segment of the process may grow;

11   the maximum size to which the user mode stack used by the process may grow;

12   the maximum size of core file that the process may produce;

13   the maximum number of pages that this process may have in memory at the one time;

14   the maximum number of child processes that this process can have in existence at one time;

15   the maximum number of files that this process can have open at one time;

16   the maximum amount of memory space which this process can lock in.

17   the maximum address space allowed to this process.

18   the maximum number of file locks that it can hold.

20   the number of resources that are limit controlled, or the size of the `rlim[]` array.

Line 377: `used_math`

The `used_math` field indicates whether or not the process has used the math co-processor. This is totally architecture-specific.

Line 378: `comm`

The name of the program being executed by the process is maintained in `comm`. This information is set up by `exec()` and is only ever used by the debugger (Chapter 22) and the accounting subsystem (Section 22.6).

2.6   Miscellaneous information

Figure 2.13 shows the information on file systems, and System V semaphores, which is maintained in the `task_struct`. These are two areas that will not be considered further in this book.

```
380  int                          link_count, total_link_count;
381  struct tty_struct            *tty;
382  unsigned int                 locks;
383
384  struct sem_undo              *semundo;
385  struct sem_queue             *semsleeping;
```

Figure 2.13 Miscellaneous information in the `task_struct`

Line 380: `link_count, total_link_count`

The number of recursive symbolic links encountered while parsing the current filename is kept in `link_count`. The number of consecutive symbolic links is maintained in `total_link_count`.

Line 381: `tty`

The structure `tty_struct` represents the terminal assigned to the process. This is where all the state associated with a terminal device is kept while it is open. This field is NULL if there is no terminal (i.e. if it is a background process). Note that this is a pointer field; more than one process may be sharing the same terminal.

Line 382: `locks`

This field indicates how many file locks the process is holding. These have to be given back when the process terminates.

Line 384: `semundo`

The `semundo` field is a pointer to a list of System V semaphores, that may have to have operations undone on them when this process terminates.

Line 385: `semsleeping`

When a process is suspended on a System V semaphore, `semsleeping` points to the particular semaphore wait queue on which the process is suspended.

2.7 Volatile environment and input–output

The three fields shown in Figure 2.14 contain a significant amount of information about the state of the process.

```
386  /* CPU-specific state of this task */
387      struct thread_struct     thread;
388  /* filesystem information */
389      struct fs_struct         *fs;
```

```
390  /* open file information */
391         struct files_struct        *files;
```

Figure 2.14   The volatile environment and input–output

Line 387: `thread`

There is really no fundamental distinction between the terms 'task', 'process', and 'thread' in Linux. However, the sources do seem to reserve the identifier 'thread' for architecture-specific details. Figure 2.15, from `<asm-i386/processor.h>`, shows the `thread_struct` used with the i386 architecture. This contains all the state information that must be saved when a process is context switched out. Context switches always occur in kernel mode. Most of the hardware register values have already been saved on entry to the kernel. So, in general, this structure contains values of some other registers that were not saved when the process entered the kernel as well as architecture-specific information.

```
365  struct thread_struct {
366         unsigned long              esp0;
367         unsigned long              eip;
368         unsigned long              esp;
369         unsigned long              fs;
370         unsigned long              gs;
371
372         unsigned long              debugreg[8];
373
374         unsigned long              cr2, trap_no, error_code;
375
376         union i387_union           i387;
377
378         struct vm86_struct         * vm86_info;
379         unsigned long              screen_bitmap;
380         unsigned long              v86flags, v86mask, v86mode,
                                                  saved_esp0;
381
382         int                        ioperm;
383         unsigned long              io_bitmap[IO_BITMAP_SIZE+1];
384  };
```

Figure 2.15   The `thread_struct`

366   even though declared as `unsigned long`, this field actually contains a pointer to the base (top) of the stack. It is always cast to be a pointer to a particular data type before being used.

367–370   these are standard i386 registers.

372   the i386 architecture has eight debugging registers, where the processor saves status information when an exception occurs. The values in these registers are saved (in `debugreg[]`) on a context switch.

374 the CR2 register is used to store the address that caused a page-fault. The page-fault handler can examine this. The generic interrupt handler saves the number of the trap or interrupt it is handling in `trap_no`. Handlers for specific interrupts put an appropriate error code in `error_code`.

376 the values in the floating point registers are saved here. See Figure 2.16 for the structure itself.

378–380 these fields are relevant only when the processor is running in virtual 8086 mode, as a result of calling the `vm86()` system service. Virtual 8086 mode, including the use made of these fields, will be discussed in detail in Section 23.4.

378 `vm86_info` is a pointer to a `struct vm86_struct`, containing information required when running in vm86 mode (see Section 24.1.1.1).

379 each bit in this field represents a page of the DOS screen memory area. The bit is set if the corresponding page is paged in.

380 the `v86flags` field is the virtual flags register, maintained by Linux while in vm86 mode (see Section 24.2). The `v86mask` defines the processor type. The `v86mode` field does not seem to be used anywhere. The `saved_esp0` field is used to save a copy of `esp0`, when changing into VM86 mode.

382–383 these fields define the I/O addresses that this process can access. They will not be considered further in this book.

Figure 2.16, from `<asm-i386/processor.h>`. shows the data structure used to store FPU information. The different formats are for different models of FPU and are described in the following figures.

```
324  union i387_union {
325       struct i387_fsave_struct      fsave;
326       struct i387_fxsave_struct     fxsave;
327       struct i387_soft_struct       soft;
328  };
```

Figure 2.16 Floating point register values

The information that needs to be saved for a standard i387 FPU is shown in Figure 2.17, from `<asm-i386/processor.h>`.

```
282  struct i387_fsave_struct {
283       long                     cwd;
284       long                     swd;
285       long                     twd;
286       long                     fip;
287       long                     fcs;
288       long                     foo;
289       long                     fos;
290       long                     st_space[20];
```

```
291      long                            status;
292  };
```

Figure 2.17   Standard FPU registers

283   the control word register of the FPU is saved here.

284   the status register of the FPU is saved here.

285   the tag word, saved here, indicates which FPU registers contain valid data.

286–287   the floating instruction pointer is a 48-bit register. The 32-bit offset is saved in fip, and the 16-bit segment selector is in `fcs`.

288–289   the floating operand is a 48-bit register. The 32-bit offset is saved in `foo`, and the 16-bit segment selector is in `fos`.

290   this relates to space to save eight floating-point registers, each 10 bytes wide.

291   this relates to software status information.

Later models of FPU, as found in Pentium processors, are more powerful and require more state to be saved. Figure 2.18, from <asm-i386/processor.h>, shows the data structure used to save this extra state. Obviously, there is much overlap with the previous figure. After all, this is only an extension of that figure.

```
294  struct i387_fxsave_struct {
295      unsigned short          cwd;
296      unsigned short          swd;
297      unsigned short          twd;
298      unsigned short          fop;
299      long                    fip;
300      long                    fcs;
301      long                    foo;
302      long                    fos;
303      long                    mxcsr;
304      long                    reserved;
305      long                    st_space[32];
306      long                    xmm_space[32];
307      long                    padding[56];
308  } __attribute__ ((aligned (16)));
```

Figure 2.18   Extended Floating point unit register

295–297   these fields are described for lines 283–285 of Figure 2.17, but note that they are now `unsigned short`. This makes sense, as they are only 16-bit registers.

298   the first two bytes of the last non-control instruction executed is stored in the last instruction opcode register and saved here.

299–302   these fields are described above for lines 286–289 of Figure 2.17.

303   this is the MXCSR register, which provides control and status bits for operations performed on the XMM registers.

305   each of the eight FPU registers is still 10-bytes wide, but they have been aligned better, on 16-byte boundaries.

306   there are also 8 XMM registers, each 16 bytes wide.

307   this is padding, to allow for future expansion.

308   each `struct i387_fxsave_struct` is aligned on a 16-byte boundary.

On very elderly machines (the original 386) without an FPU, basic floating point operations can be emulated in software. The structure used to maintain the state of the emulator is shown in Figure 2.19, from `<asm-i386/processor.h>`.

```
310   struct i387_soft_struct {
311       long                    cwd;
312       long                    swd;
313       long                    twd;
314       long                    fip;
315       long                    fcs;
316       long                    foo;
317       long                    fos;
318       long                    st_space[20];
319       unsigned char           ftop, changed, lookahead,
                                       no_update, rm, alimit;
320       struct info             *info;
321       unsigned long           entry_eip;
322   };
```

Figure 2.19   Software emulation of a floating point unit

311–318   these fields have already been seen in the standard FPU (see Figure 2.17), lines 283–290).

319–321   these fields are specific to the emulator and will not be considered further.

Line 389: `fs`

The `fs_struct` is defined in `<linux/fs_struct.h>`, as shown in Figure 2.20. It contains information about the file system associated with this process.

```
5     struct fs_struct{
6         atomic_t                count;
7         rwlock_t                lock;
8         int                     umask;
```

```
9          struct dentry              *root, *pwd, *altroot;
10         struct vfsmount            *rootmnt, *pwdmnt, *altrootmnt;
11   }
```

Figure 2.20   File system information

6   the `count` field is a reference count of processes pointing to this structure.

7   the `lock` field is a spinlock for mutual exclusion on accesses to this structure.

8   the file creation mask for the process is held in `umask`; all new files created by this process will have the permissions specified in this mask, by default.

9   the `root` field points to a structure representing the root directory, and `pwd` points to a similar structure representing the current working directory. The `altroot` field points to the alternative root directory. The current root directory is saved here by the `chroot()` system service.

10   the final three fields, `rootmnt`, `pwdmnt`, and `altrootmnt` point to the `vfsmount` structure representing the filesystem to which the root directory, current working directory, and alternate root directory, respectively, belong.

Note that `fs` is a pointer field, so this structure can be shared by different processes. It would be more typical for it to be shared by all the threads in a process, by specifying the `CLONE_FS` flag. As all of this is I/O-specific, it will not be dealt with any further in this book.

Line 391: `files`

Figure 2.21, from `<linux/sched.h>`, shows the format of an open file descriptor table for a process. It contains information about the I/O streams that this process has open. Most of the information about an individual open stream is actually contained in another structure, a `struct file`. The `files_struct` essentially gathers together the pointers to all the instances of `struct file` belonging to this process.

```
172  struct files_struct{
173      atomic_t                count;
174      rwlock_t                file_lock;
175      int                     max_fds;
176      int                     max_fdset;
177      int                     next_fd;
178      struct file             ** fd;
179      fd_set                  *close on exec;
180      fd_set                  *open_fds;
181      fd_set                  close_on_exec_init;
182      fd_set                  open_fds_init;
183      struct file             * fd_array[NR_OPEN_DEFAULT];
184  };
```

Figure 2.21   Open file table structure

173   the `count` field is a reference count of processes pointing to this structure (i.e. sharing their parents' open files).

174   the `file_lock` field is a spinlock, which provides mutual exclusion on this structure.

175   the `max_fds` field is the maximum number of files that this structure can track. It is created with a default number, `BITS_PER_LONG`, which is 32 or 64, depending on the architecture. However, this can be extended, if required.

176   `max_fdset` is the number of bits in the `fd_set` type. This is a bitmap with 1024 bits, as defined by POSIX.

177   `next_fd` is the index of the next file descriptor to be allocated. This is just a hint, for efficiency.

178   `fd` is initialised pointing to `fd_array[0]` (see line 183). If the number of open files grows beyond `NR_OPEN_DEFAULT`, a larger array of pointers to `struct file` is allocated and linked from `fd`.

179   the `close_on_exec` field is initialised pointing to `close_on_exec_init` (line 181). If provision is later made for more open files, a larger bitmap is linked from here.

180   the `open_fds` field is initialised pointing to `open_fds_init` (line 182). If provision is later made for more open files, a larger bitmap is linked from here.

181   the field `close_on_exec_init` is a bit map, with each bit indicating whether the corresponding file is to be kept open across an `exec()` or not.

182   the `open_fds_init` field is another bitmap, indicating whether a particular stream is open or not.

183   each element in the array `fd_array[]` contains a pointer to the `struct file` representing an open file. This array is created to be a standard fixed size, but it can be extended while a process is running, by replacing it with a larger array.

Note that `files` is a pointer field, so this structure can be shared by different processes. It would be more typical for it to be shared by all the threads in a process, by specifying the `CLONE_FILES` flag. As all of this is I/O-specific it will not be dealt with any further in this book.

2.8 Signal handlers

Figure 2.22, shows various items of information from the `task_struct`, to do with the handling of signals, which is dealt with in Chapter 17–19.

```
393        spinlock_t                sigmask_lock;
394        struct signal_struct      *sig;
395
396        sigset_t                  blocked;
397        struct sigpending         pending;
398
```

```
399        unsigned long              sas_ss_sp;
400        size_t                     sas_ss_size;
401        int                        (*notifier)(void *priv);
402        void                       *notifier_data;
403        sigset_t                   *notifier_mask;
```

Figure 2.22   Signal handling information in the `task_struct`

Line 393: `sigmask_lock`

First there is a spinlock, which is used to guarantee mutual exclusion on the `blocked` and `pending` fields, which come below.

Line 394: `sig`

The `sig` field is a pointer to the array of signal handlers declared in this process.

Line 396: `blocked`

This bitmap identifies signals that the process has currently masked or switched off.

Line 397: `pending`

This is a `struct sigpending`; it identifies those signals that are pending to the process.

Lines 399–400: `sas_ss_sp`, `sas_ss_size`

Signal handling can be done by using an alternate stack; the `sas_ss_sp` field is used to hold the pointer into this stack, and `sas_ss_size` gives the size of this alternate stack segment (see Section 17.6).

Line 401: `notifier`

A device driver can set up this pointer to a function to be called when any of the signals specified in `notifier_mask` (line 403) is generated. The driver can then decide whether to ignore or handle this signal (see Section 17.5).

Line 402: `notifier_data`

This is a pointer to private data in the device driver that the `notifier()` routine uses to determine whether the signal should be blocked or not.

Line 403: `notifier_mask`

This is a pointer to a signal mask in the device driver, specifying the set of signals for which the driver's permission is needed before they can be handled.

2.9 Execution domain tracking

Figure 2.23 shows the last part of the `task_struct` – information that helps to keep track of different execution domains used by this process.

```
406      u32                    parent_exec_id;
407      u32                    self_exec_id;
408
409      spinlock_t             alloc_lock;

412      void                   *journal_info;
413  };
```

Figure 2.23 Execution domain tracking information in the `task_struct`

Line 406: `parent_exec_id`

This is the domain in which the parent was executing when this process was created by `fork()` (see Section 8.2.4).

Line 407: `self_exec_id`

This is the domain in which this process is currently executing. This and `parent_exec_id` are checked by `exit()` to see if either the exiting process or its parent have changed execution domains since `fork()` (see Section 9.2.1).

Line 409: `alloc_lock`

This is a spinlock taken out when allocating or deallocating resources such as mm, `files`, `fs`, or `tty`.

Line 412: `journal_info`

This is used by the journaling extension to the Ext2 file system and will not be considered any further here.

2.10 Conclusions

It is unlikely that the meaning or use of all of the fields in the `task_struct` will be obvious at first reading. It is introduced in full here because it is so fundamental also, this chapter will serve as a point to which the reader can refer when fields in this structure are encountered in subsequent chapters; and encountered they will be. There is hardly a section in the book that does not refer to some field or other in the `task_struct`, so it is fair to say that the full implications of this chapter will only be seen only in light of the remainder of the book.

3

Organising the task structures

We have seen how Linux keeps track of an individual process. At any given time there will be many processes in existence, and hence many task structures. How does an operating system keep track of all of these? One possibility would be to use a fixed size table, an array of `struct task_struct`. A process would be inserted in this array at a position corresponding to its `pid`. This has the advantage that the information relating to a particular process can be found immediately by indexing into this array. The downside is that the `task_struct` itself is quite a large structure; a table of such structures would take up a very significant amount of memory, and there can be quite a lot of waste space if there are only a few processes running and space has been allocated for hundreds. As well as that, such an arrangement means there is a maximum number of processes that can be running at one time.

Another possibility is to allocate space dynamically, as required, and only for as long as required, usually as a linked list, even doubly linked. This means that there is never too much or too little space allocated for process control blocks. The drawback is that you cannot index into such a linked list – you have to search it sequentially. This has to be done very frequently, so it represents a significant overhead.

Linux adopts a modified version of this second approach. The `task_struct` structures themselves are allocated dynamically, as required, and kept on a doubly linked list. We have seen the links `next_task` and `prev_task`. This list is headed by `init_task`, which is created at initialisation (see Section 3.3.1), but, to avoid the overhead of searching such a sequential list, the structures are also kept on a hash table, which facilitates fast lookup.

3.1 Manipulating the linked list of task structures

This section examines the sequential list. There are three macros defined in `<linux/sched.h>` that manipulate the various links in a `task_struct`. One removes a structure, another inserts a structure, and a third follows the links from start to finish.

The Linux Process Manager. The Internals of Scheduling, Interrupts and Signals   John O'Gorman
© 2003 John Wiley & Sons, Ltd   ISBN: 0 470 84771 9

3.1.1 Removing a `task_struct`

The macro shown in Figure 3.1, from `<linux/sched.h>`, removes a descriptor p from the process structure, and from lists of siblings. Note that it does nothing about mutual exclusion. Any functions that use this macro have to guarantee they have taken out a write lock on the `tasklist_lock` (as defined in Section 7.22) beforehand.

```
847  #define REMOVE_LINKS(p) do {                                    \
848        (p)->next_task->prev_task = (p)->prev_task;              \
849        (p)->prev_task->next_task = (p)->next_task;              \
850        if ((p)->p_osptr)                                        \
851            (p)->p_osptr->p_ysptr = (p)->p_ysptr;                \
852        if ((p)->p_ysptr)                                        \
853            (p)->p_ysptr->p_osptr = (p)->p_osptr;                \
854        else                                                     \
855            (p)->p_pptr->p_cptr = (p)->p_osptr;                  \
856  } while (0)
```

Figure 3.1   Macro to remove a `task_struct`

847   the parameter is a pointer to the `task_struct` to be removed.

848–849   the first two lines remove the `task_struct` from the doubly linked list. Figure 3.2 shows the situation before and after these two lines are executed.

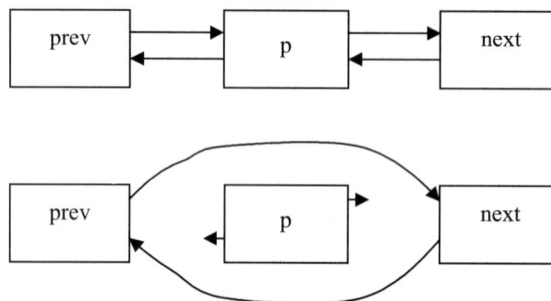

Figure 3.2   Removing a `task_struct` from the process list

850–851   if there is an older sibling, then this changes its pointer to jump over the one being removed. The reason for the 'if' here is because the `p_osptr` field may be NULL. This cannot happen with the `prev_task` and `next_task` pointers, as these maintain a circular linked list, with no NULL pointer. If there is no younger sibling, then p->ysptr will be NULL; the older sibling will then end up with a NULL pointer.

852–853   if there is a younger sibling, then this changes its back pointer to jump over the one being removed.

854–855   if there is no younger sibling, line 855 changes the parent to point to the next youngest.

Figure 3.3 shows the situation before and after lines 850–853 are executed. Figure 3.4 shows the situation before and after line 855 is executed.

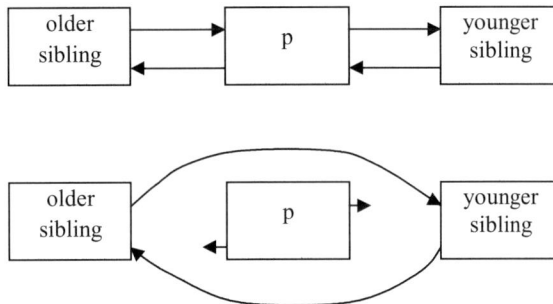

Figure 3.3   Removing a `task_struct` from the sibling list

855:   otherwise this one must be the youngest, so change the parent to point to the next youngest. Figure 3.4 shows the situation before and after line 855 is executed.

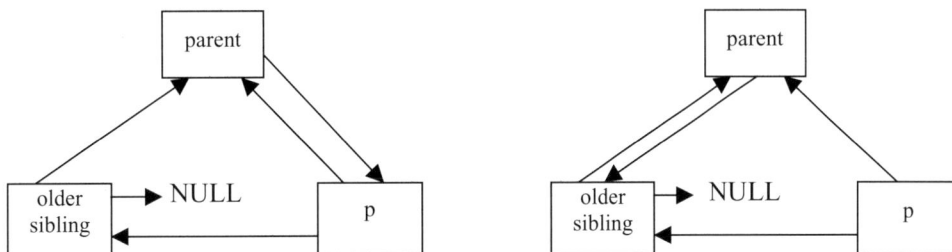

Figure 3.4   Removing a youngest child from the family tree

For the unexpected do . . while construct in this macro, see Section 1.2.1.3.

3.3.2   Inserting a `task_struct`

The macro shown in Figure 3.5, from `<linux/sched.h>`, inserts a process p in the process list, and in the sibling structure. The comments made about mutual exclusion in Section 3.1.1 apply here also.

```
858  #define SET_LINKS(p) do {                                        \
859      (p)->next_task = &init_task;                                 \
860      (p)->prev_task = init_task.prev_task;                        \
861      init_task.prev_task->next_task = (p);                        \
862      init_task.prev_task = (p);                                   \
863      (p)->p_ysptr = NULL;                                         \
864      if (((p)->p_osptr = (p)->p_pptr->p_cptr) != NULL) \
865          (p)->p_osptr->p_ysptr = p;                               \
866      (p)->p_pptr->p_cptr = p;                                     \
867  } while (0)
```

Figure 3.5   Macro to insert a new `task_struct`

859   as this new task is the last in the list, its `next_task` pointer always points back to the first `init_task`.

860   its `prev_task` should point to the one that was last – this was previously pointed to by the `prev_task` field in `init_task`.

861   the forward pointer in the previous last task (identified by the back pointer in `init_task`) is now set to point to p.

862   finally, the back pointer in `init_task` is set to p.

863–866   these lines set up the family links for this new process.

863   the new process has no younger sibling.

864   this copies the child pointer from the parent to the older sibling field of the new structure. This may be NULL if this new process is the only child process.

865   if there is an older sibling, then this points its younger sibling field to this new process.

866   in any case, this new process is set up here as the youngest child of its parent.

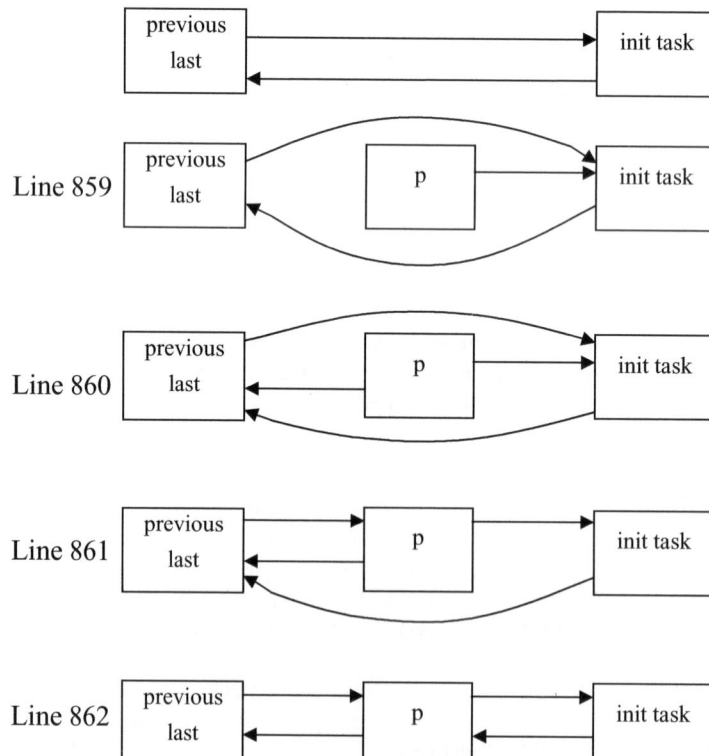

Figure 3.6   Inserting a `task_struct` into the process list

The top row in Figure 3.6 shows the situation at the beginning of this macro. Each successive row shows the change resulting from the corresponding line of code. The top row in Figure 3.7 shows the situation prior to lines 863–866. Again, each successive row shows the change resulting from the corresponding line of code.

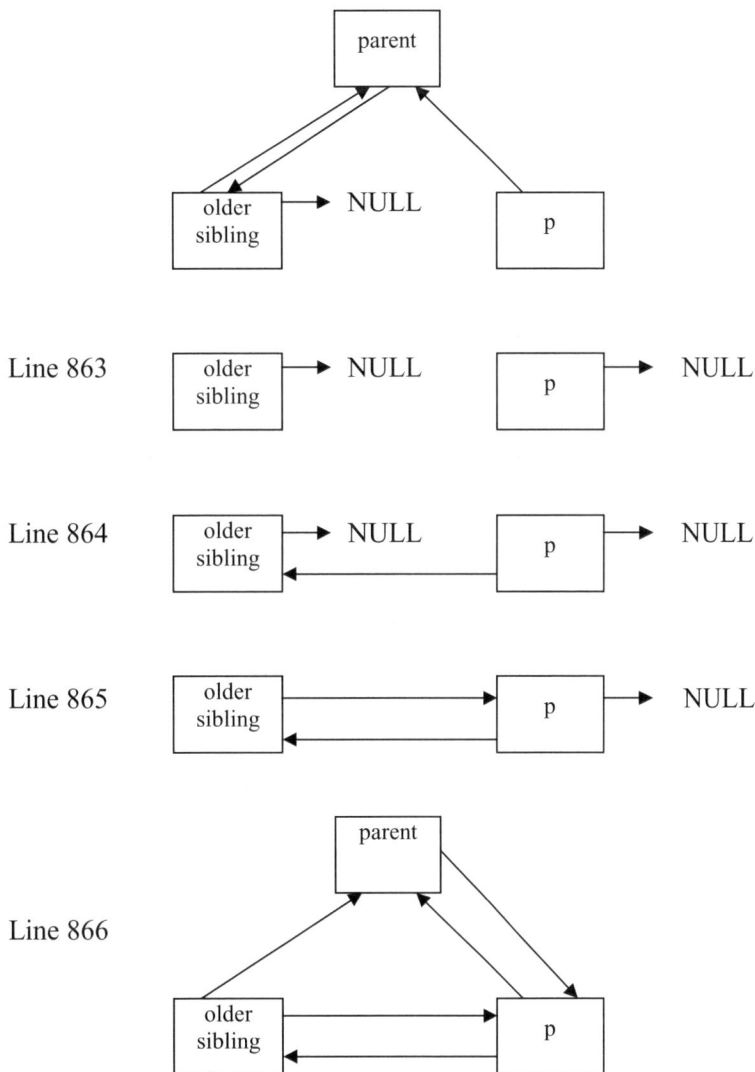

Figure 3.7 Inserting a `task_struct` into the family tree

3.1.3 Searching the process list

The macro shown in Figure 3.8, from `<linux/sched.h>`, works its way through the entire process list. Beginning with the first process, it advances the pointer p each time, until it is back at the first process again. Typically, it is used to search for a particular process, after which it jumps out of the loop. Examples of its use will be found throughout the kernel.

```
870  #define for_each_task(p)                                              \
871       for (p = &init_task ; (p = p->next_task) != &init_task;)
```

Figure 3.8   Macro to search entire process list

3.2   The hash table for task structures

As all the data structures representing processes (task_struct) are on a doubly linked list, any one can be found by searching the list linearly. This method can be time-consuming, particularly if there are a large number of processes. So, to speed things up, all the structures are also kept on hash lists, hashed on the pid of the process, and linked through the pidhash_next and pidhash_pprev fields of the task_struct. This section examines the hash structure itself, the hash function used, and how this whole mechanism is used to search for the task_struct representing a particular process.

3.2.1   The process hash table

An overview of the two sets of links holding the task_struct structures together, including the pidhash[] table, is shown in Figure 3.9. For simplicity, only the forward links are shown. The pidhash[] table is declared in kernel/fork.c as

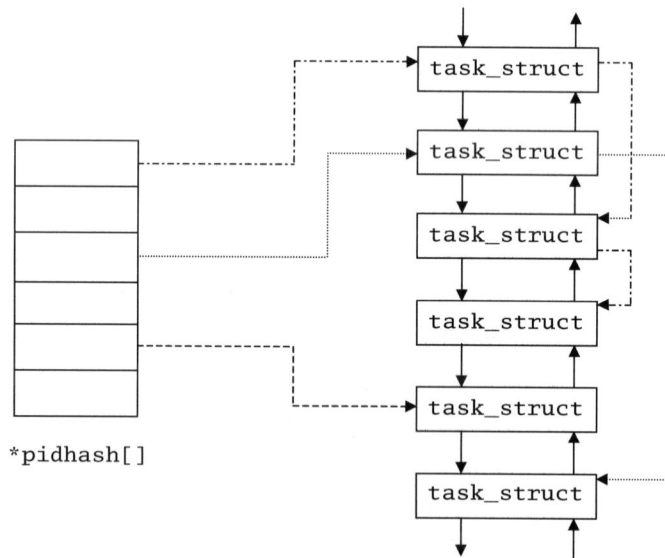

Figure 3.9   The process hash table

```
37       struct task_struct *pidhash[PIDHASH_SZ];
```

The constant PIDHASH_SZ is defined in < linux/sched.h > as:

```
522        #define PIDHASH_SZ (4096 >> 2)
```

so this table has 1024 entries. The hash table is initialised to NULL values by the function `sched_init()` (see Section 1.3.2).

3.2.2 The hash function

A simple hash function is used to spread entries evenly over this table. It is defined in <`linux/sched.h`> as:

```
525        #define pid_hashfn(x) ((((x) >> 8) ^ (x)) & (PIDHASH_SZ - 1))
```

The first part of the function tries to avoid clustering. The parameter x, the `pid`, is of type `pid_t`, which is architecture-specific, but is generally defined as an `int`, or 32 bits. However, the pid allocator uses only the low-order 16 bits of this `int`. The structure of a `pid` is shown in the top row of Figure 3.10.

x				
	zero		high byte	low byte

x>>8			
	zero		high byte

(x>>8)^x			
	zero	high byte	random

Figure 3.10 Hashing a pid

The result after shifting this right 8 bits is shown in the middle of Figure 3.10. The result of the XOR between the two of them is shown at the bottom of Figure 3.10. Performing an XOR between the low byte and the high byte produces a fairly random least-significant 8 bits.

The bitwise AND (&) in the hash function guarantees that the result will not be greater than the number of slots in the hash table, as it effectively strips off all but the 10 low-order bits. PIDHASH_SZ – 1 is 1023, or 11 1111 1111.

Because pids are given out more or less consecutively, the high byte will tend to be the same over a range of processes. The bitwise AND ignores the six most significant bits of this; these are the six most likely to be different. Despite all this, it would seem that in most cases just taking the 10 least-significant bits of the `pid` would give an adequate spread over the `pidhash[]` table.

3.2.3 Insert a `task_struct` into the hash table

Figure 3.11 from <`linux/sched.h`> shows the function `hash_pid()`, which inserts a given `task_struct` at the appropriate place in this hash table.

```
526  static inline void hash_pid(struct task_struct *p)
527  {
528       struct task_struct **htable =
529                          &pidhash[pid_hashfn(p->pid)];
```

```
530        if((p->pidhash_next = *htable) != NULL)
531            (*htable)->pidhash_pprev = &p->pidhash_next;
532        *htable = p;
533        p->pidhash_pprev = htable;
534  }
```

Figure 3.11   Function to insert a `task_struct` into the hash table

528–529   working from right to left, this hashes the `pid` to an index into the array (using the function from Section 0), and the variable `htable` is initialised to point to that entry in the hash table. At this stage `htable` points to a pointer to the first entry in the appropriate chain (see the top of Figure 3. 12).

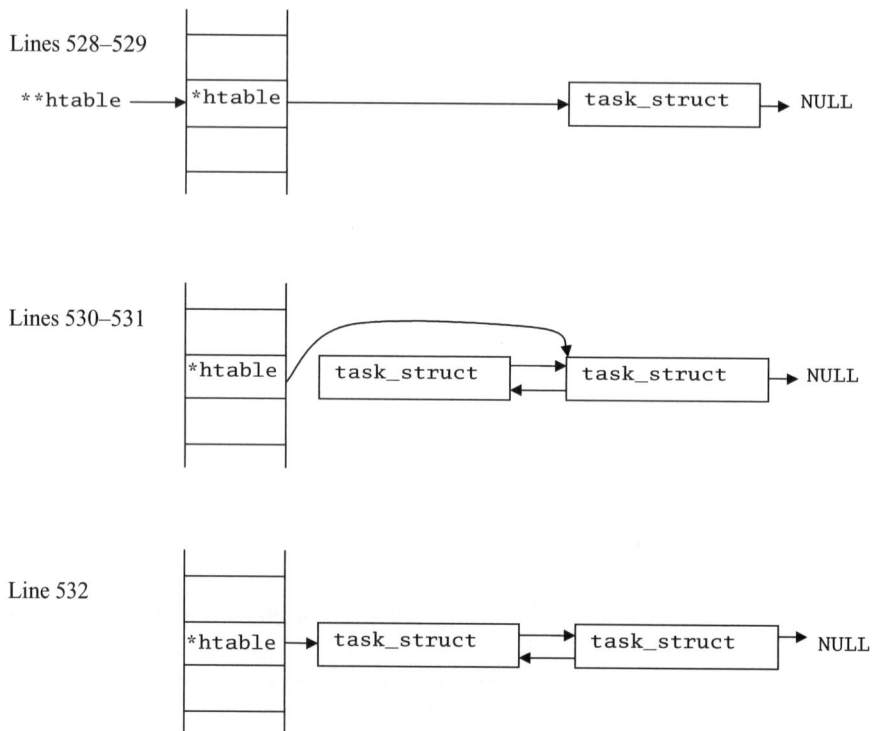

Figure 3.12   Inserting a `task_struct`

530–531   the new `task_struct` is always inserted at the head of the chain. Remember that `*htable` is the pointer in the hash table, pointing to the first entry in the chain. The value from that entry in the hash table (the head of the chain) is copied into the `pidhash_next` field of the new `task_struct`. Then, if it is a valid pointer, implying that there is at least one entry in that chain beforehand, the `pprev` pointer of the old first entry is set to point to the `pidhash_next` field of the new entry (remember that `pprev` is declared as an indirect pointer); see the middle of Figure 3.12.

532   whether there is a previous entry on the chain or not, this sets the header entry to point to the new `task_struct`; see the bottom of Figure 3.12.

533   finally, the `pprev` entry in the new `task_struct` is set to point to whatever `htable` is pointing to – the head of the chain.

3.2.4   Remove a `task_struct` from the hash table

Figure 3.13, from `<linux/sched.h>`, shows the function that unlinks a `task_struct` from the hash table. It is only ever called from `unhash_process()` (see Section 9.4.2.3).

```
536  static inline void unhash_pid(struct task_struct *p)
537  {
538        if(p->pidhash_next)
539             p->pidhash_next->pidhash_pprev = p->pidhash_pprev;
540        *p->pidhash_pprev = p->pidhash_next;
541  }
```

Figure 3.13   Remove a `task_struct` from the hash table

536   the parameter is a pointer to the `task_struct` to be removed from the table.

538–539   if the parameter is not the last entry on its chain, the back pointer of its successor is set to point to its predecessor.

540   the forward pointer of the predecessor of the parameter is always set to point to its successor. If it is the only entry on its chain, this will in fact be equal to the header entry in the hash table entry, now pointing to NULL.

Note that `pidhash_pprev` is declared as an indirect pointer in Section 2.3. It does not point to the beginning of the previous entry, but to the link field in that entry, which is itself a pointer field (see Figure 3.14).

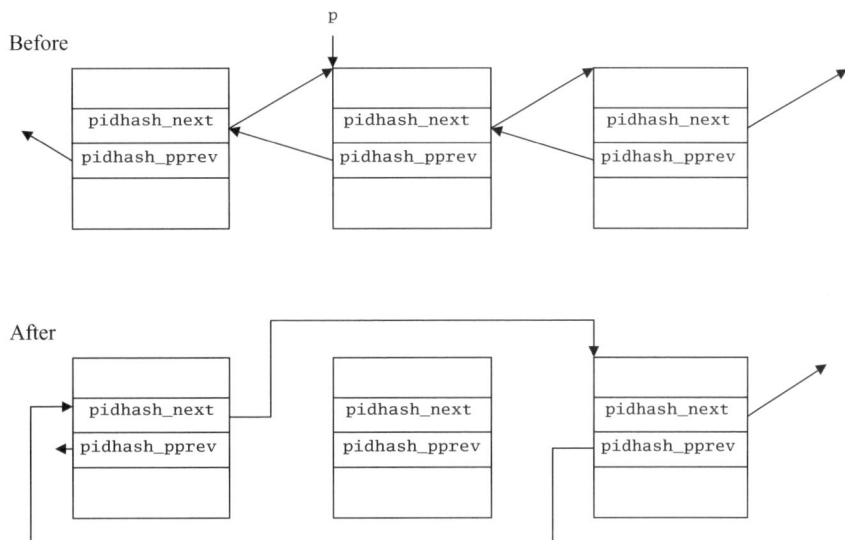

Figure 3.14   Adjusting pointers in a hash chain

3.2.5   Finding a `task_struct` using the hash table

Figure 3.15, from < linux/sched. shows the function that finds the `task_struct` corresponding to a particular `pid`.

```
543   static inline struct task_struct *find_task_by_pid(int pid)
544   {
545         struct task_struct *p,
546                           **htable = &pidhash[pid_hashfn(pid)];
547         for(p = *htable; p && p->pid != pid;
548             p = p->pidhash_next);
549
550         return p;
551   }
```

Figure 3.15   Function to find an entry in the hash table

545–546   these hash the `pid` supplied, use the result to index into the hash table, and take the address of the head pointer of the corresponding chain into `htable`.

547–548   the `for` loop works its way along the chain. It starts by putting the value in the hash table, pointing to the first entry on the chain, into p. Each time around it advances p to the next entry. It continues looping as long as p is a valid pointer (i.e. as long as it is not the last entry in the chain) *and* as long as the structure to which p is pointing is not the one being sought.

550   this returns p, which is a pointer either to the `task_struct` required or (if the `pid` supplied is invalid) is NULL .

There is no error checking; if `pid` is invalid, it will return a NULL pointer.

3.3   Setting up the initial process

In a UNIX environment, all new processes are created as clones of their parent process. The operating system creates a new `task_struct`, and copies values to it from the `task_struct` of its parent. That just leaves the question of the very first process. Where do its values come from?

3.3.1   The `task_union` of the initial process

The `task_struct` for the first process is set up statically (i.e. it is built by the compiler from declarations in the source code). As with all processes, memory space for this initial process is not allocated on its own. It is always allocated as part of a `union`, the other part of which is an array of `unsigned long`, which will be used as the kernel stack space for this process (see Figure 3.16, from `<linux/sched.h>`).

```
506   #ifndef INIT_TASK_SIZE
507   #define INIT_TASK_SIZE 2048*sizeof(long)
508   #endif
```

```
509
510  union task_union {
511      struct task_struct task;
512      unsigned long stack[INIT_TASK_SIZE/sizeof(long];
513  };
```

Figure 3.16   Allocation of `task_struct` and `stack`

506–508   as a `long` is 4 bytes, this is 8k, or 2 pages.

510–513   note this is a `union`. These areas do not come one after the other – they coincide.

An instance of this `task_union` is declared in the architecture-dependent file `arch/i386/kernel/init_task.c`. It is named `init_task_union` (see Figure 3.17, from `arch/i386/kernel/init_task.c`).

```
21   union task_union init_task_union
22       __attribute__((__section__(".data.init_task"))) =
23           { INIT_TASK(init_task_union.task) };
```

Figure 3.17   The initial task structure.

22   this structure needs to be 8192-byte aligned, because of the way process stacks are handled. This is done by having a special `".data.init_task"` linker map entry, which instructs the linker to align this section on an 8192-byte boundary.

23   the `task` part of the `union` is initialised using the `INIT_TASK` macro, which will be discussed in detail in the next section.

Now that an initial `task_struct` has been declared and initialised, in `<asm-i386/processor.h>` the directives

```
455  #define init_task              (init_task_union.task)
456  #define init_stack             (init_task_union.stack)
```

name the `task_struct` part of this union as `init_task`, under which guise it continues as the root of the linked list of `task_struct` in the system. The stack part of this union is named as `init_stack`.
In an SMP situation, each processor needs an `init_task` of its own. These are accessed through an array of pointers, declared in `kernel/sched.c` as:

```
79 struct task_struct * init_tasks[NR_CPUS] = {&init_task, };
```

The entry for the boot processor is the `task_struct` just set up. Other processors will add their own entries as they are booted.

3.3.2 The `task_struct` of the initial process

The macro shown in Figure 3.18, from `<linux/sched.h>`, initialises values for those fields of the initial `task_struct` that require initialisation. The format used here to specify initial values is not standard C; it is a gcc extension. Note that only the specified fields are initialised. Other fields default to 0. In particular, the `pid` field has a value of 0. Because it is statically declared, this `task_struct` is already in existence when the scheduler is started. The scheduler treats it as just another process.

```
462   #define INIT_TASK(tsk)                                        \
463   {                                                             \
464       state                     0,                             \
465       flags                     0,                             \
466       sigpending                0,                             \
467       addr_limit                KERNEL_DS,                     \
468       exec_domain               &default_exec_domain,          \
469       lock_depth                -1,                            \
470       counter                   DEF_COUNTER,                   \
471       nice                      DEF_NICE,                      \
472       policy                    SCHED_OTHER,                   \
473       mm                        NULL,                          \
474       active_mm                 &init_mm,                      \
475       cpus_runnable             -1,                            \
476       cpus_allowed              -1,                            \
477       run_list                  LIST_HEAD_INIT                 \
                                        (tsk.run_list),            \
478       next_task                 &tsk,                          \
479       prev_task                 &tsk,                          \
480       p_opptr                   &tsk,                          \
481       p_pptr                    &tsk,                          \
482       thread_group              LIST_HEAD_INIT                 \
                                        (tsk.thread_group),        \
483       wait_chldexit             __WAIT_QUEUE_HEAD_             \
                                           INITIALIZER             \
                                        (tsk.wait_chldexit),       \
484       real_timer {                                             \
485           function              it_real_fn                     \
486       },                                                       \
487       cap_effective             CAP_INIT_EFF_SET,              \
488       cap_inheritable           CAP_INIT_INH_SET,              \
489       cap_permitted             CAP_FULL_SET,                  \
490       keep_capabilities:        0,                             \
491       rlim                      INIT_RLIMITS,                  \
492       user                      INIT_USER,                     \
493       comm                      "swapper",                     \
494       thread                    INIT_THREAD,                   \
495       fs                        &init_fs,                      \
496       files                     &init_files,                   \
497       sigmask_lock              SPIN_LOCK_UNLOCKED,            \
```

```
498       sig                     &init_signals,          \
499       pending                 { NULL,&tsk.
                                    pending.head,{{0}}}, \
500       blocked                 {{0}},                  \
501       alloc_lock              SPIN_LOCK_UNLOCKED,     \
502       journal_info            NULL                    \
503  }
```

Figure 3.18   Initial values for `task_struct`

464   the `state` of the process is set to TASK_RUNNING (see the definition of states in Section 2.1).

465   the flags field is set to 0; this means that no flags are set, not even PF_STARTING.

466   to indicate that no signal has yet been posted to the process, `sigpending` is set to 0.

467   the address space limit is set to KERNEL DS. This is architecture-specific but is typically set to 0x FFFF FFFF, or 4 GB.

468   the execution domain is set to the default; this will be discussed in Section 21.2.2.

469   the value of `lock_depth` is initialised to −1. This is not the actual kernel lock itself; it is merely an indication of whether this process is holding the kernel lock. A value of −1 means that it is not holding the lock; a value of 0 or greater means that it is.

470   the `counter` field is the time-slice of the process, in ticks, and it is set to the default value. This is defined in <linux/sched.h> as:

```
449       #define DEF_COUNTER (10 * HZ/100)
```

For HZ of 100, this is 10. As the clock ticks every 10 ms, this gives an initial time-slice of 100 ms.

471   the default value of `nice` is defined in <linux/sched.h> as:

```
451       #define DEF_NICE (0)
```

472   the `init` process is given the normal time-sharing scheduling policy, SCHED_OTHER.

473   the `init` process does not have a memory map of its own, so the mm pointer is set to NULL.

474   this is a pointer to the `struct mm_struct` that it is to use when running. It is set up to use an architecture-specific page table, `swapper_pg_dir`, so it is effectively running the swapper program. This will not be considered any further.

475–476   as both of these fields are `unsigned long`, this sets them to 1s, meaning that this process is not currently assigned a CPU, but that it can run on any CPU.

477   the LIST_HEAD_INIT() macro is defined in Section 4.3.1. It merely sets both the forward and backwards pointers in the `struct list_head` to point to itself. The scheduler will adjust these links when it puts it on the runqueue.

478–479   as it is the only process at this stage, all the links point to it.

480–481   for the same reason (see lines 478–479), the process is set up as its own parent.

482   as it is not part of any thread group, the forward and backward pointers in the `list_head` are initialised to point to itself.

483   the macro will be discussed in Section 4.1.2.2; it initialises the wait queue headed from `wait_chldexit`.

484–486   the function field in the `struct timer_list` is initialised to point to the function `it_real_fn()`. This function will be considered in Section 15.3.3.3.

487–489   the three capabilities are set to these default values. They will be dealt with in Section 20.2.2.

490   this indicates capabilities are not to be inherited across an `exec()`.

491   the `rlim[]` array is initialised to the values defined by `INIT_RLIMITS` (see Section 3.3.3). Remember that each entry is a `struct rlimit`, which has two fields.

492:   `INIT_USER` is defined in `<linux/sched.h>` as:

```
279      #define INIT_USER (&root_user)
```

The whole area of the user cache is dealt with in Section 8.4, including the initialisation of a `user_struct` called `root_user` (Section 8.4.2).

493   the name of the program it is running is `"swapper"`. The actual code was linked in by the assignment at line 474.

494   `INIT_THREAD` is architecture-specific; its definition will be considered in Section 3.3.4.

495–496   this is a pointer to the initialised values for the `struct fs_struct` and the `struct files_struct`. These are architecture-specific, and are not relevant here.

497   the spinlock controlling access to the signal mask is initialised to the unlocked state [see Sections 5.3 (uniprocessor) and 5.4 (multiprocessor) for definitions of the macro].

498   `init_signals` is a `struct signal_struct`, declared and initialised in `arch/i386/kernel/init_task.c` as:

```
11       static struct signal_struct init_signals = INIT_SIGNALS;
```

The `INIT_SIGNALS` macro is from Section 17.1.3.2.

499   the `struct sigpending` that is being initialised here will be discussed in detail in Section 17.1.4.1; basically, it is set up with no signals pending.

500   the `blocked` bitmap is set to 0, meaning that no signals are blocked.

501   the spinlock protecting resource allocation is initialised to the unlocked state [see Sections 5.3 (uniprocessor case) and 5.4 (multiprocessor case) for definitions of the macro].

502 this pointer, for the journaling file system, is set to NULL at his stage.

3.3.3 Resource limits for the initial process

Each `task_struct` contains an `rlim[]` array, as described in Section 2.5. In the `task_struct` of the initial process, this is initialised to the values defined by `INIT_RLIMITS`, as shown in Figure 3.1, from `<asm-i386/resource.h>`. Remember that each entry is a `struct rlimit`, which has two fields.

```
26    #define RLIM_INFINITY          (~0UL)

30    #define INIT_RLIMITS                                        \
31    {                                                           \
32          { RLIM_INFINITY,          RLIM_INFINITY },            \
33          { RLIM_INFINITY,          RLIM_INFINITY },            \
34          { RLIM_INFINITY,          RLIM_INFINITY },            \
35          {_STK_LIM,                RLIM_INFINITY },            \
36          {0,                       RLIM_INFINITY },            \
37          { RLIM_INFINITY,          RLIM_INFINITY },            \
38          {0,                                  0 },            \
39          {INR_OPEN,                     INR_OPEN },            \
40          { RLIM_INFINITY,          RLIM_INFINITY },            \
41          { RLIM_INFINITY,          RLIM_INFINITY },            \
42          { RLIM_INFINITY,          RLIM_INFINITY },            \
43    }
```

Figure 3.19 Initial values for resource limits

26 this is all 1s, the largest unsigned number.

32–34 values for CPU time, filesize, and data segment size are all unlimited.

35 stack size has a limit of _STK_LIM , but can be extended ad infinitum; _STK_LIM is defined as 8 Mb in `<linux/sched.h>`:

```
447    #define _STK_LIM          (8 * 1024 * 1024)
```

36 a core file has a working limit of 0, but there is no absolute limit.

37 the resident set size is unlimited.

38 the `init` process is not allowed to create any child processes.

99 the initial setting for the number of open files is defined in `<linux/fs.h>` as:

```
44    #define INR_OPEN 1024
```

40–42 the locked memory space, address space, and the number of file locks are unlimited.

3.3.4 The `thread` field of the initial process

The `thread` field of the initial `task_struct` is, of course, architecture-specific, as is its initialising macro. Figure 3.1, from < `asm-i386/processor.h` >, shows the initial values for the `thread_struct`. As can be seen, these are almost all zero, except for `io_bitmap`, which is initialised to all ones. This means that all input–output (I/O) addresses are accessible only to processes executing at I/O privilege level, or higher. Of course, these fields are filled with realistic values as this process runs.

```
386  #define INIT_THREAD {                                            \
387      0,                                                           \
388      0, 0, 0, 0,                                                  \
389      { [0 ... 7] = 0 },         /* debugging registers */        \
390      0, 0, 0,                                                     \
391      { { 0, }, },               /* 387 state */                   \
392      0,0,0,0,0,0,                                                 \
393      0, {~0,}                   /* io permissions */              \
394  }
```

Figure 3.20 Initialization of the `thread_struct`

3.4 The idle thread

It can happen that at a particular time the runqueue is empty. All the processes in the system may be blocked, waiting for some resource or other. To cater for such a situation, operating systems use a special *idle* thread. In Linux, this is not created as a new thread. Rather, when the booting of the machine is completed, the boot-up thread metamorphoses into the idle thread (and aims for immortality), by calling the function `cpu_idle()` (see Section 1.3.3).

3.4.1 Setting up the idle thread.

Figure 3.21, from `arch/i386/kernel/process.c`, is the function executed by the idle thread. There is no useful work to be done, so it tries to conserve power, halting the processor, waiting for something to happen.

```
123  void cpu_idle (void)
124  {
125
126      init_idle();
127      current->nice = 20;
128      current->counter = -100;
129
130      while (1) {
131          void (*idle)(void) = pm_idle;
132          if (!idle)
133              idle = default_idle;
134          while (!current->need_resched)
```

```
135                    idle();
136                schedule();
137                check_pgt_cache();
138          }
139  }
```

Figure 3.21   The idle thread

126   this function will be dealt with in Section 1.3.2. It merely initialises some fields specific to the CPU on which this thread is running.

127   this gives the idle thread the lowest possible priority. So it can never monopolise the CPU, as soon as any other process becomes runable the system will preempt the idle process, because the new process is guaranteed to have a higher priority.

128   a `counter` value of -100 means it will always be the last process to be scheduled.

130–138   the idle thread then enters this infinite loop.

131–133   these lines set up a pointer to the actual function to be executed in the loop.

131   it first tries to set this up as `pm_idle()`, the power management idle function.

132   if this function is not defined, it then sets it up as `default_idle()`. This will attempt to halt the processor (see Section 3.4.3).

134–135   as long as the `need_resched` flag of this idle thread is not set, the idle function, whatever it has been set to, is called over and over again. The flag will be set by the scheduler when some other process becomes ready.

136   if a reschedule is needed (because the `need_resched` flag was set), the scheduler is called, and this thread is context switched out. The `schedule()` function will be considered in detail in Section 7.3.

137   the next time the system becomes idle, the idle process is context switched in, and takes up here. This function checks the page table cache and trims it if it has grown too large, before continuing around the loop. It is part of the memory manager and will not be considered any further.

3.4.2   Initialise the idle thread

The function shown in Figure 3.22, from `kernel/sched.c`, is called from `cpu_idle()`, (see Section 3.4.1). It initialises some scheduler data structures for the current CPU.

```
1302      void __init init_idle(void)
1303 {
1304      struct schedule_data * sched_data;
1305      sched_data = &aligned_data[smp_processor_id()].schedule_data;
1306
1307      if (current != &init_task && task_on_runqueue(current)){
1308          printk("UGH! (%d:%d) was on the runqueue,
```

```
1309                    removing.\n", smp_processor_id(), current->pid);
1310            del_from_runqueue(current);
1311    }
1312    sched_data->curr = current;
1313    sched_data->last_schedule = get_cycles();
1314    clear_bit(current->processor, &wait_init_idle);
1315 }
```

Figure 3.22   Initialise the idle thread

1305   this takes a local pointer to the `schedule_data` field corresponding to this processor (see Section 7.2.4.1). The `smp_processor_id()` is a macro defined in Section 7.2.1.4. It returns the ID of the CPU executing this code.

1307–1311   this is a sanity check, just in case the function was called by some process other than `init`, which is on the runqueue. This should not happen.

1307   the `init_task` has been described in Section 3.3.1. The `task_on_runqueue()` function, (Section 4.8.4) determines whether a particular `task_struct` is linked on the runqueue or not.

1310   this function, described in Section 4.8.3, removes the `task_struct` from the runqueue.

1312–1313   these two assignments set up fields in the `aligned_data` array.

1313   the `get_cycles()` function returns a cumulative count of cycles for this CPU.

1314   the `clear_bit()` function is from Section 5.1.2. It clears the bit corresponding to the current processor in the `wait_init_idle` bitmap, indicating that the idle process has been initialised on that CPU.

3.4.3   The default idle function

The default idle function, executed by the idle thread, is shown in Figure 3.23, from `arch/i386/kernel/process.c`.

```
79    static void default_idle(void)
80    {
81        if (current_cpu_data.hlt_works_ok && !hlt_counter) {
82            __cli();
83            if (!current->need_resched)
84                safe_halt();
85            else
86                __sti()
87        }
88    }
```

Figure 3.23   The default idle function

81   if it is possible to halt the processor then that is done. Otherwise, we just return. The `hlt_works_ok` flag in the processor descriptor indicates whether this processor can be halted or not. Apart from that, `hlt_counter` is a flag that indicates whether halting the CPU is currently allowed or not.

82 this disables maskable interrupts, so that the test in the next line can be carried out safe from interrupts. These interrupts are enabled again either as part of the macro called in line 84, or at line 86. The `_cli()` macro is just a C wrapper for the assembler `CLI` instruction (see Section 12.8.2).

83 this checks the `need_resched` field of the current (idle) process, as it may have been set by an interrupt routine in the small time window between the test in `cpu_idle()` and disabling interrupts on the previous line.

84 if it has not been set, then enable interrupts, and halts the processor, until either the reset line is activated or a maskable interrupt is requested (see Section 12.8.2 for a description of this macro).

86 if the `need_resched` flag has been set, then interrupts are turned on again, and control returns to `cpu_idle()` (Section 3.4.1). This is just a C wrapper for the assembler `STI` instruction (see Section 12.8.2).

4

Wait queues

A process may, for some reason or other, be unable to use the CPU (central processing unit), even if it is free. In general, a process in this state is waiting for some event. This may be a physical resource, such as a printer or a modem, or it may be waiting for an event such as a key to be pressed or be waiting for requested data to be delivered from a disk.

In Linux, waiting processes are kept on wait queues, one per event. For example, a process waiting for keyboard input would be linked from a pointer in the data structure representing the keyboard. When a key is pressed, the interrupt handler searches the wait queue for the appropriate entry, which it then removes from the queue. From this it finds the `task_struct` representing the waiting process, changes its state to TASK_RUNNING, and moves it to the runqueue.

4.1 Wait queue data structures

There are two main data structures used here, one to represent a wait queue itself, and another to represent an individual entry in a wait queue. There are also a number of macros for checking the (optional) debugging fields in these structures.

4.1.1 Declaring and initialising wait queue entries

This section will examine the data structure used to represent an individual entry in a wait queue and how such entries are declared and initialised. Creating a new entry for a wait queue is quite a frequent event in the kernel, so there are a number of macros and functions provided for this purpose. One declares new entries; the other fills in fields in an existing entry.

4.1.1.1 Wait queue entry

To allow more than one process to wait on the same event, a link data structure `__wait_queue` is used (see Figure 4.1, from <linux/wait.h>). A wait queue then consists of a linked list of such structures.

The Linux Process Manager. The Internals of Scheduling, Interrupts and Signals   John O'Gorman
© 2003 John Wiley & Sons, Ltd   ISBN: 0 470 84771 9

```
31    struct __wait_queue {
32        unsigned int flags;
33    #define WQ_FLAG_EXCLUSIVE     0x01
34        struct task_struct * task;
35        struct list_head task_list;
36    #if WAITQUEUE_DEBUG
37        long __magic;
38        long __waker;
39    #endif
40    };
41    typedef struct __wait_queue wait_queue_t;
```

Figure 4.1   The wait_queue_t structure

32–33   WQ_FLAG_EXCLUSIVE is the only flag defined at present. It determines whether the process is waiting exclusively or nonexclusively. When a process is waiting exclusively, then it alone will be woken up. All processes waiting nonexclusively on a wait queue are woken at the same time (see __wake_up_common(), Section 4.7.3).

34   this is a pointer to the task_struct representing the waiting process.

35   this is the link field, which maintains a doubly linked list of these structures. The generic Linux list-handling data structures and functions are used for this (see Section 4.3).

36–39   these are debugging fields and are included only if the macro WAITQUEUE_DEBUG is defined. Their use will be seen in a number of places in the following sections (in particular, Section 4.1.3 describes macros that check these fields).

41   this structure is almost always referred to in the code as wait_queue_t.

4.1.1.2   Declaring and initialising a wait queue entry

Figure 4.2, from <linux/wait.h>, shows two macros that are used to declare and initialise new wait queue entries.

```
139    #define __WAITQUEUE_INITIALIZER(name, tsk) {                        \
140        task:                        tsk,                               \
141        task_list:                   { NULL, NULL },                    \
142                                     __WAITQUEUE_DEBUG_INIT(name) }
143
144    #define DECLARE_WAITQUEUE(name, tsk)                                \
145        wait_queue_t name = __WAITQUEUE_INITIALIZER(name, tsk)
```

Figure 4.2   Macro to initialise a wait queue

139–142   this macro is passed a wait_queue_t, and a pointer to a task_struct. It points the task field to the task_struct and initialises both fields of the struct list_head to NULL. Note that it does not initialise the flags field. This is done when the entry is added to the queue. The optional debug fields are initialised by the __WAITQUEUE_DEBUG_INIT() macro (see Section

4.1.3.1). There are two different forms of this, depending on whether debugging is switched on or not.

144–145 this macro is given a name for a wait queue entry and a pointer to a `task_struct`. It declares a variable of that name, of type `wait_queue_t`, and initialises it by calling `__WAITQUEUE_INITIALIZER()` from line 139.

4.1.1.3 Initialising an existing wait queue entry

The function shown in Figure 4.3, from `<linux/wait.h>`, initialises an existing wait queue entry.

```
169  static inline void init_waitqueue_entry (wait_queue_t *q,
                                               struct task_struct *p)
170  {
171  #if WAITQUEUE_DEBUG
172      if (!q || !p)
173          WQ_BUG();
174  #endif
175      q->flags = 0;
176      q->task = p;
177  #if WAITQUEUE_DEBUG
178      q->__magic = (long)&q->__magic;
179  #endif
180  }
```

Figure 4.3 Initialise an existing wait queue entry

169 the function is passed a pointer to a structure of type `wait_queue_t`, and a second pointer to the `task_struct` representing the process that is waiting.

172–173 these lines are compiled into the code only if in debug mode. If either of the pointers passed to the function is invalid, the function calls `WQ_BUG()` (see Section 4.1.3.2).

175 the `flags` field is initialised to 0.

176 This points the `task` field to the process that is waiting.

178 this code likewise is compiled only if in debug mode. The `magic` field now contains its own address, cast as a `long`. The use of this feature will be seen in Section 4.1.3.2. Note that the `__waker` field is not initialised. This is done when the process is woken up (see Section 4.7.3).

4.1.2 Wait queue headers

A data structure of type `__wait_queue_head` is used to represent the head of a wait queue. Creating a whole new wait queue is a common enough event in the kernel, so there are a number of macros and functions provided for this: one to create a new header, another to initialise an existing header to the empty state.

4.1.2.1 Wait queue head

A wait queue is always headed by a `struct __wait_queue_head`, as shown in Figure 4.4, from `<linux/wait.h>`.

```
77   struct __wait_queue_head {
78       wq_lock_t lock;
79       struct list_head task_list;
80   #if WAITQUEUE_DEBUG
81       long __magic;
82       long __creator;
83   #endif
84   };
85   typedef struct __wait_queue_head wait_queue_head_t;
```

Figure 4.4 The wait queue header

78 this is a lock used when manipulating the wait queue (see Section 4.4).

79 this is the header of the doubly linked list of entries. It is a generic list header, as described in Section 4.3.1.

80–82 these are debugging fields. These are included only if the macro `WAITQUEUE_DEBUG` is defined. Their use will be seen in a number of places in the following sections. Section 4.1.3 in particular describes macros that check these fields.

85 this structure is almost always referred to in the code as `wait_queue_head_t`.

To show how this structure and the one described in Section 4.1.1.1 fit together, the situation where three processes are waiting for a particular event is illustrated in Figure 4.5. One of these processes is also shown as being on two wait queues. This illustrates the whole reason for using these structures, as opposed to linking wait queues directly through the `task_struct`, in which case a process could only be on one wait queue at a time.

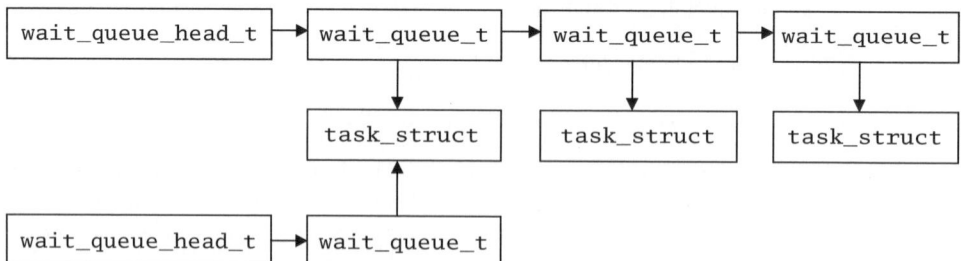

Figure 4.5 Three processes waiting for events

4.1.2.2 Declaring and initialising a wait queue head

Figure 4.6, from `<linux/wait.h>`, shows two macros that are used to declare and initialise the head of a wait queue.

```
147  #define __WAIT_QUEUE_HEAD_INITIALIZER(name){        \
148      lock:              WAITQUEUE_RW_LOCK_UNLOCKED,  \
149      task_list:         { &(name).task_list,
                            &(name).task_list},          \
150                  __WAITQUEUE_HEAD_DEBUG_INIT(name)}
151
152  #define DECLARE_WAIT_QUEUE_HEAD(name)               \
153  wait_queue_head_t name = __WAIT_QUEUE_HEAD_INITIALIZER(name)
```

Figure 4.6 Initialise a wait queue head

147–150 this macro is passed a `wait_queue_head_t` and initialises it to the empty state.

148 the `lock` field is initialised to `WAITQUEUE_RW_LOCK_UNLOCKED` (see Section 4.4 on wait queue locks).

149 both pointer fields of the `task_list` (a `struct list_head`) are initialised pointing to the `task_list` field itself, as is standard for lists linked by these generic pointer fields.

150 the optional debug fields are initialised by the `__WAITQUEUE_HEAD_DEBUG_INIT()` macro (see Section 4.1.3.1). There are two different forms of this, depending on whether debugging is switched on or not.

152–153 this macro is given a name for a wait queue, and it declares a variable of that name, of type `wait_queue_head_t`, and initialises it by calling `__WAITQUEUE_HEAD_INITIALIZER()` from line 147.

4.1.2.3 *Initialising an existing wait queue head*

The function shown in Figure 4.7, from `<linux/wait.h>`, is passed a pointer to an existing structure of type `wait_queue_head_t`, and initialises it to the empty state.

```
155  static inline void init_waitqueue_head(wait_queue_head_t *q)
156  {
157  #if WAITQUEUE_DEBUG
158      if (!q)
159          WQ_BUG();
160  #endif
161      q->lock = WAITQUEUE_RW_LOCK_UNLOCKED;
162      INIT_LIST_HEAD(&q->task_list);
163  #if WAITQUEUE_DEBUG
164      q->__magic = (long)&q->__magic;
165      q->__creator = (long)current_text_addr();
166  #endif
167  }
```

Figure 4.7 Initialise an existing wait queue head

157–160 this code is compiled only if in debug mode. If the pointer it was passed is invalid, it calls WQ_BUG() (see Section 4.1.3.2).

161 this initialises the `lock` field of the header to the unlocked state (see Section 4.4).

162 this is the generic list head initialiser, called to initialise the `task_list` field in the header (see Section 4.3.1).

163–166 This code is compiled only if in debug mode.

164 The `magic` field now contains its own address, cast as a `long`.

165 the `creator` field contains the address of the next instruction after this assignment statement, cast as a `long`. The macro is defined in `<asm-i386/processor.h>` as

```
25    #define current_text_addr()
              ({ void *pc; __asm__("movl $1f,%0\n1:":"=g" (pc)); pc; })
```

The MOVL moves the address of the label `1:` into parameter 0, the variable `pc`. This label is at the next address in the code after the MOVL, so the value in `pc` is the address of the next instruction to be executed. The `"=g"` constraint specifies that the variable `pc` can be in memory, or a register that is not a general purpose register. The macro evaluates to the value in `pc`.

4.1.3 Debugging code

In the foregoing sections it has been seen that there are a number of debugging fields that can be included in the wait queue data structures. Here, the macros that initialise and check these fields are examined.

4.1.3.1 *Initialising the debugging fields*

Figure 4.8, from `<linux/wait.h>`, gives the definitions of the initialising macros.

```
131  #if WAITQUEUE_DEBUG
132  # define __WAITQUEUE_DEBUG_INIT(name) (long)&(name).__magic, 0
133  # define __WAITQUEUE_HEAD_DEBUG_INIT(name)
                           (long)&(name).__magic, (long)&(name).__magic
134  #else
135  # define __WAITQUEUE_DEBUG_INIT(name)
136  # define __WAITQUEUE_HEAD_DEBUG_INIT(name)
137  #endif
```

Figure 4.8 Initialising the debugging fields

132–133 these are the definitions when debugging is switched on.

132 this macro is only ever used as part of the initialisation of a `wait_queue_t` structure. The `__magic` field is initialised to contain its own address, cast to be a `long`; the `__waker` field is initialised to 0.

133 this macro is only ever used as part of the initialisation of a `wait_queue_head_t` structure.

Both the __magic field and the __creator field are initialised to contain the address of the __magic field, cast to be a long.

135–136   these are the definitions when debugging is not switched on. The macros are defined, but they do nothing.

4.1.3.2   Checking the magic fields

Figure 4.9, from <linux/wait.h>, shows the macros that check these debugging fields.

```
92   #if WAITQUEUE_DEBUG
93   #define WQ_BUG() BUG()
94   #define CHECK_MAGIC(x)                                              \
95   do {                                                               \
96        if ((x) != (long)&(x)) {                                      \
97             printk("bad magic %lx (should be %lx),",                 \
98        (long)x, (long)&(x));                                         \
99             WQ_BUG();                                                \
100       }                                                             \
101  } while (0)
102  #define CHECK_MAGIC_WQHEAD(x)                                       \
103  do {                                                               \
104       if ((x)->__magic != (long)&((x)->__magic)) {                 \
105            printk("bad magic %lx (should be %lx,
                                        creator %lx),",  \
106            (x)->__magic, (long)&((x)->__magic),
                                        (x)->__creator);  \
107            WQ_BUG();                                                \
108       }                                                             \
109  } while (0)
110  #define WQ_CHECK_LIST_HEAD(list)                                    \
111  do {                                                               \
112       if (!(list)->next || !(list)->prev)                           \
113            WQ_BUG();                                                \
114  } while(0)
115  #define WQ_NOTE_WAKER(tsk)                                          \
116  do {                                                               \
117       (tsk)->__waker =(long)__builtin_return_address
                                        (0);  \
118  } while (0)
119  #else
120  #define WQ_BUG()
121  #define CHECK_MAGIC(x)
122  #define CHECK_MAGIC_WQHEAD(x)
123  #define WQ_CHECK_LIST_HEAD(list)
124  #define WQ_NOTE_WAKER(tsk)
125  #endif
```

Figure 4.9   Checking the magic fields

93–118   these are the definitions when debugging is switched on.

93   the BUG() macro is from Section 4.1.3.3.

94–101   this macro checks the __magic field in a wait_queue_t structure. Its parameter is the __magic field itself.

96   the consistency check is that its value should be the same as its address (cast to a long).

97–99   if this is not so, it prints its error message, giving the value in the __magic field, and what it should be. It then calls WQ_BUG() (line 93).

102–109   this macro checks the __magic field in a wait_queue_head_t structure. Its parameter is a pointer to the wait_queue_head_t structure.

104   the consistency check is that the value of the __magic field in that structure should be the same as its address (cast to a long).

105–107   if this is not so, it prints its error message, giving the value of the __magic field, what it should be, and the value in the __creator field. It then calls WQ_BUG(), from line 93.

110–114   this macro checks that a wait queue header is properly initialised. Its parameter is a pointer to the task_list field in the wait_queue_head_t.

112–113   if either of the pointer fields do not contain a valid pointer, WQ_BUG() is called from line 93.

115–118   this macro sets up the __waker field in a wait_queue_t, which is passed to it by reference.

117   this puts the return address from the stack into the __waker field of the wait_queue_t, using a feature of the gcc compiler. This is the address of the caller of the function in which this macro is instantiated.

120–124   these are the definitions when debugging is not switched on. The macros are defined, but they do nothing.

4.1.3.3   *The* BUG() *macro*

Whenever the kernel encounters a problem so serious that it cannot be handled, it ends up calling the BUG() macro, either directly or indirectly. This macro is shown in Figure 4.10, from <asm-i386/page.h>.

```
103   #define BUG() __asm____volatile__(".byte 0x0f,0x0b")
```

Figure 4.10   The BUG() macro

103   this specifies a two-byte opcode 0x0f0b. This is actually an invalid opcode, and is recommended by Intel as the way deliberately to generate an invalid opcode exception (see Section 10.5.5 for the handling of such an exception).

4.2 Wait queue insertion and deletion

Now that the data structures that make up wait queues are understood, the next step is to examine a number of functions that are used to manipulate wait queues, both inserting entries and removing them. Use of these functions ensures that links are kept correct.

4.2.1 Adding an entry to a wait queue

There are a number of different functions supplied for inserting an entry into a wait queue, depending on the type of entry (exclusive or nonexclusive) and where in the queue it is to be inserted (beginning or end).

4.2.1.1 Adding a nonexclusive entry under mutual exclusion

The function shown in Figure 4.11, from `kernel/fork.c`, marks an entry as nonexclusive, and adds it at the head of the queue. It is only a wrapper that protects the wait queue by taking out a lock, thus making the manipulation of the wait queue a critical section.

```
39    void add_wait_queue(wait_queue_head_t *q, wait_queue_t *wait)
40    {
41        unsigned long flags;
42
43        wq_write_lock_irqsave(&q->lock, flags);
44        wait->flags = 0;
45        __add_wait_queue(q, wait);
46        wq_write_unlock_irqrestore(&q->lock, flags);
47    }
```

Figure 4.11   Add an entry to a wait queue, with mutual exclusion

39   the first parameter is a pointer to the head of the wait queue; the second is a pointer to the new entry to be added.

43   this takes out an interrupt safe lock on this queue, using the `lock` field in the header. The value of the EFLAGS register is saved in the local `flags` variable as long as the lock is held. This macro is discussed in Section 4.4.

44   as this is a standard (nonexclusive) wait queue entry, its `flags` field is cleared. Note the two, completely different uses of the identifier `flags`.

45   this function, which does the actual work of insertion, is discussed in Section 4.2.1.3. It adds this new entry at the head of the queue.

46   this unlocks the write lock and restores the value in EFLAGS. The macro is described in Section 4.4.

4.2.1.2 Add an exclusive entry under mutual exclusion

The function shown in Figure 4.12, from `kernel/fork.c`, is almost identical to the previous one. It also is only a wrapper that makes the manipulation of the wait queue a critical section. The difference is that it sets the WQ_FLAG_EXCLUSIVE bit in the flags field of the `wait_queue_t` structure.

```
49    void add_wait_queue_exclusive(wait_queue_head_t *q,
                                                    wait_queue_t * wait)
50    {
51         unsigned long flags;
52
53         wq_write_lock_irqsave(&q->lock, flags);
54         wait->flags = WQ_FLAG_EXCLUSIVE;
55         __add_wait_queue_tail(q, wait);
56         wq_write_unlock_irqrestore(&q->lock, flags);
57    }
```

Figure 4.12　Add an entry to a wait queue, with exclusive waiting

54　By setting this bit one ensures that only this process will be woken, not all the processes on the wait queue, as usually happens. The definition of WQ_FLAG_EXCLUSIVE was given in Section 4.1.1.1.

55　this function, which does the actual work of insertion, is described in Section 4.2.1.4. Note that an exclusive entry is added to the *tail* of the wait queue.

4.2.1.3　Adding an entry at the head of the queue

The function shown in Figure 4.13, from `<linux/wait.h>`, does the actual work of insertion. It is passed a pointer to the header of the queue, and a pointer to the new entry to be inserted, and it inserts that entry immediately after the header.

```
193   static inline void __add_wait_queue(wait_queue_head_t *head,
                                                     wait_queue_t *new)
194   {
195   #if WAITQUEUE_DEBUG
196        if (!head || !new)
197             WQ_BUG();
198        CHECK_MAGIC_WQHEAD(head);
199        CHECK_MAGIC(new->__magic);
200        if (!head->task_list.next || !head->task_list.prev)
201             WQ_BUG();
202   #endif
203        list_add(&new->task_list, &head->task_list);
204   }
```

Figure 4.13　Adding an element at the head of a wait queue

195–202　these lines are compiled into the code only in the debug case. They check all pointer fields for validity and the magic fields for compatibility. All the macros used in these lines are from Section 4.1.3.2.

196–197 if either of the pointers is invalid, WQ_BUG() is called.

198 this checks the magic field in the header.

199 this checks the magic field in the structure to be inserted.

200–201 if either of the pointer fields in the header does not contain a valid pointer, WQ_BUG() is called.

203 this is a generic list-handling function. It adds the entry at the head of the list (see Section 4.3.2).

4.2.1.4 Adding an entry at the end of the queue

The function shown in Figure 4.14, from <linux/wait.h>, is passed a pointer to the header of the queue, and a pointer to the new entry to be inserted, and it inserts that entry at the tail of the queue (immediately before the header in the circular list).

```
209  static inline void __add_wait_queue_tail(wait_queue_head_t
210      *head, wait_queue_t *new)
211  {
212  #if WAITQUEUE_DEBUG
213      if (!head || !new)
214          WQ_BUG();
215      CHECK_MAGIC_WQHEAD(head);
216      CHECK_MAGIC(new->__magic);
217      if (!head->task_list.next || !head->task_list.prev)
218          WQ_BUG();
219  #endif
220      list_add_tail(&new->task_list, &head->task_list);
221  }
```

Figure 4.14   Add an element at the tail of a wait queue

212–219 these lines are compiled into the code only in the debug case (see the comments on lines 195–202 in Section 4.2.1.3).

220 this is a generic list-handling function (see Section 4.3.2). It is passed pointers to the link fields, both in the new entry, and in the head, and it adds the entry at the end of the list.

4.2.2 Removing an entry from a wait queue

As with inserting entries on a wait queue, removing is also done in two steps. First there is a function that takes out the lock on that specific wait queue. Then there is a worker function that actually removes the entry.

4.2.2.1 Lock wait queue and remove entry

The function shown in Figure 4.15, from kernel/fork.c, removes a specific entry from a wait queue. It is only a wrapper that protects the wait queue with a lock. This makes the manipulation of the wait queue a critical section.

```
59    void remove_wait_queue(wait_queue_head_t *q, wait_queue_t *wait)
60    {
61        unsigned long flags;
62
63        wq_write_lock_irqsave(&q->lock, flags);
64        __remove_wait_queue(q, wait);
65        wq_write_unlock_irqrestore(&q->lock, flags);
66    }
```

Figure 4.15   Remove an entry from a wait queue, under mutual exclusion

59   the first parameter is a pointer to the head of the wait queue; the second is a pointer to the entry to be removed.

63   this takes out a lock on this queue, using the lock field in the header. The value of the EFLAGS register is saved in the local flags. This macro is discussed in Section 4.4.

64   this function, which does the actual work of removal, is shown in Section 4.2.2.2.

65   this gives back the lock and restores the value in EFLAGS. The macro is described in Section 4.4.

4.2.2.2   *Checking for consistency and removing entry*

The function shown in Figure 4.16, from <linux/wait.h>, is the worker function that does the removal. It is passed a pointer to the header of the wait queue and a pointer to the entry to be removed. It checks for consistency and removes that entry from the queue.

```
223   static inline void __remove_wait_queue(wait_queue_head_t
224        *head, wait_queue_t *old)
225   {
226   #if WAITQUEUE_DEBUG
227        if (!old)
228            WQ_BUG();
229        CHECK_MAGIC(old->__magic);
230   #endif
231        list_del(&old->task_list);
232   }
```

Figure 4.16   Removing an element from a wait queue

226–231   these lines are compiled into the code only in the debug case. Note that the head is not checked by this function. The macros are from Section 4.1.3.2.

227–228   if the pointer to the element to be removed is invalid, WQ_BUG() is called.

229   this checks the magic field in the structure to be removed.

231   this is a generic list-handling function that deletes the specified entry from the list (see Section 4.3.3).

4.2.3 Checking for entries on a wait queue

The function shown in Figure 4.17, from `<linux/wait.h>`, is passed a pointer to the head of a wait queue and checks if there are any entries on it. It returns TRUE if there is an entry on the list, FALSE otherwise,

```
182  static inline int waitqueue_active(wait_queue_head_t *q)
183  {
184  #if WAITQUEUE_DEBUG
185      if (!q)
186          WQ_BUG();
187      CHECK_MAGIC_WQHEAD(q);
188  #endif
189
190      return !list_empty(&q->task_list);
191  }
```

Figure 4.17   Checking for entries on a wait queue

184–188   this code is compiled only if in debug mode. The macros are from Section 4.1.3.2.

185–186   this checks the pointer passed as a parameter; if invalid, WQ_BUG() is called.

187   this checks that the head structure itself is valid.

190   this is the real work. The `list_empty()` function is one of the generic list-handling functions (see Section 4.3.4.1). It returns TRUE if empty, FALSE if not. This line returns the inverse of whatever that function returns, TRUE if there is an entry on the list, FALSE if not.

4.3 Generic list handling

Manipulating doubly linked lists is a very frequent operation within an operating system. Rather than using slightly different code for lists of each different type, Linux has generalised the code to handle such lists. The link field in each constituent data structure of any linked list is the somewhat misleadingly named `struct list_head`. Generic functions, described in this section, can then manipulate entries in any sort of list, without having to know the type of the structures in the list.

4.3.1 Declaring and initialising list entries

The code shown in Figure 4.18, from `<linux/list.h>`, contains a definition of the generic link field used in these lists as well as three macros used to initialise these link fields.

```
18   struct list_head {
19       struct list_head *next, *prev;
20   };
21
22   #define LIST_HEAD_INIT(name) { &(name), &(name) }
23
```

```
24    #define LIST_HEAD(name)                                          \
25          struct list_head name = LIST_HEAD_INIT(name)
26
27    #define INIT_LIST_HEAD(ptr) do {                                 \
28          (ptr)->next = (ptr); (ptr)->prev = (ptr);                  \
29    } while (0)
```

Figure 4.18   Initialising link fields

18–20   this is the generic link field that is included in a specific data structure, such as the run_queue field of the task_struct. Note that it points backwards and forwards to the struct list_head link field, not to the beginning of the data structure itself.

22   this initialises a struct list_head pointing backwards and forwards to itself. Note that it is passed the name or identifier of a struct list_head.

24–25   the difference between this and the previous macro is that this one actually declares the link structure and then initialises the two fields in it.

27–29   the difference between this and LIST_HEAD_INIT() is that it is passed a pointer to the struct list_head, not the actual struct list_head itself.

4.3.2   Inserting entries

The code in Figure 4.19, from <linux/list.h>, shows three functions for inserting an entry into a generic linked list.

```
37    static __inline__ void __list_add(struct list_head * new,
38          struct list_head * prev,
39          struct list_head * next)
40    {
41          next->prev = new;
42          new->next = next;
43          new->prev = prev;
44          prev->next = new;
45    }


55    static __inline__ void list_add(struct list_head *new,
          struct list_had *head)
56    {
57          __list_add(new, head, head->next);
58    }
68    static __inline__ void list_add_tail(struct list_head *new,
          struct list_head *head)
69    {
70          __list_add(new, head->prev, head);
71    }
```

Figure 4.19   Inserting an entry in a list

37–45   this inserts a new entry between two known consecutive entries. This is only of use when the previous and next entries are known already! It performs the standard four assignments needed to insert an item into the middle of a doubly linked list.

55–58   this adds a new entry at the head of a list. It is passed pointers to the new item, and to the head of the list, so the item is to be inserted between `head` and `head->next`. These are the parameters passed to `__list_add()` on line 57.

68–71   this adds a new entry at the tail of a circular doubly linked list. It is passed pointers to the new item and the head of the list, so the item is to be inserted between `head->prev` and `head`. These are the parameters passed to `__list_add()` on line 70.

4.3.3 Deleting entries

The code in Figure 4.20 shows three functions for deleting an entry from a generic linked list.

```
80    static __inline__ void __list_del(struct list_head * prev,
81          struct list_head * next)
82    {
83          next->prev = prev;
84          prev->next = next;
85    }

92    static __inline__ void list_del(struct list_head *entry)
93    {
94          __list_del(entry->prev, entry->next);
95    }

101   static __inline__ void list_del_init(struct list_head *entry)
102   {
103         __list_del(entry->prev, entry->next);
104         INIT_LIST_HEAD(entry);
105   }
```

Figure 4.20   Remove an entry from a list

80–85   this removes an entry from between two known consecutive entries. This is only of use when the previous and next entries are known already! It makes the `prev` and `next` entries point to each other.

92–95   this also deletes an entry from a list. It is passed a pointer to the actual item to be deleted, which it converts to pointers to the one before and after it. These are the parameters passed to `__list_del()` on line 94. Note that it leaves the entry just removed in an undefined state.

101–105   this also deletes an entry from a list. It is passed a pointer to the actual item to be deleted, and it calls `__list_del()` to do the actual work, but, after removing the item, it calls the `INIT_LIST_HEAD()` macro (see Section 4.3.1) to reinitialise the item, pointing to itself.

4.3.4   Miscellaneous functions

Apart from those functions seen in the previous section, for inserting and deleting entries in generic linked lists, there are a number of other functions and macros supplied for manipulating such lists.

4.3.4.1   *Testing whether list is empty or not*

The function in Figure 4.21, from `<linux/list.h>`, is given a pointer to the head of a list. It checks whether that head is pointing to itself (and hence empty) or not, and returns TRUE (if empty) or FALSE.

```
111  static __inline__ int list_empty(struct list_head *head)
112  {
113        return head->next == head;
114  }
```

Figure 4.21   Test whether a list is empty

4.3.4.2   *Joining two lists*

The function shown in Figure 4.22, from `<linux/list.h>`, inserts one list into another. It can insert the first list at any position in the second.

```
121  static __inline__ void list_splice(struct list_head *list,
                                         struct list_head *head)
122  {
123        struct list_head *first = list->next;
124
125        if (first != list) {
126              struct list_head *last = list->prev;
127              struct list_head *at = head->next;
128
129              first->prev = head;
130              head->next = first;
131
132              last->next = at;
133              at->prev = last;
134        }
133
135  }
```

Figure 4.22   Joining two lists

121   the function is passed a pointer to the head of the list to be added (`list`), and a pointer to the place to add it in the first list (`head`).

123   this takes a local pointer `first` to the head of the list to be added.

125   this checks that the list being inserted is not empty. If it is empty (with the head pointing to itself) then there is nothing to insert, and the function just returns.

126–127   these two lines identify the elements that will be manipulated, as shown in Figure 4.23; `first` and `last` point to the first and last elements, respectively, of the list to be inserted.

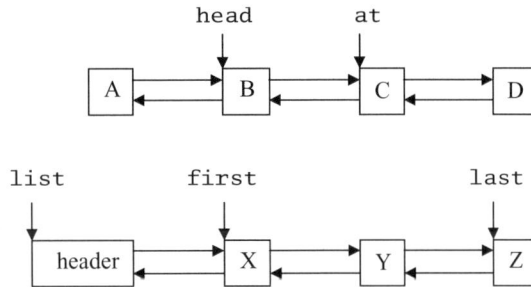

Figure 4.23   Identifiers in the two lists

129–130   the situation after these two lines have been executed is shown in Figure 4.24. The elements from `first` to `last` have now been spliced in. The list now headed by `at` is attached only by a backward link at this stage.

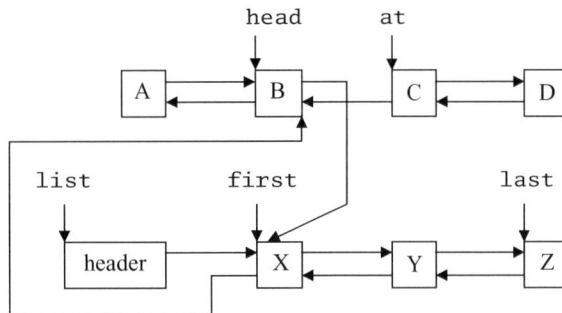

Figure 4.24   First phase of splice

132–133   The situation after these two lines have been executed is shown in Figure 4.25. The remainder of the first list, between `at` and `head`, is still there, though not shown.

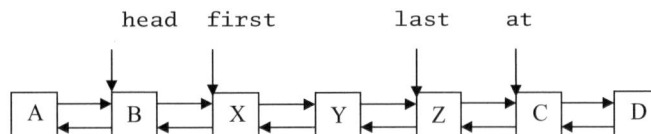

Figure 4.25   Finished splice

4.3.4.3 Miscellaneous macros

Figure 4.26, from `<linux/list.h>`, shows two further macros used for manipulating entries in generic lists. One converts a pointer to a link field to a pointer to the surrounding structure. The other works its way through all elements in a list.

```
143  #define list_entry(ptr, type, member)                              \
144  ((type *)((char *)(ptr)-(unsigned long)(&((type *)0)->member)))

151  #define list_for_each(pos, head)                                    \
152  for (pos = (head)->next, prefetch(pos->next); pos != (head);       \
153  pos = pos->next, prefetch(pos->next))
```

Figure 4.26 Miscellaneous macros

143–144 this macro converts a pointer to the `list_head` link, to a pointer to the actual structure of which it is a linked list (e.g. `task_struct`). It is passed three parameters: the `struct list_head` pointer, the type of the `struct` this is embedded in, and the name of the `struct list_head` within the `struct`.

144 `(type *)0` a is NULL pointer to a `struct` of this type;

- `((type *)0)->` member is the struct list_head within the larger structure;

- `(&((type *)0)->member)` is the address of the struct list_head;

- `(unsigned long)(&((type *)0)->member)` casts that to be an integer number; this is the number of bytes that the `list_head` is offset into the structure;

- `(char *)(ptr)` is the address of the `list_head`, interpreted as a pointer to char;

- `(char *)(ptr)-(unsigned long)(&((type *)0)->member)` this does pointer arithmetic on `ptr`, decrementing it by the number of bytes that `list_head` is offset from the beginning of the structure; finally, the result is cast to be a pointer of the correct type.

Figure 4.27 illustrates the situation. A data structure of type `type` has a `list_head` tructure embedded within it. The macro calculates the distance between the beginning of the structure and `list_head`, and subtracts that from the pointer to `list_head`, to give a pointer to the structure itself.

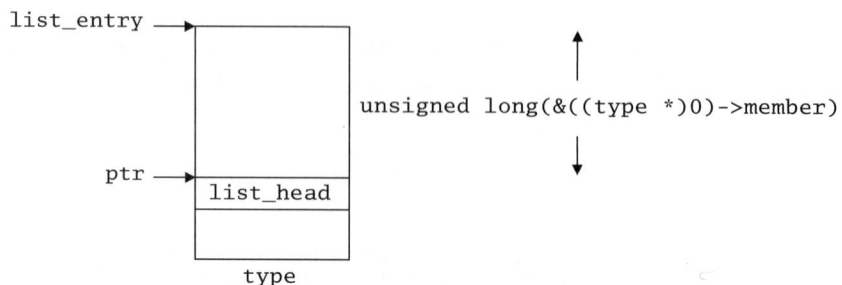

Figure 4.27 Finding the beginning of the enclosing structure

151–153   this macro iterates over all the elements in a list. The two parameters are `pos`, the address of the current `struct list_head`, and `head`, a pointer to the head of the list.

The initial value is the first element after `head`. The `prefetch()` macro is a hint to the compiler to get the element of the list into cache at this stage.

The terminating value is when it gets back to `head` again.

It advances by taking the `next` pointer each time. It also hints to the compiler to get the following element after that into cache at this stage.

4.4 Wait queue locks

We have seen in the previous sections that many of the functions that manipulate wait queues very understandably take out mutual exclusion on the particular queue while doing so. They use their own set of lock macros for this, all of which begin with the identifier `wq_`.

Linux provides what it calls a 'dual architecture' for these locks. They can be implemented either as spinlocks (`spinlock_t`) or as read–write locks (`rwlock_t`). Lightweight spinlocks are slightly faster and give smaller wait queue structure size. How this dual architecture is implemented is illustrated in Figure 4.28, from `<linux/wait.h>`.

```
49   # define USE_RW_WAIT_QUEUE_SPINLOCK 0
50
51   #if USE_RW_WAIT_QUEUE_SPINLOCK
52   # define wq_lock_t rwlock_t
53   # define WAITQUEUE_RW_LOCK_UNLOCKED RW_LOCK_UNLOCKED
54
55   # define wq_read_lock read_lock
56   # define wq_read_lock_irqsave read_lock_irqsave
57   # define wq_read_unlock_irqrestore read_unlock_irqrestore
58   # define wq_read_unlock read_unlock
59   # define wq_write_lock_irq write_lock_irq
60   # define wq_write_lock_irqsave write_lock_irqsave
61   # define wq_write_unlock_irqrestore write_unlock_irqrestore
62   # define wq_write_unlock write_unlock
63   #else
64   # define wq_lock_t spinlock_t
65   # define WAITQUEUE_RW_LOCK_UNLOCKED SPIN_LOCK_UNLOCKED
66
67   # define wq_read_lock spin_lock
68   # define wq_read_lock_irqsave spin_lock_irqsave
69   # define wq_read_unlock spin_unlock
70   # define wq_read_unlock_irqrestore spin_unlock_irqrestore
71   # define wq_write_lock_irq spin_lock_irq
72   # define wq_write_lock_irqsave spin_lock_irqsave
```

```
73    # define wq_write_unlock_irqrestore spin_unlock_irqrestore
74    # define wq_write_unlock spin_unlock
75    #endif
```

Figure 4.28   Wait queue spinlocks

49   the type of lock used is determined by the value given to the rather ungainly named USE_RW_WAIT_QUEUE_SPINLOCK macro. By default this is defined to have a value of 0, which means that it is the macros from lines 64–74 that are compiled into the code.

52–62   if USE_RW_WAIT_QUEUE_SPINLOCK is not zero, then wait queue locks are implemented as read–write locks. Read–write locks, and these macros that implement them, are dealt with fully in Sections 5.6 (uniprocessor) and 5.7 (multiprocessor).

64–74   if the macro USE_RW_WAIT_QUEUE_SPINLOCK is defined as 0, then wait queue locks are implemented as spinlocks. These spinlocks, and the macros that implement them, are dealt with fully in Sections 5.3 (uniprocessor) and 5.4 (multiprocessor).

4.5   Putting a process to sleep

Now that the low-level manipulation of wait queues has been examined, we can go on to look at the higher-level functions that actually put a process to sleep while waiting for an event (Sections 4.5 and 4.6) and wake it up again (Section 4.7).

Sometimes the delay while waiting for an event is likely to last a long time, such as when waiting for a key to be pressed or a message to come in over the network. With long-term waiting such as this, some other event may occur in the system that affects this process, possibly causing it to stop waiting, an example would be the user pressing a break key. It must be possible to wake the process up from such a wait, so it is said to be waiting interruptibly, and is in the TASK_INTERRUPTIBLE state.

If the delay is likely to be short, such as when waiting for a request for a read on a file to complete, then the process is not allowed to be interrupted. The reasoning behind this is that it is going to wake up in a short time anyway and it can then attend to whatever event has occurred. Such a process is in the TASK_UNINTERRUPTIBLE state.

There are a number of functions supplied by the kernel that put a process to sleep on a specified wait queue. These would typically be called from drivers but they may also be called from other parts of the kernel. They can be divided into two groups. The first group puts the process to sleep unconditionally. These functions will be considered in this section. All the code in this section is from kernel/sched.c. The second group of functions is always supplied with a condition as one of the parameters. Only if this condition is TRUE is the process put to sleep. These will be considered in Section 4.6.

4.5.1   Common code

As there is much code that is similar in all the following functions, the developers decided to implement this code as macros. The three macros shown in Figure 4.29 are used by the functions that follow.

```
790  #define    SLEEP_ON_VAR                                        \
791      unsigned long flags;                                       \
792      wait_queue_t wait;                                         \
793      init_waitqueue_entry(&wait, current);
794
795  #define    SLEEP_ON_HEAD                                       \
796      wq_write_lock_irqsave(&q->lock, flags);                    \
797      __add_wait_queue(q, &wait);                                \
798      wq_write_unlock(&q->lock);                                 \
799
800  #define    SLEEP_ON_TAIL                                       \
801      wq_write_lock_irq(&q->lock);                               \
802      __remove_wait_queue(q, &wait);                             \
803      wq_write_unlock_irqrestore(&q->lock, flags);
```

Figure 4.29   Macros which manipulate wait queues

790–793   the macro SLEEP_ON_VAR merely declares and initialises variables.

791   this is a local flags variable, which will be used to save the value in EFLAGS while the process is sleeping.

792   this is the basic entry in a wait queue. It has been discussed in detail in Section 4.1.1.1.

793   this function, which initialises the structure declared on the previous line to point to the current process, has been discussed in Section 4.1.1.3.

795–798   the SLEEP_ON_HEAD macro, under mutual exclusion, adds the newly defined wait_queue_t to the wait queue pointed to by q.

796   these special wait queue locks were described in Section 4.4.

797   the __add_wait_queue() function was described in Section 4.2.1.3, where it was seen that it assumes that the caller has already taken out a lock on the wait queue.

800–803   the SLEEP_ON_TAIL macro removes the entry from the wait queue, under the protection of the same lock, by using the __remove_wait_queue() function, described in Section 4.2.2.2.

4.5.2   Putting a process to sleep interruptibly

The function shown in Figure 4.30 puts the current process to sleep interruptibly on the wait queue pointed to by the parameter q.

```
805  void interruptible_sleep_on(wait_queue_head_t *q)
806  {
807      SLEEP_ON_VAR
808
809      current->state = TASK_INTERRUPTIBLE;
810
811      SLEEP_ON_HEAD
```

```
812        schedule();
813        SLEEP_ON_TAIL
814  }
```

Figure 4.30   Put a process to sleep on a wait queue

807   this sets up the required variables and links in the `task_struct` of the current process, as described in Section 4.5.1.

809   this changes the state field in the `task_struct` of the current process.

811   this links the current process onto the wait queue.

812   this calls `schedule()` (see Section 7.3), which selects another process to run and context switches to it. When this sleeping process is woken up, it is moved to the runqueue and eventually is context switched back in again. At that point `schedule()` returns and the process has the CPU and is in the TASK_RUNNING state.

813   thus, SLEEP_ON_TAIL merely has to remove this process from the wait queue. The variables declared in SLEEP_ON_VAR are local to this function, and are neither needed nor exist after this.

4.5.3   Sleeping interruptibly with a timeout

The function shown in Figure 4.31 is almost identical to that discussed in Section 4.5.2. The only extra line here is that a timeout, as specified by a parameter `timeout`, is set up before calling `schedule()`.

```
816  long interruptible_sleep_on_timeout(wait_queue_head_t *q,
                                                     long timeout)
817  {
818        SLEEP_ON_VAR
819
820        current->state = TASK_INTERRUPTIBLE;
821
822        SLEEP_ON_HEAD
823        timeout = schedule_timeout(timeout);
824        SLEEP_ON_TAIL
825
826        return timeout;
827  }
```

Figure 4.31   Sleeping interruptibly on a timeout

823   the function is described in Section 15.3.3. It puts the process to sleep for the length of time specified by `timeout`.

826   note that here the value from `schedule_timeout()` is returned to the caller.

4.5.4 Putting a process to sleep uninterruptibly

The function shown in Figure 4.32 is identical to `interruptible_sleep_on()`, from Section 4.5.2, except that the state is set so that it cannot be interrupted by a signal. It is normally used with short sleeps.

```
829  void sleep_on(wait_queue_head_t *q)
830  {
831      SLEEP_ON_VAR
832
833      current->state = TASK_UNINTERRUPTIBLE;
834
835      SLEEP_ON_HEAD
836      schedule();
837      SLEEP_ON_TAIL
838  }
```

Figure 4.32   Sleeping uninterruptibly

4.5.5 Sleeping uninterruptibly with a timeout

The function shown in Figure 4.32 is identical to `interruptible_sleep_on_timeout()`, from Section 4.5.2, except that the state is set so that it cannot be interrupted by a signal. It is normally used when it is expected that the event being waited for will occur very soon.

```
840  long sleep_on_timeout(wait_queue_head_t *q, long timeout)
841  {
842      SLEEP_ON_VAR
843
844      current->state = TASK_UNINTERRUPTIBLE;
845
846      SLEEP_ON_HEAD
847      timeout = schedule_timeout(timeout);
848      SLEEP_ON_TAIL
849
850      return timeout;
851  }
```

Figure 4.33   Sleeping uninterruptibly on a timeout

4.6 Conditionally waiting on an event

The functions examined in Section 4.5 are used to put a process to sleep unconditionally. They always end up calling `schedule()`. This section will examine a number of macros that put a process to sleep only if a specified condition is not TRUE. As before, such a sleep can be interruptible or noninterruptible.

4.6.1 Conditional uninterruptible sleep

There are three macros involved in this. The first one just checks the condition; the main macro puts the process to sleep; last, there is a worker macro to change the state of the process.

4.6.1.1 Checking the condition

The macro shown in Figure 4.34, from `<linux/sched.h>`, is the principal piece of code called to put processes to sleep uninterruptibly, depending on a condition. However, it is only a wrapper that tests the condition. Note that as this is a macro; the `condition` is actually defined in the code into which the macro is inserted.

```
812  #define wait_event(wq, condition)               \
813  do {                                            \
814      if (condition)                              \
815          break;                                  \
816      __wait_event(wq, condition);                \
817  } while (0)
```

Figure 4.34 The macro to wait conditionally on an event

814–815 if the condition is TRUE then we break out of the loop and do not wait.

816 otherwise, we call `__wait_event()` (see Section 4.6.1.2).

4.6.1.2 Putting the process to sleep

The macro shown in Figure 4.35, from `<linux/sched.h>`, puts a process to sleep on a specific wait queue until `condition` is TRUE. Its first parameter is the wait queue, represented by a `wait_queue_head_t`. The second is the condition on which it is waiting.

```
796  #define __wait_event(wq, condition)                     \
797  do {                                                    \
798      wait_queue_t __wait;                                \
799      init_waitqueue_entry(&__wait, current);            \
800                                                          \
801      add_wait_queue(&wq, &__wait);                       \
802      for (;;) {                                          \
803          set_current_state(TASK_UNINTERRUPTIBLE);       \
804          if (condition)                                 \
805              break;                                     \
806          schedule();                                    \
807      }                                                  \
```

```
808         current->state = TASK_RUNNING;                    \
809         remove_wait_queue(&wq, &__wait);                  \
810  } while (0)
```

Figure 4.35 Macro to wait on an event uninterruptibly

798   this declares a `wait_queue_t` structure, as defined in Section 4.1.1.1.

799   this sets the wait queues task field to point to the current task. The function is declared in Section 4.1.1.3.

801   this adds it to the specified wait queue. This function, which is described in Section 4.2.1.1, takes out its own lock on the queue.

802–807   putting this block of code in a loop forces a reevaluation of the condition after `schedule()` returns. If the condition is not TRUE at this stage, it sleeps again. This is for the situation where a number of processes are all sleeping on the same queue (e.g. waiting for the same resource), one gets it, and the others go back to sleep.

803   this marks the state TASK_UNINTERRUPTIBLE. On a multiprocessor this must be atomic, hence the special macro (see Section 4.6.1.3).

804–805   if the condition is TRUE at this stage, the process continues to line 808, without any context switch.

806   if the condition is FALSE, the scheduler is called. When this process next runs, it goes around the loop again and checks the condition.

808–809   eventually, when the condition is TRUE, it sets the state to TASK_RUNNING and removes the `wait_queue_t` from the queue. The function is described in Section 4.2.2.1. It takes out its own lock on the specific queue while it is manipulating it.

4.6.1.3   Changing the `state` field in the `task_struct`

A number of macros are provided for changing the `state` field in the `task_struct`, as shown in Figure 4.36, from `<linux/sched.h>`. They guarantee that in the symmetric multiprocessing (SMP) case, a change of value in the `state` variable is atomic.

```
92   #define __set_task_state(tsk, state_value)               \
93        do { (tsk)->state = (state_value); } while (0)
94   #ifdef CONFIG_SMP
95   #define set_task_state(tsk, state_value)                 \
96        set_mb((tsk)->state, (state_value))
97   #else
98   #define set_task_state(tsk, state_value)                 \
99        __set_task_state((tsk), (state_value))
100  #endif
101
102  #define __set_current_state(state_value)                 \
103        do { current->state = (state_value); } while (0)
```

```
104 #ifdef CONFIG_SMP
105 #define set_current_state(state_value)               \
106     set_mb(current->state, (state_value))
107 #else
108 #define set_current_state(state_value)               \
109     __set_current_state(state_value)
110 #endif
```

Figure 4.36 Atomically setting the state of a process

92–100 these macros set the `state` of a specified process.

92–93 this is the trivial code that does the actual assignment. It sets the state field of the `task_struct` specified by `tsk` to the value specified. It is used in the uniprocessor case.

95–96 this is the SMP case. The `set_mb()` macro is defined in `<asm-i386/system.h>` as

```
309 #define set_mb(var, value) do {xchg(&var, value); } while (0)
```

The `xchg()` macro is from Section 5.2.10 and does an atomic swap. Its parameters are the address of the `state` field in the `task_struct` and the value to be written there.

98–99 this is the uniprocessor case, which uses the macro at line 92 to do straightforward assignment instead of using the `xchg()` macro.

102–110 this is a simplified version of the foregoing, used to set the `state` field of the current process.

4.6.2 Conditional interruptible sleep

The significant difference between this section and the previous one is the value in the `state` field of the process while it is sleeping. As before, there are two macros involved in putting a process to sleep conditionally. The first just checks the condition, whereas the main one actually puts the process to sleep.

4.6.2.1 Checking the condition

The macro shown in Figure 4.37, from `<linux/sched.h>`, puts a process to sleep in the TASK_INTERRUPTIBLE state. It is only a wrapper that tests the condition before ever calling `__wait_event_interruptible()`. Note that in all cases it returns a value. This is 0 if it is returning because the condition is TRUE, or ERESTARTSYS if returning because there is a signal pending to the process.

```
840 #define wait_event_interruptible(wq, condition)          \
841 ({                                                       \
842     int __ret = 0;                                       \
843     if (!(condition))                                    \
844         __wait_event_interruptible(wq, condition, __ret); \
```

```
845          __ret;                                                        \
846  })
```

Figure 4.37 Macro to wait conditionally interruptibly

843–844 if the condition is FALSE then it calls __wait_event_interruptible() (see Section 4.6.2.2); otherwise it does not wait.

845 the whole macro evaluates to the value of __ret.

4.6.2.2 Put process to sleep

The macro shown in Figure 4.38, from <linux/sched.h>, is very similar to __wait_event() (Section 4.6.1.2). The two differences are that it sets the state field to be TASK_INTERRUPTIBLE, and if the condition is FALSE then it calls schedule() only if there is no signal pending. If there is a signal pending, then it returns ERESTARTSYS, and reverses any work done so far. This involves setting the state back to TASK_RUNNING and removing the wait_queue_t from the queue.

```
819  #define __wait_event_interruptible(wq, condition, ret)   \
820  do {                                                     \
821      wait_queue_t __wait;                                 \
822      init_waitqueue_entry(&__wait, current);             \
823                                                           \
824      add_wait_queue(&wq, &__wait);                        \
825      for (;;) {                                           \
826          set_current_state(TASK_INTERRUPTIBLE);          \
827          if (condition)                                   \
828              break;                                       \
829          if (!signal_pending(current)) {                 \
830              schedule();                                  \
831              continue;                                    \
832          }                                                \
833          ret = -ERESTARTSYS;                              \
834          break;                                           \
835      }                                                    \
836      current->state = TASK_RUNNING;                       \
837      remove_wait_queue(&wq, &__wait);                     \
838  } while (0)                                               \
```

Figure 4.38 Macro to wait interruptibly on an event

821–822 this declares a wait_queue_t structure and set the wait queues task field to point to the current process. The function is described in Section 4.1.1.3.

824 this adds the process to the specified wait queue. The function is described in Section 4.2.1.1.

825–835 this loop ensures that if the process does sleep, the condition is tested again after it wakes up.

826   this marks the state TASK_INTERRUPTIBLE. The function was described in Section 4.6.1.3.

827–828   if the condition is TRUE, we break out of the loop and go to line 836. The process is not going to sleep.

829–830   if there is no signal pending to this process, the scheduler is called to context switch the process out. The signal_pending() function is from Section 18.3.1.

831   when this process next runs, it goes around the loop again.

833–834   if there is a signal pending to the process, schedule() is not called. We set the parameter ret to a value of ERESTARTSYS and break out of the loop.

836–837   control transfers to this line either because the condition is TRUE (from line 828), or because there is a signal pending (from line 834). It sets the state to TASK_RUNNING and removes the wait_queue_t from the queue (see Section 4.2.2.1).

4.7 Waking processes up

Sections 4.5 and 4.6 examined the various functions available for putting processes to sleep on wait queues. The other side of that coin is waking them up when the event they have been sleeping through has occurred. This section examines the range of functions supplied for that purpose. There are a number of wrapper functions, and one worker.

4.7.1 Wake-up macros

At the first level, the macros shown in Figure 4.39, from <linux/sched.h>, provide a range of options for waking up a process. In all cases they take one parameter, a pointer to the head of a wait queue. They are all defined as wrappers for either __wake_up(), or __wake_up_sync() (see Section 4.7.2). The only difference between them is in the parameters they pass.

```
595  #define wake_up(x)__wake_up((x),TASK_UNINTERRUPTIBLE |
                                      TASK_INTERRUPTIBLE, 1)
596  #define wake_up_nr(x, nr)__wake_up((x),TASK_UNINTERRUPTIBLE
                                      | TASK_INTERRUPTIBLE, nr)
597  #define wake_up_all(x)__wake_up((x),TASK_UNINTERRUPTIBLE |
                                      TASK_INTERRUPTIBLE, 0)
598  #define wake_up_sync(x)__wake_up_sync((x),
               TASK_UNINTERRUPTIBLE | TASK_INTERRUPTIBLE, 1)
599  #define wake_up_sync_nr(x, nr)__wake_up_sync((x),
               TASK_UNINTERRUPTIBLE | TASK_INTERRUPTIBLE, nr)
600  #define wake_up_interruptible(x)__wake_up((x),
                                      TASK_INTERRUPTIBLE, 1)
601  #define wake_up_interruptible_nr(x, nr)
                      __wake_up((x),TASK_INTERRUPTIBLE, nr)
602  #define wake_up_interruptible_all(x)__
                      wake_up((x),TASK_INTERRUPTIBLE, 0)
```

```
603  #define wake_up_interruptible_sync(x)
                          __wake_up_sync((x),TASK_INTERRUPTIBLE, 1)
604  #define wake_up_interruptible_sync_nr(x)
                          __wake_up_sync((x),TASK_INTERRUPTIBLE, nr)
```

Figure 4.39   Wake-up macros

595   this wakes up one exclusive process on the wait queue, along with all nonexclusive processes, whether in the TASK_INTERRUPTIBLE or TASK_UNINTERRUPTIBLE state (see Section 4.7.2 for the __wake_up() function).

596   see line 595; the second parameter is the number of exclusive processes to be woken up on this call.

597   see line 595; only nonexclusive processes are to be woken.

598   as for line 595, except that the woken process must run on the CPU that woke it.

599   as for line 596, except that the woken process must run on the CPU that woke it.

600–604   as for lines 595–599, except that only processes in the TASK_INTERRUPTIBLE state are to be woken.

4.7.2   Locking the wait queue and wake up

The 10 macros discussed in the previous section all end up calling one of the two wrapper functions shown in Figure 4.40, from kernel/sched.c. These merely take out an interrupt safe read lock on the wait queue, and then call the generic __wake_up_common() function (see Section 4.7.3). The only difference between them is whether the newly awoken process is required to run on the CPU that woke it or not.

```
740  void __wake_up(wait_queue_head_t *q, unsigned int mode, int nr)
741  {
742       if (q) {
743             unsigned long flags;
744             wq_read_lock_irqsave(&q->lock, flags);
745             __wake_up_common(q, mode, nr, 0);
746             wq_read_unlock_irqrestore(&q->lock, flags);
747       }
748  }
749
750  void __wake_up_sync(wait_queue_head_t *q, unsigned int mode, int nr)
751  {
752       if (q) {
753             unsigned long flags;
754             wq_read_lock_irqsave(&q->lock, flags);
755             __wake_up_common(q, mode, nr, 1);
756             wq_read_unlock_irqrestore(&q->lock, flags);
```

```
757        }
758   }
```

Figure 4.40   Locking the wait queue and wake up

740   The parameters are as follows:

- a pointer to the head of the relevant wait queue;

- A bitmap, containing state bits (TASK_INTERRUPTIBLE and/or TASK_UNINTERRUPTIBLE); only processes waiting in a corresponding state will be considered;

- the number of exclusive processes to wake up at the same time; this may be 0.

742–747   if not passed a valid pointer to a wait queue, we return without doing anything.

744–746   these lines merely safeguard the call to __wake_up_common() with an interrupt safe read lock. The two macros are described in Section 4.4.

745   the function is described in Section 4.7.3. Note that a value of 0 is passed for the fourth parameter, implying that the woken process can run on any CPU.

750–758   the only difference between this function and the previous one is seen on line 755.

755   note that a value of 1 is passed for the fourth parameter, implying that the woken process must run on the CPU that woke it.

4.7.3   Finding a process to wake up

The function shown in Figure 4.41, from kernel/sched.c, is the main worker function for waking up a process.

```
716   static inline void __wake_up_common (wait_queue_head_t *q,
717        unsigned int mode, int nr_exclusive, const int sync)
718   {
719        struct list_head *tmp;
720        struct task_struct *p;
721
722        CHECK_MAGIC_WQHEAD(q);
723        WQ_CHECK_LIST_HEAD(&q->task_list);
724
725        list_for_each(tmp,&q->task_list) {
726             unsigned int state;
727             wait_queue_t *curr = list_entry(tmp, wait_queue_t,
                                                      task_list);
728
729             CHECK_MAGIC(curr->__magic);
730             p = curr->task;
731             state = p->state;
```

```
732            if (state & mode) {
733                WQ_NOTE_WAKER(curr);
734                if (try_to_wake_up(p, sync) &&
          (curr->flags&WQ_FLAG_EXCLUSIVE) && !-nr_exclusive)
735        break;
736            }
737        }
738  }
```

Figure 4.41   The core wake-up function

716   the first parameter is a pointer to the head of the wait queue to be searched.

The second is a mode flag (indicating TASK_INTERRUPTIBLE and/or TASK_UNINTERRUPTIBLE). The third parameter determines whether one, some, or all processes on the queue are to be woken up. If 0, then it is nonexclusive, and all are to be woken up; otherwise, the first exclusive process on the wait queue is woken along with all the nonexclusive processes. The final parameter, sync, specifies whether the process must run on the CPU that woke it up (TRUE) or whether any CPU will do (FALSE).

722   this macro checks the validity of the parameter (q) that was described in Section 4.1.3.2. If WAITQUEUE_DEBUG is not defined, this macro does nothing.

723   this macro, also described in Section 4.1.3.2, checks that the wait queue header is properly initialised. If WAITQUEUE_DEBUG is not defined, this macro does nothing.

725–737   the loop goes through each entry on the wait queue in turn. The macro was described in Section 4.3.4.3.

727   the pointer tmp is only pointing to the link field in the current entry. The list_entry() function (Section 4.3.4.3) converts that to a pointer to the beginning of the current wait_queue_t.

729   this checks that the entry has been properly initialised, using the macro from Section 4.1.3.2.

730   this takes a pointer to the task_struct of the process this entry represents.

731   this gets a copy of the state field.

732–736   if a bit corresponding to the state of the process is not set in the mode parameter, we ignore this one and go around the loop again. This process is not in the state specified by the caller. If the bit is set, then the process is a candidate for being woken.

733   this macro, from Section 4.1.3.2, fills in the __waker field in the wait_queue_t with the address of the caller of the present function (i.e. the return address on the stack at this point).

734   all three conditions (described below) must be TRUE for control to break out of the loop; otherwise it continues searching the queue.

With regard to line 734, the three conditions are as follows:

• It is a candidate, so wake it up. The try_to_wake_up() function will be described in

Section 4.7.4. It returns TRUE if it put the process on the runqueue. There are circumstances in which we can try to wake a process that is already on the runqueue; `try_to_wake_up()` returns FALSE in this (rare) case, and we handle it by continuing to scan the queue.

- WQ_FLAG_EXCLUSIVE means that this process was sleeping exclusively, so the next condition has to be checked.

- The specified number of exclusive processes have been woken up. Note that this decrement is carried out only if the previous two conditions were TRUE.

4.7.4 Trying to wake up a specific process

When a process is woken up, the waker can specify whether or not it must run on the CPU that is waking it up. The function shown in Figure 4.42, from `kernel/sched.c`, wakes up a process, and puts it on the runqueue, if it is not already there. If the caller has specified appropriately, it will even attempt to cause a reschedule on another CPU.

```
351   static inline int try_to_wake_up(struct task_struct *p,
                                              int synchronous)
352   {
353         unsigned long flags;
354         int success = 0;

359         spin_lock_irqsave(&runqueue_lock, flags);
360         p->state = TASK_RUNNING;
361         if (task_on_runqueue(p))
362             goto out;
363         add_to_runqueue(p);
364         if (!synchronous || !(p->cpus_allowed &
                                     (1 << smp_processor_id())))
365             reschedule_idle(p);
366         success = 1;
367   out:
368         spin_unlock_irqrestore(&runqueue_lock, flags);
369         return success;
370   }
```

Figure 4.42   Function to wake up a process

351   the parameters are a pointer to the process to be woken and a flag indicating whether or not the process must run on the CPU that is waking it up. TRUE indicates that it must.

354   this is set up a default return value indicating that the `task_struct` was already on the runqueue.

359–368   these lock the `runqueue_lock` spinlock and save the state of the EFLAGS register at that point. Any work on the runqueue is protected by this spinlock. The macros for acquiring and releasing the lock are introduced in Section 12.8.1.

360 the state field is changed to TASK_RUNNING; the process is now contending for the CPU.

361–362 if the process is already on the runqueue, there is nothing further to be done and a value of FALSE (0) is returned. The function is dealt with in Section 4.8.4.

363 this function does just what it says; see Section 4.8.1.

364–365 if the process is not required to, or not allowed to, run on this CPU, then an attempt is made to find a suitable idle or preemptible CPU on which to run this process now for the reschedule_idle() function, (see Section 7.6.1).

366 this sets up a return value indicating that the task_struct was put on the runqueue.

368 this releases the spinlock and restores the EFLAGS register as it was before the lock was taken out.

369 a return value of TRUE means that the process has been woken up and put on the runqueue; FALSE just means that it was on the runqueue already.

4.7.5 Waking up and trying to schedule a process

The function shown in Figure 4.43, from kernel/sched.c wakes up a process and tries to reschedule it on a suitable CPU. It is merely a wrapper for try_to_wakeup(), passing a 0 as the synchronous parameter. This means there is no requirement to run the newly woken process on the current CPU.

```
372  inline int wake_up_process(struct task_struct * p)
373  {
374      return try_to_wake_up(p, 0);
375  }
```

Figure 4.43   Waking up and trying to schedule a process

4.8 Manipulating the runqueue

This section will examine a number of functions that manipulate the runqueue. Linux is moving towards generalising functions that manipulate lists of all sorts, replacing links pointing to specific structures with links pointing to a generic link field of type struct list_head. These generic functions were dealt with in Section 4.7.4.

4.8.1 Add a task_struct to the runqueue

The function shown in Figure 4.44, from kernel/sched.c, is passed a pointer to the task_struct representing a process and it inserts at the beginning of the runqueue. It is only ever called from try_to_wake_up() (see Section 4.7.4).

```
325  static inline void add_to_runqueue(struct task_struct * p)
326  {
327        list_add(&p->run_list, &runqueue_head);
328        nr_running++;
329  }
```

Figure 4.44   Function that adds a process to the runqueue

327   this generic function is discussed in Section 4.3.2. It is passed a pointer to the link field in the `task_struct` and a pointer to the head of the particular queue, in this case the runqueue.

328   this increases the count of processes on the runqueue. The `nr_running` counter is defined in Section 8.1.1.

4.8.2   Moving a `task_struct` to the end of the runqueue

The function shown in Figure 4.45, from `kernel/sched.c`, moves a process to the end of the runqueue. It is typically used with round-robin scheduling. The `nr_running` counter is not affected.

```
331  static inline void move_last_runqueue(struct task_struct * p)
332  {
333        list_del(&p->run_list);
334        list_add_tail(&p->run_list, &runqueue_head);
335  }
```

Figure 4.45   Function to move a process to the end of the runqueue

331   the parameter is a pointer to a `task_struct` already on the runqueue.

333   this generic function is discussed in Section 4.3.3. It is passed a pointer to the link field in the `task_struct`, and it removes that entry from the list.

334   this generic function is discussed in Section 4.3.2. It is passed a pointer to the link field in the `task_struct` and a pointer to the particular queue, in this case the runqueue. It adds that entry at the tail of the list.

4.8.3   Removing a `task_struct` from the runqueue

The function shown in Figure 4.46, from `<linux/sched.h>`, is the dual of the function in Section 4.8.1. It is called to remove a process from the runqueue when it has used up its quantum or when it is waiting for a resource. It is passed a pointer to the `task_struct` to be removed.

```
876  static inline void del_from_runqueue(struct task_struct * p)
877  {
878        nr_running-;
879        p->sleep_time = jiffies;
880        list_del(&p->run_list);
```

```
881        p->run_list.next = NULL;
882 }
```

Figure 4.46   Function to remove a process from the runqueue

878   there is one less process on the runqueue, so the counter is decremented, (see Section 8.1.1).

879   this records the time (in jiffies) at which the process was put to sleep, in its own `task_struct`. The `jiffies` variable will be described in Section 15.1.1.

880   this generic function is discussed in Section 4.3.3. It is passed a pointer to the link field in the `task_struct` and it removes that entry from the list.

881   this is something the generic function does *not* do. This sets the `next` pointer in the `task_struct` to NULL. This feature is used to check whether the structure is on the runqueue or not (see Section 4.8.4).

4.8.4   Checking if a `task_struct` is on the runqueue

The code shown in Figure 4.47 is from `<linux/sched.h>`. It returns TRUE if the specified `task_struct` in on the runqueue, FALSE otherwise. It does not check the actual runqueue but merely the `next` field in the `task_struct`.

```
884 static inline int task_on_runqueue(struct task_struct *p)
885 {
886        return (p->run_list.next != NULL);
887 }
```

Figure 4.47   Checking if a `task_struct` is on the runqueue

886   this field is always set to NULL when the `task_struct` is removed and so can be used to test whether it is linked in or not.

5

Mutual exclusion with locks

In many places throughout the kernel it is necessary to prevent processes, particularly ones running on different computer processing units (CPUs), from simultaneously accessing particular data structures. There are a variety of mechanisms provided for that, ranging from atomic operations, through locks, to semaphores. This chapter examines mechanisms that use busy waiting. Chapter 6 will examine solutions that involve processes being put to sleep while waiting.

5.1 Bit manipulations

At the lowest level, there is a requirement to be able to manipulate a single bit, atomically. Linux supplies a range of functions for this. These can be used to implement a lock, but they have a much wider application and are in fact used by many different parts of the kernel.

5.1.1 Setting a bit

Figure 5.1, from <asm-generic/bitops.h>, sets a bit and returns TRUE if the bit was set beforehand, FALSE otherwise. To guarantee atomicity, it disables interrupts while it operates.

```
19   extern __inline__ int set_bit(int nr, long * addr)
20   {
21       int        mask, retval;
22
23       addr +=    nr >> 5;
24       mask = 1 << (nr & 0x1f);
25       cli();
26       retval = (mask & *addr) != 0;
27       *addr |= mask;
28       sti();
```

The Linux Process Manager. The Internals of Scheduling, Interrupts and Signals   John O'Gorman
© 2003 John Wiley & Sons, Ltd   ISBN: 0 470 84771 9

```
29          return retval;
30      }
```

Figure 5.1   Setting a bit unconditionally

19   the parameters are an `int` identifying the bit to be set, and a pointer to the data element containing the bit. Although the input parameter is a pointer to a `long`, the actual bitmap may be more than one `long` in length. The function operates by picking out the relevant `long` in the bitmap and working on the appropriate bit within that. So this function works with any length of bitmap, beginning at `addr`.

23   the right-hand side divides `nr` by 32, so giving the number of the `long` in which the required bit is found. For example, bit 90 would be in element 90/32 (or element 2) of the bitmap. Note that counting is zero-based, so this is the third element. Incrementing `addr` by this number points it to the correct `long` in the bitmap.

24   this takes the bitwise AND of `nr` with `0x1f` strips off all but the least significant 5 bits of `nr`. Another way of looking at this operation is that it is `nr` MOD 32. This gives the offset within the `long` identified on the previous line. To continue the example, for bit 90 this would result in 26 (90 MOD 32). So the bit required is bit 26 in element 2 of the bitmap. After the assignment on this line, `mask` has a bit set in the appropriate position.

25   this disables interrupts, to guarantee that no interrupt handler can interfere while the next two lines are being executed (see Section 12.8.2 for the macro).

26   this is the test line; `mask & *addr` will be 1 if the bit has been set already, 0 otherwise. So `retval` will be TRUE if the bit was set, FALSE otherwise.

27   this sets the appropriate bit, whether or not it was set beforehand.

28   Interrupts can be enabled again at this stage (see Section 12.8.2 for the macro).

29   the returned `retval` lets the caller know whether the bit was set or clear before the call.

5.1.2   Clearing a bit

The corresponding function to clear a bit is shown in Figure 5.2, from `<asm-generic/bitops.h>`. The description given in Section 5.1.1 is applicable here also. It returns TRUE if the bit was set beforehand, FALSE otherwise.

```
32      extern __inline__ int clear_bit(int nr, long * addr)
33      {
34          int      mask, retval;
35
36          addr +=   nr >> 5;
37          mask = 1 << (nr & 0x1f);
38          cli();
39          retval = (mask & *addr) != 0;
40          *addr &= ~mask;
41          sti();
```

```
42        return retval;
43    }
```

Figure 5.2 Clearing a bit

40 inverting `mask` means that the specified bit is clear all other bits are set, so the AND will not affect those. Whether the bit specified by `nr` was set or not beforehand, it will be clear after this line.

5.1.3 Testing a bit

The function shown in Figure 5.3, from `<asm-generic/bitops.h>`, simply returns the value of the specified bit. As it is not making any changes, it does not disable interrupts. If an interrupt handler alters the bit while this function is running, it will return either the old or the new value, depending on exactly when the interrupt occurs. The description given in Section 5.1.1 is directly applicable.

```
45    extern __inline__ int test_bit(int nr, long * addr)
46    {
47        int  mask;
48
49        addr += nr >> 5;
50        mask = 1 << (nr & 0x1f);
51        return ((mask & *addr) != 0);
52    }
```

Figure 5.3 Testing a bit

51 the result of 'ANDing' `mask` and `*addr` is 1 if the bit was set beforehand, 0 if it was clear beforehand. So, accordingly, it returns TRUE or FALSE.

5.1.4 Testing and setting a bit

This function atomically sets a bit and returns its old value. It has the same functionality as `set_bit()` (Section 5.1.1), but it guarantees atomicity using i386 machine instructions, not interrupt inhibition. It will be dealt with in two stages. First, there is the main function itself; then there are some macros it uses.

5.1.4.1 *Setting a bit and returning its old value*

The function shown in Figure 5.4, from `<asm-i386/bitops.h>`, sets a bit and returns its old value. This operation is guaranteed to be atomic and cannot be reordered by the compiler.

```
123   static __inline__ int test_and_set_bit(int nr, volatile void * addr)
124   {
125       int oldbit;
126
127       __asm__ __volatile__( LOCK_PREFIX
128           "btsl %2,%1\n\tsbbl %0,%0"
129           :"=r" (oldbit),"=m" (ADDR)
130           :"Ir" (nr) : "memory");
131       return oldbit;
132   }
```

Figure 5.4   Testing and setting a bit

123   the parameters are an `int` identifying the bit to be set, and a pointer to the data element containing the bit.

127   the `LOCK_PREFIX` macro is defined in Section 5.1.4.2. On a multiprocessor, it evaluates to the LOCK machine instruction, which locks the bus for the following instruction, so making it atomic. On a uniprocessor it is NULL, as the instruction is atomic anyway.

128   the bit test and set long instruction, BTS, assigns the bit specified by parameter 2, in the bitmap identified by parameter 1, to the carry flag, then sets the bit itself to 1.

- SBB is subtract with borrow. If the carry flag is set, there is a borrow into the subtraction. So this subtraction is only a way to test the carry flag.

- If the carry flag was 0 beforehand, then the result is 0 (FALSE).

- If the carry flag was 1 beforehand, then the result is all 1s (-1), or TRUE.

129   parameter 0 is `oldbit`; writable, it can be in a register ("=r"). Parameter 1 specifies the value of the bitstring to which `addr` points; it is write only ("="), and may be in memory ("m"). See Section 5.1.4.2 for the macro ADDR, which merely de-references the pointer `addr`.

130   parameter 2, an input parameter, is the number of the bit. It must be a constant in the range $1-31$ ("I"), and it may be in a general purpose register ("r"). The "memory" operand constraint tells the compiler that memory will be modified in an unpredictable manner, so it will not keep memory values cached in registers across the group of assembler instructions.

131   the value in `oldbit` is returned. This is TRUE or FALSE, depending, respectively on whether the bit was set or clear beforehand.

5.1.4.2   Auxiliary macros

The macros shown in Figure 5.5, from `<asm-i386/bitops.h>`, are used in the function described in the Section 5.1.4.1.

```
18    #ifdef CONFIG_SMP
19    #define LOCK_PREFIX "lock ; "
20    #else
```

```
21    #define LOCK_PREFIX ""
22    #endif
23
24    #define ADDR (*(volatile long *) addr)
```

Figure 5.5 Auxiliary macros

18–22 this macro is used in the inline assembly part of some of the functions that follow. It means that the LOCK macro can always be used. But sometimes (the SMP case) it invokes the machine instruction to lock the bus; other times it has no effect.

24 this macro takes the pointer `addr`, of whatever type, casts it to be a pointer to `long`; and then de-references it.

5.1.5 Testing and clearing a bit

There is a corresponding function to atomically clear a bit, and return its old value, also from `<asm-i386/bitops.h>` (see Figure 5.6).

```
162  static __inline__ int test_and_clear_bit(int nr,
                                              volatile void * addr)
163  {
164      int oldbit;
165
166      __asm__ __volatile__( LOCK_PREFIX
167          "btrl %2,%1\n\tsbbl %0,%0"
168          :"=r" (oldbit),"=m" (ADDR)
169          :"Ir" (nr) : "memory");
170      return oldbit;
171  }
```

Figure 5.6 Testing and clearing a bit

162–170 the comments made on Figure 5.4, in Section 5.1.4.1, are relevant here also.

167 the bit test and set long instruction, BTR, assigns the bit specified by parameter 2, in the bitmap identified by parameter 1, to the carry flag, then clears the bit itself to 0.

5.1.6 Finding the first bit clear

The function shown in Figure 5.7, from `<asm-i386/bitops.h>`, returns the offset of the first bit clear in the `unsigned long` it is passed as a parameter.

```
325  static __inline__ unsigned long ffz(unsigned long word)
326  {
327      __asm__("bsfl %1,%0"
328          :"=r" (word)
329          :"r" (~word));
```

```
330        return word;
331    }
```

Figure 5.7   Finding the first bit clear in a word

325   the parameter is an `unsigned long`, passed by value.

327   the `BSF` (bit scan forward) machine instruction scans parameter 1 (the inverse of `word`) for the first bit set. This is equivalent to scanning `word` for the first bit clear. The index of the first bit found is stored into parameter 0, `word`. This result is undefined if the value on entry is all 1s, so the calling code should check for this.

328   parameter 0 is the result parameter, which may be in a register (`"=r"`).

329   parameter 1 is the inverse of the supplied value. This is the bitmap scanned.

330   as `word` is passed by value, it has to be made available to the caller.

5.2   Atomic operations

The standard implementation of a lock requires incrementing and decrementing the value of a variable. It is essential that this be done in one, single, atomic operation. Typically, the value has to be copied from memory to a register, the operation performed in the register, and the result written back to memory. On a multiprocessor, another CPU could read the value from memory before the foregoing three steps are complete. Even on a uniprocessor, an interrupt could occur before the three steps are complete, and the interrupt handler could change the value in memory. To overcome these problems, Linux provides a set of macros and functions that guarantee atomic operations on variables.

5.2.1   Basic definitions

The basic definitions required by all the functions that follow in this section are shown in Figure 5.8, from `<asm-i386/atomic.h>`.

```
11    #ifdef CONFIG_SMP
12    #define LOCK "lock ; "
13    #else
14    #define LOCK ""
15    #endif

22    typedef struct { volatile int counter; } atomic_t;
23
24    #define ATOMIC_INIT(i) { (i) }

33    #define atomic_read(v) ((v)->counter)

43    #define atomic_set(v,i) (((v)->counter) = (i))
```

Figure 5.8   Basic definitions

11–15　this macro is used in the inline assembly part of some of the functions that follow. It means that the LOCK macro can always be used. But sometimes (the SMP case) it invokes the machine instruction to lock the bus; other times it has no effect.

22　the comment in the code says that this complex definition of an atomic variable is to prevent gcc becoming too clever. With a simple int, the compiler might alter some alias that contains the same information. The volatile keyword warns the compiler that the value in this variable may be changed asynchronously by another CPU or an interrupt handler.

24　having defined the atomic_t type as a structure, this more complex initialisation format is required.

33　assuming that v is a pointer to type atomic_t, this macro evaluates the value of the int counter.

43　This macro atomically sets the value of the atomic_t pointed to by v to be i.

5.2.2　Atomic addition

The function shown in Figure 5.9, from <asm-i386/atomic.h>, adds an int value to an atomic_t variable. The operation is guaranteed to be atomic, uninterruptible.

```
53    static __inline__ void atomic_add(int i, atomic_t *v)
54    {
55            __asm__ __volatile__(
56                LOCK "addl %1,%0"
57                :"=m" (v->counter)
58                :"ir" (i), "m" (v->counter));
59    }
```

Figure 5.9　Atomic addition

56　in an SMP kernel, the LOCK macro causes the LOCK machine instruction to be inserted here. This locks the bus for the duration of the following instruction, thus making it atomic with respect to other CPUs. The ADDL instruction is guaranteed to be atomic on a uniprocessor, so the LOCK macro is NULL in that case. It adds the value i to the counter field of the atomic_t to which v points.

57　parameter 0 (the counter field) is write only ("=") and may be in memory ("m").

58　parameter 1 is the input parameter i. It is expected to be an immediate integer operand and may be in a general register ("ir"). Parameter 2 is the other input, the value in (v->counter) beforehand.

5.2.3　Atomic subtraction

There is a corresponding function, shown in Figure 5.10, from <asm-i386/atomic.h>. This subtracts an int value from an atomic_t in one atomic operation. The comments on lines 56–58 for Figure 5.9 apply here also (see Section 5.2.2).

```
69    static __inline__ void atomic_sub(int i, atomic_t *v)
70    {
71          __asm__ __volatile__(
72              LOCK "subl %1,%0"
73              : "=m" (v->counter)
74              : "ir" (i), "m" (v->counter));
75    }
```

Figure 5.10   Atomic subtraction

5.2.4   Atomic subtract and test for zero

The function shown in Figure 5.11, from `<asm-i386/atomic.h>`, atomically subtracts
an `int` value from an `atomic_t` variable. It returns TRUE if the result is 0, or FALSE for
all other cases.

```
87    static __inline__ int atomic_sub_and_test(int i, atomic_t *v)
88    {
89          unsigned char c;
90
91          __asm__ __volatile__(
92              LOCK "subl %2,%0; sete %1"
93              : "=m" (v->counter), "=qm" (c)
94              : "ir" (i), "m" (v->counter) : "memory");
95          return c;
96    }
```

Figure 5.11   Atomic subtract and test

92   the SETE instruction sets parameter 1 (the unsigned char c) to 1 if the zero bit is set in
EFLAGS (i.e. if the result of the subtraction was 0).

93   parameter 0 (the counter field) is write only ("=") and may be in memory ("m"). Parameter 1
is the unsigned char c declared on line 89. It may be in a general purpose register, or in
memory ("=qm").

94   parameter 2 is the input parameter i; it is expected as an immediate integer operand and may be
in a general register ("ir") . Parameter 3 is the other input, the value in (v->counter)
beforehand. The "memory" operand constraint tells the compiler that memory will be modified
in an unpredictable manner, so it will not keep memory values cached in registers across the
group of assembler instructions.

95   the value in c is returned.

5.2.5   Atomic increment

The function shown in Figure 5.12, from `<asm-i386/atomic.h>`, atomically adds 1 to
the `atomic_t` to which its parameter is pointing.

```
105  static __inline__ void atomic_inc(atomic_t *v)
106  {
107       __asm__ __volatile__(
108           LOCK "incl %0"
109           :"=m" (v->counter)
110           :"m" (v->counter));
111  }
```

Figure 5.12 Atomic increment

108 in an SMP kernel, the LOCK macro causes the LOCK machine instruction to be inserted here. This locks the bus for the duration of the INCL instruction, thus making that instruction atomic with respect to other CPUs. The INCL instruction is guaranteed to be atomic on a uniprocessor, so the LOCK macro is NULL in that case. It increments parameter 0 (the counter field of the atomic_t to which v points) by 1.

109 the output counter field is write only, and in memory ("=m").

110 the input counter field may be in memory ("m").

5.2.6 Atomic decrement

There is a corresponding function to atomically decrement an atomic_t by 1 (see Figure 5.13, from <asm-i386/atomic.h>). The comments on Figure 5.12 (see Section 5.2.5) apply here also.

```
120  static __inline__ void atomic_dec(atomic_t *v)
121  {
122       __asm__ __volatile__(
123           LOCK "decl %0"
124           :"=m" (v->counter)
125           :"m" (v->counter));
126  }
```

Figure 5.13 Atomic decrement

5.2.7 Atomic decrement and test for zero

There is a slightly more complex version of the function from Section 5.2.6, which atomically decrements an atomic_t by 1 and returns TRUE if the result is 0 or FALSE for all other cases (see Figure 5.14, from <asm-i386/atomic.h>). The comments on lines 92–95 of Figure 5.11 apply here also (see Section 5.2.4).

```
137  static __inline__ int atomic_dec_and_test(atomic_t *v)
138  {
139       unsigned char c;
140
141       __asm__ __volatile__(
```

```
142            LOCK "decl %0; sete %1"
143            : "=m" (v->counter), "=qm" (c)
144            : "m" (v->counter) : "memory");
145        return c != 0;
146  }
```

Figure 5.14 Atomically decrementing and testing for zero

145 if the result of the decrement was 0, then c was set to 1 on line 142. In that case, c != 0 is TRUE. Otherwise, c was set to 0, and c != 0 is FALSE.

5.2.8 Atomic increment and test for zero

The function shown in Figure 5.15, from <asm-i386/atomic.h>, is the dual of that shown in Figure 5.14. It atomically increments an atomic_t by 1 and returns TRUE if the result is 0, or FALSE for all other cases. The comments on lines 91–95 of Figure 5.11 apply here also (see Section 5.2.4).

```
157  static __inline__ int atomic_inc_and_test(atomic_t *v)
158  {
159        unsigned char c;
160
161        __asm__ __volatile__(
162            LOCK "incl %0; sete %1"
163            : "=m" (v->counter), "=qm" (c)
164            : "m" (v->counter) : "memory");
165        return c != 0;
166  }
```

Figure 5.15 Atomically decrementing and testing for zero

5.2.9 Atomically add and test for negative result

The function shown in Figure 5.16, from <asm-i386/atomic.h>, adds an int value to an atomic_t variable. It returns TRUE if the result is negative, FALSE otherwise.

```
178  static __inline__ int atomic_add_negative(int i, atomic_t *v)
179  {
180        unsigned char c;
181
182        __asm__ __volatile__(
183            LOCK "addl %2,%0; sets %1"
184            : "=m" (v->counter), "=qm" (c)
185            : "ir" (i), "m" (v->counter) : "memory");
186        return c;
187  }
```

Figure 5.16 Atomically adding and testing for negative result

183 in an SMP kernel, the LOCK macro causes the LOCK machine instruction to be inserted here. This locks the bus for the duration of the ADD instruction, thus making it atomic with respect to other CPUs. The ADDL instruction is guaranteed to be atomic on a uniprocessor, so the LOCK macro is NULL in that case. It adds the value of parameter 2 (the int i) to parameter 0 (the counter field of the atomic_t to which v points), and sets the sign bit in EFLAGS if the result is negative. The SETS instruction sets parameter 1 (the unsigned char c) to 1 if the sign bit is set as a result of the addition (i.e. if the result is negative).

184 parameter 0 (the counter field) is write only ("=") and may be in memory ("m"). Parameter 1 is the unsigned char c declared on line 180. It may be in a general purpose register, or in memory ("=qm").

185 parameter 2 is the input parameter i; it is expected as an immediate integer operand and may be in a general register ("ir"). Parameter 3 is the other input, the value in (v->counter) beforehand. The "memory" operand constraint tells the compiler that memory will be modified in an unpredictable manner, so it will not keep memory values cached in registers across the group of assembler instructions.

5.2.10 Atomically exchanging a value

The classic algorithm to exchange values between two locations takes three steps. There is a very common requirement in an operating system to implement this exchange atomically. Because the types of the values requiring to be exchanged can vary so much, Linux implements such an atomic exchange in two steps: first through a macro that sorts out the type casts, and, seconds by a function that actually implements the exchange. The relevant code is shown in Figure 5.17, from <asm-i386/system.h>.

```
141  #define xchg(ptr,v) ((__typeof__(*(ptr)))__xchg((unsigned
                            long)(v),(ptr),sizeof(*(ptr))))

145  struct __xchg_dummy { unsigned long a[100]; };
146  #define __xg(x) ((struct __xchg_dummy *)(x))

203  static inline unsigned long __xchg(unsigned long x,
                            volatile void *ptr, int size)
204  {
205      switch (size) {
206          case 1:
207              __asm__ __volatile__("xchgb %b0,%1"
208                  : "=q" (x)
209                  : "m" (*__xg(ptr)), "" (x)
210                  : "memory");
211              break;
212          case 2:
213              __asm__ __volatile__("xchgw %w0,%1"
214                  : "=r" (x)
215                  : "m" (*__xg(ptr)), "" (x)
216                  : "memory");
217              break;
```

```
218                 case 4:
219                     __asm__ __volatile__("xchgl %0,%1"
220                         :"=r" (x)
221                         :"m" (*__xg(ptr)), "" (x)
222                         :"memory");
223                     break;
224             }
225         return x;
226  }
```

Figure 5.17 Atomically exchange a value

141   there is a lot packed into this line. It will atomically swap two values of any type. The first must be specified by reference, the second by value. Note that it swaps the order of the two parameters before passing them to the __xchg() function. It also casts the v parameter to be of type unsigned long. Finally, it passes a third parameter, the size of the datatype to which the other parameter is pointing.

145   this seems to be overkill, allowing for the possibility of exchanging an array 100 long.

146   the parameter x is cast to be a pointer to a struct __xchg_dummy, from line 145.

203   the first parameter is an unsigned long value, the second points to some value; these are to be swapped. The third parameter gives the size of the datatype to which the second is pointing.

205–224   the function will handle 1-byte, 2-byte, or 4-byte values. As the comment in the code notes, there is no need for a LOCK prefix, even in SMP, as the XCHG machine instruction always implies a lock anyway.

207   the low-order byte of parameter 0 (the long x) is exchanged with the low-order byte of parameter 1 (the de-referenced pointer).

208   parameter 0 is the output value of x. It must be in one of the four general purpose registers ("q").

209   parameter 1 is the de-referenced pointer ptr. It can be in memory ("m"). Parameter 2 is the input value of x.

210   memory values can be affected in unpredictable ways, so the compiler is not to keep values in registers across this group of instructions.

213   the low-order word of parameter 0 (the long x) is exchanged with the low-order word of parameter 1 (the de-referenced pointer).

214   X can be in a register.

215–216   see the comments on lines 209 and 210.

219   parameter 0 (the long x) is exchanged with parameter 1 (the de-referenced pointer).

220–222   see the comments on lines 214–216.

5.3   Single-processor version of spinlocks

So far, this chapter has considered bit manipulations and atomic operations on scalar values. The time has now come to put these together and build a locking mechanism. One way of implementing locks if to use busy waiting. If such a lock is free it is acquired immediately, but if it is not free then the requesting process continually tests the lock, waiting for it to become free, hence the name, busy waiting.

Linux provides two such mechanisms, spinlocks and read–write locks. Spinlocks are a simpler mechanism by which only one process at a time can acquire the lock, for whatever purpose. A spinlock guarantees strict mutual exclusion. It is essentially a location in memory that is checked by each process before it enters its critical section. If the value is 0, this means the lock is free, so the process sets it to 1 and proceeds. If the value is already 1, the process continually tests the value until the process holding the lock returns it to 0. The loop that implements this repeated testing is said to be spinning on the lock, hence the name.

To guarantee mutual exclusion, the testing and setting of the lock must be atomic, but in some cases this can be overrestrictive. Frequently, it is permissible for more than one process to acquire the same lock simultaneously, if all these processes are only reading the data controlled by the lock and none of them is going to write to it. Such a mechanism is known as a read–write lock. Processes can take out either a read lock (to exclude writing) or a write lock (mutually exclusive) on such a lock.

In this section I consider the implementation of spinlocks in a uniprocessor kernel. Even this is not as simple as one might expect. There are actually three different implementations of spinlocks, corresponding to three different levels of debugging. Each of these will be examined in turn. Multiprocessor versions of spinlocks will be examined in Section 5.4; read–write locks will be discussed in Sections 5.6 and 5.7.

5.3.1   Spinlocks with no debugging

The first implementation is for the case where there is no debugging; in fact, in this case no lock state is maintained and most of the macros do nothing. Remember, in the uniprocessor case there is no contention for the locks anyway. The code in Figure 5.18, from `<linux/spinlock.h>`, shows the implementation of the spinlock macros in this default implementation.

```
44    #define DEBUG_SPINLOCKS  0

45

46    #if (DEBUG_SPINLOCKS < 1)

47

48    #define atomic_dec_and_lock(atomic,lock)
                                          atomic_dec_and_test(atomic)

56    #if (__GNUC__ > 2)
57        typedef struct { } spinlock_t;
58        #define SPIN_LOCK_UNLOCKED (spinlock_t) { }
59    #else
60        typedef struct { int gcc_is_buggy; } spinlock_t;
```

```
61          #define SPIN_LOCK_UNLOCKED (spinlock_t) { 0 }
62   #endif
63
64   #define spin_lock_init(lock)      #do { } while(0)
65   #define spin_lock(lock)           (void)(lock)
66   #define spin_is_locked(lock)      (0)
67   #define spin_trylock(lock)        ({1; })
68   #define spin_unlock_wait(lock)    do { } while(0)
69   #define spin_unlock(lock)         do { } while(0)
```

Figure 5.18   Spinlocks with no debugging

44   this macro controls the level of debugging implemented. The default is 0, which means that the code in this section is compiled. A value of 1 (minimum debugging) means that the code in Section 5.3.2 is compiled. For a value of 2 (full debugging), the code in Section 5.3.3 is compiled.

46–69 this is a trivial implementation of spinlocks. As there is only one CPU, it is assumed that there can be no contention anyway.

48   this macro atomically decrements a variable (e.g. a use counter) and takes out a lock if the result is zero. It evaluates to TRUE if the result is 0, FALSE otherwise. As lock state is not being maintained, only the atomic_dec_and_test() function is needed (see Section 5.2.7).

56–62 earlier versions of gcc had a nasty bug with empty initialisers, so there are two different declarations of the spinlock_t provided.

56–57 if using a version of gcc later than 2, then it is possible to typedef the spinlock_t as a NULL structure; also, the SPIN_LOCK_UNLOCKED()-generating macro can initialise it to NULL.

60–61 for version 2 or earlier, the struct must be declared as an int, and initialised to 0. Note that, apart from initialisation to 0 by the SPIN_LOCK_UNLOCKED() macro, this int is never referenced again.

64–69 these are the actual macros. In all cases, the lock parameter is a pointer to a spinlock_t.

64   initialising such a spinlock is a NULL action.

65   taking out such a spinlock merely casts the lock pointer to be of type void.

66   as the spinlock is never, in fact, locked, this macro always evaluates to 0 (FALSE).

67   if the spinlock is free, this macro locks it. It returns TRUE if it is free beforehand, otherwise FALSE. As the spinlock is always free in the uniprocessor case, this macro always evaluates to TRUE. Note the braces and the semicolon; the value is going to populate a struct.

68   the purpose of this macro is to wait until the spinlock is unlocked. All that is required here in the uniprocessor case is a NULL action.

69   as the spinlock is never in fact locked, all that is required here is a NULL action.

5.3.2   Spinlocks with level-1 debugging

This section will consider the implementation of spinlocks at level-1 debugging. This
actually sets, tests, and clears the lock, so the lock state is maintained. The macros are
shown in Figure 5.19, which is from `<linux/spinlock.h>`.

```
71    #elif (DEBUG_SPINLOCKS < 2)
72
73    typedef struct {
74        volatile unsigned long lock;
75    } spinlock_t;
76    #define SPIN_LOCK_UNLOCKED (spinlock_t) { 0 }
77
78    #define spin_lock_init(x)    do { (x)->lock = 0; } while (0)
79    #define spin_is_locked(lock) (test_bit(0,(lock)))
80    #define spin_trylock(lock)   (!test_and_set_bit(0,(lock)))
81
82    #define spin_lock(x)         do { (x)->lock = 1; } while (0)
83    #define spin_unlock_wait(x)  do { } while (0)
84    #define spin_unlock(x)       do { (x)->lock = 0; } while (0)
```

Figure 5.19   Spinlocks with level-1 debugging

74   in this case the `spinlock_t` structure is an `unsigned long`. Note that it is declared volatile, a
warning to the compiler that its value can be asynchronously changed by another process or by
an interrupt handler.

76   in the unlocked state it has a value of 0; a value of 1 implies that it is locked.

78   the `lock` field of the `spinlock_t` is initialised to 0 (unlocked).

79   if the `lock` field is set (has a value of 1) this returns TRUE; otherwise it returns FALSE. The
macro has been discussed in Section 5.1.3.

80   the `test_and_set_bit()` function (see Section 5.1.4.1) sets (puts a 1 in) the least significant
bit (bit 0) of the `lock` field and returns TRUE if that bit was already set (locked), otherwise it
returns FALSE (unlocked). The macro evaluates to the inverse of this: TRUE if it was unlocked
beforehand, FALSE otherwise.

82   this set is the `lock` field to 1 (locked).

83   this is a NULL operation, as a process never waits in the uniprocessor situation.

84   this sets the `lock` field to 0 (unlocked).

5.3.3   Spinlocks with full debugging

This section describes an implementation of spinlocks that not only maintains lock state but
also does a significant amount of checking that the locks have been properly initialised and

properly used. Warning messages are printed if anomalies are discovered. Figure 5.20 is from <linux/spinlock.h>.

```
86    #else /* (DEBUG_SPINLOCKS >= 2) */
87
88    typedef struct {
89         volatile unsigned long lock;
90         volatile unsigned int babble;
91         const char *module;
92    } spinlock_t;
93    #define SPIN_LOCK_UNLOCKED (spinlock_t){0, 25, __BASE_FILE__}

97    #define spin_lock_init(x)     do { (x)->lock = 0; } while (0)
98    #define spin_is_locked(lock) (test_bit(0,(lock)))
99    #define spin_trylock(lock)    (!test_and_set_bit(0,(lock)))
100
101   #define spin_lock(x)           do {
            unsigned long __spinflags;
            save_flags(__spinflags);
            cli();
            if ((x)->lock && (x)->babble) {
                printk("%s:%d: spin_lock(%s:%p) already locked\n",
                    __BASE_FILE__, __LINE__, (x)->module, (x));
                (x)->babble-;
            }
            (x)->lock = 1;
            restore_flags(__spinflags);
        } while (0)
102   #define spin_unlock_wait(x)  do {
            unsigned long __spinflags;
            save_flags(__spinflags);
            cli();
            if ((x)->lock && (x)->babble) {
                printk("%s:%d: spin_unlock_wait(%s:%p)
                    deadlock\n", __BASE_FILE__, __LINE__,
                    (x)->module, (x)); (x)->babble-;
            }
            restore_flags(__spinflags);
        } while (0)
103   #define spin_unlock(x)         do {
            unsigned long __spinflags;
            save_flags(__spinflags);
            cli();
            if (!(x)->lock && (x)->babble) {
                printk("%s:%d: spin_unlock(%s:%p) not locked\n",
                    __BASE_FILE__, __LINE__, (x)->module, (x));
                (x)->babble--;
            }
            (x)->lock = 0;
```

```
                            restore_flags(__spinflags);
                        } while (0)
            104
            105  #endif    /* DEBUG_SPINLOCKS */
```

Figure 5.20   Spinlocks with full debugging

88–92   this is the fullest version of the spinlock_t.

90   the babble field, as will be seen from its use, limits the number of times that an error message is printed.

91   this is a pointer to a string containing the name of the file in which the particular spinlock_t structure was declared.

93   the lock field is initialised to 0 (unlocked) as usual. Error messages are to be printed a maximum of 25 times. The __BASE_FILE__ macro expands to the name of the source file containing the code that declares the particular instance of the structure.

97   this macro is always used with an existing spinlock_t, to which it is passed a pointer. The lock field is reinitialised to 0. None of the other fields is changed.

98   if bit 0 of the lock field is set, this returns TRUE; otherwise it returns FALSE. See Section 5.1.3 for the test_bit() function.

99   the test_and_set_bit() function was discussed in Section 5.1.4.1. It sets (puts a 1 in) the least significant bit (bit 0) of the lock field, and returns TRUE if that bit was already set (locked), otherwise FALSE (unlocked). The macro evaluates to the inverse of this: TRUE if it was unlocked beforehand, FALSE otherwise. Only the lock field is set or tested.

101–103   these three macros, for some unknown reason, are each written on one line. The normal Linux style breaks long macros over several lines. They have been broken into lines in Figure 5.20 for ease of reading.

101   the value in EFLAGS is saved in the local __spinflags. The whole purpose of this is to remember the state of the interrupt enable bit. The save_flags() function will be dealt with in Section 12.8.2. Interrupts are disabled, whether they were enabled or disabled beforehand. If already locked, and the maximum number of messages has not already been printed, a message is printed saying so. The message consists of the name of the source file, the line-number, "spin_lock" (the file which initialised the error: this is a pointer to spinlock) and "already locked". In the uniprocessor case, as there is no contention, attempting to lock an already locked spinlock implies an error in the design. This code makes sure that such an error is reported. Then babble is decremented, so that a repeated error will not generate a flood of messages. In any case, the lock is set to 1 (whether locked or not). The restore_flags() function (Section 12.8.2) restores the EFLAGS register from __spinflags, thus leaving interrupts in the state they were in beforehand, whether enabled or disabled.

102   this is very similar to line 101. On a uniprocessor, it should always find the spinlock unlocked. If locked, a similar message is printed, but the error is identified as coming from "spin_unlock_wait", and "deadlock" is announced. If unlocked, it returns immediately. This macro does not affect the value of the lock.

103   an attempt to unlock a lock which is not locked implies an error in design. If the maximum number of warning messages has not already been printed, then another one will be printed, identifying it as coming from `"spin_unlock"` and announcing `"not locked"`. In any case, the value of the lock is set to 0 (unlocked).

5.4 Multiprocessor version of spinlocks

The uniprocessor implementation of spinlocks has already been seen in Section 5.3. This section examines how spinlocks are implemented in a multiprocessor kernel.

5.4.1 Data structure

The basic structure of the `spinlock_t` data type in an SMP kernel is shown in Figure 5.21, from `<asm-i386/spinlock.h>`.

```
26    typedef struct {
27        volatile unsigned int lock;
28    #if SPINLOCK_DEBUG
29        unsigned magic;
30    #endif
31    } spinlock_t;
```

Figure 5.21   Data structure representing a spinlock

27   essentially the structure consists of an `unsigned int`, which represents the lock. This will take values of 1 (meaning unlocked) or 0 (meaning locked). This is the inverse of the convention used in the uniprocessor case. Note that it is declared `volatile`, which is a warning to the compiler that its value may be changed by routines other than the one in which it is declared.

28–30   there is also a `magic` field, used for debugging purposes. This is compiled in only if SPINLOCK_DEBUG is defined.

31   this data structure is generally referred to in the sources as `spinlock_t`.

5.4.2 Initialising a spinlock

There are a number of macros declared for initialising spinlocks; see Figure 5.22, from `<asm-i386/spinlock.h>`.

```
33    #define SPINLOCK_MAGIC   0xdead4ead
34
35    #if SPINLOCK_DEBUG
36    #define SPINLOCK_MAGIC_INIT , SPINLOCK_MAGIC
37    #else
38    #define SPINLOCK_MAGIC_INIT  /* */
39    #endif
40
41    #define SPIN_LOCK_UNLOCKED (spinlock_t) { 1 SPINLOCK_MAGIC_INIT }
```

```
42
43    #define spin_lock_init(x) do { *(x) = SPIN_LOCK_UNLOCKED; } while(0)
```

Figure 5.22　Initialising a spinlock

33　the SPINLOCK_MAGIC macro is merely a unique bit pattern most unlikely to occur by accident. If this value is found in the magic field, it implies that the spinlock has actually been initialised and so the value in the lock field can be trusted.

36　if spinlock debugging in turned on, then SPINLOCK_MAGIC_INIT is given the value of SPINLOCK_MAGIC. Note the comma; this is part of the string that will be substituted by the preprocessor.

38　otherwise SPINLOCK_MAGIC_INIT has a null value, and is simply ignored by the preprocessor.

41　the standard initialisation of a spinlock_t (the unlocked state) is a value of 1 in the lock field, and SPINLOCK_MAGIC_INIT in the magic field. Note that this may bring its own comma. The value is either {1, SPINLOCK_MAGIC}, or {1}, depending on whether SPINLOCK_DEBUG is defined or not. The (spinlock_t) here is a cast.

43　finally, there is a macro that initialises a given spinlock (x) to the SPIN_LOCK_UNLOCKED state. Note that it is passed a pointer to a spinlock_t structure, which it de-references and operates on.

5.4.3　Operations on spinlocks

Having looked at the declaration and initialisation of spinlocks, we now turn to the actual functions that operate on these locks.

5.4.3.1　Trying for a spinlock

The spin_trylock() function in Figure 5.23, from <asm-i386/spinlock.h>, does just what it says. If the spinlock is free, it locks it; otherwise, it returns without waiting. The return value distinguishes between the two cases.

```
116  static inline int spin_trylock(spinlock_t *lock)
117  {
118      char oldval;
119      __asm__ __volatile__(
120          "xchgb %b0,%1"
121          :"=q" (oldval), "=m" (lock->lock)
122          :"" (0) : "memory");
123      return oldval > 0;
124  }
```

Figure 5.23　Testing a spinlock and claiming it if free

116　the parameter is a pointer to the spinlock it is to try.

120   the byte in parameter 0 (oldval) is exchanged with parameter 1 (the lock field). For the initial value in oldval, see the description of line 122.

121   these are output parameters. The q constraint means that oldval must be in the A, B, C, or D register. Note that parameter 1, lock, is write only ("=") and may be in memory ("m"). Both of these requirements make sense for the XCHG instruction on the i386.

122   parameter 2 is specified to occupy the same location as parameter 0 and is to have an initial value of 0. The difference is that parameter 0 is output, parameter 2 is input. The "memory" directive tells the compiler that memory will be modified in an unpredictable manner, so it will not keep memory values cached in registers across the group of assembler instructions.

123   after the instruction at line 120, lock has a value of 0, and oldval now has the value that was previously in lock. If this was positive, the lock was free beforehand, so the function returns TRUE – it is locked now. If it was zero or negative beforehand, the lock was held by another process, so the function returns FALSE – it was unable to obtain the lock.

5.4.3.2   Taking out a spinlock

The spin_lock() function shown in Figure 5.24, from <asm-i386/spinlock.h>, also does just what it says. If the lock is free, it takes it; otherwise, it 'busy waits' (spins) until the lock becomes free.

```
126  static inline void spin_lock(spinlock_t *lock)
127  {
128  #if SPINLOCK_DEBUG
129        __label__ here;
130  here:
131        if (lock->magic != SPINLOCK_MAGIC) {
132              printk("eip: %p\n", &&here);
133              BUG();
134        }
135  #endif
136        __asm__ __volatile__(
137              spin_lock_string
138              :"=m" (lock->lock) : : "memory");
139  }
```

Figure 5.24   Taking out a spinlock

126   the parameter is a pointer to the spinlock it is to acquire.

128–135   this code is compiled in only if spinlock debugging is turned on.

129   a local label is declared. This is a gcc-specific extension. It will be used to identify the location of any errors that may be generated. Note that the function is declared as inline, so such an identification makes sense.

131   the debug code checks that the magic field contains the correct bit pattern. If it does not, this

implies that the lock was not properly initialised, so it should not be used or relied on. The SPINLOCK_MAGIC macro was defined in Section 5.4.2.

132   this prints the virtual address of the label `here:`. The `%p` format specifier in `printk()` is a 'pointer' type. The `&&` unary operator is a `gcc`-specific extension. It returns the address of a label, as type `char *`.

133   the `BUG()` macro is from Section 4.1.3.3. It generates an invalid opcode exception.

136–138   these lines do the real work of the function.

137   the code in `spin_lock_string` is executed. This string contains assembler instructions to test and loop, and will be discussed in Section 5.4.3.4.

138   the string itself has no parameters specified; these are supplied here. The only one is the `lock` field, which is expected to be in memory. The `"memory"` directive tells the compiler that memory will be modified in an unpredictable manner, so it will not keep memory values cached in registers across the group of assembler instructions.

5.4.3.3   Giving back a spinlock

The `spin_unlock()` function in Figure 5.25 is from `<asm-i386/spinlock.h>`. It unlocks the spinlock, returning its value to 1. Note there is another, slightly different, version of this function, and a corresponding `spin_unlock_string`, at lines 95–112. This is for particular CPU models and is not considered here.

```
80   static inline void spin_unlock(spinlock_t *lock)
81   {
82   #if SPINLOCK_DEBUG
83       if (lock->magic != SPINLOCK_MAGIC)
84           BUG();
85       if (!spin_is_locked(lock))
86           BUG();
87   #endif
88       __asm__ __volatile__(
89           spin_unlock_string
90           );
91   }
```

Figure 5.25   Giving back a spinlock

80   the parameter is a pointer to the spinlock it is to release.

82–87   these lines are compiled into the code only if debugging is turned on.

83   this checks that the `magic` field contains the correct bit pattern. If it does not, this implies that the lock was not properly initialised, so it should not be used or relied on.

84   the `BUG()` macro is from Section 4.1.3.3. It generates an invalid opcode exception.

85 the `spin_is_locked()` macro checks that it is not trying to unlock a spinlock that has not in fact been locked. It is described in Section 5.4.3.4.

89 this does the real work of the function. The assembler code in the `spin_unlock_string` macro (see Section 5.4.3.4) merely moves a literal 1 to the `lock` field. The operand specifier field is part of that macro, so no operands are specified here

5.4.3.4 Spinlock macros

Figure 5.26 shows some auxiliary macros from `<asm-i386/spinlock.h>` used elsewhere in this section. Some of the coding here is very concise; maybe more concise than it need be.

```
52   #define spin_is_locked(x) (*(volatile char *)(&(x)->lock) <= 0)
53   #define spin_unlock_wait(x)
                                 do { barrier(); } while (spin_is_locked(x))
54
55   #define spin_lock_string                            \
56        "\n1:\t"                                       \
57        "lock ; decb %0\n\t"                           \
58        "js 2f\n"                                      \
59        ".section .text.lock,\"ax\"\n"                 \
60        "2:\t"                                         \
61        "cmpb $0,%0\n\t"                               \
62        "rep;nop\n\t"                                  \
63        "jle 2b\n\t"                                   \
64        "jmp 1b\n"                                     \
65        ".previous"

75   #define spin_unlock_string                          \
76        "movb $1,%0"                                   \
77        : "=m" (lock->lock) : : "memory"
```

Figure 5.26 Auxiliary spinlock macros

52 the parameter to this macro is a pointer to a `spinlock_t`. The definition is best understood when broken down into its components, as follows:

- `(x)->lock` is the lock field.

- `&(x)->lock` is the address of the lock field.

- `(volatile char *)(&(x)->lock)` casts that address to be a pointer to `char`. This is now pointing to the first byte of the `unsigned int`, but because the i386 is little endian, this is the least significant byte.

- `*(volatile char *)(&(x)->lock)` de-references that `char` pointer, to get the value in the byte. If that value is less than or equal to zero, the spinlock is locked, and the macro evaluates to TRUE; otherwise, a value of 1 means it is unlocked, and the macro evaluates to FALSE.

53 if the lock is free, this macro returns immediately. If the spinlock is locked, the macro 'busy waits' until some other process unlocks the spinlock. The `barrier()` macro is defined in `<linux/kernel.h>` as

> 17   #define barrier() __asm__ __volatile__("":::"memory").

The `"memory"` directive to the compiler means that it must not move values from before this point to after it (or vice versa). It guarantees that the current process is seeing a coherent view of memory.

55–65 the `spin_lock_string` has been used in the `spin_lock()` function (see Section 5.4.3.2). Note that the usual operand constraints following the code are not present here. They will be supplied when this macro is instantiated, as, for example, at line 137 of Figure 5.24.

56 a new line, and a label `1:`.

57 the LOCK instruction is a prefix to the following instruction. This guarantees that the DECB (decrement byte) instruction is indivisible. This decrements the byte at parameter 0. Because the i386 is little endian, this is the least significant byte.

58 if the sign bit was set after the decrement, we jump (forwards) to label `2:`. This means the result of the decrement was negative, so the value was not 1 beforehand and the lock was not free.

59–64 this block of code is assembled into a section named `".text.lock"`, with the attributes that it is allocatable and executable. The `ax` flags must be quoted, and the quotes need a backslash, to distinguish them from the quotes at the end of the line. This code is executed only if the lock is busy. It is put in a different section, so that in the common case (lock free) the instruction cache is not filled with code that will not be used.

60–63 this is the busy waiting loop, where it spins on the lock.

61 This checks if the value in parameter 0 is now 0.

62 this is a delay loop, which repeats the NOP instruction. The number of times to repeat is taken from the ECX register. This effectively delays a random number of instructions before trying again.

63 if the result of the comparison at line 61 was less than or equal to 0, then there is a jump back to label `2:`.

64 otherwise (it is 1), there is a jump back to label `1:` and another attempt is made to take out the lock.

65 from here on, code is generated in whatever section was in force before line 59.

75–77 the `spin_unlock_string` is much simpler, it merely writes a literal value of 1 to parameter 0. This is one uninterruptible machine instruction.

77 parameter 0, the `lock` field, is write only (`"="`) and may be in memory (`"m"`). The `"memory"` directive tells the compiler that memory will be modified in an unpredictable manner, so it will not keep memory values cached in registers across the group of assembler instructions.

5.5 The kernel lock

Although most of the time processes take out locks on individual parts of the kernel, there is also a 'big' kernel lock that gives a process mutual exclusion on the whole of the kernel. This is really meant only for multiprocessor kernels; there is a trivial imlementation of it for a uniprocessor. As it is just a spinlock with a side-effect, it is best treated here.

5.5.1 Uniprocessor implementation

In a uniprocessor configuration, this lock is not needed, so the various functions that operate on it are trivially defined; see Figure 5.27, from `<linux/smp_lock.h>`.

```
6    #ifndef CONFIG_SMP
7
8        #define lock_kernel()                          do { } while(0)
9        #define unlock_kernel()                        do { } while(0)
10       #define release_kernel_lock(task, cpu)         do { } while(0)
11       #define reacquire_kernel_lock(task)            do { } while(0)
12       #define kernel_locked() 1
13
14   #else
15
16       #include <asm/smplock.h>
17
18   #endif /* CONFIG_SMP */
```

Figure 5.27   Trivial implementation of the kernel lock

6–12   this is the uniprocessor case.

8–11   these four macros do nothing; the compiler optimises them away.

12   this always evaluates to TRUE.

16   in the SMP case, this header file is included instead, and the functions shown in Section 5.5.2 are compiled in.

5.5.2 Multiprocessor implementation

This section will consider the SMP implementation of the lock. First of all, the lock itself is defined in `arch/i386/kernel/smp.c` as:

```
106  spinlock_t kernel_flag __cacheline_aligned_in_smp =
                                               SPIN_LOCK_UNLOCKED;
```

Because this lock may be acquired recursively, the kernel also keeps track of the number of times it has been acquired by a process, in the `lock_depth` field of the `task_struct`.

5.5.2.1   Acquiring the kernel lock

When a routine within the kernel needs exclusive access to the whole of the kernel, it calls the function shown in Figure 5.28, from `<asm-i386/smplock.h>`. This cannot happen asynchronously on the same CPU, so it needs to worry only about other CPUs.

```
43    static __inline__ void lock_kernel(void)
44
45    #if 1
46        if (!++current->lock_depth)
47            spin_lock(&kernel_flag);
48    #else
49        __asm__ __volatile__(
50            "incl %1\n\t"
51            "jne 9f"
52            spin_lock_string
53            "\n9:"
54            :"=m" (__dummy_lock(&kernel_flag)),
55            "=m" (current->lock_depth));
56    #endif
57    }
```

Figure 5.28   Acquiring the kernel lock

46 the 'unlocked' state of `lock_depth` is −1. As this is the initial acquiring of the lock, its value after the increment should be 0, otherwise there is something wrong.

47 the multiprocessor version of the `spin_lock()` function is from Section 5.4.3.2.

48–56 this is the remains of some debugging code which is never compiled into the kernel – just as well, as the `__dummy_lock()` macro on line 54 does not exist!

5.5.2.2   Releasing the kernel lock

The code in Figure 5.29, from `<asm-i386/smplock.h>`, releases the global kernel lock held by a process and the global interrupt lock for a specific CPU, and enables interrupts. It is used when a process wants to release the lock temporarily.

```
18    #define release_kernel_lock(task, cpu)          \
19        do   {                                      \
20            if (task->lock_depth >= 0)              \
21                spin_unlock(&kernel_flag);          \
22            release_irqlock(cpu);                   \
23            __sti();                                \
24    } while (0)
```

Figure 5.29   Releasing the global kernel lock

18 the parameters are a pointer to the `task_struct` of the releasing process and the number of the CPU on which it is running.

20 only if the `lock_depth` field of the `task_struct` is zero or positive does this release the lock; otherwise, it is not actually holding it. Note that `lock_depth` is not decremented, so if it is holding the lock it gives it back but still remembers that it was holding it.

22 this releases the interrupt lock specific to the CPU (See Section 14.5.1.3 for the function).

23 this enables interrupts; the macro is from Section 12.8.2.

5.5.2.3   Reacquiring the kernel lock

When a routine within the kernel wishes to reacquire the temporarily released kernel lock, it uses the function shown in Figure 5.30, from `<asm-i386/smplock.h>`.

```
29    #define reacquire_kernel_lock(task)                      \
30        do{                                                  \
31            if(task->lock_depth >= 0)                        \
32                spin_lock(&kernel_flag);                     \
33    } while (0)
```

Figure 5.30   Re-acquire the kernel lock

29 the parameter is a pointer to the `task_struct` of the process that wants to reacquire the lock.

31 if the `lock_depth` field of the process is not −1 then the process has been holding the kernel lock, so it is entitled to acquire it again.

32 this is multiprocessor version of the `spin_lock()` function is from Section 5.4.3.2.

5.5.2.4   Returning the kernel lock

When the kernel is finally finished with the kernel lock, it releases it by using the function shown in Figure 5.31, from `<asm-i386/smplock.h>`.

```
59    static __inline__ void unlock_kernel(void)
60    {
61        if(current->lock_depth < 0)
62            BUG();
63    #if 1
64        if (-current->lock_depth < 0)
65            spin_unlock(&kernel_flag);
66    #else
67        __asm____volatile__(
68            "decl %1\n\t"
69            "jns 9f\n\t"
70            spin_unlock_string
71            "\n9:"
```

```
72                    :"=m" (__dummy_lock(&kernel_flag)),
73                    "=m" (current->lock_depth));
74    #endif
75    }
```

Figure 5.31   Giving back the kernel lock

61–62   the kernel is not actually holding the lock, then an attempt to return it is a serious error. The BUG() macro is called (Section 4.1.3.3), which causes an invalid opcode exception.

64–65   decrementing the lock_depth field should return it to its initial value of −1. Only if this invariant is true is the lock released, using the function from Section 5.4.3.3.

66–74   this is a remnant of debugging code and is never compiled into the kernel.

5.6 Single-processor version of read–write locks

Spinlocks are a simple mechanism by which only one process at a time can acquire the lock, for whatever purpose, but in some cases this can be overrestrictive. Frequently, it is permissible for more than one process to acquire the same lock simultaneously, if all of such processes are only reading the data controlled by the lock, and none of them is going to write to it. Such a mechanism is known as a read–write lock. Processes can take out either a read lock (excluding writing) or a write lock (mutually exclusive) on such a lock, so there can be multiple readers at the same time, but only one writer with no readers.

The uniprocessor version of read–write locks is considered in this section. Figure 5.32 is from <linux/spinlock.h>.

```
119  #if (__GNUC__ > 2)
120      typedef struct { } rwlock_t;
121      #define RW_LOCK_UNLOCKED (rwlock_t) { }
122  #else
123      typedef struct { int gcc_is_buggy; } rwlock_t;
124      #define RW_LOCK_UNLOCKED (rwlock_t) { 0 }
125  #endif
126
127  #define rwlock_init(lock)     do { } while(0)
128  #define read_lock(lock)       (void)(lock)
129  #define read_unlock(lock)     do { } while(0)
130  #define write_lock(lock)      (void)(lock)
131  #define write_unlock(lock)    do { } while(0)
```

Figure 5.32   Read–write locks

119–125   earlier versions of gcc had a bug with empty initialisers, so there are two different declarations of the rwlock_t, depending on the version of the compiler in use.

120–121   if using a version of gcc later then 2, then we can typedef the rwlock_t as NULL, and also the RW_LOCK_UNLOCKED() initialising macro.

123–124   otherwise, it has to be declared as an `int` and initialised to 0. Note that apart from initialisation, this `int` is never referenced again.

127–131   in all cases, the lock parameter is a pointer to an `rwlock_t`;

127   initialising such a lock is a null action;

128   taking out such a read lock merely casts the lock pointer to be of type `void`; this prevents the compiler from complaining about 'unused variables';

129   as the read lock is never, in fact, locked, this macro is a null action;

130   taking out such a write lock merely casts the lock pointer to be of type `void`; this prevents the compiler from complaining about 'unused variables';

131   as the write lock is never, in fact, locked, all that is required here is a null action.

5.7   Multiprocessor version of read–write locks

The uniprocessor implementation of these locks has been described in Section 5.6. That treatment is now extended to examine their implementation in a multiprocessor kernel, which is somewhat similar to the code for spinlocks, as described in Section 5.4.1.

5.7.1   Data structures and initialisation

A data structure and a set of macros are also defined for multiprocessor read–write locks; but this time they actually do something.

5.7.1.1   Lock values

Read–write locks are implemented as a 25-bit counter with the high bit being the writer bit. When this is clear, it means that a write lock is held. When set, it means that no writer is holding the lock. The low-order 24 bits count the number of readers. A 0 value here means there are no readers. Every time a read lock is taken out, the value of the `lock` field is decremented. This has the side-effect of clearing the write bit as well. Figure 5.33, from `<asm-i386/rwlock.h>`, shows two macros used when setting and testing such locks.

```
22   #define RW_LOCK_BIAS        0x01000000
23   #define RW_LOCK_BIAS_STR    "0x01000000"
```

Figure 5.33   Read–write lock values

22   this macro is used to test whether or not a write lock is held.

23   this has the same value, represented as an ASCII string; it is used by `write_unlock()` (see Section 5.7.2.4).

5.7.1.2 Representing and initialising read—write locks

The data structure used to represent a read—write lock as well as some macros used to initialise them are shown in Figure 5.34, from <asm-i386/spinlock.h>.

```
152  typedef struct {
153      volatile unsigned int lock;
154  #if SPINLOCK_DEBUG
155      unsigned magic;
156  #endif
157  } rwlock_t;
158
159  #define RWLOCK_MAGIC      0xdeafleed
160
161  #if SPINLOCK_DEBUG
162  #define RWLOCK_MAGIC_INIT         , RWLOCK_MAGIC
163  #else
164  #define RWLOCK_MAGIC_INIT         /* */
165  #endif
166
167  #define RW_LOCK_UNLOCKED (rwlock_t)
                                    { RW_LOCK_BIAS RWLOCK_MAGIC_INIT }
168
169  #define rwlock_init(x) do { *(x) = RW_LOCK_UNLOCKED; } while(0)
```

Figure 5.34 read—write lock definitions

152–157 the rwlock_t is identical to the spinlock_t, as described in Section 5.4.1.

159 the RWLOCK_MAGIC macro is sufficiently different from the SPINLOCK_MAGIC macro to detect any attempt to operate on one with use of routines designed for the other.

162 if spinlock debugging in turned on, then RWLOCK_MAGIC_INIT is given the value of RWLOCK_MAGIC. Note the comma; this is part of the string that will be substituted by the preprocessor.

164 otherwise, RWLOCK_MAGIC_INIT has a null value, and is simply ignored by the preprocessor.

167 the RW_LOCK_UNLOCKED macro gives the lock field a value of either {RW_LOCK_BIAS, RW_LOCK_MAGIC}, or just {RW_LOCK_BIAS}. In either case, the write bit is set. The (rwlock_t) is a cast.

169 this macro initialises a lock field either to RW_LOCK_BIAS RW_LOCK_MAGIC, or just RW_LOCK_BIAS, depending on whether debugging is switched on or not.

5.7.2 Operations on read—write locks

The three functions which take out read—write locks are similar to those seen previously for spinlocks. Of course, there are different functions for read locks and write locks; then there are two macros for returning these locks.

5.7.2.1 Taking out a read lock

The first function, which takes out a read lock, is shown in Figure 5.35, from `<asm-i386/spinlock.h>`. The code in this function is concerned mainly with debugging; the real work is done by a subsidiary macro. If a writer is holding the lock, it busy waits.

```
182  static inline void read_lock(rwlock_t *rw)
183  {
184  #if SPINLOCK_DEBUG
185      if (rw->magic != RWLOCK_MAGIC)
186          BUG();
187  #endif
188      __build_read_lock(rw, "__read_lock_failed");
189  }
```

Figure 5.35 Taking out a read lock

182   the parameter is a pointer to the read–write lock.

184–187   the debugging code merely checks that the `magic` field has the correct bitmap. This implies that the lock was correctly initialised and can be trusted. The `BUG()` macro is described in Section 4.1.3.3.

188   the macro `__build_read_lock()` is described in Section 5.7.3.1. The parameters are a pointer to the lock and the name of a 'helper' subroutine to be called if a writer is holding the lock.

5.7.2.2 Taking out a write lock

The next function, shown in Figure 5.36, from `<asm-i386/spinlock.h>`, takes out a write lock. If it cannot get exclusive ownership of the lock, it busy waits. The comments made in Section 5.7.2.1 apply here also.

```
191  static inline void write_lock(rwlock_t *rw)
192  {
193  #if SPINLOCK_DEBUG
194      if (rw->magic != RWLOCK_MAGIC)
195          BUG();
196  #endif
197      __build_write_lock(rw, "__write_lock_failed");
198  }
```

Figure 5.36 Taking out a write lock

197   the macro `__build_write_lock()` is described in Section 5.7.4.1. The parameters are a pointer to the lock and the name of a 'helper' subroutine to be called if a reader is holding the lock.

5.7.2.3 Trying for a write lock

Figure 5.37, from <asm-i386/spinlock.h>, shows the function that tries for a write lock but does not wait if it cannot acquire it immediately. It returns 1 (TRUE) if it acquires the lock, 0 (FALSE) otherwise. Note that there is no corresponding read_trylock().

```
203  static inline int write_trylock(rwlock_t *lock)
204  {
205      atomic_t *count = (atomic_t *)lock;
206      if (atomic_sub_and_test(RW_LOCK_BIAS, count))
207          return 1;
208      atomic_add(RW_LOCK_BIAS, count);
209      return 0;
210  }
```

Figure 5.37 Testing for a write lock

205 first, we treat the lock field, defined as an unsigned int, as atomic_t, by casting the pointer.

206–207 we can then atomically subtract the RW_LOCK_BIAS and test for 0; if the result is 0, then we have acquired the lock, so we return success (1). If the write lock, or any read locks, were held beforehand, the result will not be 0. The atomic_sub_and_test() function is from Section 5.2.4.

208–209 otherwise, we atomically add the value just subtracted, which puts the lock back as it was, and we return failure (0). The atomic_add() function is from Section 5.2.2.

5.7.2.4 Returning a read–write lock

Unlocking of read and write locks is implemented by the macros given in Figure 5.38, from <asm-i386/spinlock.h>.

```
200  #define read_unlock(rw)
         asm volatile("lock ; incl %0" :"=m" ((rw)->lock) : : "memory")
201  #define write_unlock(rw)
             asm volatile("lock ; addl $" RW_LOCK_BIAS_STR ",%0":"
                                    =m" ((rw)->lock) : : "memory")
```

Figure 5.38 Unlocking read–write locks

200 the inline assembler to unlock a read lock merely locks the bus and increments parameter 0, the lock field, which may be in memory ("=m"). The "memory" directive tells the compiler that memory will be modified in an unpredictable manner, so it will not keep memory values cached in registers across the group of assembler instructions.

201 when a write lock is held, the value of the lock field is 0, so unlocking it merely returns it to its initialisation (free) value. The inline assembler to do that is more complicated – the comment in the source warns that it is not obvious, and needs thinking about. It inserts the literal "RW_LOCK_BIAS_STR" in the middle of the string it is building up, to pass to the assembler.

That literal string is defined in Section 5.7.1.1. Macro substitution does not take place within quotes, so the quoted string has to be terminated after $. Then a string representing the lock bias is concatenated to that, followed by a space. The quotes are then opened again, ",%0", so the instruction now locks the bus and adds the lock bias to parameter 0, which is the `lock` field. The finished assembler will look like this:

```
lock;
addl $01000000, %0
```

5.7.3   Macros to operate on read locks

The two functions for taking out read–write locks, as considered in the previous section, were concerned mainly with checking and debugging. They leave the actual manipulation of the locks to the macros in this section.

5.7.3.1   Checking if parameter is a compile time constant

The macro shown in Figure 5.39, from `<asm-i386/rwlock.h>`, does no work at all. It functions only as an adapter between the read lock code that calls it and common lower-lever worker (or 'helper') macros. This macro calls one of two different worker macros, depending on whether the pointer can be de-referenced at compile time or not. It is used, for example, at line 188 of Figure 5.35.

```
54   #define __build_read_lock(rw, helper) do {            \
55        if (__builtin_constant_p(rw))                    \
56             __build_read_lock_const(rw, helper);        \
57        else                                             \
58             __build_read_lock_ptr(rw, helper);          \
59   } while (0)
```

Figure 5.39   Check if parameter is a compile time constant

55   this is an internal gcc function. It is used to determine if a value is known to be constant at compile time and hence that gcc can perform constant folding on expressions involving that value. The function returns TRUE if its argument is known to be a compile time constant and FALSE otherwise.

56   if it returns TRUE, then `rw` is a compile time constant, so the specific macro for this is used, passing on the `helper` parameter.

57   otherwise, the slightly less efficient macro is used. Both of the macros here are given in Section 5.7.3.2.

5.7.3.2   Taking out a read lock

The previous section referenced two macros that a reader uses to test for a write lock before taking out a read lock. These are shown in Figure 5.40, from `<asm-i386/rwlock.h>`.

The inline assembly is particularly convoluted because of the use of the `.subsection` directive.

```
25    #define __build_read_lock_ptr(rw, helper)                             \
26        asm volatile(LOCK "subl $1,(%0)\n\t"                              \
27            "js 2f\n"                                                     \
28            "1:\n"                                                        \
29            ".subsection 1\n"                                            \
30            ".ifndef _text_lock_" __stringify(KBUILD_BASENAME) "\n" \
31            "_text_lock_" __stringify(KBUILD_BASENAME) ":\n"            \
32            ".endif\n"                                                   \
33            "2:\tcall " helper "\n\t"                                    \
34            "jmp 1b\n"                                                    \
35            ".subsection 0\n"                                            \
36            :: "a" (rw) : "memory")
37
38    #define __build_read_lock_const(rw, helper)                           \
39        asm volatile(LOCK "subl $1,%0\n\t"                               \
40            "js 2f\n"                                                     \
41            1:\n"                                                         \
42            ".subsection 1\n"                                            \
43            ".ifndef _text_lock_" __stringify(KBUILD_BASENAME) "\n" \
44            "_text_lock_" __stringify(KBUILD_BASENAME) ":\n"            \
45            ".endif\n"                                                   \
46            "2:\tpushl %%eax\n\t"                                        \
47            "leal %0,%%eax\n\t"                                          \
48            "call " helper "\n\t"                                        \
49            "popl %%eax\n\t"                                             \
50            "jmp 1b\n"                                                    \
51            ".subsection 0\n"                                            \
52            : "=m" (*(volatile int *)rw) : : "memory")
```

Figure 5.40   Reader testing for a write lock

25–36   this macro deals with the case when the lock is passed by reference. The second parameter is a string representing the name of the 'helper' routine, which is executed if a writer is holding the lock.

26   the LOCK macro was described in Section 5.2.1. In SMP, it translates to the LOCK instruction, otherwise it is NULL. This line locks the bus, and subtracts 1 from the location to which parameter 0 (the `rw` pointer) is pointing. Note the parentheses in (%0), implying indirection. Because of the bias, this cannot on its own drive a free lock, or a lock held by other readers, negative on its own.

27   if the result was negative, the sign bit was set. The value must have been 0 beforehand, implying that a writer is holding the lock, so this causes a jump to label 2: at line 33.

28   if the sign bit was not set, then the lock has been acquired. This is the end of the assembly, as the next line is in a different subsection.

29   this block of code is assembled into a section named `.subsection 1`. This code is (one hopes) seldom executed, only when a writer is holding the lock, so it is compiled into a different section to avoid filling the cache with unused code.

30–32 these lines are for the assembler. The `__stringify()` macro converts the kernel build number (e.g. 2.4.18) to a string. Then, if a label of the form `_text_lock_buildnumber` does not already exist, it is placed here in the code for the assembler. Note the colon (`:`) at the end of line 31, indicating a label definition. This label is inserted merely to help with debugging kernel code.

33   control transfers here if a writer was holding the lock. The helper routine is called, as specified by the caller.

34   when the helper routine returns, we jump unconditionally back to label `1:`, which terminates the assembly.

35   the code from here on is assembled into the main section.

36   parameter 0, the pointer to the `lock` structure, is to be in the EAX register (`"a"`), because the helper routine expects to find it there. This is an input parameter; rw itself is never written. The `"memory"` directive tells the compiler that memory will be modified in an unpredictable manner, so it will not keep memory values cached in registers across the group of assembler instructions.

38–52 this macro deals with the case when the compiler was able to determine that the rw parameter was a constant at compile time. The second parameter is a string representing the name of the 'helper' routine, which is executed if a writer is holding the lock.

39   the LOCK macro was described in Section 5.2.1. In SMP, it translates to the LOCK instruction, otherwise it is NULL. This line locks the bus, and subtracts 1 from parameter 0, which is the de-referenced pointer rw (see line 52). This is slightly more efficient than line 26. Because of the bias, this subtraction cannot drive the lock value negative on its own.

40–45 these lines are identical to lines 27–32, and the same comments apply.

46   control transfers here if a writer was holding the lock. The contents of the EAX register are saved on the stack, as that register is needed now.

47   the effective address of parameter 0 (rw) is loaded into EAX. The helper routine is expecting to find the address of the lock in that register.

48   call the helper routine is called, as specified by the caller.

49   the original value is restored to EAX.

50   we jump unconditionally back to label `1:`, which terminates the assembly.

51   the code from here on is assembled into the main section.

52   parameter 0 is the rw pointer cast to be a pointer to an `int` and then de-referenced. This output parameter, which is write only, can be in memory (`"=m"`). The `"memory"` directive tells the compiler that memory will be modified in an unpredictable manner, so it will not keep memory values cached in registers across the group of assembler instructions.

5.7.4 Macros to operate on write locks

This section describes the worker macros for write locks. Although it is just as complicated, it is very similar to the previous section. Once that is understood, there should be no difficulty with this section.

5.7.4.1 Checking if parameter is a compile time constant

The macro shown in Figure 5.41, from <asm-i386/rwlock.h>, does no work at all. It functions only as an adapter between the write lock code which calls it, and common lower-lever worker (or 'helper') macros. It merely calls one of two different worker macros, depending on whether the pointer can be de-referenced at compile time or not. It is used, for example, at line 197 of Figure 5.36.

```
90    #define __build_write_lock(rw, helper)  do {          \
91        if (__builtin_constant_p(rw))                      \
92            __build_write_lock_const(rw, helper);          \
93        else                                               \
94            __build_write_lock_ptr(rw, helper);            \
95    } while (0)
```

Figure 5.41   Check if parameter is a compile time constant

90–95   this is the code for a write lock, corresponding to that shown in Section 5.7.3.1. There is no need to repeat the comments here.

5.7.4.2 Taking out a write lock

The two macros that writers use to check for other holders of locks are shown in Figure 5.42, from <asm-i386/rwlock.h>. As with read locks, the inline assembler is complicated by the use of the .subsection directive.

```
61    #define __build_write_lock_ptr(rw, helper)                          \
62        asm volatile(LOCK "subl $" RW_LOCK_BIAS_STR ",(%0)\n\t"          \
63            "jnz 2f\n"                                                    \
64            "1:\n"                                                        \
65            ".subsection 1\n"                                             \
66            ".ifndef _text_lock_"__stringify(KBUILD_BASENAME) "\n" \
67            "_text_lock_" __stringify(KBUILD_BASENAME) ":\n"              \
68            ".endif\n"                                                    \
69            "2:\tcall " helper "\n\t"                                     \
70            "jmp 1b\n"                                                    \
71            ".subsection 0"                                               \
72            ::"a" (rw) : "memory")
73
74    #define __build_write_lock_const(rw, helper)                         \
75        asm volatile(LOCK "subl $" RW_LOCK_BIAS_STR ",(%0)\n\t"          \
76            "jnz 2f\n"                                                    \
```

```
77              "1:\n"                                                        \
78              ".subsection 1\n"                                             \
79              ".ifndef_text_lock_"_stringify(KBUILD_BASENAME) "\n"          \
80              "_text_lock_" __stringify(KBUILD_BASENAME) ":\n"              \
81              ".endif\n"                                                    \
82              "2:\tpushl %%eax\n\t"                                         \
83              "leal %0,%%eax\n\t"                                           \
84              "call " helper "\n\t"                                         \
85              "popl %%eax\n\t"                                              \
86              "jmp 1b\n"                                                    \
87              ".subsection 0"                                              \
88              :"=m" (*(volatile int *)rw) : : "memory")
```

Figure 5.42   Building a write lock

61–72   this deals with the case where the lock pointer has to be de-referenced at run time. The second parameter is a string representing the name of the 'helper' routine, which is executed if the caller cannot get an exclusive lock.

62   the LOCK macro was described in Section 5.2.1. In SMP, it translates to the LOCK instruction, otherwise it is null. This line locks the bus and subtracts the value of the bias string from the location to which parameter 0 (rw) is pointing. Note the parentheses, implying indirection.

63   if it is not 0 after this, either a write lock, or at least one read lock, is held and on jump forward is made to label 2:.

64–72   see the comments on lines 28–36 within Section 5.7.3.2.

74–88   this macro deals with the case when the lock pointer does not have to be de-referenced at run time.

75–81   these lines are identical to lines 62–68, and the same comments apply.

82–88   see the comments on lines 46–52 in Section 5.7.3.2.

5.7.5   Assembly language helper routines for read–write locks

When we considered the functions that acquire read–write locks, in Section 5.7.3, two helper routines were introduced. These are used when an attempt to take out a read–write lock fails. They are shown in Figure 5.43, from `arch/i386/kernel/semaphore.c`.

```
239   #if defined(CONFIG_SMP)
240   asm(
241   "
242   .align    4
243   .globl    __write_lock_failed
244   __write_lock_failed:
245       " LOCK "addl $" RW_LOCK_BIAS_STR ",(%eax)
246   1:  rep; nop;
247       cmpl $" RW_LOCK_BIAS_STR ",(%eax)
```

```
248        jne  1b
249
250        "LOCK"subl    $"RW_LOCK_BIAS_STR",(%eax)
251        jnz  __write_lock_failed
252        ret
253
254
255 .align   4
256 .globl    __read_lock_failed
257 __read_lock_failed:
258        lock ; incl    (%eax)
259 1:    rep; nop;
260        cmpl $1,(%eax)
261        js   1b
262
263        lock ; decl    (%eax)
264        js   __read_lock_failed
265        ret
266 "
267 );
268 #endif
```

Figure 5.43   Helper routines for read–write locks

239–268   the whole block of assembler code is only included in the SMP case, but these routines are used only in the SMP case anyway, so that makes sense.

243   this makes the symbol visible to the linker `ld.`, otherwise functions in other modules could not call this entry point.

244   this routine is called, with a pointer to the `lock` field in EAX, if either of the macros described in Section 5.7.4 failed to acquire a write lock (because a writer, or readers, are holding it).

245   the LOCK macro locks the next instruction in the SMP case; otherwise it does nothing. The bias value is added to the lock, a pointer to which is in EAX. This reverses the subtraction made in the calling macro.

246   This is a delay loop, which repeats the NOP instruction. The number of repeats is taken from the ECX register. This effectively delays a random number of instructions before trying again.

247   this check is if the value of the lock is now equal to the bias value. If it is, this means the lock is now free.

248   if not, then we spin on the lock until it is free.

250   the lock should be free at this stage. The bias value is subtracted from the value of the lock.

251   if that does not give a zero result (i.e. some other process has acquired the lock) then a further attempt should be made.

252   this line will be executed when the subtraction at line 250 gives a 0 result.

257   this routine is called, with a pointer to the `lock` field in EAX, if either of the macros in Section 5.7.3 failed to acquire a read lock because a writer was holding it.

258   the LOCK instruction macro locks the bus for the duration of the next instruction. Note that this is the assembler instruction; not the macro as used on line 245. The value of the lock is incremented as an atomic operation. This reverses the subtraction made in the calling macro. Note the parentheses for (%eax).

259   this is a delay loop, that repeats the NOP instruction. The number of times to repeat is taken from the ECX register. This effectively delays a random number of instructions before a further attempt is made.

260   this comparison instruction works by doing a dummy subtraction of 1 from the `lock` field. If the `lock` field was 0 beforehand (a writer was holding it), this will set the sign bit; otherwise (there is no writer) the sign bit is not set.

261   if the comparison sets the sign bit, there is a writer holding the lock so we jump back to label `1:` and spin on the lock until that writer exits.

263   there should be no writer at this stage. The lock is decremented as an atomic operation.

264   just in case a writer got in between lines 261 and 263, the sign bit is checked again. If it is set, we try again.

6

Mutual exclusion with waiting

The previous chapter looked at a number of kernel mechanisms for providing mutual exclusion between processes. All these relied in some way on busy waiting. But there are frequent occasions when a process has to wait for an indefinite time to acquire access to a shared resource. Busy waiting is not acceptable in such cases.

The standard approach to this is to put the process to sleep while it is waiting, using a mechanism such as a semaphore. This chapter considers the mechanisms provided by Linux for handling these situations. These include standard semaphores, a variation called read–write semaphores, and another synchronisation mechanism of its own, called a completion.

6.1 Kernel semaphores

At the user level, Linux provides both System V and POSIX semaphores, but, internally, the kernel provides an implementation of semaphores for its own use. Unlike the user-level semaphores, these are not accessed by means of system calls – they are implemented as ordinary functions within the kernel. This makes them more efficient.

For even greater efficiency, the designers decided to optimise the default case as much as possible: nonblocking waits, and signals on semaphores with empty queues. For this reason, kernel semaphores are implemented at two levels. The actual semaphore functions, down() (which implements WAIT), and up() (which implements SIGNAL) are written in assembler and are in the architecture-dependent source files. Atomicity is handled at this level. These functions test the value of the semaphore and, in the simple case, return immediately. In the rare case (one hopes), when wait queues have to be manipulated, the generic code is called to do so. This would be a WAIT on a zero-valued semaphore, or a SIGNAL on a semaphore with waiting processes.

The Linux Process Manager. The Internals of Scheduling, Interrupts and Signals   John O'Gorman
© 2003 John Wiley & Sons, Ltd   ISBN: 0 470 84771 9

6.1.1 Semaphore data structures and macros

This section will examine the data structure representing a semaphore, and the macros provided for declaring and initialising semaphores

6.1.1.1 The semaphore data structure

The data structure used to represent a semaphore to the system is shown in Figure 6.1, from `<asm-i386/semaphore.h>`.

```
44   struct semaphore {
45        atomic_t count;
46        int sleepers;
47        wait_queue_head_t wait;
48   #if WAITQUEUE_DEBUG
49        long __magic;
50   #endif
51   };
```

Figure 6.1   The semaphore data structure

45   this is the value of the semaphore. When positive, the resource is free and can be acquired. When zero or negative, the resource protected by the semaphore is in use and a requesting process must be blocked. A value of -1 indicates that there are processes sleeping on the semaphore.

46   there is no record of the *number* of processes sleeping on the semaphore. This `int` merely indicates that there are processes on the queue (value 1) or that the queue is empty (value 0).

47   waiting processes are queued from here.

49   the __magic field is given a unique identifier, which is an indication that the structure has been properly initialised (see Section 6.1.1.3).

6.1.1.2 Macros to initialise semaphores

A range of macros are supplied for declaring and initialising semaphores, as shown in Figure 6.2, from `<asm-i386/semaphore.h>`.

```
54   #if WAITQUEUE_DEBUG
55   # define __SEM_DEBUG_INIT(name)                               \
56          , (int)&(name).__magic
57   #else
58   # define __SEM_DEBUG_INIT(name)
59   #endif
60
61   #define __SEMAPHORE_INITIALIZER(name,count)                   \
62   {    ATOMIC_INIT(count), 0,
             __WAIT_QUEUE_HEAD_INITIALIZER((name).wait)           \
63           __SEM_DEBUG_INIT(name) }
```

```
64
65    #define __MUTEX_INITIALIZER(name)                                    \
66          __SEMAPHORE_INITIALIZER(name,1)
67
68    #define __DECLARE_SEMAPHORE_GENERIC(name,count)                     \
69          struct semaphore name = __SEMAPHORE_INITIALIZER(name,count)
70
71    #define DECLARE_MUTEX(name)__DECLARE_SEMAPHORE_GENERIC(name,1)
72    #define DECLARE_MUTEX_LOCKED(name)
                                 __DECLARE_SEMAPHORE_GENERIC(name,0)
```

Figure 6.2   Declaring and initialising semaphores

54–59   these lines define the value that goes into the __magic field of the semaphore.

55–56   if debugging is turned on, the address of the __magic field itself, cast as an int, is written there. Note the comma before it – when this macro is instantiated, it is the second part of the initialisation sequence.

58   when debugging is turned off, this macro is NULL.

61–63   this is a macro that initialises a given semaphore to a specified value. This is the real workhorse of the set.

62   this atomically initialises the count field to the supplied value (the count parameter), using the macro from Section 5.2.1. Note the two different uses of the identifier count here. The sleepers field is always initialised to 0. The head of the wait queue is initialised, using the macro from Section 4.1.2.2 and passing it the identifier of the appropriate field in the struct semaphore.

63   this macro, from lines 54–59, will intialise the __magic field, if it is present.

65–66   a mutex is a semaphore initialised to 1; so this merely calls the __SEMAPHORE_INITIALIZER() from line 60, passing it a parameter of 1.

68–69   this macro both declares and initialises a general semaphore. Its parameters are the name to give to the semaphore, and its initial value.

69   this declares the structure and calls the initialising macro.

71   this declares and initialises a mutex semaphore, in the unlocked state.

72   this macro declares a mutex semaphore and initialises it to the locked state.

6.1.1.3   *Function to initialise a semaphore*

Much of the functionality of the macros discussed in the previous section is duplicated by the inline functions shown in Figure 6.3, from <asm-i386/semaphore.h>.

```
74    static inline void sema_init (struct semaphore *sem, int val)
75    {

82        atomic_set(&sem->count, val);
83        sem->sleepers = 0;
84        init_waitqueue_head(&sem->wait);
85    #if WAITQUEUE_DEBUG
86        sem->__magic = (int)&sem->__magic;
87    #endif
88    }
89
90    static inline void init_MUTEX (struct semaphore *sem)
91    {
92        sema_init(sem, 1);
93    }
94
95    static inline void init_MUTEX_LOCKED (struct semaphore *sem)
96    {
97        sema_init(sem, 0);
98    }
```

Figure 6.3　Inline functions to initialise semaphores

74–88　this provides the same functionality as the __SEMAPHORE_INITIALIZER() macro from lines 61–63 of Section 6.1.1.2.

74　the parameters are a pointer to the semaphore structure to be initialised, and the initial value to be given to it.

82　this atomically sets the count field to val by using the function from Section 5.2.1.

83　this initialises sleepers to 0, as always.

84　this uses the function from Section 4.1.2.3 to initialise the head of the wait queue.

86　if debugging is turned on, this initialises the __magic field with its own address.

90–93　this function provides the same functionality as the __MUTEX_INITIALIZER() macro from lines 65–66 of Section 6.1.1.2.

92　this merely calls sema_init() with a parameter of 1.

95–98　this function initialises a mutex semaphore to the locked state.

97　this merely calls sema_init() with a parameter of 0.

6.1.2　Operations on semaphores

As well as the classic WAIT and SIGNAL, Linux provides two other versions of WAIT. One is nonblocking, and the other can be interrupted by a signal. The high-level, atomic, parts of these four operations are considered in this section.

6.1.2.1   WAIT on a semaphore

The high-level implementation of the classic WAIT operation, for which Linux uses the even more classic name down(), is shown in Figure 6.4, from <asm-i386/semaphore.h>.

```
115   static inline void down(struct semaphore * sem)
116   {
117   #if WAITQUEUE_DEBUG
118         CHECK_MAGIC(sem->__magic);
119   #endif
120
121         __asm__ __volatile__(
122             "# atomic down operation\n\t"
123             LOCK "decl %0\n\t"
124             "js 2f\n"
125             "1:\n"
126             ".section .text.lock,\"ax\"\n"
127             "2:\tcall __down_failed\n\t"
128             "jmp 1b\n"
129             ".previous"
130             :"=m" (sem->count)
131             :"c" (sem)
132             :"memory");
133   }
```

Figure 6.4   WAIT on a semaphore

118   if debugging is turned on, the macro from Section 4.1.3.2 is used to check the validity of the __magic field.

122   this line is only a comment.

123   the LOCK macro (Section 5.2.1) is only operative in an SMP kernel; it guarantees that the following instruction is atomic.

- The DECL instruction decrements the value of the count field by 1.

- If the result is negative, then the sign bit is set in the EFLAGS register. A negative result implies that the process must be put to sleep.

124   if the sign bit is set, it jumps on to label 2:, on line 126.

125   otherwise (the semaphore was positive beforehand) it falls through to here, which terminates the assembly. The process has acquired the semaphore.

126–128   these lines are assembled into a different section, .text.lock. It is hoped that they will not be used frequently, and putting them in a different section means that the cache will not be cluttered with unneeded code.

127   this routine puts the process to sleep (see Section 6.1.3.1).

128   when `__down_failed` returns, the process will have acquired the semaphore (after waiting some time), and the jump terminates the assembler routine.

129   the remainder of the code is assembled into whatever section was in use before line 125 (probably `.text`).

130   parameter 0 is the `count` field. It is written to, and it may be in, memory (`"=m"`).

131   this is the pointer to the semaphore structure. The calling convention used in all these semaphore functions requires that it must be in the ECX register.

6.1.2.2   *Code to wait interruptibly on a semaphore*

If the semaphore is free, the function shown in Figure 6.5, from `<asm-i386/semaphore.h>`, operates identically to `down()` discussed in Section 6.1.2.1. It does, however, return a success value, of 0. Only if it has to wait for the semaphore is it any different. In that case, if it acquires the semaphore after waiting, it also returns 0, but its wait can be interrupted by a signal, in which case it returns without acquiring the semaphore but with a return value of EINTR. The code is almost identical to that in Section 6.1.2.1, and only the differences will be noted here

```
142  static inline int down_interruptible(struct semaphore * sem)
143  {
144      int result;
145
146  #if WAITQUEUE_DEBUG
147      CHECK_MAGIC(sem->__magic);
148  #endif
149
150      __asm____volatile__(
151          "# atomic interruptible down operation\n\t"
152          LOCK "decl %1\n\t"
153          "js 2f\n\t"
154          "xorl %0,%0\n"
155          "1:\n"
156          ".section .text.lock,\"ax\"\n"
157          "2:\tcall __down_failed_interruptible\n\t"
158          "jmp 1b\n"
159          ".previous"
160          :"=a" (result), "=m" (sem->count)
161          :"c" (sem)
162          :"memory");
163      return result;
167  }
```

Figure 6.5   Code to WAIT interruptibly on a semaphore

154   this is an efficient way of setting `result` to 0, indicating that the semaphore has been acquired.

157   this routine is described in Section 6.1.3.2.

160 the `result` variable is to be in the EAX register. The `__down_failed_interruptible` routine on the previous line will put its return value into that register.

163 this returns 0, or the value returned by `__down_failed_interruptible`.

6.1.2.3 Trying to acquire a semaphore

The version of the `down()` operation shown in Figure 6.6, from `<asm-i386/semaphore.h>`, attempts to acquire a semaphore, and returns zero if it succeeds. If it fails, it still returns, but with a value of 1.

```
173
174  static inline int down_trylock(struct semaphore * sem)
175  {
176        int result;
177
178  #if WAITQUEUE_DEBUG
179        CHECK_MAGIC(sem->__magic);
180  #endif
181
182        __asm____volatile__(
183            "# atomic interruptible down operation\n\t"
184            LOCK "decl %1\n\t"
185            "js 2f\n\t"
186            "xorl %0,%0\n"
187            "1:\n"
188            ".section .text.lock,\"ax\"\n"
189            "2:\tcall __down_failed_trylock\n\t"
190            "jmp 1b\n"
191            ".previous"
192            :"=a" (result), "=m" (sem->count)
193            :"c" (sem)
194            :"memory");
195        return result;
196  }
```

Figure 6.6 Trying to acquire a semaphore

173–196 the code is identical to that given in Section 6.1.2.1.

189 the only difference from the code given in Section 6.1.2.1 is the assembler routine called when it cannot acquire the semaphore (see Section 6.1.3.3).

6.1.2.4 Code to signal a semaphore

The first-level code to implement a SIGNAL on a semaphore is shown in Figure 6.7, from `<asm-i386/semaphore.h>`.

```
196  static inline void up(struct semaphore * sem)
```

```
197  {
198  #if WAITQUEUE_DEBUG
199       CHECK_MAGIC(sem->__magic);
200  #endif
201       __asm__ __volatile__(
202            "# atomic up operation\n\t"
203            LOCK "incl %0\n\t"
204            "jle 2f\n"
205            "1:\n"
206            ".section .text.lock,\"ax\"\n"
207            "2:\tcall __up_wakeup\n\t"
208            "jmp 1b\n"
209            ".previous"
210            :"=m" (sem->count)
211            :"c" (sem)
212            :"memory");
213  }
```

Figure 6.7 A SIGNAL on a semaphore

198–200   if debugging is turned on, the validity of the struct semaphore supplied is checked. The macro was described in Section 4.1.3.2.

203   the LOCK macro makes the following machine instruction atomic on a multiprocessor (see Section 5.2.1). The count field in the semaphore is always incremented by an up().

204   if the value is still zero or less after this, there is at least one process sleeping on the semaphore. In that case it jumps forward to label 2: at line 207.

205   this is the trivial case – a signal on a semaphore with no sleepers. Because lines 206–208 are assembled into a different section, this is actually the end of the mainline up() code.

206–208   this is the code executed when a sleeping process has to be woken. It is assembled into a separate section, so that it will not take up space in the cache except when really needed.

207   the __up_wakeup routine is discussed in Section 6.1.3.4.

208   after a process has been woken up, control returns to the mainstream code again.

209   the remainder of the code is compiled into whatever section was in use before line 206 (probably .text).

210   parameter 0 is the count field of sem. It is write-only and can be in memory ("=m").

211   parameter 1 is the pointer sem. It is to be in the ECX register, where the assembler routine called at line 207 is expecting it.

6.1.3   Intermediate-level routines

When any of the four functions discussed in the previous section cannot acquire or release the semaphore immediately, they call routines to carry out the required manipulations of processes and queues. These routines are merely an intermediate layer, which save values in registers that may be 'clobbered' by the C worker functions, and call the appropriate one. These routines will be considered in this section, the worker functions in Section 6.1.4.

6.1.3.1 Wrapper for implementation of __down()

When down() is called to do a WAIT on a zero-valued or negative semaphore, the process has to be put to sleep. The assembler routine called to do this is shown in Figure 6.8, from arch/i386/kernel/semaphore.c. It is merely a wrapper around the __down() function.

```
180  asm(
181  ".text\n"
182  ".align 4\n"
183  ".globl __down_failed\n"
184  "__down_failed:\n\t"
185        "pushl %eax\n\t"
186        "pushl %edx\n\t"
187        "pushl %ecx\n\t"
188        "call __down\n\t"
189        "popl %ecx\n\t"
190        "popl %edx\n\t"
191        "popl %eax\n\t"
192        "ret"
193  );
```

Figure 6.8   Wrapper routine for __down()

181–182   this indicates the code is to be compiled into the .text segment, aligned on a 4-byte boundary.

183   this marks __down_failed as a global symbol. Otherwise, the linker would not be able to see it and link it into routines outside this file, for example down().

185–187   the values in these registers will be 'clobbered' by the __down routine, so they have to be saved, and restored afterwards.

187   this register contains a pointer to the semaphore structure. It is the parameter to __down().

188   the __down() worker function is described in Section 6.1.4.2.

6.1.3.2 Wrapper for implementation of __down_interruptible()

When down_interruptible() is called to do a WAIT on a zero-valued or negative semaphore, the process has to be put to sleep. The assembler routine called to do this is shown in Figure 6.9, from arch/i386/kernel/semaphore.c. It is merely a wrapper around the __down_interruptible() function.

```
195  asm(
196  ".text\n"
197  ".align 4\n"
198  ".globl __down_failed_interruptible\n"
199  "__down_failed_interruptible:\n\t"
200      "pushl %edx\n\t"
201      "pushl %ecx\n\t"
202      "call __down_interruptible\n\t"
203      "popl %ecx\n\t"
204      "popl %edx\n\t"
205      "ret"
206  );
```

Figure 6.9   Wrapper routine for __down_interruptible()

196–197   this indicates the code is to be compiled into the .text segment, aligned on a 4-byte boundary.

198   this marks __down_failed_interruptible as a global symbol. Otherwise, the linker would not be able to see it and link it into routines outside this file, for example down_interruptible().

200–201   the values in these registers will be 'clobbered' by the __down_interruptible routine, so they have to be saved and restored afterwards. The EAX register is not saved, as it will actually be used to pass back the return value.

201   this register contains a pointer to the semaphore structure. It is the parameter to __down_interruptible().

202   the __down_interruptible() worker function is described in Section 6.1.4.3.

6.1.3.3   *Wrapper routine for* __down_trylock()

When down_trylock() is called to do a WAIT on a zero-valued or negative semaphore, the process has to be put to sleep. The assembler routine called to do this is shown in Figure 6.10, from arch/i386/kernel/semaphore.c. It is merely a wrapper around the __down_trylock() function.

```
208  asm(
209  ".text\n"
210  ".align 4\n"
211  ".globl __down_failed_trylock\n"
212  "__down_failed_trylock:\n\t"
213      "pushl %edx\n\t"
214      "pushl %ecx\n\t"
215      "call __down_trylock\n\t"
216      "popl %ecx\n\t"
```

```
217        "popl %edx\n\t"
218        "ret"
219  );
```

Figure 6.10   Wrapper routine for __down_trylock()

209–210   this indicates the code is to be compiled into the .text segment, aligned on a 4-byte boundary.

211   this marks __down_failed_trylock as a global symbol. Otherwise the linker would not be able to see it and link it into routines outside this file, for example down_trylock().

213–214   the values in these registers will be 'clobbered' by the __down_trylock routine, so they have to be saved, and restored afterwards. The EAX register is not saved, as it will actually be used to pass back the return value.

214   this register contains a pointer to the semaphore structure. It is the parameter to down trylock().

215   the __down_trylock() worker function is described in Section 6.1.4.4.

6.1.3.4   *Wrapper for implementation of __up()*

When up() is called to do a SIGNAL on a negative-valued semaphore, a sleeping process has to be woken up. The assembler routine called to do this is shown in Figure 6.11, from arch/i386/kernel/semaphore.c. It is merely a wrapper around the __up() function.

```
221  asm(
222  ".text\n"
223  ".align 4\n"
224  ".globl __up_wakeup\n"
225  "__up_wakeup:\n\t"
226        "pushl %eax\n\t"
227        "pushl %edx\n\t"
228        "pushl %ecx\n\t"
229        "call __up\n\t"
230        "popl %ecx\n\t"
231        "popl %edx\n\t"
232        "popl %eax\n\t"
233        "ret"
234  );
```

Figure 6.11   Wrapper routine for __up()

222–223   this indicates the code is to be compiled into the .text segment, aligned on a 4-byte boundary.

224   this marks __up_wakeup as a global symbol. Otherwise, the linker would not be able to see it and link it into routines outside this file, for example up().

226–228　the values in these registers will be 'clobbered' by the __up routine, so they have to be saved, and restored afterwards.

228　this register contains a pointer to the semaphore structure. It is the parameter to __up().

229　the __up() worker function is described in Section 6.1.4.1.

6.1.4　Semaphore worker functions

The group of functions examined in this section are called only when a high-level semaphore operation is unable to complete. Also, they are all called through the wrapper routines introduced in Section 6.1.3. In all cases they take one parameter, a pointer to the struct semaphore. This has been pushed on the stack by the wrapper routine.

6.1.4.1　Waking up a waiting process

When the first-level up() function determines that there is one or more processes waiting on the semaphore, it calls the __up() function; see Figure 6.12, from arch/i386/kernel/semaphore.c.

```
50   void __up(struct semaphore *sem)
51   {
52         wake_up(&sem->wait);
53   }
```

Figure 6.12　Waking up a process waiting on the semaphore

52　the wake_up() macro was defined in Section 4.7.1 as a wrapper for __wake_up(). It wakes up at most one process waiting exclusively on that particular wait queue.

6.1.4.2　Putting a process to sleep uninterruptibly on a semaphore

When processes do have to wait for a semaphore, they can be put to sleep interruptibly, or uninterruptibly. Figure 6.13, from arch/i386/kernel/semaphore.c, shows the uninterruptible version.

```
55   static spinlock_t semaphore_lock = SPIN_LOCK_UNLOCKED;
56
57   void __down(struct semaphore * sem)
58   {
59         struct task_struct *tsk = current;
60         DECLARE_WAITQUEUE(wait, tsk);
61         tsk->state = TASK_UNINTERRUPTIBLE;
62         add_wait_queue_exclusive(&sem->wait, &wait);
63
64         pin_lock_irq(&semaphore_lock);
65         sem->sleepers++;
66         for (;;) {
```

```
67              int sleepers = sem->sleepers;

73              if (!atomic_add_negative(sleepers - 1, &sem->count)) {
74                   sem->sleepers = 0;
75                   break;
76              }
77              sem->sleepers = 1;
78              spin_unlock_irq(&semaphore_lock);
79
80              schedule();
81              tsk->state = TASK_UNINTERRUPTIBLE;
82              spin_lock_irq(&semaphore_lock);
83         }
84         spin_unlock_irq(&semaphore_lock);
85         remove_wait_queue(&sem->wait, &wait);
86         tsk->state = TASK_RUNNING;
87         wake_up(&sem->wait);
88    }
```

Figure 6.13   Putting a process to sleep interruptibly on a semaphore

55   this is a global spinlock, used to protect *all* semaphores, so while one process is manipulating one semaphore queue no other process can access any other semaphore queue.

59   this gets a pointer to the `task_struct` of the current process.

60   first, it creates and initialises an entry for a wait queue, pointing to the current process. The macro was described in Section 4.1.1.2.

61   then, the `state` field in the `task_struct` is changed to TASK_UNINTERRUPTIBLE.

62   the newly initialised entry is added to the wait queue for this specific semaphore, using the function from Section 4.2.1.2. It is also marked 'exclusive', meaning that only the specified number of waiting processes are to be woken up at a time.

64–84   this takes out the global semaphore lock and disables interrupts as well. The lock was declared on line 55; the macro is from Section 12.8.1. However, it should be noted that even while the lock is held, other processes can still call `up()` or `down()`. So the value of `count` can change asynchronously, even while this lock is held. It does not protect `count`, but it does protect `sleepers`.

65   this increments the `sleepers` variable. There is one extra process sleeping on this semaphore. If there was no process previously sleeping on the semaphore, `sleepers` is 0, this sets it to 1. If there are one or more processes sleeping on the semaphore already, `sleepers` will be 1, and this sets it to 2.

66–83   the infinite loop is to ensure that the process does not assume it has acquired the semaphore just because it has been woken up. The loop causes it to go around and check again.

67   this takes a local copy of the `sleepers` variable specific to this semaphore. This is done purely for efficiency. Because this process is holding the lock, no other process can write to `sleepers`.

73–76   this block of code is at the heart of this implementation of semaphores. It is checking whether the semaphore is now free (i.e. whether `count` has been changed asynchronously). Remember, it is in a loop, and a process may execute it more than once. A process can come to this test under different circumstances, and the value of `sleepers` is used to distinguish between them. In all cases we want to check `count`.

- Scenario 1: it can be the first time around the loop for the process, with no other process on the queue before it. In that case, `sleepers` is 1 (from line 65), and `count` should have been -1 after being decremented by `down()`, but, to check for the possibility that some other process may have done an `up()` since then, this test is performed. Because `sleepers` is 1, the process does not change the value of `count`, only tests it. If `count` is still negative, `sleepers` is set to 1 (to signify that there is a process waiting) and the queue is joined. If it has been incremented [by an `up()`] `sleepers` is set to 0 (to signify that there is no process waiting) and the process jumps out of the loop. It leaves `sleepers` and `count` both with a value of 0, which is correct for the situation where there is no process on the queue.

- Scenario 2: it can also be the first time around the loop for the process, but with another process or processes on the queue before it. In that case, `sleepers` is 2 (from line 65), and `count` should have been -2 after being decremented by `down()`. To check for the possibility that some other process many have done an `up()` since then, the process first undoes its own decrement of `count` and then tests `count`. If `count` is still negative, `sleepers` is set to 1 (to signify that there is a process waiting) and the queue is joined. If it has been incremented [by an `up()`] `sleepers` is set to 0, and the process jumps out of the loop. This process is going to take the semaphore and leave the previously waiting process(es) on the queue. It leaves `sleepers` and `count` both with a value of 0, which is incorrect for the situation where there are processes on the queue. This will be corrected by the effect of the `wake_up()` at line 87 (see scenario 4).

- Scenario 3: a process can be carrying out this test because it has been woken by an `up()` (at line 80), and has gone around the loop again. In that case `sleepers` is 1, and `count` has been incremented to 0 by the `up()`. The process tests `count`, finds it to be nonnegative, so it sets `sleepers` to 0 and jumps out of the loop. It leaves `sleepers` and `count` both with a value of 0. This is correct for the situation where there is no process on the queue. But if there *is* another process on the queue, this is incorrect. The values will be normalised by the effect of the `wake_up()` at line 87 (see scenario 4). Otherwise, if `count` is negative, it means that some other process has got in beforehand (typically, scenario 2), so it goes back to sleep again, leaving `sleepers` at 1, `count` at -1, the correct values when there is a process on the queue.

- Scenario 4: a process can be carrying out this test because it has been woken by the `wake_up()` at line 87. In that case `sleepers` is 0, and `count` is nonnegative. The `atomic_add_negative()` adds -1 to `count`. If `count` was merely 0, this makes it negative, so `sleepers` is set to 1 and goes back to sleep with the correct values. But if `count` was positive [because of some process doing an `up()` in the meantime] this cannot drive it negative, so the process sets `sleepers` to 0 and jumps out of the loop.

74–75   if the semaphore is free, `sleepers` is set to 0 (a process waking up) and the process breaks out of the loop. When a process breaks out of the loop, it leaves `count` nonnegative and sets `sleepers` to 0. If there is no other process on the queue, the `wake_up()` at line 87 has no effect, and `sleepers` remains at 0, correctly indicating no process on the queue, and `count` has its correct value. If there is at least one other process on the queue it is woken by the wake_up(). When it goes around the loop again, if finds sleepers at 0. The atomic_add_negative() causes it to decrement count by 1. If count is still nonnegative after this, then this process breaks out of the loop as well, and the pattern repeats. However, if the atomic_add_negative() sets count to −1, then the previous process goes back to sleep, leaving count at −1 and sleepers at 1, their correct 'resting' values.

77   otherwise, sleepers is set to 1 (a process going to sleep). Control arrives at this line when count is still negative after the atomic addition.

78   this gives back the lock (see Section 12.8.1 for the macro).

80   this calls schedule(), to give up the CPU. The process is already in the TASK_UNINTERRUPTIBLE state and on the wait queue, from lines 60–62.

81   when the process runs again, the state is set back to TASK_UNINTERRUPTIBLE, just in case it has changed in the meantime. This is to prepare it for the possibility of going back to sleep when it goes around the loop again.

82   this takes out the interrupt safe spinlock and the process goes around the loop again to check if it can acquire the semaphore now that it has been woken up.

84   control transfers here only from the break statement at line 75. Here, the spinlock is given back.

85   this removes the task_struct from the wait queue (see Section 4.2.2.1 for the function).

86   this sets the state to TASK_RUNNING.

87   this wakes up another sleeper. This is to prevent a SIGNAL being lost, if it occurs at just the wrong moment. This way, if there is another process on the wait queue it will be woken up, and go around the loop again, trying to take out the semaphore. If there is no process on the wait queue, this will have no effect.

6.1.4.3   Putting a process to sleep interruptibly on a semaphore

There is also a version of WAIT that puts a process to sleep interruptibly; see Figure 6.14, from arch/i386/kernel/semaphore.c. This is used when it is expected that the semaphore will not be available in the short term. The code here is very similar to that in Section 6.1.4.2, and only the differences will be noted

```
90    int __down_interruptible(struct semaphore * sem)
91    {
92          int retval = 0;
93          struct task_struct *tsk = current;
94          DECLARE_WAITQUEUE(wait, tsk);
95          tsk->state = TASK_INTERRUPTIBLE;
96          add_wait_queue_exclusive(&sem->wait, &wait);
97
98          spin_lock_irq(&semaphore_lock);
99          sem->sleepers ++;
```

```
100          for (;;) {
101                  int sleepers = sem->sleepers;

110                  if (signal_pending(current)) {
111                          retval = -EINTR;
112                          sem->sleepers = 0;
113                          atomic_add(sleepers, &sem->count);
114                          break;
115                  }

123                  if (!atomic_add_negative(sleepers - 1, &sem->count)) {
124                          sem->sleepers = 0;
125                          break;
126                  }
127                  sem->sleepers = 1;
128                  spin_unlock_irq(&semaphore_lock);

130                  schedule();
131                  tsk->state = TASK_INTERRUPTIBLE;
132                  spin_lock_irq(&semaphore_lock);
133          }
134          spin_unlock_irq(&semaphore_lock);
135          tsk->state = TASK_RUNNING;
136          remove_wait_queue(&sem->wait, &wait);
137          wake_up(&sem->wait);
138          return retval;
139  }
```

Figure 6.14   Putting a process to sleep interruptibly on a semaphore

90   this function returns an int value, indicating whether it is returning with the semaphore held (0) or because it was interrupted by a signal (EINTR).

92   this default value indicates that the process waited and acquired the semaphore.

95   the state field is set to TASK_INTERRUPTIBLE.

110–115   if there is a signal pending to the current process at this stage, the proces is going to abort its attempt to acquire the semaphore. This may happen on its first time around the loop but is more likely on subsequent iterations. In any case it must adjust the count field before it returns.

110   the signal_pending() function will be discussed in Section 18.3.1.

111   the value returned indicates that, while waiting, the process was interrupted by a signal.

112–113   the logic here is identical to that discussed at length for lines 73–76 of Section 6.1.4.2. A process can come to this block of code under the same four conditions identified there (scenarios 1–4), and the value of the semaphore is normalised in the same way.

113   a process can come to this line under different circumstances, and the value of sleepers is used

to distinguish between them. In all cases it wants to adjust count by the previous value of sleepers.

- It can be the first time around the loop for the process, with no other process on the queue before it. In that case, sleepers is 1, and count should have been −1 after being decremented by down_interruptible(). This line undoes the decrement, and sets count back to 0.

- It can be the first time around the loop for the process, but with another process on the queue before it. In that case sleepers is 2, and count should have been −2 after being decremented by down_interruptible(). This line undoes the decrement and sets count back to 0.

- A process can arrive at this line because it has been woken by an up() and has gone around the loop again. In that case, sleepers is 1, and count has been incremented to 0. So this line sets count to 1. In that case, the wake_up() at line 137 will cause another process to wake up and go around the loop again, resetting count to −1 at line 123.

- A process can be carrying out this test because it has been woken by the wake_up() at line 137. In that case, sleepers is 0, and count is nonnegative. So this line leaves count unchanged.

114   the process breaks out of the loop and exits.

6.1.4.4 Trying for a semaphore

The function shown in Figure 6.15, from arch/i386/kernel/semaphore.c, is called when down_trylock() fails to acquire the semaphore. Its main purpose is to correct for having decremented the count.

```
149  int __down_trylock(struct semaphore * sem)
150  {
151      int sleepers;
152      unsigned long flags;
153
154      spin_lock_irqsave(&semaphore_lock, flags);
155      sleepers = sem->sleepers + 1;
156      sem->sleepers = 0;

162      if (!atomic_add_negative(sleepers, &sem->count))
163          wake_up(&sem->wait);
164
165      spin_unlock_irqrestore(&semaphore_lock, flags);
166      return 1;
167  }
```

Figure 6.15 Adjust count when trylock fails

154–165   this takes out the semaphore spinlock, disables interrupts, and saves the value of EFLAGS. The macros will be introduced in Section 12.8.1.

155   a local copy of `sleepers` is taken, incremented to take this process into account.

156   set the `sleepers` field of the `struct semaphore` is set to 0, to indicate that the semaphore needs to be normalised again.

162–163   the high-level `sem_trylock()` failed to acquire the semaphore because some other process was holding it. If there is 'no one' else waiting on it then (the incremented) `sleepers` will be 1, and `count` will be −1 [after the decrement in `down_trylock()`]. However, if there is at least one other process waiting on it, then (the incremented) `sleepers` will be 2, and `count` will be −2 (after the decrement in `down_trylock()`). In both cases the result of the `atomic_add_negative()` will be 0 (nonnegative), and `wake_up()` will be called.

- If there is no process on the wait queue, this has no effect. Both the `count` and `sleepers` fields have a value of 0, which is correct for the situation where the semaphore is held but there are no waiters.

- If there is even one process on the wait queue, this will wake it up; the process will go around its loop again and normalise the values of `count` and `sleepers` to −1 and 1, respectively.

165   we return the spinlock and restore `EFLAGS` as it was before.

166   we always return 1, meaning that we did not acquire the lock.

6.2   Read–write semaphores

We have seen in Chapter 5 that Linux makes a distinction between standard spinlocks and read–write locks, to allow for finer granularity. The same distinction is made with semaphores. There may be occasions when it is quite permissible to allow a process of one type to do a successful WAIT on a semaphore, while a process of another type should be blocked. The classic example is readers and writers, hence the name given to the mechanism. Note the essential difference between read–write locks and read–write semaphores. Read–write locks hold up contenders by forcing them to busy wait; the latter read–write semaphores do so by putting them to sleep.

6.2.1   Data structures

As usual, we begin by considering the data structures used to represent such semaphores, and their initialisation.

6.2.1.1   *The semaphore definition*

The basic structure of a read–write semaphore is shown in Figure 6.16, from `<asm-386/rwsem.h>`.

```
54    struct rw_semaphore {
55        signed long                  count;
56    #define RWSEM_UNLOCKED_VALUE      0x00000000
57    #define RWSEM_ACTIVE_BIAS         0x00000001
```

```
58    #define RWSEM_ACTIVE_MASK          0x0000ffff
59    #define RWSEM_WAITING_BIAS         (-0x00010000)
60    #define RWSEM_ACTIVE_READ_BIAS     RWSEM_ACTIVE_BIAS
61    #define RWSEM_ACTIVE_WRITE_BIAS
                            (RWSEM_WAITING_BIAS + RWSEM_ACTIVE_BIAS)
62        spinlock_t                 wait_lock;
63        struct list_head           wait_list;
64    #if RWSEM_DEBUG
65        int                        debug;
66    #endif
67    };
```

Figure 6.16   Data structure representing a read–write semaphore

55   this field contains the value of the semaphore. As with read–write locks, it is a faceted field. The low-order word keeps track of the number of processes holding it. The high-order word counts any active writer, plus any waiting processes. This field is maintained as a negative value.

56   this is the unlocked value: no process is holding the semaphore, and no process of either type is waiting.

57   the count field is incremented by this value each time a process acquires the semaphore, either for reading or writing.

58   the low-order 16-bits count the number of processes holding the semaphore, either for reading or writing. This gives a maximum of 65,535, which should be adequate. The mask defined on this line picks out that number from the full value.

59   a writer adds this negative value each time it acquires the semaphore. In effect, it subtracts 1 from the high-order 16-bits. Each waiting process also adds this negative value.

61   this is the value representing the active writer. It indicates both that it is the active writer (RWSEM_WAITING_BIAS) and that it is holding the semaphore (RWSEM_ACTIVE_BIAS).

62   this is a spinlock used to guarantee mutual exclusion on this data structure (see Sections 5.3 and 5.4).

63   this is the head of the linked list of waiting processes (readers and writers). On generic list handling, see Section 4.3.

65   this field is included only if semaphore debugging is turned on

6.2.1.2   Initialising read–write semaphores

The code used to create and initialise read–write semaphores is shown in Figure 6.17, from <asm-i386/rwsem.h>.

```
72    #if RWSEM_DEBUG
73    #define __RWSEM_DEBUG_INIT    , 0
74    #else
```

```
75    #define __RWSEM_DEBUG_INIT    /**/
76    #endif
77
78    #define __RWSEM_INITIALIZER(name)                                      \
79    { RWSEM_UNLOCKED_VALUE, SPIN_LOCK_UNLOCKED,                             \
80         LIST_HEAD_INIT((name).wait_list) __RWSEM_DEBUG_INIT }
81
82    #define DECLARE_RWSEM(name)                                            \
83         struct rw_semaphore name = __RWSEM_INITIALIZER(name)
84
85    static inline void init_rwsem(struct rw_semaphore *sem)
86    {
87         sem->count = RWSEM_UNLOCKED_VALUE;
88         spin_lock_init(&sem->wait_lock);
89         INIT_LIST_HEAD(&sem->wait_list);
90    #if RWSEM_DEBUG
91         sem->debug = 0;
92    #endif
93    }
```

Figure 6.17   Initialising a read–write semaphore

72–76   these lines are merely setting up an initial value of 0 for the debug field, if it exists.

78–80   this macro provides initial values for a struct rw_semaphore called name.

79   the count field is set to 0, using the macro from Section 6.2.1.1, and the spinlock is initialised to the unlocked state, using the macro from Section 5.3.

80   the head of the wait queue is pointed to itself, using the macro from Section 4.3.1. If the debug field exists, it is initialised to 0. The comma between the two items on this line is provided by the __RWSEM_DEBUG_INIT macro (see line 73).

82–83   this macro creates a read–write semaphore called name, and initialises it.

85–93   this function sets an existing read–write semaphore back to initial values:

85   it is passed a pointer to the structure representing the semaphore;

87   the count field is initialised to 0 (see Section 6.2.1.1);

88   the spinlock is initialised to the unlocked state, using the macro from Section 5.3;

89   the head of the wait queue is initialised, using the macro from Section 4.3.1;

91   if this field exists, it is initialised to 0

6.2.1.3   Data structure representing a waiting process

The read–write semaphore mechanism uses its own version of the struct __wait_ queue to link a waiting process onto the queue headed from the semaphore structure. This is shown in Figure 6.18, from `lib/rwsem.c`. Compare this with the standard `struct __wait_queue` shown in Section 4.1.1.1 (see Figure 4.1).

```
10    struct rwsem_waiter {
11          struct list_head                list;
12          struct task_struct              *task;
13          unsigned int                    flags;
14    #define RWSEM_WAITING_FOR_READ    0x00000001
15    #define RWSEM_WAITING_FOR_WRITE   0x00000002
16    };
```

Figure 6.18   Data structure representing a waiting process

11   this is the link field for the list of waiting processes. The `struct list_head` was described in Section 4.3.1.

12   this is a pointer to the `task_struct` representing the waiting process.

13   this field contains the reason the process is waiting. The two possible reasons are defined on lines 14 and 15.

6.2.1.4   Tracing semaphore operations

When debugging is turned on, informational messages are printed at various points in the manipulation of read–write semaphores. The function that prints these messages is shown in Figure 6.19, from `lib/rwsem.c`.

```
18    #if RWSEM_DEBUG
19    #undef rwsemtrace
20    void rwsemtrace(struct rw_semaphore *sem, const char *str)
21    {
22          printk("sem=%p\n", sem);
23          printk("(sem)=%08lx\n", sem->count);
24          if (sem->debug)
25                printk("[%d] %s({%08lx})\n", current->pid, str,
                                                      sem->count);
26    }
27    #endif
```

Figure 6.19   Tracing semaphore operations

18–27   the whole function is included only when read–write semaphore debugging is turned on.

19   to avoid any conflict with the macro defined in `<linux/rwsem.h>`, it is undefined here.

20   the parameters are a pointer to the semaphore structure and a pointer to a message string.

22   the address of the semaphore structure is printed on the first line.

23   the value of the semaphore is printed as an 8-digit hex number.

24–25   if the debug field of this particular semaphore has a value other than its initial 0, then a third line
of information is printed, as follows:

[process id] message string ({value of semaphore}).

6.2.2   High-level manipulation of read–write semaphores

The kernel provides four high-level functions for acquiring and releasing read–write
semaphores, as shown in Figure 6.20, from <linux/rwsem.h>. These are only wrappers
around the real worker functions, discussed in Section 6.2.3. The wrapper function used in
all cases is for debugging, and was discussed in Section 6.2.1.4.

```
41    static inline void down_read(struct rw_semaphore *sem)
42    {
43        rwsemtrace(sem,"Entering down_read");
44        __down_read(sem);
45        rwsemtrace(sem,"Leaving down_read");
46    }


51    static inline void down_write(struct rw_semaphore *sem)
52    {
53        rwsemtrace(sem,"Entering down_write");
54        __down_write(sem);
55        rwsemtrace(sem,"Leaving down_write");
56    }


61    static inline void up_read(struct rw_semaphore *sem)
62    {
63        rwsemtrace(sem,"Entering up_read");
64        __up_read(sem);
65        rwsemtrace(sem,"Leaving up_read");
66    }


71    static inline void up_write(struct rw_semaphore *sem)
72    {
73        rwsemtrace(sem,"Entering up_write");
74        __up_write(sem);
75        rwsemtrace(sem,"Leaving up_write");
76    }
```

Figure 6.20   Locking and unlocking read–write semaphores

44   this worker function is described in Section 6.2.3.1.

54   this worker function is described in Section 6.2.3.2.

64   this worker function is described in Section 6.2.3.3.

74   this worker function is described in Section 6.2.3.4.

6.2.3   Acquiring and releasing a read–write semaphore

Two worker functions are provided for acquiring a read–write semaphore, and two more for releasing such a semaphore. All these are implemented by using inline assembler.

6.2.3.1   *Acquiring the semaphore for reading*

The function shown in Figure 6.21, from `<asm-i386/rwsem.h>`, attempts to acquire a read–write semaphore for reading. The calling process will be put to sleep only if a writer is holding the semaphore.

```
98    static inline void __down_read(struct rw_semaphore *sem)
99    {
100        __asm__ __volatile__(
101        "# beginning down_read\n\t"
102        LOCK_PREFIX " incl (%%eax)\n\t"
103        " js  2f\n\t"
104        "1:\n\t"
105        ".subsection 1\n"
106        ".ifndef _text_lock_" __stringify(KBUILD_BASENAME) "\n"
107        "_text_lock_" __stringify(KBUILD_BASENAME) ":\n"
108        ".endif\n"
109        "2:\n\t"
110        " pushl    %%ecx\n\t"
111        " pushl    %%edx\n\t"
112        " call     rwsem_down_read_failed\n\t"
113        " popl     %%edx\n\t"
114        " popl     %%ecx\n\t"
115        " jmp 1b\n"
116        ".subsection 0\n"
117        "# ending down_read\n\t"
118        : "+m"(sem->count)
119        : "a"(sem)
120        : "memory", "cc");
121    }
```

Figure 6.21   Acquire a semaphore for reading

102   the `LOCK_PREFIX` macro was defined in Section 5.1.4.2. On a multiprocessor, it evaluates to the `LOCK` machine instruction, which locks the bus for the following `INCL` instruction, so making it atomic. On a uniprocessor it is a null operation, as the instruction is atomic anyway. A reader always increments the value of the semaphore, whether it has to wait or not. This increment will be reversed if it finds later that it has to wait. Doing it this way means that the default path (semaphore-free) is as short as possible. The pointer to the semaphore structure is in the `EAX` register (see line 119). The present line makes use of the fact that the `count` field is the first field in the semaphore structure, and so EAX is effectively pointing to count. The sign bit is set in the EFLAGS register, depending on the result of the increment.

103 if the most significant bit is set, the semaphore is held by a writer, and control jumps on to label 2: at line 109. As the next block of code is compiled into a different subsection, if the most significant bit is clear, control falls through to the end of the assembler code and the function terminates, with the caller holding the semaphore.

105–115 this block of code, which should be needed less frequently than the previous lines, is compiled into subsection 1. This is an optimisation to save putting unused code into the cache.

106–108 these lines are for the assembler. The __stringify() macro converts the kernel build number (e.g. 2.4.18) to a string. Then, if a label of the form _text_lock_*buildnumber* does not already exist, it is placed here in the code for the assembler. Note the colon at the end of line 107, indicating a label definition. This label is inserted merely to help with debugging kernel code.

110–111 these registers will be used by the routine called at line 112, so they are saved here, and restored at lines 113–114.

112 this routine, as described in Section 6.2.4.2, adjusts the count field and arranges for the process to sleep. It expects its parameter in the EAX register. It will return only when the process has acquired the semaphore.

113–114 these remove values pushed on the stack at lines 110–111.

115 at this stage the process has acquired the semaphore; it returns to the mainline code and exits the function.

116 the code from here on is assembled into the main section.

118 this output parameter may be in memory. The "+" means that this operand is both read and written by the INCL instruction.

119 this input parameter, the pointer sem, must be in the EAX register, "a".

120 the "memory" operand constraint means that memory may be modified in an unpredictable manner. The "cc" warns the assembler that the EFLAGS register may be altered by the INCL instruction.

6.2.3.2 Acquiring the semaphore for writing

The function shown in Figure 6.22, from <asm-1386/rwsem.h>, attempts to acquire a read–write semaphore for writing. The calling process will be put to sleep if any other process (reader or writer) is currently holding the semaphore.

```
126  static inline void __down_write(struct rw_semaphore *sem)
127  {
128      int tmp;
129
130      tmp = RWSEM_ACTIVE_WRITE_BIAS;
```

```
131        __asm__ __volatile__(
132        "# beginning down_write\n\t"
133        LOCK_PREFIX    " xadd          %0,(%%eax)\n\t"
134        " testl        %0,%0\n\t"
135        " jnz          2f\n\t"
136        "1:\n\t"
137        ".subsection 1\n"
138        ".ifndef _text_lock_" __stringify(KBUILD_BASENAME) "\n"
139        "_text_lock_" __stringify(KBUILD_BASENAME) ":\n"
140        ".endif\n"
141        "2:\n\t"
142        " pushl    %%ecx\n\t"
143        " call     rwsem_down_write_failed\n\t"
144        " popl     %%ecx\n\t"
145        " jmp      1b\n"
146        ".subsection 0\n"
147        "# ending down_write"
148        : "+d"(tmp), "+m"(sem->count)
149        : "a"(sem)
150        : "memory", "cc");
151  }
```

Figure 6.22   Acquiring a semaphore for writing

130   the local `tmp` variable is initialised to 1 – 00010000, which is FFFF 0001, This indicates one active lock and one active writer.

133   the `LOCK_PREFIX` macro is defined in Section 5.1.4.2. On a multiprocessor, it evaluates to the LOCK machine instruction, which locks the bus for the following XADD instruction, so making it atomic. On a uniprocessor it is NULL, as the instruction is atomic anyway.
   The first parameter to XADD is `tmp` (line 148); the second is the `count` field of the semaphore structure itself. This instruction first exchanges the values, putting the previous value of `count` into `tmp`, and then puts the sum of the two into `count`, so it increments the total number of requests (in the bottom half of `count`) and also increments the (negative) top half of `count`.

134   for the semaphore to be granted for writing, `count` must have been 0 beforehand, (i.e. no readers and no writers). The local `tmp` now has the previous value of `count`, so on comparing that with itself it will set the zero flag in EFLAGS if it has a value of 0.

135   if the result of the test on the previous line was not 0, control jumps to label `2:` at line 141. Otherwise, as the next block of code is compiled into a different section, control falls through to the end of the assembler code, and the function terminates, with the caller holding the semaphore for writing. In such a case, the `count` field always has a value of FFFF0001.

137–145   this block of code, which should be needed less frequently than the previous lines, is compiled into `subsection 1`. This is an optimisation to save putting unused code into the cache.

138–140   see lines 106–108 of Section 6.2.3.1.

142   this register will be used by the routine called at line 143, so it is saved here and restored at line 144.

143   this routine, as described in Section 6.2.4.3, adjusts the count field and arranges for the process to sleep waiting for the semaphore. It expects its parameter in the EAX register. It will return only when the process has acquired the semaphore for writing.

145   control returns to the mainline code and the function is exited.

146   the code from here on is assembled into the main section.

148   the output parameter 0 (tmp) must be in the EDX register ("d") and Parameter 1 (the count field) may be in memory ("m"); both of these will be both read and written by the XADD instruction ("+").

149   this input parameter, the pointer sem, must be in the EAX register, "a".

150   the "memory" operand constraint means that memory may be modified in an unpredictable manner. The "cc" warns the assembler that the EFLAGS register may be altered by the XADD instruction.

6.2.3.3   Releasing a semaphore held for reading

The function shown in Figure 6.23, from <asm-i386/rwsem.h>, gives back a semaphore held for reading.

```
156   static inline void __up_read(struct rw_semaphore * sem)
157   {
158         __s32 tmp = -RWSEM_ACTIVE_READ_BIAS;
159         __asm__ __volatile__(
160         "# beginning __up_read\n\t"
161         LOCK_PREFIX    " xadd     %%edx, (%%eax)\n\t"
162         " js        2f\n\t"
163         "1:\n\t"
164         ".subsection 1\n"
165         ".ifndef _text_lock_" __stringify(KBUILD_BASENAME) "\n"
166         "_text_lock_" __stringify(KBUILD_BASENAME) ":\n"
167         ".endif\n"
168         "2:\n\t"
169         " decw     %%dx\n\t"
170         " jnz      1b\n\t"
171         " pushl    %%ecx\n\t"
172         " call     rwsem_wake\n\t"
173         " popl     %%ecx\n\t"
174         " jmp      1b\n"
175         ".subsection 0\n"
176         "# ending __up_read\n"
```

```
177            : "+m"(sem->count), "+d"(tmp)
178            : "a"(sem)
179            : "memory", "cc");
180  }
```

Figure 6.23   Release a semaphore held for reading

158   the `tmp` variable is initialised to a value of -1. This will be used to decrement the count of processes holding the semaphore.

161   the `LOCK_PREFIX` macro was defined in Section 5.1.4.2. On a multiprocessor, it evaluates to the `LOCK` machine instruction, which locks the bus for the following XADD instruction, so making it atomic. On a uniprocessor it is NULL, as the instruction is atomic anyway. The first parameter to XADD is `tmp` (see line 177); the second is the `count` field of the semaphore structure itself (see line 178). This instruction first exchanges the values, putting the previous value of `count` into `tmp`, and then puts the sum of the two into `count`. So, it adds -1 to (decrements) the number of processes holding the semaphore (in the bottom half of `count`).

162   if the sign bit was set after the previous operation, then one or more writers were waiting. Control transfers to label `2:` at line 168. Otherwise, as the next block of code is compiled into a different section, control falls through to the end of the assembler code, and the function terminates. There was no process waiting, so there is nothing more to be done.

164–174   this block of code, which should be needed less frequently than the previous lines, is compiled into the `subsection 1`. This is to save putting unused code into the cache.

165–167   see lines 106–108 of Section 6.2.3.1.

169   a waiting writer has been found at line 162. This line checks if the present process was the *last* reader and decrements the low-order 16-bits of `tmp` (i.e. the number of users as recorded in `count` before line 161). Note that this does not affect the value of `count`.

170   if there are still some active readers left, there is nothing further to be done, do control jumps back to the mainstream at label `1:`, and the function is exited.

171–174   if this was the last reader, then these lines are executed.

171   this register will be used by the routine called at line 172, so it is saved here and restored at line 173.

172   this routine, as described in Section 6.2.4.5, will wake up one waiting writer process. It expects its single parameter (the `sem` pointer) to be in the EAX register.

174   returns to the mainline code and the function is exited.

177   output parameter 0 (the `count` field) may be in memory (`"m"`) and parameter 1 (`tmp`) must be in the EDX register (`"d"`); both of these will be both read and written by the XADD instruction (`"+"`).

178   this input parameter, the pointer `sem`, must be in the EAX register, `"a"`.

179   the `"memory"` operand constraint means that memory may be modified in an unpredictable manner. The `"cc"` warns the assembler that the EFLAGS register may be altered by the XADD instruction.

6.2.3.4   Releasing a semaphore held for writing

The function shown in Figure 6.24, from `<asm-i386/rwsem.h>`, gives back a semaphore held for writing.

```
185   static inline void __up_write(struct rw_semaphore *sem)
186   {
187         __asm__ __volatile__(
188         "# beginning __up_write\n\t"
189         " movl    %2,%%edx\n\t"
190         LOCK_PREFIX    " xaddl    %%edx,(%%eax)\n\t"
191         " jnz      2f\n\t"
192         "1:\n\t"
193         ".subsection 1\n"
194         ".ifndef _text_lock_" __stringify(KBUILD_BASENAME) "\n"
195         "_text_lock_" __stringify(KBUILD_BASENAME) ":\n"
196         ".endif\n"
197         "2:\n\t"
198         " decw     %%dx\n\t"
199         " jnz      1b\n\t"
200         " pushl    %%ecx\n\t"
201         " call     rwsem_wake\n\t"
202         " popl     %%ecx\n\t"
203         " jmp      1b\n"
204         ".subsection 0\n"
205         "# ending __up_write\n"
206         : "+m"(sem->count)
207         : "a"(sem), "i"(-RWSEM_ACTIVE_WRITE_BIAS)
208         : "memory", "cc", "edx");
209   }
```

Figure 6.24   Releasing a semaphore held for writing

189   parameter 2 is the immediate value −RWSEM_ACTIVE_WRITE_BIAS (see line 207), and it is copied to the EDX register.

190   this value is added to count and the original value of count in EDX is returned. If there are no processes waiting on the semaphore, the value of count beforehand will be FFFF0001. Adding −RWSEM_ACTIVE_WRITE_BIAS (-FFFF0001) to this would result in count being 0. If there are any waiting processes, then the result would not be 0.

191   if the semaphore is being waited on, control jumps to label 2: in the next section. Otherwise this function terminates.

193–203   this block of code, which should be needed less frequently than the previous lines, is compiled into subsection 1. This is to save putting unused code into the cache.

194–196 see lines 106–108 of Section 6.2.3.1.

198 control transfers here if there is even one process waiting. The low-order 16 bits of EDX (i.e. the number of users as recorded in count before line 190) is decremented.

199 if there is even one process holding the semaphore, there is nothing further to be done and the process jumps back to the mainstream at label 1: and exits the function. This could not happen on a uniprocessor; but on a multiprocessor, another process could have woken the waiter identified at line 191.

200–203 if no process is holding the semaphore, then these lines are executed.

200 this register will be used by the routine called at line 201, so it is saved here, and restored at line 202.

201 this routine, as described in Section 6.2.4.5, will wake up a process or processes at the head of the wait queue. It expects its one parameter, a pointer to the semaphore structure, to be in the EAX register.

203 control returns to the mainline code and the function is exited.

206 this output parameter may be in memory. The "+" means that this operand is both read and written by the XADD instruction.

207 input parameter 1, the pointer sem, must be in the EAX register, "a", and parameter 2 is the immediate value –RWSEM_ACTIVE_WAIT_BIAS.

208 the "memory" operand constraint means that memory may be modified in an unpredictable manner. The "cc" warns the assembler that the EFLAGS register may be altered by the XADD instruction. The "edx" warns that the EDX register will be altered by the XADD instruction

6.2.4 Interaction with the scheduler

The critical part of the implementation of read–write semaphores was examined in the previous section. The noncritical part, involving manipulation of wait queues, and inter-action with the scheduler, is described in this section.

6.2.4.1 Parameter passing optimisation

The three functions discussed in this section each take one parameter, a pointer to the semaphore structure. They are optimised to expect this pointer in the EAX register, not on the stack. The declarations to effect this are shown in Figure 6.25, from <asm-i386/rwsem.h>.

```
47    extern struct rw_semaphore
              *FASTCALL(rwsem_down_read_failed(struct rw_semaphore *sem));
48    extern struct rw_semaphore
              *FASTCALL(rwsem_down_write_failed(struct rw_semaphore *sem));
```

```
49   extern struct rw_semaphore
                     *FASTCALL(rwsem_wake(struct rw_semaphore *sem));
```

Figure 6.25 Optimising parameter passing

6.2.4.2 *Waiting for the semaphore to be granted for reading*

When the code in Section 6.2.3.1 is unable to acquire a semaphore for reading, it calls the wrapper function shown in Figure 6.26, from `lib/rwsem.c`, which arranges for the process to sleep.

```
155  struct rw_semaphore
                     *rwsem_down_read_failed(struct rw_semaphore *sem)
156  {
157        struct rwsem_waiter waiter;
158
159        rwsemtrace(sem, "Entering rwsem_down_read_failed");
160
161        waiter.flags = RWSEM_WAITING_FOR_READ;
162        rwsem_down_failed_common(sem, &waiter,
                           RWSEM_WAITING_BIAS-RWSEM_ACTIVE_BIAS);
163
164        rwsemtrace(sem, "Leaving rwsem_down_read_failed");
165        return sem;
166  }
```

Figure 6.26 Waiting for the semaphore to be granted for reading

155 the parameter is a pointer to the semaphore structure.

157 read–write semaphores use this structure (see Section 6.2.1.3) instead of the standard `struct __wait_queue`.

159 this function, described in Section 6.2.1.4, will print a debugging message, if debugging is switched on.

161 this sets up the flags field in the `rwsem_waiter` structure declared at line 157, to indicate why this process is waiting. The symbolic constant is defined in Section 6.2.1.3.

162 this calls the generic waiting function, described in Section 6.2.4.4. The parameters are a pointer to the semaphore structure, a pointer to the `rwsem_waiter` structure, and the adjustment to be made to the `count` field of the semaphore, which reverses the increment made to the value of the semaphore at line 102 of `__down_read()` (Section 6.2.3.1) and increments the number of waiters (in the high-order word of `count`).

164 when the process wakes up after waiting, it returns here, holding the semaphore. This function, described in Section 6.2.1.4, will print a debugging message, if debugging is switched on.

165 the pointer to the semaphore structure is returned (in the EAX register, as usual).

6.2.4.3 Waiting for the semaphore to be granted for writing

When the code in Section 6.2.3.2 is unable to acquire a semaphore for writing, it calls the wrapper function shown in Figure 6.27, from lib/rwsem.c, which arranges for the process to sleep. It is very similar to the code described in Section 6.2.4.2, and only the differences will be noted here.

```
171   struct rw_semaphore
                    *rwsem_down_write_failed(struct rw_semaphore *sem)
172   {
173       struct rwsem_waiter waiter;
174
175       rwsemtrace(sem, "Entering rwsem_down_write_failed");
176
177       waiter.flags = RWSEM_WAITING_FOR_WRITE;
178       rwsem_down_failed_common(sem, &waiter,
                                            RWSEM_ACTIVE_BIAS);
179
180       rwsemtrace(sem, "Leaving rwsem_down_write_failed");
181       return sem;
182   }
```

Figure 6.27   Waiting for the semaphore to be granted for writing

177   the flags value identifies this as waiting for a write lock; see Section 6.2.1.3 for the definition.

178   the adjustment this time reverses the increment made to count at line 133 of __down_write() (Section 6.2.3.2). The other change made there, incrementing the (negative) value in the high-order word of count, is not reversed. It now indicates one extra waiting process.

6.2.4.4 Sleep waiting for the semaphore

When either or the two foregoing functions find that a request for a semaphore, either read or write, cannot be granted, and the process has to wait, then the function shown in Figure 6.28, from lib/rwsem.c, is called.

```
113   static inline struct rw_semaphore
114       *rwsem_down_failed_common(struct rw_semaphore *sem,
115           struct rwsem_waiter *waiter, signed long adjustment)
116   {
117       struct task_struct *tsk = current;
118       signed long count;
119
120       set_task_state(tsk, TASK_UNINTERRUPTIBLE);
121
123       spin_lock(&sem->wait_lock);
124       waiter->task = tsk;
125
```

```
126             list_add_tail(&waiter->list,&sem->wait_list);

129             count = rwsem_atomic_update(adjustment,sem);

134             if (!(count & RWSEM_ACTIVE_MASK))
135                 sem = __rwsem_do_wake(sem);
136
137             spin_unlock(&sem->wait_lock);

140             for (;;) {
141                 if (!waiter->flags)
142                 break;
143                 schedule();
144                 set_task_state(tsk, TASK_UNINTERRUPTIBLE);
145             }
146
147             tsk->state = TASK_RUNNING;
148
149             return sem;
150     }
```

Figure 6.28   Sleep waiting for the semaphore

114   the first parameter is a pointer to the semaphore structure.

115   the second parameter is a pointer to a specialised type of wait queue structure used only with these semaphores. The third is the adjustment to be made to the value of the semaphore while this process is waiting.

117   this gets a pointer to the task_struct of the current (calling) process, using the macro from Section 7.2.1.3.

120   this marks the current process as sleeping uninterruptibly (i.e. short term), using the macro described in Section 4.6.1.3.

123–137   fields in the semaphore structure are going to be manipulated, so the semaphore is locked, using the macro from Section 5.3 (5.4 if dealing with an SMP system).

124   the rwsem_waiter structure is pointed to the task_struct of the waiting process. Remember, this is being used in place of the standard struct __wait_queue (see Chapter 4 for the general mechanism).

126   the rwsem_waiter structure is added to the tail of the queue of processes waiting on this semaphore, using the function from Section 4.3.2.

129   the value of the semaphore is adjusted, using the function from Section 6.2.5.2. This returns the resulting value into count. The adjustment was specified by the caller and is different for a read and a write. For a read, it increments the (negative) count of waiters. In both cases it decrements the number of active processes, as this one is not active (even though that count was incremented earlier on).

134–135   if the bottom half of the semaphore now has a value of 0, a process (or processes) (readers only) is (are) woken from the front of the queue. The function to do this is described in Section 6.2.4.6. This could only happen on a multiprocessor, but, in such a case, it could even take the current process off the wait queue.

137   in any case, the spinlock is given back, and we go on.

140–145   we loop here until the semaphore is acquired.

141–142   if the `flags` field in the `rwsem_waiter` structure is 0, we break out of the loop. The semaphore has been acquired. This could not happen the *first* time around the loop.

143   otherwise, the scheduler is called (Section 7.3). As this process is in the `TASK_UNINTERRUPTIBLE` state, it will be context-switched out.

144   when this process runs again, its state is set back to `TASK_UNINTERRUPTIBLE`, using the macro from Section 4.6.1.3, and it goes around the loop again. This is taking the pessimistic view that it will be put to sleep again.

147   control arrives here by breaking out of the foregoing loop at line 142. The process has acquired the semaphore; its state is set to `TASK_RUNNING`.

149   the pointer is returned to the semaphore structure (in the EAX register, as usual).

6.2.4.5   *Checking if a waiting process needs to be woken*

When either of the functions described in Sections 6.2.3.3 or 6.2.3.4 finds that the semaphore is now free, it calls `rwsem_wake()` to check if a waiting process needs to be woken. This function is shown in Figure 6.29, from `lib/rwsem.c`. The state of the `count` field on entry to this function is that the number of active holders has been decremented (in both the read case and the write case), and, in the writer case, that the negative value representing the active writer has also been removed.

```
188   struct rw_semaphore *rwsem_wake(struct rw_semaphore *sem)
189   {
190       rwsemtrace(sem,"Entering rwsem_wake");
191
192       spin_lock(&sem->wait_lock);

195       if (!list_empty(&sem->wait_list))
196           sem = __rwsem_do_wake(sem);
197
198       spin_unlock(&sem->wait_lock);
199
200       rwsemtrace(sem,"Leaving rwsem_wake");
201
202       return sem;
203   }
```

Figure 6.29   Waking up a waiter on the semaphore

190   this function, described in Section 6.2.1.4, will print a debugging message, if debugging is switched on.

192–198   fields in the semaphore structure are going to be manipulated, so a spinlock is taken out on it, using the macro from Section 5.3.

195–196   if there is a least one process waiting on this semaphore, the waker is called, (see Section 6.2.4.6); otherwise nothing is done.

200   this function, described in Section 6.2.1.4, will print a debugging message, if debugging is switched on.

6.2.4.6   Waking up a sleeping process

When a read–write semaphore is released, and there is a process or processes blocked waiting on it, the function shown in Figure 6.30, from `lib/rwsem.c`, is called to wake up one or more of these processes. The caller of this function has determined that there is some process on the queue and that it is holding a spinlock on the semaphore data structure.

```
38    static inline struct rw_semaphore
                       * __rwsem_do_wake(struct rw_semaphore *sem)
39    {
40          struct rwsem_waiter *waiter;
41          struct list_head *next;
42          signed long oldcount;
43          int woken, loop;
44
45          rwsemtrace(sem, "Entering __rwsem_do_wake");

48    try_again:
49          oldcount =
                       rwsem_atomic_update(RWSEM_ACTIVE_BIAS, sem) -
                                           RWSEM_ACTIVE_BIAS;
50          if (oldcount & RWSEM_ACTIVE_MASK)
51              goto undo;
52
53          waiter = list_entry(sem->wait_list.next,
                                   struct rwsem_waiter, list);
59          if (!(waiter->flags & RWSEM_WAITING_FOR_WRITE))
60              goto readers_only;
61
62          list_del(&waiter->list);
63          waiter->flags = 0;
64          wake_up_process(waiter->task);
65          goto out;
71    readers_only:
72          woken = 0;
73          do {
74              woken++;
```

```
75
76                    if (waiter->list.next==&sem->wait_list)
77                        break;
78
79                    waiter = list_entry(waiter->list.next,
                                              struct rwsem_waiter,list);
80
81            } while (waiter->flags & RWSEM_WAITING_FOR_READ);
82
83            loop = woken;
84            woken *= RWSEM_ACTIVE_BIAS - RWSEM_WAITING_BIAS;
85            woken -= RWSEM_ACTIVE_BIAS;
86            rwsem_atomic_add(woken,sem);
87
88            next = sem->wait_list.next;
89            for (; loop>0; loop-) {
90                    waiter = list_entry(next, struct rwsem_waiter,list);
91                    next = waiter->list.next;
92                    waiter->flags = 0;
93                    wake_up_process(waiter->task);
94            }
95
96            sem->wait_list.next = next;
97            next->prev = &sem->wait_list;
98
99     out:
100            rwsemtrace(sem,"Leaving __rwsem_do_wake");
101            return sem;
102
104    undo:
105            if (rwsem_atomic_update(-RWSEM_ACTIVE_BIAS,sem)!=0)
106                    goto out;
107            goto try_again;
108    }
```

Figure 6.30   Waking up sleeping processes

38   the parameter is a pointer to the semaphore structure.

45   if debugging is turned on, this function, from Section 6.2.1.4, will print an information message.

49   the call to `rwsem_atomic_update()` (Section 6.2.5.2) has the effect of incrementing the `count` field of the semaphore by 1, indicating that there is one more process holding the semaphore. As this function returns the resultant value in `count`, `oldcount` will now have the previous value.

50−51   if this previous value shows that the number of active processes was not 0 beforehand, we jump to line 104, undo the adjustment made on the previous line, and return. A sleeping process should only be woken up when the semaphore is free.

53   at this stage we know that it is legal to wake up a process and have in fact marked the semaphore as having one active process. a local pointer is taken to the `struct rwsem_waiter` of the first entry on the wait queue, using the `list_entry()` macro from Section 4.3.4.3.

59–60 if the first process waiting is a reader, then a jump is made to line 71 to handle readers. Otherwise, lines 62–64 are used to handle a single writer.

62   one waiting writer is removed from the wait queue, using the function from Section 4.3.3.

63   its `flags` field is marked to indicate that it is active, not waiting.

64   it is moved to the run queue, using the function described in Section 4.7.5.

65   the standard exit from this function is taken.

71–97 the semaphore is granted to all waiting readers clustered together at the head of the queue. This stops when the first waiting writer is encountered.

73–81 this loop merely counts the number of consecutive waiting readers at the head of the queue.

76–77 at this stage, we have got to the end of the list, so we jump out of the loop.

79   otherwise, the `waiter` is advanced to point to the next entry in the list.

81   the loop is terminated when the `flags` field of the next entry is not RWSEM_WAITING_FOR_ READ.

84   the count of active processes (RWSEM_ACTIVE_BIAS) is incremented and the count of waiting processes (RWSEM_WAITING_BIAS) by the number of processes found waiting.

85   the count of active processes is decremented by 1, to compensate for the increment made at line 49.

86   the value in the semaphore structure is now adjusted accordingly, using the function described in Section 6.2.5.1.

88   the selected process(es) is (are) set to be woken by pointing `next` to the first process.

89–94 these lines count backwards, while moving forwards over the list.

90   this line gets a pointer to the entry, using the macro from Section 4.3.4.3.

91   this advances the `next` pointer.

92   this marks the `flags` field of the current entry to indicate that it is active, not waiting.

93   this moves it to the run queue, using the function from Section 4.7.5.

96   this points the header field in the semaphore structure to the next entry after the last one processed in the loop, effectively unlinking the whole block from the list.

97   this points the new first entry in the list back to the semaphore structure.

99   control either falls through to here from line 97, jumps to here from line 65, when finished with a writer, or from line 106, when finished undoing adjustments to `count`. It is the standard exit path.

100   if debugging is turned on, this function, from Section 6.2.1.4, will print an information message.

104   control transfers here from line 51 if no process should be woken up. It undoes the change to `count` made at line 49, but, if things have changed in the meantime (as could happen on a multiprocessor), it goes back and tries again.

105–106   if, after undoing the change to `count`, the semaphore is still in active use, a return to the caller is made.

107   otherwise, we go back to line 48 and begin all over again.

6.2.5   Atomic operations on read–write semaphore values

Two worker functions are provided for operating atomically on the value of a read–write semaphore. Both add to the `count` field, but the second also returns the updated value.

6.2.5.1   *Atomically adding to the value of a semaphore*

The function shown in Figure 6.31, from `<asm-i386/rwsem.h>`, implements an atomic add on a read–write semaphore.

```
214  static inline void rwsem_atomic_add(int delta,
                                         struct rw_semaphore *sem)
215  {
216       __asm__ __volatile__(
217  LOCK_PREFIX   "addl %1,%0"
218                "=m"(sem->count)
219                "ir"(delta), "m"(sem->count));
220  }
```

Figure 6.31   Atomically adding to the value of a semaphore

214   the first parameter is the change to be made to the value of the semaphore; the second is a pointer to the semaphore structure itself.

217   the `LOCK_PREFIX` macro was defined in Section 5.1.4.2. On a multiprocessor, it evaluates to the LOCK machine instruction, which locks the bus for the following instruction, so making it atomic. On a uniprocessor it is a null operation, as the instruction is atomic anyway. The first parameter to ADDL is `delta`; the second is the `count` field of the semaphore structure itself.

218   output parameter 0 (the `count` field) is in memory, (`"m"`).

219   parameter 1 (`delta`) must be in a register; parameter 2 is the value of the `count` field beforehand.

6.2.5.2 *Atomically updating a semaphore value*

The function shown in Figure 6.32, from `<asm-i386/resem.h>`, uses exchange and add to update the value of a read–write semaphore atomically. It returns the resultant value of the semaphore.

```
225  static inline int rwsem_atomic_update(int delta,
                                   struct rw_semaphore *sem)
226  {
227      int tmp = delta;
228
229      __asm__ __volatile__(
230  LOCK_PREFIX  "xadd %0,(%2)"
231                   : "+r"(tmp), "=m"(sem->count)
232                   "r"(sem), "m"(sem->count)
233                   : "memory");
234
235      return tmp+delta;
236  }
```

Figure 6.32   Atomically updating a semaphore value

225   the first parameter is the change to be made to the value of the semaphore; the second is a pointer to the semaphore structure itself.

230   the LOCK_PREFIX macro was defined in Section 5.1.4.2. On a multiprocessor, it evaluates to the LOCK machine instruction, which locks the bus for the following XADD instruction, so making it atomic. On a uniprocessor it is NULL, as the instruction is atomic anyway. The first parameter to XADD is tmp, the change to be made; the second is the count field of the semaphore structure itself. This instruction first exchanges the values, putting the previous value of count into tmp, and then puts the sum of the two into count.

231   output parameter 0 (tmp) must be in a register, and it will be both read and written by the XADD instruction ("+r"). Parameter 1 (the count field) may be in memory ("=m").

232   input parameter 2, the pointer sem, must be in a register, "r", parameter 3 is the input value of the count field.

233   the "memory" operand constraint means that memory may be modified in an unpredictable manner.

234   this line returns the old value of the semaphore, plus the change; this is equivalent to the new value.

6.3 Completions

This is a final synchronisation mechanism supplied by Linux. It is effectively a simplified implementation of a semaphore, suitable for a situation where there are only two processes synchronising. It is much used by device drivers. The only place the process manager uses a completion is when implementing the `vfork()` system service (see Section 8.2).

6.3.1 Data structures and macros

The code shown in Figure 6.33, from `<linux/completion.h>`, shows the data structure representing a completion and a number of macros used to initialise such structures.

```
13   struct completion {
14       unsigned int            done;
15       wait_queue_head_t       wait;
16   };
17
18   #define COMPLETION_INITIALIZER(work)                              \
19       { 0, __WAIT_QUEUE_HEAD_INITIALIZER((work).wait) }
20
21   #define DECLARE_COMPLETION(work)                                  \
22       struct completion work = COMPLETION_INITIALIZER(work)
23
24   static inline void init_completion(struct completion *x)
25   {
26       x->done = 0;
27       init_waitqueue_head(&x->wait);
28   }
29
30   extern void FASTCALL(wait_for_completion(struct completion *));
31   extern void FASTCALL(complete(struct completion *));
32
33   #define INIT_COMPLETION(x)    ((x).done = 0)
```

Figure 6.33   Completion data structure and initialisation

13–16   this is the data structure representing a completion. Like a semaphore, it consists of an `int` and the head of a wait queue.

18–19   this macro initialises an existing `struct completion`, putting 0 in the `done` field and using the macro from Section 4.1.2.2 to initialise the wait queue header.

21–22   this macro declares and initialises a `struct completion` called `work`.

24–28   this inline function initialises a `struct completion` passed to it by reference, using the function from Section 4.1.2.3 to initialise the wait queue header.

30–31   these lines declare the functions described in the next two sections as having the `FASTCALL` attribute. They expect their parameters in the EAX register, not on the stack.

33   this macro merely initialises the `done` field to 0, without affecting the wait queue.

6.3.2 Signalling a completion

The function shown in Figure 6.34, from `kernel/sched.c`, is called when the event being waited for has occurred. Its only parameter is a pointer to the appropriate struct completion. It notes that the event has occurred and tries to wake up a process if one is sleeping on the completion.

```
745   void complete(struct completion *x)
746   {
747       unsigned long flags;
748
749       spin_lock_irqsave(&x->wait.lock, flags);
750       x->done++;
751       __wake_up_common(&x->wait,
                  TASK_UNINTERRUPTIBLE | TASK_INTERRUPTIBLE, 1, 0);
752       spin_unlock_irqrestore(&x->wait.lock, flags);
753   }
```

Figure 6.34　Signalling a completion

749–752 this block of code is protected by a spinlock specific to the wait queue header in the struct completion and interrupts are disabled. The EFLAGS register is saved, so that the interrupt state can be restored just as it was beforehand.

750 this increments the done field in the struct completion.

751 this call to __wake_up_common() (Section 4.7.3) wakes up any processes on the wait queue associated with the struct completion, in either the TASK_INTERRUPTIBLE or the TASK_UNINTERRUPTIBLE state. The third parameter specifies that only one process waiting exclusively is to be woken up. The final parameter specifies that the newly woken process does not have to run on the current CPU.

6.3.3 Waiting for completion

When a process wants to wait for some event, it calls the function shown in Figure 6.35, from kernel/sched.c. Its only parameter is a pointer to a struct completion.

```
755   void wait_for_completion(struct completion *x)
756   {
757       spin_lock_irq(&x->wait.lock);
758       if (!x->done) {
759           DECLARE_WAITQUEUE(wait, current);
760
761           wait.flags |= WQ_FLAG_EXCLUSIVE;
762           __add_wait_queue_tail(&x->wait, &wait);
763           do {
764               __set_current_state(TASK_UNINTERRUPTIBLE);
765               spin_unlock_irq(&x->wait.lock);
766               schedule();
767               spin_lock_irq(&x->wait.lock);
768           } while (!x->done);
769           __remove_wait_queue(&x->wait, &wait);
770       }
```

```
771        x->done-;
772        spin_unlock_irq(&x->wait.lock);
773  }
```

Figure 6.35   Waiting for completion

757–772   the whole function is bracketed by this interrupt safe spinlock, specific to the wait queue header in the `struct completion`.

758–770   this block of code is executed only if the `done` field of the `struct completion` is 0, and the process has to wait.

759   this declares a `wait_queue_t`, called `wait`, and initialises it pointing to the `task_struct` of the current process (see Section 4.1.1.2 for the macro).

761   this sets the exclusive bit in the `flags` field of that `wait_queue_t`.

762   this adds it at the tail of the wait queue headed from the `struct completion`. The function was described in Section 4.2.1.4.

763–768   this loop is executed at least once and is repeated as long as the `done` field is still zero (i.e. as long as the event has not occurred).

764   this sets the state of the process to be TASK_UNINTERRUPTIBLE, using the macro from Section 4.6.1.3.

765–766   these give back the lock and call `schedule()`.

767   when the process next runs, it takes out the lock again.

768   if `done` is still zero, the process goes around the do loop again and sleeps.

769   now that the process has finished waiting, it is removed from the wait queue, using the function from Section 4.2.2.2.

771   the `done` field is decremented. One occurrence of this event has been dealt with.

772   the spinlock is returned to for the final time.

7

Scheduling

Chapter 2 examined how Linux keeps track of individual processes. This process structure, as it is called, is something very static. It merely records that the process exists. Scheduling determines *which* process will be next to run on a processor. Now that mechanisms such as queues and locks are available, this chapter can go on to examine the scheduler itself.

7.1 Introduction

The main objective of the scheduler is to see that the computer processor unit (CPU) is shared among all contending processes as fairly as possible. But fairness can mean different things in different situations:

- In real time systems, the scheduler will have to be able to guarantee that response time will never exceed a certain maximum. For example, a multimedia system handling video and audio must have access to the processor at predefined intervals.

- A batch system will not be concerned with response time, but with maximising the use of expensive peripherals. Many different scheduling algorithms have been developed for such systems.

- In an interactive system, there is no way to predict in advance how many processes will be running, or how long they will want to run for. They could be scheduled on a first-come first-served basis, but this way some unimportant processes could monopolise the system, while urgent processes languish on a queue.

7.1.1 Scheduling policies in Linux

Linux implements three different scheduling policies, and any particular process can choose to be dealt with under the policy that best suits it. The policy in use is recorded in the `policy` field of the `struct task_struct`.

The Linux Process Manager. The Internals of Scheduling, Interrupts and Signals   John O'Gorman
© 2003 John Wiley & Sons, Ltd   ISBN: 0 470 84771 9

- SCHED_RR is fixed-priority. An RR (for round robin) process is given its priority when it is created, and it does not change throughout its lifetime. Such a process runs until one of the following three events occurs:

    - it blocks itself, in which case it moves to the wait queue;

    - it is preempted because a higher-priority process has become runable; in this case, it stays on the runqueue;

    - it uses up its quantum, in which case it is given a new quantum and moved to the end of the runqueue.

- SCHED_FIFO is also fixed priority, but it has no quantum. It runs until it blocks or is preempted.

- SCHED_OTHER is the normal time-sharing policy, which is the default. It adjusts process priorities to favour interactive ones over compute-intensive ones.

The first two specialised policies are used by real-time applications and by some system processes within the kernel.

In an interactive system, the scheduler tries to make the response time as short as possible. A typical target would be 50–150 ms. Users can find it quite off-putting if the response time varies wildly, say from 10 ms to 1000 ms. If one keystroke is echoed immediately and the next is not echoed for a second a user is inclined to press the key again, with all the consequent errors.

7.1.2 The Linux scheduler

Scheduling in Linux works in two phases that could be called short-term and medium-term scheduling. Each process is given a certain time-slice on the processor. This is called the quantum, and is maintained in the count field of the task_struct. Each time the hardware timer interrupts, the count field of the running process is decremented until it gets to zero.

The size of the time-slice can have an effect on performance. On the one hand, if it is too large, interactive processes will find themselves spending long periods of time waiting for the CPU. Time sharing will become very obvious to the user. On the other hand, as the time slice is decreased, the overhead of context switching grows, so, if the time-slice is too small, the machine could spend most of its time context switching instead of doing productive work.

The short-term scheduler is called frequently, every time a process waits for some event. Each time it is called, it examines all the processes on the runqueue and selects the most suitable to run next. Eventually, the short-term scheduler will find that all the processes on the runqueue have used up their quantum and it is not able to find any candidate to run. This is where the second phase comes in, the medium-term scheduler. At this stage all processes are given a new allocation of time, even those on wait queues. How much their quantum is topped up is determined by the value in their priority field.

A question arises as to where to put the current or running process. It could be at the head of the queue. Another possibility is that it could be taken off the queue altogether and pointed to directly from some location in the kernel. Linux, for example, keeps the `task_struct` of the running process on the runqueue but supplies a macro `current` (see Section 7.2.1.3, that evaluates to a pointer to that `task_struct`.

7.1.3 Multiprocessor scheduling

Scheduling for machines with more than one CPU brings in extra difficulties of its own. Two big decisions that have to be made are: should the operating system be given a processor of its own or should it run on whichever processor is free; and should there be individual queues for each processor, or should there be systemwide queues?

Linux is capable of running on a multiprocessor architecture. Following the Unix philosophy of having very few system processes, most kernel code is executed in the context of the process that calls a system service, so the question of whether or not the kernel should have a processor of its own does not arise; but, now, more than one process can be executing kernel code at the same time. This introduces the need for locks within the kernel. As all processes are equal and can run on any CPU there is only one systemwide runqueue.

7.2 Data structures used by the scheduler

Before beginning to examine the code of the scheduler there are a number of widely used data structures and macros that must be described. The i386-specific task state segment (TSS) is also introduced here. Finally, the structure used by the kernel to record performance statistics is examined.

7.2.1 Scheduler-related data structures and macros

This section introduces data structures, functions, and macros used extensively throughout the kernel. Even in the SMP case they are relatively trivial, but it is still necessary to introduce them.

7.2.1.1 Number of computer processing units

Some information needed for SMP management is shown in Figure 7.1 from `arch/i386/kernel/smpboot.c`.

```
57    int smp_num_cpus = 1;

60    int smp_num_siblings = 1;

978   int cpu_sibling_map[NR_CPUS] __cacheline_aligned;
```

Figure 7.1   Number of computer processing units

57   this global variable contains the total count of active CPUs. It is statically initialised to 1, as there must always be at least one CPU to begin with. It is incremented as each new one CPU booted.

60   this is the number of sibling CPUs packaged together. It is also statically initialised to 1; it may be incremented to 2 if a dual package is encountered at bootup.

978   each CPU has an entry in this array. If there are siblings packaged together, then each entry in this array contains the number of its sibling.

7.2.1.2   Mapping of computer processing unit numbers

Each active CPU is identified in Linux by an identification (ID) number. Although on the i386 architecture these are sequential, they may not be so on all architectures, so the two functions shown in Figure 7.2 from <asm-i386/smp.h>, have to be supplied for mapping between logical and physical numbering.

```
57    extern unsigned long cpu_online_map;

75    static inline int cpu_logical_map(int cpu)
76    {
77         return cpu;
78    }
79    static inline int cpu_number_map(int cpu)
80    {
81         return cpu;
82    }
```

Figure 7.2 Numbering of computer processing units

57   this is a bitmap, with bits set corresponding to CPUs that are currently on-line, not disabled.

77   although this is an identity mapping on an i386, on another architecture it could map between the physical CPU number, corresponding to its place on the motherboard, and its logical number, as used within the kernel.

81   although this is also an identity mapping on an i386, on another architecture it could map between the logical number by which a CPU is identified within the kernel and its physical place on the motherboard.

7.2.1.3   Identifying the current process

Figure 7.3, from <asm-i386/current.h>, shows a function that returns a pointer to the task_struct of the currently executing process (i.e. the process executing the code that calls it). There is also a macro that simplifies the use of this function, by condensing it down to one word. This macro is used extensively throughout the kernel.

```
6    static inline struct task_struct * get_current(void)
7    {
8         struct task_struct *current;
9         __asm__("andl %%esp,%0;":"=r" (current) : "" (~8191UL));
10        return current;
```

```
11    }
12
13    #define current get_current()
```

Figure 7.3   Identifying the current process

9 the value of the kernel stack pointer is somewhere within the `task_union`; 8191 decimal is 0001 1111 1111 1111. Inverting that gives 1110 0000 0000 0000. This effectively strips off the low-order 13 bits of the stack pointer value, aligning it at the beginning of the `task_union`. This is also the beginning of the `task_struct`.

7.2.1.4   Identifying the current processor

The macro shown in Figure 7.4 from `<asm-i386/smp.h>`, returns the ID of the processor on which the current process is executing. It gets this information from the `processor` field of its `task_struct`. The `current` macro is defined in Section 7.2.1.3.

```
107  #define smp_processor_id() (current->processor)
```

Figure 7.4 Identifying the current process

7.2.2   Global scheduler structures

Figure 7.5, from `kernel/sched.c`, shows some global structures used by the scheduler.

```
79    struct task_struct * init_tasks [NR_CPUS] = {&init_task, };

92    spinlock_t    runqueue_lock __cacheline_aligned =
                                       SPIN_LOCK_UNLOCKED; /* inner */
93    rwlock_t tasklist_lock __cacheline_aligned =
              RW_LOCK_UNLOCKED; /* outer */

95    static LIST_HEAD (runqueue_head);
```

Figure 7.5   Statically initialised data structures

79 this array of pointers has one element per CPU. Each is initialised pointing to `init_task`, defined in Section 3.3.1. It effectively records the idle process for each CPU.

92 the `runqueue_lock` spinlock protects those parts of the code that actually access and change the runqueue and have to be interrupt-safe. It is initialised to the unlocked state. Spinlocks are described in Sections 5.3 (for the uniprocessor) and 5.4 (for the multiprocessor) .

93 the `tasklist_lock` read–write lock protects the doubly linked list of `struct task_struct`. It is initialised to the unlocked state. Read–write locks are described in Sections 5.6 (for the uniprocessor) and 5.7 (for the multiprocessor). If both locks are to be held concurrently, the `runqueue_lock` nests inside the `tasklist_lock`.

95 this macro declares a `static list_head` structure called `runqueue_head` and initialises the backward and forward pointers in it to point to itself. This is the head of the runqueue [see Section 4.3.1 for the LIST_HEAD() macro].

7.2.3 Task state segment

The task state segment (TSS) is specific to the i386 architecture. It is Intel's layout for the volatile environment of a process. The TR register in the CPU always points to the TSS of the current process. Intel intended that each process would have its own TSS and that the volatile environment of a process would be saved there when it was context switched out. Linux does not implement things that way, preferring to save most of the volatile environment on the kernel stack of the process and the remainder in the thread structure. However, the CPU expects to find a valid value in its TR, and a valid TSS as well. So Linux provides one TSS, shared by all processes, to keep the CPU happy. On a multiprocessor system, there is an array of these, one per CPU.

7.2.3.1 Structure of the task state segment

Figure 7.6, from <asm-i386/processor.h>, shows the structure of the TSS.

```
334  struct tss_struct {
335      unsigned short      back_link, __blh;
336      unsigned long       esp0;
337      unsigned short      ss0, __ss0h;
338      unsigned long       esp1;
339      unsigned short      ss1, __ss1h;
340      unsigned long       esp2;
341      unsigned short      ss2, __ss2h;
342      unsigned long       __cr3;
343      unsigned long       eip;
344      unsigned long       eflags;
345      unsigned long       eax, ecx, edx, ebx;
346      unsigned long       esp;
347      unsigned long       ebp;
348      unsigned long       esi;
349      unsigned long       edi;
350      unsigned short      es, __esh;
351      unsigned short      cs, __csh;
352      unsigned short      ss, __ssh;
353      unsigned short      ds, __dsh;
354      unsigned short      fs, __fsh;
355      unsigned short      gs, __gsh;
356      unsigned short      ldt, __ldth;
357      unsigned short      trace, bitmap;
358      unsigned long       io_bitmap[IO_BITMAP_SIZE+1];

362      unsigned long       __cacheline_filler[5];
363  };
```

Figure 7.6   The task state segment – one per computer processing unit

335 this is a link field that allows more than one TSS to be linked together. As each TSS is a segment in its own right, this is only a 16-bit selector (an index into the segment table), so __blh (for back link high) is a filler. It is not used by Linux.

336–337 the esp0 field is a 32-bit pointer to the top of the register save area on the stack used when operating at protection level 0 (kernel mode in Linux); ss0 is a 16-bit selector for the segment containing the level-0 stack; __ss0h is a filler.

338–341 this is similar information for the level-1 and level-2 stacks. These are not used by Linux.

342 the CR3 register in the CPU holds a pointer to the page table of the process.

343–349 these are standard CPU registers.

350–355 these are the standard segment registers. As these are all 16-bit values (selectors), each is padded out with an unused unsigned short.

356 the value of the LDT register is saved here. This register contains the selector for the local descriptor table of the current process. This is the concern of the i386-specific part of the memory manager and will not be considered further here.

357 the trace field is available to indicate special attributes of the process. The only one used is the T (debug trap) flag, in bit 0. This lets the context switcher know if the debug registers contain valid information or not. The bitmap field contains the offset within this present structure at which the input–output (IO) bitmap can be found.

358 this is the IO bitmap itself. It defines the IO addresses that this process can access. Its size is determined by the constant in <asm-i386/processor.h> as

```
278  #define IO_BITMAP_SIZE 32
```

It is really the province of the IO manager.

362 this is a dummy 5 longs, to bring the size of the structure up to a multiple of 32 bytes, the size of a cacheline. With these 20 bytes added, the size of a struct tss_struct is now 256 bytes, or 8 cachelines.

7.2.3.2 The task state segment array

There is an array of these tss_struct structures, one per CPU. See Figure 7.7 from arch/i386/kernel/init_task.c. They are statically initialised at compile time.

```
32    struct tss_struct init_tss[NR_CPUS] __cacheline_aligned
                              = { [0 ... NR_CPUS-1] = INIT_TSS };
```

Figure 7.7   The initial task state segment array

32 as the TSS size has been kept to a multiple of a cacheline, there is no problem keeping each one cacheline aligned. The initialising macro is described in the next section.

7.2.3.3   Initial values for an entry in the task state segment

The macro to initialise a TSS entry is found in `<asm-i386/processor.h>` (see Figure 7.8).

```
396  #define INIT_TSS {                                                    \
397       0,0,                              /* back_link, __blh */     \
398       sizeof(init_stack) + (long) &init_stack,                    \
399       __KERNEL_DS, 0,                   /* ss0 */                  \
400       0,0,0,0,0,0,                      /* stack1, stack2 */       \
401       0,                               /* cr3 */                   \
402       0,0,                             /* eip, eflags */           \
403       0,0,0,0,                         /* eax, ecx, edx, ebx */    \
404       0,0,0,0,                         /* esp, ebp, esi, edi */    \
405       0,0,0,0,0,0,                     /* es, cs, ss */            \
406       0,0,0,0,0,0,                     /* ds, fs, gs */            \
407       __LDT(0),0,                      /* ldt */                   \
408       0, INVALID_IO_BITMAP_OFFSET,                                 \
409       {~0, }                           /* ioperm */                \
410  }
```

Figure 7.8   Initialisation values for the TSS

397   the link field is 0, as it is unused by Linux.

398   the TSS is initialised for the `init` process. This is the `esp0` field. It takes the address of the beginning of the stack space (`&init_stack`; see Section 3.3.1) and adds the size of the stack space to it, so giving the top of the stack. So the initial value is pointing to an empty stack.

399   all kernel stacks are in the kernel data segment.

400   level-2 and level-3 stacks are not used by Linux, so these fields are initialised to 0.

401–406   the save areas for all these registers are initialised to 0.

407   the `__LDT()` macro, part of the memory manager, evaluates to a selector for the local descriptor table.

408   the `trace` field is set to 0. The value supplied for the `bitmap` field is from `<asm-i386/processor.h>`:

```
280  #define INVALID_IO_BITMAP_OFFSET 0x8000
```

This puts it outside the TSS. It will actually cause a segment fault if ever referenced. It can then be filled out with valid values.

409   the initial setting is that all IO ports are protected.

7.2.4   Kernel statistics

The operating system maintains a significant amount of statistical information about what is going on in the kernel. As much of this is maintained by the scheduler, this is a suitable place to introduce it.

7.2.4.1   Scheduler-specific information

Figure 7.9, from `kernel/sched.c`, shows some data structures used to record scheduling statistics.

```
101  static union {
102      struct schedule_data {
103          struct task_struct * curr;
104          cycles_t last_schedule;
105          } schedule_data;
106          char __pad [SMP_CACHE_BYTES];
107  } aligned_data [NR_CPUS] __cacheline_aligned = {{{&init_task,0}}};
108
109  #define cpu_curr(cpu) aligned_data[(cpu)].schedule_data.curr
110  #define last_schedule(cpu)
                         aligned_data[(cpu)].schedule_data.last_schedule
111
112  struct kernel_stat kstat;
```

Figure 7.9   Recording scheduling information

101–107   this array contains scheduling data on a per-CPU basis.

103   this contains a pointer to the `task_struct` of the process currently running on that CPU.

104   this is the clock cycle count when that process began on that CPU.

106   each element is padded out to fill one line in the cache.

107   all elements are initialised pointing to `init_task` (Section 3.3.1), with a count of 0, aligned on a cacheline boundary, to prevent cacheline 'ping pong'.

109   this macro converts a CPU number into a pointer to the `task_struct` representing the current process assigned to that CPU.

110   this macro converts a CPU number into the machine cycle count on that CPU at the time of the last context switch.

112   this structure contains kernel-wide statistics. It is described in detail in Section 7.2.4.2.

7.2.4.2   Kernel statistics

The structure `kernel_stat` is declared in `<linux/kernel_stat.h>` (see Figure 7.10). It is used to maintain statistics on a kernel-wide basis. Most of the fields deal with IO, memory management, and networking. Only those relevant to the process manager will be discussed here.

```
15    #define DK_MAX_MAJOR 16
16    #define DK_MAX_DISK 16
17
18    struct kernel_stat {
19        unsigned int   per_cpu_user[NR_CPUS],
20                       per_cpu_nice[NR_CPUS],
21                       per_cpu_system[NR_CPUS];
22        unsigned int dk_drive[DK_MAX_MAJOR][DK_MAX_DISK];
23        unsigned int dk_drive_rio[DK_MAX_MAJOR][DK_MAX_DISK];
24        unsigned int dk_drive_wio[DK_MAX_MAJOR][DK_MAX_DISK];
25        unsigned int dk_drive_rblk[DK_MAX_MAJOR][DK_MAX_DISK];
26        unsigned int dk_drive_wblk[DK_MAX_MAJOR][DK_MAX_DISK];
27        unsigned int pgpgin, pgpgout;
28        unsigned int pswpin, pswpout;
29    #if !defined(CONFIG_ARCH_S390)
30        unsigned int irqs[NR_CPUS][NR_IRQS];
31    #endif
32        unsigned int ipackets, opackets;
33        unsigned int ierrors, oerrors;
34        unsigned int collisions;
35        unsigned int context_swtch;
36    };
```

Figure 7.10   Structure for storing kernel statistics

15–16   these are constants that determine the size of arrays used to maintain information about the IO subsystem.

19–21   these three fields are updated by the update_process_times() function (see Section 15.1.3.1).

19   this is the total amount of time each CPU has spent running in user mode.

20   this is the total amount of time each CPU has spent running in user mode, with reduced priority.

21   this is the total amount of time each CPU has spent running in system mode.

22–26   cumulative statistics for the IO manager are maintained in these fields.

27–28   cumulative statistics for the memory manager are maintained in these fields.

30   cumulative statistics for each interrupt line on each CPU are maintained in these fields (see Section 12.4.1).

32–34   cumulative statistics for the network manager are maintained in these fields.

35   this gives the number of context switches executed since the system was booted. See Section 7.3.4, where this field is updated.

7.2.5 Scheduler locks

The `alloc_lock` of a process is manipulated so frequently that there are two special functions supplied; `task_lock()` and `task_unlock()`. These are simply wrappers for `spin_lock()` and `spin_unlock()`, respectively; see Figure 7.11, from `<linux/sched.h>`.

```
901  static inline void task_lock(struct task_struct *p)
902  {
903      spin_lock(&p->alloc_lock);
904  }
905
906  static inline void task_unlock(struct task_struct *p)
907  {
908      spin_unlock(&p->alloc_lock);
909  }
```

Figure 7.11   The process allocation lock

7.3 The main scheduler

The `schedule()` function is at the heart of the Linux process manager. It is called from many places in the kernel, any time a process gives up the CPU. But these cases can be grouped into two. System calls may call `schedule()`, but they usually do this by calling `sleep_on()` (Section 4.5.4), which then calls `schedule()`. Also, after every system call, the `ret_from_sys_call()` routine checks the `need_resched` flag of the calling process and, if it is set, calls `schedule()`. This is described in Section 10.6. The remainder of this chapter will be devoted to the `schedule()` function, from `kernel/sched.c`, and the worker functions that support it. Later chapters will illustrate the different occasions when it is called.

The main outline of the scheduler is presented as follows:

- checking for exceptions: Section 7.3.1;

- removing caller from runqueue, if necessary: Section 7.3.2;

- selecting next process to run: Section 7.3.3;

- recording scheduling decision: Section 7.3.4;

- context switching: Section 7.3.5.

7.3.1 Eliminating exceptions

The first few lines of `schedule()` are shown in Figure 7.12 This deals with preliminaries that have little or nothing to do with scheduling. It merely declares some local variables and checks for some exceptions that have to be handled.

```
549   asmlinkage void schedule(void)
550   {
551         struct schedule_data * sched_data;
552         struct task_struct *prev, *next, *p;
553         struct list_head *tmp;
554         int this_cpu, c;

557         spin_lock_prefetch(&runqueue_lock);
558
559         if (!current->active_mm) BUG();
560   need_resched_back:
561         prev = current;
562         this_cpu = prev->processor;
563
564         if (unlikely(in_interrupt())) {
565               printk("Scheduling in interrupt\n");
566               BUG();
567         }
568
569         release_kernel_lock(prev, this_cpu);
```

Figure 7.12 Checking for errors and software interrupts

557 this macro hints that the CPU should move the data representing the runqueue_lock from memory into cache, in preparation for its use at line 577 (see Figure 7.13).

559 if the current process does not have an active memory context there is something seriously wrong. The BUG() macro (see Section 4.1.3.3) prints a warning message then executes an illegal instruction that halts the operating system.

561 the current macro (Section 7.2.1.3) always evaluates to a pointer to the task_struct representing the currently running process. Confusingly, the pointer to the current process used throughout the scheduler is called prev, but remember that it is the current process that called schedule() and it is very quickly going to become the previous one.

562 the ID number of the processor on which the current process is running is recorded in the local this_cpu.

564 the in_interrupt() macro is architecture-dependent and will be dealt with in Section 16.5.3.1. Wrapping it with unlikely() (Section 1.2.1.2) gives a hint to the compiler that it is unlikely to return TRUE, so the compiler can optimise code layout. If it returns TRUE, that means that the scheduler was called from within an interrupt handler. This should not happen.

565–566 thus, it prints a warning message and calls BUG() (section 4.1.3.3), which halts the operating system.

569 the macro release_kernel_lock()was discussed in Section 5.5. The lock was acquired when the process entered the kernel. Releasing it here allows processes running on other CPUs to enter the kernel. The scheduler takes out locks on individual parts of the kernel as it needs them. This 'big' kernel lock is reacquired in line 701, before leaving the scheduler (see Section 7.3.5).

7.3.2 Scheduling preliminaries

Now that the incidentals are taken care of, the code shown in Figure 7.13 gets down to the actual scheduling.

```
575            sched_data = & aligned_data[this_cpu].schedule_data;
576
577            spin_lock_irq(&runqueue_lock);

580            if (unlikely(prev->policy == SCHED_RR))
581                if (!prev->counter) {
582                    prev->counter = NICE_TO_TICKS(prev->nice);
583                    move_last_runqueue(prev);
584                }
585
586            switch (prev->state) {
587                case TASK_INTERRUPTIBLE:
588                    if (signal_pending(prev)) {
589                        prev->state = TASK_RUNNING;
590                        break;
591                    }
592                default:
593                    del_from_runqueue(prev);
594                case TASK_RUNNING:
595            }
596            prev->need_resched = 0;
```

Figure 7.13   Scheduling preliminaries

575   the `aligned_data` structure has been discussed in Section 7.2.4. It contains information about the last process to run on this CPU. Here a local pointer is set up to the `struct schedule_` data for the CPU on which we are running. Even though the process is not holding the kernel lock, it can still read and write that field safely, as it is protected by the fact that there can be only one process per CPU. No other CPUs should ever deal with this element of the array `aligned_ data[]`.

577   the runqueue can be accessed by another CPU, or even by an interrupt being serviced on this one, so it must be protected with an interrupt safe spinlock. This lock is held until the process is finished with the runqueue, at line 637 of Figure 7.15. The spinlock macro is defined in Section 12.8.1; the spinlock itself was declared in Section 7.2.2.

580–584   this block of code is executed only for a SCHED_RR process. The `unlikely()` macro, see Section 1.2.1.2, is a hint to the compiler that the result of the comparison is most likely to be FALSE, and the code can be optimised accordingly.

581–584   if such a process called `schedule()` because it has used up its quantum, it is given a full quantum and moved to the end of the runqueue. FIFO (first-in first-out) processes are not treated this way – they run to completion in one go, not in a number of quanta.

582 the process is given a full quantum. The `NICE_TO_TICKS()` macro is described in Section 7.4.3.

583 the process is moved to the end of the runqueue. The function is described in Section 4.8.2.

587–590 if the current process has just requested that it be put to sleep interruptibly, then a check is made for a pending signal. If there is one, it should be handled immediately, so the process is marked as running. The `signal_pending()` function is described in Section 18.3.1.

592–593 otherwise (i.e. the process has moved to TASK_INTERRUPTIBLE, TASK_ZOMBIE, or TASK_STOPPED state) the process is removed from the runqueue. It will not be considered for selection after this. The function will be described in Section 4.8.3.

594 if the process is in the TASK_RUNNING state, nothing is done, as the scheduler may decide to leave it running. This means that the process actually stays on the runqueue.

596 the current process is being rescheduled, so its flag is cleared.

7.3.3 Selecting the next process to run

Now we come to the real heart of the scheduler. Each time it is called, the scheduler examines the whole runqueue and calculates a factor called the 'goodness' for each process on it. For a SCHED_RR or SCHED_FIFO process, goodness is always `priority + 1000`. This will boost it way above any SCHED_OTHER (interactive) process. Otherwise, goodness is just the value of the `counter` field in the `task_struct`. The process with the highest goodness is the next to run. Figure 7.14 shows how the scheduler selects the next process to run.

```
602  repeat_schedule:

606      next = idle_task(this_cpu);
607      c = -1000;
608      list_for_each(tmp, &runqueue_head) {
609          p = list_entry(tmp, struct task_struct, run_list);
610          if (can_schedule(p, this_cpu)) {
611              int weight = goodness(p, this_cpu, prev->active_mm);
612              if (weight > c)
613                  c = weight, next = p;
614          }
615      }

618      if (unlikely(!c)) {
619          struct task_struct *p;
620
621          spin_unlock_irq(&runqueue_lock);
622          read_lock(&tasklist_lock);
623          for_each_task(p)
624              p->counter = (p->counter >> 1) +
                                        NICE_TO_TICKS(p->nice);
625          read_unlock(&tasklist_lock);
```

```
626            spin_lock_irq(&runqueue_lock);
627            goto repeat_schedule;
628    }
```

Figure 7.14 Selecting the next process to run

606 the macro `idle_task()`, as described in Section 7.4.1, returns a pointer to the idle task for a particular CPU. This is taken as the default (it will be chosen if nothing better can be found), but if and when a more suitable process is found `next` will be pointed to it.

607 a default `goodness` of -1000 is set. If and when a more suitable process is found, its goodness will be recorded here.

608–615 the code shown in these lines examines each process on the runqueue and records the most suitable found so far.

608 the macro `list_for_each()` is described in Section 4.3.4.3. The first parameter, a pointer to a `struct list_head`, is a running pointer to each element in turn. The second parameter is the head of the runqueue (see Section 7.2.2). The loop works its way along the runqueue, performing lines 609–614 each time until it gets back to the `runqueue_head` at the beginning.

609 this line gets a pointer to the current entry. The `list_entry()` macro was described in Section 4.3.4.3. It converts a pointer to the `list_head` link to a pointer to the actual structure of which it is a linked list (e.g. `task_struct`). The second parameter describes the type of the enclosing structure; the third identifies the link field within the `task_struct` itself.

610 for each process `can_schedule()` is called, (see Section 7.4.1). In the uniprocessor case, this always returns TRUE; every process is eligible to continue – even the one running. In the SMP case, it returns TRUE only if both of the following conditions are fulfilled:

- the process does not have a CPU assigned: an SMP kernel will consider scheduling a process only if it is not currently running on a CPU; remember a running process is still on the runqueue.

- the process is eligible to run on the CPU under consideration, as defined by the `cpus_allowed` field of its `task_struct`.

611–613 this block of code, in which a more suitable process may be selected, is executed only if `can_schedule()` returns TRUE.

611 now the goodness is calculated for this process. The first parameter, p, is the process being considered. The third parameter is rather misleadingly named. It really refers to the current process. The `goodness()` function is described in Section 7.4.2.

612 if the goodness is better than the current best, then this new goodness is taken as the running value, and the process that returned this goodness is recorded in `next`. Note that if (`weight == c`), no change is made.

615 in all cases we go on to the next process on the runqueue. After this loop, c should hold the weight of the most suitable process to run, and `next` should point to its `task_struct`.

619–628 this block of code is executed if, after going through all the processes on the runqueue, none was found with a positive quantum. In that case, the counter field of all processes is updated, including those on wait queues. This is called rescheduling.

621–622   the scheduler is not going to be dealing with the runqueue for a while now, so it releases the runqueue spinlock, which it acquired at line 577 of Figure 7.13, but, as it is going to be reading each element of the process list, it takes out a read lock on the process list.

623   the macro has been discussed in Section 3.1.3. It goes through each element in the process structure.

624   the counter field is recalculated. The formula used is as follows:

$$counter = (counter)/2 + priority.$$

For a process on the runqueue, as its counter is 0 at this stage, its counter value is set back to the value determined by the NICE_TO_TICKS() macro (Section 7.4.3). For a process on a wait queue, the counter value is actually increased, but, to prevent a long-waiting process from acquiring an unreasonably high counter value, half of the previous value is forgotten each time. This means that the value continues to increase, but more slowly each time it is rescheduled.

625–626   afterwards the read lock on the process structure is released, and the process reacquires the runqueue spinlock.

627   the scheduler goes back to line 602. In this way it avoids all the preliminaries, and tries again to select the next process to run.

7.3.4 Recording a scheduling decision

Now that the best process to run has been found, some book-keeping that has to be done before that process is actually run needs to be done (see Figure 7.15).

```
635         sched_data->curr = next;
636         task_set_cpu(next, this_cpu);
637         spin_unlock_irq(&runqueue_lock);
638
639         if (unlikely(prev == next)) {
640
641               prev->policy &= ~SCHED_YIELD;
642               goto same_process;
643         }
644
645 #ifdef CONFIG_SMP

653         sched_data->last_schedule = get_cycles();

661 #endif /* CONFIG_SMP */
662
663         kstat.context_swtch++;
```

Figure 7.15 Record scheduling decision

635   the sched_data field is changed to point to the new process.

636   this function, from Section 7.4.4, notes in the task_struct that the process has been assigned a CPU.

637   at this stage the process is finished with the runqueue, so it can give back the lock.

639–643   if the decision was to continue with the current process, these lines take a short cut. The unlikely() function (Section 1.2.1.2) hints to the compiler that this is unlikely to happen, and it can organise its code accordingly.

641   the SCHED_YIELD bit in the policy field is cleared, just in case it was set. The call to the scheduler might have been a result of the process yielding the CPU.

642   this line jumps over the context switching code, to line 700 (Section 7.3.5).

653   this code is used only on SMP systems. The function get_cycles()returns the cycle count for this CPU to date. This is a very precise measure of when the context switch occurred. The current cycle count is saved in the struct schedule_data, which is CPU-specific and was discussed in Section 7.2.4.1.

663   as a context switch is about to be carried out, the global count of context switches performed is updated. The data structure is discussed in Section 7.2.4.2.

7.3.5   Context switching

The code shown in Figure 7.16 begins actually to switch the context of the CPU. However, much of the work is done in out-of-line functions, examined in Section 7.5.

```
673        prepare_to_switch();
674        {
675            struct mm_struct *mm = next->mm;
676            struct mm_struct *oldmm = prev->active_mm;
677            if (!mm) {
678                if (next->active_mm) BUG();
679                next->active_mm = oldmm;
680                atomic_inc(&oldmm->mm_count);
681                enter_lazy_tlb(oldmm, next, this_cpu);
682            } else {
683                if (next->active_mm != mm) BUG();
684                switch_mm(oldmm, mm, next, this_cpu);
685            }
686
687            if (!prev->mm) {
688                prev->active_mm = NULL;
689                mmdrop(oldmm);
690            }
```

```
691        }

697            switch_to(prev, next, prev);
698            __schedule_tail(prev);
699
700  same_process:
701            reacquire_kernel_lock(current);
702            if (current->need_resched)
703                goto need_resched_back;
704            return;
```

Figure 7.16 Switch the context of the CPU

673   this macro is architecture-specific. On the i386 it does nothing. Other architectures may need some work done here.

674–691   this block of code changes the memory context of the CPU. As it really pertains to the memory manager, it will not be examined in full detail here. Remember prev is the current process; next is the one being switched in.

675–676   taking local copies of these pointers is more efficient than following the path through the task_struct each time. The mm pointer is used three times, oldmm four times. This more than outweighs the overhead of these two lines. Also, these pointers may be needed after task_struct values have been changed.

678–681   these lines are executed if the next process has no mm (i.e. if it is a kernel process).

678   if the process being switched in still has an active_mm, there is something seriously wrong. It should have dropped that when it was context switched out. BUG() prints an error message and executes an illegal instruction, so stopping the kernel (see Section 4.1.3.3).

679   the active_mm is set to be the active_mm of the process being switched out. A kernel thread has no memory context of its own; it borrows that of the previous process, but only while it is actually executing. It gives it back when it is context switched out (see line 688).

680   there is now an extra process sharing this memory map, so the count field is incremented. The atomic_inc() function is from Section 5.2.5.

681   this function is specific to the memory manager; it sets the translation lookaside buffer for this CPU to be 'lazy', so that it only propagates updates to other processors when required. On a uniprocessor, it does nothing.

683–684   the new process does have an mm field, so it is a user process.

683   if the mm of the process is not the same as its active_mm, there is something badly wrong, so a warning message is printed and the operating system is stopped, using the BUG() macro from Section 4.1.3.3.

684   this changes the memory context of the process, including the page tables. It is architecture-specific. Also, as it pertains to the memory manager, it will not be discussed further here.

687–689   these lines are executed if the process that is being switched out does not have an mm (i.e. it is a kernel thread).

688   the `active_mm` of the process is set to NULL. It was executing with the memory context of the process it succeeded; now it disassociates itself from that.

689   this function decrements the count field in the `mm_struct` it was using. If it is now zero, it frees the memory. As it is part of the memory manager, it will not be considered further in this book.

697   the macro `switch_to()` is machine-specific; it triggers the actual context switch by switching the register state and the stack. Passing the same parameter twice to a macro is unusual, but it may help to understand what is going on here to note that in the definition of the macro itself (see Section 7.5.1) these three parameters are named `prev`, `next`, and `last`. Also, the macro arranges that whatever value was in `prev` beforehand will be in `last` afterwards. Once this call returns, the CPU is executing in the context of the new process.

698   the function `__schedule_tail()` is described in Section 7.5.4. It is relevant only in the SMP case. It tries to find a suitable CPU on which to run the process just switched out.

700   we come here directly from line 642 of Figure 7.15 if the current process is still the most suitable; otherwise we fall through after the context switch.

701   the `current` macro (Section 7.2.1.3) always evaluates to a pointer to the `task_struct` reresenting the currently running process. The macro to reacquire the lock has been described in Section 5.5.2.3.

702–703   if the `need_resched` flag is set in the (new) current process, then we go back to line 560 at the beginning of the scheduler (see Section 7.3.1). It is no longer suitable, and the scheduler must run again.

704   the call to `schedule()` returns here. Control goes back to the new process, at the line after its call to `schedule()`. It takes up seamlessly from there.

7.4 Functions used by the scheduler

In Section 7.3 the scheduler was examined in some detail. In the course of that examination, a number of functions that the scheduler called were passed over merely with a description. This section will now examine the code of these functions.

7.4.1 Scheduling macros

At different times, the main scheduler needs to determine the appropriate idle process corresponding to a particular CPU or if a given process can be scheduled onto a particular CPU. Figure 7.17, from `kernel/sched.c`, shows alternate forms of these two macros, one for the SMP case, the other for the uniprocessor case.

```
115  #ifdef CONFIG_SMP
116
117  #define idle_task(cpu) (init_tasks[cpu_number_map(cpu)])
```

```
118   #define can_schedule(p,cpu) ((!(p)->has_cpu) &&          \
119               ((p)->cpus_allowed & (1 << cpu)))
120
121   #else
122
123   define idle_task(cpu) (&init_task)
124   #define can_schedule(p,cpu) (1)
125
126   #endif
```

Figure 7.17 Macros used by the scheduler

117 the `idle_task()` macro converts a CPU number into a pointer to the `task_struct` of the idle process for that CPU. The `init_tasks[]` array was described in Section 3.3.1. On the i386 architecture the `cpu_number_map()` function merely returns the number it was passed as parameter (see Section 7.2.1.2).

118 the `can_schedule()` macro converts a pointer to `task_struct` into TRUE or FALSE. In the SMP case, the result is TRUE only if a CPU is not currently assigned to the process (if the `has_cpu` field of the `task_struct` is NULL) and the process can be scheduled onto that CPU (the bit corresponding to that CPU is set in the `cpus_allowed` field of the `task_struct`).

123 in the single CPU case, the idle task is always `init_task`, declared in Section 3.3.1.

124 any sort of CPU affinity is meaningless in the uniprocessor case, so this macro always returns TRUE.

7.4.2 Calculating the goodness of a process

The function shown in Figure 7.18, from `kernel/sched.c`, decides how desirable a process is to run. It attempts to weigh different processes against each other depending on their scheduling policy, priority, and the CPU on which they ran last. It takes into account penalties due to cache and translation lookaside buffer misses. Possible return values are:

−1: not to be selected, it has just yielded the CPU;

0: not to be selected, it has used its full quantum;

>1: the 'goodness' value (the larger, the better);

+1000: a real-time process, select this.

```
144   static inline int goodness(struct task_struct * p,
                              int this_cpu, struct mm_struct *this_mm)
145   {
146       int weight;

153       weight = -1;
154       if (p->policy & SCHED_YIELD)
```

```
155                 goto out;

160        if (p->policy == SCHED_OTHER){

168               weight = p->counter;
169               if (!weight)
170                   goto out;
171
172  #ifdef CONFIG_SMP

175               if (p->processor -- this_cpu)
176                   weight += PROC_CHANGE_PENALTY;
177  #endif

180               if (p->mm == this_mm || !p->mm)
181                   weight += 1;
182               weight += 20-p->nice;
183               goto out;
184         }

191        weight = 1000 + p->rt_priority;
192  out:
193        return weight;
194  }
```

Figure 7.18   Function that decides how desirable a process is

144   the first parameter is a pointer to the process being evaluated; the second identifies the CPU on which the current process is executing; the third identifies the memory context of the current process.

153   the return value will be built up in the local variable `weight`, which is given a default initial value of −1.

154–155   if the SCHED_YIELD bit is set in the `policy` field of the `task_struct`, then this process does not want to be considered, so a goodness of −1 is returned.

160–184   this code is executed only if it is an interactive process (SCHED_OTHER), so the common time-sharing case is dealt with first.

168   the process is given a first approximation weight of the number of clock ticks it has left.

169–170   if the `counter` value is 0, this means the process has used up its quantum. The function returns immediately, with a `goodness` of 0.

175–176   this is relevant only to the SMP case. If the process being considered last ran on this CPU then there may still be entries relevant to this process in the cache and translation lookaside buffer, so it is a particularly suitable candidate to run and is given a large boost. PROC_CHANGE_PENALTY is machine-specific, defined in <asm/smp.h>. Values vary from 15 to 20.

180–181   if the process being considered is using the same memory context as the current one, or if it does not have a memory context of its own, it is given a boost of 1. In the first case, it is a thread in the same process; in the second case, it is a kernel thread. In both cases there would be no need to change the memory context, if selected.

182   this line adds the priority of the process as calculated from `nice`. Because `nice` can range from −20 (a high-priority process) to +19, (the lowest-priority process) this will be a value from 40 (highest priority) to 1 (lowest).

183   the `goto` jumps over the weighting for real-time processes in line 191, and returns the result just calculated.

191   if the process is not a SCHED_OTHER process, then it must be SCHED_FIFO or SCHED_RR. These are real-time, fixed-priority, processes. In that case, the function returns the real-time priority of the process, boosted by 1000. This guarantees that no interactive process can get ahead of it. So, effectively, the process with the highest `rt_priority` will be scheduled next.

7.4.3   Determining the quantum for a process

Every time a reschedule is performed, all processes, whether ready or waiting, have their `counter` field, or quantum, topped up. The code in Figure 7.19, from `kernel/sched.c`, shows how the quantum to be given to any particular process is determined.

```
59    #if HZ < 200
60    #define TICK_SCALE(x)     ((x) >> 2)
61    #elif HZ < 400
62    #define TICK_SCALE(x)     ((x) >> 1)
63    #elif HZ < 800
64    #define TICK_SCALE(x)     (x)
65    #elif HZ < 1600
66    #define TICK_SCALE(x)     ((x) << 1)
67    #else
68    #define TICK_SCALE(x)     ((x) << 2)
69    #endif
70
71    #define NICE_TO_TICKS(nice)  (TICK_SCALE(20-(nice))+1)
```

Figure 7.19   Determining the quantum

59–69   the quantum is measured in ticks, or interrupts by the system clock, so when a quantum is determined for a particular process it has to be scaled in proportion to the frequency of the interrupting clock. Faster machines should be given more ticks. The `TICK_SCALE()` macro does this.

59–60   for HZ of less than 200, the quantum is divided by 4.

61–62   for HZ between 200 and 400, the quantum is divided by 2.

63–64   for HZ between 400 and 800, the quantum is not adjusted.

65–66 for HZ between 800 and 1600, the quantum is multiplied by 2.

67–68 for HZ over 1600, the quantum is multiplied by 4.

71 each process has a `nice` field in its `task_struct`, which can be set by the `nice()` system service. The value in this field gives an indication of the priority of the process. This value can range from −20 (a high-priority process) to +19, (the lowest-priority process). This macro converts the `nice` value for the process into the size of the quantum in clock ticks. The first part of the calculation, 20−(`nice`), produces values from 40 (highest priority) to 1 (lowest priority). This value is then scaled by the `TICK_SCALE()` macro, with a result depending on the frequency of the interrupting clock. For slower clocks, it is divided by 4, or 2; for faster clocks, it is multiplied by 2 or 4. The 1 added at the end guarantees that no matter how low the priority, or how slow the interrupting clock, the quantum will always be at least 1 tick.

7.4.4 Noting the central processing unit assigned

The trivial function shown in Figure 7.20, from `<linux/sched.h>`, notes in the `task_struct` that the particular process has been assigned a CPU.

```
553   #define task_has_cpu(tsk) ((tsk)->cpus_runnable != ~0UL)

556   static inline void task_set_cpu(struct task_struct *tsk,
                                                unsigned int cpu)
557   {
558         tsk->processor = cpu;
559         tsk->cpus_runnable = 1UL << cpu;
560   }
```

Figure 7.20 Noting that a computer processing unit has been assigned

553 if a process is not assigned a CPU, then the `cpus_runnable` field in its `task_struct` is set to all 1s. When assigned a CPU, only the bit corresponding to that CPU is set.

558 this notes the number of the assigned CPU in the `processor` field.

559 this sets the bit in `cpus_runnable` corresponding to the assigned processor. All other bits are cleared.

7.5 Context switching

When considering the scheduler in Section 7.3, we broke the discussion down into five main parts. The last part of these was context switching between processes. The mainstream code for that part of the scheduler is concerned mostly with changing the memory context of the machine (see Section 7.3.5). It leaves the work of switching stacks and registers to two further routines. There are a number of steps in this, to be examined here. First, we have a macro that prepares things by switching stack pointers. Then we have a function that actually completes the context switch. The first code executed by the newly running process sees to it that the previous one is resting happily and announces to the rest of the system that it has actually ceded the CPU.

The i386 CPU does have a hardware context-switching mechanism, but Linux does not use it, preferring to do it in software. It seems that this is not for performance reasons but to avoid problems in recovering from errors caused by stale state. The comment in the code says that doing it like this gives much more flexibility.

There are still some traces of the hardware mechanism left, however. The CPU uses a struct tss to save the volatile environment, and each process would have had one of these. Even when not using hardware context switching, the CPU has a TR register, pointing to the current struct tss, and it expects to find a valid value in it. So Linux supplies one struct tss per CPU, to keep it happy. This was examined in Section 7.2.3.

7.5.1 Preparing to context switch

The code in Figure 7.21, from <asm-i386/system.h>, is a wrapper that sets things up for actually switching the CPU between two processes.

```
12    extern void FASTCALL(__switch_to(struct task_struct *prev,
                                        struct task_struct *next));

13
14    #define prepare_to_switch()  do { } while(0)
15    #define switch_to(prev,next,last) do {                      \
16        asm volatile("pushl %%esi\n\t"                          \
17            "pushl %%edi\n\t"                                    \
18            "pushl %%ebp\n\t"                                    \
19            "movl %%esp,%0\n\t"                                 \
20            "movl %3,%%esp\n\t"                                 \
21            "movl $1f,%1\n\t"                                   \
22            "pushl %4\n\t"                                       \
23            "jmp __switch_to\n"                                 \
24            "1:\t"                                              \
25            "popl %%ebp\n\t"                                    \
26            "popl %%edi\n\t"                                    \
27            "popl %%esi\n\t"                                    \
28            :"=m" (prev->thread.esp),                           \
29                "=m" (prev->thread.eip), "=b" (last)            \
30            :"m" (next->thread.esp),                            \
31                "m" (next->thread.eip), "a" (prev),             \
32                "d" (next), "b" (prev));                         \
33    } while (0)
```

Figure 7.21 Context switcher

12 the FASTCALL means that this function, described in Section 7.5.2, is expecting its parameters in the EAX and EDX registers, not on the stack.

14 this macro has nothing to do on the i386 architecture.

15 the parameters are pointers to the task_struct of the process to switch out (in the EAX and EBX registers), the one to switch in (in the EDX register), and an output parameter (in the EBX register) which will contain a pointer to the process switched out.

16–18   this pushes the source and destination index registers, and the base pointer register, onto the stack (the kernel mode stack of prev). The compiler assumes that they are going to remain unchanged until the end of this block of assembly code, but, in fact, many other processes may execute between lines 22–24.

19   the current contents of ESP (the stack pointer register) are moved to the destination represented by parameter 0. That is the esp field in the thread structure of prev, the process being switched out. Note that this is different from the value saved on the kernel stack when that process entered the kernel. The three previous instructions have altered the stack pointer.

20   the ESP register is loaded from the source represented by parameter 3. This is the esp field of the thread structure of next, so these two instructions have switched the stack pointer register. The processor is now operating on the kernel stack of the new process.

21   the address of label 1: is moved into the destination represented by parameter 1. This is the eip field of the thread structure of prev, so this is saving the instruction pointer, pointing to line 24. When prev runs again, some time in the future, it will take up here.

22   parameter 4 is pushed onto the stack (the kernel stack of the next process). This is the eip field of the thread structure of next, or the address at which the next process will resume execution.

23   see the description of line 679 in Section 7.5.2 for this function. It is expecting its parameters in EAX and EDX. According to the operand specifiers on lines 31–32, the EAX register on entry contains a pointer to the task_struct of the process being switched out, EDX the one being switched in.

24   this is where a process takes up after it is context switched in, so these lines are being executed by the next process.

25–27   these lines pop the base pointer, destination index, and source index to their appropriate hardware registers. These values were pushed on the stack before it was switched out, at lines 16–18. This is the end of the assembly code; control returns to line 697 of schedule() (see Section 7.3.5).

28   parameter 0 is the esp field of the process being switched out. It is write only ("=") and may be in memory ("m").

29   parameter 1 is the eip field of the process being switched out. It is write only ("="), and may be in memory ("m"). Parameter 2 is the last parameter; an output parameter, in the EBX register. Since the EBX register contains the pointer prev on entry to the macro this is an instruction to the compiler that the pointer last is to have the same value as prev, on exit.

30   parameter 3 is the esp field of the process being switched in. It is an input parameter and may be in memory ("m").

31   parameter 4 is the eip field of the process being switched in. It is an input parameter and may be in memory ("m"). Parameter 5 is a pointer to the task_struct of the process being switched out. It must be in the EAX register, the first parameter to __switch_to() (see line 23).

32   parameter 6 is a pointer to the task_struct of the process being switched in. It must be in the EDX register, the second parameter to __switch_to() (see line 23). Parameter 7 is a pointer to the `task_struct` of the process being switched out. This input parameter must be in the EBX register. It is aliased onto parameter 2.

7.5.2 Switching the computer processing unit context

The code shown in Figure 7.22 from `arch/i386/kernel/process.c`, should switch tasks from `prev_p` to `next_p`. When this function is called, the scheduler is already running on the stack of the new process.

```
679  void __switch_to(struct task_struct *prev_p,
                                          struct task_struct *next_p)
680  {
681        struct thread_struct *prev = &prev_p->thread,
682        *next = &next_p->thread;
683        struct tss_struct *tss = init_tss + smp_processor_id();
684
685        unlazy_fpu(prev_p);

690        tss->esp0 = next->esp0;

696        asm volatile("movl %%fs,%0":"=m" (*(int *)&prev->fs));
697        asm volatile("movl %%gs,%0":"=m" (*(int *)&prev->gs));

702        loadsegment(fs, next->fs);
703        loadsegment(gs, next->gs);

708        if (next->debugreg[7]){
709              loaddebug(next, 0);
710              loaddebug(next, 1);
711              loaddebug(next, 2);
712              loaddebug(next, 3);
713              /* no 4 and 5 */
714              loaddebug(next, 6);
715              loaddebug(next, 7);
716        }
717
718        if (prev->ioperm || next->ioperm) {
719              if (next->ioperm) {

728                    memcpy(tss->io_bitmap, next->io_bitmap,
729                          IO_BITMAP_SIZE*sizeof(unsigned long));
730                    tss->bitmap = IO_BITMAP_OFFSET;
731              } else

738                    tss->bitmap = INVALID_IO_BITMAP_OFFSET;
739        }
740  }
```

Figure 7.22 The actual context switcher

679	the parameters are pointers to the `task_struct` of the previous and next processes.
681–682	these lines take local pointers to the `thread` field of each `task_struct`.
683	this takes a local pointer to the `tss` field corresponding to this CPU, (see Section 7.2.3.2).
685	this checks if the process has used the floating point unit (FPU) (see Section 11.10.2.2 for the function).
690	this copies the stack pointer from the `thread` of the incoming process into the appropriate field in the `struct tss`, overwriting the previous value there.
696–697	this saves away the FS and GS hardware registers into the `thread` of the previous process. There is no need to save ES and DS, as they are always kernel segments while inside the kernel.
702–703	this restores FS and GS hardware register values from the `thread` of the new process. The macro is from Section 19.6.2.
708–716	if the saved `debugreg[7]` (the debug control register) of the new process indicates that there is valid information saved, then the hardware debug registers are loaded from the `thread` structure. The `loaddebug()` function is described in Section 7.5.3.
718–739	this block of code is executed only if the `ioperm` field of either the old or new process is valid, indicating that a process is allowed direct access to IO ports. It is really the province of the IO manager.
728–730	if the `ioperm` field of the new process is valid, then the `io_bitmap` field is copied from `thread.io_bitmap` to the `tss`.
730	the `bitmap` field of the `tss` is set up as the offset of the `io_bitmap` field just copied in the previous line.
738	this line is executed if the `ioperm` field is set in the previous process, but not in the new one. It sets up an invalid bitmap offset in the `tss`, pointing outside the limit of the segment, which causes a SIGSEGV if a process tries to use an IO port instruction. Any subsequent call to `sys_ioperm()` will then set up the bitmap properly.
740	the function terminates in a rather unusual way. The return address on the stack does not point back to the caller. In fact, this function was never called, rather it was jumped to, at line 23 of `switch_to()` (see Section 7.5.1). Because it is declared as a standard C function, the compiler generates an RET instruction at the end of this. When this instruction is executed, it pops a value from the stack to the EIP register. This value, pushed on the stack at line 22 of `switch_to()`, points to the instruction at which to resume the new process.

7.5.3 Loading a debug register

The macro shown in Figure 7.23, from `arch/i386/kernel/process.c`, will load a value from memory into one of the debugging registers in the CPU.

```
651   #define loaddebug(thread,register)                    \
652          __asm__("movl %0,%%db" #register               \
653        : /* no output */                                 \
654                :"r" (thread->debugreg[register]))
```

Figure 7.23   Loading a debugging register

651   the parameters are a pointer to the `thread` structure containing the value to be loaded, and the number of the register.

652   this machine instruction moves the value from parameter 0 into the specified register. Note that it prefixes the register number with `"db"`.

654   the only operand constraint is the element of the array `debugreg[]` in the `thread` structure, as specified by the register parameter.

7.5.4   Cleaning up after the context switch

The function `__schedule_tail()`, shown in Figure 7.24, is from `kernel/sched.c`. It is called from line 698 of `schedule()`, immediately after the context switch (see Section 7.3.5). That means it is the first code executed by a process when it is context switched back onto a CPU. The pointer `prev` is really pointing to the process that has just been switched out. Most of the code is only of relevance to the SMP case. The uniprocessor case is trivial.

```
467   static inline void __schedule_tail (struct task_struct *prev)
468   {
469   #ifdef CONFIG_SMP
470          int policy;

482          policy = prev->policy;
483          prev->policy = policy & ~SCHED_YIELD;
484          wmb();

491          task_lock(prev);
492          task_release_cpu(prev);
493          mb();
494          if (prev->state == TASK_RUNNING)
495                goto needs_resched;
496
497   out_unlock:
498          task_unlock(prev);
499          return;

511   needs_resched:
512          {
513          unsigned long flags;

519          if ((prev == idle_task(smp_processor_id())) ||
520          (policy & SCHED_YIELD))
```

```
521              goto out_unlock;
522
523       spin_lock_irqsave(&runqueue_lock, flags);
524       if (prev->state == TASK_RUNNING)&& !task_has_cpu(prev))
525            reschedule_idle(prev);
526       spin_unlock_irqrestore(&runqueue_lock, flags);
527       goto out_unlock;
528       }
529  #else
530       prev->policy &= ~SCHED_YIELD;
531  #endif /* CONFIG_SMP */
532  }
```

Figure 7.24   Cleaning up after scheduling

482   this takes a local copy of the `policy` of the previous process. This is needed because the `policy` field is going to be changed in the next line, and the old value of `policy` will be needed at line 520.

483   this clears the SCHED_YIELD bit, if it was set. The process may have yielded the CPU just now, but it wants to be considered for further selection. It is safe to write to the `task_struct` of the old process at this stage without a lock, because its `has_cpu` field has not yet been changed, and so no other processor will take it.

484   this guarantees that the write has been propagated to memory, before going on. The `wmb()` macro is architecture-specific. On the 386 it does not actually do anything, as Intel CPUs guarantee that all writes are seen by other CPUs in the order in which they are executed.

491–499   this is a critical section, guarded by the `task_lock()` function (see Section 7.2.5), which takes out a lock on the `task_struct` using the `alloc_lock` field. This is needed for the case when `prev` is in the TASK_ZOMBIE state. The parent is held up on this lock in `release_task()` (Section 9.4.2.1). Otherwise, it could try to release the `task_struct` much earlier on, find that its child still has a CPU, and become very confused.

492   this function merely sets the `cpus_runnable` field of the `task_struct` of the old process to all 1s, meaning that it does not have a CPU now. From here on, the rest of the system can see this (see Section 7.5.5).

493   the memory barrier `mb()` guarantees that the write is propagated to main memory before the test in the next line is executed.

494–495   if the previous process is still in the TASK_RUNNING state, then an attempt is made to find a CPU for it to run on.

498–499   otherwise, the spinlock is given back to that process and we return to line 491.

512–528   this block of code is executed if the process that has just been swapped out is still in the TASK_RUNNING state.

519   one reason why the process may be in the TASK_RUNNING state is because it is the idle process on its CPU, which is always runable. The macro `idle_task()` is described in Section 7.4.1. It evaluates to a pointer to the idle process on the specified CPU. The macro `smp_processor_id()`, which has been described in Section 7.2.1.4, evaluates to the ID of the current process.

520 another reason the process is in this state is because it has yielded the CPU just for now, and the scheduler has set its state back to `TASK_RUNNING`. Note that this is testing the local copy of `policy`, taken at line 482, before the `SCHED_YIELD` bit was cleared.

521 in either of the above cases no attempt should be made to reschedule. We just go back, release the lock on the `task_struct`, and return to `schedule()`.

523–526 so, the process is genuinely interested in running. The other CPUs are tried to see if any of them is idle. An interrupt safe spinlock is taken out on the runqueue lock and the value of `EFLAGS` is saved in flags. This lock must be held before calling `reschedule_idle()` at line 525. Having more than one CPU at a time manipulate the runqueue would be a recipe for trouble.

524 this is playing very safe, to avoid any possibility of allocating the same process to two CPUs at the same time. The previous process was found to be in the `TASK_RUNNING` state at line 494; between that and line 523 some other processor could have taken it on, so its `state` field is checked again, as well as its ownership of a CPU, all under the protection of the runqueue lock. The `task_has_cpu()` macro is from Section 7.4.4.

525 if the process is still in the `TASK_RUNNING` state, but not actually running, `reschedule_idle()` is called (Section 7.6.1) which will attempt to find a new processor for it (but it might preempt the current process as well).

526 the `EFLAGS` value is restored and the runqueue spinlock is released.

527 we unlock the `task_lock` and return. This lock on the `task_struct` was held throughout `needs_resched` (lines 512–528).

530 this one line is all that is done in the uniprocessor case. The `SCHED_YIELD` bit is cleared, if it was set. The process may have yielded the CPU just now, but it wants to be considered for further selection. Note there is an implicit `return` after this.

7.5.5 Releasing a computer processing unit

The trivial function shown in Figure 7.25, from `<linux/sched.h>`, announces to the rest of the system that a process has actually given up the CPU.

```
561  static inline void task_release_cpu(struct task_struct *tsk)
562  {
563          tsk->cpus_runnable = ~0UL;
564  }
```

Figure 7.25 Releasing a computer processing unit

561 the parameter is a pointer to the `task_struct` of the process that has just released the CPU.

563 the `cpus_runnable` field of the `task_struct` is set to all 1s, indicating that it does not have a CPU now.

7.6 Finding an idle processor

This section describes the kernel function that attempts to find a suitable CPU for a particular process. This is the inverse of normal scheduling, which tries to find a process to run on a particular CPU. This function is called when the scheduler finds that the process it has just switched out is still runable. It is also called when a process is woken up by a CPU on which it is not allowed to run.

This is a long and complex function, so the code is broken down into three parts, for ease of explanation. The first two sections, Sections 7.6.1 and 7.6.2, cover the SMP case; Section 7.6.3 covers the uniprocessor case.

7.6.1 Trying the computer processing unit on which the process last ran

The code in Figure 7.26, from `kernel/sched.c`, shows the first part of the function, which tries to reschedule the process onto the CPU on which it last ran.

```
212  static void reschedule_idle(struct task_struct * p)
213  {
214  #ifdef CONFIG_SMP
215      int this_cpu = smp_processor_id();
216      struct task_struct *tsk, *target_tsk;
217      int cpu, best_cpu, i, max_prio;
218      cycles_t oldest_idle;

224      best_cpu = p->processor;
225      if (can_schedule(p, best_cpu)) {
226          tsk = idle_task(best_cpu);
227          if (cpu_curr(best_cpu) == tsk) {
228              int need_resched;
229  send_now_idle:

235              need_resched = tsk->need_resched;
236              tsk->need_resched = 1;
237              if ((best_cpu != this_cpu) && !need_resched)
238                  smp_send_reschedule(best_cpu);
239              return;
240          }
241      }
```

Figure 7.26 Trying the last computer processing unit on which the process last ran

215 this finds the ID of the CPU which is executing this code. The function has been discussed in Section 7.2.1.4.

224 the ideal CPU for this process is the one on which it last ran, as recorded in its `task_struct`. This would make best use of the cache.

226–241 this block of code is executed if it is still permissible to schedule the process on the CPU on which it last ran. For the `can_schedule()` macro, see Section 7.4.1.

226 this finds the address of the idle task for that CPU. The `idle_task()` macro is from Section 7.4.1.

228–239 only if that CPU is running its idle task is the block of code in lines 228–239 executed. The `cpu_curr()` macro, discussed in Section 7.2.4, returns a pointer to the `task_struct` of the process currently running on a CPU.

235 this takes a temporary copy of the `need_resched` field of the idle process running on that CPU, as it is going to be changed on the next line, and the old value will be tested at line 237.

236 this sets the `need_resched` flag of the idle process running on that CPU.

237–238 if the CPU it last ran on is *not* the current one, and the idle task was not already marked for reschedule, then an interprocessor interrupt (IPI) is sent to that CPU. The `smp_send_reschedule()` function is dealt with in Section 13.5.1. Otherwise, setting the `need_resched` flag of the idle process should be sufficient, as the idle function continuously checks its `need_resched` flag (see Section 3.4), so it can skip the IPI.

239 the function returns at this stage.

To recap: the most suitable CPU for this process (the one it last ran on) is now running its idle process. So that idle process was marked for rescheduling; if on another CPU, an IPI was sent to that CPU for good measure.

7.6.2 Finding another computer processing unit

The code shown in Figure 7.27, from `kernel/sched.c`, is executed only if the process cannot be scheduled onto the CPU on which it last ran, because that CPU now has a process that has built up a lot of cache. Thus an attempt is made to try to find another idle CPU for it. The idle CPU with the smallest cycle count is selected (as that one will have the least active cache context). Also, the executing process that has the least priority is found. Then the selected idle process (if there is one) is marked for rescheduling, otherwise, the lowest-priority process is marked as such.

```
250         oldest_idle = (cycles_t) -1;
251         target_tsk = NULL;
252         max_prio = 0;
253
254         for (i = 0; i < smp_num_cpus; i++) {
255             cpu = cpu_logical_map(i);
256             if (!can_schedule(p, cpu))
257                 continue;
258             tsk = cpu_curr(cpu);

264             if (tsk == idle_task(cpu)) {
265 #if defined(__i386__) && defined(CONFIG_SMP)

270                 if (smp_num_siblings == 2) {
271                     if (cpu_curr(cpu_sibling_map[cpu]) ==
```

```
272                    idle_task(cpu_sibling_map[cpu])) {
273                        oldest_idle = last_schedule(cpu);
274                        target_tsk = tsk;
275                        break;
276                    }
277
278                }
279  #endif
280                if (last_schedule(cpu) < oldest_idle) {
281                        oldest_idle = last_schedule(cpu);
282                        target_tsk = tsk;
283                }
284            } else {
285                if (oldest_idle == -1ULL) {
286                    int prio = preemption_goodness(tsk,cpu);
287
288                    if (prio > max_prio) {
289                        max_prio = prio;
290                        target_tsk = tsk;
291                    }
292                }
293            }
294        }
295    tsk = target_tsk;
296    if (tsk) {
297        if (oldest_idle != -1ULL){
298            best_cpu = tsk->processor;
299            goto send_now_idle;
300        }
301        tsk->need_resched = 1;
302        if (tsk->processor != this_cpu)
303            smp_send_reschedule(tsk->processor);
304    }
305    return;
```

Figure 7.27   Finding an idle computer processing unit

250–252   each CPU is to be tried in turn. Account is taken of the priority of the process executing on each CPU and how long the process has been executing (this is an indication of how much cache state it has built up). The three variables initialised here will be used as running counters to record the 'best yet encountered'.

250   the cycles_t type is machine-specific but is always unsigned, so initialising it to −1 means setting it to its maximum value, of all 1s.

254–294   this loop tries each of the CPUs in turn. The smp_num_cpus variable is from Section 7.2.1.

255   the loop counter is converted to a CPU identifier, using cpu_logical_map(), as described in Section 7.2.1.2. CPUs may not be numbered consecutively 0–max.

256–257   if this process should not be run on the particular CPU (for whatever reason), we go around again, and try the next one. The `can_schedule()` macro is described in Section 7.4.1.

258   this gets a pointer to the `task_struct` of the process currently running on the CPU under consideration (see Section 7.2.4.1).

264–283   this code is executed if the CPU being considered is running its idle task.

265–279   this code is only compiled into an SMP kernel on the i386 architecture. It checks if two sibling CPUs in the same physical package are idle.

270   the `smp_num_siblings` was defined in Section 7.2.1.1. It indicates the number of sibling CPUs packaged together. Only if there are two of them is the block of code executed.

271–272   these lines check if the sibling of this CPU is also running its idle task. If so, this one is picked. The `cpu_sibling_map[]` array, from Section 7.2.1.1, identifies the sibling of each CPU.

273   `oldest_idle` is updated to the cycle count of the new most suitable processor.

274   which process this is is remembered by putting its `task_struct` pointer into `target_task`.

275   this CPU is definitely the best choice, so we break out of the `for` loop and go on to line 295.

280   the algorithm is trying to select the least recently active CPU – the one that will have the least active cache content. If the process on this one has been running for less time than the previous smallest, then this one is chosen and the swap is done in the next two lines. The `last_schedule()` macro, from Section 7.2.4 gives the cycle count of the processor identified by its parameter `cpu`.

281   this updates `oldest_idle` to the cycle count of the new most suitable processor.

282   we remember which process this is by putting its `task_struct` pointer into `target_task`. We then jump on to line 294 and go around the loop again.

285–293   this code is executed if the CPU being examined is not running its idle task, so it is looking at the possibility of preempting a CPU from a low-priority process.

285–292   if `oldest_idle` still has its initialisation value of −1, then a suitable CPU has not yet been found. Otherwise one has, and we are not interested in stealing a CPU from a low-priority process. In that case, we just go around the loop again.

286   should the running process be preempted in favour of this one? The first parameter `tsk` is a pointer to the process currently running on the CPU being considered. The second, `p`, is the process we are trying to place, and `cpu` is the processor we are considering. The return value is the difference between the goodness of both processes. A positive value means 'replace', 0 or negative means 'don't', see Section 7.6.4 for the function.

288   if `prio` is positive and is greater than any found in previous iterations of the loop then this is a more suitable CPU than any found before.

289   the goodness is remembered in `max_prio`, the best found so far.

290   which process it is is remembered by saving its `task_struct` pointer in `target_task`.

295   control arrives here after having tried all CPUs (including the current one, which is executing this code).

296   if no suitable process to preempt has been found at this stage, `target_tsk` and hence `tsk` will still be NULL, as it was initialised in line 251, so we just skip on to line 305 and return. Otherwise, the code at lines 297–303 is executed.

297–300   as `oldest_idle` no longer has its initialisation value, it is an idle CPU that has been found.

298   the process to be preempted is identified by `tsk`; `best_cpu` is the processor `tsk` last ran on.

299   control goes back to `send_now_idle` at line 229 of `reschedule_idle()` (see Section 7.6.1). This will arrange for the idle process on that CPU to be preempted.

301   if it was not an idle CPU, then a CPU has been found running a less important process. That one is going to be preempted, so its `need_resched` flag is set.

302–303   if it is running on another CPU, an IPI is sent, using the function from Section 13.5.1.

7.6.3 The uniprocessor case

Despite the fact that its whole purpose is to find another CPU on which to run a process, the `reschedule_idle()` function does have something to do in the uniprocessor case as well. The code shown in Figure 7.28 is executed if there is only one CPU. Note the UP in the comment stands for uniprocessor, not a semaphore operation. It decides whether the currently running process should be marked for rescheduling or not. This depends on the value returned by `preemption_goodness()`.

```
308  #else /* UP */
309       int this_cpu = smp_processor_id();
310       struct task_struct *tsk;
311
312       tsk = cpu_curr(this_cpu);
313       if (preemption_goodness(tsk, p, this_cpu) > 0)
314            tsk->need_resched = 1;
315  #endif
316  }
```

Figure 7.28   The uniprocessor case

308   the macro `smp_processor_id()` has been discussed in Section 7.2.1.4. It returns the ID of the processor executing this code.

312   for `cpu_curr()` see Section 7.2.4; this returns a pointer to the `task_struct` of the process currently running on that CPU.

313   this function decides whether the currently running process should be preempted in favour of p. The function is discussed in Section 7.6.4.

314   if so, it sets the `need_resched` flag of the currently running process.

7.6.4   Comparing suitabilities of two processes

At the heart of the `reschedule_idle()` function that has just been considered is a decision as to whether the process running on a particular CPU should be allowed to continue or should be preempted. The function shown in Figure 7.29, from `kernel/sched.c`, decides the 'goodness value' of replacing a process on a given CPU.

```
199  static inline int preemption_goodness (struct task_struct
                                    * prev, struct task_struct * p, int cpu)
200  {
201        return goodness(p, cpu, prev->active_mm) -
                              goodness(prev, cpu, prev->active_mm);
202  }
```

Figure 7.29   Function to decide on replacing a process

199   the first parameter is a pointer to the process currently running on the CPU in question; the second is the process being considered; the third is the CPU in question.

201   this calculates the goodness of both the processes and returns the difference between them. A positive return value means 'replace'; zero or negative means 'don't'. The `goodness()` function was described in Section 7.4.2.

8

Process creation

All operating systems have some way of creating new processes. A process control block representing the new process is created and linked onto the process structure, where it is indistinguishable from the others already there and competes with them for a share of CPU time.

With most operating systems, the name of an executable program is required as a parameter to the relevant system service. In Unix the system service that creates a new process, fork(), takes no parameters. It creates an exact copy of the running process. So immediately after the call to fork() there are two processes, each executing the same program. Each of them is at exactly the same point in the program – the next instruction after the fork() – and both will continue on from there. This is not very useful. Normally, one of them then asks the operating system to run another program, so the end result is one process executing one program and the second process executing the other.

Linux also has a nonstandard system service, clone(). This is similar to fork() but it has a number of parameters specifying which resources are to be shared with its parent. Depending on the parameters passed to clone() it can share memory (including program), file systems (root and current directory), open files, signal handlers, even identification (ID) number. In Linux, the pthread library creates new threads by a call to clone(). This effectively creates a new process, identical to its parent in everything except the volatile environment, the thread field.

8.1 Data structures and initialisation

This chapter will begin, as do other chapters, by considering the data structures used and their initialisation.

8.1.1 Process manager variables

The variables shown in Figure 8.1, from kernel/fork.c, are used by the process manager to track process creation and termination.

The Linux Process Manager. The Internals of Scheduling, Interrupts and Signals   John O'Gorman
© 2003 John Wiley & Sons, Ltd   ISBN: 0 470 84771 9

```
30   int            nr_threads;
31   int            nr_running;
32
33   int            max_threads;
34   unsigned long  total_forks;
35   int            last_pid;
```

Figure 8.1 Global variables used by the process manager

30 this variable keeps track of the total number of processes that currently exist in the system.

31 this tracks the number of processes on the runqueue at any given time.

33 this is the maximum number of processes allowed.

34 this gives the total number of processes that have been created since the system booted. An unsigned long is used, to allow for a large number of forks.

35 this keeps track of the pid assigned by the last fork. It is used when allocating new process IDs (pids).

8.1.2 Initialisation routine

There is a short initialisation routine; see Figure 8.2, from kernel/fork.c. It is called from start_kernel() (see Section 1.3.1).

```
68   void __init fork_init(unsigned long mempages)

75       max_threads = mempages /(THREAD_SIZE/PAGE_SIZE) / 2;
76
77       init_task.rlim[RLIMIT_NPROC].rlim_cur = max_threads/2;
78       init_task.rlim[RLIMIT_NPROC].rlim_max = max_threads/2;
79   }
```

Figure 8.2 Initialisation routine

68 the parameter passed is the total number of page frames present in the system.

75 the literal constant THREAD_SIZE is defined in <asm-i386/processor.h> as 2 * PAGE_SIZE. It is the amount of kernel memory allocated to a process – the task_struct plus the kernel stack. So THREAD_SIZE/PAGE_SIZE is the size of this in pages (2). Then mempages /(THREAD_SIZE/PAGE_SIZE) is the number of processes that could be created using the whole memory. As each process needs 2 pages, this is half the number of physical pages available. To allow room for code and data as well, the default maximum number of threads is set to half of this again, or a quarter of the number of physical pages.

77–78 the limits for the init_task are set at half of this again, or a maximum of one eighth of the number of physical pages.

8.2 Creating a new process

When the `fork()` system service is called, the Linux kernel first checks if the user has the required permissions to create a new process. It then checks if the maximum number of processes has been exceeded; if so, the request is refused. If not, then a new `task_struct` is allocated and linked with the already existing structures, through `next_task` and `prev_task`. It is assigned a new `pid`, but the pointers `fs`, `files`, `mm`, and `sig` are copied from its parent.

The worker function that creates a new process is `do_fork()`, from `kernel/fork.c`. It copies the process information from the parent and sets up the necessary registers. It also copies the data segment in its entirety. As it is quite a long function, the discussion is broken down into several parts, in Sections 8.2.1–8.2.6.

8.2.1 Checking permissions and allocating data structure

The first block of code, shown in Figure 8.3, checks that the caller has the requisite permission to create a new process and allocates a new `task_struct`.

```
565  int  do_fork(unsigned long clone_flags,
566       unsigned long stack_start, struct pt_regs *regs,
          unsigned long stack_size)
567  {
568       int retval;
569       struct task_struct *p;
570       struct completion vfork;
571
572       retval = -EPERM;

578       if (clone_flags & CLONE_PID) {
579            if (current->pid)
580                 goto fork_out;
581       }
582
583       retval = -ENOMEM;
584       p = alloc_task_struct();
585       if (!p)
586            goto fork_out;
```

Figure 8.3   Checking permissions and allocating data structure

565   the `clone_flags` parameter specifies those attributes of the parent that the child is to inherit. These are described in Section 8.3.1.

566   the `stack_start` parameter is the value in the ESP register when `fork()` was called. It is pointing into the user stack of the parent. The `regs` parameter is a pointer to a `struct pt_regs` built on the parent's kernel stack on entry to the `fork()` or `clone()` system service. It contains copies of all the parent's hardware registers, which will be the initial values for the child process. Finally, `stack_size` is the size of the parent's stack, which will also be that of the child. This parameter is unused in the i386 architecture, so it is always passed a value of 0.

570   this struct completion will be used to synchronise between the parent and child (see Section 6.3.1 for the definition of the structure).

572   permissions are going to be checked later (see line 597–599 of Figure 8.4), so a default return value of EPERM is set for the moment.

578–581   for a definition of the CLONE_PID flag, see Section 8.3.1. It specifies that the new process is to have the same pid as the parent. Only a process with a pid of 0 (the boot up process) can use the CLONE_PID flag.

579–580   if the process has a pid other than 0, then the error exit with the current value in retval (i.e. EPERM) is taken. The calling process does not have permission to use the CLONE_PID flag (see Section 8.2.6 for the error exit).

579   the current macro (Section 7.2.1.3) always evaluates to a pointer to the task_struct representing the currently running process.

583   this sets up a default return value of ENOMEM, which will be returned if it is not possible to allocate any of the data structures involved.

584   this allocates a block from the slab cache to hold a struct task_struct and keeps the pointer returned in p. This is part of memory management, and will not be considered further here.

585–586   if the pointer is not valid (i.e. it is unable to allocate this much memory) then the error exit with the current value in retval (i.e. ENOMEM) is taken (see Section 8.2.6 for the error exit).

8.2.2   Initialising fields in the new task_struct

The next block of code (see Figure 8.4) initialises a number of fields in the new task_struct. For the moment its state is set to TASK_UNINTERRUPTIBLE. Flags are set to indicate that the new process has not yet done an exec() and that it cannot be swapped out to secondary storage (there is nothing to swap yet). It is assigned a unique ID number.

```
588        *p = *current;
589
590        retval = -EAGAIN;

597        if (atomic_read(&p->user->processes) >=
                    p->rlim[RLIMIT_NPROC].rlim_cur
598                && !capable(CAP_SYS_ADMIN)
                    && !capable(CAP_SYS_RESOURCE))
599            goto bad_fork_free;
600
601        atomic_inc(&p->user->__count);
602        atomic_inc(&p->user->processes);

609        if (nr_threads >= max_threads)
610            goto bad_fork_cleanup_count;
611
612        get_exec_domain(p->exec_domain);
```

```
613
614        if (p->binfmt && p->binfmt->module)
615              __MOD_INC_USE_COUNT(p->binfmt->module);
616
617        p->did_exec = 0;
618        p->swappable = 0;
619        p->state = TASK_UNINTERRUPTIBLE;
620
621        copy_flags(clone_flags, p);
622        p->pid = get_pid(clone_flags);
623
624        p->run_list.next = NULL;
625        p->run_list.prev = NULL;
626
627        p->p_cptr = NULL;
628        init_waitqueue_head(&p->wait_chldexit);
629        p >vfork_donc = NULL;
630        if (clone_flags & CLONE_VFORK) {
631              p->vfork_done = &vfork;
632              init_completion(&vfork);
633        }
634        spin_lock_init(&p->alloc_lock);
635
636        p->sigpending = 0;
637        init_sigpending(&p->pending);
```

Figure 8.4   Initialise fields in new `task_struct`

588   the new descriptor, which up to this was just a blank piece of memory, is now made to be an exact copy of the descriptor of the current process. The `current` macro (Section 7.2.1.3) always evaluates to a pointer to the `task_struct` representing the currently running process. The code then goes on to change some fields in it, customising them to suit the new process.

590   the next few lines are going to check on limits, so this line sets up a new default return value of `EAGAIN`, which means that limits are currently exceeded, try again later.

597–599   both the new and the old process belong to the same user, so there is only one `user_struct` (see Section 8.4). If the limit on the total number of processes this user can create has been exceeded, the error exit is taken (see Section 8.2.6).

597   the `atomic_read()` function was described in Section 5.2.1. The `rlim[]` array was introduced in Section 2.5.

598   there are two exceptional cases in which the restrictions of line 597 do not apply. If the creating process has either the `CAP_SYS_ADMIN` or the `CAP_SYS_RESOURCE` capability, then, irrespective of limits, it can create the new process (see Section 20.1.1 for a description of capabilities; the `capable()` function itself is discussed in Section 20.4.1).

601–602   otherwise, the `__count` field and the `processes` field of the `user_struct` are incremented using the `atomic_inc()` function from Section 5.2.5. The meaning of both of these fields will be explained in Section 8.4.1.

609–610   if the maximum number of processes allowed in the whole system has been exceeded, the error exit is taken (see Section 8.2.6). Note that the `fork()` currently in progress does not increase `nr_threads` until line 729 (see Section 8.2.5; the `nr_threads` variable was introduced in Section 8.1.1).

612   this function increments the count of processes running in the execution domain used by the parent (see Section 21.3.3).

614–615   if the `binfmt` field is valid, and also the `module` subfield in the `binfmt` is valid, then the use count is incremented. Binary formats are the concern of the file manager and will not be considered further in this book.

617   the new process has never called `exec()` at this stage.

618   the new process is not swappable at this stage.

619   the new process is not yet ready to be scheduled or to handle signals, so its state is set to `TASK_UNINTERRUPTIBLE`.

621   the function, from Section 8.3.2, copies the `flags` field from the parent and then does some adjustments.

622   a `pid` number is allocated (see Section 8.3.3) and written to the appropriate field. The value of `clone_flags` is passed to this function so that it can determine whether it should use the same ID as the parent or find another ID.

624–625   the process is not on the runqueue (unlike its parent), so these fields are changed to `NULL`.

627   the new process cannot have any children at this stage.

628   however, the mechanism by which it will wait for eventual children to exit is initialised (see Section 4.1.2.3 for the function).

629   the child's copy of this field is set to `NULL`. This is the default value, which may be changed in the next block of code.

630   the `CLONE_VFORK` bit is set if the parent wants the child to wake it up when it calls `exec()` or terminates.

631   this is a pointer to the `struct completion`, declared at line 570 (see Section 8.2.1).

632   this initialises the `struct completion` to a value of 0 (see Section 6.3.1).

634   the purpose of this spinlock was explained in Section 2.9. The `spin_lock_init()` function is from Sections 5.3 (for a uniprocessor) and 5.4 (for a multiprocessor).

636   the signal pending flag is cleared, as there can be no signals pending for the new process.

637   this function is discussed in Section 17.1.4.2. It clears all bits in the `pending` field in the `task_struct` to show that there are no pending signals.

8.2.3 Initialising time-related fields

Various timer fields in the `task_struct` of the new process are initialised next, as shown in Figure 8.5.

```
639        p->it_real_value = p->it_virt_value = p->it_prof_value
                                                            = 0;
640        p->it_real_incr = p->it_virt_incr = p->it_prof_incr = 0;
641        init_timer(&p->real_timer);
642        p->real_timer.data = (unsigned long) p;
643
644        p->leader = 0;
645        p->tty_old_pgrp = 0;
646        p->times.tms_utime = p->times.tms_stime = 0;
647        p->times.tms_cutime = p->times.tms_cstime = 0;
648  #ifdef CONFIG_SMP
649        {
650            int i;
651            p->cpus_runnable = ~0UL;
652            p->processor = current->processor;
653
654            for(i = 0; i < smp_num_cpus; i++)
655                p->per_cpu_utime[i] = p->per_cpu_stime[i] = 0;
656            spin_lock_init(&p->sigmask_lock);
657        }
658  #endif
659        p->lock_depth = -1;
660        p->start_time = jiffies;
661
662        INIT_LIST_HEAD(&p->local_pages);
```

Figure 8.5   Initialising time related fields

639–640   for the three interval timers, both the initial value and the increment field are initialised to 0. Timers are dealt with in Chapter 15.

641   the function `init_timer()` is called to initialise the real-time timer (see Section 15.3.2.1).

642   remember p is a pointer, so a pointer to the `task_struct` will be made available to the timer function when it expires.

644   this line is just in case the creating process was a session leader; children do not inherit this property.

645   the child has inherited its process group from its parent. This field may have had a value in its parent's `task_struct`, so it is cleared to 0 here. It will be used in the future if this new process changes its process group.

646–647   fields in the `struct tms` are initialised to 0. The new process counts its own times.

649–657   this code is only compiled into a multiprocessor kernel.

651   this field is set to all 1s, to indicate that this process (the child) is not presently running on any computer processing unit (CPU).

652   its processor of choice is set to be the one the parent is using. The `current` macro (Section 7.2.1.3) always evaluates to a pointer to the `task_struct` representing the currently running process.

654–655   the fields recording the time spent by the new process on each CPU (in user and kernel mode) are initialised to 0.

656   the `sigmask_lock` field of the `task_struct` is initialised. Apparently, this lock is used only in SMP. Different versions of the `spin_lock_init()` function are described in Sections 5.3 (for a uniprocessor) and 5.4 (for a multiprocessor).

659   as the new process is not holding the big kernel lock, the `lock_depth` field is initialised to −1.

660   the time at which the new process began is copied in from the system clock, so it is timed from here even though it is not fully set up yet.

662   this initialises the list header, using the macro from Section 4.3.1. This is part of the memory manager.

8.2.4   Copying external process information

The `task_struct` of the parent was copied in the code Section 8.2.2. The code shown in Figure 8.6 copies all the state of the process that exists outside the `task_struct`.

```
664        retval = -ENOMEM;
665
666        if (copy_files(clone_flags, p))
667              goto bad_fork_cleanup;
668        if (copy_fs(clone_flags, p))
669              goto bad_fork_cleanup_files;
670        if (copy_sighand(clone_flags, p))
671              goto bad_fork_cleanup_fs;
672        if (copy_mm(nr, clone_flags, p))
673              goto bad_fork_cleanup_sighand;
674        retval = copy_thread (0, clone_flags, stack_start,
                                              stack_size, p, regs);
675        if (retval)
676              goto bad_fork_cleanup_mm;
677        p->semundo = NULL;

682        p->parent_exec_id = p->self_exec_id;

685        p->swappable = 1;
686        p->exit_signal = clone_flags & CSIGNAL;
687        p->pdeath_signal = 0;
```

Figure 8.6   Copying all the process information

664   the only problem anticipated here is not being able to allocate memory to hold these structures, so a default error return value of ENOMEM is set up.

666–667   first, we have the open files. This is part of the file manager and will not be considered any further here. If we are unable to copy, then we go to the cleanup routine, which undoes everything done so far (see Section 8.2.6).

668–669   the function to copy the file system information from the parent is also part of file system management and is not considered here. If it is unable to copy, then goes to the appropriate part of the cleanup routine, which undoes everything done so far, including the open file information (see Section 8.2.6).

670–671   the function to copy the signal handlers from the parent will be considered in Section 8.3.4. If it is unable to copy, then it goes to the cleanup routine, which undoes everything done so far, including the file system information (see Section 8.2.6).

672–673   the function to copy the memory management information from the parent is part of the memory manager and is not considered here. If it is unable to copy, then it goes to the cleanup routine, which undoes everything done so far, including the signal handlers (see Section 8.2.6).

674   the copy_thread() function, which is architecture-specific and initialises the values in the thread structure of the child, is described in Section 8.3.5. The first parameter is unused on the i386, so a 0 is passed.

675–676   the i386 version of the copy_thread() function only returns 0, so this check is redundant here, but this is generic code and other architectures do return a value. If we are unable to initialise the thread structure, we go to the exit code in Section 8.2.6, which undoes everything done so far, including the memory management information.

677   at this stage, there are no semaphore operations that could be undone, so a NULL pointer is put in here. This is specific to the implementation of System V semaphores, which is not considered in this book.

682   the parent_exec_id of the child is set to the value of the self_exec_id field in the parent. The child inherits the execution domain of its parent, which it may change later.

685   the process data structures are now in such a state that the process can be swapped out if necessary.

686   the low-order 8 bits of clone_flags are reserved for the number of the signal to be sent to the parent when this process exits. The CSIGNAL mask clears all the other bits in clone_flags.

687   this is the signal to be sent to this process when its parent dies. The default is none.

8.2.5   Linking into process structure

Now the new process is all ready to go. The code in Figure 8.7 links it on to the scheduler's structures.

```
695        p->counter = (current->counter + 1) >> 1;
696        current->counter >>= 1;
697        if (!current->counter)
698            current->need_resched = 1;
```

```
706        retval = p->pid;
707        p->tgid = retval;
708        INIT_LIST_HEAD(&p->thread_group);

711        write_lock_irq(&tasklist_lock);

714        p->p_opptr = current->p_opptr;
715        p->p_pptr = current->p_pptr;
716        if (!(clone_flags & (CLONE_PARENT | CLONE_THREAD))) {
717            p->p_opptr = current;
718            if (!(p->ptrace & PT_PTRACED))
719                p->p_pptr = current;
720        }
721
722        if (clone_flags & CLONE_THREAD) {
723            p->tgid = current->tgid;
724            list_add(&p->thread_group, &current->thread_group);
725        }
726
727        SET_LINKS(p);
728        hash_pid(p);
729        nr_threads++;
730        write_unlock_irq(&tasklist_lock);
731
732        if (p->ptrace & PT_PTRACED)
733            send_sig(SIGSTOP, p, 1);
734
735        wake_up_process(p);
736        ++total_forks;
737        if (clone_flags & CLONE_VFORK)
738            wait_for_completion(&vfork);
```

Figure 8.7 Linking the new task_struct into the existing process structure

695–696 any time remaining of the parent's time-slice is shared with the child process. This affects only the first time-slice; in the long run, the scheduling behaviour is unchanged.

695 the child is given an initial assignment of clock cycles equal to half that remaining to the parent, with a minimum of 1.

696 the parent's time remaining is also halved.

697–698 if that would reduce the parent to 0, the parent is marked as requiring a reschedule.

706 the default retval is set up, the pid of the newly created process. This is the value returned to the parent. Remember, this code is being executed by the parent.

707 the thread group ID field of the child is also set to its pid. The default assumption is that it is a process in its own right, not a thread in its parent's process, but this may be changed at line 723.

708 the link field for the thread group is initialised. The macro is described in Section 4.3.1.

711–730 these lines of code write to the process list, so this interrupt safe writelock is needed. The read–write lock itself was defined in Section 7.2.2, and the locking macro is from Section 12.8.1.

714–715 the child is given the same parent and original parent as its own parent (it is a sibling of its parent). These are default values, which may be changed in the following lines.

716–720 this block of code is executed if neither CLONE_PARENT nor CLONE_THREAD was set in the clone_flags passed in. It is not to be a sibling nor a thread but a standard child process.

717 the creating process is set up as its original parent.

718–719 if it is not being traced, then the creating process is set up as its parent. Otherwise, the assignment from line 715 stands.

722–725 this block of code is executed if the clone_flags passed in specify that the new process is to be a thread of its parent.

723 the thread group ID field of the new process is set to be that of its parent.

724 the new process is added to the list of threads headed from its parent (see Section 4.3.2 for the function).

727 the macro has been described in Section 3.1.2. It inserts the new process onto the process list and the sibling structure.

728 this function, described in Section 3.2.3, inserts the task_struct into the hash table.

729 this increment is the count of the total number of processes in the system. This variable was declared in the code in Section 8.1.1.

732–733 if the child process is being traced (because it inherited that condition from its parent), it is now sent the SIGSTOP signal. As soon as it runs, this signal will be delivered.

735 the function wake_up_process() has been described in Section 4.7.5. It sets the state of the child to TASK_RUNNING and puts it on the runqueue, so making it visible to the rest of the system. When the child eventually runs, it will begin at the value in its EIP register, as set up by copy_thread() at line 674 (Section 8.2.4).

736 the running total of forks is incremented at this late stage so that there is no danger of it having to be undone. The global variable was declared in the code in Section 8.1.1.

737–738 if the appropriate flag was set, the parent sleeps here (see Section 6.3.3 for the function). It will be woken when the child deallocates its reference to the memory map of the parent as part of the implementation of exec().

8.2.6 Error handling

An error can occur at a number of different places when setting up a new process. Obviously, any work done up to the point where the error occurs must be undone, so the error handling is arranged in reverse order, as shown in Figure 8.8.

```
740 fork_out:
741     return retval;
742
743 bad_fork_cleanup_mm:
744     exit_mm(p);
745 bad_fork_cleanup_sighand:
746     exit_sighand(p);
747 bad_fork_cleanup_fs:
748     exit_fs(p);
749 bad_fork_cleanup_files:
750     exit_files(p);
751 bad_fork_cleanup:
752     put_exec_domain(p->exec_domain);
753     if (p->binfmt && p->binfmt->module)
754         __MOD_DEC_USE_COUNT(p->binfmt->module);
755 bad_fork_cleanup_count:
756     atomic_dec(&p->user->processes);
757     free_uid(p->user);
758 bad_fork_free:
759     free_task_struct(p);
760     goto fork_out;
761 }
```

Figure 8.8   Error handling

740   the entry point fork_out: is entered normally (fall-through) or if there is a permission problem (line 580; Section 8.2.1) or a problem allocating memory for the task_struct (line 586; Section 8.2.1). At that stage no other setting up has been done. The value in retval distinguishes between the cases. In the first, it is the (positive) pid of the child; in the others, it is the (negative) EPERM or ENOMEM.

741   we return to the system service code and, ultimately, to the caller.

743   control transfers here from line 676 (Section 8.2.4) if the system was unable to copy the register values from parent to child.

744   this function, part of the memory manager, undoes any memory management data structures set up in the child by copy_mm() at line 672 (Section 8.2.4). The function itself will not be considered any further here.

745–746   if the system is unable to copy the memory management information from parent to child, this is the error exit taken. The function is described in Section 17.4.1.

747–748   this entry would be taken if a problem arose allocating space for signal handlers. It goes on to call cleanup functions for all the allocations made before it. The function itself is part of the input–output (IO) manager and is not considered in this book.

749–750   this entry would be taken if a problem arose allocating space for file system information. It undoes any changes made to open file descriptors and goes on to call cleanup functions for all the allocations made before it. The function itself is part of the IO manager and is not considered in this book.

751 this entry would be taken if a problem arose allocating space for descriptors of open files (line 667; Section 8.2.4).

752 this decrements the execution domain count, incremented at line 612 (Section 8.2.2). The function is described in Section 21.3.3.

753–754 the decrements the binary format count, incremented at line 615 (Section 8.2.2).

755 the `bad_fork_cleanup_count:` entry is taken from line 610 (Section 8.2.2) if the maximum number of processes allowed in the system has been exceeded.

756 this atomically decrements the number of processes belonging to this user, incremented at line 602 (Section 8.2.2). The function is from Section 5.2.6.

757 this function from Section 8.4.4.1 atomically decrements the `__count` field of the `user_struct`, thus reversing the increment at line 601 (Section 8.2.2). If there are no further processes belonging to this user, it will release the `user_struct`.

758 `bad_fork_free:` is called from line 599 (Section 8.2.2), if the user has exceeded its maximum number of processes.

759 this function frees the allocated `task_struct`. The function is part of the memory manager and will not be considered any further in this book.

760 control then returns to `fork_out:` at line 740, from which the whole `do_fork()` function exits.

Figure 8.9 illustrates the flow of control through this section.

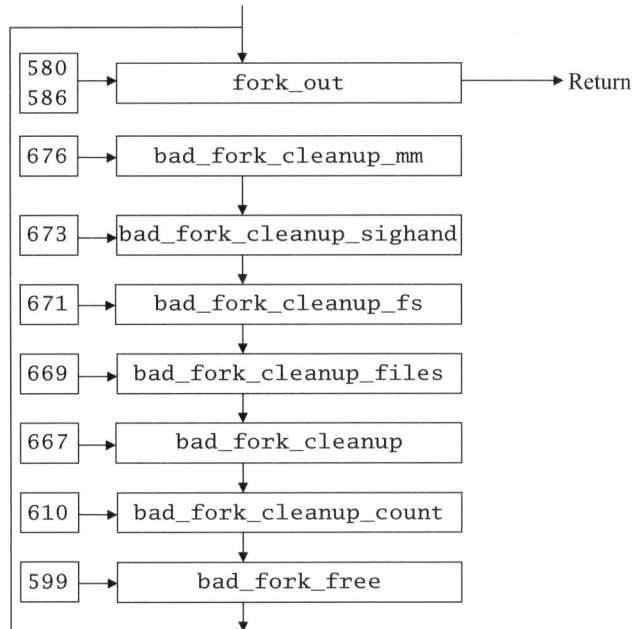

Figure 8.9 Flowchart of control through the error handling code

8.3 Subsidiary functions

The previous section considered the do_fork() function in some detail. A number of subsidiary functions were used at various places in that section. These functions will now be discussed.

8.3.1 Clone flags

The clone flags determine a whole range of properties of the child process. They are defined in <linux/sched.h>, as shown in Figure 8.10.

```
35   #define   CSIGNAL              0x000000ff
36   #define   CLONE_VM             0x00000100
37   #define   CLONE_FS             0x00000200
38   #define   CLONE_FILES          0x00000400
39   #define   CLONE_SIGHAND        0x00000800
40   #define   CLONE_PID            0x00001000
41   #define   CLONE_PTRACE         0x00002000
42   #define   CLONE_VFORK          0x00004000
43   #define   CLONE_PARENT         0x00008000
44   #define   CLONE_THREAD         0x00010000
45
46   #define   CLONE_SIGNAL   (CLONE_SIGHAND | CLONE_THREAD)
```

Figure 8.10   Clone flags

35   the number of the signal to be sent to the parent process when the child exits is encoded in the low-order 8 bits of the clone flag value. This mask clears the rest of the value.

36   the parent and child are to share the same virtual memory mapping.

37   file system information is to be shared.

38   open files are to be shared.

39   signal handlers are shared.

40   even the pid is shared.

41   the child process is to inherit the traced attribute of its parent (i.e. if the parent was being traced when the child was created, the child will also be traced).

42   this bit is set if it is expected that the child is going to call exec() immediately after the fork(). In that case the parent sleeps on the vfork completion. When the child releases its link to the memory it shares with the parent, as part of the implementation of exec(), then it signals that completion and wakes up the parent.

43   this is set if the child is to have the same parent as the cloner (i.e. if it is to be a sibling, not a child).

44 this is set if the call to `clone()` is actually creating a new thread in an existing process.

46 this is a common combination, so it is given a name of its own. It means that the new thread is to share signal handlers with the creating thread.

8.3.2 Setting up the flags field in the new process

The function shown in Figure 8.11, from `kernel/fork.c`, sets up the flags field in the `task_struct` of the new process.

```
545  static inline void copy_flags(unsigned long clone_flags,
                                               struct task_struct *p)
546  {
547       unsigned long new_flags = p->flags;
548
549       new_flags &= ~(PF_SUPERPRIV | PF_USEDFPU);
550       new_flags |= PF_FORKNOEXEC;
551       if (!(clone_flags & CLONE_PTRACE))
552           p->ptrace = 0;
553       p->flags = new_flags;
554  }
```

Figure 8.11 Setting up the flags field in the new process

545 the function is passed a copy of the `clone_flags` specified by the caller, and a pointer to the `task_struct` of the new process. At this stage the flags field in that structure is an exact copy of the parent's.

547 we begin by copying the flags field inherited from the parent into a local variable. This is just for efficiency. Then we go on to make adjustments.

549 the flags for `PF_SUPERPRIV` and `PF_USEDFPU` are turned off, whether or not they were set in the parent. The new process has not used superuser privilege, nor the floating point unit (FPU).

550 set the `PF_FORKNOEXEC` flag is set, whether it was set in the parent or not. The new process which is being forked cannot have called `exec()` at this stage, so by definition it must be running the same program as its parent.

551–552 if the `CLONE_PTRACE` bit was clear in `clone_flags`, then the `ptrace` field is cleared. If the `CLONE_PTRACE` bit was set, then the `ptrace` field remains as it was copied from the parent. In that case the child will be traced, or not, depending on whether its parent was being traced or not.

553 finally, the `new_flags` field just built is copied to the `task_struct` of the new process.

8.3.3 Allocating a process identification number

Each process must be allocated an ID number that is unique in the system. The function to do that is shown in Figure 8.12, from `kernel/fork.c`. Although this is quite a complicated piece of code, in essence it takes a very simple approach: it picks a number and checks every process to see if that number is in use. The complexity arises from attempts to pick a 'likely' number and handling overflow.

```
82   spinlock_t lastpid_lock = SPIN_LOCK_UNLOCKED;
83
84   static int get_pid(unsigned long flags
85   {
86        static int next_safe = PID_MAX;
87        struct task_struct *p;
88        int pid;
89
90        if (flags & CLONE_PID)
91             return current->pid;
92
93        spin_lock(&lastpid_lock);
94        if ((++last_pid) & 0xffff8000) {
95             last_pid=300;
96             goto inside;
97        }
98        if (last_pid >= next_safe) {
99   inside:
100            next_safe = PID_MAX;
101            read_lock(&tasklist_lock);
102       repeat:
103            for_each_task (p) {
104                 if (p->pid == last_pid ||
105                      p->pgrp == last_pid ||
106                      p->tgid == last_pid ||
107                      p->session == last_pid) {
108                           if(++last_pid >= next_safe {
109                                if(last_pid & 0xffff8000)
110                                     last_pid = 300;
111                                next_safe = PID_MAX;
112                           }
113                 goto repeat;
114                 }
115                 if(p->pid > last_pid && next_safe > p->pid)
116                      next_safe = p->pid;
117                 if(p->pgrp > last_pid && next_safe > p->pgrp)
118                      next_safe = p->pgrp;
119                 if(p->session > last_pid && next_safe > p->session);
120                      next_safe = p->session;
121            }
122            read_unlock(&tasklist_lock);
123       }
124       pid = last_pid;
125       spin_unlock(&lastpid_lock);
126
```

```
127        return pid;
128  }
```

Figure 8.12 Assigning a unique process identification (pid) number

82 this spinlock is used to prevent more than one process picking the same number. It is initialised here to the unlocked state. The macro is defined in Sections 5.3 (for the uniprocessor case) and 5.4 (for the multiprocessor case).

84 the flags parameter is passed solely to check if CLONE_PID is set (see line 90).

86 in an attempt to save on repeated searches, the system tries to remember a range of pid numbers that it has recently searched and found not to be in use. The ceiling of this range is kept in the static int next_safe, so it retains its value over successive calls to get_pid(). It is initialised to its maximum value here and will be repeatedly reduced by the algorithm until it is valid. The literal constant is defined in <linux/tasks.h> as

```
23    #define PID_MAX     0x8000
```

90–91 if the appropriate bit was set in flags requesting the same pid as the parent, then the current pid is returned (see Section 8.3.1 for the clone flags). This test could have been done in do_fork() and saved the overhead of calling this function, but doing it this way makes this function more generic.

93–125 a spinlock is now taken out to prevent two processes getting the same pid. That spinlock is declared and initialised at line 82. It protects next_safe (static) and the global last_pid, which was declared in the code in Section 8.1.1.

94–96 the condition will only be true when the incremented last_pid has a value greater than 0x7fff; so we increment last_pid modulo 0x8000 and then go back to start at a value of 300 again. The reason for not going back to 0 is because it can be assumed that there are a number of daemon processes running with low pids, and it would be wasting time to check these. The code here is rather unstructured. Because a number (300) has just been picked out of 'thin air', the checks on lines 99–123 have to be made to ensure that it is not in use, irrespective of the value of next_safe.

98 this line is executed if the pid selected did not roll over. If it is also less than next_safe, then it is safe to allocate it, and control goes straight to line 124. Otherwise, it has to be checked against all existing processes. As each one is checked, next_safe is pulled down to the floor of its current value or the value being checked. In this way, once the for loop is finished, next_safe is set to the lowest value currently in use. This may save work for the next call to get_pid().

99–123 all numbers less than next_safe are guaranteed to be free, so this code is executed only on two conditions:

- if after incrementing last_pid it is greater than or equal to next_safe;

- if last_pid has been reset back to 300.

- It checks if the number chosen is in use already, or if it is safe to allocate it.

100   `next_safe` is set up as the maximum valid number.

101–122   because all entries in the process table are going to be checked, it is important that another process does not change it in the meantime, so a readlock is taken out on this table (see Section 5.6 for the uniprocessor version of the function; the multiprocessor version is given in Section 5.7.2.1).

103–121   then the `for_each_task()` macro (Section 3.1.3) is used to go through all the processes to check that this number is not presently in use as an identifier for a process, a process group, a thread group, or a session. Only when it finds a number that is not already in use will this loop terminate; otherwise it will try another number. The indentation is important here, to match up where each `if` ends.

104–107   if the number is not in use by the process currently being considered, a command is given to go to line 115.

108   control comes here only if the number is in use. The number is incremented, and the next one tried. If that number is still less than `next_safe`, then it cannot have rolled over, so the function goes back to `repeat:`, and all processes are checked against this new number, beginning again with the first one.

109–110   if it has rolled over, `last_pid` is reset to 300.

111   the number chosen at line 108 was greater than `next_safe`; so `next_safe` is reset to `PID_MAX`.

113   the previous number chosen was in use; so a new number has been chosen. Now we go back to the beginning of the process list and start checking all over again.

115–120   the number `last_pid` is not in use by this process. These lines are an optimisation that adjusts `next_safe`, for the next iteration of the loop.

115–116   if this process has a `pid` in the range between `last_pid` and `next_safe`, then `next_safe` is reduced to the `pid` of this process.

117–120   it is ultimately reduced to the lowest of the pid, group, or session ID of the process being considered, so `next_safe` is reduced each time a process is checked. By line 122, no process will be using IDs in the range from `last_pid` to `next_safe`.

122   all processes have been checked by this stage, so the readlock on the process table can be released.

124   this is the value that is going to be returned. The copy is taken before the lock on it is released in case some other process (in SMP mode) increments it immediately.

125   finally, the spinlock protecting the `next_safe` and `last_pid` variables can be released.

The foregoing discussion is presented in the form of an algorithm in Figure 8.13. The heart of the algorithm is in the lines annotated with bold line numbers. The remainder is optimisation.

```
98     IF number outside safe range THEN
100        Reset next_safe to MAX
103        FOR each process DO
104            IF in use THEN
108                Try next number
                   IF outside safe range THEN
111                    Reset next_safe to MAX
112                ENDIF
113                JUMP out of loop, begin it again
114            ENDIF
115            IF current is between new number and next_safe THEN
116                next_safe = current
120            ENDIF
121        ENDFOR
123    ENDIF
```

Figure 8.13   Algorithm for assigning a unique process identification number

8.3.4   Copying signal handlers

The function shown in Figure 8.14, from `kernel/fork.c`, sets up the signal handlers in a new process.

```
527   static inline int copy_sighand(unsigned long clone_flags,
                                          struct task_struct * tsk)
528   {
529       struct signal_struct *sig;
530
531       if (clone_flags & CLONE_SIGHAND) {
532           atomic_inc(&current->sig->count);
533           return 0;
534       }
535       sig = kmem_cache_alloc(sigact_cachep, GFP_KERNEL);
536       tsk->sig = sig;
537       if (!sig)
538           return -1;
539       spin_lock_init(&sig->siglock);
540       atomic_set(&sig->count, 1);
541       memcpy(tsk->sig->action, current->sig->action,
                                      sizeof(tsk->sig->action));
542       return 0;
543   }
```

Figure 8.14   Copying signal handlers

527   the parameters are the clone flags passed to `do_fork()` and a pointer to the `task_struct` of the new process.

531–534 if the `clone_flags` parameter specifies that the new process is to share the signal handlers of its parent then there is no need to change anything, as the information on handlers has already been copied by default. However, the number of references to the parent's table of handlers is incremented atomically (see Section 5.2.5); a success value is returned.

535 the new process is to have its own handlers, so a `struct signal_struct` is allocated for it. The function is part of the memory manager and will not be considered further here.

536 this sets up the appropriate field in the `task_struct` of the new process pointing to this new `signal_struct`.

537–538 an inability to allocate the memory returns an error indication.

539 each `struct signal_struct` has its own spinlock (`siglock`) to protect the `signal` and `blocked` bitmaps. The spinlock in the new `struct signal_struct` is initialised here; the macro is discussed in Sections 5.3 (for a uniprocessor) and 5.4.2 (for a multiprocessor).

540 the reference count on the new `struct signal_struct` is set to 1 atomically; see Section 5.2.1 for the function.

541 the values of the handlers (the `action` field, which is an array of pointers) is then copied from the parent (`current`) to the newly allocated structure in the child, so the child begins life with the same handlers as its parent, but it can change them later, independently of the parent. The `memcpy()` function is part of the memory manager and will not be considered further here.

542 a success value is returned.

8.3.5 Setting up the `thread` structure for a child process

When a new process is created, most of its volatile environment, including register values, is inherited from the parent, but some of it has to be set up by hand. This section considers the function that copies and adjusts these values and some of the worker functions it uses.

8.3.5.1 Copying register and `thread` values from the parent

The function to set up register values for a new process on its stack is architecture-specific and is shown in Figure 8.15, from `arch/i386/kernel/process.c`.

```
581  int copy_thread(int nr, unsigned long clone_flags,
582          unsigned long esp, unsigned long unused,
583          struct task_struct * p, struct pt_regs * regs)
584  {
585          struct pt_regs * childregs;
586
587          childregs = ((struct pt_regs *) (THREAD_SIZE +
                                          (unsigned long) p)) - 1;
588          struct_cpy(childregs, regs);
589          childregs->eax = 0;
590          childregs->esp = esp;
```

```
591
592          p->thread.esp = (unsigned long)childregs;
593          p->thread.esp0 = (unsigned long)(childregs+1);
594
595          p->thread.eip = (unsigned long)ret_from_fork;
596
597          savesegment(fs,p->thread.fs);
598          savesegment(gs,p->thread.gs);
599
600          unlazy_fpu(current);
601          struct_cpy(&p->thread.i387, &current->thread.i387);
602
603          return 0;
604  }
```

Figure 8.15   Setting up register values for a child process

581–583   the first two parameters, nr and clone_flags, are unused in the i386 architecture. The esp parameter is the value in the ESP register when fork() was called. The fourth parameter is unused in the i386 architecture. The fifth parameter, p, is a pointer to the task_struct to be filled in. The final parameter points to the saved values of the parent's registers on the stack.

587   this casts the pointer to the new task_struct (p) to be an integer value and adds THREAD_SIZE, using ordinary integer addition. THREAD_SIZE is 2 pages. The result is cast to be a pointer to pt_regs. This is now pointing to the first byte *after* the area allocated to the new process (i.e. after the task_struct and after the kernel stack area). Decrementing this by 1 leaves it pointing a distance down the stack equivalent to the size of a struct pt_regs, so it ends up pointing to an empty struct pt_regs at the top of the kernel stack of the new process. Figure 8.16 shows how this line converts from a pointer to the task_struct to a pointer to the correct place on the stack for the new struct pt_regs.

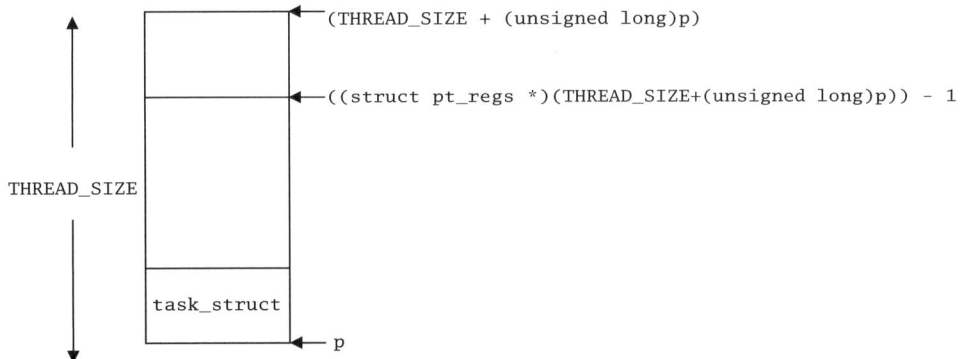

Figure 8.16   Position of struct pt_regs on the stack

588   the register values of the parent, as saved on entry to the system call, are copied to the top of the child's stack. The struct_cpy() macro is given in Section 8.3.5.2.

589   by convention, EAX contains the return value, and the child process always returns 0.

590   the saved value of the stack pointer is the `stack_size` parameter passed in to `do_fork()`. Despite its name, this is actually the value in the ESP register when `fork()` was called. It points into the user mode stack.

592–601   the remainder of the function is concerned with setting up values in the architecture-specific `thread` field of the `task_struct`.

592   the `thread.esp` field always points to the beginning of the register save area on the stack.

593   the `thread.esp0` field points one full `struct pt_regs` beyond this, to the top of the stack. Remember, `childregs` is a pointer, so `childregs + 1` is using pointer arithmetic.

595   the saved value of the instruction pointer is set to the routine `ret_from_fork` (see Section 8.3.6.1). When the child process first runs, it will begin there.

597–598   these save the value from the hardware FS and GS registers into the `thread.fs` and `thread.gs` fields, respectively. These registers are not part of the stack frame. The function is described in Section 8.3.5.3.

600   the macro, defined in Section 11.10.2.2, checks if the parent has used the FPU during its current time-slice. If it has, then it saves the values in the hardware FPU registers to the `thread` field of the parent.

601   any floating point information in the parent's `thread` is copied to the child. The generic macro to copy a structure is described in Section 8.3.5.2.

8.3.5.2   Copying a structure

The macro shown in Figure 8.17, from `<asm-i386/string.h>`, copies the whole contents of one `struct` to another. Both have to be exactly the same size, though not necessarily of the same type.

```
337  #define struct_cpy(x,y)                            \
338  ({                                                 \
339       if (sizeof(*(x)) != sizeof(*(y)))             \
340            __struct_cpy_bug;                         \
341       memcpy(x, y, sizeof(*(x)));                   \
342  })
```

Figure 8.17   Copying a structure

339–340   the source and destination must be exactly the same size, otherwise an error message is printed. The `__struct_cpy_bug` is declared as an `extern` procedure.

341   this is a memory management function that copies a specified number of bytes.

8.3.5.3 Saving a segment register

The macro shown in Figure 8.18, from `arch/i386/kernel/process.c`, saves the value of the hardware segment register indicated by `seg` into the memory area specified by `value`.

```
578  #define savesegment(seg,value)                                          \
579       asm volatile("movl %%" #seg ",%0":"=m" (*(int *)&(value)))
```

Figure 8.18 Saving a segment register

578 the `seg` parameter is the identifier of the register; `value` is the identifier of a memory location (not a pointer to it).

579 output parameter 0 is the address of `value`, cast as a pointer to `int` (32 bit) and then dereferenced. It may be in memory (`"=m"`).

8.3.6 The child's return path

The final point to consider is how the child process moves from kernel mode (in which it was created) back to user mode.

8.3.6.1 Returning from `fork()`

When the child process is first scheduled onto a CPU the value in its `EIP` register is the address of the `ret_from_fork` routine; see Figure 8.19, from `arch/i386/kernel/entry.S`. This value was set up in its `thread` structure by the code in Section 8.3.5.1.

```
178  ENTRY(ret_from_fork)
179       pushl %ebx
180       call SYMBOL_NAME(schedule_tail)
181       addl $4,%esp
182       GET_CURRENT(%ebx)
183       testb $0x02,tsk_ptrace(%ebx)
184       jne tracesys_exit
185       jmp ret_from_sys_call
```

Figure 8.19 First code executed by a child process

179 at this stage, all the other registers contain values inherited from the parent. The EBX register contains a pointer to the `task_struct` of the parent. This is the parameter to the function called on the next line, being pushed here in preparation for the call.

180 this function, described in Section 8.3.6.2, does some cleaning up of the `task_struct` of its parent.

181 after returning from the call, the immediate addition of value of 4 to the ESP register discards the value pushed on the stack at line 179.

182 this macro, from Section 10.3.4, gets a pointer to the `task_struct` of the child process into the EBX register.

183 this checks if the child is being traced. The `tsk_ptrace` offset is defined in Section 10.3.5; it identifies the `ptrace` field of the `task_struct`. Bit 1 in this field is the `PT_TRACESYS` bit (see Figure 2.4, page 17). It means that the child process is being traced but is only to be interrupted at each system call.

184 if that bit was set, then the zero flag will be clear in `EFLAGS`, so the special code for handling traced system calls is executed (Section 10.4.3.3). This merely lets the tracer know that the child is exiting the `fork()` system call before jumping to `ret_from_sys_call`.

185 otherwise, the standard entry from a system call is taken (Section 10.6.1). This starts the execution of the child process.

8.3.6.2 Cleaning up after the parent

The function shown in Figure 8.20, from `kernel/sched.c`, is only a wrapper around a call to the `__schedule_tail()` function, as described in Section 7.5.4. It is always the first code executed by a process when it wakes up after a context switch. It does some cleaning up of the `task_struct` of the previous process, in this case of its parent.

```
534  asmlinkage void schedule_tail(struct task_struct *prev)
535  {
536      __schedule_tail(prev);
537  }
```

Figure 8.20 Cleaning up after the parent

8.4 The user cache

Each `task_struct` contains a field pointing to a `user_struct`, which identifies the user or owner of the process. As one user will typically have a number of processes in existence at the same time, this `user_struct` is shared. This section examines the `user_struct`, and the functions provided for manipulating it.

8.4.1 User identification structures

The basic data structure representing a user is shown in Figure 8.21, from `<linux/sched.h>`. It is still only skeletal; the comment in the code indicates that it is eventually intended to maintain much more information about the user in this structure.

```
263  struct user_struct {
264      atomic_t __count;
265      atomic_t processes;
266      atomic_t files;
```

```
269         struct user_struct *next, **pprev;
270         uid_t uid;
271    };
```

Figure 8.21   The user structure

264   this is a count of how many references this user has to this structure. This is incremented at each log-on session.

265   this is a count of how many processes this user has. This is incremented at each `fork()`.

266   this is a count of how many files this user has opened.

269   as will be seen in following subsections, these structures are maintained on a hash table. These are the link fields for that hash structure.

270   this is the actual `uid` of the user represented by this structure.

8.4.2   The user hash structure

To facilitate easy access to any particular `user_struct`, and to avoid having to search the entire process list each time a new process is created, these structures are also kept on a hash table. The data structures involved in the implementation of this are shown in Figure 8.22, from `kernel/user.c`.

```
19   #define UIDHASH_BITS          8
20   #define UIDHASH_SZ            (1 << UIDHASH_BITS)
21   #define UIDHASH_MASK         (UIDHASH_SZ - 1)
22   #define __uidhashfn(uid)     (((uid >> UIDHASH_BITS) ^ uid)
                                              & UIDHASH_MASK)
23   #define uidhashentry(uid)    (uidhash_table + __uidhashfn(uid))
24
25   static kmem_cache_t          *uid_cachep;
26   static struct user_struct    *uidhash_table[UIDHASH_SZ];
27   static spinlock_t uidhash_lock   = SPIN_LOCK_UNLOCKED;
28
29   struct user_struct root_user =   {
30       __count:       ATOMIC_INIT(1),
31       processes:     ATOMIC_INIT(1),
32       files:         ATOMIC_INIT(0)
33   };
```

Figure 8.22   The user hash structure

19–20   the size of the hash table for `user_struct` is determined by these two lines, currently `0x100`, or 256 entries. This is only a quarter of the size of the hash table for pids. This is based on the assumption that a typical user would have an average of four processes.

21   this is `0x100 – 1`, or `0xFF`. It will be used in the hash function to mask off all but the low-order 8 bits.

22   this macro attempts to spread the user identification (uid) numbers as evenly as possible over the `uidhash` array. It is almost identical to the hash function described in Section 3.2.2.

23   the hash function returns an index into the hash table; this macro converts that index into a pointer to the appropriate entry.

25   the system maintains a supply of free `user_struct` structures, to avoid the overhead of having to involve the kernel memory allocator each time one is required or is returned. This is headed from `uid_cachep`. This slab cache is set up by the memory manager and will not be considered further.

26   the hash table is declared statically as an array of pointers to `struct user_struct`.

27   to protect this structure, a spinlock `uidhash_lock` is declared and initialised to the `SPIN_LOCK_UNLOCKED` state.

29–33   the structure representing the root user is set up statically at compile time. It is linked into the `task_struct` representing the `init` process (see Section 3.3.2).

30–32   there is one reference to this structure; that user is running one process, and currently there are zero files open. The `ATOMIC_INIT()` macro is from Section 5.2.1.

8.4.3 Allocating a user structure

When a new user creates a process (e.g. at log-on), a user structure is required. Such a structure may exist already. Otherwise, it has to be allocated, initialised, and linked into the hash table. The processing involved is described in this section.

8.4.3.1 Adding a user

The function shown in Figure 8.23, from `kernel/user.c`, is called to allocate a new user. It searches for a corresponding `user_struct` and, if one is not found, it allocates and initialises one.

```
85    struct user_struct * alloc_uid(uid_t uid)
86    {
87        struct user_struct **hashent = uidhashentry(uid);
88        struct user_struct *up;
89
90        spin_lock(&uidhash_lock);
91        up = uid_hash_find(uid, hashent);
92        spin_unlock(&uidhash_lock);
93
94        if (!up) {
95            struct user_struct *new;
96
97            new = kmem_cache_alloc(uid_cachep, SLAB_KERNEL);
98            if (!new)
99                return NULL;
```

```
100                 new->uid = uid;
101                 atomic_set(&new->__count, 1);
102                 atomic_set(&new->processes, 0);
103                 atomic_set(&new->files, 0);

109                 spin_lock(&uidhash_lock);
110                 up = uid_hash_find(uid, hashent);
111                 if (up) {
112                     kmem_cache_free(uid_cachep, new);
113                 } else {
114                     uid_hash_insert(new, hashent);
115                     up = new;
116                 }
117                 spin_unlock(&uidhash_lock);
118
119             }
120         return up;
121 }
```

Figure 8.23   Adding a user

85   the function is passed a uid by which the new structure will be identified and it returns a pointer to the new structure.

87   this hashes the uid value to get a pointer to the head of the appropriate hash chain (see Section 8.4.2 for the uidhashentry() macro).

90–92   a search of the hash table is protected by a spinlock, declared in the code in Section 8.4.2.

91   this searches for an entry corresponding to this user. The function is in Section 8.4.3.2. If it exists already, this will return a pointer to it; otherwise, NULL.

94–119   only if there is no corresponding user_struct do we have to go into the main body of the routine and insert a new one, otherwise, we can skip on to line 120 and return a pointer to the existing entry. Note that up here is a pointer variable; it has nothing to do with semaphores.

97   first memory is allocated for the new structure. The function is part of the memory manager and will not be considered further here.

98–99   if we are unable to allocate memory, then we return immediately with a NULL pointer.

100–103   it fills in the uid field of the newly allocated structure and atomically sets its __count field to 1 and the processes and files fields to 0. The macro is from Section 5.2.1.

109–117   this is to check whether another CPU has added the same user since the lock was released at line 92. All of this is because two processes could have checked the table at lines 130–132, have found no entry for this user, and have decided to insert a new entry. This piece of code is designed to cover that slight possibility.

109   the spinlock on the hash table is taken out again.

110 this searches for an entry corresponding to this one.

111–112 if another processor has already created the hash entry, then it returns the memory requested in line 97.

114–115 otherwise, it calls `uid_hash_insert()` (see Section 8.4.3.3) to insert the new one in the hash table and sets its own up variable to point to the new one, in preparation for the `return` on line 120.

8.4.3.2 Searching a user identification hash chain

The function shown in Figure 8.24, from `kernel/user.c`, searches a hash chain in the uid hash table. It returns a pointer to the corresponding `struct user_struct`, if found; otherwise, it returns NULL.

```
59    static inline struct user_struct *uid_hash_find(uid_t uid,
                                         struct user_struct **hashent)
60    {
61          struct user_struct *next;
62
63          next = *hashent;
64          for (;;) {
65                struct user_struct *up = next;
66                if (next) {
67                      next = up->next;
68                      if (up->uid != uid)
69                            continue;
70                      atomic_inc(&up->__count);
71                }
72                return up;
73          }
74    }
```

Figure 8.24 Searching a user identification (uid) hash chain

59 the function is passed both the `uid` itself, and a double indirect pointer to the first entry on the chain to which it hashes.

63 this converts the input parameter to be a direct pointer to the first entry in the chain.

64–73 the chain is searched until the NULL pointer at the end.

65 this takes a copy of the pointer to this entry.

66 if still searching, and this is a NULL pointer, then the entry being sought does not exist, so jump on to line 72 and return this NULL pointer.

67 we otherwise, it takes a pointer to the next entry.

68–69 the current entry is checked. If it is not the target, we go around the loop again, with `next` pointing to the next entry to be checked.

70 the entry required has been found. We atomically increment its __count field before returning it (see Section 5.2.5 for the function).

8.4.3.3 Inserting an entry in the hash table

The function shown in Figure 8.25, from `kernel/user.c`, inserts an entry at the head of a chain in the uid hash table. It must be called with the uidhash spinlock held.

```
38    static inline void uid_hash_insert(struct user_struct *up,
                                         struct user_struct **hashent)
39    {
40          struct user_struct *next = *hashent;
41
42          up->next = next;
43          if (next)
44                next->pprev = &up->next;
45          up->pprev = hashent;
46          *hashent = up;
47    }
```

Figure 8.25   Function to insert an entry in the user identification (uid) hash table

38 the function is passed a pointer to a `struct user_struct`, and a pointer to the head of the `uidhash` chain to which it hashes.

40 this converts the input parameter to be a direct pointer to the first entry in the chain.

42 this sets the forward pointer of the new structure to point to the (old) first entry in the chain. This may be NULL.

43–44 if there was a previous first entry, then its backward pointer is set to the new structure.

45 the `pprev` field of the new structure is set to point back to the entry in the array.

46 finally, the array is set to point to this new entry.

8.4.4 Deallocating a user structure

When the last process associated with a particular user terminates, the corresponding user structure is no longer required and can be returned to the memory manager. The processing involved is described in this section.

8.4.4.1 Freeing a user structure

When a process exits the use count on its `user_struct` has to be decremented, and, if 0, the structure itself is returned to the memory manager. The function to do this is shown in Figure 8.26, from `user.c`.

```
76   void free_uid(struct user_struct *up)
77   {
78       if (up && atomic_dec_and_lock(&up->__count, &uidhash_lock)) {
79           uid_hash_remove(up);
80           kmem_cache_free(uid_cachep, up);
81           spin_unlock(&uidhash_lock);
82       }
83   }
```

Figure 8.26   Freeing a `user_struct`

76   the function is passed a pointer to the `user_struct` to be deallocated.

78   first of all, there must be a valid `user_struct` assigned. The second part of the `if` is executed only if the pointer is valid. In that case, the `atomic_dec_and_lock()` macro, described in Section 5.3, decrements the `__count` field of the specified entry. If the decremented result was zero it locks the hash table spinlock and returns a positive value. Only if it returns a zero value is the structure actually removed.

79   the function to remove an entry from the hash table is discussed in Section 8.4.4.2.

80   the function to return the structure to the slab cache is part of memory management and will not be considered further here.

81   this returns the lock on the hash table, taken out by the successful completion of the `atomic_dec_and_lock()` on line 78.

8.4.4.2   Removing an entry from the hash table

The function shown in Figure 8.27, from `kernel/user.c`, removes an entry from the uid hash table. The caller is presumed to be holding a lock on this table.

```
49   static inline void uid_hash_remove(struct user_struct *up)
50   {
51       struct user_struct *next = up->next;
52       struct user_struct **pprev = up->pprev;
53
54       if (next)
55           next->pprev = pprev;
56       *pprev = next;
57   }
```

Figure 8.27   Removing an entry in the user identification (uid) hash table

51–52   these likes take local copies of the forwards and backwards links in the structure to be removed.

54–55   if the entry is not the last entry in its chain, then the `pprev` of its successor is set to point to its predecessor. If it is the last one, this step is unnecessary.

56 in all cases the field to which pprev points (either the previous entry or the head) is set pointing to the successor (which may be NULL).

8.5 Creating a kernel thread

Closely allied to the creation of a new process is the creation of a kernel thread. Figure 8.28, from `arch/i386/kernel/process.c`, shows the code that creates such a thread. It calls `sys_clone()` and, ultimately, `do_fork()` to create the thread, arranges for the specified function to run, and, if and when it returns, calls `sys_exit()` to terminate the thread.

```
487  int kernel_thread(int (*fn)(void*), void* arg, unsigned long flags)
488  {
489      long retval, d0;
490
491      __asm__ __volatile__(
492          "movl %%esp,%%esi\n\t"
493          "int $0x80\n\t"
494          "cmpl %%esp,%%esi\n\t"
495          "je 1f\n\t"

499          "movl %4,%%eax\n\t"
500          "pushl %%eax\n\t"
501          "call *%5\n\t"
502          "movl %3,%0\n\t"
503          "int $0x80\n"
504          "1:\t"
505          :"=&a" (retval), "=&S" (d0)
506          :"" (__NR_clone), "i" (__NR_exit),
507          "r" (arg), "r" (fn),
508          "b" (flags | CLONE_VM)
509          : "memory");
510      return retval;
511  }
```

Figure 8.28 Creating a kernel thread

487 the code is passed a pointer to a function that the thread is to execute, a `void` pointer to the argument for this function, as well as a `flags` bitmap, made up of clone flags.

492 the current value of the stack pointer is temporarily stored in the `ESI` register. This will be used at line 494 to distinguish between the existing process and the new one.

493 this is the Linux system call entry (see Section 10.4.3). The operand constraint on line 506 specifies that the EAX register is to contain the number corresponding to `clone()`, which creates a new thread. The `clone()` system service expects to find its operand in the EBX register. The value in that register is specified by the operand constraint on line 508 as the `flags` parameter.

494   the new thread will have its own stack; this is used to distinguish it from its parent. Remember that the parent's ESP was saved in ESI at line 492.

495   if the stack pointer still has the same value it had before the new thread was created, then this is the parent process, so control jumps forward to the label 1: at line 504. This is the last assembler instruction, so control goes on to line 510.

499   this code is only executed by the new thread and arranges for it to run the specified function. Operand 4 in a zero-based list is the void pointer arg, so this input parameter is loaded into EAX.

500   this value is now pushed on the stack, so that it will be available to the called function.

501   this calls operand 5. This is the pointer fn to the function to be executed by the new thread.

502   this line is only executed if and when fn() terminates. Operand 3 is __NR_exit, and this is moved to operand 0, which is specified as the EAX register.

503   this calls sys_exit() as __NR_exit is in the EAX register. This system call terminates the kernel thread. It does not return.

504   this is merely a target label for the jump in line 495.

505   these are operand constraints, or instructions to the compiler on how to treat these operands. The two on this line, between the first and second colons, are the output operands. The "=" means that the operand is write only for this context. The "&" tells the compiler that the operand may be written before the group of instructions is finished with the input operands. Parameter 0 is retval; the "a" specifies the EAX register. Parameter 1 is d0; the "S" specifies the ESI register. The variable d0 is never actually used; this is just a way of letting the compiler know that the ESI register will be written to (at line 492).

506   the next five parameter are input operands, terminated by the third colon. Parameter 2 is initialised with the number of the clone() system service. For parameter 3, the "i" means that it is an immediate integer operand, the number of the exit() system service.

507   the "r" constraint tells the compiler that a general register can be used for storing the operands. Parameter 4 is the void pointer arg, and parameter 5 is the function pointer fn.

508   the "b" tells the compiler that parameter 6 must be put in the EBX register. The clone() system service expects to find its parameter in this register. If the CLONE_VM bit was not set in flags, it is to be set when flags is moved into the EBX register. The new thread is to share the same memory mapping as its parent.

509   this is an instruction to the assembler not to keep any memory values in registers across the foregoing series of machine instructions. The inline assembler finishes here.

510   this line is only ever executed by the parent. Because retval is mapped to the EAX register, it returns whatever value the clone() system service planted there. This is in fact the pid of the newly created kernel thread.

9

Process termination

A Unix process terminates when the program it is running comes to an end. There is a special system service, exit(), by which a child process can let its parent know that it has finished, and also pass back some information about why it finished – whether this was normal or abnormal. This is one of the few system services that does not return a value. This makes sense, as there is not going to be any process around to receive or check a return value. A byte of status information can be included as a parameter to exit(), and the system sees to it that that byte is delivered to the parent. The compiler includes a call to exit(), if the programmer does not.

Because of the use of a system call, a process always terminates from kernel mode. It deallocates resources, such as memory or open files. It then moves to a new state, TASK_ZOMBIE. At this stage it has no memory or program, just its task_struct, the exit_code field of which holds the information it wants to pass back to its parent. The scheduler is then called to schedule a new process onto the CPU.

When eventually the parent calls the wait() system service and picks up this status information the task_struct is deallocated and so the last trace of the terminating process is removed from the system. If the child has already done an exit() before the parent does a wait(), then the parent just picks up the status information and goes on. However, if the parent does a wait() before the child exits then the parent process is held up until the child does so.

If a parent process terminates before its child processes, these are adopted by the init process, which always has a pid of 1. The init process periodically does a wait() to get rid of any such adopted processes that may have exited.

9.1 Terminating a process

The decision to terminate a process can be made at many places in the kernel, not just when implementing the exit() system call. In all cases the function do_exit() is called, as shown in Figure 9.1, from kernel/exit.c.

The Linux Process Manager: The Internals of Scheduling, Interrupts and Signals   John O'Gorman
© 2003 John Wiley & Sons, Ltd   ISBN: 0 470 84771 9

```
432  NORET_TYPE void do_exit(long code)
433  {
434       struct task_struct *tsk = current;
435
436       if (in_interrupt())
437            printk("Aiee, killing interrupt handler\n");
438       if (!tsk->pid)
439            panic("Attempted to kill the idle task!");
440       if (tsk->pid == 1)
441            panic("Attempted to kill init!");
442       tsk->flags |= PF_EXITING;
443       del_timer_sync(&tsk->real_timer);
444
445  fake_volatile:
446  #ifdef CONFIG_BSD_PROCESS_ACCT
447       acct_process(code);
448  #endif
449       __exit_mm(tsk);
450
451       lock_kernel();
452       sem_exit();
453       __exit_files(tsk);
454       __exit_fs(tsk);
455       exit_sighand(tsk);
456       exit_thread();
457
458       if (current->leader)
459            disassociate_ctty(1);
460
461       put_exec_domain(tsk->exec_domain);
462       if (tsk->binfmt && tsk->binfmt->module)
463            __MOD_DEC_USE_COUNT(tsk->binfmt->module);
464
465       tsk->exit_code = code;
466       exit_notify();
467       schedule();
468       BUG();
469
482       goto fake_volatile;
483  }
```

Figure 9.1 Terminate a process

432   the return value is always in bits 8–15 of code; the low-order 8 bits may contain further information. When this function is called by exit(), these low-order bits are cleared to 0. NORET_TYPE is defined in <linux/kernel.h> as

```
46   #define NORET_TYPE  /**/
```

so it is really only a comment, or a reminder.

434   this gets a pointer to the `task_struct` of the current (exiting) process.

436–437   if called to exit while running an interrupt handler, then we print a warning message (see Section 16.5.3 for `in_interrupt()`), but we still terminate the process.

438–441   if it is called to exit the idle process (pid 0), or the `init` process (pid 1), it prints a panic message. This actually reboots the whole operating system.

442   the `PF_EXITING` bit is set in the flags of the exiting process. This lets other processes know that it is exiting. However, it is not yet a zombie.

443   the `del_timer_sync()` function removes any real timer that may have been set by that process. Timers will be described in Chapter 15.

447   the `acct_process()` function is called only if BSD-style accounting is enabled. It writes information about the terminating process to the accounting file. This is described in Section 23.3.1.

449   this function releases the memory context of the current process. It will not be considered any further here.

451   the `lock_kernel()` function is described in Section 5.5.2.1.

452   the `sem_exit()` function is specific to System V semaphores and will not be considered in this book.

453–454   the `__exit_files()` and `__exit_fs()` functions are part of the file manager and will not be considered here.

455   for `exit_sighand()`, see Section 17.4.1. It deallocates the data structures used to keep track of signal handlers.

456   the `exit_thread()` function is architecture-dependent. On the i386, it has nothing to do.

458–459   if the exiting process is a session leader, then it is disassociated from its controlling terminal. The function sends a `SIGHUP` and `SIGCONT` signal to the foreground process group and clears the terminal from controlling the session. Parameter 1 means it is being called because the process is exiting. The function is part of the inputs/output (IO) manager and will not be considered any further here.

461   this decrements the use count and possibly deallocates the execution domain structure. There is one less process executing in this domain. The function will be discussed in Section 21.3.3.

462–463   if the process has been using a binary format module, this decrements the use count on that module. There is one less process using this module.

465   this set's up the `exit_code` field in the `task_struct`, with the value supplied by the input parameter (see the comment on line 432).

466   the `exit_notify()` function is described in Section 9.2.1. It notifies other interested processes that this one is terminating and changes its state to `TASK_ZOMBIE`.

467 this call's the scheduler to run some other process (see Section 7.3 for the `schedule()` function). As this one is now in the zombie state, it should never be run again.

468 if the scheduler should run this process again then there is a serious problem. The `BUG()` macro is from Section 4.1.3.3.

482 this is slightly paranoid code. Just in case something *really* bad happens, and the scheduler returns, this jump will try again.

9.2 Subsidiary functions used when exiting

The `do_exit()` function described in Section 9.1 uses a number of subsidiary functions, which will be considered in this section.

9.2.1 Notifying other processes of termination

A process may have a special relationship with other processes, particularly its parent, children, and those in its own process group. When it exits, it may need to inform these others of that fact, so that, as the comment in the source says, they know to mourn it properly. The function shown in Figure 9.2, from `kernel/exit.c`, sends signals to all the closest relatives of the exiting process. It is called by `do_exit()` (see Section 9.1). It checks to see if any process groups have become orphaned as a result of this process exiting and, if there are any stopped processes in that group, it sends them a `SIGHUP` and then a `SIGCONT`. This behaviour is required by POSIX 3.2.2.2.

```
338   static void exit_notify(void)
339   {
340       struct task_struct * p, *t;
341
342       forget_original_parent(current);

353       t = current->p_pptr;
354
355       if ((t->pgrp != current->pgrp) &&
356           (t->session == current->session) &&
357           will_become_orphaned_pgrp(current->pgrp, current) &&
358           has_stopped_jobs(current->pgrp)) {
359               kill_pg(current->pgrp, SIGHUP, 1);
360               kill_pg(current->pgrp, SIGCONT, 1);
361       }

379       if(current->exit_signal != SIGCHLD &&
380       (current->parent_exec_id != t->self_exec_id ||
381           current->self_exec_id != current->parent_exec_id)
382       && !capable(CAP_KILL))
383               current->exit_signal = SIGCHLD;

395       write_lock_irq(&tasklist_lock);
```

```
396          current->state = TASK_ZOMBIE;
397          do_notify_parent(current, current->exit_signal);
398          while (current->p_cptr != NULL) {
399               p = current->p_cptr;
400               current->p_cptr = p->p_osptr;
401               p->p_ysptr = NULL;
402               p->ptrace = 0;
403
404               p->p_pptr = p->p_opptr;
405               p->p_osptr = p->pptr->p_cptr;
406               if (p->p_osptr)
407                    p->p_osptr->p_ysptr = p;
408               p->p_pptr->p_cptr = p;
409               if (p->state == TASK_ZOMBIE)
410                    do_notify_parent(p, p->exit_signal);

417               if ((p->pgrp != current->pgrp) &&
418          (p->session == current->session) {
419                    int pgrp = p->pgrp;
420
421                    write_unlock_irq(&tasklist_lock);
422                    if (is_orphaned_pgrp(pgrp) &&
                                              has_stopped_jobs(pgrp)) {
423                         kill_pg(pgrp,SIGHUP,1);
424                         kill_pg(pgrp,SIGCONT,1);
425                    }
426                    write_lock_irq(&tasklist_lock);
427               }
428          }
429     write_unlock_irq(&tasklist_lock);
430 }
```

Figure 9.2 Notifying other processes of termination

342 first of all we deal with any child processes that may exist. The call to `forget_original_parent()` notifies such processes of the death of their parent and puts a pointer to their adoptive parent (usually `init`) into the original parent (`p_opptr`) field of their `task_struct` (see Section 9.2.2 for a description of the function).

355–361 if the exiting process is a group leader, it must notify the members of the group. The exact conditions under which it does so are complex; the following four conditions must all be true.

- The exiting process must be in a different group from its parent.

- The exiting process must be in the same session as its parent.

- The exiting process is the leader of its process group, which will then become orphaned (see Section 9.2.3.1 for the `will_become_orphaned_pgrp()` function). It checks all of the other processes in the group.

- There is at least one process in the group in the TASK_STOPPED state (see Section 9.2.4 for the has_stopped_jobs() function).

359–360   the kill_pg() function sends a signal to each process in a specified group. It is described in Section 18.2.7. These two lines send all processes in the group a SIGHUP followed by a SIGCONT. The default action for SIGHUP is to terminate the process, but it can be ignored, or handled. The default action for SIGCONT is to wake up a stopped process; otherwise, it is ignored. So if the default action is taken for SIGHUP then there is no process around to receive the SIGCONT, but if the SIGHUP is ignored then the SIGCONT will wake up that stopped process.

379–383   the next section decides on the signal to be sent to the parent process, to indicate that this one has terminated. If the following three conditions are true, then the exit_signal of the current (exiting) process is set to be SIGCHLD. Otherwise, it is left as it is.

379   condition 1 – the signal is currently set to something other than SIGCHLD.

380   condition 2 – the parent_exec_id of the exiting process was set to the self_exec_id of its parent by fork() and has not been changed since. If these two do not match now, then the parent has changed execution domain (such domains are described in full in Chapter 21).

381   condition 3 – the parent_exec_id and self_exec_id of the exiting process were set to the same value by fork(). If these two do not match now, then the exiting process has changed execution domain.

382   the exiting process does not have the CAP_KILL capability, which would allow it to ignore restrictions on sending signals. The capable() function is described in Section 20.4.1.

383   in summary, either the parent or child has changed execution domain since they went their separate ways. So the child is forced to send SIGCHLD, nothing else.

385–429   this block of code is modifying the process list, so it takes out an interrupt safe write lock on it, to guarantee mutual exclusion.

396   the state of the exiting process is set to TASK_ZOMBIE. It can never be selected to run again after this, but its task_struct will remain on the process list.

397   a death notice is sent to the parent; the function is described in Section 18.2.6.1.

398–428   finally, it deals with child processes. The code loops through them all, beginning with the youngest, doing three things. It:

- unlinks it from the family tree (lines 399–402);

- relinks it into the family tree at its new, adoptive, position (lines 404–410);

- checks to see if any process groups have become orphaned as a result of this adoption; and, if they have any stopped jobs, sends them a SIGHUP and then a SIGCONT, as required by POSIX (lines 417–427).

399   this remembers the child process being dealt with in this iteration of the loop. Each time around, it is the (current) youngest.

400   this changes the child pointer of the exiting process from the youngest to the next-youngest child. From here on, the one being dealt with is no longer a child of the exiting process.

401   this marks the new youngest as having no younger sibling. The first one dealt with never had a younger sibling, but this loop may be traversed several times.

402   this turns off tracing in the child process being dealt with (if turned on), as the adoptive parent will not be interested in tracing.

404   this arranges for the child being dealt with to be adopted by its original parent. This was set to `child_reaper` (normally `init`) by the call to `forget_original_parent()` at line 342.

405   its older sibling is now the (previously) youngest child of its adoptive parent. This will be NULL if the adoptive parent was childless.

406–407   if the adoptive parent did have a child previously, that process, whatever it was, is set to point to this one as its younger sibling.

408   the adoptive parent is set to point to this one as its youngest child.

409–410   if this child is a zombie, then this lets the new, adoptive, parent know it died, by calling `do_notify_parent()`. This function is described in Section 18.2.6.1.

417–427   this block of code checks again for orphaned process groups, this time as a result of abandoning child processes. It is executed only if the child is in a different process group from the exiting process, but in the same session.

419   this line is merely an optimisation, using a local copy of the process group identification (ID).

421–426   the process list write lock is released across these lines, because the `is_orphaned_pgrp()` function will attempt to take out a read lock on it at line 422. This would lead to deadlock if it were not released here.

422–425   if the process group of this child is now orphaned (see Section 9.2.3.2), and there is at least one process in the group in the TASK_STOPPED state (see Section 9.2.4), then SIGHUP is sent to each process in the child's process group, then SIGCONT (the `kill_pg()` function is from Section 18.2.7). The default action for SIGHUP is to terminate the process, but it can be ignored or handled. The default action for SIGCONT is to wake up a stopped process; otherwise, it is ignored.

426   the process list write lock is acquired again, preparatory to looping back to line 398.

9.2.2   Notifying child processes of the death of the parent

When a process exits, it must take care of any children it may have. This involves sending each one a signal and arranging for that child to be adopted by some other process, usually `init`. The function shown in Figure 9.3, from `kernel/exit.c`, is called from `exit_notify()`. It is passed a pointer to the current (exiting) process and it finds any children that consider this one as their original parent. It does this by scanning through the whole task list, looking for any process having a pointer to this one in its `p_opptr` field. It changes this `p_opptr` field to point to the process nominated as `reaper`.

```
158   static inline void forget_original_parent(struct task_struct * father)
159   {
160       struct task_struct * p, *reaper;
161
162       read_lock(&tasklist_lock);

165       reaper = next_thread(father);
166       if (reaper == father)
167           reaper = child_reaper;
168
169       for_each_task(p) {
170           if (p->p_opptr == father) {
171
172               p->exit_signal = SIGCHLD;
173               p->self_exec_id++;

176               if (p == reaper)
177                   p->p_opptr = child_reaper;
178               else
179                   p->p_opptr = reaper;
180
181               if (p->pdeath_signal) send_sig(p->pdeath_signal, p, 0);
182           }
183       }
184       read_unlock(&tasklist_lock);
185   }
```

Figure 9.3   Notifying children of the parent's demise

162–184   a read lock is taken out on the process list so that it cannot be changed by another process while this one is checking it.

165   the `next_thread()` macro is from Section 9.4.1. It evaluates to a pointer to the `task_struct` of the next child thread of the exiting process. This process will now become the parent of all the other children, a fact recorded in the `reaper` variable, defined on line 160.

166–167   if the exiting process has no child threads, then `next_thread()` returned the father process itself; in that case, it defaults to the process nominated `child_reaper`, normally `init`. The variable `child_reaper` is defined in `init/main.c` as

```
646   struct task_struct *child_reaper = &init_task;
```

169–183   this loop goes through each process in turn. The `for_each_task()` macro is from Section 3.1.3.

170–182   this code is executed only for a process claiming the exiting one as its original parent.

172   it sets the `exit_signal` field in any such child process to `SIGCHLD`. Presumably, the reaper expects `SIGCHLD` and is prepared to handle it. So, just in case the child has changed the `exit_signal` to some other signal that the reaper is not prepared for, it is reset here.

173   the `self_exec_id` of the child is incremental. It is moving to a new place in the family tree and so is changing domain.

176–177   these lines make sure that a process is not set up as its own parent. This could happen if the eldest child thread of the exiting parent is chosen as `reaper`. It will rightly claim the exiting process as its original parent and so `child_reaper` is set up as *its* new parent, not `reaper` itself.

179   the `p_opptr` field is set to `reaper`. This line is nominating the adoptive parent; the adoption is actually done later in `exit_notify()`.

181   if the child has specified a signal it is to receive on the death of its parent, it is sent that signal now. The `send_sig()` function is from Section 18.2.7.

9.2.3   Determining if a process group is orphaned

In a process group only one of the processes is connected to a controlling terminal and so can receive signals from the outside world. If this process terminates, the others cannot receive controlling signals; they are 'orphaned'. So, whenever a process terminates it must check whether it is creating such orphans; and, if it is, it must let them know so that they can do something about it. Such a check can consider all processes or it can ignore some particular process. Two different functions are supplied for this.

9.2.3.1   Checking for orphans, excluding one process

The function shown in Figure 9.4, from `kernel/exit.c`, determines if a process is 'orphaned', according to the POSIX definition. It will ignore one specified process (usually itself).

```
108   static int will_become_orphaned_pgrp(int pgrp,
                                     struct task_struct * ignored_task)
109   {
110       struct task_struct *p;
111
112       read_lock(&tasklist_lock);
113       for_each_task(p) {
114           if ((p == ignored_task) || (p->pgrp != pgrp) ||
115               (p->state == TASK_ZOMBIE) ||
116               (p->p_pptr->pid == 1))
117               continue;
118           if ((p->p_pptr->pgrp != pgrp) &&
119           (p->p_pptr->session == p->session)) {
120               read_unlock(&tasklist_lock);
121               return 0;
122           }
123       }
124       read_unlock(&tasklist_lock);
```

```
125        return(1);     /* (sighing) "Often!" */
126  }
```

Figure 9.4   Determine if a process group is orphaned

108   it is passed the ID number of the process group to be checked and a pointer to the `task_struct` of a process that is not to be considered. This is typically the caller; it may meet all of the other conditions but, as it is exiting, it cannot really become orphaned.

112–124   it needs a read lock on the process list all the time it is working, so that no other process can change this list.

113–123   it goes through each `task_struct` on the process list. The `for_each task()` macro is from Section 3.1.3.

114–117   any process in this first group cannot be involved. These are the specified `ignored_task`, a process in another process group, a zombie process, or a process that has been adopted by `init`. So the next one is tried.

118–121   these lines are executed (by falling through from above) only if none of the foregoing conditions is true. In particular, the process being checked is in the specified process group, so it is a candidate. If the parent of the process being is returned examined is not in this process group but is in the same session as its parent then FALSE; it will not become orphaned.

125   only if all processes have been tried and no match found is TRUE returned, so this process group will become orphaned.

9.2.3.2   Checking for orphans with no exception

Sometimes a whole process group, with no exception, needs to be checked for orphans. The wrapper function shown in Figure 9.5, from `kernel/exit.c`, passes a NULL pointer for `ignored_task` to `will_become_orphaned_pgrp()`.

```
128  int is_orphaned_pgrp(int pgrp)
129  {
130      return will_become_orphaned_pgrp(pgrp, 0);
131  }
```

Figure 9.5   Checking for orphans, with no exception

9.2.4   Checking if there is a stopped process in a group

Sometimes it is necessary to identify if any process in a particular group is in the TASK_STOPPED state. The function shown in Figure 9.6, from `kernel/exit.c`, is called from `exit_notify()`. It returns TRUE if at least one process in the group is in the TASK_STOPPED state; otherwise, it returns FALSE. It does not identify to its caller *which* process is stopped.

```
133  static inline int has_stopped_jobs(int pgrp)
134  {
135      int retval = 0;
136      struct task_struct * p;
137
138      read_lock(&tasklist_lock);
139      for_each_task(p) {
140          if (p->pgrp != pgrp)
141              continue;
142          if (p->state == !TASK_STOPPED)
143              continue;
144          retval = 1;
145          break;
146      }
147      read_unlock(&tasklist_lock);
148      return retval;
149  }
```

Figure 9.6   Checking if any process in a group is stopped

133   the parameter is the ID number of the process group to be searched.

135   this is the default (none found) value of retval.

138–147   as we are going to read through the whole process list, we take out a read lock to prevent any other process changing it [see Section 5.6 for the uniprocessor version and Section 5.7.2.1 for the multiprocessor version of the read_lock() function].

139–146   this loop goes through each task_struct on the process list. The for_each_task() macro is from Section 3.1.3.

140–143   if the process is not in the specified process group or is not in the TASK_STOPPED state it is of no interest, so we go on to the next one.

144–145   control only comes here if the process being considered is in the specified process group, and is stopped. At least one stopped process has been found, so the success return value is set and control breaks out of the loop.

147   this returns the read lock [see Section 5.6 for the uniprocessor version and Section 5.7.2.4 for the multiprocessor version of the read_unlock() macro].

148   this returns a value of 1 (TRUE) for success; otherwise, all processes have been tried and none in the group is stopped, so the default retval of 0 (FALSE) is returned.

9.3   Waiting for a child process to exit

A parent process can synchronise with the termination of a child process, using some version of the wait() system service. The parent may wait for the child to exit, in which case the parent is put to sleep and is woken up when the child calls exit(). The other possibility is that the parent calls wait() *after* the child has called exit(). In that case, the parent is not held up but immediately picks up the waiting information and continues.

Although there are a number of different versions of the wait() system service, internally they are all implemented by the sys_wait4() function, from kernel/exit.c, which will be considered in this section. As it is a fairly long function, the discussion is broken down into three parts.

9.3.1 Parameter checking and initial setup

The first part of the function is shown in Figure 9.7. It checks the parameters, constructs a struct wait_queue, and inserts it in a queue.

```
498  asmlinkage int sys_wait4(pid_t pid, unsigned int * stat_addr,
                                     int options, struct rusage * ru)
499  {
500      int flag, retval;
501      DECLARE_WAITQUEUE(wait, current);
502      struct task_struct *tsk;
503
504      if (options &
              ~(WNOHANG|WUNTRACED|__WNOTHREAD|__WCLONE|__WALL))
505          return -EINVAL;
506
507      add_wait_queue(&current->wait_chldexit,&wait);
508  repeat:
509      flag=0;
510      current->state = TASK_INTERRUPTIBLE;
```

Figure 9.7 Initial processing of the wait4() system service

498   the function is passed four parameters:

Parameter 1   this is the pid of the child process to wait for; this parameter is interpreted as follows:

- if it is −1, then wait for any child process,

- if less than −1, then its absolute value represents a group; wait for any child process with this group ID,

- if 0, then wait for any child process with the same group ID as the parent.

- if positive, wait for the process with this ID.

Parameter 2   a pointer to an int in user space into which a status value will be written.

Parameter 3   this is an options field. Allowable options are:

- WNOHANG, which causes it to return with 0 if status is not available for any child process;

- WUNTRACED, which causes it to report the status of any child processes that are stopped and whose status has not been reported since they stopped (this feature is normally used by the shell to support job control);

- __WNOTHREAD, which specifies that only children of the current process are to be checked, not any children of other processes in the same thread group;

- __WCLONE, which causes it to synchronise even with a child process that reports to its parent with a signal other than SIGCHLD;

- __WALL, which causes it to wait for any child, without restrictions.

Parameter 4 A pointer to a struct rusage in user space, into which usage statistics will be written.

501 this initialises a struct wait_queue called wait for the current process (see Section 4.1.1.2 for the macro).

504–505 if an invalid option was supplied, then EINVAL is returned.

507 this puts the wait_queue structure representing the current process on the wait queue linked from its wait_chldexit field. If it does have to be put to sleep later, this is where it rests. The function was described in Section 4.2.1.1.

508 if the process is put to sleep, then when it wakes up it comes back here and begins its checking all over again; see line 587, in Section 9.3.3.

509 this flag will be used to signify that a child process has been found, but it is neither stopped nor a zombie, so the possibility of waiting for it will have to be considered. Setting it to 0 means nothing has been found yet.

510 again, this is preparing for a potential sleep, when its state will be TASK_INTERRUPTIBLE.

9.3.2 Searching for a zombie child

The sys_wait4() function then goes on to find a suitable child process. The do loop shown in Figure 9.8 works its way through the thread list of the calling process. For each one, its inner for loop checks any children that that thread may have created.

```
511        read_lock(&tasklist_lock);
512        tsk = current;
513        do {
514            struct task_struct *p;
515            for (p = tsk->p_cptr ; p ; p = p->p_osptr){
516                if (pid>0) {
517                    if (p->pid != pid)
518                        continue;
519                } else if (!pid) {
520                    if (p->pgrp != current->pgrp)
521                        continue;
522                } else if (pid != -1) {
523                    if (p->pgrp != -pid)
```

```
524                          continue;
525              }

531              if (((p->exit_signal != SIGCHLD) ∧ ((options &
532                              __WCLONE) != 0)) && !(options & __WALL))
533                  continue;
534          flag = 1;
535          switch (p->state) {
536          case TASK_STOPPED:
537              if (!p->exit_code)
538                  continue;
539              if (!(options & WUNTRACED)
                                    && !(p->flags & PF_PTRACED))
540                  continue;
541              read_unlock(&tasklist_lock);
542              retval = ru ? getrusage(p, RUSAGE_BOTH, ru) : 0;
543              if (!retval && stat_addr)
544                  retval = put_user((p->exit_code << 8) | 0x7f,
                                        stat_addr);
545              if (!retval) {
546                  p->exit_code = 0;
547                  retval = p->pid;
548              }
549              goto end_wait4;
550          case TASK_ZOMBIE:
551              current->times.tms_cutime +=
                        p->times.tms_utime + p->times.tms_cutime;
552              current->times.tms_cstime +=
                        p->times.tms_stime + p->times.tms_cstime;
553              read_unlock(&tasklist_lock);
554              retval = ru ? getrusage(p, RUSAGE_BOTH, ru) : 0;
555              if (!retval && stat_addr)
556          retval = put_user(p->exit_code, stat_addr);
557              if (retval)
558                  goto end_wait4;
559              retval = p->pid;
560              if (p->p_opptr != p->p_pptr) {
561                  write_lock_irq(&tasklist_lock);
562                  REMOVE_LINKS(p);
563                  p->p_pptr = p->p_opptr;
564                  SET_LINKS(p);
565                  do_notify_parent(p, SIGCHLD);
566                  write_unlock_irq(&tasklist_lock);
567              } else
568                  release_task(p);
569              goto end_wait4;
570          default:
571              continue;
572          }
```

```
573                    }
574                    if (options & __WNOTHREAD)
575                          break;
576                    tsk = next_thread(tsk);
577            } while (tsk != current);
578            read_unlock(&tasklist_lock);
```

Figure 9.8   Search for child process

511   the next section of code reads the process list, so this read lock is taken out to guarantee no changes are made it is read (see Section 5.6 for the uniprocessor version of the `read_lock()` function; the multiprocessor version is given in Section 5.7.2.1).

512–577   on each iteration of the do loop, `tsk` points to the process whose children are being checked. The loop terminates when it gets back to the current (waiting) process again.

515–573   the `for` loop works its way back through all the children, beginning with the youngest, changing back to the next older sibling each time, until it comes to the oldest surviving one. This will have a NULL in its `p_osptr` field.

516–518   if we are waiting on a specific `pid` and this `pid` is not the one currently being checked, we go around the `for` loop again (i.e. trying the next oldest).

519–521   if waiting on a 0 pid (looking for any child in the same group as the parent), and the one being checked is in a different process group, we skip on to the next one.

522–524   positive and zero valued pids have already been ruled out, so this case is looking for any child process in the specified process group. If the process we are currently looking at is not in the specified process group (`-pid`), then we go around the `for` loop again.

531–533   all that is left is the −1 case (any process). The logic here is very condensed. The input parameter (−1) has specified synchronisation with *any* suitable child, but there are some that are not suitable. A 'clone' child is one that reports to its parent using a signal other than SIGCHLD. Normally, a parent does not wait for such children, unless the __WCLONE bit is set in `options`. However, overriding all of that, it waits for *all* children, clone or not, if the __WALL bit is set in `options`. Otherwise, we ignore this process and go around the `for` loop again.

534   at this stage the child processes are still being checked one by one. The current one might be a candidate, and is being checked further. This is indicated by setting `flag`.

535–572   only if the process is stopped or a zombie can the wait go ahead immediately, so these are the two cases in the `switch` structure.

536–549   the process being waited on is in the TASK_STOPPED state. This code merely reports to the caller; it does not clean up any data structures, and the process continues to exist.

537–538   if a stopped process has no value in `exit_code` (that means it does not want to report, or its report has already been picked up), we go around the `for` loop again and try the next one.

539–540   if the WUNTRACED bit is *not* set in options, and the PF_PTRACED bit is *not* set in the task_struct, then the function goes around the for loop again. The process is stopped, but the caller did not specifically ask for it to be reported, and it is not being traced – so it is not a candidate for synchronisation.

541   by this stage a stopped child with which to synchronise has been found. The process list is no longer needed, so the lock (taken out at line 511) can be given back (see Section 5.6 for the uniprocessor version of the read_unlock() macro; the multiprocessor version is given in Section 5.7.2.4).

542   if the supplied parameter ru is valid, then this puts usage statistics into the location it specifies in user space, using the getrusage() function, which is described in Section 9.4.3.2. This function returns the success (0) or failure (EFAULT) of the attempt to write to user space. If a NULL parameter was supplied, a 0 is written to retval.

543–544   if retval is in fact zero, indicating there was no problem writing to user space on the previous line, and the caller has supplied an address for a return value, then this shifts the exit code left 8 bits, sets the least significant 7 bits, and writes it to stat_addr in user space. The put_user() function is part of the memory manager code and returns 0 on success.

545–548   note that retval is being used for a double purpose here. If the write on the previous line did succeed, the exit code in the child is reset to 0, and the child's number is set up as the return value from sys_wait4().

549   a candidate process has been found and dealt with, so we jump out of the for loop and the enclosing do loop, to end_wait4 at line 590 (see Section 9.3.3).

550–569   this block of code is executed if a child is found in the zombie state. This is the normal occurrence. It will actually remove the task_struct from memory.

551–552   this adds the child's cumulative times, both in user and kernel mode, to the parent's counts.

553   at this stage the process list is no longer needed, so the lock taken out at line 511 can be given back (see Section 5.6 for the uniprocessor version of the read_unlock() macro; the multi-processor version is given in Section 5.7.2.4).

554   if the supplied parameter ru is valid, then this puts usage statistics into the location it specifies in user space, using the getrusage() function which is described in Section 9.4.3.2. This function returns the success (0) or failure (EFAULT) of the attempt to write to user space. If a NULL parameter was supplied, a 0 is written to retval.

555–556   if retval is, in fact, zero, indicating that there was no problem writing to user space on the previous line, and the caller has supplied an address for a status value, then this writes the exit_code to stat_addr in user space. The put_user() function is part of the memory manager code and returns 0 on success.

557–558   if that write failed, we jump out of the for loop and the enclosing do loop to end_wait4 at line 590 (see Section 9.3.3). Invalid parameters have been supplied, and the system call returns, sending the error value in retval back to the caller.

559   otherwise (given success) retval is set to be the number of the child process currently being dealt with.

560–566 this block of code is executed only if the child is temporarily reparented (fostered? its current parent is not its original parent). Before being removed, it is given back to its original parent.

561–566 this time an exclusive interrupt safe write lock is taken out on the process list, as changes are going to be made to it.

562 this removes the links of the process to its foster parent and the other processes in its foster family [for the REMOVE_LINKS() macro, see Section 3.1.1].

563 this gives it back its original parent.

564 this sets up the appropriate links [for the SET_LINKS() macro, see Section 3.1.2].

565 sends a SIGCHLD signal to the parent. The function was described in Section 18.2.6.1. The original parent is now charged with cleaning up the zombie. The present call to sys_wait4() returns the pid of this zombie process.

568 if the child has not been reparented, then the release_task() function, as described in Section 9.4.2, is called. It removes the task_struct from the table, removes links, and so on.

569 we jump out of the for loop, and the enclosing do loop, to line 590 (see Section 9.3.3).

570–571 if the child process is in any state other than TASK_STOPPED or TASK_ZOMBIE then we go around the for loop again and try another child.

574–575 this code is executed only when all children of a particular process have been checked and no match found. If the __WNOTHREAD bit was specified by the caller, then we break out of the do loop and go to line 578.

576 this looks for the next thread on the thread list of the caller. The macro is described in 9.4.1.

577 The do loop goes through each thread in the thread group of the caller, until it gets back to the beginning again.

578 no suitable child has been found, so the lock on the task table is given back and control falls into the following line (see Section 5.6 for the uniprocessor version of the read_unlock() macro; the multiprocessor version is given in Section 5.7.2.4).

9.3.3   Waiting for a child to exit

The final part of the sys_wait4() function is shown in Figure 9.9. It is always executed – from the beginning if no suitable child has been found, or from the end_wait4: entry if one has been found.

```
579        if (flag) {
580            retval = 0;
581            if (options & WNOHANG)
582                goto end_wait4;
583            retval = -ERESTARTSYS;
584            if (signal_pending(current))
585                goto end_wait4;
```

```
586                    schedule();
587                    goto repeat;
588            }
589            retval = -ECHILD;
590    end_wait4:
591            current->state = TASK_RUNNING;
592            remove_wait_queue(&current->wait_chldexit,&wait);
593            return retval;
594    }
```

Figure 9.9   Waiting for a child to exit

579–588   if flag is set, this means that the `switch` statement was executed at least once (that is, at least one child exists, but it is not stopped or a zombie, so the possibility of waiting for it has to be considered.

580   this sets up a default `retval` of 0 (no child available yet).

581–582   if the `WNOHANG` bit is set in `options`, the process is not to wait for a suitable child to become available, so we go to end_wait4 with 0 in `retval`.

583   this sets up a default `retval` of ERESTARTSYS. This is setting up for the check for a pending signal on the next line.

584–585   before putting the waiter to sleep, a check is made here to see if there are some signals pending for the current process, that are not blocked (the `signal_pending()` function will be described in Section 18.3.1). If so, then we go to end_wait4 with ERESTARTSYS in `retval`. This value will be trapped on the way out of system call handling, and the `sys_wait4()` tried again.

586   at this stage no eligible child has been found, so the scheduler is called to run another process, leaving this one in the `TASK_INTERRUPTIBLE` state. Remember it has been put into this state, and on a wait queue, in the code given in Section 9.3.1. It will remain on the wait queue until a child calls `exit()`, when it will be woken by a signal.

587   when the scheduler returns (i.e. when this process is woken up again) it may be because some child has exited in the meantime, so we go back and start the checking all over again, at line 508 of the code in Section 9.3.1.

589   this line is executed only if flag was still 0 after checking, that is, it has not found any child alive, and has never been into the `switch` statement. It sets `retval` to ECHILD (meaning no child is alive).

590   this is the generic exit path, taken both on success and failure. The only difference is the value in `retval`.

591   the parent has finished checking, it can now return to the caller, so the state is set to TASK_RUNNING.

592   the process was put on the wait queue at line 507 of Section 9.3.1.

9.4 Subsidiary functions used when waiting

The sys_wait4() function examined in Section 9.3 uses a number of worker functions.
These are described in this section.

9.4.1 Finding the next entry in the thread group list

A macro is supplied in <linux/sched.h> to find the next entry on a thread group list
(see Figure 9.10).

```
872  #define next_thread(p)                                          \
873      list_entry((p)->thread_group.next, struct task_struct,
                                                      thread_group)
```

Figure 9.10 Finding the next entry in a thread group list

873 the list_entry() macro was described in Section 4.3.4.3. It converts a pointer to the
list_head link, to a pointer to the actual structure of which it is a linked list (e.g.
task_struct). The first parameter is a pointer to the list_head field in the next
task_struct. The second parameter identifies the type of structure (task_struct). The
third parameter identifies the link field within the task_struct.

9.4.2 Removing the task_struct

When the sys_wait4() function finds a child in the zombie state, it deallocates its
task_struct and any substructures still associated with it. This is handled by the
release_task() function, which in turn calls a number of subsidiary functions. All these
will be examined in this section.

9.4.2.1 Master function to release a task_struct

The function shown in Figure 9.11, from kernel/exit.c, first checks that the process
being removed is not running on another CPU and calls a number of subfunctions to release
various data structures.

```
28   void release_task(struct task_struct * p)
29   {
30       if (p != current) {
31   #ifdef CONFIG_SMP

36           for (;;) {
37               task_lock(p);
38               if (!task_has_cpu(p))
39                   break;
40               task_unlock(p);
41               do {
42                   cpu_relax();
43                   barrier();
```

```
44                      } while (task_has_cpu(p));
45                  }
46                  task_unlock(p);
47  #endif
48                  atomic_dec(&p->user->processes);
49                  free_uid(p->user);
50                  unhash_process(p);
51
52                  release_thread(p);
53                  current->cmin_flt += p->min_flt + p->cmin_flt;
54                  current->cmaj_flt += p->maj_flt + p->cmaj_flt;
55                  current->cnswap += p->nswap + p->cnswap;

65                  current->counter += p->counter;
66                  if (current->counter >= MAX_COUNTER)
67                      current->counter = MAX_COUNTER;
68                  p->pid = 0;
69                  free_task_struct(p);
70              } else {
71                  printk("task releasing itself\n");
72              }
73      }
```

Figure 9.11   Remove a `task_struct`

28   the parameter is a pointer to the `task_struct` to be released.

30   if the current process is trying to release its own `task_struct` then it skips over everything, prints an error message (line 71) and returns.

31–47   the SMP code checks that the process being released is not currently active on some other CPU.

36–45   the infinite loop keeps testing until it is not active.

37   the code in this loop is checking the `cpus_runnable` field, which is only changed by the scheduler (see Section 7.4.4). To avoid it being changed by another CPU while this one is checking it, a lock is taken out on it (the function is given in Section 7.2.5).

38–39   if this process does not have a CPU assigned, then it jumps out of the `for` loop. Because its state has been set to `TASK_ZOMBIE` before this function was called, there is no possibility of its being given a CPU *after* this (the `task_has_cpu()` function is given in Section 7.4.4).

40   the lock is given back, to give another CPU a chance to release the process.

41–44   if the process is running on a CPU at the moment, then the process wait until the CPU gives it up, and then goes around the `for` loop again.

42   this macro inserts a pause in a busy waiting loop (see Section 9.4.2.2).

43   the `barrier()` guarantees that any writes by other CPUs have been flushed to main memory and so are visible to this CPU.

46 this line is needed for the case when the process is not currently running on any CPU (the `break` on line 39; see Section 7.2.5 for the function).

48 this atomically decrements the `processes` field in the `user_struct`. There is one process less sharing this structure. The function was described in Section 5.2.6.

49 if this is the last process belonging to the particular user (i.e. the result of the previous line was 0), then the `user_struct` is released (see Section 8.4.4.1).

50 the `task_struct` is removed from the pid hash table. The function is discussed in Section 9.4.2.3.

52 the function `release_thread()` is architecture-specific. It is misleadingly named, as all it does is to check if the memory context of the child process has indeed been released. It is really part of the memory manager and will not be considered any further.

53–55 these add the counts of minor and major page faults and the number of swaps of the task being released, and its children, to the appropriate fields in the `task_struct` of the caller.

65–67 the parent recovers any time-slices still available to the child process. This way, the parent is not penalised for creating many (short-lived) processes.

65 this adds any remaining value in the child's `counter` to the parent's `counter`.

66–67 if this would result in the parent having more than the maximum time-slice, the value is trimmed back. The maximum is defined in `<linux/sched.h>` as

```
450   #define MAX_COUNTER (20 * HZ/100)
```

For HZ of 100, this is 20 ticks.

68 this sets the `pid` field of the child being released to 0.

69 the memory taken by the `task_struct` is freed. The routine is in the architecture-specific part of the memory manager so will not be considered any further.

71 this message is printed if the process is trying to release its own `task_struct`.

9.4.2.2 Pausing in a busy wait loop

To insert a pause in a busy waiting loop, Linux provides the macro shown in Figure 9.12, from `<asm-i386/processor.h>`.

```
474   static inline void rep_nop(void)
475   {
476        __asm____volatile__("rep;nop");
477   }
478
479   #define cpu_relax() rep_nop()
```

Figure 9.12   Pausing in a busy wait loop

476   the REP instruction repeats the NOP a number of times specified by the value in the ECX register. This is effectively a random number of times.

479   the cpu_relax() macro is just an alias for the rep_nop() function.

9.4.2.3 Unlinking a task_struct

The function shown in Figure 9.13, from <linux/sched.h>, is called to remove a task_struct from the hash table and also from the process structure. It is really only a wrapper that takes out a lock and calls a number of other routines to do the work.

```
888  static inline void unhash_process(struct task_struct *p)
889  {
890      if (task_on_runqueue(p)) BUG();
891      write_lock_irq(&tasklist_lock);
892      nr_threads--;
893      unhash_pid(p);
894      REMOVE_LINKS(p);
895      list_del(&p->thread_group);
896      write_unlock_irq(&tasklist_lock);
897  }
```

Figure 9.13   Unlinking a task_struct

888   the parameter is a pointer to the task_struct to be unlinked.

890   if an attempt is made to unlink the data structure representing a process actually on the runqueue there is something seriously wrong, so the BUG() macro is called (see Section 4.1.3.3). It causes an invalid opcode exception. The function task_on_runqueue() has been described in Section 4.8.4.

891–896 the process list is going to be changed, so an interrupt safe write lock is needed; see Section 12.8.1 for the macro.

892   this decrements the running total of processes in the system. This global variable was introduced in Section 8.1.1.

893   this removes the task_struct from the hash table (see Section 3.2.4).

894   this removes all the links of this process to the process structure (see Section 3.1.1).

895   this removes the process from the thread list of its parent. This is a relatively new linkage, not catered for by REMOVE_LINKS; the function is given in Section 4.3.3.

9.4.3 Usage statistics

As part of the procedure involved in terminating a process, information about its resource usage is passed back to the parent. The process manager maintains usage statistics for each process in its task_struct. When such statistics are being passed to a user, they are encapsulated in a `struct rusage`. This section considers that structure and the function used to export such statistics to user space.

9.4.3.1 *The* `rusage` *structure*

When the process manager exports usage statistics, it encapsulates them in a `struct rusage`, as shown in Figure 9.14, from `<linux/resource.h>`. This is taken directly from BSD 4.3. Linux does not support all these fields yet, but it probably will. If they were not included now, each time new items are added, programs that depend on this structure would crash, so having them all here now reduces the chances of that happening.

```
17   #define   RUSAGE_SELF         0
18   #define   RUSAGE_CHILDREN     (-1)
19   #define   RUSAGE_BOTH         (-2)
20
21   struct    rusage {
22             struct timeval ru_utime;
23             struct timeval ru_stime;
24             long      ru_maxrss;    /* maximum resident set size */
25             long      ru_ixrss;     /* integral shared memory size */
26             long      ru_idrss;     /* integral unshared data size */
27             long      ru_isrss;     /* integral unshared stack size */
28             long      ru_minflt;    /* page reclaims */
29             long      ru_majflt;    /* page faults */
30             long      ru_nswap;     /* swaps */
31             long      ru_inblock;   /* block input operations */
32             long      ru_oublock;   /* block output operations */
33             long      ru_msgsnd;
34             long      ru_msgrcv;
35             long      ru_nsignals;
36             long      ru_nvcsw;
37             long      ru_nivcsw;
38   };
```

Figure 9.14   The `rusage` structure

17–19   these three literal constants are used by kernel code to determine just which subset of the statistics are to be passed back to the caller. The names are self-descriptive.

22   this is the total time spent in user mode. The `struct timeval` is described in Section 15.2.2.1.

23   this is the total time spent in kernel or system mode.

24–27   these are fields for memory management statistics, currently unused by Linux. The comments in the code give some hint as to their purpose.

28–30   these are further memory management statistics, which *are* used by Linux.

31–37   the remaining fields are not currently used by Linux.

31–32   these are fields for IO manager statistics.

33–34   these are cumulative totals of messages sent and received.

35   this is the total number of signals received by the process.

36–37   these give the number of voluntary and involuntary context switches that have occurred since the process was created.

9.4.3.2   *Returning usage statistics to the user*

The process manager provides a function that gathers up usage statistics from the `task_struct` and writes them back to user space (see Figure 9.15, from `kernel/sys.c`). The comment in the code says that this is SMP safe. Either a process calls this function for its own statistics, in which case no other process can interfere, or it is called from `sys_wait4()` on a process that is either stopped or zombied. In both of these cases the process being examined is in a frozen state so the counters will not change.

```
1153 int getrusage(struct task_struct *p, int who, struct rusage *ru)
1154 {
1155     struct rusage r;
1156
1157     memset((char *) &r, 0, sizeof(r));
1158     switch (who) {
1159     case RUSAGE_SELF:
1160         r.ru_utime.tv_sec = CT_TO_SECS(p->times.tms_utime);
1161         r.ru_utime.tv_usec =   CT_TO_USECS(p->times.tms_utime);
1162         r.ru_stime.tv_sec = CT_TO_SECS(p->times.tms_stime);
1163         r.ru_stime.tv_usec = CT_TO_USECS(p->times.tms_stime);
1164         r.ru_minflt = p->min_flt;
1165         r.ru_majflt = p->maj_flt;
1166         r.ru_nswap = p->nswap;
1167         break;
1168     case RUSAGE_CHILDREN:
1169         r.ru_utime.tv_sec = CT_TO_SECS(p->times.tms_cutime);
1170         r.ru_utime.tv_usec = CT_TO_USECS(p->times.tms_cutime);
1171         r.ru_stime.tv_sec = CT_TO_SECS(p->times.tms_cstime);
1172         r.ru_stime.tv_usec = CT_TO_USECS(p->times.tms_cstime);
1173         r.ru_minflt = p->cmin_flt;
1174         r.ru_majflt = p->cmaj_flt;
1175         r.ru_nswap = p->cnswap;
1176         break;
1177     default:
1178         r.ru_utime.tv_sec =
1179             CT_TO_SECS(p->times.tms_utime + p->times.tms_cutime);
         r.ru_utime.tv_usec =
             CT_TO_USECS(p->times.tms_utime + p->times.tms_cutime);
1180         r.ru_stime.tv_sec =
             CT_TO_SECS(p->times.tms_stime + p->times.tms_cstime);
```

```
1181                    r.ru_stime.tv_usec =
                            CT_TO_USECS(p->times.tms_stime + p->times.tms_cstime);
1182                    r.ru_minflt = p->min_flt + p->cmin_flt;
1183                    r.ru_majflt = p->maj_flt + p->cmaj_flt;
1184                    r.ru_nswap = p->nswap + p->cnswap;
1185                    break;
1186            }
1187            return copy_to_user(ru, &r, sizeof(r)) ? -EFAULT : 0;
1188 }
```

Figure 9.15   Return usage statistics to the user

1153   the first parameter points to the `task_struct` from which the information is to be read. The second specifies whether information about the process itself, about its children, or about both is to be passed back. The third is the address of a `struct rusage` in user space, where the information is to be written.

1155   the information is built up in this local `struct rusage`, which will then be copied to user space.

1157   the `struct rusage` as declared on line 1155 is initialised to all zeroes. This might seem paranoid but, as was seen in Section 9.4.3.1, there are many unused fields in this structure. The `memset()` function is part of the memory manager; it fills the specified memory area with 0 in this case.

1158   there are three possible sets of statistics that can be returned: those for the process itself, the cumulative times for its children, or the sum of both of these (see Section 9.4.3.1 for the definition of the literal constants). The who parameter specifies which set to return.

1160–1161   the `tms_utime` field of the `task_struct` maintains the time the process has spent on the CPU in user mode. The `CT_TO_SECS()` macro converts it to an integer number of seconds. The `CT_TO_USECS()` macro returns the remainder in microseconds. See Section 15.2.5.3 for these macros.

1162–1163   these lines do the same as lines 1160–1161 for the time the process has spent in kernel or system mode.

1164–1166   this set of code copies memory management statistics for the process.

1169–1176   these lines fill in the same fields in the `struct rusage` as did lines 1160–1166, but they read from the fields in the `task_struct` containing cumulative values for the child processes, not the parent.

1178–1184   these lines fill in the sum of the values for the parent and the child processes.

1187   the `copy_to_user()` function, part of the memory manager, attempts to copy the `struct rusage` just filled in to the location in user space specified by the parameter ru. If it fails, it returns an error value, in which case the function returns EFAULT; otherwise, if the information is successfully returned to user space, the `copy_to_user()` function returns a success value of 0 and the `getrusage()` function returns 0 to its caller.

10

Interrupting Linux

The concept of an interrupt is fundamental to any modern computer system. Numerous events occur within the running system, at unpredictable times, which need to be handled immediately. The central processing unit (CPU) suspends whatever it is doing, switches control to a block of code specially tailored to deal with the specific event, and then returns seamlessly to take up whatever it was doing beforehand. The whole procedure is known as interrupt handling.

The CPU needs help from the operating system in all of this. There has to be some way of keeping track of which service routine to execute when a particular interrupt occurs. This is very heavily influenced by the hardware architecture, and, of course, the operating system must provide each of these handlers or interrupt service routines.

Interrupts are divided into different categories, depending on what caused them. Some are actually generated by the CPU itself when it encounters some unusual condition while executing an instruction. These are known as exceptions and will be the subject matter of this chapter and the next. Then there are interrupts that are caused by hardware outside the CPU, such as disk drives or network cards looking for attention. Such hardware interrupts will be the study of Chapters 12–15.

Concentrating now on exceptions, some are coded into programs deliberately. Examples would be the setting of breakpoints in a program for debugging, or a programmed interrupt that transfers control to the operating system to execute a system service. Other exceptions are generated by the CPU, for example when it encounters an invalid opcode or when an arithmetic operation overflows a register.

The Intel documentation distinguishes exceptions into faults, traps, and aborts.

- A fault (such as a page fault) is reported before the instruction that causes it. The saved value of `EIP` on the stack points to the instruction causing the fault. A fault is fully restartable.

- A trap (such as `INT n`) is reported after the instruction that caused it. The saved value of `EIP` on the stack points to the next instruction after the faulting one. For this reason it is not generally possible to identify the instruction that caused the trap.

The Linux Process Manager. The Internals of Scheduling, Interrupts and Signals   John O'Gorman
© 2003 John Wiley & Sons, Ltd   ISBN: 0 470 84771 9

- An abort (such as the double fault exception) denotes a very serious problem. The instruction that caused it may not be identifiable. The running program cannot be resumed and the operating system may even have to be rebooted.

This terminology is not followed very strictly in the Linux process manager. As will be seen in Section 10.5, the handlers for faults, traps, and aborts are all contained in the file `arch/i386/kernel/traps.c`, without any distinction, so in this chapter and the next the generic term exception will be used throughout.

10.1 The interrupt descriptor table

Intel i386 processors have a privileged interrupt descriptor table register (IDTR) which points to a table of up to 256 interrupt descriptors in memory. This table has to be set up and the IDTR register loaded by the operating system.

10.1.1 Data structures

In Linux, this interrupt descriptor table (IDT) is declared in `arch/i386/kernel/traps.c` as

```
65    struct desc_struct idt_table[256]
          __attribute__((__section__(".data.idt"))) = { {0, 0}, };
```

In Linux, the IDT is page-aligned. This is implemented by using a special link section, `".data.idt"`. Each entry in the table is initialised to 0 by the compiler.

An entry in this table contains information about one specific interrupt. As can be seen from the declaration above, each is a `struct desc_struct`, as shown in Figure 10.1, from `<asm-i386/desc.h>`. This declaration of a descriptor as two longs ensures that each `desc_struct` is 64 bits, but it does not tell the full story. The internal structure of a descriptor is more complicated than this.

```
44    struct desc_struct {
45        unsigned long a,b;
46    };
```

Figure 10.1 An entry in the interrupt descriptor table

An entry in the IDT is an instance of a more generic data type used by Intel hardware, known as a gate. There are a number of different types of gate defined by Intel, of which only three are valid in the IDT. Of these, only two are actually used by Linux, known as interrupt gates (type 0xE) and trap gates (type 0xF). The names do not correspond directly to the use made of these gates. Interrupts, traps, or exceptions can be handled by either of these types of gates. The essential difference between them is as follows:

- Interrupt gates set the IF bit in EFLAGS to 0, to mask interrupts on entry to the handler. So interrupt gates are used for handling INTR interrupts.

- Trap gates do not change the state of IF, so they are used for exceptions (including software traps).

Figure 10.2 shows the internal structure of a gate. The offset fields between them contain the full 32-bit address of the handler for the particular interrupt. The offset is divided into two parts, for backward compatibility with 80286 descriptors.

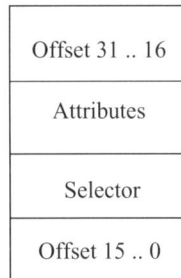

Offset 31 .. 16
Attributes
Selector
Offset 15 .. 0

Figure 10.2   Format of a descriptor

The 16 bits in the attributes field are used as follows:

Bits 0–7   these bits are not used with IDT entries.

Bits 8–11   this is the type of the gate; 4 bits allow for 16 types, but only 1110 and 1111 are used by Linux.

Bit 12   this bit is always 0 in a gate.

Bits 13–14   these bits specify the descriptor privilege level (dpl; 0–3) required to execute the handler. The dpl is used to prevent an application program calling just any old handler.

Bit 15   this is the present bit and is set to 1 if the gate is valid.

The selector field in the gate specifies an entry in the global descriptor table (GDT). This entry must be a descriptor for an executable segment. The dpl field in this descriptor is compared with the dpl in the gate. If this comparison indicates a transfer to a procedure at an inner level (e.g. user mode to kernel mode) then the CPU automatically pushes the current SS and ESP on the stack. If the comparison indicates a transfer to a procedure at the same privilege level, there is no need to save these values, and IRET will do a normal return from interrupt by restoring EFLAGS, CS, and EIP with values saved on the stack. It will not change stacks. In either case, the CPU pushes the value of EFLAGS at this stage. The trap-enable bit TF in EFLAGS is also cleared to 0 at this stage. If single stepping was enabled, this clears it. If the entry in the IDT is an interrupt gate, IF is cleared to 0; this disables further interrupts on the INTR line. For a trap gate, IF is unchanged. After this, the CPU pushes CS and EIP. Depending on the interrupt, it may or may not push an error code.

10.1.2 Initialising the interrupt descriptor table

In the first stages of boot up, the system is running in real mode and uses the real mode IDT at address 0x0000. Each entry in this is a 4-byte segment:offset address. There is no further information in the descriptor. Then, as part of the work of setting up the kernel, an assembly language routine called `setup_idt` is run.

The `setup_idt` routine builds a protected mode IDT, as described in Section 10.1.1. To begin with, it fills all entries with the same interrupt gate, pointing to the `ignore_int` interrupt handler, which will be described in Section 10.1.3. At a later stage in the boot procedure, the `trap_init()` function customises many of these gates, as described in Section 10.2.2.

The assembly code shown in Figure 10.3, from `arch/i386/kernel/head.S`, sets up 256 interrupt gates in the IDT, each pointing to `ignore_int`. It does not actually load the IDTR register – that is done as part of the `startup_32` routine, also in `head.S`.

```
306  setup_idt:
307        lea ignore_int,%edx
308        movl $(__KERNEL_CS << 16),%eax
309        movw %dx,%ax
310        movw $0x8E00,%dx
311
312        lea SYMBOL_NAME(idt_table),%edi
313        mov $256,%ecx
314  rp_sidt:
315        movl %eax,(%edi)
316        movl %edx,4(%edi)
317        addl $8,%edi
318        dec %ecx
319        jne rp_sidt
320        ret
```

Figure 10.3 Initialising the interrupt descriptor table

307 this puts the 32-bit address of the `ignore_int` routine into the EDX register. This routine will be discussed shortly (see Section 10.1.3).

308 the effect of this instruction is that the high-order 16 bits of EAX contain the selector for the kernel code segment (`__KERNEL_CS`).

309 this puts the low-order 16 bits of the address of `ignore_int` into the low-order 16 bits of EAX. This is to fit in with the storage ordering of information within a descriptor.

310 writing to DX leaves the high-order 16 bits of EDX unchanged. This still contains the high-order 16 bits of the address of `ignore_int`. The bit pattern written is 1000 1110 0000 0000. This sets the present bit (bit 15), with a dpl (bits 13–14) of 0, a gate (bit 12) of type 0x0E [i.e. an interrupt gate (bits 8–11)].

312 the destination index register is pointed to the beginning of the IDT; see Section 10.1.1 for the declaration of `idt_table`.

313 the code is now going to iterate 256 times around a loop. The ECX register is the loop counter in the i386 architecture.

315 the value in EAX is copied to the address pointed to by EDI (the IDT table). This copies bits 0–15 of the offset and the selector field (see Figure 10.2).

316 the high-order 4 bytes of the descriptor are filled from EDX, that is, the attributes, and bits 16–31 of the offset (see Figure 10.2).

317 the destination index register is pointed to the next entry in the IDT.

318 this decrements the loop counter.

319 we go around again, unless the counter (ECX) is 0.

320 in that case, we finish.

10.1.3 The default interrupt handler

The `ignore_int` routine shown in Figure 10.4, from `arch/i386/kernel/head.S`, is a protected mode wrapper for the IRET instruction with which the IDT is populated. All it does is to print a message saying 'unknown interrupt'.

```
327  int_msg:
328       .asciz "Unknown interrupt\n"
329       ALIGN
330  ignore_int:
331       cld
332       pushl %eax
333       pushl %ecx
334       pushl %edx
335       pushl %es
336       pushl %ds
337       movl $(__KERNEL_DS),%eax
338       movl %eax,%ds
339       movl %eax,%es
340       pushl $int_msg
341       call SYMBOL_NAME(printk)
342       popl %eax
343       popl %ds
344       popl %es
345       popl %edx
346       popl %ecx
347       popl %eax
348       iret
```

Figure 10.4 The default interrupt handler

328 this is the text of the message that is to be printed should this handler ever be called. It is used at line 340.

329   this macro was described in Section 1.2.2.1.

332–336   like all interrupt handlers, this must save values currently in the registers it is likely to use. These are restored after the message is printed (lines 343–347).

337–339   these three lines together load the DS and ES registers with the selector for the kernel data segment. The ASCII string from line 328 is stored in this segment.

340   this is the parameter to printk() – a pointer to the message string (within the kernel data segment).

341   this calls the printk() routine to output the message 'Unknown interrupt'.

342   this is removing the address of int_msg from the stack, where it was pushed at line 340. This is effectively discarding it, as the register will be overwritten at line 347.

343–347   these lines restore the registers saved on entry to this routine.

347   note that this overwrites the value popped at line 342 with the value in EAX on entry to this interrupt handler.

348   we return from the interrupt context. The EIP, CS, and EFLAGS registers are restored to the values they had before the interrupt occurred (by popping them from the stack). If the interrupt handler interrupted code is running at an outer level (e.g. ring 3), then ESP and SS are also popped.

10.2   Customising the interrupt descriptor table

After the code in Section 10.1.2 has been executed, the interrupt descriptor table is set up, with each of the 256 entries pointing to a default handler, ignore_int. The next step in the boot procedure is to put real working values into the appropriate slots in the IDT. The first 32 entries are reserved by Intel. These are for handling exceptions generated by the CPU. The remaining entries are available to an operating system designer, although there are certain conventions about the use of some of them established by the PC architecture. This section will examine the worker functions that insert entries of different types into the IDT and how these are used to set up entries for the defined exceptions.

10.2.1   Setting up gates

There are actually two levels of worker function for inserting entries into the IDT. There is one generic macro (with four parameters) and then, a level up from that, there are functions for inserting specific types of entries, which use that macro.

10.2.1.1   *Creating an entry in the descriptor table*

The macro shown in Figure 10.5, from arch/i386/kernel/traps.c, actually sets up an individual entry in the interrupt descriptor table (or, indeed, in any descriptor table).

```
755  #define _set_gate(gate_addr,type,dpl,addr)                    \
756  do {                                                          \
757      int __d0, __d1;                                           \
758      __asm____volatile__ ("movw %%dx,%%ax\n\t"                \
759          "movw %4,%%dx\n\t"                                    \
760          "movl %%eax,%0\n\t"                                   \
761          "movl %%edx,%1"                                       \
762          :"=m" (*((long *)(gate_addr))),                      \
763          "=m" (*(1+(long *)(gate_addr))), "=&a" (__d0),
                                              "=&d" (__d1)  \
764          :"i" ((short)(0x8000+(dpl<<13)+(type<<8))),  \
765          "3" ((char *)(addr)),"2" (__KERNEL_CS << 16));  \
766  } while (0)
```

Figure 10.5 Inserting a descriptor into the interrupt descriptor table (IDT)

755 the macro is passed the address of the gate that it is to fill in, the type of entry, the dpl, and the address of the handler function that it is to set up in that gate.

758 the constraint on line 765 specifies that parameter 5, the pointer addr, is to occupy the same storage as parameter 3, __d1; this has already been specified (by "=&d" on line 763) as the EDX register. Also, parameter 6, __KERNEL_CS << 16, is to occupy the same storage as parameter 2, __d0; this has already been specified (by "=&a" on line 763) as the EAX register. The initial state of the registers is shown in Figure 10.6, so the instruction on this line copies the 16 bits in DX into AX. This is the 16 low-order bits of the address of the handler. The high-order 16 bits in EAX is __KERNEL_CS.

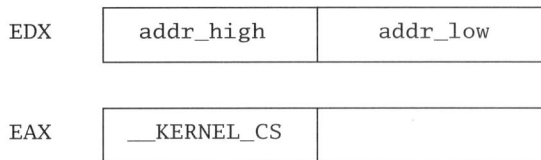

EDX	addr_high	addr_low

EAX	__KERNEL_CS	

Figure 10.6 State of registers on entry to macro

759 Parameter 4 is copied into the low-order 16 bits of DX. Line 764 specifies that parameter 4 is the immediate 16-bit (short) operand formed by adding together the following three values:

- 0x8000: this sets bit 15, the presence bit;

- (dpl<<13): this moves the two dpl bits into locations 14 and 13;

- (type<<8): this moves the four type bits into locations 11–8.

The state of the registers after these two MOV instructions have been executed is shown in Figure 10.7.

EDX	addr_high	attributes

EAX	__KERNEL_CS	addr_low

Figure 10.7   State of registers after line 759 of the code in Figure 10.5

760   EAX is copied into the first 32 bits of the descriptor. Parameter 0 is `gate_addr`, cast as a pointer to `long` and then de-referenced.

761   EDX is copied into the next 32 bits of the descriptor. Parameter 1 is `gate_addr`, cast as a pointer to `long`, incremented by 1 and then de-referenced.

These last two instructions set up the four fields in the gate, in order `addr_low`, `__KERNEL_CS` (selector), attributes, `addr_high` (see Figure 10.2).

10.2.1.2   *Creating interrupt descriptor table entries of different types*

The four functions shown in Figure 10.8, from `arch/i386/kernel/traps.c`, use the `_set_gate()` macro to set up four different types of descriptor. Each is passed the number of the descriptor (or a pointer to it, in the last case) and a pointer to the handler function corresponding to that descriptor. Note that all except the first have the `__init` property; it is assumed that such gates will be set up only at initialisation time and never thereafter.

```
775  void set_intr_gate(unsigned int n, void *addr)
776  {
777        _set_gate(idt_table+n,14,0,addr);
778  }
779
780  static void __init set_trap_gate(unsigned int n, void *addr)
781  {
782        _set_gate(idt_table+n,15,0,addr);
783  }
784
785  static void __init set_system_gate(unsigned int n, void *addr)
786  {
787        _set_gate(idt_table+n,15,3,addr);
788  }
789
790  static void __init set_call_gate(void *a, void *addr)
791  {
792        _set_gate(a,12,3,addr);
793  }
```

Figure 10.8   Creating gates of different types

777 for an interrupt gate, the type field is 14 (0xE) and the dpl is 0, so it cannot be called from user mode. This is used for hardware interrupts.

782 for a trap gate, the type field is 15 (0xF) and the dpl is 0, so it cannot be called from user mode. This is used for trap or exception handlers.

787 for a system gate, the type field is 15 (0xF), and the dpl is 3. A system gate can be called from user mode. There are only four of these, corresponding to the assembler instructions INT3 (3), INTO (4), BOUND (5), and INT 0x80 (128).

792 call gates are specific to Intel hardware. When a program transfers control to a call gate, the CPU recognises that this is not executable code. Instead, it uses the information that it reads from the call gate to transfer control to a routine in the specified code segment. Call gates are not used in the IDT. For a call gate, the first parameter is a pointer to void, not an int. The type field is 12 or 0xC, and the dpl is 3. Such call gates can be called from user mode.

10.2.2 System entries in the interrupt descriptor table

After the code in Section 10.1.2 has been executed, the IDT is set up, with each of the 256 entries pointing to a default handler, ignore_int. At a later stage in the boot procedure, the trap_init() function shown in Figure 10.9, from arch/i386/kernel/traps.c, is called from line 556 of init_kernel(). It overwrites a number of specific entries in the IDT, pointing them to more appropriate handlers. These are the entries associated with exceptions, the subject of this chapter and the next. All other entries retain their default values, for the moment (but see Chapter 12).

```
916  void __init trap_init(void)
917  {
918  #ifdef CONFIG_EISA
919      if (isa_readl(0x0FFFD9) == 'E'+('I'<<8)+('S'<<16)+('A'<<24))
920          EISA_bus = 1;
921  #endif
922
923      set_trap_gate(0,&divide_error);
924      set_trap_gate(1,&debug);
925      set_intr_gate(2,&nmi);
926      set_system_gate(3,&int3);
927      set_system_gate(4,&overflow);
928      set_system_gate(5,&bounds);
929      set_trap_gate(6,&invalid_op);
930      set_trap_gate(7,&device_not_available);
931      set_trap_gate(8,&double_fault);
932      set_trap_gate(9,&coprocessor_segment_overrun);
933      set_trap_gate(10,&invalid_TSS);
934      set_trap_gate(11,&segment_not_present);
935      set_trap_gate(12,&stack_segment);
936      set_trap_gate(13,&general_protection);
937      set_trap_gate(14,&page_fault);
938      set_trap_gate(15,&spurious_interrupt_bug);
```

```
939        set_trap_gate(16,&coprocessor_error);
940        set_trap_gate(17,&alignment_check);
941        set_trap_gate(18,&machine_check);
942        set_trap_gate(19,&simd_coprocessor_error);
943
944        set_system_gate(SYSCALL_VECTOR,&system_call);

950        set_call_gate(&default_ldt[0],lcall7);
951        set_call_gate(&default_ldt[4],lcall27);

956        cpu_init();
957
958  #ifdef CONFIG_X86_VISWS_APIC
959        superio_init();
960        lithium_init();
961        cobalt_init();
962  #endif
963  }
```

Figure 10.9 Initialising specific entries in the interrupt descriptor table (IDT)

918–921 this bit of initialisation has to be done somewhere, but it still seems out of place here. It looks for the EISA signature and, if this is found, it sets the EISA_bus variable to 1. As this is relevant to the input–output (IO) manager it will not be considered further here.

923–942 these lines of code customise the first 20 entries in the IDT. Most of them are set up as trap gates, so interrupts are still enabled when the handler is entered. Entry 2, the handler for the nonmaskable interrupt, is set up as an interrupt gate. In this way, interrupts are automatically masked on entry to the handler. Entries 3, 4, and 5 are set up as system gates. This means that these interrupts can be called from a program running in user mode. They are typically used for debugging. The 20 first-level handler routines will be considered in detail in Section 10.5.

944 this sets up interrupt 0x80 as the system call handler. The first parameter is the number of the interrupt vector to be set; SYSCALL_VECTOR is defined in <asm-i386/hw_irq.h> as

```
25    #define SYSCALL_VECTOR    0x80
```

The second parameter is the address of the handler to be set for that vector. This handler is at the assembly language entry point system_call, which will be considered in Section 10.4.3.

950–951 these are two alternative entries into the kernel, one for the Intel binary compatibility specification, the other for Solaris x86 binaries. The former will be considered in Section 10.4.1, the latter in Section 10.4.2. These are set up as call gates in the local descriptor table, not as entries in the interrupt descriptor table. First of all, a table of five call gates is set up and statically initialised to 0, in arch/i386/kernel/traps.c:

```
56    struct desc_struct default_ldt[] = { { 0, 0 }, { 0, 0 },
57                          { 0, 0 }, { 0, 0 }, { 0, 0 } };
```

Then, line 950 initialises the first of these to point to the `lcall7` routine (see Section 10.4.1). Line 951 initialises the last one to point to the `lcall27` routine (see Section 10.4.2).

956   this function initialises state specific to the particular CPU. As it is part of hardware initialisation it will not be considered further here.

958–962   then, if a Visual Workstation APIC is installed, there is some further initialisation carried out. Again, this is part of hardware initialisation and will not be considered any further here.

10.3 Interrupt handling

After the foregoing introduction to how the IDT is actually set up, we now turn our attention to the substantive issue of what actually happens when any particular interrupt occurs. Handling an interrupt is a three-phase operation, as follows.

- Entry phase: this is largely concerned with manipulating and saving values in registers. For this reason it is written in assembler. The code for the entry phase of all exception handlers is in the appropriately named `arch/i386/kernel/entry.S`, and will be considered in Section 10.5. The code for the entry phase of all hardware interrupts is built by macros declared in `<asm-i386/hw_irq.h>` (see Section 12.3.2).

- Service phase: the code for this phase is normally written in C, and is to be found in various files in the `arch/i386/kernel` directory. In particular, we will examine the service routines for each of the exceptions in turn in Chapter 11.

- Exit phase: this is almost totally concerned with restoring values to registers. There are slight differences in the exit phases for system calls, exceptions, or hardware interrupts. All of these are also written in assembler, and are to be found in `entry.S`.

The remainder of this chapter will cover the entry and exit phases of all the handlers set up in Section 10.2.2. In general, it will follow the order of the file `entry.S`. The early part of that file sets up a number of constants and macros that will be used frequently throughout the remainder of this chapter. Because these first-level handlers are concerned mainly with setting up the stack properly, they really should be read in conjunction with a copy of the `struct pt_regs` (see Section 10.3.1.1), but remember that this is actually upside down – the last item in the `struct` is the first pushed, and vice versa (see Figure 10.1.1).

10.3.1 Format of saved registers on the stack

The entry phase of every interrupt handler is concerned largely with saving the current values in the hardware registers. These are restored in the exit phase. Meanwhile, they are saved on the kernel stack. A number of data structures are supplied for accessing this stack frame, both from C and from assembler.

10.3.1.1 *The* struct pt_regs

The order in which registers are saved on the stack conforms to that in the struct pt_regs – see Figure 10.10, from <asm-i386/ptrace.h> – so when they are on the stack they actually constitute a struct pt_regs. Note that the stack grows downwards (towards lower addresses) in the i386 architecture whereas data items (such as a struct) grow upwards. This means that the last item pushed is actually the first in the structure (see Figure 10.11). If the interrupt involves a change of privilege level, the hardware automatically pushes the SS and SP registers. In all cases the hardware pushes EFLAGS, CS, and EIP.

```
26    struct pt_regs {
27         long ebx;
28         long ecx;
29         long edx;
30         long esi;
31         long edi;
32         long ebp;
33         long eax;
34         int xds;
35         int xes;
36         long orig_eax;
37         long eip;
38         int xcs;
39         long eflags;
40         long esp;
41         int xss;
42    };
```

Figure 10.10   Registers stored on the stack during interrupt handling

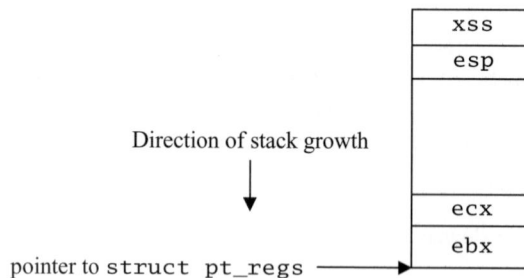

Figure 10.11   The stack and the struct pt_regs

The orig_eax value (line 36) is not really from a hardware register; rather, it is a value that the entry phase handler wants to pass on to the service phase. With some exceptions, the hardware actually pushes this value onto the stack. We will note this when it happens. Sometimes this value is pushed by the entry phase handler. Examples would be a system service number (taken from EAX, hence the name of the field) or an error code pushed by an exception handler. The remaining values on the stack are pushed by the entry phase code, using the macro described in Section 10.3.2.

10.3.1.1   Offsets into the stack frame

The whole stack frame is frequently referenced in C functions as a `struct pt_regs`. However, assembler code refers to these items on the stack by numeric offsets from the stack pointer, which, of course, points to the bottom (the beginning) of this structure. These offsets are defined in Figure 10.12, from `entry.S`.

```
49    EBX        = 0x00
50    ECX        = 0x04
51    EDX        = 0x08
52    ESI        = 0x0C
53    EDI        = 0x10
54    EBP        = 0x14
55    EAX        = 0x18
56    DS         = 0x1C
57    ES         = 0x20
58    ORIG_EAX   = 0x24
59    EIP        = 0x28
60    CS         = 0x2C
61    EFLAGS     = 0x30
62    OLDESP     = 0x34
63    OLDSS      = 0x38
```

Figure 10.12   Offsets from the stack pointer

10.3.1.2   The EFLAGS register

The assembly code that implements first-level interrupt handlers is frequently checking bits in the EFLAGS register. To facilitate these checks, a number of masks are set up, as shown in Figure 10.13, from `entry.S`.

```
65    CF_MASK    = 0x00000001
66    IF_MASK    = 0x00000200
67    NT_MASK    = 0x00004000
68    VM_MASK    = 0x00020000
```

Figure 10.13   Bits in the EFLAGS register

65   The carry flag is set to 1 if an arithmetic operation generates a carry out of the most significant bit.

66   the CPU accepts external interrupts if the interrupt enable flag is set to 1.

67   the nested task bit controls the operation of the IRET instruction. If set to 1, then the return from interrupt involves a change of privilege level and must change stacks. Otherwise, IRET restores only EIP, CS, and EFLAGS.

68   if the VM bit is set to 1, the CPU operates in virtual 8086 mode (see Section 23.4); otherwise, it operates in normal protected mode.

10.3.1.3 *Determining the mode of a process*

When an interrupt handler needs to determine whether or not a process was running in kernel mode when an interrupt occurred, it uses the macro shown in Figure 10.14, from `<asm-i386/ptrace.h>`.

```
58   #define user_mode(regs) ((VM_MASK & (regs)->eflags) || (3 & (regs)->xcs))
```

Figure 10.14   Determining the mode of a process before the interrupt

58   If the `VM_MASK` bit was set in `EFLAGS` before the interrupt, then the process was running in vm86 mode (see Section 23.4). If the two least significant bits were set in the `CS` register before the interrupt, then the process was running in user mode. If either of these conditions is TRUE, the macro evaluates to TRUE; otherwise, it evaluates to FALSE.

10.3.2   Saving registers

All interrupt handlers need to save the general purpose CPU registers on the stack. The macro shown Figure 10.15, from `entry.S`, does that.

```
85    #define SAVE_ALL                     \
86        cld;                             \
87        pushl %es;                       \
88        pushl %ds;                       \
89        pushl %eax;                      \
90        pushl %ebp;                      \
91        pushl %edi;                      \
92        pushl %esi;                      \
93        pushl %edx;                      \
94        pushl %ecx;                      \
95        pushl %ebx;                      \
96        movl $(__KERNEL_DS),%edx;        \
97        movl %edx,%ds;                   \
98        movl %edx,%es;
```

Figure 10.15   Macro to save registers

86   This clears the direction flag bit in `EFLAGS` to 0. After this, string instructions will increment the index registers `ESI` and `EDI` (as opposed to decrementing them).

87–95   the registers are pushed one by one. The order conforms to that in a `struct pt_regs`. Note that the values on the stack before `SAVE_ALL` is called constitute the remainder of the structure. The whole stack frame is frequently referenced as a `struct pt_regs`. Also note that in reverse order the last three are EBX, ECX, and EDX. These contain parameters (if any) for the handler function being called to service the exception.

96–98 the data segment register (DS) and the extra segment register (ES) are set to point to the kernel data segment. This may seem a roundabout way of doing things, but the segment registers cannot be loaded directly; they can only be loaded from another register. We are, after all, about to execute kernel code, so it is logical that we should be using the kernel data segment.

10.3.3 Restoring registers

Of course, registers must be popped in exactly the reverse order. The macro shown in Figure 10.16, from `arch/i386/kernel/entry.S`, restores all the registers saved on entry to the exception handler.

```
100  #define RESTORE_ALL       \
101       popl %ebx;           \
102       popl %ecx;           \
103       popl %edx;           \
104       popl %esi;           \
105       popl %edi;           \
106       popl %ebp;           \
107       popl %eax;           \
108       popl %ds;            \
109       popl %es;            \
110       addl $4,%esp;        \
111       iret;
```

Figure 10.16   Macro to restore all saved registers.

101–109 the registers are popped in reverse order to that in which they were pushed. EBX was the last register saved, at line 96 of Figure 10.15, so it is the first restored. Note that some of these values may have been changed in the meantime by a particular exception handler.

110 the stack pointer is incremented by 4, which effectively discards the bottom value now on the stack. This is the `orig_eax`, pushed there either by the hardware or by the first-level handler before calling SAVE_ALL. This spoils the symmetry between SAVE_ALL and RESTORE_ALL, but, as long as all handlers observe this convention and ensure that *some* value is on the stack before calling SAVE_ALL, everything will work fine.

111 when the kernel is finished, it uses another special machine instruction, IRET. This restores the EIP, CS, and EFLAGS values from the stack to the hardware registers. If the original interrupt involved a change in privilege level (i.e. from user to kernel mode) then the original values of ESP and SS are also restored from the stack by IRET.

10.3.4 Finding the current `task_struct`

In the entry phase, all interrupt handlers need to find the `task_struct` of the current process. The macro shown in Figure 10.17, from `entry.S`, puts a pointer to this `task_struct` into the specified register.

```
131  #define GET_CURRENT(reg)         \
132         movl $-8192, reg;         \
133         andl %esp, reg
```

Figure 10.17 Macro to find the `task_struct` of the current process

132 as discussed in Section 3.3.1, the `task_struct` and kernel stack for each process are allocated together, aligned on a 8192-byte boundary (0x2000), so the starting address of a `task_struct` will always be 0xN000, where N is even (i.e. the least significant 13 bits of the address will be 0). All addresses within the `task_struct` and on the stack will have the same high order bits – only these 13 low-order bits will change.

133 the value in `reg` is now −8192, or 0xFFFFE000. ANDing this with the stack pointer effectively zeros the least significant 13 bits of the value in ESP and puts the result in `reg`. This means that `reg` is now pointing to the beginning of the `task_struct` of the current process.

10.3.5 Offsets into the `task_struct`

Interrupt handlers may need to reference the `task_struct` of the current process, which is declared as a C `struct` (see Chapter 2). Assembly language routines cannot access that directly. When they do need to access the `task_struct` they use byte offsets to identify the fields. This, of course, means that the position and size of the fields should be constant. We have seen in Section 2.1 that the fields accessed that way are gathered together at the beginning of the `task_struct`. Figure 10.18, from `entry.S`, shows the byte offsets corresponding to these fields.

```
73     state          = 0
74     flags          = 4
75     sigpending     = 8
76     addr_limit     = 12
77     exec_domain    = 16
78     need_resched   = 20
79     tsk_ptrace     = 24
80     processor      = 52
81
82     ENOSYS         = 38
```

Figure 10.18 Offsets into the `task_struct`

73–80 the meaning of all of these fields has been explained in Section 2.1.

80 the way the code is presently set up requires that some of the scheduling fields after `tsk_ptrace` have to be at fixed positions. It seems a prime candidate to be moved up to offset 28.

82 this is not part of the `task_struct`, it is, in fact, an error number required in the code in Sections 10.4.3.3 and 10.4.3.4.

10.4 System call entry

As has been seen in Section 10.2.2, there are three different interrupts set up to allow entry into the kernel, and our examination of interrupt handlers will begin with these. Following the order of the code, we first of all examine two alternative entry points provided for compatibility with binaries created on other systems, then we examine the standard Linux entry INT 0x80.

10.4.1 The Intel binary specification entry point

The Intel family binary compatibility specification (iBCS) defines a system interface for application programs that are compiled for various Unix implementations. It was designed to enable binary application compatibility and migration between different operating system environments on the i386 architecture.

The assembly language routine shown in Figure 10.19, from entry.S, is the kernel entry point used by the iBCS. This is the target of the call gate set up in Section 10.2.2. The layout of the registers on the stack is different from the Linux layout. Because of this, it begins by moving things around, so that the stack is arranged as a struct pt_regs. The reader should refer to Section 10.3.1.1 while reading the following.

```
135  ENTRY(lcall7)
136      pushfl
137      pushl %eax
138      SAVE_ALL
139      movl EIP(%esp),%eax
140      movl CS(%esp),%edx
141      movl EFLAGS(%esp),%ecx
142      movl %eax,EFLAGS(%esp)
143      movl %edx,EIP(%esp)
144      movl %ecx,CS(%esp)
145      movl %esp,%ebx
146      pushl %ebx
147      andl $-8192,%ebx
148      movl exec_domain(%ebx),%edx
149      movl 4(%edx),%edx
150      pushl $0x7
151      call *%edx
152      addl $4,%esp
153      popl %eax
154      jmp ret_from_sys_call
```

Figure 10.19 The lcall7 system entry point

136 on entry through the call gate, the hardware has pushed CS and EIP on the stack, in that order. The software now pushes the 32-bit EFLAGS. This is different from the order in a struct pt_regs, which would be EFLAGS, CS, EIP.

137 the number of the system service requested is in the EAX register on entry. It goes into the `orig_eax` slot on the stack.

138 this saves the current values in the other hardware registers on the stack. These are saved in the standard Linux format (see Section 10.3.2).

139–144 the three values at the top of the stack are now going to be put into their proper order. We begin by copying (not popping) all three into registers. The offsets from the stack pointer used here (e.g. EIP) have been described in 10.3.1.2.

139 owing to call gates, this is in fact the EFLAGS value, not EIP.

140 this is EIP, not CS as the code says.

141 this is CS, not EFLAGS as the code says.

142–144 these three lines are putting the values in their normal Linux positions on the stack; see Figure 10.20, which attempts to illustrate all this.

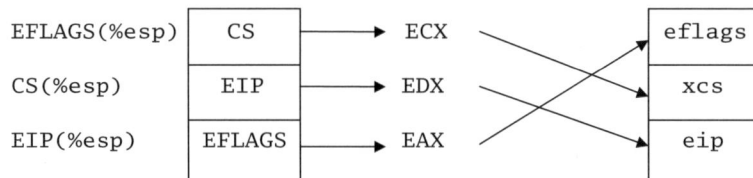

Figure 10.20 Adjusting values on the stack

145–146 these push the current value of the stack pointer, which is pointing to the `struct pt_regs`. This register cannot be pushed directly; it must first be moved to a general purpose register. This is a parameter to the handler that will be called at line 151.

147 the way in which this instruction gets a pointer to the `task_struct` of the current process into EBX has been described in Section 10.3.4.

148 because it is using call gates, the executing program is not part of a standard Linux binary, so the data structure representing this particular type of binary must be found. There is a pointer to this in the `exec_domain` field of the `task_struct`, which is copied into EDX. The offset `exec_domain` has been defined in Section 10.3.5. Execution domains will be discussed in Chapter 21.

149 the address of the `lcall7` handler for that domain is 4 bytes into the `struct exec_domain`. This line takes a copy of that into EDX. The format of a `struct exec_domain` is described in Section 21.2.1.

150 this pushes an immediate value of 7 onto the stack. It is padded out to 32 bits on the stack to keep it aligned. This is a parameter to the `lcall7` handler.

151 this calls the `lcall7` handler for that domain, which will execute the system call.

152 control returns here when the system call has executed. The bottom value on the stack is discarded. This is the 7 pushed at line 150.

153 this pops the next value up into EAX. This was a pointer to the `struct pt_regs` on the stack, pushed at line 146.

154 this takes the standard return from system call handling, with EAX pointing to the `struct pt_regs` on the stack (see Section 10.6.1 for the `ret_from_sys_call` routine).

10.4.2 The Solaris X86 binary entry point

The code shown in Figure 10.21, from `entry.S`, is the system entry point used by Solaris binaries that have been compiled for the i386 architecture. The code is almost identical to that discussed in Section 10.4.1. The only difference is at line 171, where an immediate value of `0x27` is pushed onto the stack.

```
156  ENTRY(lcall27)
157      pushfl
158      pushl %eax
159      SAVE_ALL
160      movl EIP(%esp),%eax
161      movl CS(%esp),%edx
162      movl EFLAGS(%esp),%ecx
163      movl %eax,EFLAGS(%esp)
164      movl %edx,EIP(%esp)
165      movl %ecx,CS(%esp)
166      movl %esp,%ebx
167      pushl %ebx
168      andl $-8192,%ebx
169      movl exec_domain(%ebx),%edx
170      movl 4(%edx),%edx
171      pushl $0x27
172      call *%edx
173      addl $4,%esp
174      popl %eax
175      jmp ret_from_sys_call
```

Figure 10.21 The `lcall27` system entry point

10.4.3 The Linux system call entry

Before we get into the internals of this, it may be useful to look at how a Linux user program enters the kernel – the system call interface. This involves changing the CPU to run in kernel mode and changing it back to user mode afterwards. Then we will examine the mainline entry code. The section concludes with two branches from the mainline, one taken when a process is being traced, the other when the call specifies an invalid system service.

10.4.3.1 Overview

Each system service is known to the programmer by name, and is called by name, such as read() or write(). This is understandable for the programmer side of the interface, but, internally, the operating system identifies each service by number. The numbers corresponding to each one can be found in the file <asm-i386/unistd.h>. The names and addresses of the functions that implement each of these are also listed at the entry point sys_call_table in entry.S, lines 398–636. Each of the functions declared there is the kernel implementation of the particular system service.

The actual C library function that the application calls does very little work. It puts the appropriate system call number into the EAX register, puts the parameters into registers beginning with EBX, and then executes a special machine instruction, INT x, which generates an interrupt. As we have seen in Section 10.1.1, there are 256 possible interrupts in the i386 architecture; the one reserved for entry to the Linux kernel is INT 0x80. When this instruction is executed, the CPU goes to the appropriate entry in the IDT and reads the 8-byte descriptor stored there. Reading this descriptor has a number of effects on the CPU. First of all, it changes the processor to execute in kernel mode. The value in the SS register is changed – the machine is now working on the kernel stack, but, most importantly, it causes the CPU to read in its next instruction from a different place in memory – a sort of implied jump. It transfers control to a common system call handler in the kernel code segment, at the assembly language entry point system_call.

When the system call handler terminates, it executes an IRET instruction, which changes the mode back to user and takes up execution at the line after the INT 0x80 instruction in the C library code. This in turn arranges that any data to be returned to the user are in the expected format. It will also determine what value the C function itself is to return. If the call failed, it would put an appropriate value into errno and return −1 to the user program.

10.4.3.2 Mainstream entry to a system service

The code shown in Figure 10.22, from entry.S, is the first-level handler for interrupt 0x80. It is always called with the number of the system service being requested in the EAX register.

```
194  ENTRY(system_call)
195       pushl %eax
196       SAVE_ALL
197       GET_CURRENT(%ebx)
198       testb $0x02,tsk_ptrace(%ebx)
199       jne tracesys
200       cmpl $(NR_syscalls),%eax
201       jae badsys
202       call *SYMBOL_NAME(sys_call_table)(,%eax,4)
203       movl %eax,EAX(%esp)
```

Figure 10.22 Common code to call a system service

195   a copy of the number of the system service being called is saved on the kernel stack, in the

orig_eax position. Here it is available to the system service code, if required. It is removed at the end of RESTORE_ALL, as noted in Section 10.3.3.

196   all the general purpose CPU registers are saved, to make sure this routine does not overwrite any information the user may have in these registers. Parameters to the system call (if any) will be in EBX, ECX, and EDX. Also, the system call may result in a process being context switched out. In this case, the values it has in all the hardware registers are safely stored on its own kernel stack. The macro SAVE_ALL was discussed in Section 10.3.2.

197   the macro GET_CURRENT() gets a pointer to the task_struct of the current process. In this instance it puts it into the EBX register. This macro was discussed in Section 10.3.4.

198–199   after the call to GET_CURRENT() on line 197, EBX now contains the address of the task_struct of the current process. Offsetting that by tsk_ptrace gives us the ptrace field in the task_struct (see Section 10.3.5 for this offset). The PT_TRACESYS bit in this field is defined as 0x02 (see Section 2.1). If this bit is set then the process calling the system service is being traced and is to be stopped before and after each system call. The special handling for this case is discussed in Section 10.4.3.3.

200–201   NR_syscalls is defined in <linux/sys.h> as

        7   #define NR_syscalls 256

If the service requested is numbered 256 or greater then it is invalid, and the program jumps to the label badsys:. It might seem better to do this test before saving any registers, but this way a standard 'return from system call' routine is employed. The error handling code at badsys: is discussed in Section 10.4.3.4.

202   this is the line that actually transfers control to the system service code. The macro is defined in <linux/linkage.h> as

        21   #define SYMBOL_NAME(X) X

It is merely a device to help the linker find the particular entry point in an assembly program. In this particular case, SYMBOL_NAME() returns a pointer to the beginning of sys_call_table. This is offset by the value in EAX (the system call number), multiplied by 4. Each entry in sys_call_table is the address of the kernel code that executes that particular system service. Each is defined as .long, or 4 bytes. Finally, the address found in that location is the target of the call instruction. There are two tables involved here, which may lead to some confusion. Only one entry in the first table, the IDT, is relevant to a Linux system service call, that is entry 0x80. This contains the address of the system_call routine. The second table, sys_call_table, has one entry for each possible system service; each entry contains the address of the operating system function that carries out that system service. The system_call routine uses the value in the EAX register to index into this second table and find the address of the appropriate code. Any parameters required by the function being called are on the stack, in the ebx, ecx, and edx positions. From Figure 10.10 it can be seen that these are the three last items on the stack.

203   this line is executed after the return from the system call code. The system call always puts its return value into the EAX register. The destination operand EAX(%esp) means the stack pointer offset by the constant EAX, which has been defined in Section 10.3.1.2, so the destination operand is the position on the stack where the EAX register was saved by SAVE_ALL at line 196. At this stage, the previous value in the copy of EAX on the stack, the number of the system service called, is no longer needed. After this, control falls into the next line of code, ret_from_sys_call, which is considered in Section 10.6.1.

10.4.3.3 System call entry when a process is being traced

The whole area of process tracing will be dealt with in detail in Chapter 22. Figure 10.23, from arch/i386/kernel/entry.S, shows how a system call is handled for a process that is being traced. Control transfers here from line 199 of Figure 10.22.

```
232  tracesys:
233       movl $-ENOSYS,EAX(%esp)
234       call SYMBOL_NAME(syscall_trace)
235       movl ORIG_EAX(%esp),%eax
236       cmpl $(NR_syscalls),%eax
237       jae tracesys_exit
238       call *SYMBOL_NAME(sys_call_table)(,%eax,4)
239       movl %eax,EAX(%esp)
240  tracesys_exit:
241       call SYMBOL_NAME(syscall_trace)
242       jmp ret_from_sys_call
```

Figure 10.23 System call handling when tracing is in effect

233 ENOSYS has been defined in Section 10.3.5. This is set up as the return value in the copy of EAX on the stack (see the comment on the next line).

234 this function will be discussed in Section 22.5. Basically, it lets the tracing parent know that the current process has hit a breakpoint. The same function is called both before and after the system call is executed, and a rather subtle device is used to allow the parent to distinguish between them. On this first call, the copy of EAX on the stack contains ENOSYS. No actual system call can return this value, so the parent can determine that it is before the system call.

235 now we are ready to process the system call. We cannot assume that the system call number is still in EAX, but we have another copy of it. ORIG_EAX has been defined in the code in Figure 10.12. This is the copy of EAX that was pushed on the stack in line 195 of Figure 10.22.

236–237 if it is an invalid system call number, then the exit at line 240 is taken.

238 otherwise, the system service is called, as usual. This has been explained in detail in Section 10.4.3.2.

239 all system services return a status code in the EAX register. This is saved in the copy of the EAX register located on the stack, so it will be in the hardware EAX register when we return from the system call.

241 this is the same function as called in line 234 and is described in Section 22.5. This time, the actual return value from the system call is in the saved EAX on the stack. The tracing process can use this to determine that it is after the system call.

242 this is the standard return path, which will be examined in Section 10.6.1.

10.4.3.4 Short circuit on invalid system call number

When the system detects that an invalid system call number has been supplied (line 201 of the code in Figure 10.22), the code shown in Figure 10.24, from `arch/i386/kernel/entry.S`, is executed.

```
243 badsys:
244     movl $-ENOSYS,EAX(%esp)
245     jmp ret_from_sys_call
```

Figure 10.24 Invalid system call number

244 the error number ENOSYS has been defined in the code in Figure 10.18. This writes to the copy of the EAX register saved on the stack.

245 this is the standard return path, which will be examined in Section 10.6.1.

10.5 Exception handler entry

The entry phase of the handlers for system calls has just been examined in some detail. This section will now consider the entry phase of the 20 other interrupts set up in Section 10.2.2.

The entry phase is written in assembler. Although it varies slightly from one to another, it always:

- puts the address of the second-level handler on the stack;

- builds a register save frame on the stack, in `pt_regs` format;

- sets DS and ES to point to the kernel data segment; the service function may use kernel data structures;

- gets a pointer to the `task_struct` of the current process (into EBX); the service function may write information into this;

- calls the service function.

The reader should refer to Section 10.3.1.1 while reading the following.

10.5.1 Divide error

The first-level handler for the divide error exception (number 0) is the assembly language routine shown in Figure 10.25, from `entry.S`. This occurs if the result of a divide instruction is too big to fit into the result operand or if the divisor is 0. The CS and EIP values on the stack point to the instruction that caused the exception. The CPU does not push any error code on the stack corresponding to this exception.

```
262  ENTRY(divide_error)
263      pushl $0
264      pushl $ SYMBOL_NAME(do_divide_error)
265      ALIGN
266  error_code:
267      pushl %ds
268      pushl %eax
269      xorl %eax,%eax
270      pushl %ebp
271      pushl %edi
272      pushl %esi
273      pushl %edx
274      decl %eax
275      pushl %ecx
276      pushl %ebx
277      cld
278      movl %es,%ecx
279      movl ORIG_EAX(%esp), %esi
280      movl ES(%esp), %edi
281      movl %eax, ORIG_EAX(%esp)
282      movl %ecx, ES(%esp)
283      movl %esp,%edx
284      pushl %esi
285      pushl %edx
286      movl $(__KERNEL_DS),%edx
287      movl %edx,%ds
288      movl %edx,%es
289      GET_CURRENT(%ebx)
290      call *%edi
291      addl $8,%esp
292      jmp ret_from_exception
```

Figure 10.25 Handler for the divide error exception

263 because the hardware does not automatically put an error code on the stack, an immediate value of 0 is pushed here, at the orig_eax position, to keep all the handlers compatible.

264 this pushes the address of the routine do_divide_error() onto the stack, at the xes position (see Section 11.1 for this function, regarding carrying out the actual handling of the exception). Note, however, that because of this the contents of ES are not saved (but see lines 278–282).

265 this macro was described in Section 1.2.2.1.

266–292 this code is common to all the exception handlers. It is dealt with here in the context of the first exception discussed but it is relevant to all the others, as they all jump to the `error_code:` label.

267–276 these build a register save frame on the stack, in `pt_regs` format (see Section 10.3.1.1). The interrupt mechanism itself has already pushed `SS` and `ESP`, followed by `EFLAGS`, `CS`, and `EIP`. Then either the hardware pushed an error code on the stack or the first-level interrupt handler pushed 0 (e.g. line 263). This takes the `orig_eax` place in the `struct pt_regs`. The first-level exception handler always pushes the address of the second-level handler (e.g. `do_divide_error` at line 264). This takes the `xes` place. These lines now push the remaining values to complete the `struct pt_regs`. Note that exception handlers do not use the SAVE_ALL macro.

268–269 the current contents of `EAX` are saved, and then `EAX` is zeroed.

274 `EAX` now has a value of -1. This is setting up an error code, which will be used at line 281.

278–282 the next part of the code is adjusting the values in `orig_eax` and `xes` on the stack.

278 the value in the `ES` segment register is saved temporarily in `ECX`, to be used at line 282.

279 the `orig_eax` field on the stack is the error code on the stack, pushed there either by the hardware or by the first-level handler. This is one of the parameters to the second-level handler, and we want to get it into the correct place on the stack for this. Here it is temporarily stored in a register (`ESI`), preparatory to pushing it back on the stack at line 284.

280 this gets the address of the second-level handler from the stack, into a register (`EDI`), preparatory to calling it at line 290.

281 the `orig_eax` location on the stack is set to -1. This is the default error code that will be passed back on return from the first-level handler.

282 the `xes` location on the stack now contains the value from the `ES` register, on entry. This is the value that should have been there all the time. It might seem more straightforward to have done a `pushl %es` at line 264, and then a `pushl $SYMBOL_NAME` at line 285, but remember that `error_code:` is a common routine used by all the exception handlers, each of which wants to call a different second-level handler. This causes the extra complexity.

283 this saves the current value of the stack pointer in `EDX`. As the stack was last adjusted at line 276, this is pointing to the beginning of the `pt_regs` structure on the stack.

284 this pushes the error code on entry (see line 279). This is the second parameter for the handler.

285 this pushes the pointer to the `struct pt_regs`. This is the first parameter for the handler.

286–288 this sets `DS` and `ES` to point to the kernel data segment. The handler may use kernel data structures.

289 this gets a pointer to the `task_struct` of the current process into `EBX`. This macro is described in Section 10.3.4.

290 this calls the second-level handler.

291   this throws away the last 8 bytes on the stack. These are the two 4-byte parameters pushed at lines 284 and 285.

292   this takes the standard return from exception handling (see Section 10.6.2).

10.5.2   Co-processor errors

The x87 co-processor can generate three different exceptions. The assembly language routines in Figure 10.26, from entry.S, show the first-level handlers for these.

```
294  ENTRY(coprocessor_error)
295      pushl $0
296      pushl $ SYMBOL_NAME(do_coprocessor_error)
297      jmp error_code
298
299  ENTRY(simd_coprocessor_error)
300      pushl $0
301      pushl $ SYMBOL_NAME(do_simd_coprocessor_error)
302      jmp error_code
303
304  ENTRY(device_not_available)
305      pushl $-1
306      SAVE_ALL
307      GET_CURRENT(%ebx)
308      movl %cr0,%eax
309      testl $0x4,%eax
310      jne device_not_available_emulate
311      call SYMBOL_NAME(math_state_restore)
312      jmp ret_from_exception
313  device_not_available_emulate:
314      pushl $0
315      call SYMBOL_NAME(math_emulate)
316      addl $4,%esp
317      jmp ret_from_exception
```

Figure 10.26   Exceptions raised by the co-processor

294–297   the co-processor error (number 16) means that a numeric error such as underflow or overflow has occurred in the floating point unit. It is reported by the *next* floating point instruction after the one that caused the error. The address on the stack points to the floating point instruction that was about to be executed. This is not the one that caused the exception; its address is in the floating point unit (FPU) instruction pointer register.

295   no error code is pushed on the stack by the CPU; the x87 FPU provides its own error information, so this line pushes a 0 to keep things consistent.

296   this puts the address of the do_coprocessor_error() function on the stack. The function itself is given in Section 11.8.1.

297   this is a common entry path to exception handlers (see Section 10.5.1).

299–302   Pentium processors have MMX instructions that act in an SIMD mode on 64-bit MMX registers. For example, the one instruction could treat the register as eight separate bytes and carry out the same operation on each byte in parallel. Errors in this part of the CPU generate the SIMD co-processor error (number 19). The saved address on the stack points to the faulting instruction in which the error condition was detected.

300   as no error code is provided by the hardware, a 0 is pushed to keep things consistent.

301   the handler will be described in Section 11.9.1.

302   this is a common entry path to exception handlers (see Section 10.5.1).

304–317   this is the first-level handler for the device-not-available exception (number 7). This interrupt is generated by the CPU when a floating point opcode is encountered in the instruction stream and it cannot be immediately executed. The saved address on the stack points to the floating point instruction that caused the exception.

305   the hardware does not supply an error code, so we supply −1, in the `orig_eax` position. The comment in the code says that this marks it as an interrupt, but it does not seem to be used anywhere.

306   see Section 10.3.2 for this macro. The previous line pushed a value into the `orig_eax` position on the stack. This macro pushes registers from ES to EBX, and loads DS and ES with a selector for the kernel data segment.

307   this gets a pointer to the `task_struct` of the current process into EBX (see Section 10.3.4).

308   the CR0 register contains bits that, among other things, control the operation of the floating point co-processor.

309   this checks if the math emulation (EM) bit is set in CR0. This is bit 2, 0100. If set to 1, then floating point instructions will raise a device-not-available interrupt. If cleared to 0 they will be sent to the co-processor to be executed. The TESTL instruction does a logical AND. It sets the zero bit in EFLAGS if the result is 0; otherwise, the zero bit is cleared.

310   if the math emulation bit was set (the exception was raised because there is no FPU), the zero flag will not be set, and this branch will be taken. The routine is at line 313.

311   otherwise, the bit was clear (the exception was raised because the state of the FPU was invalid). The `math_state_restore` routine is called. This function is described in Section 11.7.2. It writes appropriate values to the FPU registers.

312   this is the standard exit from exception handling (see Section 10.6.2).

313–317   this code is executed if the exception was raised because no hardware FPU is available.

314   if the math emulation bit is clear, then a 0 is pushed onto the stack. This is the parameter for the function called on the next line. However, it is not used by the `math_emulate()` function.

315   this calls the `math_emulate()` function, described in Section 11.7.1. This is badly named, as in fact it only prints a message saying no math emulation is available.

316   on return, the bottom 4 bytes on the stack are discarded. This is the parameter pushed at line 314.

317   this is the standard exit from exception handling (see Section 10.6.2).

10.5.3 Debug

The i386 architecture provides a facility for a programmer to set up and monitor a number of breakpoints in a program. When execution transfers to one of these addresses, the debug exception (number 1) is raised. The assembly language routine shown in Figure 10.27, from entry.S, is the first-level handler for this. The saved CS and EIP point to the instruction that generated the exception (e.g. single stepping, or data breakpoint) or to the following instruction (e.g. instruction breakpoint).

```
319  ENTRY(debug)
320      pushl $0
321      pushl $ SYMBOL_NAME(do_debug)
322      jmp error_code
```

Figure 10.27   Setting up to handle the debug exception.

320   as no error code is provided by the hardware, a 0 is pushed in order to keep things consistent.

321   this function is described in Section 11.2.2.

322   this code is used by all the exception handlers (see Section 10.5.1).

10.5.4 The nonmaskable interrupt

The source of this interrupt, unlike all the others considered in this chapter, is not the CPU. It is triggered by an electrical signal put on one of the CPU pins by some hardware outside the CPU, but, for historical reasons, it has always been treated as an exception, even though it really is a hardware interrupt. It is used to indicate a catastrophic error in the system, typically a memory parity error.

The assembly language routine shown in Figure 10.28, from entry.S, is the first-level handler for the nonmaskable interrupt (nmi; number 2). The saved CS and EIP on the stack point to the next instruction to be executed.

```
324  ENTRY(nmi)
325      pushl %eax
326      SAVE_ALL
327      movl %esp,%edx
328      pushl $0
329      pushl %edx
330      call SYMBOL_NAME(do_nmi)
331      addl $8,%esp
332      RESTORE_ALL
```

Figure 10.28   First-level handler for the nonmaskable interrupt

325 the hardware does not provide an error code. To keep the stack compatible, the contents of EAX are pushed, into the orig_eax position on the stack. This value is never used and is discarded by RESTORE_ALL at line 332.

326 this macro is described in Section 10.3.2. It pushes the remaining values to complete the struct pt_regs, beginning with ES and finishing with EBX. It also sets up DS and ES pointing to the kernel data segment.

327 this puts a copy of the stack pointer as it is at this stage – pointing to the register block on the stack – into EDX. This is needed a few lines later on, after another value has been pushed onto the stack.

328 this immediate value of 0 is an error code, the second parameter passed to the handler function called at line 330.

329 this is a pointer to the struct pt_regs on the stack, the first parameter to the handler function called at line 330.

330 this runs the second-level handler for the nmi (see Section 11.3.1).

331 this discards the bottom two entries on the stack after returning. These are the two parameters pushed at lines 328 and 329. This is really setting up for the next line, so that RESTORE_ALL will begin at the correct place on the stack.

332 this macro is described in Section 10.3.3. It restores values from the stack, beginning with EBX, up to ES, and discards orig_eax, so, when it calls IRET, the next item on the stack is EIP.

10.5.5 Exceptions requiring trivial handling

There are a number of exceptions that require only the most trivial entry phase. The first-level handlers for these exceptions are shown in Figure 10.29, from entry.S. No error code is provided by the CPU for any of them, so they all push a 0 on the stack to keep things compatible. The service functions called by all these are so similar that they are all generated by macros, as described in Section 11.1. They all use the standard entry to exception handling, as described in Section 10.5.1.

```
334  ENTRY(int3)
335      pushl $0
336      pushl $ SYMBOL_NAME(do_int3)
337      jmp error_code
338
339  ENTRY(overflow)
340      pushl $0
341      pushl $ SYMBOL_NAME(do_overflow)
342      jmp error_code
343
344  ENTRY(bounds)
345      pushl $0
346      pushl $ SYMBOL_NAME(do_bounds)
347      jmp error_code
348
```

```
349  ENTRY(invalid_op)
350      pushl $0
351      pushl $ SYMBOL_NAME(do_invalid_op)
352      jmp error_code
353
354  ENTRY(coprocessor_segment_overrun)
355      pushl $0
356      pushl $ SYMBOL_NAME(do_coprocessor_segment_overrun)
357      jmp error_code

387  ENTRY(machine_check)
388      pushl $0
389      pushl $ SYMBOL_NAME(do_machine_check)
390      jmp error_code
391
392  ENTRY(spurious_interrupt_bug)
393      pushl $0
394      pushl $ SYMBOL_NAME(do_spurious_interrupt_bug)
395      jmp error_code
```

Figure 10.29   Exceptions for which the computer processing unit provides no error code

334–337   the breakpoint exception (number 3) is generated by the INT3 instruction. This is a single-byte version of the generic INT x software interrupt. The CS and EIP values on the stack point to the next instruction after the INT3.

339–342   this is the first-level handler for the overflow exception (number 4). This exception is caused by the INTO machine instruction if the OF bit in EFLAGS is set to 1. This means that the last arithmetic instruction generated a result too large to fit into the destination register. The CS and EIP values on the stack point to the next instruction after the INTO.

344–347   the bounds-range-exceeded exception (number 5) is raised by the BOUND machine instruction if the value it is testing is outside the range specified. The CS and EIP values on the stack point to the BOUND instruction.

349–352   this is the first-level handler for the invalid-opcode exception (number 6). The address saved on the stack points to the first byte of the invalid instruction.

354–357   the co-processor segment overrun exception (number 9) is caused by a page or segment violation while handling an FPU instruction. The saved CS and EIP point to the instruction that caused the exception. This is only relevant on a 386. Later processors use the general protection exception instead (see Section 10.5.6).

387–390   this is the first-level handler for the machine-check exception (number 18). Pentium processors have a facility for detecting and reporting hardware errors, such as bus, parity, cache, and translation lookaside buffer errors. Saved values on the stack may not be associated with the error. The service function is discussed in Section 11.6.

392–395   this is the first-level handler for the spurious interrupt bug exception (number 15). This was only ever relevant with advanced programmable interrupt controllers (APICs); it is now gone from the Intel documentation. There is still a stub service function (see Section 11.5).

10.5.6 Exceptions with error code provided by the computer processing unit

There are seven exceptions for which the CPU itself pushes an error code on the stack, and the handling of these is even simpler; see Figure 10.30, from `entry.S`.

```
359  ENTRY(double_fault)
360        pushl $ SYMBOL_NAME(do_double_fault)
361        jmp error_code
362
363  ENTRY(invalid_TSS)
364        pushl $ SYMBOL_NAME(do_invalid_TSS)
365        jmp error_code
366
367  ENTRY(segment_not_present)
368        pushl $ SYMBOL_NAME(do_segment_not_present)
369        jmp error_code
370
371  ENTRY(stack_segment)
372        pushl $ SYMBOL_NAME(do_stack_segment)
373        jmp error_code
374
375  ENTRY(general_protection)
376        pushl $ SYMBOL_NAME(do_general_protection)
377        jmp error_code
378
379  ENTRY(alignment_check)
380        pushl $ SYMBOL_NAME(do_alignment_check)
381        jmp error_code
382
383  ENTRY(page_fault)
384        pushl $ SYMBOL_NAME(do_page_fault)
385        jmp error_code
```

Figure 10.30 Exceptions for which the computer processing unit provides an error code on the stack

359–361 the double-fault exception (number 8) means that a segment or page fault has occurred while the CPU is trying to report some other exception. It normally means that system tables have become corrupted. The saved values of CS and EIP on the stack are undefined. An error code of 0 is pushed on the stack by the hardware. The service function is described in Section 11.1.

363–365 the invalid TSS exception (number 10) can be raised when loading a selector from the task state segment (TSS; see Section 7.2.3). The address on the stack points to the instruction causing the fault. If the fault occurs as part of a task switch then it will point to the first instruction of the task. An error code (the index of the faulting selector) is pushed on the stack by the hardware. The service function is described in Section 11.1.

367–369 as the name implies, the segment-not-present exception (number 11) results from the presence bit being cleared in a segment descriptor being loaded into a segment register other than SS. There is a special exception for that; see the stack segment exception at line 371. The address on the stack points to the instruction causing the fault. If the fault occurs as part of a task switch, then it will point to the first instruction of the task. An error code is pushed on the stack by the hardware, the index of the faulting selector. The service function is described in Section 11.1.

371–373 the stack segment exception (number 12) results from the CPU detecting problems with the segment addressed by the SS register. The address saved on the stack points to the instruction that caused the exception. If it happened as part of a task switch, then it points to the first instruction of the new task. The specific problem is represented by the error code pushed on the stack by the CPU. This is the index of the faulting selector. If it is a limit violation, the error code is 0. This exception, with an error code of 0, can be used to indicate that the stack needs to be expanded. The service function is described in Section 11.1.

375–377 the general protection exception (number 13) is caused by some violation of the protection model not covered by more explicit exceptions. The address saved on the stack points to the instruction that caused the exception. If it happened as part of a task switch, then it points to the first instruction of the new task. The system also supplies an error code on the stack. If the fault condition was detected while loading a selector, this is the index of the selector; otherwise it is 0. The service function is considered in Section 11.4.

379–381 the alignment check exception (number 17) occurs when the processor detects an unaligned memory operand, while alignment checking was enabled. The saved address on the stack points to the instruction that caused the exception. An error code of 0 is always pushed on the stack by the CPU. The service function is described in Section 11.1.

383–385 this is the first-level handler for the page fault exception (number 14). The address on the stack points to the faulting instruction. This instruction is restartable, by an IRET. The CR2 register contains the address causing the fault, and an error code is also pushed on the stack. As this pertains to the memory manager it will not be considered any further here.

10.6 Returning from an interrupt

There is also generalised code provided for exiting from an interrupt, but this is much more complicated than the entry path. The obvious work, such as restoring the state of the machine as it was before the interrupt occurred, is relatively trivial. However, the designers decided that as this return path is traversed fairly frequently, it is a good place to do other tasks, unrelated to the interrupt, but that need to be done fairly frequently. These include checking for pending signals or if a reschedule is needed.

As a first cut at understanding this, there are three starting points and only one finishing point (see Figure 10.31), so we will look at each of these elements in turn and then try to put it all together.

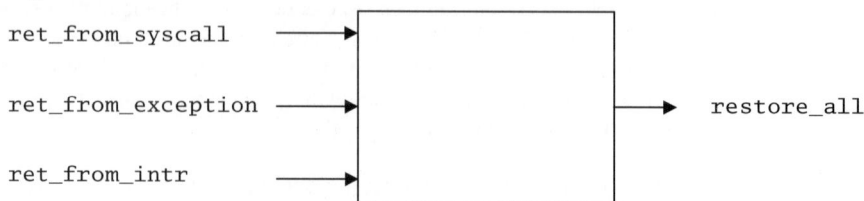

Figure 10.31 Exiting from interrupt handling

10.6.1 Returning from a system call

After a system call has been completed, and before a return to user mode, the code shown in Figure 10.32, from entry.S, is executed. Control either falls into this code segment when the system call returns to the first-level handler, from line 203 of Figure 10.22, or transfers here from other places on the return path from interrupt or exception handling. Basically, this code checks for two different conditions:

- The handling of the interrupt or system service may have caused the need_reschedule flag of the current process to be set. If so, the scheduler is called.

- There may be a signal pending for the current process. In that case, the signal handler is executed.

```
204  ENTRY(ret_from_sys_call)
205      cli
206      cmpl $0,need_resched(%ebx)
207      jne reschedule
208      cmpl $0,sigpending(%ebx)
209      jne signal_return
210  restore_all:
211      RESTORE_ALL
```

Figure 10.32   The default return path after a system call

In all cases, the code jumps out of the mainstream to handle these conditions, but it always returns again to some point on the mainstream, so control always leaves through the macro RESTORE_ALL, which finishes with the IRET instruction.

205   disabling interrupts means that the tests that follow are guaranteed to be atomic.

206–207   the need_resched offset has been defined in Section 10.3.5. If the need_resched field of the task_struct is not 0, then a reschedule is needed, so the scheduler is called. This code is discussed in Section 10.6.4.

208–209   the sigpending offset has been defined in Section 10.3.5. If the sigpending field of the task_struct is not 0, then a signal is pending and needs to be handled (Section 10.6.3).

211   this is the normal exit. The macro RESTORE_ALL was discussed in Section 10.3.3. It restores all the registers saved on the stack on entry, and executes IRET. This restores the EIP, CS, and EFLAGS values from the stack to the hardware registers. Restoring the EFLAGS value sets interrupt recognition to the state it was in before this interrupt occurred.

10.6.2 Returning from exceptions and interrupts

Up to this point, the assembler code being considered has dealt with system service calls. The exception handlers discussed in Section 10.5 also have exit phases of their own. Although these make use of some of the code already described, they do not use the ret_from_system_call entry point. Instead, they all use ret_from_exception;

hardware interrupt handlers use `ret_from_intr`. The code for both of these is shown in Figure 10.33, from `entry.S`.

```
248   ENTRY(ret_from_intr)
249        GET_CURRENT(%ebx)
250   ret_from_exception:
251        movl EFLAGS(%esp),%eax
252        movb CS(%esp),%al
253        testl $(VM_MASK | 3),%eax
254        jne ret_from_sys_call
255        jmp restore_all
```

Figure 10.33   Returning from an exception or an interrupt

248   a hardware interrupt handler can call this entry point directly.

249   the only purpose of this macro is to get the `task_struct` of the current process. For this macro, see Section 10.3.4.

250   an exception handler will already have a pointer to the `task_struct` in the EBX register, so it can begin here. The only purpose of this piece of code is to determine whether the CPU was already running in kernel mode before the interrupt or not. If so, we are dealing with a nested interrupt and want to terminate the processing of it as quickly as possible.

251   the value of EFLAGS saved on the stack is copied to EAX. This represents the state of the machine when the interrupt or exception occurred.

252   the CS offset has been defined in Section 10.3.1.2. The value in the CS register was not pushed by SAVE_ALL but was automatically put on the stack by the interrupt. Note that it is only moving the low-order byte into the low half of the AX register (AL). The three high-order bytes of EAX are now from the saved EFLAGS; the low byte is from the saved CS. The comment in the code refers to mixing EFLAGS and CS. This is setting up to test pieces of both at the same time.

253   we want to determine if the saved machine status on the stack shows that the CPU was in user mode when the interrupt or exception occurred. In protected mode, the value in CS is not a segment address; rather, it is a selector, or an index into a descriptor table. Only the high-order bits are used as an index; the two low-order bits indicate the protection level. If both of these are set then we are in user mode; otherwise we are in kernel mode. But there is one exception. If the machine was in vm86 mode, then CS contains a segment address, not a selector. The two low-order bits of this are just address bits – they have nothing to do with protection levels, so only if the VM_MASK bit is not set and the two low-order bits of CS are not set are we in kernel mode. The test does a bitwise AND between these 3 bits and the mixture in EAX. It sets the zero flag if the result is zero. Note that this test is not being performed on the current state of the processor, but on its state when the interrupt occurred. If the processor was either in vm86 mode, or user mode, or both, the result will be nonzero, so the zero flag will be clear. Only if the processor was in kernel mode will the result be 0; in that case the zero flag will be set.

254   this is an instruction to jump if the zero flag is clear. The machine was in vm86 or user mode when the interrupt occurred. The jump is to `ret_from_sys_call` (Section 10.6.1), which checks if the process should be rescheduled or has a signal pending.

255   the machine was already in kernel mode when the interrupt occurred; so this is a nested interrupt. In this case we do not check for reschedules or pending signals but jump directly to `restore_all` at line 210, shown in Figure 10.32.

The flow of control through this section is illustrated in Figure 10.34.

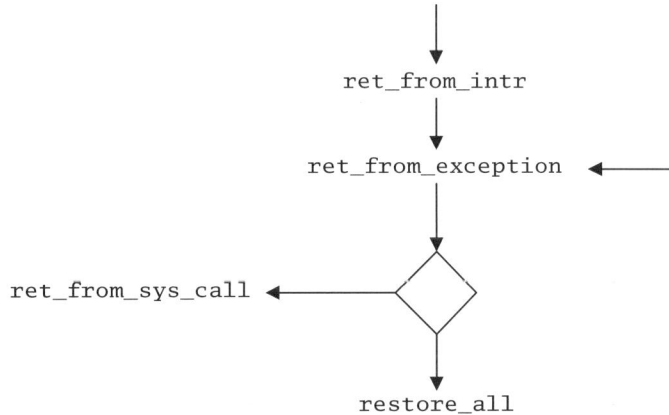

Figure 10.34   Returning from interrupts and exceptions

10.6.3   Detecting a pending signal

If a signal was found to be pending on the return from a system call (see Section 10.6.1), then the code shown in Figure 10.35, from `entry.S`, is executed.

```
214  signal_return:
215       sti
216       testl $(VM_MASK),EFLAGS(%esp)
217       movl %esp,%eax
218       jne v86_signal_return
219       xorl %edx,%edx
220       call SYMBOL_NAME(do_signal)
221       jmp restore_all
222
223       ALIGN
224  v86_signal_return:
225       call SYMBOL_NAME(save_v86_state)
226       movl %eax,%esp
227       xorl %edx,%edx
228       call SYMBOL_NAME(do_signal)
229       jmp restore_all
```

Figure 10.35   Signal handling when returning from system call

215 control normally transfers to this routine from line 209 in Figure 10.32, with interrupts disabled. Interrupts are enabled while signals are being handled.

216 VM_MASK was defined in Section 10.3.1.3. This is the virtual 8086 mode bit. EFLAGS is the offset of the saved EFLAGS register value on the stack frame, so this is checking if the VM_MASK bit was set in the flags register before the interrupt. If set, the processor was executing in virtual 8086 mode. If clear, the processor was executing in normal protected mode.

217 the stack pointer is copied to the EAX register. This line is setting up the first parameter for the call to do_signal() a few lines on.

218 if the processor was executing in virtual 8086 mode before the interrupt, then there is extra work to be done. The code for this is at line 224.

219 this has the effect of clearing the EDX register to 0. This is setting up the second parameter for the call to do_signal().

220 the prototype of the do_signal() function is given in arch/i386/kernel/signal.c as

```
31   asmlinkage int FASTCALL(do_signal(struct pt_regs *regs,
                                       sigset_t *oldset));
```

The FASTCALL macro is defined in <linux/kernel.h> as

```
51   #define FASTCALL(x) x __attribute__((regparm(3)))
```

This means that do_signal() has the regparm(3) attribute, that is, the compiler will pass it a maximum of three integer parameters in EAX, EDX, and ECX, instead of on the stack. As ESP has just been copied to EAX in line 217, the first parameter is the stack pointer, interpreted as a pointer to a struct pt_regs. This makes sense, as the last thing pushed on the stack is the registers, in the format specified by struct pt_regs. As EDX has just been zeroed on line 219, the second parameter is 0, interpreted as a pointer to sigset_t, so this is a NULL pointer. The function is not expecting a third parameter, so the value in ECX is irrelevant. The do_signal() function itself is described in Section 18.4.1.

221 this transfers control back to the normal return path, restore_all, back at line 210 of Figure 10.32.

223 this macro was described in Section 1.2.2.1.

224–229 there is an extra complication if a signal was found to be pending while the processor was running in virtual 8086 mode before the interrupt.

225 the save_v86_state() function, from Section 24.8.2, does just what it says. It is defined as FASTCALL, taking one parameter, a pointer to struct kernel_vm86_regs. This pointer should be in EAX and, in fact, the stack pointer was copied there at line 217. It copies saved values from the stack to the vm86_info field of the thread structure. The whole area of virtual 8086 mode will be dealt with in Section 23.4.

226 the stack pointer cannot be trusted to remain undisturbed across the call to save_v86_state, but EAX on return is still pointing to the bottom of the stack. This is also the first parameter for the do_signal() function.

227–229 these are as the protected mode code, at lines 219–221.

10.6.4 Rescheduling the current process

If the current process cannot continue after the interrupt, then the code in Figure 10.36, from
entry.S, is executed.

```
258  reschedule:
259      call SYMBOL_NAME(schedule)
260      jmp ret_from_sys_call
```

Figure 10.36 Current process needs to be rescheduled

258 we come here from line 207 of Figure 10.32 if the current process needs to be rescheduled.

259 the function schedule() is the main scheduler, as described in Section 7.3.

260 this jump is taken the next time the process is context switched in (see Section 10.6.1).

10.6.5 Summary

The flow of control throughout the whole of Section Figure 10.6 is illustrated in Figure
10.37. The bullets (•) indicate the three possible entry points. There is only one exit,
restore_all.

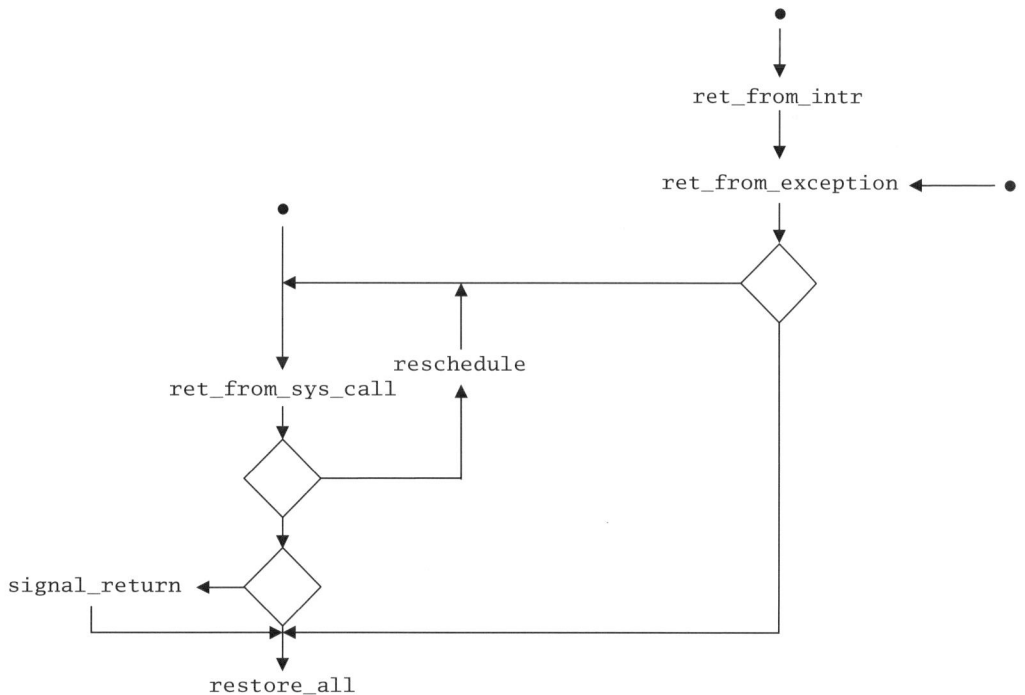

Figure 10.37 Exit path from interrupt handling

11

Exception handlers

The previous chapter examined the first-level handlers for the different exceptions that can be generated by the CPU. This chapter examines the second-level handlers supplied in the Linux kernel for each of these exceptions.

The general pattern of a exception handler is that it interrogates the hardware to learn as much as it can about the reason for the exception. Then it does as much as it can (if anything) to recover from whatever fault caused the exception. Finally, it sends a signal to the process running when the exception was generated, passing it back the information acquired from the hardware. This gives the user process the option of doing its own handling if it has an appropriate signal handler registered.

Twelve of these exceptions have such rudimentary second-level handling that almost identical code is used for them. This code is produced by a number of parameterised macros. This chapter will begin by looking at the handlers for these 12 'simple' exceptions. The remainder of the chapter will deal with the other 8 exceptions.

11.1 Generating generic exception handlers

As just stated, the second-level handling required for a number of the exceptions is very similar, so the developers have taken a shortcut and use macros to generate these handlers. This section examines how they are generated and what they do.

11.1.1 Generating the handlers

Individual second-level exception handlers are generated by using a number of macros. Figure 11.1, from `arch/i386/kernel/traps.c`, shows the 12 handlers involved. The first thing to remember here is that these are not macro definitions – each of these lines is expanded into the full macro code by the preprocessor, so, if you examine the code output by the preprocessor, you will find a full C function for each of these handlers.

```
338  DO_VM86_ERROR_INFO( 0, SIGFPE, "divide error", divide_error,
                                     FPE_INTDIV, regs->eip)
```

The Linux Process Manager. The Internals of Scheduling, Interrupts and Signals   John O'Gorman
© 2003 John Wiley & Sons, Ltd   ISBN: 0 470 84771 9

```
339  DO_VM86_ERROR( 3, SIGTRAP, "int3", int3)
340  DO_VM86_ERROR( 4, SIGSEGV, "overflow", overflow)
341  DO_VM86_ERROR( 5, SIGSEGV, "bounds", bounds)
342  DO_ERROR_INFO( 6, SIGILL, "invalid operand", invalid_op,
                                        ILL_ILLOPN, regs->eip)
343  DO_VM86_ERROR( 7, SIGSEGV, "device not available",
                                        device_not_available)
344  DO_ERROR( 8, SIGSEGV, "double fault", double_fault)
345  DO_ERROR( 9, SIGFPE, "coprocessor segment overrun",
                                    coprocessor_segment_overrun)
346  DO_ERROR(10, SIGSEGV, "invalid TSS", invalid_TSS)
347  DO_ERROR(11, SIGBUS, "segment not present",
                                        segment_not_present)
348  DO_ERROR(12, SIGBUS, "stack segment", stack_segment)
349  DO_ERROR_INFO(17, SIGBUS, "alignment check",
                            alignment_check, BUS_ADRALN, get_cr2())
```

Figure 11.1   Macros to generate 12 interrupt handlers

As will be seen shortly, the code generated by each of these macros essentially sends a signal to the current process. The parameters passed to the macro determine the signal that will be sent.

- The first parameter is the number of the exception. This always ends up in the `trap_no` field of `thread`.

- The second parameter is the signal to be sent to the current process.

- The third parameter is an error message. This will be output to the console by the handler if it has to abort the process.

- The fourth parameter is the specific part of the name to be given to the generated function. The full name will always be of the form do_*name*().

On lines 338, 342, and 349 there are two extra parameters. In these cases, the handlers use the extended signal mechanism to pass back extra information to the signal handler. These two parameters supply this extra information, which is copied into the `siginfo_t` structure passed to the signal handler. For the relevant background on signals, see Chapter 17.

11.1.2   The generating macros

There are four different generating macros shown in Figure 11.1, and each of these is now considered in turn.

11.1.2.1   Function sends a simple signal

The simplest of these generating macros is shown in Figure 11.2, from `arch/i386/kernel/traps.c`. This is provided with four parameters: the number of the exception for which it is a handler, the number of the signal to be sent by the handler, an error message to be output by the handler, and the name to be given to the handler function that it generates. The effect of this macro is to generate a C function called do_*name*, which, like all exception handlers, will be passed a pointer to a struct pt_regs, and an error code. This function merely calls do_trap(), passing it the appropriate parameters. These, and the do_trap() function itself, will be discussed in Section 11.1.3.

```
304  #define DO_ERROR(trapnr, signr, str, name)                          \
305  asmlinkage void do_##name(struct pt_regs * regs, long error_code)   \
306  {                                                                    \
307      do_trap(trapnr, signr, str, 0, regs, error_code, NULL)          \
308  }
```

Figure 11.2   Generating a wrapper function to send a simple signal

When do_trap() returns, this function returns to the first-level handler, always at line 291 of the error_code assembler routine (see Section 10.5.1). As can be seen from Figure 11.1, this macro is used to generate handlers for exceptions number 8, 9, 10, 11, and 12.

11.1.2.2   Function sends extra information with the signal

A slightly more complicated version of the generating macro is shown in Figure 11.3, from arch/i386/kernel/traps.c. This takes the extra step of setting up the fields in a siginfo_t structure and passing a pointer to this structure to do_trap(), as described in Section 11.1.3. The do_trap() function in turn makes this information available to the user-level signal handler. This macro is used to generate handlers for exceptions number 6 and 17.

```
310  #define DO_ERROR_INFO(trapnr, signr, str, name, sicode, siaddr)     \
311  asmlinkage void do_##name(struct pt_regs * regs, long error_code)   \
312  {                                                                    \
313      siginfo_t info;                                                  \
314      info.si_signo = signr;                                           \
315      info.si_errno = 0;                                               \
316      info.si_code = sicode;                                           \
317      info.si_addr = (void *)siaddr;                                   \
318      do_trap(trapnr, signr, str, 0, regs, error_code, &info);         \
319  }
```

Figure 11.3   Generating a wrapper function to send a signal with extra information

11.1.2.3   Exceptions that can occur in vm86 mode

There are versions of these generating macros used with exceptions that can occur in vm86 mode; see Figure 11.4, from arch/i386/kernel/traps.c.

```
321  #define DO_VM86_ERROR(trapnr, signr, str, name)                     \
322  asmlinkage void do_##name(struct pt_regs * regs, long error_code)   \
```

```
323  {                                                                        \
324      do_trap(trapnr, signr, str, 1, regs, error_code, NULL);             \
325  }
326
327  #define DO_VM86_ERROR_INFO(trapnr, signr, str, name, sicode, siaddr)\
328  asmlinkage void do_##name(struct pt_regs * regs, long ;error_code)   \
329  {                                                                        \
330      siginfo_t info;                                                     \
331      info.si_signo = signr;                                              \
332      info.si_errno = 0;                                                  \
333      info.si_code = sicode;                                              \
334      info.si_addr = (void *)siaddr;                                      \
335      do_trap(trapnr, signr, str, 1, regs, error_code, &info);            \
336  }
```

Figure 11.4   Generating wrapper functions for exceptions which can occur in vm86 mode

These are identical to the functions shown in the previous two figures, except for the fourth parameter, where they pass a 1 to do_trap(). The significance of this parameter will be seen in Section 11.1.3, when the do_trap() function is considered. These macros are used to generate handlers for exceptions number 0, 3, 4, 5, and 7.

11.1.3   The generic handler function

Each of the four macros described in the previous section generates a stub, which ends up calling one generic handler, do_trap(); see Figure 11.5, from arch/i386/kernel/traps.c.

```
269  static void inline do_trap(int trapnr, int signr, char *str,
270              int vm86, struct pt_regs * regs, long error_code,
             siginfo_t *info)
271  {
272      if (vm86 && regs->eflags & VM_MASK)
273          goto vm86_trap;
274      if (!(regs->xcs & 3))
275          goto kernel_trap;
276
277      trap_signal: {
278          struct task_struct *tsk = current;
279          tsk->thread.error_code = error_code;
280          tsk->thread.trap_no = trapnr;
281          if (info)
282              force_sig_info(signr, info, tsk);
283          else
284              force_sig(signr, tsk);
285          return;
286      }
287
```

```
288        kernel_trap: {
289              unsigned long fixup = search_exception_table
                                                    (regs->eip);
290              if (fixup)
291                    regs->eip = fixup;
292              else
293                    die(str, regs, error_code);
294              return;
295        }
296
297        vm86_trap: {
298              int ret = handle_vm86_trap ((struct kernel_vm86_
                                    regs *)regs, error_code, trapnr);
299              if (ret) goto trap_signal;
300              return;
301        }
302   }
```

Figure 11.5   Generic exception handler

269–270   One of the drawbacks of generic functions is that they usually require a large number of parameters, and this one is no exception. It is passed:

- the number of the exception it is handling;

- the number of the signal it is to send to the interrupted process;

- a pointer to an error message string;

- a flag indicating whether the particular exception can occur in vm86 mode (1) or not (0);

- a pointer to the saved register values on the stack;

- an error code;

- a pointer to a siginfo_t structure; if not NULL, this contains extended information for handling the signal.

272–273   if the vm86 parameter was 1, and the processor was running in vm86 mode when the interrupt occurred, then the special code for vm86 exceptions is executed, at line 297.

274–275   in a kernel mode selector, the two least significant bits are always 0. This is used to test if the computer processing unit (CPU) was running in kernel mode when the interrupt occurred. If so, then the special code for exceptions in the kernel is executed, at line 288.

277–286   this is the body of the function, the default exception handler.

278   this gets a pointer to the task_struct of the current process.

279–280   these fill in the error code and exception number fields of the thread structure, from the parameters passed in to this function.

281–284   these send the signal specified by the `signr` parameter to the current process. Either `force_sig_info()` (Section 18.2.1) or `force_sig()` (Section 18.2.7) is used for this, depending on whether extra information was supplied via the `info` parameter, or not.

285   however the signal was delivered, we return to the second-level exception handler, which called `do_trap()`.

288–295   this block of code is executed if the CPU was running in kernel mode when the exception occurred. In this case, no signal is sent. As the exception occurred in kernel mode, the user-level process knows nothing about it and cannot be expected to handle it.

289   this checks for predefined fixup code for a exception occurring at this point in the kernel code. As this table is maintained by the memory manager, we will not consider it any further here.

290–291   if there is such fixup code, then these lines adjust the `EIP` value on the stack so that after the return from interrupt, execution will continue at the new location.

292–293   otherwise, the process is killed, and the message passed in the `str` parameter, the values in the registers saved on the stack, and the error code are printed. For the `die()` function, see Section 11.10.4.2.

294   this line is reached only if it was possible to fix things up. It returns to the second-level handler, and hence to the first-level handler, but with a doctored-value of `EIP` saved on the stack.

297–301   this block of code is executed if the interrupt is one that can occur in vm86 mode and the CPU was running in vm86 mode when the interrupt occurred.

298   this special handler is described in Section 24.5.

299   if a nonzero value is returned, the normal processing path is taken, at line 277, a signal is sent, and so on.

300   otherwise, control returns directly to the second-level interrupt handler, which in all cases returns immediately to the appropriate first-level handler.

11.2 Debug

The i386 architecture provides a facility for a programmer to set up and monitor up to four breakpoints in a program. Whenever execution transfers to one of these addresses, the debug exception (number 1) is raised.

11.2.1 Debug registers

The CPU has a number of special registers, known as the debug registers. As these are manipulated by the exception handler it is necessary to understand something about them:

- DR0–DR3 each contain the address of one of the breakpoints.

- DR6 is the debug status register; after the exception is raised, it can be interrogated to determine the exception type and which of the four breakpoints raised this exception.

- DR7 is the debug control register. It controls the enabling and disabling of the four breakpoints, as well as the protection on all the other debug registers.

Figure 11.6, from `<asm-i386/debugreg.h>`, shows the definitions for various bits in the status register. The other bits are either reserved or are not of interest here.

```
17    #define DR_TRAP0      (0x1)
18    #define DR_TRAP1      (0x2)
19    #define DR_TRAP2      (0x4)
20    #define DR_TRAP3      (0x8)
21
22    #define DR_STEP       (0x4000)
```

Figure 11.6   Bits in the debug status register

17–20   these bits correspond to breakpoints 0–3, respectively. When a breakpoint raises an exception, the corresponding bit is set.

22   this is the single-step bit. When set (by the CPU) it indicates that the debug exception was raised by single stepping.

11.2.2 The debug exception handler

The function that actually handles the debug exception is shown in Figure 11.7, from `arch/i386/kernel/traps.c`. It checks for several unusual situations, before sending a signal to the current process.

```
477  asmlinkage void do_debug(struct pt_regs * regs, long error_code)
478  {
479      unsigned int condition;
480      struct task_struct *tsk = current;
481      siginfo_t info;
482
483      __asm____volatile__("movl %%db6,%0" : "=r" (condition));

486      if (condition & (DR_TRAP0|DR_TRAP1|DR_TRAP2|DR_TRAP3)) {
487          if (!tsk->thread.debugreg[7])
488              goto clear_dr7;
489      }
490
491      if (regs->eflags & VM_MASK)
492      goto debug_vm86;

495      tsk->thread.debugreg[6] = condition;

498      if (condition & DR_STEP) {

508      if ((tsk->ptrace & (PT_DTRACE|PT_PTRACED)) == PT_DTRACE)
509          goto clear_TF;
```

```
510        }

513        tsk->thread.trap_no = 1;
514        tsk->thread.error_code = error_code;
515        info.si_signo = SIGTRAP;
516        info.si_errno = 0;
517        info.si_code = TRAP_BRKPT;

522        info.si_addr = ((regs->xcs & 3) == 0) ?
523                (void *)tsk->thread.eip : (void *)regs->eip;
524        force_sig_info(SIGTRAP, &info, tsk);

529  clear_dr7:
530        __asm__("movl %0,%%db7"
531            : /* no output */
532            : "r"(0));
533        return;
534
535  debug_vm86:
536        handle_vm86_trap((struct kernel_vm86_regs *) regs,
                                                     error_code, 1);
537        return;
538
539  clear_TF:
540        regs->eflags &= ~TF_MASK;
541        return;
542  }
```

Figure 11.7   Handling the debug exception

480   this gets a pointer to the `task_struct` of the current process.

483   the information in the DR6 (status) register is moved into output parameter 0, the local `condition` variable, where it can be manipulated from now on. Note that in the Intel documentation these are DR registers; the AT&T mnemonic is db.

486–489   the four least significant bits of DR6 indicate which breakpoint caused the exception. Note that these bits are set by the CPU, even if the breakpoint condition has not been enabled by DR7. This block of code is executed only if at least one of the breakpoints raised the exception. It is designed to mask out spurious debug exceptions. These may result from a delay in setting or clearing DR7.

487–488   if the `debugreg[7]` field of the `thread` structure belonging to the current process is 0, then the program intended to turn off debugging, but this one slipped through before the control register was set. So this clears the hardware DR7 register, which turns off debugging, and returns to the first-level handler, see Section 10.5.1. For more on turning debugging on and off, see Chapter 22.

491–492   if the CPU was running in virtual 8086 mode when the exception occurred, then these lines execute a special handler for this and return to the first-level handler (see Section 10.5.1).

495 there is another bit of housekeeping to dispose of before handling the exception. This line saves the value of the debug status register DR6 into the `debug[6]` field of `thread`, where the debugger can see it (see Chapter 22 for more on debugging).

498–510 this block of code checks for a process single stepping itself.

498 `DR_STEP` is the single-step bit in the debug status register. When in single-step mode, the CPU will generate a debug exception after every instruction and set this bit to indicate the reason for the exception.

508 the i386 CPU has a TF (trap enable) bit in the `EFLAGS` register. When this bit is set, the CPU generates a debug exception after *every* instruction. This is known as single-stepping mode. The i386 TF flag can be modified by the process itself in user mode, allowing programs to debug themselves without the `ptrace()` interface. For this condition to be TRUE, the PT_DTRACE bit must be set (the TF flag has been set previously by the process) and the PT_PTRACED bit must be clear (the current process is not being traced) in the `ptrace` field of the current process. So, if the condition is TRUE, we have a process single stepping itself. In that case, the only handling done is to clear the TF bit in the saved copy of EFLAGS and return to the first-level handler. When the `EFLAGS` register is restored from the stack before the `IRET`, we want the TF bit to be clear. Otherwise, we just fall into the standard handling.

513–533 finally we have an exception we can handle. This is the heart of the function – sending a signal to the process.

513 the `trap_no` field in `thread` is set to 1, the number of the debug exception.

514 the error code value passed as a parameter is copied into `thread`.

515–523 this block of code sets up a `siginfo_t` to send to the current process. The signal to be sent is `SIGTRAP`, the error number is 0, and the code is `TRAP_BRKPT`, a breakpoint exception (see Chapter 17 on signals).

522–523 if the two low-order bits in the `xcs` field of the `regs` structure are 0, the process was executing in kernel mode when the exception occurred. In that case, we pass to the signal handler the value in the `eip` field of `thread`. This is the user `IP` on entry to the kernel; that is what the debugger can make sense of. Otherwise, the process was executing in user mode when the exception occurred, in which case we pass the saved `EIP` value on the stack.

524 this sends the `SIGTRAP` signal to the current process. The function is described in Section 18.2.1.

529–533 this block of code disables additional debug exceptions. They will be reenabled when the signal is delivered (see Section 18.4.5). Note that this is also done if it was a spurious exception.

530 this clears `DR7` by putting a 0 in it. This turns off debugging.

533 this returns to line 291 of the `error_code` routine (see Section 10.5.1).

535–537 this block of code is executed only if the CPU was running in virtual 8086 mode before the exception occurred.

536 this function is described in Section 24.5. As its name implies, it is a generic handler for exceptions which occur while in vm86 mode. Note that the saved registers on the stack are now being treated as a `struct kernel_vm86_regs`. The final parameter indicates the number of the exception – in this case 1.

539–541   this block of code is executed only if the handler was called by a single-stepping exception.

540   this clears the single-step bit in the saved copy of EFLAGS. If the user program wants to continue single stepping, it will have to explicitly set this bit again (in the signal handler).

11.3   Nonmaskable interrupt

The source of this interrupt, unlike all the others considered in this chapter, is not the CPU. It is triggered by an electrical signal put on one of the CPU pins by some hardware outside the CPU, but, for historical reasons, it has always been treated as a exception, even though it really is a hardware interrupt. It is used to indicate a catastrophic error in the system, typically a memory parity error.

The handling of this interrupt is quite complicated, and the discussion will be broken down into a number of parts. It begins with the second-level handler. That handler in turn uses a number of worker functions, which are also described.

11.3.1   Second-level handler for the nonmaskable interrupt

The function that actually handles the nonmaskable interrupt (nmi) is shown in Figure 11.8, from `arch/i386/kernel/traps.c`.

```
421   asmlinkage void do_nmi(struct pt_regs * regs, long error_code)
422   {
423        unsigned char reason = inb(0x61);
424
425        ++nmi_count(smp_processor_id());
426
427        if (!(reason & 0xc0)) {
428   #if CONFIG_X86_IO_APIC

433             if (nmi_watchdog) {
434                  nmi_watchdog_tick(regs);
435                  return;
436             }
437   #endif
438             unknown_nmi_error(reason, regs);
439             return;
440        }
441        if (reason & 0x80)
442             mem_parity_error(reason, regs);
443        if (reason & 0x40)
444             io_check_error(reason, regs);

449        outb(0x8f, 0x70);
450        inb(0x71);
```

```
451        outb(0x0f, 0x70);
452        inb(0x71);
453  }
```

Figure 11.8   The handler for the nonmaskable interrupt

421   although passed an error code by the first-level handler, the function never actually uses it.

423   input−output (IO) port 0x61, port B in the PC, has bits indicating the source or reason for an nmi (among other things):

- Bit 2 is for system board parity error checking; 0 means that it is enabled, 1 means that it is reset but disabled. It is a read−write bit.

- Bit 3 is for expansion board parity error checking; 0 for enabled, 1 for reset but disabled. It is also a read−write bit.

- Bit 6 is set to 1 when an expansion board parity error generates an nmi. Such an nmi is also known as an IOCHK error. If cleared to 0, this means that the expansion board has not generated an nmi. This bit is read only. It is reset by writing a 1 to bit 3.

- Bit 7 is set to 1 when a system memory parity error generates an nmi. If cleared to 0, this means that the system board has not generated an nmi. This bit is also read only. It is reset by writing a 1 to bit 2.

This line reads in the value from that port, using the function from Section 12.9.1.2.

425   this increments the cumulative count of non maskable interrupts on this CPU, using a macro described in Section 16.5.1.2. The smp_processor_id() macro, from Section 7.2.1.4, identifies the CPU on which this code is running.

427−440   this block of code deals with an unexplained nmi. The mask is 1100 0000. If both bits 6 and 7 are cleared in reason, then this nmi is not due to any parity error, so we go on to eliminate some other possible sources, before giving up. The logic of the code is complicated here by the preprocessor directives. The whole area of IO advanced programmable interrupt controllers (APICs) is dealt with in 13.7.6. It can be summarised as:

```
IF (not parity error) THEN
    IF (an IO APIC is installed) THEN
        IF (nmi_watchdog) THEN
            nmi_watchdog_tick (line 434)
            return
        ENDIF
    ENDIF
    unknown_nmi_error (line 438)
    return
ENDIF
```

433   if set to 1 by the initialisation code, this indicates that the IO APIC is broadcasting timer ticks, which are counted by a function described in Section 13.7.3.1.

434   in that case, the nmi may be a 'watchdog' interrupt, to check if the CPU is locked up. The function to check this is described in Section 11.3.2.2.

438   The next possibility is seen here. The function is described in Section 11.3.6. If a microchannel architecture (MCA) bus is present, this function checks that; otherwise, it prints an error message and returns.

441–442   control only comes here if either bit 6 or bit 7 of port 0x61 are set. Note that it is possible (though highly unlikely) for both to be set. If bit 7 is set, it indicates a memory parity error on the system board. The function to handle this is discussed in Section 11.3.3. It prints a warning message, and reenables parity detection.

443–444   if bit 6 is set, it indicates an IO check error – that is a parity error on an expansion board. The function to handle this is discussed in Section 11.3.4. It prints a warning message and reenables parity detection.

449–452   ports 0x70 and 0x71 are a peculiarity of the PC. Used together, they provide a way of reading or writing the CMOS chip. A write to port 0x70 indicates which location to access in the CMOS. A subsequent read or write to port 0x71 actually reads or writes the specified location in the CMOS. So far, this is no concern of ours here, but internal CMOS addresses are only 7 bits, leaving the most significant bit of port 0x70 unused, and, incredibly, the PC designers decided to use this bit for a totally unrelated purpose – to enable and disable nonmaskable interrupts. Bit 7 clear (0) means that nonmaskable interrupts are enabled. When set (1), nonmaskable interrupts are disabled. So, even an nmi can be blocked out, not by a software instruction within the CPU but by toggling external hardware that prevents the interrupt signal ever getting to the CPU. Lines 449–452 reenable nmi reporting.

449   setting bit 7 to 1 disables the nmi interrupt. The inb() and outb() functions are from Section 12.9.1.

450–452   these dummy reads are delays, to allow the hardware to settle down.

451   setting bit 7 to 0 enables the nmi interrupt.

11.3.2   Checking if the computer processing unit is locked up

The code in this section is compiled in (and is only called) only if there is an IO APIC in the system (see 13.7.6 for a full discussion of the IO APIC). Such an APIC can be used to broadcast timer ticks to each CPU, and a cumulative count of these is maintained on a per CPU basis. When in this mode, the APIC periodically broadcasts watchdog interrupts on the nmi line to all CPUs in the system. It is these nonmaskable interrupts that are being dealt with here.

11.3.2.1   Data structures

The global data structures shown in Figure 11.9, from arch/i386/kernel/nmi.c, are used by the function discussed next, in Section 11.3.2.2.

```
27    unsigned int              nmi_watchdog = NMI_NONE;
```

```
28  static unsigned int      nmi_hz = HZ;
29  unsigned int             nmi_perfctr_msr;

229 static spinlock_t        nmi_print_lock = SPIN_LOCK_UNLOCKED;

246 static unsigned int
247                          last_irq_sums [NR_CPUS],
248                          alert_counter [NR_CPUS];
```

Figure 11.9 Data structures for nonmaskable interrupt (nmi) watchdog

27 this is a flag to indicate whether the watchdog is enabled or not. It is statically initialised to NMI_NONE (not enabled) but would be set to some other value (indicating the source of the interrupt) by the startup code.

28 this is the frequency at which the watchdog nmi will be generated. It is statically initialised here to HZ (50), but after startup checks it is reduced to a more reasonable value of 1.

29 the address of the machine-specific performance counter register which is to be reset by the watchdog nmi handler is written to this variable by the startup code.

229 this spinlock is used to guarantee mutual exclusion in the handler function while it is writing to the console.

246–248 These arrays maintain statistics for the handler function on a per CPU basis. Note they are static – they retain information across successive calls to the function.

247 the last_irq_sums[] array contains the cumulative number of watchdog nonmaskable interrupts received by each CPU at the last time the handler was called.

248 the alert_counter[] array is used to track the number of times the handler function has been called by specific CPU.

11.3.2.2 Handler for the watchdog nonmaskable interrupt

The function shown in Figure 11.10, from arch/i386/kernel/nmi.c, is called by the nmi handler when it cannot identify any other reason for an nmi. It checks if the count for this CPU is incrementing. If not, then the CPU has some problem.

```
262 void nmi_watchdog_tick(struct pt_regs * regs)
263 {

269     int sum, cpu = smp_processor_id();
270
271     sum = apic_timer_irqs[cpu];
272
273     if (last_irq_sums[cpu] == sum) {

278         alert_counter[cpu]++;
279         if (alert_counter[cpu] == 5*nmi_hz) {
```

```
280                        spin_lock(&nmi_print_lock);

285                        bust_spinlocks(1);
286                        printk("NMI Watchdog detected LOCKUP on CPU%d,
                                                  registers:\n", cpu);
287                        show_registers(regs);
288                        printk("console shuts up Ò.\n");
289                        console_silent();
290                        spin_unlock(&nmi_print_lock);
291                        bust_spinlocks(0);
292                        do_exit(SIGSEGV);
293                    }
294          } else {
295              last_irq_sums[cpu] = sum;
296              alert_counter[cpu] = 0;
297          }
298          if (nmi_perfctr_msr)
299              wrmsr(nmi_perfctr_msr,-(cpu_khz/nmi_hz*1000),-1);
300  }
```

Figure 11.10   Checking if the computer processing unit is locked up

269   this gets the identification (ID) number of the CPU on which we are running (see Section 7.2.1.4).

271   this array is updated every time an APIC timer interrupt is received (see Section 13.7.3.1).

273   if the value has not changed since the last time this function was called, then it looks like this CPU is stuck, so the block of code at lines 278–293 is executed.

278   this increments the alert counter for this CPU. It will wait for a number of irqs to come in and check the count of timer interrupts each time before taking serious action.

279–292   if this interrupt has occurred 5 * nmi_hz (5) times, then this code takes action and tries to get a message out; otherwise, do nothing.

280   the lock is declared in Section 11.3.2.1. It is used to make lines 285–289 a critical section so that no other CPU executing this function at the same time can get in there. In that way a coherent console message is guaranteed.

285   this function, part of the IO subsystem, unlocks any spinlocks that might prevent a message getting to the console.

286–288   this message identifies the CPU that has locked up and prints the values of the registers as saved on the stack. The show_registers() function is described in Section 22.6.4.

289   the console_silent() function turns the console loglevel down, so that everything is filtered out. This is part of IO subsystem so it will not be considered further here.

291   when called with a parameter of 0, this function ensures that the kernel logging daemon klogd is woken up, to take note of the message just printed.

292 this terminates the process, sending a `SIGSEGV` code back to its parent (see Section 9.1).

295–296 this block of code is executed if the test at line 273 is `FALSE` (i.e. if the current sum of irqs is greater than the previous sum). The CPU is not stuck, so it just updates the static variables and returns.

295 this remembers the most recent total of irqs for this CPU is in `sum`, from line 271. That value is saved in the static array, ready for the next time the function is called by this CPU.

296 this sets the alert counter for this CPU back to 0. The next time this function is called by the current CPU, it will wait another 5 times before printing a warning message.

298–299 these lines are executed only if the processor has a nmi performance counter machine-specific register. It writes the number of CPU cycles between watchdog ticks.

11.3.3 Parity error on main memory board

If the non maskable interrupt was caused by a memory parity error on the main board, the function shown in Figure 11.11, from `arch/i386/kernel/traps.c`, is called. It prints a warning message and reenables parity error detection.

```
380  static void mem_parity_error(unsigned char reason, struct
                                                       pt_regs * regs)
381  {
382       printk("Uhhuh. NMI received. Dazed and confused, but
                                              trying to continue\n");
383       printk("You probably have a hardware problem with your RAM
                                                         chips\n");

386       reason = (reason & 0xf) | 4;
387       outb(reason, 0x61);
388  }
```

Figure 11.11 Clearing and disabling the memory parity bit

380 the `reason` parameter is a byte read from port `0x61`, port B of the PC. The `pt_regs` structure on the stack is never used.

386 the four high-order bits of `reason` are cleared. These are read-only bits anyway. The four low-order bits are not affected. Bit 2 is set. This clears system board parity detection (bit 7) but leaves it disabled. The user has been warned that there is a problem; we do not want to be overwhelmed with repetitions of the same interrupt.

387 then this value is then written to IO port `0x61`, port B of the PC.

11.3.4 Parity error on an expansion card

If an nmi is caused by an IO check error (parity error on an expansion card), then the code in Figure 11.12, from `arch/i386/kernel/traps.c`, is executed.

```
390  static void io_check_error(unsigned char reason,
                                              struct pt_regs * regs)
391  {
392      unsigned long i;
393
394      printk("NMI: IOCK error (debug interrupt?)\n");
395      show_registers(regs);

398      reason = (reason & 0xf) | 8;
399      outb(reason, 0x61);
400      i = 2000;
401      while (-i) udelay(1000);
402      reason &= ~8;
403      outb(reason, 0x61);
404  }
```

Figure 11.12   Processing an input–output check error

390   the `reason` parameter is a byte read from port 0x61, port B of the PC.

395   this function prints the saved contents of the CPU registers on the console. It is described in Section 22.6.4.

398   this clears the four high-order bits in `reason`. These are read-only bits anyway. The four low-order bits are not affected. Bit 3 is set. This clears expansion board parity detection (bit 6), but leaves it disabled. It will be enabled at line 403.

399   this writes that value to IO port 0x61, port B of the PC.

400–401   each call to `udelay()` is 1000 microseconds, or 1 millisecond, so the whole loop delays for 2000 ms, or 2 seconds. Expansion board parity detection is left disabled for this time, in the hope that a transient fault may clear itself.

402–403   this clears bit 3 in `reason` and writes it to port 0x61. This enables parity detection again.

11.3.5   Unidentifiable reason for nonmaskable interrupt

Sometimes the operating system just will not be able to determine what has caused an nmi interrupt (line 438 of Section 11.3.1). The code shown in Figure 11.13, from `arch/i386/kernel/traps.c`, shows how that case is handled.

```
406  static void unknown_nmi_error(unsigned char reason,
                                              struct pt_regs * regs)
407  {
408  #ifdef CONFIG_MCA

411      if( MCA_bus ) {
412          mca_handle_nmi();
413          return;
414      }
```

```
415 #endif
416     printk("Uhhuh. NMI received for unknown reason %02x.\n",
                                                    reason);
417     printk("Dazed and confused, but trying to continue\n");
418     printk("Do you have a strange power saving mode
                                              enabled?\n");
419 }
```

Figure 11.13 Handling an unknown nonmaskable interrupt (nmi) error

406 The reason parameter is a copy of PC port B (port 0x61). The pointer to the registers on the stack is never used.

408–415 if there is an MCA bus (as used in the PS/2) in the machine, that may be the cause of the interrupt, so that is checked. This is a last-ditch effort, but it might actually be able to figure out who the 'guilty party' is.

412 the function is part of the IO manager and will not be considered here.

416–418 if there is not an MCA bus installed, then a message is printed.

416 this prints the `reason` bitmap, in hexadecimal. It might have been more meaningful to print it in binary.

11.4 General protection

The general protection exception (number 13) is caused by some violation of the protection model that is not covered by the more explicit exceptions. The address saved on the stack points to the instruction that caused the exception. If it happened as part of a context switch, then it points to the first instruction of the new process. Figure 11.14, from `arch/i386/kernel/traps.c`, shows the function that actually handles the general protection exception. It singles out two special cases; otherwise it sends a SIGSEGV signal to the current process.

```
351 asmlinkage void do_general_protection(struct pt_regs * regs,
                                          long error_code)
352 {
353     if (regs->eflags & VM_MASK)
354         goto gp_in_vm86;
355
356     if (!(regs->xcs & 3))
357         goto gp_in_kernel;
358
359     current->thread.error_code = error_code;
360     current->thread.trap_no = 13;
361     force_sig(SIGSEGV, current);
362     return;
363
364 gp_in_vm86:
```

```
365              handle_vm86_fault((struct kernel_vm86_regs *) regs,
                                                        error_code);
366              return;
367
368  gp_in_kernel:
369          {
370          unsigned long fixup;
371          fixup = search_exception_table(regs->eip);
372          if (fixup) {
373                  regs->eip = fixup;
374                  return;
375          }
376          die("general protection fault", regs, error_code);
377          }
378  }
```

Figure 11.14   Handler for the general protection exception

351   the error_code parameter was originally supplied by the CPU. If the fault condition was detected while loading a selector, this is the index of the selector; otherwise, it is 0.

353–354   if the VM_MASK bit is set in the copy of EFLAGS on the stack, then the CPU was running in virtual 8086 mode when the exception occurred. There is special handling for this case at line 364.

356–357   if the two least significant bits are clear (0) in the copy of CS (the selector for the code segment) on the stack, then the CPU was running in kernel mode when the exception occurred. There is special handling for this case at line 368.

359–362   this is the normal handling for this exception.

359–360   these copy the error code supplied by the CPU and the number of this exception (13) into the thread structure of the current process.

361   this sends SIGSEGV to the current process. This function, which delivers the signal even if the process has it blocked out, is described in Section 18.2.7.

362   this returns to line 291 of the error_code routine (see Section 10.5.1).

364–366   this block of code is only executed if the CPU was running in vm86 mode when the interrupt occurred. The function will be considered in Section 24.6. It then returns to the error_code routine at line 291 (see Section 10.5.1).

368–377   this block of code is executed only if the CPU was running in kernel mode when the interrupt occurred.

371   this function is specific to the memory manager and so will not be considered in detail. A table of kernel instructions that can potentially generate general protection violations is maintained, and for each one there is a corresponding routine to recover from the error. This function returns the address of the appropriate fixup function, if there is one.

372–375   if it can be fixed up, these lines adjust the value of EIP on the stack and return to the error_code routine that called this function. The eventual IRET there will resume execution at the fixup function.

376 if a NULL pointer was returned at line 371, the error cannot be fixed up – so the process is killed off. The die() function is described in Section 11.10.4.2.

11.5 Spurious interrupt

Figure 11.15, from arch/i386/kernel/traps.c, shows the trivial handler for the spurious interrupt bug. Because there is no need to warn about this any longer, it compiles to a NULL procedure – the printk() line is not compiled into the code.

```
682  asmlinkage void do_spurious_interrupt_bug(struct pt_regs
683                               *regs, long error_code)
684  {
685  #if 0
686
687  printk("Ignoring P6 Local APIC Spurious Interrupt Bug...\n");
688  #endif
689  }
```

Figure 11.15 Handling the spurious interrupt bug

11.6 Machine check

Pentium processors have a facility for detecting and reporting hardware errors, such as bus, parity, cache, and translation lookaside buffer errors. The CPU has several banks of registers for recording such errors, and it reports them by means of the machine check exception. It is not generally possible to restart the processor reliably after such an exception; but the handler can collect information from the banks of registers and display it. Saved register values on the stack may not be associated with the error.

Different handlers are provided for different hardware configurations. To link these into the kernel, a static global pointer is provided that is assigned the address of the handler actually installed. This section describes that linking mechanism and then the generic handler for the Intel architecture, which is somewhat complex. Finally, there is a description of the worker functions used to read and write the machine-specific registers involved in handling this exception.

11.6.1 Wrapper for machine check handler

Figure 11.16, from arch/i386/kernel/bluesmoke.c, shows the mechanism which allows different machine check handlers to be configured into the kernel, for different models of CPU.

```
96  static void unexpected_machine_check(struct pt_regs * regs,
                               long error_code)
97  {
```

```
98          printk(KERN_ERR "CPU#%d: Unexpected int18
                        (Machine Check).\n", smp_processor_id());
99     }

105  static void (*machine_check_vector)(struct pt_regs *,
                        long error_code) = unexpected_machine_check;
106
107  asmlinkage void do_machine_check(struct pt_regs * regs,
                                            long error_code)
108  {
109      machine_check_vector(regs, error_code);
110  }
```

Figure 11.16   Wrapper for machine check handler

96–99   this is the default machine check handler, which merely prints a warning message. It should never be called in practice.

105   this function pointer is statically initialised pointing to the unexpected_machine_check() function (lines 96–99). It is normally overwritten by the initialisation code and pointed to intel_machine_check() (see Section 11.6.2).

107–110   this function is called by the first-level handler for the machine check exception. It in turn calls whatever function has been assigned to the machine_check_vector function pointer on line 105.

11.6.2   Second-level handler for machine check

Figure 11.17, from arch/i386/kernel/bluesmoke.c, shows the generic handler for the machine check exception. It prints debugging information on the console and, depending on the seriousness of the problem, either shuts down or continues.

```
15   static int banks;
16
17   void intel_machine_check(struct pt_regs * regs, long error_code)
18   {
19       int recover=1;
20       u32 alow, ahigh, high, low;
21       u32 mcgstl, mcgsth;
22       int i;
23
24       rdmsr((MSR_IA32_MCG_STATUS, mcgstl, mcgsth);
25       if(mcgstl&(1<<0))
26           recover=0;
27
28       printk(KERN_EMERG "CPU %d: Machine Check Exception:
                        %08x%08x\n", smp_processor_id(), mcgsth, mcgstl);
29
30       for(i=0;i<banks;i++)
```

```
31     {
32          rdmsr(MSR_IA32_MC0_STATUS+i*4,low,high);
33          if(high&(1<<31))
34          {
35              if(high&(1<<29))
36                  recover|=1;
37              if(high&(1<<25))
38                  recover|=2;
39              printk(KERN_EMERG "Bank %d: %08x%08x", i, high, low);
40              high&=~(1<<31);
41              if(high&(1<<27))
42              {
43                  rdmsr(MSR_IA32_MC0_MISC+i*4, alow, ahigh);
44                  printk("[%08x%08x]", alow, ahigh);
45              }
46              if(high&(1<<26))
47              {
48                  rdmsr(MSR_IA32_MC0_ADDR+i*4, alo, ahigh);
49                  printk(" at %08x%08x",
50     high, low);
51              }
52              printk("\n");
53
54              wrmsr(MSR_IA32_MC0_STATUS+i*4, 0UL, 0UL);
55
56              wmb();
57          }
58     }
59
60     if(recover&2)
61          panic("CPU context corrupt");
62     if(recover&1)
63          panic("Unable to continue");
64     printk(KERN_EMERG "Attempting to continue.\n");
65     mcgstl&=~(1<<2);
66     wrmsr(MSR_IA32_MCG_STATUS,mcgstl, mcgsth);
67     }
```

Figure 11.17   Handler for the machine check exception

15   the value of banks has been set at boot time. There are 4, 5, or 6 banks of registers, depending on the model of processor.

19   bits in this recover variable will be set to designate the level of seriousness encountered as the banks are read. Action will then be taken, depending on the bits set. The default is set up here as not recoverable (bit 0 set).

24   the rdmsr()macro reads from a machine-specific register (see Section 11.6.4). Here it reads two 32-bit values from the machine check status register, which describes the state of the CPU after a machine check exception has occurred. The high-order 32 bits are written to `mcgsth`; the low-order 32 bits to `mcgstl`.

25   this checks the value just read, to determine if it is possible to recover from the fault. Bit 0 is the restart IP valid flag. When set, the program can be restarted at the address pushed on the stack; otherwise, it cannot. The remaining 63 bits of this register are not defined.

26   if it is possible to recover, this changes the default value for `recover` to 0.

28   this prints a warning message at emergency priority, giving the ID of the CPU on which we are running (see Section 7.2.1.4) and the high-order and low-order 32 bits of the machine check status register. These are printed as 16 consecutive hex nibbles. This is information overload – only one of all of these bits is defined.

30–58   there are 4, 5, or 6 banks of registers, depending on the model of processor. This loop will interrogate all of them.

32   each bank contains four 64-bit registers. The second register in each bank is the bank status register. The symbolic constant gives the address of that register for bank 0; the `i*4` points to the corresponding register in each successive bank. It contains valid information if its valid flag (bit 63) is set. For the `rdmsr()` macro, which reads from a machine-specific register, see Section 11.6.4.

33   the most significant bit of `high` is the valid bit. If this is clear, the particular bank has no information about any error. We just go around the loop again and check the next bank.

34–57   otherwise, this bank has valid error information; this block of code deals with it.

35–36   bit 29 of `high` is the error uncorrected bit. When set, it means that the CPU did not correct the error condition. In that case we are unable to continue, so we set bit 0 of `recover`, whether set or not beforehand (from a previous iteration of the loop). Remember, bit 0 set in `recover` means we are unable to recover.

37–38   bit 25 of `high` is the processor context corrupt bit; when set, it indicates that the state of the processor might have been corrupted by the error condition, so it cannot be reliably restarted. In that case, we set bit 1 of `recover`, whether set or not (from a previous iteration of the loop). Bit 1 in `recover` is the 'cannot restart' bit.

39   this prints a warning message, identifying the bank, and the high-order and low-order 32 bits of the bank status register. Again, these are printed as 16 consecutive hex nibbles.

40   we have recognized the problem; this line clears the most significant bit of `high` (the valid bit).

41–45   this code is executed only if bit 27 of `high` is set. This is the `MISCV` flag. It means that the fourth machine-specific register in the bank, `MISC`, contains valid information.

43   this reads from the `MISC` register. This contains additional information describing the machine check error. Note that, as with all these reads, the low-order 32 bits come first.

44   this prints the values in the `MISC` register as 16 consecutive hex nibbles.

46–51   this code is executed only if bit 26 of `high` is set, the `ADDRV` flag. It means that the third machine-specific register (ADDR) contains valid information.

48   this reads from the ADDR register. This register contains the address of the code or data memory location that produced the machine check error.

49–50   these lines print the values in the ADDR register as 16 consecutive hex nibbles, so the format of the message is `[error code] at address`, but the code here is actually printing `high` and `low`, the contents of the bank status register.

52   this terminates the information about this bank with a new line.

54   this clears all 64 bits in the status register for this bank. Intel insists that operating system software is responsible for clearing these status registers by explicitly writing all 0 values after handling an error.

56   this guarantees that all the assignments have actually been written to memory before going around the loop again. The `wmb()` macro is architecture specific. On the 386 it does not actually do anything, as Intel CPUs guarantee that all writes are seen in program order.

60–61   this only happens if the processor context corrupt bit was set in one or more of the bank status registers (see line 38). If the CPU context is corrupt and we cannot continue then we exit with the message. The `panic()` function reboots the machine.

62–63   this is a slightly less serious situation. We still are unable to continue, but at least the CPU context is not corrupt. We exit with the message.

64   we only get to this line if all bits are clear in `recover`; we try to continue. This handler is unusual in that it does not send a signal to the user process.

65   this clears bit 2 of `msgstl`. This, the 'machine check in progress' flag, can be written to. It is left set while handing the exception to prevent another machine check event overwriting the data in the banks. If such an event occurs while this bit is set, it will cause the processor to shut down.

66   this write to the machine-check status register changes only 1 bit. The `wrmsr()` macro is described in Section 11.6.4.

11.6.3   Machine-specific registers

The addresses of all the machine-specific registers used by Linux are defined as literal constants in `<asm-i386/msr.h>`. The ones used in the previous section are shown in Figure 11.18.

```
57    #define MSR_IA32_MCG_STATUS        0x17a

70    #define MSR_IA32_MC0_STATUS        0x401
71    #define MSR_IA32_MC0_ADDR          0x402
72    #define MSR_IA32_MC0_MISC          0x403
```

Figure 11.18   Machine-specific registers

57 this is the machine check status register, which describes the state of the CPU after a machine check exception has occurred:

- Bit 0 indicates whether the program can be restarted (1) or not (0).

- Bit 2 set indicates that a machine check exception was generated; this bit can be (and is) cleared by software.

70 this is the bank status register for bank 0:

- Bit 25 indicates whether the CPU context has been corrupted (1) or not (0).

- Bit 26 indicates whether the third register in the bank has valid information (1) or not (0).

- Bit 27 indicates whether the fourth register in the bank has valid information (1) or not (0).

- Bit 29 indicates whether the CPU corrected the error (0) or not (1).

- Bit 31 is a status bit; only if this is set are any of the other bits valid.

71 this is the ADDR register for bank 0. It may contain the address of the code or data memory location that produced the machine check error.

72 this is the MISC register for bank 0. This may contain additional information describing the machine check error.

11.6.4   Reading and writing machine-specific registers

Two macros are provided in <asm-i386/msr.h> for reading and writing machine-specific registers (see Figure 11.19).

```
10   #define rdmsr(msr,val1,val2)                \
11         __asm____volatile__("rdmsr"     \
12         : "=a" (val1), "=d" (val2)            \
13         : "c" (msr))
14
15   #define wrmsr(msr,val1,val2)                \
16         __asm____volatile__("wrmsr"     \
17         : /* no outputs */                    \
18         "c" (msr), "a" (val1), "d" (val2))
```

Figure 11.19   Macros to read and write machine-specific registers

11 The RDMSR instruction reads from a machine-specific register. The register to read is specified by the value in ECX. The contents of the machine-specific register is copied into EDX:EAX.

12 this line specifies the two output parameters: val1 mapped onto EAX ("a"), and val2 mapped onto EDX ("d").

13 there is one input parameter, msr, mapped onto ECX ("c").

16 the WRMSR instruction writes to a machine-specific register. The register to be written is specified by ECX. The value to be written is in EDX:EAX.

17 this macro has no output parameters.

18 this line specifies the three input parameters: `msr` mapped onto ECX, `val1` mapped onto EAX, and `val2` mapped onto EDX.

11.7 Device not available

This interrupt is generated by the CPU when a floating point opcode is encountered in the instruction stream and it cannot be immediately executed. There are two possible reasons for this:

- The floating point co-processor is not installed. This would be very rare. It would occur on a 386 that did not have a corresponding 387 floating point unit (FPU). The operating system handles this situation by printing a warning message and sending SIGFPE to the process.

- This interrupt is more typically generated when the FPU detects that the values in its registers are not valid. Such a situation results from the lazy policy adopted by the Linux context switcher.

The first-level handler (Section 10.5.2) determined the reason for the interrupt and called the appropriate second-level handler. Each of these is now examined in turn.

11.7.1 No floating point unit present

If the math emulation bit is clear in CR0, there is no FPU, or math emulation. In that case the function shown in Figure 11.20, from `arch/i386/kernel/traps.c`, is called directly by the first-level handler for the device not available exception. It prints a warning message and sends SIGFPE to the current process, so the name of the function is rather misleading.

```
712  asmlinkage void math_emulate(long arg)
713  {
714      printk("math-emulation not enabled and no coprocessor
                                                      found.\n");
715      printk("killing %s.\n", current->comm);
716      force_sig(SIGFPE, current);
717      schedule();
718  }
```

Figure 11.20 Killing the current process for lack of floating point unit

712 although the function is actually passed an argument, it does not use it.

715   the `comm` field in the `task_struct` contains the name of the program being executed by the current process.

716   the `force_sig()` function, described in Section 18.2.7, sends the signal even if the process has it blocked out.

11.7.2   Floating point unit registers not valid

The `math_state_restore()` function shown in Figure 11.21, from `arch/i386/kernel/traps.c`, handles the lazy context switch case. There are two further possibilities. The process may have used the FPU at some previous stage in its execution, in which case valid values for the FPU registers are stored in its `thread` structure. It is also possible that it has not used the FPU before, in which case the FPU registers have to be loaded with initial values. These two possibilities are dealt with in later subsections.

```
698   asmlinkage void math_state_restore(struct pt_regs regs)
699   {
700           __asm____volatile__("clts");
701
702           if (current->used_math) {
703                   restore_fpu(current);
704           } else {
705                   init_fpu();
706           }
707           current->flags |= PF_USEDFPU;
708   }
```

Figure 11.21   Updating the floating point register values

698   note that the parameter `struct pt_regs` is passed by value. This is what is actually on the stack, it did not have to be pushed there by the caller. But note also that the function never actually uses it.

700   the CLTS instruction clears the task-switched flag in the CR0 register. It is used to minimise the overhead of context switching when the FPU is used. On a context switch, although all values pertaining to the old process are saved, only the general purpose registers are restored – the FPU registers are not (see Section 7.5, on context switching). They will be restored only when needed, but it is vital to be able to determine whether they are valid or not, and this is where the `task_switched` bit in CR0 comes in. Normally, it is set to 0. Every time a context switch occurs, it is set to 1 by the hardware. If set to 1, and the new task attempts to use the FPU, a fault will occur. This is the fault we are handling here, so by clearing it here we are announcing that the values in the FPU registers are now valid (or will be when this function returns).

702–703   if the current process has used the FPU any time since it began, then the values for the FPU registers at the time it was last context switched out will be saved in its `thread` structure. These can now be restored to the hardware registers. The function is discussed in Section 11.10.2.5.

705   if this is the first time the current process has used the FPU, then the hardware registers need to be set to their initial values. The function to do this is discussed in Section 11.10.2.1.

707 this sets the `PF_USEDFPU` bit in the flags field of the `task_struct` of the current process. This will cause the FPU registers to be saved at the next context switch.

11.8 Co-processor error

The co-processor error (number 16) means that a numeric error such as underflow or overflow has occurred in the FPU. It is reported by the *next* floating point instruction after the one that caused the error. The address on the stack points to the floating point instruction that was about to be executed. This is not the one that caused the exception; its address is in the FPU instruction pointer register.

The handling of this exception will be dealt with in two steps. We begin with the second-level handler, which is trivial. Then we go on to consider the function that actually does the work, `math_error()`. A number of auxiliary functions, for example to save the FPU state, or read values from specific FPU registers, will be described in Section 11.10.

11.8.1 Second-level handler for co-processor error

Figure 11.22, from `arch/i386/kernel/traps.c`, shows the trivial second-level handler for a co-processor error. It is really only a link between the assembly language routine that calls it and the C function that handles the error.

```
604  asmlinkage void do_coprocessor_error(struct pt_regs * regs,
                                          long error_code)
605  {
606      ignore_irq13 = 1;
607      math_error((void *)regs->eip);
608  }
```

Figure 11.22 Handling the co-processor error exception

606 this variable is defined in `arch/i386/kernel/setup.c` as type `char`. Irq13 is the hardware interrupt from the math co-processor. If exception 16 (co-processor error) is working, then irq13 should be ignored.

607 this is the function that does the actual work, and will be dealt with in Section 11.8.2. It is passed a `void` pointer to the value of `EIP` on the stack.

11.8.2 The main handler for a co-processor error

The function that actually handles errors in the FPU is shown in Figure 11.23, from `arch/i386/kernel/traps.c`. Basically, it sends a `SIGFPE` to the current process, but, before that, it tries to determine the cause of the error and passes as much information as it can to the user-defined handler for `SIGFPE`.

```
549  void math_error(void *eip)
550  {
```

```
551          struct task_struct * task;
552          siginfo_t info;
553          unsigned short cwd, swd;

558          task = current;
559          save_init_fpu(task);
560          task->thread.trap_no = 16;
561          task->thread.error_code = 0;
562          info.si_signo = SIGFPE;
563          info.si_errno = 0;
564          info.si_code = __SI_FAULT;
565          info.si_addr = eip;

576          cwd = get_fpu_cwd(task);
577          swd = get_fpu_swd(task);
578          switch ((((~cwd) & swd & 0x3f) | (swd & 0x240)) {
579              case 0x000:
580              default:
581                  break;
582              case 0x001:
583              case 0x040:
584              case 0x240:
585                  info.si_code = FPE_FLTINV;
586                  break;
587              case 0x002:
588              case 0x010:
589                  info.si_code = FPE_FLTUND;
590                  break;
591              case 0x004:
592                  info.si_code = FPE_FLTDIV;
593                  break;
594              case 0x008:
595                  info.si_code = FPE_FLTOVF;
596                  break;
597              case 0x020:
598                  info.si_code = FPE_FLTRES;
599                  break;
600          }
601          force_sig_info(SIGFPE, &info, task);
602  }
```

Figure 11.23 The floating point error handler

549 the function is passed a pointer to the saved value of EIP on the stack. This is pointing to the instruction that was about to be executed when the exception was reported, not the one that caused the error.

558 this gets a pointer to the task_struct of the current process.

559 this function, which is described in Section 11.10.2.4, saves the state of the FPU registers in the `thread` structure of the current process.

560–561 this saves the exception number (16) and the error code (0) in the `thread` field of the `task_struct`, where the signal handler can access them if it wishes.

562–565 these lines set up a `siginfo_t` with the relevant information, which will be made available to the signal handler. The `si_code` field is given a default value of `__SI_FAULT` (see Section 17.1.5.5 for these codes). This may be changed before the signal is sent.

565 this is the address of the next instruction, not the one that caused the error.

576–577 these functions, described in Section 11.10.3.1, copy the values of the FPU control word and status word registers from the `thread` structure, where they were saved at line 559.

578 this switch statement is trying to figure out exactly what caused the exception. The low-order 6 bits of `cwd` (control word) are masks for exceptions, as follows:

- Bit 0: IM, invalid operation;

- Bit 1: DM, denormal;

- Bit 2: ZM, divide by zero;

- Bit 3: OM, overflow;

- Bit 4: UM, underflow;

- Bit 5: PM, precision.

When set to 1, the particular exception is to be dealt with by the default handler within the FPU; when cleared to 0, the exception is to be passed to a software error handler. The corresponding low-order 6 bits of `swd` (status word) are set by the FPU if an exception is detected while executing a floating point instruction. They must be explicitly cleared by software. For a bit to be set in `((~cwd) & swd & 0x3F)` it must be one of the low-order 6 bits (`0x3f`), clear in `cwd` (handle in software) and set in `swd` (this particular exception has occurred). For a bit to be set in (`swd & 0x240`), bit 6 and/or bit 9 of `swd` must be set. Bit 6 is the stack fault bit. When set, the internal FPU stack is invalid; otherwise, the fault was caused by an invalid opcode. In the case of a stack fault, bit 9 distinguishes between underflow (0) and overflow (1) of the stack. Thus, we are switching on combinations of bits 0–6, and bit 9.

579–581 if no bits are set in either half of the combination, or some unforeseen combination occurs, then these lines break out of the switch, with default value `__SI_FAULT` in `info.si_code`.

582 this is the invalid operation bit. It is set either by an invalid arithmetic operation or by a stack fault.

583 this is the stack fault bit (6). If this bit on its own is set, the internal FPU stack under flowed.

584 if both bits 6 *and* 9 are set, then the stack overflowed.

585   all the previous three are classed as invalid operations. In that case, the `si_code` is
        `FPE_FLTINV` (see Section 17.1.5.5).

587   bit 1 is the denormal bit. This exception occurs if an arithmetic instruction attempts to operate on
        an operand that is not normalised.

588   bit 4 is the underflow bit. This exception occurs if the result of an arithmetic instruction is less
        than the smallest possible value that can be represented in the FPU.

589   if either of the previous two occurs, then the `si_code` is `FPE_FLTUND` (see Section 17.1.5.5).

591–592 if the divide-by-zero bit (2) is set, then the `si_code` is `FPE_FLTDIV` (see Section 17.1.5.5).

594–595 this is the overflow bit (3). This bit is set if the result of an arithmetic instruction is greater than
        the largest possible value that can be represented in the FPU. In this case, the `si_code` is
        `FPE_FLTOVF` (see Section 17.1.5.5).

597–598 if the precision bit (5) is set, then the `si_code` is `FPE_FLTRES` (see Section 17.1.5.5). This
        exception occurs if the result of an operation cannot be represented exactly in the destination
        format.

601   in all cases, a `SIGFPE` signal is sent, with the appropriate extra information, to the current
        process. The function is described in Section 18.2.1. It will deliver the signal even if it is blocked
        by the destination process.

11.9   SIMD co-processor interrupt

Pentium processors have MMX instructions that act in an SIMD mode on 64-bit MMX
registers. For example, the one instruction could treat the register as 8 separate bytes and
carry out the same operation on each byte in parallel. Errors in this part of the CPU generate
the SIMD co-processor error (number 19). The saved address on the stack points to the
faulting instruction in which the error condition was detected.

There are really two second-level handlers for this, depending on the type of CPU. One
possibility is a standard Pentium, which has the extra MMX instructions, and so can raise
the simd co-processor error, but more advanced Pentiums have streaming SIMD extensions
(SSE) with 128-bit XMM registers and the corresponding MXCSR register. The handling of
an SIMD co-processor error from one of these is more complicated and is dealt with in a
separate function.

There are then a number of worker functions used by all the exception handlers dealing
with the FPU. These are considered in the following section.

11.9.1   Error in a non-SIMD co-processor

Figure 11.24, from `arch/i386/kernel/traps.c`, shows the function called directly by
the first-level handler for the SIMD co-processor error exception. This determines the type
of CPU present and either handles the exception itself or passes control onto the appropriate
handler function.

```
658   asmlinkage void do_simd_coprocessor_error(struct pt_regs * regs,
```

```
659          long error_code)
660  {
661          if (cpu_has_xmm) {
662
663                  ignore_irq13 = 1;
664                  simd_math_error((void *)regs->eip);
665          } else {

670                  if (regs->eflags & VM_MASK) {
671                          handle_vm86_fault((struct
672                                  kernel_vm86_regs *)regs, error_code);
673                          return;
674                  }
675                  die_if_kernel("cache flush denied", regs, error_code);
676                  current->thread.trap_no = 19;
677                  current->thread.error_code = error_code;
678                  force_sig(SIGSEGV, current);
679          }
680  }
```

Figure 11.24   Second-level handler for the SIMD co-processor error exception

661–664   this code is specific to the Pentium III and later processors.

661   the macro is defined in Section 11.10.1. It evaluates to TRUE if the CPU has SSE capability.

663   this ignores any future occurrences of the co-processor hardware interrupt, on irq13. These should not occur on a Pentium.

664   the function for handling SSE FPU exceptions is described in Section 11.9.2. Note that it is passed the saved value of EIP on the stack, cast as a pointer to void. This is the instruction in which the error was detected.

665–679   if there is no SSE capability, then the exception is handled by this block of code

670   maybe the exception was perhaps caused by some strange fault in vm86 mode. If the VM_MASK bit is set in the copy of EFLAGS on the stack, the CPU was running in virtual 8086 mode when the exception occurred.

671–672   thus the standard function for vm86 faults is called. This is dealt with in Section 24.6.

673   this returns to the error_code routine, which will eventually exit from interrupt mode.

675–678   if not in virtual 8086 mode, then we are really into undocumented behaviour.

675   this function checks if the exception occurred while running in kernel mode. If so, it kills the process. The comment in the code says this can be caused by some sort of a strange cache flush from user space, hence the error message. The die_if_kernel() function is described in Section 11.10.4.1.

676   if control returns from the function at line 675 then the process was not in kernel mode. All that can be done is to alert the user by sending a signal. Some information is passed to the signal handler by putting the number of this exception into the `trap_no` field of the `thread` structure belonging to the current process.

677   this puts the error code into the `error_code` field. This is 0, as the CPU does not supply an error code.

678   this sends a `SIGSEGV` signal to the current process. The `force_sig()` function, described in Section 18.2.7, will deliver the signal even if the destination process has it blocked.

11.9.2   SIMD co-processor errors

The function that actually handles errors in the SIMD co-processor is shown in Figure 11.25, from `arch/i386/kernel/traps.c`.

```
610   void simd_math_error(void *eip)
611   {
612          struct task_struct * task;
613          siginfo_t info;
614          unsigned short mxcsr;

619          task = current;
620          save_init_fpu(task);
621          task->thread.trap_no = 19;
622          task->thread.error_code = 0;
623          info.si_signo = SIGFPE;
624          info.si_errno = 0;
625          info.si_code = __SI_FAULT;
626          info.si_addr = eip;

633          mxcsr = get_fpu_mxcsr(task);
634          switch (~((mxcsr & 0x1f80) >> 7) & (mxcsr & 0x3f)) {
635              case 0x000:
636              default:
637                  break;
638              case 0x001:
639                  info.si_code = FPE_FLTINV;
640                  break;
641              case 0x002:
642              case 0x010:
643                  info.si_code = FPE_FLTUND;
644                  break;
645              case 0x004:
646                  info.si_code = FPE_FLTDIV;
647                  break;
648              case 0x008:
649                  info.si_code = FPE_FLTOVF;
650                  break;
651              case 0x020:
```

```
652                         nfo.si_code = FPE_FLTRES;
653                         break;
654       }
655       force_sig_info(SIGFPE, &info, task);
656  }
```

Figure 11.25 Handling an SIMD co-processor error

610 the function is passed a `void` pointer to the instruction that caused the error.

619–626 the first block of code saves the information for the signal handler that will eventually try to deal with the problem in user mode.

619 this gets a pointer to the `task_struct` of the current process.

620 this function, described in Section 11.10.2.4, copies values from the FPU registers to the `thread` field of the `task_struct`.

621–622 the number of this trap (19) and the error code associated with it are also copied to the `thread` structure.

625 the `si_code` field is set to a default value of `__SI_FAULT`; this may be changed later if a specific reason is found for the fault. The various fault codes used here are described in Section 17.1.5.5.

626 the `si_addr` field is pointed to the instruction that caused the error.

633 there is only a single status/control register for SIMD extensions to the FPU, MXCSR. This function reads information from the `thread` – the saved value of the combined control/status register. This information was written there at line 620. If there is no SSE capability, it returns `0x1f80`. The function is described in Section 11.10.3.2.

634 this switch statement is trying to figure out exactly what caused the exception. In order to make sense of this, it is necessary to understand the meaning of the bits in the MXCSR register. Bits $0-5$ are exception bits, as follows:

- Bit 0: IM, invalid operation – an invalid arithmetic operand.

- Bit 1: DM, denormal – an attempt to operate on an operand that is not normalised.

- Bit 2: ZM, zero divide – an attempt to divide by zero.

- Bit 3: OM, overflow – result would overflow destination operand.

- Bit 4: UM, undeflow – result smaller than FPU can represent.

- Bit 5: PM, precision – result not exactly representable in destination format.

Bits $7-12$ are corresponding mask bits. When set to 1, the exception is to be dealt with by the default handler within the FPU; when cleared to 0, the exception is to be passed to a software error handler. In order to determine which unmasked exception was caught, the mask bits must be compared with the exception bits.

- 0x1f80 is 0001 1111 1000 0000 in binary, so (mxcsr & 0x1f80) clears all except the mask bits. Then ((mxcsr & 0x1f80) >> 7) are the mask bits moved to the rightmost positions. By negating this, any bit set in ~((mxcsr & 0x1f80) >> 7) means that the corresponding exception is to be passed to a software error handler.

- (mxcsr & 0x3F) clears all bits, except the exception bits. Finally, (~((mxcsr & 0x1f80) >> 7) & (mxcsr & 0x3f)) is ANDing the inverted mask bits and the exception bits. The only bits set in the result will correspond to an occurring exception which is to be handled in software.

The remainder of the switch statement takes one at a time.

635–637   if no bits are set in the combination, or an unforeseen combination occurs, we break out of the switch, with default value __SI_FAULT in info.si_code.

638–639   this is the invalid operation bit (0). The si_code is set to FPE_FLTINV.

641   this is the denormal bit (1).

642   this is the underflow bit (4).

643   if either of the previous two bits are set, then the si_code is FPE_FLTUND.

645–646   if the divide-by-zero bit (2) is set, then the si_code is FPE_FLTDIV.

648–649   if the overflow bit (3) is set, then the si_code is FPE_FLTOVF.

651–652   if the precision bit (5) is set, then the si_code is FPE_FLTRES.

655   this sends a signal to the current process, even if the process has it blocked. The function is described in Section 18.2.1.

11.10 Auxiliary functions for co-processor error handling

The three previous sections have dealt with the handlers for the different exceptions that can be raised by the co-processor. All of these make use of a number of utility functions, which are considered together in this section. Some of these are wrappers for machine instructions that manipulate FPU registers, others are concerned with terminating the process.

11.10.1 Checking for additional features

Owing to the range of i386 processors available, various features can be present, or not. Macros are provided to check for the presence of these features, as shown in Figure 11.26, from <asm-i386/processor.h>. The test_bit() function used in all of them has been described in Section 5.1.3. In all cases it is testing a data structure set up at boot time, after probing the installed hardware.

```
89   #define cpu_has_fxsr    (test_bit(X86_FEATURE_FXSR,
                                 boot_cpu_data.x86_capability))
90   #define cpu_has_xmm     (test_bit(X86_FEATURE_XMM,
                                 boot_cpu_data.x86_capability))
91   #define cpu_has_fpu     (test_bit(X86_FEATURE_FPU,
                                 boot_cpu_data.x86_capability))
92   #define cpu_has_apic    (test_bit(X86_FEATURE_APIC,
                                 boot_cpu_data.x86_capability))
```

Figure 11.26   Checking for additional computer processing unit (CPU) features

89   this bit is set if the CPU has FXSR functionality (i.e. if it supports the FXSAVE and FXRSTOR instructions).

90   this bit is set if the CPU has SSEs (streaming SIMD extensions).

91   this bit is set if the CPU has an integrated FPU (i486 or later).

92   this bit indicates that the CPU has an integrated APIC (see Chapter 13).

11.10.2   Manipulating floating point unit registers

Later models of the i386 architecture have more FPU registers than do earlier ones. The streaming SIMD extensions were introduced with the Pentium III. They are of use in areas such as image processing and word recognition. SSE uses 128-bit registers, called XMM registers. There is also an MXCSR register, containing control and status bits for operating the XMM registers.

11.10.2.1   Initialising floating point unit registers

When the current process uses the FPU for the first time, the function shown in Figure 11.27, from `arch/i386/kernel/i387.c`, is called. It initialises the registers and, if SSE is supported, sets the MXCSR to its default value. It also notes that the current process now has valid values in the FPU.

```
33   void init_fpu(void)
34   {
35        __asm__("fninit");
36        if (cpu_has_xmm)
37             load_mxcsr(0x1f80);
38
39        current->used_math = 1;
40   }
```

Figure 11.27   Initialising the hardware floating point unit registers

35   this executes the machine instruction to initialise the hardware FPU registers to default values, without checking for error conditions.

36–37 the macro to determine if the CPU has SSE capability is from Section 11.10.1. If so, this code sets the MXCSR register to its default value, 0001 1111 1000 0000. The 6 bits set in this mean that all six error types are enabled. This has been considered in more detail when discussing the handling of SIMD error conditions in the FPU (see Section 11.9.2). The load_mxcsr() macro is from Section 11.10.2.3.

39 this initialisation routine should be run only once for each process, the first time it attempts to use the FPU. The used_math field in the task_struct notes that this initialisation has been done.

11.10.2.2   Checking if a process has used the floating point unit

Whenever a process uses the FPU, the PF_USEDFPU flag is set in the task_struct. The macro shown in Figure 11.28, from <asm-i386/i387.h>, checks this flag and, if it is set, saves the FPU context to the thread structure. For this it uses the save_init_fpu() function, from Section 11.10.2.4.

```
30    #define unlazy_fpu( tsk ) do {              \
31          if ( tsk->flags & PF_USEDFPU )        \
32                save_init_fpu( tsk );           \
33    } while ( 0 )
```

Figure 11.28   Checking if a process has used the floating point unit

11.10.2.3   Loading the MXCSR register

The macro shown in Figure 11.29, from <asm-1386/i387.h>, loads the supplied value into the MXCSR register.

```
56    #define load_mxcsr( val ) do {                                      \
57          unsigned long __mxcsr = ((unsigned long)(val) & 0xffbf); \
58          asm volatile( "ldmxcsr %0" : : "m" (__mxcsr) );             \
59    } while ( 0 )
```

Figure 11.29   Loading the MXCSR register

57 0x ffbf is 1111 1111 1011 1111, so this line ensures that bit 6 of the supplied value is clear. This bit was introduced in the Pentium 4, and attempts to set it on any other type of CPU will cause a general protection exception.

58 this loads the value from __mxcsr into the MXCSR register.

11.10.2.4   Saving state of floating point unit registers

The state of FPU registers is saved to the thread structure by the functions shown in Figure 11.30, from arch/i386/kernel/i387.c.

```
46    static inline void __save_init_fpu( struct task_struct *tsk )
47    {
```

```
48          if ( cpu_has_fxsr ) {
49              asm volatile( "fxsave %0 ; fnclex"
50                          : "=m" (tsk->thread.i387.fxsave) );
51          } else {
52              asm volatile( "fnsave %0 ; fwait"
53                          : "=m" (tsk->thread.i387.fsave) );
54          }
55          tsk->flags &= ~PF_USEDFPU;
56      }
57
58      void save_init_fpu( struct task_struct *tsk )
59      {
60          __save_init_fpu(tsk);
61          stts();
62      }
```

Figure 11.30   Saving floating point unit register values

46   this function saves values from the FPU registers to the `thread` field of the specified `task_struct`.

48   this checks whether the CPU supports the FXSAVE instruction or not (see Section 11.10.1).

49   the FXSAVE instruction saves the x87 state, along with the state of the MMX, XMM, and MXCSR registers. The information is copied to parameter 0, which is the architecture-specific `thread` structure of the process, where it can be used by system software. The actual values in the registers are not altered. The FNCLEX instruction clears the floating point exception flags in the FPU status word, without checking for error conditions.

52   for older CPUs, FNSAVE is used. This instruction stores x87 FPU state information, including data registers, in `thread`, where it can be used by system software. It also initialises the FPU to the same default values as FNINIT. Then the FWAIT instruction checks for and handles pending unmasked x87 FPU exceptions. It does not wait for the *next* instruction, as usual.

55   in all cases, we clear the `PF_USEDFPU` bit in the flags field of the `task_struct`. The registers have been saved and, as long as this bit remains clear, they will not be saved again at a context switch.

58–62   this is just a wrapper function which calls `__save_init_fpu()` from line 46 and sets the TS bit in CR0.

61   this macro, described in Section 11.10.2.6, sets the TS bit in the CR0 register, whether set beforehand or not. This bit allows context switches to be speeded up by swapping the FPU registers only when necessary. The CPU sets it to 1 every time a context switch occurs. An FPU instruction will raise an exception if it is set to 1. Setting it at this point means that a subsequent FPU instruction will raise a 'device not available' exception. Ideally, by the time this happens, the signal handler would have fixed up the saved values in the `thread` structure, so, when the handler for the 'device not available' exception reloads the hardware registers from there, execution should proceed correctly.

11.10.2.5 Restoring floating point unit register values

Figure 11.31, from `arch/i386/kernel/i387.c`, shows the function that restores values to the FPU registers from the `thread` structure of the current process. It is not called on every context switch but only when required.

```
75   void restore_fpu( struct task_struct *tsk )
76   {
77        if (cpu_has_fxsr) {
78             asm volatile( "fxrstor %0"
79        : : "m" (tsk->thread.i387.fxsave) );
80        } else {
81             asm volatile( "frstor %0"
82                            : : "m" (tsk->thread.i387.fsave);
83        }
84   }
```

Figure 11.31   Restoring the hardware floating point unit registers

77 depending on whether the CPU has this extra functionality or not, this code executes the appropriate machine instruction to restore the register values from the `thread` structure of the current process.

78 this restores FPU state, as well as the XMM registers, and the MXCSR register, from parameter 0. This is the appropriate element of the `i387_union` in `thread`.

81 this restores the simpler FPU state from parameter 0. This is the appropriate element of the `i387_union` in `thread`.

11.10.2.6 Manipulating the CR0 register

Several macros are defined to operate on the CR0 register. These are shown in Figure 11.32, from `<asm-i386/system.h>`.

```
104   #define clts() __asm__ __volatile__ ("clts")
105   #define read_cr0() ({                            \
106        unsigned int __dummy                        \
107        __asm__ (                                    \
108             "movl %%cr0,%0\n\t"                     \
109             :"=r" (__dummy));                       \
110        __dummy;                                     \
111   })
112   #define write_cr0(x)                             \
113        __asm__("movl %0,%%cr0": :"r" (x));

124   #define stts() write_cr0(8 | read_cr0())
```

Figure 11.32   Macros to manipulate the TS bit in CR0

104 the CLTS machine instruction clears the TS bit in CR0. Here it is converted to a C macro of the same name. This bit is set by the CPU on every context switch.

105–111 the macro evaluates to the value in the CR0 register.

108 the value in the CR0 register is moved to parameter 0, the local variable __dummy.

110 the macro evaluates to the value of __dummy.

112–113 this macro copies the value of parameter 0 (x) to the CR0 register.

124 this macro reads the value in CR0, using the macro from line 104. It then sets bit 3 (TS), whether it was set beforehand or not, and writes the result back to CR0, using the macro from line 111.

11.10.3 Retrieving values from `thread` structure

The process manager maintains copies of the values in FPU registers in the thread structure of the process. As some of these data structures are nested up to four deep, a number of functions are provided to simplify reading the control and status register values from the thread structure.

11.10.3.1 Retrieving floating point unit control and status words

Two functions are provided for returning the saved values of the FPU control word and the FPU status word. These are shown in Figure 11.33, from `arch/i386/kernel/i387.c`.

```
153  unsigned short get_fpu_cwd( struct task_struct *tsk )
154  {
155      if ( cpu_has_fxsr ) {
156          return tsk->thread.i387.fxsave.cwd;
157      } else {
158          return (unsigned short)tsk->thread.i387.fsave.cwd;
159      }
160  }
161
162  unsigned short get_fpu_swd( struct task_struct *tsk )
163  {
164      if ( cpu_has_fxsr ) {
165          return tsk->thread.i387.fxsave.swd;
166      } else {
167          return (unsigned short)tsk->thread.i387.fsave.swd;
168      }
169  }
```

Figure 11.33 Providing saved values of floating point unit registers

155 the macro to check if the CPU supports the FXSAVE instruction is from Section 11.10.1.

156   this returns the control word saved in the `thread` structure of the current process (see the description of the `thread` structure, in Section 2.7).

158   otherwise, the older version of the control word is returned, cast to be `unsigned short`.

164–165   the macro to check if the CPU supports the FXSAVE instruction is from Section 11.10.1. This code returns the status word saved in the `thread` structure of the current process.

167   otherwise, the older version of the status word is returned.

11.10.3.2   Retrieving the MXCSR value

The function shown in Figure 11.34, from `arch/i386/kernel/i387.c`, retrieves the value of the combined control/status register of the MMX FPU from the `thread` structure of a process.

```
180  unsigned short get_fpu_mxcsr(struct task_struct *tsk)
181  {
182       if (cpu_has_xmm) {
183            return tsk->thread.i387.fxsave.mxcsr;
184       } else {
185            return 0x1f80;
186       }
187  }
```

Figure 11.34   Getting MMX control and status values

182   this macro checks if the CPU has SSE extensions. It is defined in Section 11.10.1.

183   if the CPU has SSE extensions, then the value of the combined control/status register is returned, as saved in the `thread` structure.

185   otherwise, 0001 1111 1000 0000 is returned, which would be the value in the `mxcsr` register corresponding to all exceptions masked out and none actually occurring.

11.10.4   Terminating a process

A number of the second-level handlers discussed in the previous sections actually terminate a process if the exception is severe enough.

11.10.4.1   Checking for kernel mode and terminating a process

If certain exceptions occur while in kernel mode, then something very strange is going on. Figure 11.35, from `arch/i386/kernel/traps.c`, shows the function that checks if the saved value of EFLAGS shows kernel mode and, if so, kills the process.

```
254  static inline void die_if_kernel(const char * str,
                                struct pt_regs * regs, long err)
255  {
```

```
256        if (!(regs->eflags & VM_MASK) && !(3 & regs->xcs))
257            die(str, regs, err);
258 }
```

Figure 11.35   Killing the process if in kernel mode

254   the first parameter is a pointer to an error message string; the second is a pointer to the saved registers on the stack; the third is an error code, provided by the caller.

256   the condition is: (not in vm86 mode) AND (in kernel mode). If the process was in either vm86 mode or in user mode when the interrupt occurred, then the function does nothing and returns to the error handler.

257   the die() function prints a message and terminates the process (see Section 11.10.4.2).

11.10.4.2   Terminating a process

The function shown in Figure 11.36, from arch/i386/kernel/traps.c, prints an information message and terminates the process.

```
240  spinlock_t die_lock = SPIN_LOCK_UNLOCKED;
241
242  void die(const char * str, struct pt_regs * regs, long err)
243  {
244      console_verbose();
245      spin_lock_irq(die_lock);
246      bust_spinlocks(1);
247      printk("%s: %04lx\n", str, err & 0xffff);
248      show_registers(regs);
249      bust_spinlocks(0);
250      spin_unlock_irq(&die_lock);
251      do_exit(SIGSEGV);
252  }
```

Figure 11.36   Terminating the calling process

240   this spinlock is used to guarantee that the message output by this function is not interleaved with messages from any other dying process, and so remains coherent.

244   this sets the console loglevel to 15, which is the highest level. As this function is part of the IO subsystem, we will not consider it any further here.

245–250   this is a critical section. It wants mutual exclusion on the console so that it can output a meaningful message. It does not want to be interrupted by any other dying process. The lock and unlock macros are described in Section 12.8.1. The spinlock is defined and initialised at line 240.

246   this function, part of the IO subsystem, unlocks any spinlocks that might prevent a message getting to the console.

247   this prints the error message on the console, along with the error code. The format string specifies a minimum of 4 hex nibbles, left padded with 0. The parameter to be formatted is treated as a 32-bit value, but masking it with `0xffff` ensures that the high-order 16 bits will be 0 anyway.

248 the `show_registers()` function is described in Section 22.6.4.

249 when called with a parameter of 0, this function ensures that the kernel logging daemon `klogd` is woken up, to take note of the message just printed.

251 this terminates the process, sending a `SIGSEGV` code back to its parent (see Section 9.1).

12

Hardware interrupts

Chapter 10 described how the interrupt descriptor table is used to dispatch CPU-generated exceptions, as well as the programmed interrupt, `INT 0x80`. The same interrupt descriptor table is also used to dispatch hardware interrupts which originate outside the CPU. How that is done is the subject of this chapter.

12.1 Programmable interrupt controller

A hardware interrupt line is an electrical connection between a device and the CPU. The device can put an electrical signal on this line and so get the attention of the CPU. Because devices use these lines to request interrupts they are commonly referred to as an irq line, or just an irq.

The Intel 8080 was designed at a time when the number of transistors that could be integrated onto one chip was quite limited. The designers only had space in the CPU to implement one interrupt line. For compatibility reasons, all the successor CPUs, including the Pentium, still have only the one interrupt line. At first sight, this means that the CPU knows only that *some* device has interrupted. It would have to poll to find out which one. But the designers automated the polling, which enables it to be done sufficiently quickly.

The devices are not connected directly to the CPU but to another chip called an interrupt controller. This in turn is connected to the CPU via the single interrupt line (see Figure 12.1). The controller is then programmed with information about each device that is connected to it. With this architecture, when a device interrupts the CPU saves the `EFLAGS`, `CS`, and `EIP` register values on the stack, just as with an exception. It then sends a signal back to the controller on another line, the acknowledge line (not shown). The controller hears the acknowledgement and in turn puts an 8-bit number on the data bus, corresponding to the particular interrupting device. The CPU reads this number and then uses it as an index into the interrupt descriptor table.

The Linux Process Manager. The Internals of Scheduling, Interrupts and Signals   John O'Gorman
© 2003 John Wiley & Sons, Ltd   ISBN: 0 470 84771 9

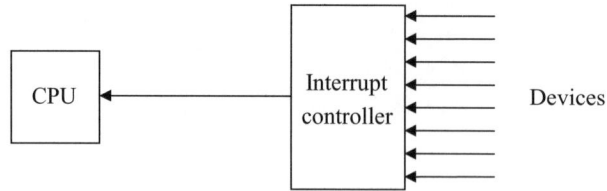

Figure 12.1 An interrupt controller

Figure 12.2, from <linux/irq.h>, shows the data structure that represents an interrupt controller. This contains pointers to all the functions needed to control the low-level hardware. Each particular type of interrupt controller will have its own implementation of these functions.

```
39    struct hw_interrupt_type {
40         const char     * typename;
41         unsigned int (*startup)(unsigned int irq);
42         void      (*shutdown)(unsigned int irq);
43         void      (*enable)(unsigned int irq);
44         void      (*disable)(unsigned int irq);
45         void      (*ack)(unsigned int irq);
46         void      (*end)(unsigned int irq);
47         void      (*set_affinity)(unsigned int irq, unsigned long mask);
48    };
49
50    typedef struct hw_interrupt_type hw_irq_controller;
```

Figure 12.2 Interrupt controller descriptor

40 this is a pointer to an ASCII string, giving the name of the device (e.g. "XT_PIC").

41 this function initialises the controller for a particular irq line.

42 this function shuts down the specified irq line.

43 after this function has been called, the particular line on the controller is enabled. Interrupt signals on that line will now be acted on by the controller.

44 after this function has been called, the particular interrupt line is disabled. Even if a device puts an interrupt signal on that line, the controller will not pass it on to the CPU.

45 this function acknowledges to the controller that the operating system has been notified about the interrupt. This is different from the hardware acknowledgement that the CPU sends automatically, to let the controller know it has received the electrical signal on the interrupt line.

46 this lets the controller know that the processing of a particular interrupt is finished.

47 this function is relevant only to multiprocessors. It establishes which CPUs are to receive a particular interrupt.

50 the foregoing structure is frequently known as hw_irq_controller.

12.2 Data structures for hardware interrupts

As we have seen so often in other parts of the kernel, there is a network of data structures used to record information about each of the possible interrupt lines that can trigger a hardware interrupt in the system.

12.2.1 Descriptor for an interrupt line

Each hardware line on which an interrupt can be received is represented in the kernel by a descriptor, which contains various items of information about that line, including what kind of hardware handling it has, whether it is disabled, and so on Figure 12.3 from <linux/irq.h>, shows the format of such a descriptor.

```
59    typedef struct {
60        unsigned int          status;
61        hw_irq_controller     *handler;
62        struct irqaction      *action;
63        unsigned int          depth;
64        spinlock_t            lock;
65    } ____cacheline_aligned irq_desc_t;
```

Figure 12.3   Data structure representing a hardware interrupt line

60   this field reports the status of the particular irq. The various values possible are given in Section 12.2.2.

61   this is a pointer to the struct hw_interrupt_type representing the particular hardware interrupt controller to which this interrupt line is connected, as shown in Figure 12.2.

62   this is a header for a linked list of struct irqaction, each specifying some action to be taken when this interrupt occurs (see Section 12.2.3). This allows for physical irq lines to be shared between devices. In such a case, there will be one entry on this list for each device.

63   this field is used to prevent already disabled irqs being disabled again. Its normal value is 0, denoting an enabled irq line. It is incremented by the disable_irq() function (see Section 12.6.3.2). Only if the value is 0 beforehand will that function actually disable the irq line. It is decremented by the enable_irq() function (see Section 12.6.4). Only when the value gets to 0 is the irq line actually enabled.

64   a spinlock is taken out while manipulating this descriptor.

65   this is padded out to a cacheline boundary for cache performance and indexing reasons.

12.2.2 Status bits

Figure 12.4, from <linux/irq.h>, shows the meaning of the different bits in the status field of the irq_desc_t structure.

```
25    #define IRQ_INPROGRESS   1
26    #define IRQ_DISABLED     2
27    #define IRQ_PENDING      4
28    #define IRQ_REPLAY       8
29    #define IRQ_AUTODETECT   16
30    #define IRQ_WAITING      32
31    #define IRQ_LEVEL        64
32    #define IRQ_MASKED       128
33    #define IRQ_PER_CPU      256
```

Figure 12.4   Status values for the irq descriptor

25   on a multiprocessor system, each hardware interrupt is sent to every CPU. Of course, we want only one CPU to handle any one interrupt, so this bit is used to mark whether an irq is actually being serviced or not. If a CPU receives an interrupt, but finds this bit set, it knows that some other CPU is handling it, and does nothing. Otherwise, it sets this bit, and handles that interrupt itself.

26   this bit is set when the irq is disabled. In this state, even if the device interrupts, the hardware controller will not pass it on to the CPU.

27   this irq is pending. It has been acknowledged to the controller, but the handler has not yet begun to execute.

28   sometimes the function to enable an irq line (Section 12.6.4) asks for the irq to be resent to itself. This bit is set to indicate that such a request is in progress. It is cleared by the second-level hardware interrupt handler (see Section 12.4.1).

29   this irq line is used at startup to autodetect the presence of a particular hardware device.

30   this irq is used for autodetection, but no interrupt has yet been raised on this line.

31   when set, this means the irq is level triggered; otherwise, it is edge triggered. This is very hardware-specific, but there are some differences in the handlers for both types.

32   this irq is masked so in fact it should not occur. It does not seem to be used anywhere in the code.

33   this bit marks an irq as specific to a particular CPU.

12.2.3   Descriptor for an interrupt handler

When a particular interrupt occurs some specific action has to be carried out. All the information about this action is encapsulated in a data structure, shown in Figure 12.5, from `<linux/interrupt.h>`.

```
14   struct irqaction {
15        void (*handler)(int, void *, struct pt_regs *);
16        unsigned long      flags;
17        unsigned long      mask;
18        const char         *name;
19        void               *dev_id;
20        struct irqaction   *next;
21   };
```

Figure 12.5 Data structure representing the action corresponding to an interrupt

15   this is a pointer to a function to be executed when this interrupt is generated. The first parameter is the number of the irq, the second is a pointer to the major and minor numbers assigned by the input–output (IO) system to the device associated with this irq, and the third is a pointer to the saved registers on the stack.

16   these flags are defined in the chapter on signal handling (see Section 17.1.3.4).

17   this is a new addition to the structure, intended to hold SMP affinity information, but it is initialised to 0 and is never used.

18   this is a pointer to the name of the device associated with this irq.

19   this is a pointer to the major and minor numbers assigned to this device in the IO system.

20   it is possible to associate more than one device with a particular irq, so a series of struct irqaction can be strung together on a linked list, one per device. This is the link field. When an interrupt occurs, these functions will be executed in turn to find the device that actually interrupted.

12.2.4   Table of hardware interrupt line descriptors

Finally, to tie all the foregoing together, there is an array of irq_desc_t, irq_desc[], declared in arch/i386/kernel/irq.c (see Figure 12.6). The size of this array is defined in <asm-i386/irq.h> as

```
26   #define NR_IRQS 224.
```

```
67   irq_desc_t irq_desc[NR_IRQS] __cacheline_aligned =
68        { [0 ... NR_IRQS-1] = { 0, &no_irq_type, NULL, 0,
                                             SPIN_LOCK_UNLOCKED}};
```

Figure 12.6 Table of descriptors for all interrupt sources

Since vectors 0x00-0x1f are reserved for use by the CPU, the usable vector space is 0xff-0x20 (224 vectors). Each element in this array is statically initialised with a status of 0 (no bits set), its handler field pointing to no_irq_type (see Section 12.2.5.1), a NULL pointer in its action field, a nesting depth of 0, and its lock field unlocked. Figure 12.7 outlines the relationship between these data structures.

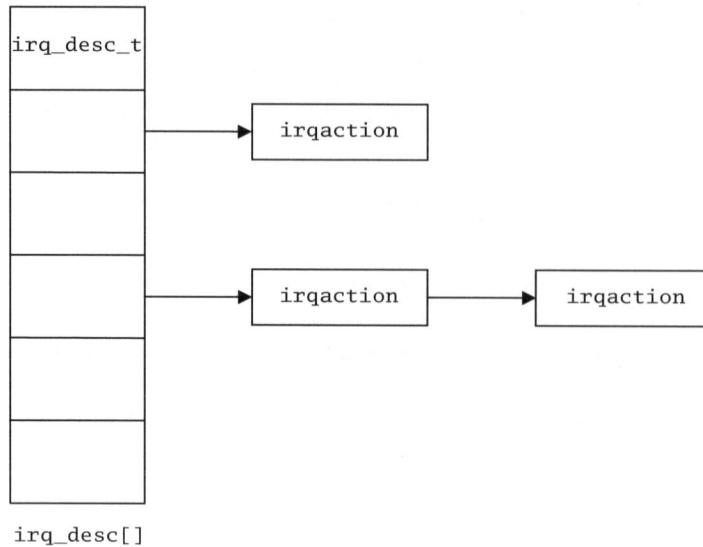

irq_desc[]

Figure 12.7   Recording information about hardware interrupts

12.2.5   Default functions for an interrupt controller.

In Section 12.2.4 we saw that the irq_desc[] table is initialised with a handler field pointing to no_irq_type. This is a struct hw_interrupt_type representing a virtual or nonexistent controller. Just in case control should ever transfer to one of these unused 'fillers' in the irq_desc[] table, dummy functions are provided. We look first at the no_irq_type structure, and then at the individual functions provided.

12.2.5.1   The no_irq_type structure

Figure 12.8, from arch/i386/kernel/irq.c, shows the struct hw_interrupt_type for a dummy controller. Note that there is no entry corresponding to set_affinity, but as this is the last entry it does not matter as long as nobody ever calls it.

```
113  struct hw_interrupt_type no_irq_type = {
114       "none",
115       startup_none,
116       shutdown_none,
117       enable_none,
118       disable_none,
119       ack_none,
120       end_none
121  };
```

Figure 12.8   Description for dummy interrupt controller

12.2.5.2 Dummy controller handling functions

We now go on to consider the trivial implementation of these functions, which is given in Figure 12.9, from `arch/i386/kernel/irq.c`. It may seem to be overkill to provide these NULL functions, but if an unexpected interrupt should occur, they will prevent the machine from crashing.

```
83    static void enable_none(unsigned int irq) { }
84    static unsigned int startup_none(unsigned int irq) {return 0; }
85    static void disable_none(unsigned int irq) { }
86    static void ack_none(unsigned int irq)
87    {

93    #if CONFIG_X86
94        printk("unexpected IRQ trap at vector %02x\n", irq);
95    #ifdef CONFIG_X86_LOCAL_APIC

104       ack_APIC_irq();
105   #endif
106   #endif
107   }

110   #define shutdown_none    disable_none
111   #define end_none         enable_none
```

Figure 12.9   Dummy handlers for unregistered irqs

83–85   the `enable`, `startup`, and `disable` handlers are just NULL functions. Note that `startup` does return a value, as its prototype requires.

86–107   it is always possible that a malfunctioning interrupt controller will signal an irq on an illegal vector. The software should not just ignore this.

94   on the i386 architecture, a warning is printed as is the number of the irq line.

104   currently unexpected vectors happen only when using an advanced programmable interrupt controller (APIC; see Chapter 13). These *must* be acknowledged because a hanging, unacknowledged (unacked) irq holds up a slot in the APIC, and every local APIC has a limited number of these slots. If many unexpected interrupts were to occur, that might lock up the APIC completely. The function is described in Section 13.3.2.4.

110   the `shutdown` handler is aliased onto `disable`, which is a NULL function anyway.

111   the end handler is aliased onto `enable`, which is also a NULL function.

12.3 First-level handlers for hardware interrupts

The generic interrupt mechanism used in Linux on the i386 architecture was examined in Chapter 10. In particular we saw the role of the interrupt description table (IDT), the role of first-level and second-level interrupt handlers, and the common code used on the return path from all interrupt handlers. Hardware interrupts also fit into this generic mechanism. They have their entries in the IDT, and their first-level and second-level handlers. We now go on to discuss this aspect of hardware interrupt processing.

12.3.1   Table of first-level handlers

The IDT represents the operating system's view of hardware interrupts, where they are integrated with all the traps and exceptions that may also interrupt the normal running of the CPU. But hardware interrupts also have their own numbering scheme, based on the physical irq line with which each one is associated.

12.3.1.1   Generating the table

First of all we have a table of first-level handlers for each irq. Figure 12.10 shows the definition of this table, from `arch/i386/kernel/i8259.c`.

```
109  void (*interrupt[NR_IRQS])(void) = {
110                          IRQLIST_16(0x0),
111
112  #ifdef CONFIG_X86_IO_APIC
113                          IRQLIST_16(0x1), IRQLIST_16(0x2), IRQLIST_16(0x3),
114      IRQLIST_16(0x4), IRQLIST_16(0x5), IRQLIST_16(0x6), IRQLIST_16(0x7),
115      IRQLIST_16(0x8), IRQLIST_16(0x9), IRQLIST_16(0xa), IRQLIST_16(0xb),
116      IRQLIST_16(0xc), IRQLIST_16(0xd)
117  #endif
118  };
```

Figure 12.10   The table of first-level hardware interrupt handlers

109   for a standard PC, there are 16 entries in this `interrupt[]` table. The generating macro `IRQLIST_16()`, which sets up 16 entries, is discussed in Section 12.3.1.2.

111–117   if several IO APICs are installed (see Section 13.7.6), then there can be many more hardware interrupt lines, so a further 208 entries are set up (13 groups of 16), for a total of 224.

12.3.1.2   Generating names for first-level handlers

The macros shown in Figure 12.11, from `arch/i386/kernel/i8259.c`, generate entries in the `interrupt[]` table.

```
100  #define IRQ(x,y)                                        \
101          IRQ##x##y##_interrupt
102
103  #define IRQLIST_16(x)                                   \
104          IRQ(x,0), IRQ(x,1), IRQ(x,2), IRQ(x,3),        \
```

```
105        IRQ(x,4), IRQ(x,5), IRQ(x,6), IRQ(x,7),    \
106        IRQ(x,8), IRQ(x,9), IRQ(x,a), IRQ(x,b),    \
107        IRQ(x,c), IRQ(x,d), IRQ(x,e), IRQ(x,f)
```

Figure 12.11   Macros to generate entries in the hardware interrupt table

100–101   this macro generates a name for one handler. For example, if passed (0, 1) as parameters, then the macro evaluates to IRQ01_interrupt.

103–107   this macro generates a set of 16 handler names. For example, if passed a parameter of 0, then the macro evaluates to IRQ00_interrupt, IRQ01_interrupt, ... IRQ0f_interrupt. These values are used to populate the array of pointers set up in Section 12.3.1.1.

12.3.2   Generating first-level interrupt handlers

In Section 12.3.1 an array of pointers to first-level handlers for hardware interrupts was initialised. The handler stubs themselves are built using some ugly macros, which create the low-level assembly routines that save register context and call the second-level handler, do_IRQ(). The do_IRQ() function then does all the operations that are needed to keep the hardware interrupt controller happy.

12.3.2.1   Building all the handler stubs

Figure 12.12, from arch/i386/kernel/i8259.c, shows the code that builds handler stubs for hardware interrupts.

```
53    BUILD_16_IRQS(0x0)
54
55    #ifdef CONFIG_X86_IO_APIC

66    BUILD_16_IRQS(0x1)    BUILD_16_IRQS(0x2)    BUILD_16_IRQS(0x3)
67    BUILD_16_IRQS(0x4)    BUILD_16_IRQS(0x5)    BUILD_16_IRQS(0x6)
                                                  BUILD_16_IRQS(0x7)
68    BUILD_16_IRQS(0x8)    BUILD_16_IRQS(0x9)    BUILD_16_IRQS(0xa)
                                                  BUILD_16_IRQS(0xb)
69    BUILD_16_IRQS(0xc)    BUILD_16_IRQS(0xd)
70    #endif
```

Figure 12.12   Building handler stubs for the hardware interrupts

53   this actually instantiates the first 16 stubs, to handle interrupts from the standard hardware configuration in a PC. The generating macro is discussed in Section 12.3.2.2. When the preprocessor encounters this line, it actually outputs 16 blocks of code, each with its own entry point.

55–70   the IO APIC gives many more interrupt sources. Most of these are unused but they may arise (mostly because of hardware bugs), so a system should be prepared for all of these. Plus, more powerful systems might have more than one IO APIC, so another 13 groups of 16 are built, for a total of 224.

12.3.2.2 Building a block of 16 stubs

Figure 12.13, from `arch/i386/kernel/i8259.c`, shows the macros used in Section 12.3.2.1 to generate the first-level handler stubs.

```
38    BUILD_COMMON_IRQ()
39
40    #define BI(x,y)                                              \
41          BUILD_IRQ(x##y)
42
43    #define BUILD_16_IRQS(x)                                     \
44          BI(x,0) BI(x,1) BI(x,2) BI(x,3)                        \
45          BI(x,4) BI(x,5) BI(x,6) BI(x,7)                        \
46          BI(x,8) BI(x,9) BI(x,a) BI(x,b)                        \
47          BI(x,c) BI(x,d) BI(x,e) BI(x,f)
```

Figure 12.13   Building a block of 16 stubs

38 this macro is described in Section 12.3.2.3. When the macro is actually instantiated at this point it provides the common entry point code for all hardware interrupt handling.

40–41 this builds one stub. For example, if passed (`1,1`) as parameters, it evaluates to the macro `BUILD_IRQ(11)`. That further macro is described in Section 12.3.2.4.

43–47 this builds 16 stubs. For example, if passed a parameter of 0, it evaluates to `BUILD_IRQ(00)`, `BUILD_IRQ(01)`, ... `BUILD_IRQ(0f)`.

12.3.2.3 Common entry point

At the bottom level, the actual interrupt handlers themselves are generated by using a macro from `<asm-i386/hw_irq.h>` (see Figure 12.14). This macro merely saves registers on the stack, calls `do_IRQ()`, and then takes the `ret_from_intr` exit.

```
155   #define BUILD_COMMON_IRQ()                                   \
156   asmlinkage void call_do_IRQ(void);                          \
157   __asm__(                                                     \
158         "\n" __ALIGN_STR"\n"                                   \
159         "common_interrupt:\n\t"                               \
160         SAVE_ALL                                               \
161         SYMBOL_NAME_STR(call_do_IRQ)":\n\t"                   \
162         "call " SYMBOL_NAME_STR(do_IRQ) "\n\t"                \
163         "jmp ret_from_intr\n");
```

Figure 12.14   Common entry point to hardware interrupt handling

156 this line is merely setting up the assembler label at line 161 so that it can be called from within a C program, with the `regparm(0)` attribute. However, it never seems to be used this way.

158 this macro was described in Section 1.2.2.1.

159   this line is just declaring a target label. All the handler stubs jump to this label.

160   this macro pushes register values onto the stack, beginning with ES, down to EBX. It has been described in Section 10.3.2.

161   this is another label in the code; this entry point never seems to be used.

162   this calls the do_IRQ() function (see Section 12.4.1).

163   the ret_from_intr routine was described in Section 10.6.2.

12.3.2.4   Individual stubs

The foregoing code is called by all the stubs. Finally, we come to the parameterised macro used in Section 12.3.2.2 to generate each of these stubs. This is given in Figure 12.15, from <asm-i386/hw_irq.h>.

```
175  #define BUILD_IRQ(nr)                                    \
176  asmlinkage void IRQ_NAME(nr);                           \
177  __asm__(                                                 \
178        "\n"__ALIGN_STR"\n"                                \
179        SYMBOL_NAME_STR(IRQ) #nr "_interrupt:\n\t"         \
180        "pushl $"#nr"-256\n\t"                             \
181        "jmp common_interrupt");
```

Figure 12.15   Macro to build a common irq handler

175   this is the actual first-level stub, parameterized by nr.

176   the IRQ_NAME() macro is defined in <asm-i386/hw_irq.h> as:

```
113  #define IRQ_NAME2(nr) nr##_interrupt(void)
114  #define IRQ_NAME(nr) IRQ_NAME2(IRQ##nr)
```

So, for example, if given a parameter of 01, IRQ_NAME(01) evaluates to IRQ_NAME2 (IRQ01), which in turn evaluates to IRQ01_interrupt(void). The asmlinkage macro sets up this entry point so that it can be called from a C program, with the regparm(0) attribute.

178   this macro was described in Section 1.2.2.1.

179   to continue the example, if passed a parameter of 01, this sets up a label IRQ01_interrupt: . This is the address that will be inserted into the IDT.

180   this is going into the orig_eax field on the stack. Both system calls and random hardware interrupts want to have small integer numbers in orig_eax, and the syscall code has won the optimisation conflict. Thus we have to put a negative value into orig_eax here. The high-order 24 bits of orig_eax are all 1s; the low-order 8 bits represent the irq number.

181   this jumps to the common_interrupt entry point, which was discussed in Section 12.3.2.3.

12.3.2.5 Summary

To illustrate exactly what is going on here, Figure 12.16 is an example of the code that would be generated when parameter 12 is passed to the BUILD_IRQ() macro. When irq12 is eventually set up, the entry in the IDT points to the IRQ12_interrupt: label. The handler pushes a negative number, specific to this irq, onto the stack, in the orig_eax position. Then it jumps to the common_interrupt: label, where all the hardware registers are saved. Finally, control transfers to the do_IRQ() routine. When this returns, it jumps to ret_from_interrupt.

```
common interrupt:
        SAVE_ALL
call_do_irq:
        call do_IRQ
        jmp ret_from_interrupt

IRQ12_interrupt:
        pushl $ -244
        jmp common_interrupt
```

Figure 12.16   Example of generated code

12.4   The second-level hardware interrupt handler

In the previous section we saw how individual first-level interrupt handler stubs are generated. These are almost identical to each other, but they all go on to call a common second-level interrupt handler, which is considered in this section. Even that handler is broken into two parts: first there is the generic do_IRQ(), which repeatedly calls handle_IRQ_event() for every handler registered for that irq line.

12.4.1   Generic second-level interrupt handling

The function shown in Figure 12.17 (from arch/i386/kernel/irq.c) is effectively the second-level hardware interrupt handler in Linux. It is called by all the first-level handlers.

```
563   asmlinkage unsigned int do_IRQ(struct pt_regs regs)
564   {

575           int irq = regs.orig_eax & 0xff;
576           int cpu = smp_processor_id();
577           irq_desc_t *desc = irq_desc + irq;
578           struct irqaction * action;
579           unsigned int status;
580
581           kstat.irqs[cpu][irq]++;
582           spin_lock(&desc->lock);
583           desc->handler->ack(irq);

588           status = desc->status & ~(IRQ_REPLAY | IRQ_WAITING);
```

```
589            status |= IRQ_PENDING;

595            action = NULL;
596            if (!(status & (IRQ_DISABLED | IRQ_INPROGRESS))) {
597                    action = desc->action;
598                    status &= ~IRQ_PENDING;
599                    status |= IRQ_INPROGRESS;
600            }
601            desc->status = status;

609            if (!action)
610                    goto out;

622            for (;;) {
623                    spin_unlock(&desc->lock);
624                    handle_IRQ_event(irq, &regs, action);
625                    spin_lock(&desc->lock);
626
627                    if (!(desc->status & IRQ_PENDING))
628                            break;
629                    desc->status &= ~IRQ_PENDING;
630            }
631            desc->status &= ~IRQ_INPROGRESS;
632  out:

637            desc->handler->end(irq);
638            spin_unlock(&desc->lock);
639
640            if (softirq_pending(cpu))
641                    do_softirq();
642            return 1;
643  }
```

Figure 12.17   The generic second-level interrupt handler

---

563   the function is passed a `struct pt_regs` as parameter. Note this is passed by value, not by reference, as is more common. Passing a value parameter to a C function means the parameter is on the stack – which it is in this case.

575   ANDing the `orig_eax` field with `0xFF` clears the high-order 24 bits to 0. This gives the irq number (see Section 12.3.2.4).

576   this gets the identification (ID) number of the CPU on which we are running, using the macro from Section 7.2.1.4.

577   beginning with `irq_desc`, a pointer to the beginning of the table, and adding the irq number, generates a pointer to the element in the `irq_desc[]` table corresponding to this irq. All the information relevant to handling an irq is encapsulated there (see Section 12.2.4 for a description of the `irq_desc[]` table).

581 this increments the running total of hardware interrupts handled on this CPU. The array was defined in Section 7.2.4.2.

582 a spinlock is taken out on the descriptor for this interrupt. This lock is held until line 638. The `lock` field is in the descriptor, as described in Section 12.2.1.

583 this acknowledges the irq to the controller by calling the appropriate function in the controller descriptor (see Section 12.1). This allows the controller go on to handle the next interrupt.

588 this takes a local copy of the bits from the `status` field of the descriptor, except that these two bits are cleared.

- `IRQ_REPLAY` means that the most recent occurrence of this irq has not yet been acknowledged to the programmable interrupt controller (PIC). As it has just been acknowledged in the previous line, this is no longer true.

- `IRQ_WAITING` is used at boot time to mark irqs that are being tested but have not yet occurred. As it is being handled now, it must have occurred, so this is no longer true.

589 this sets the `IRQ_PENDING` bit in the local `status`. This announces that it has been noticed and is about to be handled.

595 this initialises the local `action` pointer with a default value of `NULL`. In most cases this will be replaced by a specific pointer, but if the irq is disabled for whatever reason, this will abort processing at line 609.

596–600 these check both the `IRQ_DISABLED` and `IRQ_INPROGRESS` bits in `status`, and if neither of them is set, then this block of code is executed, which sets up for handling the irq. If either of these bits is set, then this irq should not be handled. By not entering this scope, a valid pointer is not assigned to `action`, and this is picked up at line 609.

597 this gets a pointer to the (first) handler into the local `action`, from the `action` field of the descriptor.

598 this clears the `IRQ_PENDING` bit in the local `status` – we have committed to handling this interrupt, so it is no longer pending.

599 this sets the `IRQ_INPROGRESS` bit in the local `status` – it is actually being handled.

601 this copies the local `status` into the `status` field of the descriptor for this irq, with any changes that may have been made to it since it was read at line 588.

609–610 if the irq was disabled, or was in progress (on another CPU), then line 597 was not executed and `action` is still `NULL` from line 595; so we exit early. Since `IRQ_PENDING` was set in line 589, if another processor is handling a different instance of this same irq, the other processor will take care of this instance (in its `for` loop at lines 622–630).

622–630 this code deals with any hardware interrupts that allow a second instance of the same irq to arrive while a previous instance is in `do_IRQ()` or in the handler.

623 this lock was taken out on line 582. Giving it back allows another instance of the interrupt to register itself.

624   the function `handle_IRQ_event()` is described in Section 12.4.2. It runs all the handlers associated with this irq line. The parameters are the number of the irq currently being handled (from line 575), a pointer to the saved registers on the stack, and a pointer to the head of the linked list of handlers for this interrupt.

625   this takes out the lock again, as the descriptor is now going to be manipulated.

627–628   if the `IRQ_PENDING` bit has not been set in the meantime (by some other CPU), then the handling for this interrupt has finished and we break out of the loop.

629   otherwise, we clear the `IRQ_PENDING` bit in the descriptor, and go around the loop again to handle this next instance of the interrupt.

631   this interrupt has now been handled, so we clear the `IRQ_INPROGRESS` bit in the descriptor when finally out of the loop.

632–642   this block of code is always executed on the way out, whether the interrupt was handled or not.

637   this calls the `end()` function in the controller descriptor, to let the hardware know that the operating system has finished handling this interrupt.

638   finally, we give back the lock on that irq descriptor.

640   if there are any software interrupts pending, these are executed (see Section 16.5.1.2 for the macro).

641   the function to handle software interrupts will be described in Section 16.1.3.

642   the comment in the code says that a 0 return value means that this irq is already being handled by some other CPU (or is disabled), but it is hard to see how it can return a 0 value.

12.4.2   Running the handlers for a hardware interrupt

Figure 12.18, from `arch/i386/kernel/irq.c`. shows the function that actually handles each occurrence of an irq, working its way through the linked list of handlers to be executed. It is called from line 624 of Figure 12.17.

```
437  int handle_IRQ_event(unsigned int irq, struct pt_regs * regs,
                                           struct irqaction * action)
438  {
439      int status;
440      int cpu = smp_processor_id();
441
442      irq_enter(cpu, irq);
443
444      status = 1;
445
446      if (!(action->flags & SA_INTERRUPT))
```

```
447                __sti();
448
449        do {
450             status |= action->flags;
451             action->handler(irq, action->dev_id, regs);
452             action = action->next;
453        } while (action);
454        if (status & SA_SAMPLE_RANDOM)
455             add_interrupt_randomness(irq);
456        __cli();
457
458        irq_exit(cpu, irq);
459
460        return status;
461   }
```

Figure 12.18   Handling one occurrence of a hardware interrupt request

437   the parameters passed are the number of the irq, a pointer to the register values saved on the stack, and a pointer to the head of the list of `struct irqaction` corresponding to this irq.

440   this gets the ID of the CPU on which we are running, using the macro from Section 7.2.1.4.

442   the `irq_enter()` macro increments the count of the number of irqs currently being handled by this CPU. It is defined in Section 16.5.3.1.

444   this sets the least significant bit in the local `status`. This is the 'do bottom halves' bit. Information will be built up in this `status` variable as we go along, and finally it will be returned to the caller.

446–447   if the `SA_INTERRUPT` bit is not set in the flags field of the `struct irq_action`, then this enables interrupts on the CPU. This means that other (higher-priority) interrupts can be acknowledged and handled while this one is being handled.

449–453   this loop works its way through each element in the chain of handlers for this interrupt until it comes to the `NULL` pointer at the end. Only in the case of a shared irq will there be more than one entry in this list, but the kernel must execute all of them as it cannot tell which device interrupted.

450   this adds the flag s bits corresponding to this handler to the local `status` variable.

451   here, we run that handler, passing it the irq number, the device ID field, and the pointer to the register values on the stack.

452   this moves on to the next handler in the chain.

454–455   if the `SA_SAMPLE_RANDOM` bit was set by any of the handlers, this function is called. It helps to keep the random number generator random. This has nothing to do with interrupt handling, so it will be ignored here.

456 this disables interrupts, in case they were enabled at line 447. They were disabled on entry to the function, and the caller is expecting things that way.

458 the `irq_exit` macro decrements the `__local_irq_count` field for the current CPU. It is defined in Section 16.5.3.1. This is complementary to line 442.

460 this returns the sum of all the bits set in the descriptors of all the handlers run, as well as the 'do bottom halves' bit. The comment in the code says that ideally it should return information about whether bottom-half handling is required, but, in fact, the return is not checked in either of the two places in the kernel that call this function. The caller *always* makes an independent check for pending software interrupts, which is a waste of time and is not what some drivers would prefer.

12.5 Hardware interrupts and the interrupt descriptor table

In Section 12.3.1 a table of pointers to first-level handlers for hardware interrupts was set up. The final piece of the jigsaw puzzle is the connection between this `interrupt[]` table set up there and the interrupt descriptor table (IDT) itself. This initialisation is done at various levels, and we will work through each of them in turn.

12.5.1 Initialising hardware interrupts

The root of the whole setup is `init_IRQ()`, from `arch/i386/kernel/i8259.c` (see Figure 12.19). This function is called at boot time, from line 560 of `init/main.c`.

```
443  void __init init_IRQ(void)
444  {
445      int i;
446
447  #ifndef CONFIG_X86_VISWS_APIC
448      init_ISA_irqs();
449  #else
450      init_VISWS_APIC_irqs();
451  #endif
452
457      for (i = 0; i < NR_IRQS; i++) {
458          int vector = FIRST_EXTERNAL_VECTOR + i;
459          if (vector != SYSCALL_VECTOR)
460              set_intr_gate(vector, interrupt[i]);
461      }
462
```

```
463   #ifdef CONFIG_SMP

468        set_intr_gate(FIRST_DEVICE_VECTOR, interrupt[0]);

474        set_intr_gate(RESCHEDULE_VECTOR, reschedule_interrupt);

477        set_intr_gate(INVALIDATE_TLB_VECTOR, invalidate_interrupt);

480        set_intr_gate(CALL_FUNCTION_VECTOR,
                                          call_function_interrupt);
481   #endif
482
483   #ifdef CONFIG_X86_LOCAL_APIC
484
485        set_intr_gate(LOCAL_TIMER_VECTOR, apic_timer_interrupt);

488        set_intr_gate(SPURIOUS_APIC_VECTOR, spurious_interrupt);
489        set_intr_gate(ERROR_APIC_VECTOR, error_interrupt);
490   #endif

496        outb_p(0x34,0x43);
497        outb_p(LATCH & 0xff , 0x40);
498        outb(LATCH >> 8 , 0x40);
499
500   #ifndef CONFIG_VISWS
501        setup_irq(2, &irq2);
502   #endif

508        if(boot_cpu_data.hard_math && !cpu_has_fpu)
509             setup_irq(13, &irq13);
510   }
```

Figure 12.19   Initialising the interrupt vectors

448   this is for the traditional hardware setup, with 16 irqs. It initialises entries in the irq_desc[] table. The function will be described in Section 12.5.2.

450   this function is called instead if the Visual Workstation APIC is installed. It will not be considered in this book.

457–461   in Section 10.2.2 the first 32 entries in the IDT were filled in. This loop fills in the remainder of the vector space, after the exceptions. Some of these entries will be overwritten later in this function, by SMP interrupts.

457   NR_IRQS is defined as 224 (see Section 12.2.4). This is the number of entries after the first 32, reserved by Intel.

458   the values for vector begin at 0x20 (see the definition in Section 12.5.3). Vectors 00 – 1F, which are reserved by Intel, have already been filled in.

459   this is to avoid overwriting interrupt `0x80`, which has already been set up as the system call entry.

460   this sets up all the other interrupt descriptors to point to default handlers. The `set_intr_gate()` function was described in Section 10.2.1.2. The `interrupt[]` array of pointers to first-level handlers was described in Section 12.3.1.1.

463–481   these lines are only compiled into a multiprocessor kernel. In that case there will be an IO APIC installed. They set up four special entries in the IDT, which are used for interprocessor interrupts (IPI). The vector number of each entry is defined in Section 12.5.3.

468   an entry for irq0 (the system timer) has already been assigned and initialised in the loop at lines 457–461. Another entry is set up at `FIRST_DEVICE_VECTOR` (see Section 12.5.3) for when time signals are sent by the IO APIC.

474   the reschedule interrupt is an IPI, driven by `reschedule_idle()` (see Section 7.6.1. The handler is described in Section 13.6.1).

477   this is an IPI for invalidating the translation lookaside buffers. The handler will be mentioned in Section 13.6.1.

480   this is the IPI for executing a function on another CPU. The handler will be described in Section 13.6.1.

483–490   these lines are compiled only if there is a local APIC in the CPU. They set up three special entries in the IDT, used for interrupts generated by the local APIC. The vector number of each entry is defined in Section 12.5.3.

485   this interrupt is self-generated by the local APIC timer. The handler will be described in Section 13.6.1.

488   the handler for spurious interrupts from a local APIC will be described in Section 13.6.1.

489   the handler for the APIC error interrupt will be discussed in Section 13.6.1.

496–498   at this stage the vector for the clock interrupt has been set up as irq0. In a uniprocessor this is `0x20`, `FIRST_EXTERNAL_VECTOR`. In a multiprocessor it is also `FIRST_DEVICE_VECTOR`, `0x31`. In either case the clock hardware can be initialised. The clock is set to interrupt at HZ Hz. It has to be done somewhere, so this is as good a place as any. Each 8254 timer chip has three timers or counters (at ports `0x40`, `0x41`, and `0x42`). Each has a 16-bit counter register, which always counts down. There is also one control register (at port `0x43`), which controls these three counters.

496   this writes `0011 0100` to the control register.

- Bits 6 and 7 are the counter select bits; here they select counter 0.

- Bits 4 and 5 are the read–load bits. To access a 16-bit counter register through an 8-bit IO port needs two writes. The read–load bits control the access method; 11 means load the least significant byte first, then the most significant byte.

- Bits 1, 2 and 3 are the mode bits; here they select mode 2. This uses the 8254 as a rate generator. The output is low for one clock cycle and high for a number of clock cycles corresponding to the value in the counter.

- Bit 0 is the counter type: here it selects a binary counter.

The `outb_p()` function (Section 12.9.1.3) writes a byte, and pauses to allow the hardware to react.

497   this line writes to the least significant byte of counter 0 (port 0x40). The value of LATCH is declared in `<linux/timex.h>` as

> 155   #define LATCH ((CLOCK_TICK_RATE + HZ/2) /HZ)

HZ is 100, and from `<asm-i386/timex.h>` the CLOCK_TICK_RATE is

> 15   #define CLOCK_TICK_RATE 1193180

So the value of LATCH is `((1193180 + 100/2) /100)` or 11932 (decimal). ANDing with 0xFF takes only the low-order 8 bits of LATCH.

498   this line is writing to the most significant byte of counter 0 (second write to port 0x40). This moves LATCH 8 bits to the right, bringing the high-order 8 bits into the low-order byte, and writes them to port 0x40. There is no need for a pausing version of `outb()` this time, as there are no further instructions. After this strange manoeuvre, we now have LATCH in counter register 0 of the 8254 timer chip, so the timer will interrupt every 11932 clock ticks.

500–502   these lines are not compiled if the kernel was configured to run on an SGI visual workstation. This is setting up irq2, the cascade interrupt on the master PIC. The `setup_irq()` function is described in Section 12.6.1.2. The second parameter is a `struct irqaction`, initialised as discussed in Section 12.5.4. This irq should never be sent to the CPU, but, just in case it is, there is a NULL function there to handle it.

508   this is for the case where an external floating point unit (FPU) (387) has been detected at boot time. In that case, irq13 has to be set up so that it can communicate with the CPU.

509   the `setup_irq()` function is described in Section 12.6.1.2. The second parameter is a `struct irqaction`, initialised in Section 12.5.4.

12.5.2   Initialising the `irq_desc[]` array for a programmable interrupt controller

There is a software and a hardware side to this. The `irq_desc[]` table has to be initialised with default values for all the possible irqs. But before that, the PIC itself has to be set to an initial state. The function shown in Figure 12.20, from `arch/i386/kernel/i8259.c`, is for the traditional hardware setup, with an external PIC. It is called from `init_IRQ`, at line 448 of the same file (see Section 12.5.1), before the vectors for hardware interrupts are set up in the IDT.

```
415  void __init init_ISA_irqs (void)
416  {
```

```
417        int i;
418
419  #ifdef CONFIG_X86_LOCAL_APIC
420        init_bsp_APIC();
421  #endif
422        init_8259A(0);
423
424        for (i = 0; i < NR_IRQS; i++) {
425              irq_desc[i].status = IRQ_DISABLED;
426              irq_desc[i].action = 0;
427              irq_desc[i].depth = 1;
428
429              if (i < 16) {

433                    irq_desc[i].handler = &i8259A_irq_type;
434              } else {

438                    irq_desc[i].handler = &no_irq_type;
439              }
440        }
441  }
```

Figure 12.20 Initialising the `irq_desc[]` array for a programmable interrupt controller

420 if a local APIC is installed, it is initialised at this stage (see Section 13.2.5 for the function).

422 this initialises the 8259A PIC. The parameter controls the mode in which the controller will work, as described in Section 12.7.3.

424–440 this loop goes through each possible irq and sets up default data structures for each one. The `irq_desc[]` array has already been statically initialised in Section 12.2.4. Here some of the fields are reinitialised.

425 no bits were set in this field in Section 12.2.4; here, the `IRQ_DISABLED` bit is set, so each irq line is initialised to the disabled state.

426 the `action` field heads the list of handlers for a particular irq. It is initialised with no handlers, but as it is declared as a pointer type, should this not be NULL? It was statically initialised to NULL in Section 12.2.4.

427 a nesting depth of 1 implies that the line is currently disabled (see Section 12.2.1).

429–433 if this is one of the traditional 16 interrupts, dealt with by the PIC, the handler field is initialised to `i8259A_irq_type` (see Section 12.7.2.1 for this).

438 for any other interrupts, up to `NR_IRQS`, we initialise them for now to `no_irq_type` (see Section 12.2.5.1 for this). They can be filled in as required later.

Note that no assignment is made here to the `lock` field. This retains its statically allocated value of `SPIN_LOCK_UNLOCKED`.

12.5.3 Reserved interrupt vectors

Figure 12.21, from <asm-i386/hw_irq.h>, shows the definitions of a number of special interrupt vectors.

```
23    #define FIRST_EXTERNAL_VECTOR      0x20

25    #define SYSCALL_VECTOR             0x80

40    #define SPURIOUS_APIC_VECTOR       0xff
41    #define ERROR_APIC_VECTOR          0xfe
42    #define INVALIDATE_TLB_VECTOR      0xfd
43    #define RESCHEDULE_VECTOR          0xfc
44    #define CALL_FUNCTION_VECTOR       0xfb

51    #define LOCAL_TIMER_VECTOR         0xef

58    #define FIRST_DEVICE_VECTOR        0x31
59    #define FIRST_SYSTEM_VECTOR        0xef

62    #define IO_APIC_VECTOR(irq)        irq_vector[irq]
```

Figure 12.21 Irq vectors used by the SMP architecture

23 this is the offset in the IDT where the first irq can be placed, after the slots reserved by Intel. It is usually assigned to the timer interrupt.

25 this is the entry point for Linux system calls (see Section 10.4.3).

40–41 these are two interrupts that can be generated by a local APIC (see Section 13.6).

42–44 these are interprocessor interrupts (see Section 13.6).

51 the local APIC timer irq vector is on a different priority level from the others – e as opposed to f. There is a problem with local APIC interrupts being lost if more than 2 irq sources are configured per level.

58 this is the offset in the IDT for the timer vector, when it is generated by the IO APIC rather than by an 8254 timer chip.

59 this is only ever used as a place marker in the IDT.

62 this macro evaluates to the value of the appropriate element of the irq_vector[] array, defined in Section 14.2.3.3.

12.5.4 Initialising irq13 and irq2

Figure 12.22, from arch/i386/kernel/i8259.c, shows the code that statically initialises a struct irqaction for irq13, and one for irq2. Note these are interrupt lines 13 and 2, not to be confused with exceptions 13 and 2.

```
404  static struct irqaction irq13 = { math_error_irq, 0,
                                0, "fpu", NULL, NULL };

410  #ifndef CONFIG_VISWS
411  static struct irqaction irq2 =
                        { no_action, 0, 0, "cascade", NULL, NULL};
412  #endif
```

Figure 12.22   Initialising irq13 and irq2

404   the handler function for irq13 is described in Section 12.5.5.

- The flags and mask fields are cleared to 0. No flags are set.

- The name field points to "fpu", which makes sense.

- The dev_id field is initialised to NULL. This will not cause any problem, as irq13 is never shared.

- As with all new handlers, the link field is NULL.

410–412   these lines provide the initialisation for irq2, the cascade interrupt from the slave PIC. This is done in all configurations, except on Visual Workstations.

411   the handler, no_action, is declared in arch/i386/kernel/irq.c as

```
77   void no_action(int cpl, void *dev_id, struct pt_regs *regs) { }
```

- The flags and mask fields are cleared to 0. No flags are set.

- The name field points to "cascade", which makes sense.

- The dev_id field is initialised to NULL; again, irq2 will never be shared.

- As with all new handlers, the link field is NULL.

12.5.5 Handler for irq13

The handler function for irq13 is shown in Figure 12.23, from arch/i386/kernel/i8259.c.

```
391  static void math_error_irq(int cpl, void *dev_id, struct
                                                pt_regs *regs)
392  {
393      extern void math_error(void *);
394      outb(0,0xF0);
395      if (ignore_irq13 || !boot_cpu_data.hard_math)
396          return;
```

```
397          math_error((void*)regs->eip);
398  }
```

Figure 12.23   Handler for irq13

394   typically, in the PC environment an IO access to port 0xf0 clears the external x87 FPU exception interrupt request.

395–397   if ignore_irq13 is set, or there is no co-processor, then we simply return. The ignore_irq13 flag is set on any machine on which exception 16 works correctly. Otherwise, the second-level handler for a co-processor error is called, which has been seen in Section 11.8.2. This will send a SIGFPE to the current process.

12.6   Requesting and releasing an interrupt line

At this stage, all the data structures are in place and some specific interrupts (0, 2, and 13) have been fully set up. Of course, the whole purpose of the interrupt mechanism is to enable arbitrary devices to associate themselves with specific irq lines. The kernel exports two functions for this, which are typically used by drivers.

12.6.1   Requesting an interrupt line

The processing involved in this is broken down into two functions. The first checks the validity of the request, particularly in the case of sharing an irq. Then, if that test is passed, it calls the second function, which allocates the irq by setting up the appropriate data structures and then enables the irq on the interrupt controller.

12.6.1.1   *Checking a request for an interrupt line*

The function shown in Figure 12.24, from arch/i386/kernel/irq.c, checks the validity of the request and creates a new struct irqaction. It then calls setup_irq() to insert the struct irqaction into the linked list of handlers for that irq. Once this function is called, the supplied handler function may be invoked. So, before a driver calls this function, it is important that its hardware is properly initialised.

```
677  int request_irq(unsigned int irq,
678          void (*handler)(int, void*, struct pt_regs*),
679          unsigned long irqflags,
680          const char* devname,
681          void*dev_id)
682  {
683      int retval;
684      struct irqaction* action;
685
686  #if 1

693      if (irqflags & SA_SHIRQ) {
694          if (!dev_id)
```

```
695                         printk("Bad boy: %s (at 0x%x) called us without a
                                dev_id!\n", devname, (&irq)[-1]);
696       }
697  #endif
698
699       if (irq >= NR_IRQS)
700           return -EINVAL;
701       if (!handler)
702           return -EINVAL;
703
704       action = (struct irqaction *)
705       kmalloc(sizeof(struct irqaction), GFP_KERNEL);
706       if (!action)
707           return -ENOMEM;
708
709       action->handler = handler;
710       action->flags = irqflags;
711       action->mask = 0;
712       action->name = devname;
713       action->next = NULL;
714       action->dev_id = dev_id;
715
716       retval = setup_irq(irq, action);
717       if (retval)
718           kfree(action);
719       return retval;
720  }
```

Figure 12.24 Check a request for an irq line

677 the `irq` parameter is the number of the interrupt line to allocate.

678 the `handler` parameter is a pointer to the function to be called when the irq occurs. Such a function takes three parameters: the irq number, a pointer to the device identifier, and a pointer to the saved register values.

679 the third parameter to `request_irq()` is irqflags, which specifies the type of handling required by this irq. These flags are formally defined in Section 17.1.3.4, when dealing with signals. For the present context the following information is sufficient.

- SA_INTERRUPT: the handler must execute with interrupts disabled.

- SA_SHIRQ: this irq is shared.

- SA_SAMPLE_RANDOM: it is possible to use the random nature of interrupts to keep the random number generator random. But, because this adds an overhead to the processing of each interrupt, it is possible to specify whether the interrupt can be used for this or not. When set, this interrupt can be used.

- SA_PROBE: the kernel is using this line while probing for devices during setup.

680   the fourth parameter, `devname`, is a pointer to an ASCII name for the device that is associating itself with this irq line.

681   the final parameter, `dev_id`, is a pointer to an identifier that will be passed on to the handler function as its second parameter during an interrupt. It must be globally unique. Normally, the address of the data structure representing the device is used for this.

693–696   If the interrupt is to be shared it is absolutely essential that the request should pass in a non-NULL `dev_id`, otherwise there will be trouble later trying to figure out which interrupt is which. In particular, it messes up the interrupt freeing logic. So a sanity check is done. Such a request is still accepted, but it is given a rap on the knuckles.

695   the error message gives the name of the device claiming the interrupt, and the address from which this function was called. The `(&irq)` is a pointer to the first parameter on the stack. Below this on the stack is the return address. So `(&irq)[-1]` is a pointer to the return address on the stack (i.e. the next instruction after the one that called this function).

699–700   a request for an irq line greater than the maximum catered for is invalid, so `EINVAL` is returned to the caller.

701–702   a handler must be supplied; otherwise `EINVAL` is returned to the caller.

704–705   this books out a block of kernel memory large enough to hold a `struct irqaction`.

706–707   if unable to acquire this memory, `ENOMEM` is returned to the caller.

709–714   this code fills in the six fields in the `struct irqaction`. Most of these are copied from the input parameters, except for `mask` and `next`.

711   the `mask` field is set to 0, and is never used later. This is a very new field in the structure, intended to hold SMP affinity information.

713   the link field is set to `NULL`. This entry will always be at the end of the chain, even if it is the only one.

716   finally, we are ready to set up that irq. For the `setup_irq()` function, see Section 12.6.1.2.

717–718   if `setup_irq()` does not return 0, it was unable to set up the entry, so the `struct irqaction` is freed. Otherwise, it was successful, and the `irqaction` is now linked into the table.

719   a nonzero value in `retval` is an error code, indicating why it was unable to set up the entry, so this is passed back to the caller.

12.6.1.2   Inserting an entry on the linked list of handlers

When a device requests the use of an irq line, a `struct irqaction` representing this request must be linked into the existing network of data structures. The function to do this is shown in Figure 12.25, from `arch/i386/kernel/irq.c`.

```
976  int setup_irq(unsigned int irq, struct irqaction * new)
977  {
```

```
978        int shared = 0;
979        unsigned long flags;
980        struct irqaction *old, **p;
981        irq_desc_t *desc = irq_desc + irq;

988        if (new->flags & SA_SAMPLE_RANDOM) {

997            rand_initialize_irq(irq);
998        }

1003       spin_lock_irqsave(&desc->lock, flags);
1004       p = &desc->action;
1005       if ((old = *p) != NULL) {
1006
1007           if (!(old->flags & new->flags & SA_SHIRQ)) {
1008               spin_unlock_irqrestore(&desc->lock, flags);
1009               return -EBUSY;
1010           }
1011
1013           do {
1014               p = &old->next;
1015               old = *p;
1016           } while (old);
1017           shared = 1;
1018       }
1019
1020       *p = new;
1021
1022       if (!shared) {
1023           desc->depth = 0;
1024           desc->status &= ~(IRQ_DISABLED | IRQ_AUTODETECT |
                                                 IRQ_WAITING);
1025           desc->handler->startup(irq);
1026       }
1027       spin_unlock_irqrestore(&desc->lock, flags);
1028
1029       register_irq_proc(irq);
1030       return 0;
1031 }
```

Figure 12.25   Insert an entry into the interrupt descriptor table

978   the variable shared is initialised to a default value of not shared; this may be changed if in fact the requested irq is already allocated, in a mode that allows sharing.

981   beginning with irq_desc, a pointer to the beginning of the table, and adding the irq number, generates a pointer to the element in the irq_desc[] table corresponding to this irq (see Section 12.2.4).

988   it is possible to use the random nature of calls to this function to keep the random number generator random. Only some interrupts allow themselves to be used this way, by setting the SA_SAMPLE_RANDOM flag in the `struct irqaction` we are trying to insert. Some drivers use `request_irq()` heavily, and this would slow them down significantly, so they can specify that they are not to be used in this way, by clearing the SA_SAMPLE_RANDOM bit in the `flags` field of the `struct irqaction`.

997   this is not part of interrupt handling and will not be considered further.

1003–1027   because the descriptor being manipulated may be shared, this block of code has to be executed atomically. The lock is in the element of the `irq_desc[]` table corresponding to this irq. For the interrupt-safe spinlock macros, see Section 12.8.1.

1004   this sets up an indirect pointer to the first entry on the linked list of handlers in the descriptor of this irq. This sets p pointing to the `action` field of the descriptor, which is itself a pointer to a `struct irqaction`.

1005–1018   this block of code is executed only if the `action` field of the descriptor is not NULL; that is, if there is some action declared, meaning that this irq is already allocated. So, this code is investigating the possibility of sharing the irq.

1005   note that `old` is set pointing to that `action` field, the head pointer in the descriptor. If this is NULL (that irq is not currently assigned), we skip on to line 1020.

1007–1010   this block of code is executed only if SA_SHIRQ is not set in the `flags` field of both `old` and `new`. Interrupts cannot be shared unless both agree to it.

1008–1009   if not, the spinlock is given back, and EBUSY is returned.

1013–1016   to recap: we have got to this point because the irq is already assigned, but sharing is allowed. So now we run down the linked list of handlers (one for each sharing device) until we get to the end.

1014   first time around this loop, `old` is pointing to the first entry, `old->next` is the pointer field in the first entry, pointing to the second one, so p is set to point indirectly to the second entry.

1015   this points `old` to the second entry, so `old` is advanced each time around.

1016   when we get to the end, `old` will be NULL.

1017   note that we are about to insert a shared irq, so we set the local `shared` flag; this is needed at line 1022.

1020   at this stage p is either pointing to the pointer field in the descriptor (if not shared) or the pointer field in the last entry in the chain (if shared). This assignment links `new` onto the chain in either case, so inserting the supplied `struct irqaction` at the end of the linked list.

1022–1026   if the new request is sharing with a previously set up irq, then this block of code is not needed as these fields are already filled in.

1023   the `depth` field is set to 0, denoting this irq line as enabled (see Section 12.2.1).

1024   the IRQ_DISABLED, IRQ_AUTODETECT, and IRQ_WAITING bits are cleared in the `status` field. It is not disabled; we are about to call `startup()` for it on the next line. The other two bits are only set at boot time, for autodetection of devices, which is certainly not what is going on here. All other bits in the `status` field are unaffected.

1025 the interrupt controller `startup()` function is called for this irq. At the least, this enables the specified irq.

1027 we are finished with the descriptor, so we return the spinlock (see Section 12.8.1).

1029 this function registers the irq in the `/proc/irq` file system It will not be considered further here, but note in passing that there is no corresponding deregistration in the function that deallocates an irq, in Section 12.6.2.

12.6.2 Freeing an interrupt line

The function shown in Figure 12.26, from `arch/i386/kernel/irq.c`, deallocates an interrupt line. The handler is removed and the interrupt line is not available for use by any driver; it is disabled and shutdown. If the irq was shared, then the caller must ensure that the interrupt is disabled on the card that issues this irq before calling this function. This function may be called from interrupt context, but note that attempting to free an irq in a handler for the same irq hangs the machine.

```
740  void free_irq(unsigned int irq, void *dev_id)
741  {
742      irq_desc_t *desc;
743      struct irqaction **p;
744      unsigned long flags;
745
746      if (irq >= NR_IRQS)
747              return;
748
749      desc = irq_desc + irq;
750      spin_lock_irqsave(&desc->lock, flags);
751      p = &desc->action;
752      for (;;) {
753          struct irqaction * action = *p;
754          if (action) {
755              struct irqaction **pp = p;
756              p = &action->next;
757              if (action->dev_id != dev_id)
758                  continue;

761              *pp = action->next;
762              if (!desc->action) {
763                  desc->status |= IRQ_DISABLED;
764                  desc->handler->shutdown(irq);
765              }
766              spin_unlock_irqrestore(&desc->lock, flags);
767
```

```
768  #ifdef CONFIG_SMP
769
770                    while (desc->status & IRQ_INPROGRESS) {
771                        barrier();
772                        cpu_relax();
773                    }
774  #endif
775                    kfree(action);
776                    return;
777                }
778                printk("Trying to free free IRQ%d\n",irq);
779                spin_unlock_irqrestore(&desc->lock,flags);
780                return;
781        }
782  }
```

Figure 12.26   Freeing an irq line

740   the function is passed the number of the interrupt line to free and a pointer to the structure representing the device that generates this interrupt. Note that it is declared as void; it gives no indication of whether it was successful or not.

746–747   if trying to free an impossibly numbered irq, we simply return immediately.

749   this constructs a pointer to the entry corresponding to this irq in irq_desc[] (see Section 12.2.4).

750   mutual exclusion is needed while working on the descriptor, to protect from any other interrupts while doing so. The interrupt safe spinlock functions are described in Section 12.8.1.

751   this takes a local pointer p to the action field of the descriptor, which is itself a pointer to a struct irqaction (see the definition of p on line 743).

752–781   this loop is working its way along the chain of handlers for this irq.

753   the first time around this loop, the local action variable has the same value as action in the descriptor – that is, it points to the first struct irqaction in the list. On each subsequent iteration of the loop, it will point to the next entry. On any iteration, action points directly to the one we are considering, p points indirectly to the same entry.

754–777   this block of code is executed if there is a valid struct irqaction (i.e. if there is at least one more to try). Otherwise, we skip on to line 778.

755   this takes a local indirect pointer pp to the struct irqaction being considered.

756   this advances p to point to the next entry in the list.

757–758   if the dev_id field in the current entry does not match the dev_id passed as parameter, then we do not want to deallocate this one. We go around the loop again (with an updated value for p).

761–776   we have found the one we were looking for – now we remove it from the list of entries.

761   from line 755, pp is an indirect pointer to the entry we are considering, through the link field of the previous one. So *pp is the link field in the previous entry. By copying the next field of the entry we are considering into that we ensure that this entry is being removed from the list.

762–765   after the previous line, if there are no entries at all on the list, then this irq is no longer in use by any device.

763   this sets the disabled bit in the status field of the descriptor.

764   this runs the controller shutdown() function for that irq.

766   we are finished with the descriptor, so we give back the lock (see Section 12.8).

768–774   there is one extra complication for a multiprocessing kernel. We have to wait to make sure that the interrupt is not being processed, or that the descriptor is in use by another CPU.

770–773   if the IRQ_INPROGRESS bit is set in the status field of the descriptor, we synchronise memory to make sure that other CPUs see the disabled bit and that we know as soon as possible that the other CPU is finished. So this function will not return until any executing interrupts for this IRQ have completed.

772   this function inserts a pause in a busy waiting loop (see Section 9.4.2.2).

775–776   in any case, we give back the memory occupied by the struct irqaction, and return.

778   control only comes here if action was found to be NULL at line 754 (i.e. we got to the end of the list and found no entry corresponding to the interrupt we are trying to deallocate). The message is not the most helpful.

12.6.3   Disabling an irq

After an irq line has been set up, a driver may wish temporarily to disable it and reenable it later without the extra overhead of shutting it down and then setting it up again. So functions are provided for this. However, calls to disable_irq() and enable_irq() must be paired, and the depth field in the irq_desc_t is provided for this.

There are two functions provided for disabling an irq line. One just goes ahead and disables it; the other is a synchronous version; it waits until any instances of this irq that might be running on any other CPU are finished before returning to the caller.

12.6.3.1   Disabling an irq line without waiting

The function shown in Figure 12.27, from arch/i386/kernel/irq.c, does not ensure existing instances of the irq handler have completed before returning.

```
482   inline void disable_irq_nosync(unsigned int irq)
483   {
484         irq_desc_t *desc = irq_desc + irq;
485         unsigned long flags;
486
487         spin_lock_irqsave(&desc->lock, flags);
```

```
488        if (!desc->depth++) {
489             desc->status |= IRQ_DISABLED;
490             desc->handler->disable(irq);
491        }
492        spin_unlock_irqrestore(&desc->lock, flags);
493  }
```

Figure 12.27   Disabling an irq line without waiting

484   this uses the irq number supplied as a parameter to get a pointer to the entry in the `irq_desc[]` table (Section 12.2.4) corresponding to this irq.

487–492   this code takes out an interrupt-safe spinlock on that element of the table. The macros to manipulate the spinlock are in Section 12.8; the lock itself is part of the descriptor in the table.

488–491   only if the `depth` field in the descriptor was 0 before the increment will this block of code be executed.

489   this sets the `IRQ_DISABLED` flag in the descriptor, so that all other handlers know this. However, the controller still thinks it is enabled and many send interrupts until the next line.

490   this calls the `disable()` function appropriate to the hardware controller from which the interrupt originated.

12.6.3.2   *Disabling an irq line and waiting*

The `disable_irq()` function, from `arch/i386/kernel/irq.c`, is shown in Figure 12.28. It disables the selected interrupt line. This function waits for any pending irq handlers for this interrupt to complete before returning.

```
508  void disable_irq(unsigned int irq)
509  {
510       disable_irq_nosync(irq);
511
512       if (!local_irq_count(smp_processor_id())) {
513            do {
514                 barrier();
515                 cpu_relax();
516            } while (irq_desc[irq].status & IRQ_INPROGRESS);
517       }
518  }
```

Figure 12.28   Disabling an irq line and wait

510   this function, described in Section 12.6.3.1, does most of the work. It is the nonwaiting version.

512–517   this code is executed only if there are no irqs currently being handled by the local CPU.

512   the `smp_processor_id()` macro is from Section 7.2.1.4; the `local_irq_count()` macro is from Section 16.5.1.2. If there are other irqs in progress, then this function must have been called from a higher priority and so preempted one of them. We do not want to go into a busy waiting loop in that situation.

513–516   the loop delays until any occurrence of this irq being handled on any other CPU has finished.

514   the `barrier()` macro guarantees that the current process is seeing a coherent view of memory.

515   the `cpu_relax()` macro, from Section 9.4.2.2, introduces a delay into this busy waiting loop.

516   we loop until some other CPU clears the `IRQ_INPROGRESS` flag for this irq.

12.6.4   Enabling an irq line

The `enable_irq()` function is shown in Figure 12.29, from `arch/i386/kernel/irq.c`. It undoes the effect of one call to `disable_irq()`. If this matches the last disable, processing of interrupts on this irq line is reenabled.

```
531  void enable_irq(unsigned int irq)
532  {
533      irq_desc_t *desc = irq_desc + irq;
534      unsigned long flags;
535
536      spin_lock_irqsave(&desc->lock, flags);
537      switch (desc->depth) {
538      case 1: {
539          unsigned int status = desc->status & ~IRQ_DISABLED;
540          desc->status = status;
541          if ((status & (IRQ_PENDING | IRQ_REPLAY)) == IRQ_PENDING) {
542              desc->status = status | IRQ_REPLAY;
543              hw_resend_irq(desc->handler, irq);
544          }
545          desc->handler->enable(irq);
546
547      }
548      default:
549          desc->depth--;
550          break;
551      case 0:
552          printk("enable_irq(%u) unbalanced from %p\n", irq,
553          __builtin_return_address(0));
554      }
555      spin_unlock_irqrestore(&desc->lock, flags);
556  }
```

Figure 12.29   Enabling an irq line

533   this uses the irq number supplied as a parameter to get a pointer to the entry in the `irq_desc[]` table (Section 12.2.4) corresponding to this irq.

536–555	this code takes out an interrupt-safe spinlock on that element of the table. The macros to manipulate the spinlock are in Section 12.8; the lock itself is part of the descriptor in the table.
537–554	the effect of this function depends on the value in the `depth` field of the descriptor, so this `switch` statement considers the different possibilities.
538–547	a value of 1 means that the irq has been disabled exactly once, so the function can enable it.
539	this clears the `IRQ_DISABLED` bit in the local copy of the `status` field.
540	this writes that changed value back to the global field, so that the whole system can see that the irq is now enabled.
541–544	when disabling an irq, there is a small gap between setting the `IRQ_DISABLED` bit and calling `disable()` on the controller (lines 489–490 in Section 12.6.3.1). An interrupt could arrive during this gap. When `do_IRQ()` is called for that interrupt, it sets the `IRQ_PENDING` flag but notices that the irq is disabled and does nothing further, but it leaves the `IRQ_PENDING` flag set. When `enable_irq()` is called and finds `IRQ_PENDING` set it will ask for this irq to be resent so that it is not lost to the system. Of course, it will do this only if it has not been resent already (`IRQ_REPLAY` is clear).
542	this sets the `IRQ_REPLAY` bit in the global field, as it is going to be replayed on the next line.
543	on a uniprocessor, this is a null function. On a multiprocessor, it resends this interrupt to itself, as an interprocessor interrupt (IPI; see Section 13.7.6).
545	this lets the interrupt controller know that this irq line is reenabled.
547	note that there is no `break` here; control falls through to line 549, where the value of `depth` is decremented to 0.
548–550	any value higher than 1 means that enables have not yet matched disables. We decrement the `depth` counter, but take no other action.
551–554	this indicates an attempt to enable an already enabled irq line, so something is wrong.
552–553	these print a warning message giving the number of the irq and the address from which this function was called, but no action is taken, nor is `depth` adjusted.

12.7 The 8259A programmable interrupt controller

So far in this chapter we have been dealing with the software side of the interrupt mechanism, but there is a hardware interrupt controller somewhere in the picture, and now we have to turn our attention to that.

A number of different interrupt controllers are handled by the Linux process manager. At present these include the 8259 PIC, the Pentium II X4 internal 8259 PIC, the local APIC, IO APIC, and SGI's Visual Workstation Cobalt IO APIC.

The simplest piece of hardware to understand is the original 8259A PIC, which was present in the majority of PC/AT-type computers, so we will begin with that. The following chapter will look at the advanced programmable interrupt controller, or APIC.

Individual devices are not connected directly to the CPU but to this PIC chip. The 8259 PIC can handle up to eight input lines (see Figure 12.30). The PIC in turn is connected to the CPU via the single interrupt line. The PIC is then programmed with information about each device that is connected to it.

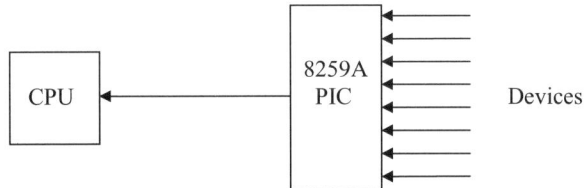

Figure 12.30   A programmable interrupt controller

The eight input lines in a PIC limit any particular computer built around this architecture to eight devices, which is rather inhibiting, so Intel arranged that PICs could be cascaded. The PIC connected directly to the CPU in Figure 12.30 is known as the master PIC. Instead of having devices connected directly to this, it is possible to connect slave PICs to any or all of its input lines. This allows for a maximum of 64 devices. In the standard PC design, there is only one slave PIC, connected to input 2 of the master. This allows for 15 devices, each with its own unique interrupt line (see Figure 12.31).

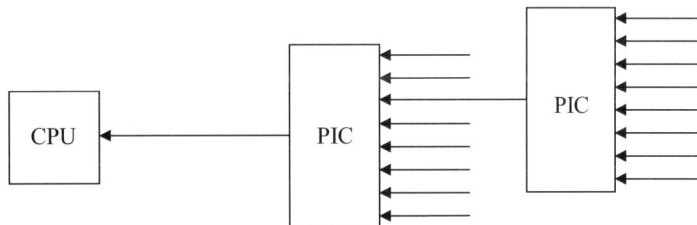

Figure 12.31   Two programmable (PICs) cascaded together

With this architecture, when the master PIC interrupts, the CPU saves the EFLAGS, CS, and EIP register values on the stack, just as with an exception. It then sends a signal back to the PIC on another line, the acknowledge line (not shown). The PIC hears the acknowledgement and in turn puts an 8-bit number on the data bus, corresponding to the particular interrupting device. The CPU reads this number and then uses it as an index into the interrupt descriptor table.

12.7.1   Programming the programmable interrupt controller

Programming the PIC is a complex topic in its own right. Here we will introduce the minimum necessary to understand what is going on in the remainder of this section.

The PIC has a number of internal registers:

* interrupt mask register (IMR): a bit set to 0 in this register means that the corresponding irq is enabled; otherwise it is disabled;

- interrupt request register (IRR): a bit set in this register means that the corresponding irq line has signalled an interrupt;

- in-service register (ISR): a bit set in this register means that a request from the corresponding irq line is being serviced; the end of interrupt command clears the appropriate bit in this register.

The programming complexity arises from the fact that these registers are not directly accessible to the programmer, as they would be if each were mapped into its own IO port. Instead, the PIC has only two IO ports and accesses to the three internal registers are multiplexed over these.

These ports are always contiguous in the IO address space of the PC. The first one always has an even address, and the second one odd. The standard allocation on a PC is ports 0x20 and 0x21 for the master PIC, ports 0xA0 and 0xA1 for the slave. Intel does not give names to these ports, but it is common to refer to port 0x20 as the interrupt control port. This is a dual purpose port. It is used to switch between internal registers in the PIC. Which register is returned depends on a value previously written to this port. By default, it is set to read from the IRR:

- To select the ISR, write to port 0x20, with bits 0 and 1 both set to 1.

- To select the IRR, write to port 0x20, with bit 0 cleared to 0, and bit 1 set to 1.

Port 0x21 is commonly referred to as the interrupt mask port. After initialisation, it is mapped to the IMR and can be used to read and write that register, but, in the initialisation phase, it has other uses. Linux supplies a number of functions for reading and writing IO ports. These will be discussed in Section 12.9.

12.7.2 Data structures

As usual, the process manager represents external realities, such as the PIC in this case, by means of data structures.

12.7.2.1 Data structure representing a programmable interrupt controller

As we have seen in Section 12.1, an interrupt controller is represented in software by a struct hw_interrupt_type. The instance of this specific to an 8259A PIC is shown in Figure 12.32, from arch/i386/kernel/i8259.c.

```
132   spinlock_t i8259A_lock = SPIN_LOCK_UNLOCKED;

150   static struct hw_interrupt_type i8259A_irq_type = {
151         "XT-PIC",
152         startup_8259A_irq,
153         shutdown_8259A_irq,
154         enable_8259A_irq,
155         disable_8259A_irq,
```

```
156        mask_and_ack_8259A,
157        end_8259A_irq,
158        NULL
159  };
```

Figure 12.32 Descriptor for an 8259A programmable interrupt controller (PIC)

132 there is a spinlock for manipulating this data structure, initialised to the unlocked state (see Section 5.3 for the uniprocessor version and Section 5.4.1 for the multiprocessor version of `spinlock_t`).

151–158 the first field contains the name of the controller, `"XT-PIC"`. The last field, `set_affinity`, is not relevant to this type of controller and so is set to NULL. Each of the functions specified on lines 152–157 of this descriptor will be described in detail in the remainder of this section.

12.7.2.2 Representing the state of the irq lines

Figure 12.33, from `arch/i386/kernel/i8259.c`, shows some variables and macros used by the following functions.

```
168  static unsigned int cached_irq_mask = 0xffff;
169
170  #define __byte(x,y) (((unsigned char *)&(y))[x])
171  #define cached_21 (__byte(0,cached_irq_mask))
172  #define cached_A1 (__byte(1,cached_irq_mask))

183  unsigned long io_apic_irqs;
```

Figure 12.23 Variables and macros used by the 8259A functions

168 each PIC has an 8-bit internal mask register. A bit clear (0) in this means that the corresponding irq line is enabled. A bit set (1) means that it is disabled. The `cached_irq_mask` field contains the irq mask for both 8259A controllers. It is declared `static`, so it is a permanent software copy of the interrupt mask registers in both controllers. It is initialised to all 1s, meaning all irqs disabled.

170 this macro evaluates to a pointer to `char`. Its value is the address of a byte within the variable passed as the second parameter. The particular byte is specified by the first parameter.

171 this evaluates to a pointer to byte 0 in `cached_irq_mask`. This byte is the operating system copy of the value in the interrupt mask register of the master PIC, at port `0x21`. Bits cleared to 0 in this byte correspond to enabled irqs.

172 this evaluates to a pointer to byte 1 in `cached_irq_mask`. This is a copy of the interrupt mask register of the slave PIC, at port `0xA1`.

183 not all irqs can be routed through the IO APIC. For example, on certain (older) boards the timer interrupt is not really connected to any IO APIC pin, it is fed to the irq0 line of the master 8259A only. Any bit set (1) in this mask means the corresponding irq is routed through the IO APIC. This mask is set up at boot time.

12.7.3 Initialising the programmable interrupt controller

At boot time, the 8259A PIC has to be initialised. The code for this is shown in Figure 12.34, from `arch/i386/kernel/i8259.c`.

```
336  void __init init_8259A(int auto_eoi)
337  {
338      unsigned long flags;
339
340      spin_lock_irqsave(&i8259A_lock, flags);
341
342      outb(0xff, 0x21);
343      outb(0xff, 0xA1);

348      outb_p(0x11, 0x20);
349      outb_p(0x20 + 0, 0x21);
350      outb_p(0x04, 0x21);
351      if (auto_eoi)
352          outb_p(0x03, 0x21);
353      else
354          outb_p(0x01, 0x21);

356      outb_p(0x11, 0xA0);
357      outb_p(0x20 + 8, 0xA1);
358      outb_p(0x02, 0xA1);
359      outb_p(0x01, 0xA1);

362      if (auto_eoi)

367          i8259A_irq_type.ack = disable_8259A_irq;
368      else
369          i8259A_irq_type.ack = mask_and_ack_8259A;
370
371      udelay(100);
372
373      outb(cached_21, 0x21);
374      outb(cached_A1, 0xA1);
375
376      spin_unlock_irqrestore(&i8259A_lock, flags);
377  }
```

Figure 12.34 Initialise the 8259A PIC

336 the parameter can be 0 or 1. If 1, then the PIC is to be initialised to the auto end-of-interrupt (EOI) mode. In this mode, the bit in the in-service register is cleared automatically when the CPU sends an ACK (acknowledgement). If the parameter is 0 (the Linux default), then the PIC is to be initialised so that a bit in the in-service register is only cleared when an EOI command is sent by software.

340   this spinlock, which guarantees mutual exclusion while programming the PIC, was introduced in Section 12.7.2.1.

342–343   writing all 1s to the interrupt control ports of both PICs disables or masks all 16 interrupts. These settings will be set to specific values when initialisation is complete (lines 373 and 374). The `outb()` function is from Section 12.9.1.3.

348–354   this block of code initialises the master PIC. The `outb_p()` is similar to `outb()`, but it introduces a delay, to allow the hardware to react. It is described in Section 12.9.1.3.

348   the bit pattern written to port `0x20` (the interrupt control port of the master PIC) is `0001 0001`.

- Bit 4 set means this is initialisation command word 1.

- Bit 0 set means that there are going to be a total of four initialisation command words.

- Bit 1 clear means operate in cascade mode (i.e. there is a second PIC behind this).

- Bit 3 clear means operate in edge detect mode (as opposed to level triggered).

349   this is command word 2. It is written to port `0x21`, the mask register, but, because it comes immediately after command word 1, it is interpreted differently. It does not instruct the PIC to set its mask, as on line 342. Instead, it tells the PIC to map its irqs to interrupt vectors beginning at `0x20`. So irq0 will request interrupt `0x20`, irq1 will request interrupt `0x21`, and so on.

350   this is command word 3. The bit pattern written is `0000 0100`. Bit 2 set tells the master PIC that there is a slave attached to input 2.

351–354   this code determines whether the master PIC is to reset itself automatically after an interrupt (`auto_eoi == 1`) or whether it is to wait for an EOI from software (`auto_eoi == 0`).

352   this is command word 4. Bit 0 set tells the PIC that it is connected to an i386 system. Bit 1 set tells the PIC to do auto EOI.

354   in this case, bit 0 set tells the PIC that it is connected to an i386 system. Bit 1 clear tells the master to expect EOI from software.

356–359   this block of code initialises the slave PIC.

356   the bit pattern written to port `0xA0` (the interrupt control port of the slave PIC) is `0001 0001`.

- Bit 4 set means this is initialisation command word 1.

- Bit 0 set means that there are going to be a total of four initialisation command words.

- Bit 1 clear means operate in cascade mode.

- Bit 3 clear means operate in edge detect mode.

357   this instruction tells the slave PIC to map its irqs to interrupt vectors beginning at `0x28`. So irq8 will request interrupt `0x28`, irq9 will request interrupt `0x29`, and so on.

358   this is command word 3. The three least-significant bits here are telling the slave its ID, that it is a
slave on the master's irq2.

359   this is command word 4. Bit 0 set tells the slave it is connected to an i386 system. Bit 1 clear
means that the slave is expecting an EOI from software. There is no provision for auto EOI on the
slave.

362–369   some changes are made to the `ack` field in the `i8259A_irq_type` (defined in Section
12.7.2.1), depending on whether auto EOI is set up on the master or not.

367   if auto EOI mode is requested, then the PIC could send another instance of this irq request before
the first one has finished, so the `ack` function is aliased onto `disable`. This means that the
interrupt is disabled while it is being handled.

369   this is the default value anyway (see Section 12.7.2.1).

371   we wait 100 microseconds for the 8259A to initialise.

373–374   this sets up the master and slave irq masks, from the copies maintained by the operating system
(see Section 12.7.2.2).

12.7.4   Startup and shutdown

Figure 12.35, from `arch/i386/kernel/i8259.c`, shows the trivial startup and shutdown routines for the 8259A PIC.

```
140   #define shutdown_8259A_irq   disable_8259A_irq

144   static unsigned int startup_8259A_irq(unsigned int irq)
145   {
146         enable_8259A_irq(irq);
147         return 0;
148   }
```

Figure 12.35 Initialising the 8259A programmable interrupt controller (PIC)

140   both of these are of type `void`, so a simple macro is sufficient. The `disable_8259A_irq()`
function itself is described in Section 12.7.6.

144   it is really aliased onto `enable_8259A_irq()` (see Section 12.7.5), but this is defined as
`void`, whereas `startup()` is expected to return an `unsigned int` to indicate whether there is
an interrupt pending when it was started up. Hence the need for this wrapper function, which
always returns 0, as by definition nothing can be pending.

12.7.5   Enable

The function shown in Figure 12.36, from `arch/i386/kernel/i8259.c`, enables a
particular irq line on the appropriate PIC.

```
199  void enable_8259A_irq(unsigned int irq)
200  {
201      unsigned int mask = ~(1 << irq);
202      unsigned long flags;
203
204      spin_lock_irqsave(&i8259A_lock, flags);
205      cached_irq_mask &= mask;
206      if (irq & 8)
207          outb(cached_A1, 0xA1);
208      else
209          outb(cached_21, 0x21);
210      spin_unlock_irqrestore(&i8259A_lock, flags);
211  }
```

Figure 12.36 Enabling a particular irq line

201 the `mask` variable is declared as an `unsigned int`, or 32 bits, so there is a maximum of 32 irqs. Note that the function as written will handle a maximum of 16. This mask is set to all 1s, except for the bit corresponding to the specific irq line to be enabled, which is 0.

204–210 the value of EFLAGS at this point is saved in the local flags and restored when the spinlock is given back (see Section 12.8 for the macros).

205 the bit corresponding to this irq line in `cached_irq_mask` is cleared.

206 if the irq number is between 8 and 15 (i.e. it is in the slave PIC), then bit 3 of `irq` will always be set.

207 this writes the second byte of the `cached_irq_mask` to port 0xA1, the interrupt mask register of the slave PIC [see Section 12.9.1.3 for the `outb()` function].

209 this writes the first byte of the `cached_irq_mask` to port 0x21, the interrupt mask register of the master PIC.

12.7.6 Disable

The function which disables a particular irq on the PIC is shown in Figure 12.37, from `arch/i386/kernel/i8259.c`.

```
185  void disable_8259A_irq(unsigned int irq)
186  {
187      unsigned int mask = 1 << irq;
188      unsigned long flags;
189
190      spin_lock_irqsave(&i8259A_lock, flags);
191      cached_irq_mask |= mask;
192      if (irq & 8)
193          outb(cached_A1, 0xA1);
194      else
195          outb(cached_21, 0x21);
```

```
196          spin_unlock_irqrestore(&i8259A_lock, flags);
197 }
```

Figure 12.37   Disabling a particular irq line

187   this sets the bit in mask corresponding to the irq number. All the other bits are clear.

190   the value of EFLAGS at this point is saved in the local flags and restored when the spinlock is given back (see Section 12.8 for the macro).

191   this sets the appropriate bit in cached_irq_mask, without affecting any others. A bit set means the corresponding irq line is disabled.

192–195   these are identical to lines 206–209 in Figure 12.36, and the same comments apply.

12.7.7 Acknowledge

There is both a hardware and a software acknowledgement cycle in the i386 architecture. The CPU takes care of the hardware acknowledgement automatically; it is no concern of the operating system. However, the PIC may be set up in non-automatic EOI mode. In this case, even after the PIC has received this hardware acknowledgement from the CPU, it will not send any further interrupts until it receives a formal acknowledgement from the software that it is safe to do so.

This section is broken down into two parts. First, there is the straightforward acknowledgement, which is covered in Section 12.7.7.1. However, on the rare occasions that the software detects that the interrupt is spurious (e.g. from an irq line that is not in use), then it has to interrogate the PIC further in an attempt to find out what is going on. This is dealt with in Section 12.7.7.2.

12.7.7.1 *Acknowledging receipt of an interrupt to the programmable interrupt controller*

The code shown in Figure 12.38, from arch/i386/kernel/i8259.c, shows the function that actually acknowledges to the 8259A that an interrupt has been received and is being handled. The comment in the code warns that the 8259A is a fragile beast; it pretty much *has* to be done exactly like this (mask it first, *then* send the EOI; and the order of the EOIs to the two 8259As is important).

```
266 void mask_and_ack_8259A(unsigned int irq)
267 {
268          unsigned int irqmask = 1 << irq;
269          unsigned long flags;
270
271          spin_lock_irqsave(&i8259A_lock, flags);

287          if (cached_irq_mask & irqmask)
288                  goto spurious_8259A_irq;
289          cached_irq_mask |= irqmask;
290
```

```
291  handle_real_irq:
292      if (irq & 8) {
293          inb(0xA1);
294          outb(cached_A1,0xA1);
295          outb(0x60+(irq&7),0xA0);
296          outb(0x62,0x20);
297      } else {
298          inb(0x21);
299          outb(cached_21,0x21);
300          outb(0x60+irq,0x20);
301      }
302      spin_unlock_irqrestore(&i8259A_lock, flags);
303      return;
304
305  spurious_8259A_irq:

309      if (i8259A_irq_real(irq))

314          goto handle_real_irq;
315
316      {
317      static int spurious_irq_mask;

322      if (!(spurious_irq_mask & irqmask)) {
323          printk("spurious 8259A interrupt: IRQ%d.\n", irq);
324          spurious_irq_mask |= irqmask;
325      }
326      atomic_inc(&irq_err_count);

332      goto handle_real_irq;
333      }
334  }
```

Figure 12.38   Acknowledging an interrupt to the 8259A programmable interrupt controller (PIC)

268   the number of the irq to acknowledge has been passed as a parameter. This line creates a mask in which the only bit set is the one corresponding to the irq.

271   the value of EFLAGS at this point is saved in the local flags and restored when the spinlock is given back, at line 302. The lock itself has been declared in the code in Section 12.7.2.1, and the macros that operate on the interrupt-safe spinlock are from Section 12.8.

287–288   this code checks if the irq being acknowledged is masked out. If the bit corresponding to this irq is set in cached_irq_mask, then that irq line is actually disabled. In that case the irq being acknowledged would seem to be spurious. There is special code to handle this at line 305.

289   this adds the bit corresponding to the irq we are handling to the cached mask. This now marks it as disabled in the mask. We do not want another instance of this irq until we are finished with this one.

293–296   this block of code is dealing with an irq on the slave PIC. Because of the way the PICs are cascaded, when an interrupt signal is sent to the slave both of the PICs have to process interrupts so both have to be sent an acknowledgement. The appropriate irq has to be acknowledged to the slave, and irq2 has to be acknowledged to the master.

293   as described in Section 12.7.1, this is a read from an internal register of the slave PIC, by default the IRR. This dummy read is apparently needed by the PIC. Apart from the time it takes to do this read, it makes no difference.

294   this writes to the interrupt mask register of the slave, using the functions from Section 12.9.1.3. This is writing the change made at line 287 out to the hardware.

295   this sends an EOI command for a specific irq to the interrupt control port of the slave PIC. Because irqs on this PIC are numbered between 8 and 15, bit 3 of their binary representation will always be set. The (irq&7) clears bit 3, so its value is between 0 and 7. Bit 3 cleared also specifies the format of the remainder of the byte being written, namely, that it is operation command word 2. The other part of the value being written, 0x60, is 0110 0000 in binary, so it is writing 0110 0xxx, where xxx is the irq number on the slave. In operation command word 2 format, a value of 011 in the three most significant bits means that the whole byte is to be interpreted as an EOI command for the irq specified in the least three significant bits.

296   this sends an EOI command specifically for irq2 of the master PIC. This is writing 0110 0010 to the master.

298–300   this block of code is dealing with an irq on the master PIC.

299   this writes to the interrupt mask register of the master. This is writing the change made at line 289 out to the hardware.

300   this sends an EOI command for a specific irq to the interrupt control port of the master PIC. Because irqs on this PIC are numbered between 0 and 7, bit 3 of their binary representation will always be clear. Bit 3 cleared specifies the format of the remainder of the byte being written; namely, that it is operation command word 2. The other part of the value being written, 0x60, is 0110 0000 in binary, so it is writing 0110 0xxx, where xxx is the irq number on the master. In operation command word 2 format, a value of 011 in the three most significant bits means that the whole byte is to be interpreted as an EOI command for the irq specified in the least three significant bits.

302   this gives back the spinlock taken out at line 269 and restores the value in EFLAGS.

305–333   this is spurious IRQ handling. Control comes here from line 288 if, according to the local data structures, this irq is masked out and so should not occur.

309   this function, described in Section 12.7.7.2, interrogates the in-service register of the 8259A. It returns 1 if the bit corresponding to this irq is set, meaning that it is currently being serviced; otherwise, it returns 0.

314   it was not spurious, so we go back and acknowledge it.

316–333   at this point the irq has been determined to be spurious. This is the real spurious handling scope. Such a spurious irq is usually a sign of hardware problems so not much can be done. We report it and then go back and acknowledge it.

317   this `static` mask remains from call to call. It records irqs that were previously reported as spurious.

322   if the bit corresponding to the irq being handled (`irqmask`) is not set in the `static spurious_irq_mask`, the message is printed, so each spurious irq is reported the first time it occurs.

324   this sets the bit in the static mask so that it will not be reported again.

326   this variable is declared in Section 14.5.1.1. It tracks the total number of spurious irqs that have accumulated since boot time. It is only ever read in the `get_irq_list()` function, which is used by the `/proc` file system.

332   theoretically, this irq does not have to be handled, but in Linux this does not cause problems, so why not do so. Also, the spinlock is given back on the way out.

12.7.7.2   Determining if an interrupt is being serviced

The function shown in Figure 12.39 interrogates the PIC to determine if a specified irq is currently being serviced. It switches between 8259A internal registers, which is slow. This function expects its caller to be holding the interrupt controller spinlock.

```
243  static inline int i8259A_irq_real(unsigned int irq)
244  {
245       int value;
246       int irqmask = 1<<irq;
247
248       if (irq < 8) {
249            outb(0x0B,0x20);
250            value = inb(0x20) & irqmask;
251            outb(0x0A,0x20);
252            return value;
253       }
254       outb(0x0B,0xA0);
255       value = inb(0xA0) & (irqmask >> 8);
256       outb(0x0A,0xA0);
257       return value;
258  }
```

Figure 12.39   Determining if an interrupt is being serviced

246   this creates a mask in which the only bit set is the one corresponding to the irq that is being checked.

248–252   if the irq number is less than 8 then it is on the master PIC.

249   this writes 0000 1011 to the interrupt control register. Bit 3 set specifies the format of the whole byte as operation control word 3. This control word specifies which internal register will be returned by the next read from the interrupt control register. The register is specified by bits 0 and 1. The value 11 there specifies that future reads from this port will return the value in the in-service register (ISR). Bits set in this register specify irqs that are currently being serviced.

250   this reads from the ISR and masks out all the other bits except the one of interest. After this, value is 1 if the irq in question is currently being serviced; otherwise, it is 0, no matter what other irqs are being serviced.

251   this writes 0000 1010 to port 0x20. This changes future reads back to the interrupt request register (IRR). This is the default.

252   this returns TRUE if this irq is being serviced; otherwise, it returns FALSE.

254–257   this code is executed if the irq in question belongs to the slave PIC.

254   this writes to the internal control register of the slave, to change the source of the next read.

255   this reads from the ISR and masks that with the bit corresponding to this irq (shifted to the lower byte position). The resulting value is 1 if the bit corresponding to this irq is set, 0 otherwise 0.

256   this writes 0000 1010 to port 0xA0. This changes future reads back to the IRR register.

257   this returns TRUE if this irq is being serviced; otherwise, FALSE.

12.7.8 End

The code shown in Figure 12.40, from arch/i386/kernel/i8259.c, shows the function that is called when an interrupt has been handled. It enables future occurrences of that irq.

```
134  static void end_8259A_irq (unsigned int irq)
135  {
136      if (!(irq_desc[irq].status & (IRQ_DISABLED|IRQ_INPROGRESS)))
137          enable_8259A_irq(irq);
138  }
```

Figure 12.40   Interrupt handling is finished

136   if the irq in question is neither disabled nor in progress (on another CPU) then we enable it by using the function from Section 12.7.5.

12.7.9 Determining if an interrupt is pending

Sometimes it is necessary to check whether or not a particular irq is pending. The function shown in Figure 12.41, from arch/i386/kernel/i8259.c, interrogates the PIC and returns TRUE or FALSE. It is only ever called in the code in Section 14.3.1.2 but as it communicates with the PIC discussion of the function belongs here. Note that this function reads from the interrupt control port of the PIC. This is a dual function port. By default it is set so that reads return the value in the interrupt request register. This register records interrupt signals that have arrived at the PIC but have not yet been sent on to the CPU.

```
213  int i8259A_irq_pending(unsigned int irq)
214  {
215      unsigned int mask = 1<<irq;
216      unsigned long flags;
217      int ret;
218
219      spin_lock_irqsave(&i8259A_lock, flags);
220      if (irq < 8)
221          ret = inb(0x20) & mask;
222      else
223          ret = inb(0xA0) & (mask >> 8);
224      spin_unlock_irqrestore(&i8259A_lock, flags);
225
226      return ret;
227  }
```

Figure 12.41   Checking for pending interrupt

215   this sets the bit in `mask` corresponding to the irq number. All the other bits are clear.

219   The value of EFLAGS at this point is saved in the local `flags` and restored when the spinlock is given back. The macros for manipulating the interrupt safe spinlock are given in Section 12.8.

220–221   if the number of the irq being checked is less than 8 then it is on the master PIC. We get the value from its interrupt request register. ANDing this with `mask` will result in TRUE if the corresponding bit is set in IRR (irq pending), FALSE if not.

223   otherwise, the irq is on the slave PIC, so we get the value from its interrupt request register and move the `mask` down to the lower byte position.

226   this returns TRUE if this irq is pending.

12.8   Interrupt-safe locks

There is a particular problem with a data structure that can be accessed by a routine in the kernel and that can also be written by an interrupt handler. There are occasions when it is not good enough to prevent another CPU from accessing the data structure (using locks); interrupts must also be disabled. Of course, when finished with the critical section, not only must the lock be released but interrupts must also be enabled. A set of spinlocks and read–write locks are defined specifically for this, known as interrupt-safe locks. These are built up of combinations of macros, some of which manipulate locks, while others disable or enable interrupts.

As well as these hardware interrupts, Linux, like other operating systems, also has a mechanism known as software interrupts, or bottom halves. These will be dealt with in detail in Chapter 16. Here it is sufficient to know that they exist and that special versions of the standard locks must be provided to cater for them.

12.8.1 Macros for interrupt-safe locks

The extra locking macros are all shown in Figure 12.42, from `<linux/spinlock.h>`. There are 19 macros defined in this block of code. These 19 definitions are completely made up of calls to a further 13 macros. Seven of these deal with locking and unlocking spinlocks and read–write locks, which have been examined in great detail in Sections 5.3–5.7. Of the other 6, `local_irq_save()` and `local_irq_restore()` take care of saving and restoring the value in the EFLAGS register (see Section 12.8.2). Then `local_irq_disable()` and `local_irq_enable()`, also from Section 12.8.2, arrange for enabling and disabling hardware interrupts. Finally, `local_bh_disable()` and `local_bh_enable()`, from Section 16.5.2, disable and enable bottom-half processing.

```
10   #define spin_lock_irqsave(lock, flags)
         do {local_irq_save(flags);    spin_lock(lock); }    while (0)
11   #define spin_lock_irq(lock)
         do {local_irq_disable();    spin_lock(lock); }    while (0)
12   #define spin_lock_bh(lock)
         do {local_bh_disable();    spin_lock(lock); }    while (0)
13
14   #define read_lock_irqsave(lock, flags)
         do {local_irq_save(flags);    read_lock(lock); }    while (0)
15   #define read_lock_irq(lock)
         do {local_irq_disable();    read_lock(lock); }    while (0)
16   #define read_lock_bh(lock)
         do {local_bh_disable();    read_lock(lock); }    while (0)
17
18   #define write_lock_irqsave(lock, flags)
         do {local_irq_save(flags);    write_lock(lock); }    while (0)
19   #define write_lock_irq(lock)
         do {local_irq_disable();    write_lock(lock); }    while (0)
20   #define write_lock_bh(lock)
         do {local_bh_disable();    write_lock(lock); }    while (0)
21
22   #define spin_unlock_irqrestore(lock, flags)
     do {spin_unlock(lock); local_irq_restore(flags);    }    while (0)
23   #define spin_unlock_irq(lock)
     do {spin_unlock(lock); local_irq_enable();          }    while (0)
24   #define spin_unlock_bh(lock)
     do {spin_unlock(lock); local_bh_enable();           }    while (0)
25
26   #define read_unlock_irqrestore(lock, flags)
     do {read_unlock(lock); local_irq_restore(flags);    unsigned    long
     stack_start, }      while (0)
27   #define read_unlock_irq(lock)
     do {read_unlock(lock); local_irq_enable();          }    while (0)
28   #define read_unlock_bh(lock)
     do {read_unlock(lock); local_bh_enable();           }    while (0)
29
30   #define write_unlock_irqrestore(lock, flags)
```

```
        do {write_unlock(lock);local_irq_restore(flags);   }     while (0)
31   #define write_unlock_irq(lock)
        do {write_unlock(lock);local_irq_enable();          }     while (0)
32   #define write_unlock_bh(lock)
        do {write_unlock(lock);local_bh_enable();           }     while (0)
33   #define spin_trylock_bh(lock)({ int __r; local_bh_disable();         \
34                                  __r = spin_trylock(lock);             \
35                                  if (!__r) local_bh_enable();          \
36                                  __r; })
```

Figure 12.42   Interrupt-safe locking macros

12.8.2 Generic interrupt macros

First of all we examine the macros which control interrupts; see Figure 12.43, from
`<asm-i386/system.h>`.

```
313  #define __save_flags(x)
             __asm__ __volatile__("pushfl ; popl %0":"=g" (x):)
314  #define __restore_flags(x)
              __asm__ __volatile__("pushl %0 ; popfl": :"g" (x):"memory")
315  #define __cli()     __asm__ __volatile__("cli": : :"memory")
316  #define __sti()     __asm__ __volatile__("sti": : :"memory")
317
318  #define safe_halt()
             __asm__ __volatile__("sti; hlt": : :"memory")

321  #define local_irq_save(x)
         __asm__ __volatile__("pushfl ; popl %0 ; cli":"=g" (x): :"memory")
322  #define local_irq_restore(x) __restore_flags(x)
323  #define local_irq_disable() __cli()
324  #define local_irq_enable()  __sti()

326  #ifdef CONFIG_SMP

332  #define cli() __global_cli()
333  #define sti() __global_sti()
334  #define save_flags(x) ((x)=__global_save_flags())
335  #define restore_flags(x) __global_restore_flags(x)
336
337  #else
338
339  #define cli() __cli()
340  #define sti() __sti()
341  #define save_flags(x) __save_flags(x)
```

```
342  #define restore_flags(x) __restore_flags(x)
343
344  #endif
```

Figure 12.43 Interrupt macros

313   the value in the EFLAGS register is pushed on the stack and then popped to parameter 0 (x), which can either be a general purpose register or be a memory location.

314   parameter 0 (the saved EFLAGS value, in a register or in memory) is pushed on the stack and then popped to the EFLAGS register. The "memory" directive tells the compiler that memory will be modified in an unpredictable manner so it will not keep memory values cached in registers across the group of assembler instructions.

315   this merely executes the CLI machine instruction, disabling maskable interrupts. The "memory" constraint is an indication to the assembler that memory may be modified in an unpredictable fashion, so it is not to keep memory values cached in registers.

316   this merely executes the STI machine instruction, enabling maskable interrupts on the local CPU.

318   this macro is used in the idle loop. It first enables interrupts then halts the processor. If halted while interrupts are disabled, the processor could not be woken again, short of a reboot. It remains halted until either the reset line is activated or a maskable interrupt is requested.

321   the value in the EFLAGS register is pushed on the stack and then popped to parameter 0 (x), which can either be a general purpose register or be in memory. Then interrupts are disabled.

322–324   these are just aliases for other macros, defined earlier.

332–335   in the multiprocessor case, these macros are aliased onto the global ones (see Sections 14.5.2 and 14.5.3, where they are described in detail).

334   the __global_save_flags() function will be described in Section 14.5.3.1. It returns a value representing the interrupt handling disposition of the system, which is then assigned to x.

339–342   in the uniprocessor case, the macros are aliased onto the standalone ones, which have just been examined.

12.9 Functions for reading and writing input–output ports

At the hardware level, the i386 architecture has only two basic instructions for input and output, IN and OUT. These move one byte at a time. There are also string versions of these instructions, INS and OUTS, which move a sequence of bytes between an IO port and memory. Linux provides a whole series of functions and macros to wrap these instructions. There are also 'pausing' versions which, as the name implies, give slow hardware time to react to the IO operation.

The comment (from Linus) says the code is not meant to be obfuscating: it is just complicated to:

- handle it all in a way that makes GNU C able to optimise it as well as possible and

- avoid writing the same thing over and over again with slight variations and possibly making a mistake somewhere.

Maybe it is not meant to be obfuscating, but it is certainly very condensed and takes a lot of teasing out.

Some 18 assembly language routines are provided for reading and writing IO ports – four each for 8-bit, 16-bit, and 32-bit operations, and six for string operations – but these are not provided as assembler code nor as clearly written inline assembler but rather as a nested set of macros that are some of the most difficult parts of the whole kernel to understand. The comment in the code says 'talk about misusing macros ...', and I agree.

12.9.1 Single input–output functions

The first 12 functions transfer a single data element to or from the IO port. First, we will examine how these functions are actually instantiated in the code and then the macros used to generate them.

12.9.1.1 Instantiating the input–output functions

The block of code shown in Figure 12.44, from <asm-i386/io.h>, generates the functions to read and write IO ports. The preprocessor converts this into the actual code for the 12 functions. There are only two macros involved here, __IN() and __OUT(), each of which generates two functions. These will now be examined in turn. As RETURN_TYPE is used in all of them, it is given three different definitions.

```
308  #define RETURN_TYPE unsigned char
309  __IN(b,"")
310  #undef RETURN_TYPE
311  #define RETURN_TYPE unsigned short
312  __IN(w,"")
313  #undef RETURN_TYPE
314  #define RETURN_TYPE unsigned int
315  __IN(l,"")
316  #undef RETURN_TYPE
317
318  __OUT(b,"b",char)
319  __OUT(w,"w",short)
320  __OUT(l,,int)
```

Figure 12.44 Macros for reading and writing input–output ports

12.9.1.2 Reading from an input–output port

The macros on lines 308–316 of Figure 12.44 are expanded by using the macros given in Figure 12.45, from <asm-i386/io.h>.

```
280  #define __IN1(s)                                                          \
281  static inline RETURN_TYPE in##s(unsigned short port) {RETURN_TYPE _v;
282
283  #define __IN2(s,s1,s2)                                                    \
284  __asm____volatile__ ("in" #s " %" s2 "1,%" s1 "0"

293  #define __IN(s,s1,i...)                                                   \
294  __IN1(s) __IN2(s,s1,"w") : "=a" (_v) : "Nd" (port) ,##i );
                                                             return _v; }    \
295  __IN1(s##_p) __IN2(s,s1,"w") __FULL_SLOW_DOWN_IO :
                                    "=a" (_v) : "Nd" (port) ,##i ); return _v; }
```

Figure 12.45 Reading from an input–output port

280–281 this macro produces the first part of the function definition.

283–284 this macro produces the inline assembler to be included in the function definition.

293–295 this macro produces two function definitions. Note that the third parameter to __IN() is given as i.... This is a feature of GNU C, known as a **rest argument**. It consists of zero or more arguments, as many as the caller provides. Then, when it is used (e.g. on line 294 or 295) it is preceded by ##. This is another feature of the GNU C preprocessor: ## before an empty rest argument discards the unnecessary comma immediately preceding it.

Probably the best way to understand what is going on here is to expand a sample macro fully. The most suitable one is the macro on line 309 of Figure 12.44, as this is the most frequently used one. Using lines 293–295 of Figure 12.45 to expand __IN(b,"") gives the result shown in Figure 12.46. Using lines 280–284 of Figure 12.45, each of these lines in Figure 12.46 can now be expanded in turn, with the results as shown in Figure 12.47.

```
__IN1(b) __IN2(b, "", "w") : "=a" (_v) : "Nd" (port)); return _v} \
__IN1(b_p) __IN2(b, "", "w") __FULL_SLOW_DOWN_IO :
                                  "=a" (_v) : "Nd" (port)); return _v; }
```

Figure 12.46 First-level expansion of the read macro

```
static inline unsigned char inb(unsigned short port) {
    unsigned char _v;
    __asm____volatile__ ("in"b " %" "w" "1,%" "" "0"
                            : "=a" (_v) : "Nd" (port));
    return _v
}
static inline unsigned char inb_p(unsigned short port) {
    unsigned char _v;
    __asm____volatile__ ("in"b " %" "w" "1,%" "" "0"
                            __FULL_SLOW_DOWN_IO
                            : "=a" (_v) : "Nd" (port));
```

```
        return _v
}
```

Figure 12.47   Second-level expansion of the read macro

This gives two functions for reading a byte from a port. The first function, inb(), executes the assembler instruction inb %w1, %. Parameter 1 is port. In AT&T syntax, opcodes can be suffixed with one-character modifiers that specify the size of operands, in this case a byte. The IN instruction always reads into the EAX register, in this case the AL part of it, which is aliased onto the unsigned char _v. This is the value returned by the function. "d" is the EDX register; "N" specifies that the value is to be a constant in the range 0–255, specially for IN and OUT instructions. The second function, inb_p(), is identical to the first, except that it adds the macro __FULL_SLOW_DOWN_IO. This is just a dummy operation, to give slow hardware time to react to the instruction just executed. The __FULL_SLOW_DOWN_IO macro is discussed in Section 12.9.3.

The macro on line 312 of Figure 12.44 expands in a similar fashion, producing functions inw() and inw_p(). These contain a version of the IN instruction, which transfers a word (2 bytes) from the specific port into the AX register. The function then returns that value as an unsigned short. The macro on line 315 of Figure 12.44 expands into the functions inl() and inl_p(). These transfer a long (4 bytes) from the specific port into the EAX register and then return that value as a long.

12.9.1.3   Writing to an input–output port

The macros on lines 318–320 of Figure 12.44 also expand, using the further macros given in Figure 12.48, from <asm-i386/io.h>. The remarks made about Figure 12.45 are also relevant here. Again, the best way to understand what is going on here is to expand a sample macro fully. The macro on line 318 of Figure 12.44 is taken, as this is the most frequently used one.

```
243  #define __OUT1(s,x)                                                       \
244  static inline void out##s(unsigned x value, unsigned short port)     {
245
246  #define __OUT2(s,s1,s2)                                                   \
247  __asm__ __volatile__ ("out" #s " %" s1 "0,%" s2 "1"

257  #define __OUT(s,s1,x)                                                     \
258  __OUT1(s,x) __OUT2(s,s1,"w") :: "a" (value), "Nd" (port)); }           \
259  __OUT1(s##_p,x) __OUT2(s,s1,"w") __FULL_SLOW_DOWN_IO ::
                                        "a" (value), "Nd" (port)); }
```

Figure 12.48   Writing to an input–output port

Using lines 257–259 of Figure 12.48 to expand __OUT(b,"b",char) gives the result shown in Figure 12.49. We now expand each of these lines in turn, with the result shown in Figure 12.50.

```
__OUT1(b, char)     __OUT2(b, "b", "w") : : "a"(value),
                                           "Nd"(port)); }        \
__OUT1(b_p, char)   __OUT2(b, "b", "w") __FULL_SLOW_DOWN_IO : :
                                "a"(value), "Nd"(port));}         \
```

Figure 12.49   First level of expansion of the write macro

```
static inline void outb(unsigned char value, unsigned short port)
{
        __asm__ __volatile__ ("out"b " %" "b" "0,%" "w" "1"
        : : "a"(value), "Nd"(port));
}


static inline void outb_p(unsigned char value,unsigned short port)
{
        __asm__ __volatile__ ("out"b " %" "b" "0,%" "w" "1"
        __FULL_SLOW_DOWN_IO
        : : "a"(value), "Nd"(port)) ;
}
```

Figure 12.50   Second-level expansion of the write macro

So, we end up with two almost identical functions. Both execute the same machine instruction, outb %b0, %w1. This writes a byte from parameter 0 (value, mapped onto the AL register) to the 16-bit port number specified by parameter 1 (port), mapped into the DX register. The only difference in the second function is that it pauses before returning to the caller, to allow the IO operation to take effect.

The macro on line 319 of Figure 12.44 expands in a similar fashion, giving two functions outw() and outw_p(). Line 320 of that Figure generates the functions outl() and outl_p().

12.9.2   String input–ouput functions

The final group of six functions transfer a sequence of data items to or from an IO port. They are instantiated by the block of code in Figure 12.51, from <asm-i386/io.h>. There are no pausing versions – it would not make sense. If the hardware is slow, you cannot expect to stream data to or from it.

```
322  __INS(b)
323  __INS(w)
324  __INS(l)
325
326  __OUTS(b)
327  __OUTS(w)
328  __OUTS(l)
```

Figure 12.51   Macros for string input–output

12.9.2.1 Reading a string from an input–output port

The macros on lines 322–324 of Figure 12.51 expand, using the further macro given in Figure 12.52, from `<asm-i386/io.h>`, in the code given in Figure 12.53. The `insb()` function will be discussed in detail. The three parameters are the port number to read from, a pointer to the location in memory where the data is to be written, and the number of bytes to transfer. This function uses the standard string operations in the i386 CPU. The REP instruction means 'repeat the following instruction, decrementing ECX each time, until ECX is zero'. The INSB instruction transfers a byte from the port specified by EDX into the memory location specified by the ES segment register, offset by DI; it also increments DI. All of this has to be set up appropriately with the operand specifiers.

```
298  #define __INS(s)                                                    \
299  static inline void ins##s(unsigned short port, void * addr,
                                          unsigned long count)     \
300  { __asm__ __volatile__ ("rep ; ins" #s                             \
301       : "=D" (addr), "=c" (count)
302       : "d" (port),"0" (addr),"1" (count)); }
```

Figure 12.52   Macro for reading from an input/output port

```
static inline void insb(unsigned short port, void * addr,
                                          unsigned long count)
{ __asm__ __volatile__ ("rep ; ins"b
     : "=D" (addr), "=c" (count)
     : "d" (port),"0" (addr),"1" (count));
}
static inline void insw(unsigned short port, void * addr,
                                          unsigned long count)
{ __asm__ __volatile__ ("rep ; ins"w
     : "=D" (addr), "=c" (count)
     : "d" (port),"0" (addr),"1" (count));
}
static inline void insl(unsigned short port, void * addr,
                                          unsigned long count)
{ __asm__ __volatile__ ("rep ; ins"l
     : "=D" (addr), "=c" (count)
     : "d" (port),"0" (addr),"1" (count));
}
```

Figure 12.53   Reading a string from an inut–output port

- Parameter 0 is addr, aliased onto the DI register. The operand specifier "=D" means it is write-only for this operation; the previous value is discarded and replaced by output data. This is the updated value of DI, after the increment. The INS machine instruction takes its destination memory address from ES:DI.

- Parameter 1 is count, aliased onto the ECX register. Again, this is the updated value after the increment.

- Parameter 2 is `port`, aliased onto the EDX register.

- Parameter 3 is the input version of `addr`. This is to be in the same location as the output version, the DI register.

- Parameter 4, is the input version of `count`. This is to have the same location as parameter 1, the ECX register.

The `insw()` function is similar, the only difference being that it transfers a word at a time. Likewise, the `insl()` function transfers a long, or 4 bytes, at a time.

12.9.2.2   Writing a string to an input–output port

The macro in Figure 12.54, from `<asm-i386/io.h>`, is used to instantiate the three functions on lines 326–328 of Figure 12.51. This produces the final three functions, `outsb()`, `outsw()`, and `outsl()`. The only differences to note from Section 12.9.2.1 are:

- the parameter `addr` to the functions has the attribute `const`;

- parameter 0 to the assembler instruction has the operand constraint `"=S"`. On the i386 this specifies the `SI` register. The `OUTS` machine instruction takes its source memory address from `ES:DI`.

```
303  #define __OUTS(s)                                                    \
304  static inline void outs##s(unsigned short port, const void *
                                           addr, unsigned long count)    \
305  { __asm__ __volatile__ ("rep ; outs" #s                            \
306       : "=S" (addr), "=c" (count) : "d" (port),"0" (addr),"1"
                                                      (count)); }
```

Figure 12.54   Writing a string to an input–output port

12.9.3   Pausing an input–output operation

Some hardware takes an appreciable time to react to data that have been written to it or to prepare the next data item after one has been read. So, pausing versions of the reading and writing functions have been provided, as seen in the previous sections. All of these pause by including the macro `__FULL_SLOW_DOWN_IO`. The definition of this is in Figure 12.55, from `<asm-i386/io.h>`.

```
224  #ifdef SLOW_IO_BY_JUMPING
225  #define __SLOW_DOWN_IO "\njmp 1f\n1:\tjmp 1f\n1:"
226  #else
227  #define __SLOW_DOWN_IO "\noutb %%al,$0x80"
228  #endif
229
```

```
230  #ifdef REALLY_SLOW_IO
231  #define __FULL_SLOW_DOWN_IO  __SLOW_DOWN_IO __SLOW_DOWN_IO
                                  __SLOW_DOWN_IO __SLOW_DOWN_IO
232  #else
233  #define __FULL_SLOW_DOWN_IO  __SLOW_DOWN_IO
234  #endif
```

Figure 12.55 Pausing an input—output operation

224–228 first, we have the definition of the macro __SLOW_DOWN_IO. There are two possible ways to implement this. One is by jumping; the other by writing to an arbitrary port.

225 this generates the assembler code:

```
        jmp  1f
1:      jmp  1f
1:
```

The idea is that executing these two jumps takes a finite time, but the delay timing is not accurate: it is less on a faster machine than on a slow one. Note the __volatile__ stops the compiler from removing these jumps from the code.

227 this writes the contents of AL to port 0x80. This is just a dummy, delaying, operation. Linus comments:

Using OUTB to a nonexistent port seems to guarantee better timings than the two short jumps: even on fast machines. On the other hand, I'd like to be sure of a nonexistent port: I feel a bit unsafe about using 0x80 (should be safe, though).

231–234 now we come to the definition of __FULL_SLOW_DOWN_IO. Whether REALLY_SLOW_IO is defined or not is decided by the speed of the machine at boot time. The macro expands to four executions of __SLOW_DOWN_IO or is just aliased onto __SLOW_DOWN_IO.

13

Advanced programmable interrupt controllers

With the advent of the Pentium version of the i386 architecture, Intel introduced the advanced programmable interrupt controller (PIC), or APIC. This comes in two flavours. All Pentium processors have a local APIC, on the same chip as the CPU, though not strictly part of it. The presence of such an APIC is determined by `CONFIG_X86_LOCAL_APIC`. Like the 8259A PIC (see Section 12.7), it provides facilities for queuing, nesting, and masking interrupts. It can be disabled and used in conjunction with an 8259A.

There may also be an input–output (IO) APIC, which takes the place of the 8259A. This will certainly be present in a multiprocessor system, where it is responsible for routing interrupts between central processing units (CPUs). The IO APIC will be dealt with in Chapter 14.

The local APIC can receive interrupts from a number of sources.

- It has two local pins of its own, to which hardware devices can be connected directly. Such a device is then specific to this CPU and cannot interrupt any other. These pins are known as `LINT0` and `LINT1`. They can be edge or level triggered.

- It has a built in timer, which can be programmed to generate periodic interrupts.

- It can also generate an interrupt when an error occurs. The local APIC has an error status register (ESR) which records errors.

- External devices can be connected to a PIC in the usual way, and the PIC connected to the `LINT0` pin of the local APIC.

- The IO APIC can send interrupts to the local APIC. This is done over a hardware bus; no software is involved.

13.1 APIC registers

The APIC contains a large number of registers, which are mapped into the physical address space of the computer, starting at 0x FEE0 0000. Each register is aligned on a 16-byte boundary, even though not 16 bytes long. The APIC address space extends up to 0x FEE0 03ff, giving a space of 0x 0400 bytes. These APIC registers are always accessed using 32 bit loads/stores.

Only those registers actually used by Linux code will be discussed here. For ease of handling, the definitions are broken down into four blocks.

13.1.1 Identification and priority

Figure 13.1, from <asm-i386/apicdef.h>, shows constants used to manipulate the first block of registers, dealing with the identification of the APIC, and arbitration between interrupts.

```
11    #define   APIC_DEFAULT_PHYS_BASE      0xfee00000
12
13    #define   APIC_ID                 0x20
14    #define       APIC_ID_MASK            (0x0F<<24)
15    #define       GET_APIC_ID(x)          (((x)>>24)&0x0F)
16    #define   APIC_LVR                0x30
17    #define       APIC_LVR_MASK           0xFF00FF
18    #define       GET_APIC_VERSION(x)     ((x)&0xFF)
19    #define       GET_APIC_MAXLVT(x)      (((x)>>16)&  0xFF)
20    #define       APIC_INTEGRATED(x)      ((x)&0xF0)
21    #define   APIC_TASKPRI            0x80
22    #define       APIC_TPRI_MASK          0xFF

26    #define   APIC_EOI                0xB0
27    #define       APIC_EIO_ACK            0x0
```

Figure 13.1 Identification and arbitration registers

11 by default, the APIC is wired into physical memory at this location. All other registers are identified by offsets from this.

13 this is the offset of the local APIC identification (ID) register.

14 the mask is 0x 0f00 0000. The ID number of the APIC is contained in bits 24–27. While set by default at power up, system software can give each APIC a unique ID.

15 this macro is passed the value in the APIC_ID register. It shifts the input value right 24 bits (6 hex nibbles) and strips off all but the last four bits. It evaluates to the ID number of the APIC, from bits 24–27.

16 this is the local APIC version register, at offset 0x30. This is a read-only register.

17   as this mask implies, only bits 0–7 and 16–23 are used. The version is in bits 0–7. Bits 4–7 distinguish a local APIC (1) from an external IO APIC (0). Bits 16–23 contain the highest-numbered entry in the local vector table (LVT; see Section 13.1.4).

18   by stripping off all but the lower 8 bits, this returns the APIC version field, which is in bits 0–7.

19   this macro returns the highest-numbered entry in the LVT. This information is in bits 16–23. For example, if there are 5 entries, the macro returns 4.

20   this macro checks bits 4–7. If 1, it evaluates to TRUE, this is a local APIC integrated into the CPU; otherwise, it is an external 82489DX APIC.

21   this is the task priority register (TPR), which tracks the priority of the CPU. Only irqs (interrupt requests) whose priority is higher than the value in the TPR will be serviced. Others are recorded and dealt with as soon as possible.

22   only bits 0–7 are defined. This is the task priority.

26   the end-of-interrupt (EOI) register: software indicates that it has completed handling of an interrupt by writing an arbitrary value to this register; however, for future compatibility, a 0 is written. This write informs the local APIC that it can issue the next interrupt to the CPU. The APIC then checks the highest-priority bit in IRR (see line 40 in Figure 13.2) and selects the next irq. If the irq just handled was level triggered, the local APIC then sends an EOI to all IO APICs in the system, containing the number of the level triggered interrupt just serviced.

27   this value is written to the EOI register to indicate that an interrupt has been accepted by software.

13.1.2   Interrupt handling registers

The next block of definitions are shown in Figure 13.2, from `<asm-i386/apicdef.h>`. These are concerned with incoming interrupts from all sources.

```
29   #define   APIC_LDR 0xD0
30   #define      APIC_LDR_MASK             (0xFF<<24)
31   #define      GET_APIC_LOGICAL_ID(x) (((x)>>24)&0xFF)
32   #define      SET_APIC_LOGICAL_ID(x) (((x)<<24))
33   #define      APIC_ALL_CPUS             0xFF
34   #define   APIC_DFR      0xE0
35   #define   APIC_SPIV     0xF0
36   #define      APIC_SPIV_FOCUS_DISABLED         (1<<9)
37   #define      APIC_SPIV_APIC_ENABLED           (1<<8)
38   #define   APIC_ISR      0x100
39   #define   APIC_TMR      0x180
40   #define   APIC_IRR      0x200
41   #define   APIC_ESR      0x280
42   #define      APIC_ESR_SEND_CS        0x00001
43   #define      APIC_ESR_RECV_CS        0x00002
44   #define      APIC_ESR_SEND_ACC       0x00004
```

```
45   #define        APIC_ESR_RECV_ACC       0x00008
46   #define        APIC_ESR_SENDILL        0x00020
47   #define        APIC_ESR_RECVILL        0x00040
48   #define        APIC_ESR_ILLREGA        0x00080
```

Figure 13.2 Interrupt handling registers

29   this is the offset for the logical destination register (LDR). The destination of an interrupt can be specified logically, using an 8-bit destination address. Each local APIC is given a unique logical ID by software, set in `setup_local_APIC()` (see Section 13.2.1). This is stored in the LDR.

30   the logical ID is in bits 24–31.

31   this macro shifts bits 24–31 of its parameter into position 0–7, clearing all other positions, so it then evaluates to the contents of bits 24–31, the logical ID of the local APIC.

32   this macro merely moves bits 0–7 into positions 24–31, clearing all other positions, so it moves its parameter into the part of the bit map corresponding to the logical ID of the local APIC. It is used when writing to the register.

33   this is a broadcast mask.

34   this is the destination format register (DFR). The only relevant bits are 28–31. This defines the interpretation of the logical destination information. It can be unique or it can be clustered.

   • If bits 28–31 are set to all 1s, then the APIC is in flat mode. In this way, a particular bit in the ID field of the LDR represents each APIC, so an arbitrary group can be selected by setting the appropriate bits. In this mode, a broadcast can be performed by setting all 8 bits in the message destination address to one.

   • If bits 28–31 are all 0s, then the APIC is in cluster mode. The bits of the logical ID field are interpreted as a unique address.

35   this is the spurious interrupt vector register, which is discussed in detail in Section 13.7.5. However, there are two bits in this register that have nothing to do with spurious interrupts.

36   this enables (0) or disables (1) focus processor checking. This facility allows a local APIC to announce to all the others that it is going to handle (is the focus of) a particular irq, and the others just ignore it.

37   strange as it may seem, this bit enables the APIC (1) or disables it (0).

38–40   the next three registers are involved in the acceptance of an interrupt by the APIC. Each is 256 bits, one per entry in the IDT.

38   this is the in-service register (ISR). It is read-only. It records interrupts accepted by the CPU but not yet fully serviced, as no EOI has been received from the software. The appropriate bit is set when INTA is received from the CPU. If the interrupt is level triggered (indicated by the corresponding bit set in the TMR) then an EOI is sent to the IO APIC. It is a 256-bit register, each bit representing one interrupt. There are 0x80 (128) bytes here, but apparently only the first 32 are used.

39   this is the trigger mode register (TMR), again with one bit per interrupt. It is read-only. When an interrupt is accepted by the APIC, the corresponding bit is cleared for edge triggered or set for level triggered interrupts. If set, the local APIC sends an EOI to the IO APIC.

40   this is the interrupt request register (IRR), again with one bit per interrupt. This contains actual interrupt requests that have been accepted by the APIC but not dealt with. The highest-priority one is sent to the CPU next. The corresponding bit is cleared when the INTA cycle is generated by the CPU.

41   this is the error status register (ESR). The local APIC sets bits in this register (7 bits are defined) to record errors it detects (see the following lines). The ESR is reset (cleared) after being written to. Whenever one of the bits is set, an error interrupt is generated.

42   bit 0 indicates that the local APIC detected a checksum error on a message it sent.

43   bit 1 represents a checksum error for an incoming message.

44   bit 2 indicates that a message sent was not accepted by any other APIC.

45   bit 3 shows an incoming message was not accepted by any APIC, including this one. Note that bit 4 is reserved by Intel.

46   bit 5 indicates there is an illegal interrupt vector number in the message it is sending.

47   bit 6 shows there is an illegal vector number in the message it has received.

48   bit 7 indicates an attempt has been made to access an unimplemented APIC register.

13.1.3 Interrupt command register

This section considers the definitions for the 64-bit interrupt command register, as shown in Figure 13.3, from <asm-i386/apicdef.h>. A CPU sends an interprocessor interrupt (IPI) by writing to this register.

```
49    #define   APIC_ICR        0x300
50    #define      APIC_DEST_SELF          0x40000
51    #define      APIC_DEST_ALLINC        0x80000
52    #define      APIC_DEST_ALLBUT        0xC0000

57    #define      APIC_INT_LEVELTRIG      0x08000
58    #define      APIC_INT_ASSERT         0x04000
59    #define      APIC_ICR_BUSY           0x01000
60    #define      APIC_DEST_LOGICAL       0x00800
61    #define      APIC_DM_FIXED           0x00000
62    #define      APIC_DM_LOWEST          0x00100

65    #define      APIC_DM_NMI             0x00400
66    #define      APIC_DM_INIT            0x00500
67    #define      APIC_DM_STARTUP         0x00600
68    #define      APIC_DM_EXTINT          0x00700
```

```
69   #define        APIC_VECTOR_MASK          0x000FF
70   #define   APIC_ICR2    0x310
71   #define        GET_APIC_DEST_FIELD(x)    (((x)>>24)&0xFF)
72   #define        SET_APIC_DEST_FIELD(x)    ((x)<<24)
```

Figure 13.3 The interrupt command register

49   this is the low-order 32 bits of the interrupt command register. The remaining 32 bits are defined at line 70.

50–52   bits 18 and 19 can be used as a shortcut to represent the destination for an IPI. If set to 00, then an explicit destination is programmed into bits 56–63 of APIC_ICR2 (see line 70).

50   the value in the destination field, bits 18–19, is 01, meaning the interrupt is to be sent to the sending CPU itself.

51   the value in the destination field is 10, meaning it is to be sent to all, including self.

52   the value in the destination field is 11, meaning it is to be sent to all, excluding self.

57   bit 15 represents the trigger mode. When set, it means the IPI is level triggered; cleared means edge triggered.

58   bit 14 is only for level triggered IPIs; 1 means it is asserted, 0 means not.

59   bit 12 indicates the delivery status. A 0 means the ICR register is idle; there is no activity for the current interrupt, or the previous interrupt from this source has completed; 1 means there is an IPI being sent, it has not yet been completely accepted.

60   bit 11 indicates the destination mode: 0 means 'physical', that is, the local APIC of the destination CPU is identified by its physical address; 1 means 'logical', that is, the destination local APIC is identified by its logical address.

61–68   bits 8–10 are the delivery mode bits. This specifies how the APICs listed in the destination set should act when this interrupt is received.

61   fixed: this delivers the interrupt to all processors listed in the destination field. The fixed interrupt is always treated as edge triggered, even if programmed as level triggered.

62   lowest priority: in this case, the interrupt is delivered to only one processor in the destination set, the one that is executing at lowest priority.

65   this delivers the interrupt as an nonmaskable interrupt (nmi) to all processors listed in the destination field. The vector information is irrelevant in this case.

66   this delivers the interrupt as an INIT signal to all processors listed in the destination field. As a result, all addressed APICs will assume their initial state. The vector information is ignored.

67   start up: this sends a special message between processors. The vector contains the address of the multiprocessor startup code.

68   such an interrupt is delivered as if it were an external hardware interrupt.

69   bits 0–7 are the vector field, identifying the interrupt being sent.

70   this is the high-order 32 bits of ICR. Only bits 56–63 are defined, as the destination field. This field is used only when the destination shorthand field (bits 18–19 of APIC_ICR) is set to 00. If the destination mode (bit 11 of APIC_ICR; see line 60) is set to physical (0), then bits 56–59 of this register contain the APIC ID; otherwise (logical destination mode, 1), the interpretation of the 8-bit destination field (bits 56–63) depends on the values in DFR and LDR of the local APIC (see Section 13.1.2).

71   this brings these 8 bits to the least significant positions and masks out everything else, so the macro evaluates to the value of the destination field.

72   this moves the parameter (the destination address) to the most significant positions (the destination field).

13.1.4   The local vector table

Each local APIC has a range of registers known as the local vector table (LVT). The definitions for these registers are shown in Figure 13.4, from <asm-i386/apicdef.h>.

```
73   #define    APIC_LVTT            0x320
74   #define    APIC_LVTPC           0x340
75   #define    APIC_LVT0            0x350
76   #define        APIC_LVT_TIMER_BASE_MASK    (0x3<<18)
77   #define        GET_APIC_TIMER_BASE(x)      (((x)>>18)&0x3)
78   #define        SET_APIC_TIMER_BASE(x)      (((x)<<18))
79   #define        APIC_TIMER_BASE_CLKIN       0x0
80   #define        APIC_TIMER_BASE_TMBASE      0x1
81   #define        APIC_TIMER_BASE_DIV         0x2
82   #define        APIC_LVT_TIMER_PERIODIC     (1<<17)
83   #define        APIC_LVT_MASKED             (1<<16)
84   #define        APIC_LVT_LEVEL_TRIGGER      (1<<15)

90   #define        APIC_MODE_FIXED             0x0
91   #define        APIC_MODE_NMI               0x4
92   #define        APIC_MODE_EXINT             0x7
93   #define    APIC_LVT1            0x360
94   #define    APIC_LVTERR          0x370
95   #define    APIC_TMICT           0x380
96   #define    APIC_TMCCT           0x390
97   #define    APIC_TDCR            0x3E0
98   #define        APIC_TDR_DIV_TMBASE         (1<<2)
99   #define        APIC_TDR_DIV_1              0xB
100  #define        APIC_TDR_DIV_2              0x0
101  #define        APIC_TDR_DIV_4              0x1
102  #define        APIC_TDR_DIV_8              0x2
103  #define        APIC_TDR_DIV_16             0x3
104  #define        APIC_TDR_DIV_32             0x8
105  #define        APIC_TDR_DIV_64             0x9
```

```
106  #define          APIC_TDR_DIV_128              0xA
107
108  #define   APIC_BASE (fix_to_virt(FIX_APIC_BASE))
109
110  #define   MAX_IO_APICS 8
```

Figure 13.4   Constants for the local vector table

73–94   these registers constitute the LVT, which specifies delivery and status information for local interrupts. There are five 32-bit entries in this table, one each for timer, a performance-monitoring counter, LINT0, LINT1, and the error interrupt. There are a number of features common to all of these registers:

- Bits 0–7 are the vector number associated with the interrupt.

- Bits 8–10 specify the delivery mode for the interrupt.

- Bit 12 is the delivery status; 0 means idle, 1 means there is an interrupt pending.

73   this is the LVT timer register. The local APIC has a 32-bit programmable timer, configured through this register. The timebase is the bus clock of the CPU, divided by the value in the divide configuration register (see line 97). It can be programmed to interrupt on an arbitrary vector, specified in bits 0–7. The timer is started by writing to the initial count register (TMICT; see line 95).

74   note that the register at 0x330 is not defined, as it was not present in the earlier APICs. This one at 0x340 is the performance counter register. It is never manipulated by Linux, apart from masking it out at bootup. Bit 16 is the mask bit.

75   this is the LVT entry for the LINT0 pin. This is one of the two local pins on the APIC.

76–92   these are definitions for various fields in the three foregoing registers and for the following one, LINT1.

77   this moves right, so that bit 18 is in the rightmost position, and masks off all but the two rightmost bits, so the macro evaluates to bits 18 and 19 of the supplied parameter (i.e. the timer base). However, it is never used in Linux.

78   this moves the values supplied into bits 18 and 19, the timer base position.

79–81   these are three possible values for the timer base field. Only APIC_TIMER_BASE_DIV is ever used by Linux, at bootup.

82   the timer supports one shot or periodic modes, controlled by bit 17. One shot means that it counts down to 0, interrupts, then stops. This is denoted by a 0 here. Periodic mode means that after the timer expires and interrupts, it begins counting with the same initial value again. This is denoted by a 1 here.

83   bit 16 is the mask bit; 0 for not masked (enabled), 1 for masked (disabled).

84   bit 15 is the trigger mode bit; 0 for edge triggered, 1 for level triggered.

90–92 bits 8–10 are the delivery mode. This specifies how an interrupt will be delivered.

90 fixed delivery mode is 000. The corresponding local interrupt is delivered to the local CPU, with the specified vector

91 the nmi delivery mode is 100. An interrupt received on a LINT pin is delivered as an nmi; the vector is meaningless.

92 the ExtInt delivery mode is 111. The APIC responds as if the interrupt originated from a PIC. This includes an INTA cycle to the external controller. Vector information should come from the controller. There can only be one ExtInt source in the system.

93 this is the LVT register for the LINT1 pin. The foregoing definitions are also relevant to this.

94 this is the LVT error register, for the error interrupt, not to be confused with ESR at 0x280. This one is specific to the LVT. The only valid fields are vector, delivery status, and mask. It specifies the interrupt to generate when a bit is set in ESR and it also allows the error interrupt to be masked.

95 this is the initial count register for the timer. It is a read–write register. The timer is started by writing to this. The value written is copied to TMCCT, and the countdown begins.

96 this is the current count register for the timer. It is read only. After this reaches 0, if in one-shot mode, it interrupts and stops. If in periodic mode, it is reloaded from TMICT and begins counting down again.

97 note that registers 0x 3A0 through 0x 3D0 are reserved. This is the timer divide configuration register. Only bits 0–3 of this register are valid, and bit 2 is hardwired to 0. So bits 0, 1, and 3 are the operative ones, giving values from 0–7. These specify the size of the divide factor, as $2^{\text{significant bits}+1}$. This value is the number of CPU clock ticks that constitute one tick of the local APIC timer.

98 this is just a mask for bit 2.

99 0xB is 1011. The meaningful bits give 111, which means divide by 2^0, or 1.

100 0000 means divide by 2^1, or 2.

101 0001 means divide by 2^2, or 4.

102 0x2 is 0010. This means divide by 2^3, or 8.

103 0x3 is 0011. This means divide by 2^4, or 16.

104 0x8 is 1000. This means divide by 2^5, or 32.

105 0x9 is 1001. This means divide by 2^6, or 64.

106 0xA is 1010. The significant bits are 110, meaning divide by 2^7, or 128.

108 this macro defines the beginning of the 4k virtual address space allocated to the local APIC. It is part of the memory manager and will not be considered further here.

13.2 Initialising the local APIC

The previous section introduced the internal structure of the local APIC. Many of these registers need to be initialised before the interrupt system can function properly. The code to do that, in `setup_local_APIC()`, assumes that there is an IO APIC in the system. It is rather long, so the explanation will be broken down into four subsections.

13.2.1 Sanity checks and APIC identification

The first part of the code, as shown in Figure 13.5, from `arch/i386/kernel/apic.c`, consists of some sanity checks, and setting up of the ID of the APIC.

```
263  void __init setup_local_APIC (void)
264  {
265      unsigned long value, ver, maxlvt;

268      if (esr_disable) {
269          apic_write(APIC_ESR, 0);
270          apic_write(APIC_ESR, 0);
271          apic_write(APIC_ESR, 0);
272          apic_write(APIC_ESR, 0);
273      }
274
275      value = apic_read(APIC_LVR);
276      ver = GET_APIC_VERSION(value);
277
278      if ((SPURIOUS_APIC_VECTOR & 0x0f) != 0x0f)
279          __error_in_apic_c();

285      if (!clustered_apic_mode &&
286      !test_bit(GET_APIC_ID(apic_read(APIC_ID)), &phys_cpu_present_map))
287          BUG();

295      if (!clustered_apic_mode) {

301          apic_write_around(APIC_DFR, 0xffffffff);

306          value = apic_read(APIC_LDR);
307          value &= ~APIC_LDR_MASK;
308          value |= (1<<(smp_processor_id()+24));
309          apic_write_around(APIC_LDR, value);
310      }

316      value = apic_read(APIC_TASKPRI);
317      value &= ~APIC_TPRI_MASK;
318      apic_write_around(APIC_TASKPRI, value);
```

Figure 13.5   Sanity checks and APIC (advanced programmable interrupt controller) identification

268–273   the `esr_disable` variable will be defined on high-specification multiprocessors, which seem to cause some trouble to the error status register (ESR) in the local APIC. Writing any value to this register clears all the bits. The function to write to an APIC register is from Section 13.4.1. The comment in the code says 'Pound the ESR really hard over the head with a big hammer'.

275   this reads the value from the APIC version register (lines 16–20 of the code in Section 13.1.1). The function to read from an APIC register will be described in Section 13.4.1.

276   this macro, described in Section 13.1.1, extracts the 8-bit version number from the full 32-bit field.

278–279   if the low-order 4 bits are not all set in the definition of the vector for the spurious APIC interrupt, then there is an error in the code. It is normally defined as `0xff` (see Section 12.5.3).

285–287   clustered mode is only relevant on high-specification multiprocessors, where CPUs are clustered together and each such cluster is individually identified. This test is meaningless in that mode, so it is skipped.

286–287   this double checks that the APIC is really registered. The `GET_APIC_ID()` macro, from Section 13.1.1, returns the ID of the local APIC for this CPU, represented by its bit position; `test_bit()` is described in Section 5.1.3. If the corresponding bit is not set in `phys_cpu_present_map` (see Section 14.1.1.1) then there is some problem. This is a sanity check, so the `BUG()` macro is called from the code in Section 4.1.3.3.

295–310   some registers in the APIC are set to meaningful values before it is enabled, but in clustered mode this is done by the firmware and can be skipped.

301   this writes all 1s to the destination format register (DFR); see line 34 of Section 13.1.2. This puts the APIC into flat delivery mode (i.e. each bit in the logical APIC ID field of the LDR represents one APIC). The function is described in Section 13.4.2.

306–309   this is setting up the logical destination register for the APIC.

306–307   the value of the logical destination register is read, and bits 24–31 are cleared. See Section 13.1.2 for this register and mask. The `apic_read()` function is from Section 13.4.1.

308   this sets a bit in the logical destination register corresponding to this CPU, as determined by the `smp_processor_id()` macro (see Section 7.2.1.4).

309   this new value is now written back to the logical destination register, using the function from Section 13.4.2.

316–318   this sets the task priority to 'accept all'. It gets the value from the task priority register, clears bits 0–7, the task priority field, and writes the new value back. We never change this later on. See Section 13.1.1 for this register and the mask.

13.2.2   Enabling the APIC

Now that we are all set up, the next part of the code, as shown in Figure 13.6, from `arch/i386/kernel/apic.c`, enables the APIC. For some strange reason, the enable–disable bit is in the spurious interrupt vector register (see Section 13.1.2).

```
323        value = apic_read(APIC_SPIV);
324        value &= ~APIC_VECTOR_MASK;

328        value |= APIC_SPIV_APIC_ENABLED;

349  #if 1
350
351        value &= ~APIC_SPIV_FOCUS_DISABLED;
352  #else
353
354        value |= APIC_SPIV_FOCUS_DISABLED;
355  #endif

359        value |= SPURIOUS_APIC_VECTOR;
360        apic_write_around(APIC_SPIV, value);
```

Figure 13.6   Enabling the APIC (advanced programmable interrupt controller)

323–324 this code reads the value from the spurious interrupt vector register and clears the low-order 8 bits, just in case there was a vector value there. The APIC_VECTOR_MASK was defined in Section 13.1.3.

328 this sets the enable bit, as defined in Section 13.1.2.

349–355 this is a workaround for an APIC bug. If high-frequency interrupts are happening on a particular IO APIC pin, and the IO APIC routing entry is masked and unmasked at a high rate as well, then sooner or later the IO APIC line gets 'stuck' and no more interrupts are received from that device. If the focus CPU check is disabled, then the problem goes away. A processor is the focus of an interrupt if it is currently servicing that interrupt or if it has a pending request for that interrupt. By clearing bit 9, the check for a focus CPU when delivering that interrupt is disabled.

359 this sets the spurious irq vector in bits 0–7.

360 finally, this writes the new value back to the spurious interrupt vector register, using the macro from Section 13.4.2.

13.2.3   The local interrupt pins

The next part of the code, as shown in Figure 13.7, from arch/i386/kernel/apic.c, sets up the two local interrupt pins, LINT0 and LINT1.

```
372        value = apic_read(APIC_LVT0) & APIC_LVT_MASKED;
373        if (!smp_processor_id() && (pic_mode || !value)) {
374            value = APIC_DM_EXTINT;
375            printk("enabled ExtINT on CPU#%d\n", smp_processor_id());
376        } else {
377            value = APIC_DM_EXTINT | APIC_LVT_MASKED;
378            printk("masked ExtINT on CPU#%d\n", smp_processor_id());
```

```
379          }
380          apic_write_around(APIC_LVT0, value);

385          if (!smp_processor_id())
386              value = APIC_DM_NMI;
387          else
388              value = APIC_DM_NMI | APIC_LVT_MASKED;
389          if (!APIC_INTEGRATED(ver))  /* 82489DX */
390              value |= APIC_LVT_LEVEL_TRIGGER;
391          apic_write_around(APIC_LVT1, value);
```

Figure 13.7 The local interrupt pins

372–380 this block of code is concerned with setting up LINT0 on the local APIC.

372 this reads the current value in the LINT0 register of the local vector table, using the function from Section 13.4.1. It clears everything except the mask bit for this interrupt, which is left in whatever state it was in. The register and the mask were described in Section 13.1.4.

373–379 this code sets up ExtInt as the delivery mode – enabled or masked depending on the condition on line 373.

373–375 the smp_processor_id() macro was discussed in Section 7.2.1.4. LINT0 is only enabled if running on logical processor 0 (the boot processor), and then only if the configuration variable pic_mode was set or the LVT0 register was previously marked as enabled. This code sets ExtInt as the delivery mode with mask 0 (enabled) and prints the message.

377 otherwise, this line sets the delivery mode as ExtInt, but sets the masked bit so that this interrupt is masked out. Note that the vector field is not filled in for ExtInt delivery mode. The vector will be supplied by the external PIC.

378 this prints the appropriate message.

380 this writes the value just built up to the LVT0 register of the APIC. The macro is from Section 13.4.2.

385–391 these lines set up the LINT1 pin.

385–386 if running on logical processor 0 (boot processor), the delivery mode is set to nmi, with all other fields set to 0. The nmi line is connected to LINT1, which is unmasked, or enabled.

388 otherwise, if running on any other processor, the mask bit is set to 1, so this pin is masked. Only the boot processor should see the LINT1 nmi signal, obviously.

389 this line is checking whether the APIC in question is a local APIC, integrated into the CPU, or an external APIC. The macro has been described in Section 13.1.1.

390 if not a local APIC, then it must be an 82489DX APIC controller. This is level triggered, so the appropriate bit is set, defined at line 84 of Section 13.1.4.

391 all this is written to the LVT1 register of the APIC, using the macro from Section 13.4.2.

13.2.4 Error handling on a local APIC

The final block of code, as shown in Figure 13.8, from `arch/i386/kernel/apic.c`, is relevant only to an integrated local APIC, not an 82489DX. It is setting up the ESR (error status register).

```
393        if (APIC_INTEGRATED(ver) && !esr_disable) {
394            maxlvt = get_maxlvt();
395            if (maxlvt > 3)
396                    apic_write(APIC_ESR, 0);
397            value = apic_read(APIC_ESR);
398            printk("ESR value before enabling vector: %08lx\n", value);
399
400            value = ERROR_APIC_VECTOR;
401            apic_write_around(APIC_LVTERR, value);

405            if (maxlvt > 3)
406                    apic_write(APIC_ESR, 0);
407            value = apic_read(APIC_ESR);
408            printk("ESR value after enabling vector: %08lx\n", value);
409        } else
410            if (esr_disable)

417                printk("Leaving ESR disabled.\n");
418            else
419                printk("No ESR for 82489DX.\n");
420        }
421
422        if (nmi_watchdog == NMI_LOCAL_APIC)
423            setup_apic_nmi_watchdog();
424 }
```

Figure 13.8 Error handling on a local APIC

393–408 this block of code is executed only if dealing with an integrated local APIC and the error status register is enabled. The `APIC_INTEGRATED()` macro was described in Section 13.1.1. The `esr_disable` flag is set on high-specification multiprocessors, which seem to cause some trouble to the ESR register.

394 this function, discussed in Section 13.3.2.1, returns the highest-numbered entry in the local vector table.

395 if the macro returns 4 or more, then there are 5 or more entries, so there is an error status register (ESR).

396 this dummy write causes the values in the ESR to be updated by the hardware. It seems odd, but this is how it works.

397–398 now the updated error status register is read and the message is printed.

400   this is the vector number for the APIC error interrupt, `0xfe`, defined in Section 12.5.3.

401   writing this value to the error register in the LVT, as defined in Section 13.1.4, implies writing a 0 to the mask field. This enables the sending of error interrupts. The `apic_write_around()` macro is from Section 13.4.2.

405–406   after enabling the error vector, the error register is updated again, using this dummy write.

407–408   this code reads the updated value from the error status register and prints the message.

409–420   otherwise, either the ESR was disabled or it was dealing with an external 82498DX APIC.

410–417   the ESR was disabled. This is only likely to happen with high-end multiprocessors.

419   the external APIC has no ESR.

422   if at setup time it was determined that the nmi watchdog timer ticks are to be provided by the local APIC, this function sets it up by writing to machine-specific registers.

13.2.5   Setup virtual wire mode

If there is no IO APIC present, then external devices are connected to a PIC, which in turn is connected to a local APIC. In this case the local APIC is set into virtual wire mode, merely providing a connection to the CPU. All arbitration between interrupts and provision of vectors is done by an 8259A PIC.

The code shown in Figure 13.9, from `arch/i386/kernel/apic.c`, sets up a local APIC in this mode.

```
224  void __init init_bsp_APIC(void)
225  {
226        unsigned long value, ver;

232        if (smp_found_config || !cpu_has_apic)
233            return;
234
235        value = apic_read(APIC_LVR);
236        ver = GET_APIC_VERSION(value);

241        clear_local_APIC();

246        value = apic_read(APIC_SPIV);
247        value &= ~APIC_VECTOR_MASK;
248        value |= APIC_SPIV_APIC_ENABLED;
249        value |= APIC_SPIV_FOCUS_DISABLED;
250        value |= SPURIOUS_APIC_VECTOR;
251        apic_write_around(APIC_SPIV, value);

256        apic_write_around(APIC_LVT0, APIC_DM_EXTINT);
257        value = APIC_DM_NMI;
```

```
258        if(!APIC_INTEGRATED(ver)) /* 82489DX */
259            value |= APIC_LVT_LEVEL_TRIGGER;
260        apic_write_around(APIC_LVT1, value);
261  }
```

Figure 13.9　Setting up local APIC (advanced programmable interrupt controller) in virtual wire mode

232–233　if we have a multiprocessor machine, then there will certainly be an IO APIC present, and virtual wire mode will have been set up through this IO APIC by the hardware detection code. In this case, or if there is no local APIC present, the remainder of this code should not be executed.

235–236　this gets the value from the version register and then extracts the version from the low-order 8 bits, using the macro from Section 13.1.1.

241　we do not trust the registers of the local APIC to be empty at boot time, so this line clears it, using the function from Section 13.3.2.2.

246–251　now we go on and enable the local APIC. The code is identical to that in Section 13.2.2.

256–260　this code sets up virtual wire mode.

256　this sets up the LINT0 pin as an external interrupt. The 8259A PIC is connected to this pin in virtual wire mode.

257–260　this is setting up the nmi on LINT1. The vector field is irrelevant for nmi.

258–259　if dealing with an external APIC chip, the level triggered bit must be set.

260　this writes the value just built up to the LVT1 register, using the macro from Section 13.4.2.

13.3　High-level operations on a local APIC

There are a number of special functions supplied for manipulating a local APIC. First of all, there are the standard functions for interfacing with an interrupt controller, as introduced in Section 12.1. Then there are a number of generic functions, not specific to any irq.

13.3.1　Interface functions for a local APIC

As with all interrupt controllers, there is a struct hw_interrupt_type, which specifies the appropriate functions for handling an irq on an APIC pin. The implementation of these functions is relatively trivial.

13.3.1.1　Controller structure

The structure shown in Figure 13.10, from arch/i386/kernel/io_apic.c, shows the hw_interrupt_type associated with a local APIC.

```
1370 static struct hw_interrupt_type lapic_irq_type = {
1371      "local-APIC-edge",
1372      NULL,
1373      NULL,
1374      enable_lapic_irq,
1375      disable_lapic_irq,
1376      ack_lapic_irq,
1377      end_lapic_irq
1378 };
```

Figure 13.10 Controller structure for a local APIC (advanced programmable interrupt controller)

1372–1373   it is not envisaged that devices will be starting up and shutting down irq lines on the local APIC, so these functions are not required.

1374–1377   see Section 13.3.1.2 for the implementation of these functions.

13.3.1.2 Controller functions

Figure 13.11, from `arch/i386/kernel/io_apic.c`, shows the functions used by interrupt handlers when servicing an irq routed through the LINT0 pin of a local APIC.

```
1347 static void enable_lapic_irq (unsigned int irq)
1348 {
1349      unsigned long v;
1350
1351      v = apic_read(APIC_LVT0);
1352      apic_write_around(APIC_LVT0, v & ~APIC_LVT_MASKED);
1353 }
1354
1355 static void disable_lapic_irq (unsigned int irq)
1356 {
1357      unsigned long v;
1358
1359      v = apic_read(APIC_LVT0);
1360      apic_write_around(APIC_LVT0, v | APIC_LVT_MASKED);
1361 }
1362
1363 static void ack_lapic_irq (unsigned int irq)
1364 {
1365      ack_APIC_irq();
1366 }
1367
1368 static void end_lapic_irq (unsigned int i) {}
```

Figure 13.11 Controller functions for a local APIC (advanced programmable interrupt controller)

1351   this reads the LINT0 register of the local vector table, using the function from Section 13.4.1.

1352   this clears the APIC_LVT_MASKED bit (line 83 of the code in Section 13.1.4) in the value just read and writes it back, using the macro from Section 13.4.2, so the irq is not masked, it is enabled.

1359–1360   these are as lines 1351–1352, except that this time the bit is set, so the irq is masked, or disabled.

1365   this is just a call to the generic function (see Section 13.3.2.4).

1368   the end() function does nothing.

13.3.2 Generic functions for manipulating a local APIC

There are a number of functions that are concerned with manipulating a local APIC itself, as opposed to any irq on that APIC.

13.3.2.1 Getting the number of entries in the local vector table

The function shown in Figure 13.12, from arch/i386/kernel/apic.c, returns the maximum number of entries in the local vector table of the APIC.

```
40   int get_maxlvt(void)
41   {
42        unsigned int v, ver, maxlvt;
43
44        v = apic_read(APIC_LVR);
45        ver = GET_APIC_VERSION(v);
46
47        maxlvt = APIC_INTEGRATED(ver) ? GET_APIC_MAXLVT(v) : 2;
48        return maxlvt;
49   }
```

Figure 13.12   Getting the number of entries in the local vector table (LVT)

44   this reads from the version register of the local APIC. The function is from Section 13.4.1.

45   this gets the 8-bit version field from the foregoing read. The macro is from Section 13.1.1.

47   the APIC_INTEGRATED() macro, from Section 13.1.1, returns TRUE if it is an integrated local APIC. In that case, the maximum number of entries in the LVT is assigned, using the macro GET_APIC_MAXLVT(), from Section 13.1.1. Otherwise, if dealing with an 82489DX external APIC, which does not report the number of LVT entries, a value of 2 is assigned, as there are always at least that number of entries.

13.3.2.2 Clearing local vector table registers in the local APIC

Sometimes it is necessary to clear all the registers in the LVT of an APIC. Figure 13.13, from arch/i386/kernel/apic.c, shows the code to do this. The function first of all masks all potential interrupt sources, then it clears the entries in the LVT, leaving each one masked.

```
51    static void clear_local_APIC(void)
52    {
53        int maxlvt;
54        unsigned long v;
55
56        maxlvt = get_maxlvt();

62        if (maxlvt >= 3) {
63            v = ERROR_APIC_VECTOR;
64            apic_write_around(APIC_LVTERR, v | APIC_LVT_MASKED);
65        }

70        v = apic_read(APIC_LVTT);
71        apic_write_around(APIC_LVTT, v | APIC_LVT_MASKED);
72        v = apic_read(APIC_LVT0);
73        apic_write_around(APIC_LVT0, v | APIC_LVT_MASKED);
74        v = apic_read(APIC_LVT1);
75        apic_write_around(APIC_LVT1, v | APIC_LVT_MASKED);
76        if (maxlvt >= 4) {
77            v = apic_read(APIC_LVTPC);
78            apic_write_around(APIC_LVTPC, v | APIC_LVT_MASKED);
79        }

84        apic_write_around(APIC_LVTT, APIC_LVT_MASKED);
85        apic_write_around(APIC_LVT0, APIC_LVT_MASKED);
86        apic_write_around(APIC_LVT1, APIC_LVT_MASKED);
87        if (maxlvt >= 3)
88            apic_write_around(APIC_LVTERR, APIC_LVT_MASKED);
89        if (maxlvt >= 4)
90            apic_write_around(APIC_LVTPC, APIC_LVT_MASKED);
91        v = GET_APIC_VERSION(apic_read(APIC_LVR));
92        if (APIC_INTEGRATED(v)) {
93            if (maxlvt > 3)
94                apic_write(APIC_ESR, 0);
95            apic_read(APIC_ESR);
96        }
97    }
```

Figure 13.13 Clearing local APIC (advanced programmable interrupt controller) registers

56   this is the highest-numbered entry in the LVT. The function was described in Section 13.3.2.1. Different CPU models have 3, 4 or 5 entries in the LVT, and the code must clear all of them and yet not attempt to clear a nonexistent register.

62–65   if there are more than three entries in the LVT (if maxlvt is 3 or greater), then we set the mask bit in the LVT error register (APIC_LVTERR), so masking it out. This is done temporarily (line

94 re-enables error interrupts) while initialising the state of the local APIC registers; otherwise, some local APICs would flag errors during this operation.

70–75   this sets the APIC_LVT_MASKED bit in the timer register (APIC_LVTT), the LINT0 register (APIC_LVT0), and the LINT1 register (APIC_LVT1), which are always present. So interrupts from these three sources are now masked out. The read function is in Section 13.4.1; the apic_write_around macro is in Section 13.4.2.

76–79   if there is a fifth register, we set the mask bit in the performance counter register (APIC_LVTPP).

84–90   these lines write to the same registers as previously, but now only the APIC_LVT_MASKED bit is set in all the registers. This cleans the state of the APIC, leaving all interrupts masked.

91   this gets the version of the APIC, using the macro from Section 13.1.1.

92–96   using the macro from Section 13.1.1, this code checks that this is an APIC integrated into the CPU, and not an external 82489DX.

93–94   if there are at least 4 registers in the LVT, then the fourth one, the error status register, is cleared. This has the effect of re-enabling error interrupts from the local apic.

95   the hardware seems to require this dummy read.

13.3.2.3   Disabling a local APIC

When a CPU is shutdown, the local APIC on that CPU must be disabled. A disabled local APIC sets all mask bits in the LVT. The code for this is shown in Figure 13.14, from arch/i386/kernel/apic.c.

```
131  void disable_local_APIC(void)
132  {
133        unsigned long value;
134
135        clear_local_APIC();

141        value = apic_read(APIC_SPIV);
142        value &= ~APIC_SPIV_APIC_ENABLED;
143        apic_write_around(APIC_SPIV, value);
144  }
```

Figure 13.14   Disabling the local APIC (advanced programmable interrupt controller)

135   this function clears all the registers in the LVT of the local APIC (see Section 13.3.2.2).

141   this reads from the spurious interrupt vector register (APIC_SPIV; see Section 13.1.2 for the register).

142   this clears bit 8 of value. This marks it as disabled. Writing a 1 to bit 8 enables the APIC. The mask is defined in Section 13.1.2.

143   writing this value to APIC_SPIV has the effect of disabling the APIC.

13.3.2.4 Acknowledging an irq to an APIC

The function shown in Figure 13.15, from `<asm-i386/apic.h>`, signals completion of interrupt servicing to the APIC. It does not specify any particular irq.

```
53    static inline void ack_APIC_irq(void)
54    {

63         apic_write_around(APIC_EOI, 0);
64    }
```

Figure 13.15 Acknowledging an irq (interrupt request) to an APIC (advanced programmable interrupt controller)

63 see Section 13.4.2 for this macro. It writes 0 to the EOI register of the APIC, thus signalling completion of interrupt processing in the handler, see line 26 of Section 13.1.1 for the register.

13.4 Low-level operations on a local APIC

Earlier sections made use of the functions that actually manipulate APIC registers. These will be described here. Some are straightforward, others are for older APICs that require a read-before-write sequence.

13.4.1 Basic functions for accessing APICs

At the lowest level, a number of functions are defined in `<asm-i386/apic.h>` for manipulating registers in a local APIC. These are shown in Figure 13.16.

```
23    static __inline void apic_write(unsigned long reg,unsigned long v)
24    {
25        *((volatile unsigned long *)(APIC_BASE+reg)) = v;
26    }
27
28    static __inline void apic_write_atomic(unsigned long reg,
                                                   unsigned long v)
29    {
30        xchg((volatile unsigned long *)(APIC_BASE+reg), v);
31    }
32
33    static __inline unsigned long apic_read(unsigned long reg)
34    {
35        return *((volatile unsigned long *)(APIC_BASE+reg));
36    }
37
38    static __inline__ void apic_wait_icr_idle(void)
39    {
```

```
40          do { } while ( apic_read( APIC_ICR) & APIC_ICR_BUSY);
41     }
```

Figure 13.16 Basic functions for accessing APICs (advanced programmable interrupt contollers)

25 APIC_BASE is the virtual address of the first register in the APIC (see line 108 of Figure 13.4). Adding reg to the base value then points it to the specified register. Casting it to be a pointer to unsigned long means that each register is treated as 32 bits. Finally, it is de-referenced and the specified value assigned to the register.

30 the calculation of the address of the register is done as on line 25. Then the xchg() macro (see Section 5.2.10) is used atomically to swap the input parameter and the previous value in the register. Note that the previous value is not returned to the caller.

35 the calculation of the address of the register is done as on line 25. Then it is de-referenced and the value in the register is returned to the caller. The single memory read is guaranteed to be atomic, so there is no need for a special atomic version.

38 this function idles until bit 12 in the APIC interrupt control register (ICR) is clear. When set, it means that the APIC is in the process of sending an IPI.

40 this reads the register specified by APIC_ICR (the interrupt control register, at offset 0x300) and checks the APIC_ICR_BUSY bit. As long as that bit is set, the APIC is in the process of sending an IPI. The while condition is TRUE, so the do loops.

13.4.2 An APIC needing read before write

Some APICs need a read before they can be written to. If such an APIC is not identified at bootup (P6 and later), then CONFIG_X86_GOOD_APIC is defined. The code shown in Figure 13.17, from <asm-i386/apic.h>, defines three macros differently, depending on whether an earlier or later APIC version has been found.

```
44    #ifdef CONFIG_X86_GOOD_APIC
45    # define FORCE_READ_AROUND_WRITE 0
46    # define apic_read_around(x)
47    # define apic_write_around(x,y) apic_write((x),(y))
48    #else
49    # define FORCE_READ_AROUND_WRITE 1
50    # define apic_read_around(x) apic_read(x)
51    # define apic_write_around(x,y) apic_write_atomic((x),(y))
52    #endif
```

Figure 13.17 Medium-level reading–writing an APIC (advanced programmable interrupt controller)

44–47 this code is executed if the APIC is considered 'good' (i.e. P6 and later).

45 the macro FORCE_READ_AROUND_WRITE is defined as FALSE (0), so it is not necessary to read from an APIC register before writing to it.

46 in this case, although the `apic_read_around()` macro is defined, it does nothing.

47 the `apic_write_around()` macro is defined as a direct call to `apic_write()` (see Section 13.4.1).

48–51 this code is executed if the APIC is not considered 'good' (i.e. it is an older APIC, which needs a read before write).

49 this time, the FORCE_READ_AROUND_WRITE macro is defined as TRUE (1).

50 the `apic_read_around()` macro actually does perform a read on the specified APIC. Note that no value is returned to the caller. The `apic_read()` function is described in Section 13.4.1.

51 this translates to an atomic write to the APIC (see Section 13.4.1).

13.5   Sending interprocessor interrupts

An interprocessor interrupt (IPI) is generated by writing to the interrupt command register (`ICR`) of the local APIC. A CPU can even interrupt itself in this way. The kernel provides functions for sending each of the different IPIs, two of which are considered in this section. The interrupt for invalidating translation lookaside buffers on other processors is considered to be part of the memory manager. Generic functions for sending IPIs are also considered.

13.5.1   The reschedule interrupt

The function in Figure 13.18 from `arch/i386/kernel/smp.c` sends a reschedule IPI to another CPU.

```
494  void smp_send_reschedule(int cpu)
495  {
496        send_IPI_mask(1 << cpu, RESCHEDULE_VECTOR);
497  }
```

Figure 13.18   Sending a reschedule interprocessor interrupt to another processor

417 the `send_IPI_mask()` function is discussed in Section 13.5.4.2. It instructs the APIC to send the RESCHEDULE_VECTOR interrupt to `cpu`. See Section 12.5.3 for a definition of this vector.

13.5.2   The call function interrupt

The discussion of how to send an interrupt to execute a function on another CPU will begin with the wrapper function that marshals the parameters, sends the interrupt, and waits for the remote function to run. Then the `call_data_struct`, which is used to pass information between the CPUs, will be examined.

13.5.2.1   Sending a call function interrupt

The function shown in Figure 13.19, from `arch/i386/kernel/smp.c`, sends a generic call function IPI to all other CPUs in the system.

```
520  int smp_call_function (void (*func) (void *info), void *info,
                                              int nonatomic, int wait)

534  {
535       struct call_data_struct data;
536       int cpus = smp_num_cpus-1;
537
538       if (!cpus)
539           return 0;
540
541       data.func = func;
542       data.info = info;
543       atomic_set(&data.started, 0);
544       data.wait = wait;
545       if (wait)
546           atomic_set(&data.finished, 0);
547
548       spin_lock_bh(&call_lock);
549       call_data = &data;
550       wmb();
551
552       send_IPI_allbutself(CALL_FUNCTION_VECTOR);

555       while (atomic_read(&data.started) != cpus)
556           barrier();
557
558       if (wait)
559           while (atomic_read(&data.finished) != cpus)
560               barrier();
561       spin_unlock_bh(&call_lock);
562
563       return 0;
564  }
```

Figure 13.19   Running a function on all other computer processing units

521   this runs a specified function on all the other CPUs.

- The first parameter, `func`, is a pointer to the function to run. This should be fast and nonblocking. It must take one parameter, a pointer to `void`.

- The second parameter, `info`, is an arbitrary pointer to pass to the function.

- The third parameter, `nonatomic`, is currently unused.

- The fourth parameter, `wait`, specifies whether the caller will wait until the function has completed on all the other CPUs, or not.

The return value is 0 on success, otherwise a negative status code, but it does not return until remote CPUs are nearly ready to execute `func` or have executed it.

535 this structure will be used to encapsulate the extra control information that will be made available to other CPUs. It is described in Section 13.5.2.2.

536 this calculates the number of *other* CPUs by using the global variable from Section 7.2.1.1.

538–539 if there are no other CPUs, then there is nothing to be done, so the success code is returned.

541–546 this code sets up various fields in `data`.

543 this keeps track of the number of other CPUs that have started to execute the function. Because it will be incremented by each one of them as they start, mutual exclusion is needed when writing to it. It is declared as type `atomic_t`, so this function is used to initialise it (see Section 5.2.1).

544 the caller of this function has specified whether it is to wait or not, by means of the fourth parameter (see line 520). This value is passed on unchanged to the other CPUs.

545–546 the `finished` field will be incremented by each CPU as it finishes the function, so mutual exclusion is needed when writing to it, but it is only ever used if `wait` is TRUE. The `atomic_set()` function is from Section 5.2.1.

548–561 this is a critical section to guarantee that only one call function IPI can be in progress at a time. It also wants to guarantee that no bottom-half processing (see Section 16.3) will begin on any CPU until all CPUs have finished. The declaration of the lock is covered in Section 13.5.2.2. The macros for manipulating bottom-half safe spinlocks are in Section 12.8.1.

549 the `call_data` variable is a `static` global pointer (see its declaration in Section 13.5.2.2). In this way, all the CPUs can see `data`.

550 this line guarantees that all CPUs now see the foregoing assignments.

552 this sends the `CALL_FUNCTION_VECTOR` interrupt to all other CPUs. See Section 13.5.3.1 for the function.

555–556 this code waits until all the others indicate that they have started. The `barrier()` function guarantees that the test is always performed using up-to-date values.

558–560 if specified by the input parameter `wait`, we wait until all the other CPUs also signify that they have finished.

563 success is returned.

13.5.2.2 The `call_data_struct` data structure

Figure 13.20, from `arch/i386/kernel/smp.c`, contains the data structure used by `smp_call_function()` in the previous subsection to pass control information to all the other CPUs.

```
503   static spinlock_t call_lock = SPIN_LOCK_UNLOCKED;
504
505   struct call_data_struct {
506        void (*func) (void *info);
507        void *info;
508        atomic_t started;
509        atomic_t finished;
510        int wait;
511   };
512
513   static struct call_data_struct * call_data;
```

Figure 13.20   Data structure to record a call function

503   this lock is used by `smp_call_function()` (Section 13.5.2.1) to guarantee that only one call function request can be in progress at any time.

506   this is a pointer to the function to be executed. It takes one parameter, a pointer to void.

507   this is an optional pointer that can be used to pass data to that function.

508   this is initialised to 0 by the caller and is incremented atomically by each CPU when it begins to execute the function, so the sender can check when all have begun and is free to invalidate the `struct` at that point.

509   this is initialised to 0 by the caller and is incremented atomically by each CPU when it has executed the function, so the sender can check when all have finished.

510   this specifies whether the caller wants confirmation that the function is finished on the other CPUs or not. In the former case, each CPU will increment `finish` when finished, and the caller will wait for all of them to do so; in the latter case, `finished` is not used.

513   this is a static pointer to such a structure. The structure itself is declared within the scope of the `smp_call_function()` code (see Section 13.5.2.1).

13.5.3   Shortcut addressing for sending interprocessor interrupts

Because there is a frequent requirement to send IPIs to groups of CPUs, three shortcut functions are provided for this that do not require specific addresses to be supplied. The first one sends a particular interrupt to all the other CPUs (excluding itself). The second sends to all CPUs, including itself. The final one sends only to itself. The symbolic constants representing these three groups were defined at lines 50–52 of Figure 13.3.

13.5.3.1   Sending an interrupt to all others

The function that sends an interrupt to all other processors is shown in Figure 13.21, from `arch/i386/kernel/smp.c`.

```
242  static inline void send_IPI_allbutself(int vector)
243  {

249      if (!(smp_num_cpus > 1))
250          return;
251
252      if (clustered_apic_mode) {
253
254          int cpu;
255
256          if (smp_num_cpus > 1) {
257              for (cpu = 0; cpu < smp_num_cpus; ++cpu) {
258                  if (cpu != smp_processor_id())
259                      send_IPI_mask(1 << cpu, vector);
260              }
261          }
262      } else {
263          __send_IPI_shortcut(APIC_DEST_ALLBUT, vector);
264          return;
265      }
266  }
```

Figure 13.21   Sending an interprocessor interrupt (IPI) to all other computer processing
units (CPUs)

249–250   if there are no other CPUs in the system then an attempt to broadcast an interrupt will result in an
APIC send error, so no IPIs should be sent in this case.

252–262   this is for the case when APICs are identified by using the clustered addressing model. In that
case, shortcuts cannot be used and the IPIs have to be sent one by one.

256–261   these lines provide a second check that there is more than one CPU in the system.

257–260   these go through each CPU one by one.

258   this skips over the sender.

259   this uses the function from Section 13.5.4.2 to send the interrupt identified by vector to cpu.

263   otherwise, this shortcut function is used to send the IPI (see Section 13.5.4.1). The first parameter,
as defined in Section 13.1.3, specifies the destination group; the second specifies the interrupt to
send.

13.5.3.2   *Sending an interrupt to all, including sender*

The function shown in Figure 13.22, from arch/i386/kernel/smp.c, sends the
specified interrupt to all CPUs, including the sender.

```
268  static inline void send_IPI_all(int vector)
269  {
```

```
270            if (clustered_apic_mode) {
271
272                int cpu;
273
274                for (cpu = 0; cpu < smp_num_cpus; ++cpu) {
275                    send_IPI_mask(1 << cpu, vector);
276                }
277            } else {
278                __send_IPI_shortcut(APIC_DEST_ALLINC, vector);
279            }
280    }
```

Figure 13.22   Send an interprocessor interrupt (IPI) to all, including the sender

268   the destination parameter specifies the interrupt to send.

270–277   if in clustered addressing mode, the shortcut addressing will not work and the IPIs will have to be sent one by one to the destination CPUs.

274–276   this code goes through each CPU one by one, even if the CPU is the sender.

275   this uses the function from Section 13.5.4.2 to send the interrupt identified by vector to cpu.

278   otherwise, this shortcut function is used to send the IPI (see Section 13.5.4.1). The first parameter, as defined in Section 13.1.3, specifies the destination group; the second specifies the interrupt to send.

13.5.3.3   *Sending an interrupt to the sender only*

The function shown in Figure 13.23, from arch/i386/kernel/smp.c, sends the specified interrupt to the sending CPU.

```
153  void send_IPI_self(int vector)
154  {
155        __send_IPI_shortcut(APIC_DEST_SELF, vector);
156  }
```

Figure 13.23   Sending the interprocessor interrupt (IPI) to the sender only

155   the destination parameter (Section 13.1.3) specifies the current CPU as the destination of the interrupt. The function is from Section 13.5.4.1.

13.5.4   Low-level functions to send an interprocessor interrupt

Finally, the low-level functions used for sending IPIs, both in the previous section and elsewhere, will be examined here.

There are several functions for sending IPIs between CPUs. The destination can be one, some, or all of the CPUs in the system. It is also possible for a CPU to send an IPI to itself. The destination can be specified either physically or logically.

In physical mode, the destination processor is specified by the 4-bit hardware-assigned ID (8-bit for Pentium 4 and Xeon) of the local APIC. A broadcast to all local APICs is specified by 0xF (0xFF for Pentium 4 and Xeon). In logical mode, destinations are specified by using an 8-bit destination mode address, which is compared with the 8-bit logical ID field in the logical destination register (LDR) of the local APIC. This can be programmed by software to have a value that is unique, or not.

The interpretation of a logical address is determined by the destination format register (DFR). Bits 28–31 determine the mode. If set to 1111, then it is using the flat model. This way, a particular one of the 8 bits in the logical ID field of the LDR is set for each APIC, so an arbitrary group can be selected by setting the appropriate bits of the destination mode address. IPIs can be broadcast by setting it to all 1s.

There is also a cluster model, bits 28–31 of the DFR set to 0000. In this case, the 8-bit logical ID field of the LDR is viewed as two nibbles. The higher nibble identifies one of 15 clusters, whereas the lower nibble identifies target processors within the cluster.

13.5.4.1 Sending an interprocessor interrupt with use of shortcut addressing

The function shown in Figure 13.24, from arch/i386/kernel/smp.c, is passed parameters specifying the CPUs to which the interrupt is to be sent, and which interrupt to send, and it writes appropriate commands to the APIC.

```
126  static inline void __send_IPI_shortcut(unsigned int shortcut,
                                                        int vector)
127  {

135       unsigned int cfg;

140       apic_wait_icr_idle();

145       cfg = __prepare_ICR(shortcut, vector);

150       apic_write_around(APIC_ICR, cfg);
151  }
```

Figure 13.24 Worker functions to send an interprocessor interrupt (IPI)

126 the first parameter specifies the destination CPU or CPUs (e.g. all, all but itself, self). The second specifies the interrupt to send.

140 this function waits for the APIC to be idle (see Section 13.4.1). Any previous IPI must be fully handled before writing new information to the APIC registers.

145 this line prepares a command word that will be written to the ICR register at line 148. It does not write to the APIC (see Section 13.5.4.5 for the function).

150 this macro, from Section 13.4.2, writes the command word calculated at line 143 to the APIC_ICR register. This actually sends the interrupt specified by vector to the CPUs identified by shortcut.

13.5.4.2   *Sending an interprocessor interrupt to a set of central processing units*

The function shown in Figure 13.25, from arch/i386/kernel/smp.c, is used to send an IPI to a group of CPUs. The destination CPUs are specified by the parameter mask. Depending on whether clustered addressing mode is in use or not, it calls send_IPI_mask_sequence() (Section 13.5.4.4) or send_IPI_mask_bitmask() (Section 13.5.4.3). These interpret mask in different ways.

```
234  static inline void send_IPI_mask(int mask, int vector)
235  {
236      if (clustered_apic_mode)
237          send_IPI_mask_sequence(mask, vector);
238      else
239          send_IPI_mask_bitmask(mask, vector);
240  }
```

Figure 13.25   Sending an interprocessor interrupt (IPI) to a set of computer processing units

13.5.4.3   *Sending an interprocessor interrupt with use of flat addressing*

The function shown in Figure 13.26, from arch/i386/kernel/smp.c, sends instructions to an APIC to transmit the interrupt specified by vector to the target CPUs specified by the bits set in mask. An IPI is actually generated by writing to the interrupt command register (ICR) of the local APIC. This command register was discussed in Section 13.1.3.

```
158  static inline void send_IPI_mask_bitmask(int mask, int vector)
159  {
160      unsigned long cfg;
161      unsigned long flags;
162
163      __save_flags(flags);
164      __cli();

170      apic_wait_icr_idle();

175      cfg = __prepare_ICR2(mask);
176      apic_write_around(APIC_ICR2, cfg);

181      cfg = __prepare_ICR(0, vector);

186      apic_write_around(APIC_ICR, cfg);
187
188      restore_flags(flags);
189  }
```

Figure 13.26   Worker function to send an interprocessor interrupt (IPI)

163   the value in the EFLAGS register is saved in the local flags by using the macro from Section 12.8.2.

164   interrupts are disabled on the local CPU using the macro from Section 12.8.2.

170   this waits for the local APIC to become idle (see Section 13.4.1 for the function).

175   this prepares a command word to write to the ICR2 register of the APIC; see Section 13.5.4.5 for this function, which just moves mask into the destination field.

176   this line writes this command word to the ICR2 register in the APIC (see Section 13.4.2).

181   this prepares a command word (specifying the interrupt) for the APIC (see Section 13.5.4.5). The first parameter specifies no shortcut, the destination field just set up is to be used instead.

186   writing this command word to the ICR register of the APIC fires off the interrupt (see Section 13.4.2).

188   this restores EFLAGS, thus setting interrupts to the state they were in before line 164.

13.5.4.4   Sending an interprocessor interrupt with use of clustered addressing

The function shown in Figure 13.27, from arch/i386/kernel/smp.c, also sends an IPI to a specified CPU or CPUs, but in this case clustered mode addressing is used, so there is no broadcast, rather a unicast to each CPU instead.

```
191  static inline void send_IPI_mask_sequence(int mask, int vector)
192  {
193        unsigned long cfg, flags;
194        unsigned int query_cpu, query_mask;

202        __save_flags(flags);
203        __cli();
204
205        for (query_cpu = 0; query_cpu < NR_CPUS; ++query_cpu) {
206            query_mask = 1 << query_cpu;
207            if (query_mask & mask) {

212                apic_wait_icr_idle();

217                cfg = __prepare_ICR2(cpu_to_logical_
                                                apicid(query_cpu));
218                apic_write_around(APIC_ICR2, cfg);

223                cfg = __prepare_ICR(0, vector);

228                apic_write_around(APIC_ICR, cfg);
```

```
229                    }
230            }
231            __restore_flags(flags);
232 }
```

Figure 13.27 Sending an interprocessor interrupt (IPI) by using clustered addressing

202 the value in the EFLAGS register is saved in the local flags, using the macro from Section 12.8.2.

203 interrupts are disabled on the local CPU by using the macro from Section 12.8.2.

205–230 this code loops through all the CPUs that are actually installed.

206 this sets a bit in this mask corresponding to the number of the CPU being considered.

207–229 if that bit is also set in the mask passed in as a parameter, then this code sends the IPI to that CPU.

212 this waits for any previous interrupt to finish (see Section 13.4.1 for the function).

217 this prepares a command word to write to the ICR2 register of the APIC (see Section 13.5.4.5), but first the CPU number must be converted to a logical APIC ID.

218 this writes this command word to the ICR2 register in the APIC (see Section 13.4.2).

223 this prepares a command word (specifying no shortcut, and the vector) for the APIC (see Section 13.5.4.5).

228 writing this command word to the ICR register of the APIC fires off the interrupt (see Section 13.4.2).

231 this restores EFLAGS, thus setting interrupts to the state they were in before line 203.

13.5.4.5 *Calculating command words for the APIC*

Two functions are provided for constructing the command words necessary to set up an APIC to send an IPI. One calculates the low-order 32 bits for ICR, the other calculates the high-order 32 bits for ICR2 of the APIC, thus setting up the destination of the interrupt. Both of these functions are shown in Figure 13.28, from arch/i386/kernel/smp.c.

```
116  static inline int __prepare_ICR (unsigned int shortcut, int vector)
117  {
118  return APIC_DM_FIXED | shortcut | vector | APIC_DEST_LOGICAL;
119  }
120
121  static inline int __prepare_ICR2 (unsigned int mask)
122  {
123  return SET_APIC_DEST_FIELD(mask);
124  }
```

Figure 13.28 Calculating command words for the APIC (advanced programmable interrupt controller)

116 the `shortcut` parameter specifies whether the destination is all, all but itself, or self. A value of 0 means that shortcut addressing is not being used. The `vector` parameter specifies the interrupt to send.

118 this calculates a command word to write to the `ICR` register of the APIC. It specifies fixed destination mode, using logical addressing (see Section 13.1.3 for the macros). The values passed in as parameters are written to the `shortcut` and `vector` fields.

123 the macro is given in Section 13.1.3. It moves the `mask` parameter into the most significant positions (the destination field).

13.6 First-level handlers for APIC interrupts

Now that the basic mechanisms for programming an APIC have been dealt with, we go on to consider the new interrupts that are introduced with the APIC. Some of these are generated by the APIC itself. In a multiprocessor, interrupts can also originate from another CPU. Although these always come through the IO APIC, which is the subject of the next chapter, they are always sent or received by the local APIC, so they are properly considered here.

13.6.1 Instantiating first-level handlers for APIC interrupts

Figure 13.29, from `arch/i386/kernel/i8259.c`, shows the code that instantiates handlers for these APIC interrupts, by calling macros described in Section 13.6.2.

```
81   #ifdef CONFIG_SMP
82   BUILD_SMP_INTERRUPT(reschedule_interrupt,RESCHEDULE_VECTOR)
83   BUILD_SMP_INTERRUPT (invalidate_interrupt,INVALIDATE_TLB_VECTOR)
84   BUILD_SMP_INTERRUPT(call_function_interrupt,
                                        CALL_FUNCTION_VECTOR)
85   #endif
94   #ifdef CONFIG_X86_LOCAL_APIC
95   BUILD_SMP_TIMER_INTERRUPT(apic_timer_interrupt,
                                        LOCAL_TIMER_VECTOR)
96   BUILD_SMP_INTERRUPT(error_interrupt,ERROR_APIC_VECTOR)
97   BUILD_SMP_INTERRUPT(spurious_interrupt,SPURIOUS_APIC_VECTOR)
98   #endif
```

Figure 13.29   Interprocessor and local APIC interrupts

81–85 these are relevant only in an SMP environment. They are not, strictly speaking, hardware interrupts; there is no hardware irq pin equivalent for them; rather they are IPIs. These three lines generate first-level handler code. The generating macro is described in Section 13.6.2.1.

82 this line generates a first-level handler for the reschedule interrupt, which does typical first-level handling and then calls the second-level handler, `smp_reschedule_interrupt()` (see Section 13.7.1).

83 this line generates a handler for the invalidate interrupt, which in turn calls `smp_invalidate_interrupt()`. This function is part of the memory manager and is not discussed in this book.

84   this line generates a handler for the call function interrupt, which in turn calls `smp_call_function_interrupt()` (see Section 13.7.2).

94–98 every Pentium local APIC can generate two interrupts of its own. One of these is a timer interrupt, the other is for error counter overflow. There may also be spurious interrupts detected, and these must be handled as well.

95   this line generates a handler for the APIC timer interrupt, which in turn calls `smp_apic_timer_interrupt()` (see Section 13.7.3).

96   this line generates a handler for the error interrupt, which in turn calls `smp_error_interrupt()` (see Section 13.7.4).

97   this line generates a handler for the spurious interrupt, which in turn calls `smp_spurious_interrupt()` (see Section 13.7.5).

The IDT vectors allocated to these interrupts have been defined in Section 12.5.3. Note that they are all of very high priority.

13.6.2   Macros to build first-level handlers for APIC interrupts

The previous section described how handlers are instantiated for six interrupts generated by APICs. Two different generating macros were used in that section, and here both of these are examined in turn.

13.6.2.1   Generic-first level handlers

Figure 13.30, from `<asm-i386/hw_irq.h>`, shows the macro that generates first-level handlers for most of the APIC interrupts.

```
126   #define BUILD_SMP_INTERRUPT(x,v) XBUILD_SMP_INTERRUPT(x,v)
127   #define XBUILD_SMP_INTERRUPT(x,v)                        \
128   asmlinkage void x(void);                                 \
129   asmlinkage void call_##x(void);                          \
130   __asm__(                                                 \
131       "\n"__ALIGN_STR" n"                                  \
132       SYMBOL_NAME_STR(x) ":\n\t"                           \
133       "pushl $"#v"-256\n\t"                                \
134       SAVE_ALL                                             \
135       SYMBOL_NAME_STR(call_##x)":\n\t"                     \
136       "call "SYMBOL_NAME_STR(smp_##x)"\n\t"                \
137       "jmp ret_from_intr\n");
```

Figure 13.30   Macro to build first level interrupt handler for APIC interrupts

126   there is a second layer of macro, which seems to be overkill. The comment in the code says that this change is for RTLinux.

127   the first parameter is the name to give to the entry point of the handler function; the second is the IDT vector to be assigned to the interrupt.

128   this is for the compiler. It enables the assembler entry point at line 132 to be called as a C function.

129   likewise, this enables the alternate entry point at line 135 to be called as a C function.

131   this macro, to align the code which follows, was described in Section 1.2.2.1.

132   this sets up a label corresponding to the first parameter, the entry point name.

133   this subtracts 256 from the second parameter and pushes the negative result on the stack as an immediate value. This is still a unique number but distinguished from the numbers used to represent system calls. It goes into the `orig_eax` slot on the stack.

134   this pushes all the other registers, from ES to EBX (see Section 10.3.2 for the SAVE_ALL macro).

135   this sets up the alternate entry point, as a label.

136   this prefaces the first parameter by `smp_` and calls the function with that name. This is the second-level handler. These handlers will be considered in Section 13.7.

137   this is the standard exit from interrupt handling (see Section 10.6.2).

13.6.2.2 *First-level handler for the APIC timer interrupt*

The macro to build the first-level handler for the APIC timer interrupt is slightly different from the previous macro. It is shown in Figure 13.31, from `<asm-i386/hw_irq.h>`.

```
139   #define BUILD_SMP_TIMER_INTERRUPT(x,v)
                                  XBUILD_SMP_TIMER_INTERRUPT(x,v)
140   #define XBUILD_SMP_TIMER_INTERRUPT(x,v)         \
141   asmlinkage void x(struct pt_regs * regs);       \
142   asmlinkage void call_##x(void);                 \
143   __asm__(                                        \
144       "\n"__ALIGN_STRING" n"                      \
145       SYMBOL_NAME_STR(x) ":\n\t"                  \
146       "pushl $"#v"-256\n\t"                       \
147       SAVE_ALL                                    \
148       "movl %esp,%eax\n\t"                        \
149       "pushl %eax\n\t"                            \
150       SYMBOL_NAME_STR(call_##x)":\n\t"            \
151       "call "SYMBOL_NAME_STR(smp_##x)"\n\t"       \
152       "addl $4,%esp\n\t"                          \
153       "jmp ret_from_intr\n");
```

Figure 13.31   Macro to build a first-level interrupt handler for timer interrupts

139   there is also a second-level macro used here (cf. line 126 in Section 13.6.2.1). Again, the comment in the code says this change is for RTLinux.

140   the first parameter is the name to give to the entry point of the handler function, the second is the IDT vector to be assigned to the interrupt.

141   this is for the compiler. It enables the assembler entry point at line 145 to be called as a C function. Note the difference between this and the macro in Section 13.6.2.1. This C function is expecting one parameter on the stack, a pointer to a `struct pt_regs`. The second-level handlers for the interrupts dealt with in Section 13.6.2.1 are declared as `void`.

142   likewise, this enables the alternate entry point at line 150 to be called as a C function.

144   this macro was described in Section 1.2.2.1.

145   this sets up a label corresponding to the first parameter.

146   this subtracts 256 from the second parameter and pushes the negative result on the stack as an immediate value. This distinguishes it from a system call. It goes into the `orig_eax` slot on the stack.

147   this pushes all the other registers, from ES to EBX (see Section 10.3.2 for the SAVE_ALL macro).

148–149   these two lines push the current ESP onto the stack. After the previous line, it is now pointing to the `struct pt_regs` on the stack. This is the parameter to the function called at line 151.

150   this sets up the alternate entry point, as a label.

151   this calls the second-level handler function. Its name is the first parameter, prefaced by `smp_`. The function itself will be discussed in Section 13.7.

152   this removes the parameter pushed at line 149.

153   this is the standard return path from interrupt handling (see Section 10.6.2).

13.7   Second-level handlers for APIC interrupts

The previous section examined how first-level handlers for APIC interrupts were generated. Each of these called a specific second-level service function, which will now be examined in this section.

13.7.1   The reschedule interrupt

This is sent to a specific CPU in order to force the execution of the `schedule()` function on that CPU. The handler has nothing to do; all the work on the target machine is done automatically on return from interrupt handling. Figure 13.32, from `arch/i386/kernel/smp.c`, shows the trivial function.

```
601  asmlinkage void smp_reschedule_interrupt(void)
602  {
603      ack_APIC_irq();
604  }
```

Figure 13.32   Second-level handler for the APIC (advanced programmable interrupt controller) reschedule interrupt

603   this acknowledges receipt of the interrupt to the APIC (see Section 13.3.2.4 for the function).

13.7.2   The call function interrupt

In a multiprocessor configuration it is possible for one CPU to request all the others to execute a specified function. This request is transmitted by means of the call function IPI. The sending of that interrupt was discussed in Section 13.5.2. Figure 13.33, from arch/i386/kernel/smp.c, shows the second-level handler for this interrupt on the destination CPU.

```
606  asmlinkage void smp_call_function_interrupt(void)
607  {
608      void (*func)(void *info) = call_data->func;
609      void *info = call_data->info;
610      int wait = call_data->wait;
611
612      ack_APIC_irq();

617      mb();
618      atomic_inc(&call_data->started);

622      (*func)(info);
623      if (wait)
624          mb();
625          atomic_inc(&call_data->finished);
626      }
627  }
```

Figure 13.33   Second-level handler for the APIC (advanced programmable interrupt controller) call function interrupt

608   the call_data global structure (see Section 13.5.2.2) has been set up by the calling CPU with all the relevant information. The func field in this structure contains a pointer to the function to be executed. As all the other CPUs only read this data there is no need for them to worry about mutual exclusion.

609   the info field contains an optional pointer to data required by the called function.

610   the wait field is TRUE if the calling CPU wants to be notified when the function terminates; otherwise it is FALSE.

612   this acknowledges receipt of the interrupt to the local APIC of the target machine (see Section 13.3.2.4).

617   this makes sure that this CPU has a consistent view of memory, before writing to shared data.

618   this notifies the initiating CPU that one other CPU has read the data and is about to execute the function. All the CPUs write to this field, so mutual exclusion is required. See Section 5.2.5 for the `atomic_inc()` function. Note that if the `wait` field has a value of 0 (FALSE), then after the `started` field has been incremented by all the CPUs the caller is free to remove the `info` structure, so it cannot be presumed valid after this.

622   this calls the requested function. Note that it must be of type `void`.

623   this is executed only if the calling CPU asked to be notified when the function had terminated.

624   this makes sure that this CPU has a consistent view of memory, before writing to shared data.

625   the `finished` field in `call_data` is incremented atomically, using the function from Section 5.2.5. The calling CPU spins on this, waiting for all the others to increment it.

13.7.3   Local APIC timer interrupt

The second-level handler for this increments the running count of timer ticks and acknowledges the irq. Then it calls a third-level handler, which does the sort of housekeeping work associated with timer interrupts.

13.7.3.1   Second-level timer handling

Each local APIC generates a timer interrupt. Figure 13.34, from `arch/i386/kernel/apic.c`, shows the second-level handler for this interrupt.

```
1021 unsigned int apic_timer_irqs [NR_CPUS];
1022
1023 void smp_apic_timer_interrupt(struct pt_regs * regs)
1024 {
1025      int cpu = smp_processor_id();
1030      apic_timer_irqs[cpu]++;
1036      ack_APIC_irq();
1042      irq_enter(cpu, 0);
1043      smp_local_timer_interrupt(regs);
1044      irq_exit(cpu, 0);
1045
1046      if (softirq_pending(cpu))
1047           do_softirq();
1048 }
```

Figure 13.34   Second-level handler for the APIC (advanced programmable interrupt controller) timer

1021   this array maintains a separate total of APIC timer interrupts for each CPU.

1025 this gets the ID of the currently executing CPU (see Section 7.2.1.4).

1030 this increments the count of APIC timer interrupts for this CPU. The nonmaskable interrupt deadlock detection uses this count (see Section 11.3.2.2).

1036 the irq is acknowledged at this stage, because timer handling (line 1043) can be slow. The acknowledging function was described in Section 13.3.2.4.

1042 this macro, and its companion on line 1044, keeps track of the number of (nested) interrupts currently in progress on this CPU. The macros are defined in Section 16.5.3. The second parameter is not used by either of the macros, so it is set to 0.

1043 this function handles work that needs to be done on every timer tick (see Section 13.7.3.2).

1046 the macro that checks if there are software interrupts waiting to be executed is from Section 16.5.1.2.

1047 software interrupts are run at least every timer tick, using the function from Section 16.1.3.

13.7.3.2 Third-level timer handling

The local timer interrupt handler, from `arch/i386/kernel/apic.c`, is shown in Figure 13.35. It does both profiling and process statistics/rescheduling. Profiling is done on every local tick, statistics/rescheduling happen only after a fixed number of ticks, although the default for this is 1. It can be changed by writing the new multiplier value into `/proc/profile`.

```
967  inline void smp_local_timer_interrupt(struct pt_regs * regs)
968  {
969       int user = user_mode(regs);
970       int cpu = smp_processor_id();

978       if (!user)
979            x86_do_profile(regs->eip);
980
981       if (--prof_counter[cpu] <= 0) {

990            prof_counter[cpu] = prof_multiplier[cpu];
991            if (prof_counter[cpu] != prof_old_multiplier[cpu]){
992            __setup_APIC_LVTT(calibration_result/prof_counter[cpu]);
993                 prof_old_multiplier[cpu] = prof_counter[cpu];
994            }
995
996  #ifdef CONFIG_SMP
997       update_process_times(user);
998  #endif
999       }

1011 }
```

Figure 13.35 The local timer interrupt handler

969   this macro evaluates to TRUE if the CPU was running in user mode, or in vm86 mode, when the interrupt occurred (see Section 10.3.1.4).

970   this gets the ID of the currently executing processor (see Section 7.2.1.4).

978–979   if the CPU was running in kernel mode when the timer ticked, then there is a special profiling function called (see Section 13.7.3.3).

981–999   this code is not executed on every interrupt but only at a frequency determined by the multiplier. The copy of the multiplier maintained in `prof_counter[cpu]` is decremented each tick.

990   as the running counter has expired, it needs to be set up again.

991–994   the multiplier may have changed since the last time this line was executed, as a result of the user writing to /proc/profile. This user intervention changes the value in the appropriate element of `prof_multiplier[]`; it does not change the corresponding element in `prof_old_multiplier[]`. The APIC timer needs to know this and has to be adjusted accordingly.

992   the function is from Section 13.7.3.4. Because the multiplier (in `prof_counter[cpu]`) has changed, the APIC timer has to be recalibrated.

993   now that the hardware has been recalibrated, the old multiplier is not relevant and that field is updated.

996–998   in a multiprocessor system, process times are updated at this less frequent interval as well (see Section 15.1.3.1). Otherwise, on a uniprocessor system, this function is called from `do_timer()` (see Section 15.1.2).

13.7.3.3   Profiling function

The function that does profiling in Linux is shown in 13.36, from `<asm-i386/hw_irq.h>`. It is called only when a timer tick occurs in kernel mode, and it profiles only kernel usage.

```
192   static inline void x86_do_profile (unsigned long eip)
193   {
194       if (!prof_buffer)
195           return;

201       if (!((1<<smp_processor_id()) & prof_cpu_mask))
202           return;
203
204       eip -= (unsigned long) &_stext;
205       eip >>= prof_shift;

211       if (eip > prof_len-1)
212           eip = prof_len-1;
213       atomic_inc((atomic_t *)&prof_buffer[eip]);
214   }
```

Figure 13.36   Profiling kernel usage

192 the function is passed a pointer to the saved value of EIP on the stack (i.e. a pointer to where it was in kernel code when the interrupt occurred).

194–195 if a buffer for profiling information has not been set up by start_kernel(), we return.

201–202 if the current CPU is not set up to be profiled, we return.

204 subtracting the address of _stext (the beginning of the kernel code segment) from the EIP value converts an absolute address to an offset into kernel code.

205 this determines the granularity of the profiling, by taking only high-order bits of the offset into account.

211–212 if the resultant value is out of bounds, it is converted so that it belongs in the last entry in the table. In this way, such values will stand out.

213 this increments the appropriate entry in the profiling table.

13.7.3.4 Setting up the local APIC timer

The function shown in Figure 13.37, from arch/i386/kernel/apic.c, sets up the local APIC timer. This is done at initialisation but may also be called if the user changes the multiplier value in /proc/profile.

```
761  void __setup_APIC_LVTT(unsigned int clocks)
762  {
763      unsigned int lvtt1_value, tmp_value;
764
765      lvtt1_value = SET_APIC_TIMER_BASE(APIC_TIMER_BASE_DIV)
766              | APIC_LVT_TIMER_PERIODIC | LOCAL_TIMER_VECTOR;
767      apic_write_around(APIC_LVTT, lvtt1_value);

772      tmp_value = apic_read(APIC_TDCR);
773      apic_write_around(APIC_TDCR, (tmp_value
774                  & ~(APIC_TDR_DIV_1 | APIC_TDR_DIV_TMBASE))
775                                  | APIC_TDR_DIV_16);
776
777      apic_write_around(APIC_TMICT, clocks/APIC_DIVISOR);
778  }
```

Figure 13.37 Setting up the local APIC (advanced programmable interrupt controller) timer

761 the parameter is the interval at which the timer is to interrupt.

765–766 the SET_APIC_TIMER_BASE() macro sets up the timer base field (bits 18–19) with APIC_TIMER_BASE_DIV (10 binary). APIC_LVT_TIMER_PERIODIC is bit 17, the timer mode field. This code is setting it to be periodic. These three macros are from Section 13.1.4. LOCAL_TIMER_VECTOR is defined in Section 12.5.3. This is the least significant 8 bits, so the whole thing builds up a value for the local timer register in lvtt1_value.

767   this value is written to the `APIC_LVTT` register, using the macro from Section 13.4.2.

772   this reads the current value in the timer divide configuration register (`APIC_TDCR`).

773–775   this clears the `APIC_TDR_DIV_1` (bits 0, 1 and 4) and `APIC_TDR_DIV_TMBASE` (bit 2) and sets `APIC_TDR_DIV_16` (bits 0 and 1); it then writes all this back to the timer divide configuration register.

777   the `APIC_TMICT`, the initial count register field of the timer, is set up by using the function described in Section 13.4.2. The input parameter is divided by the value from `arch/i386/kernel/apic.c`:

```
759   #define APIC_DIVISOR 16
```

13.7.4 The local error interrupt

This interrupt should never happen with the current SMP architecture, using APICs, but in case it does, the second-level handler in Figure 13.38, from `arch/i386/kernel/apic.c`, is there to catch it.

```
1075 asmlinkage void smp_error_interrupt(void)
1076 {
1077       unsigned long v, v1;

1080       v = apic_read(APIC_ESR);
1081       apic_write(APIC_ESR, 0);
1082       v1 = apic_read(APIC_ESR);
1083       ack_APIC_irq();
1084       atomic_inc(&irq_err_count);

1096       printk(KERN_ERR "APIC error on CPU%d:%02lx(%02lx)\n",
1097               smp_processor_id(), v, v1);
1098 }
```

Figure 13.38   Second-level handler for the error interrupt

1080   this reads from the error status register (`APIC_ESR`), using the function from Section 13.4.1.

1081   this clears that register by writing a zero to it, using the function from Section 13.4.1.

1082   again, we read from `APIC_ESR`.

1083   now the interrupt to the APIC is acknowledged by using the function from Section 13.3.2.4.

1084   this increments the global count of interrupt errors (see Section 14.5.1.1).

1096–1097   this code prints the error message. It prints *first value (second value)*. The meaning of the APIC error bits were defined in Section 13.1.2. The `smp_processor_id()` macro is from Section 7.2.1.4.

13.7.5 The spurious interrupt

If, at the moment an interrupt is sent to the CPU, it is running at higher priority than the interrupt level, there may be a delay in issuing the INTA cycle. If that interrupt has been masked by software in the meantime, then, when INTA finally does arrive, the local APIC does not issue the vector corresponding to the masked interrupt but the spurious interrupt vector. No bit is set in the ISR corresponding to this, so the handler for this vector does not issue an EOI.

The second-level handler for the spurious interrupt is shown in Figure 13.39, from arch/i386/kernel/apic.c. This interrupt should *never* happen with the present APIC/SMP architecture.

```
1053 asmlinkage void smp_spurious_interrupt(void)
1054 {
1055     unsigned long v;

1062     v = apic_read(APIC_ISR + ((SPURIOUS_APIC_VECTOR & ~0x1f) >> 1));
1063     if (v & (1 << (SPURIOUS_APIC_VECTOR & 0x1f)))
1064         ack_APIC_irq();

1067     printk(KERN_INFO "spurious APIC interrupt on CPU#%d,
1068         should never happen.\n", smp_processor_id());
1069 }
```

Figure 13.39   Second-level handler for the spurious interrupt

1062–1064   because spurious interrupts should not be acknowledged to the APIC, this code checks if this really is a spurious interrupt. If the corresponding bit is set in the ISR, then it was actually serviced, so it is acknowledged.

1062   this determines the part of the ISR corresponding to this vector and reads it in. The SPURIOUS _APIC_VECTOR is 0xff. 0x1f is 0001 1111; ~0x1f is 1110 0000. Thus (SPURIOUS_APIC_VECTOR & ~0x1f) is 1110 0000. This always clears the 5 least significant bits. In this way we divide a vector into one of eight classes, each corresponding to a 32-bit block in the ISR. Finally, ((SPURIOUS_APIC_VECTOR & ~0x1f) >> 1) is 0111 0000. So we read from APIC_ISR + 0x70 , the part of the ISR corresponding to vectors E0 – FF.

1063   (SPURIOUS_APIC_VECTOR & 0x1f) is 0001 1111 or 0x1f, or the low-order 5 bits of the vector. 1 << (SPURIOUS_APIC_VECTOR & 0x1f) sets bit 1f, or the most significant bit. If this bit is set in v, then this is acknowledged.

1067–1068   this code prints a warning message, identifying the CPU. The smp_processor_id() macro is from Section 7.2.1.4.

13.7.6 Resending an irq

As has been seen in Section 12.6.4, when attempting to reenable an irq, if the IRQ_PENDING flag is found to be set then it is possible to resend that interrupt to the same

CPU, using the IO APIC. Figure 13.40, from `<asm-i386/hw_irq.h>`, shows the function to do this.

```
216  #ifdef CONFIG_SMP
217  static inline void hw_resend_irq(struct hw_interrupt_type *h,
                                                unsigned int i) {
218       if (IO_APIC_IRQ(i))
219             send_IPI_self(IO_APIC_VECTOR(i));
220  }
221  #else
222  static inline void hw_resend_irq(struct hw_interrupt_type *h,
                                                unsigned int i) {}

223  #endif
```

Figure 13.40　Resending an irq (interrupt request)

216–220　on a multiprocessor system, there will always be an IO APIC, so interprocessor interrupts can be sent.

217　the first parameter, a pointer to the `hw_interrupt_type` representing the controller that delivered the interrupt in the first instance, is not used. The second parameter is the vector associated with the interrupt.

218–219　the `IO_APIC_IRQ()` macro is defined in `<asm-i386/hw_irq.h>` as:

```
93   #define IO_APIC_IRQ(x) (((x) >= 16) || ((1<<(x)) & io_apic_irqs))
```

It returns TRUE if either the irq is not one of the original 16 or the bit corresponding to this irq is set in `io_apics_irqs` (i.e. the irq is routed through the IO APIC).

219　the `IO_APIC_VECTOR()` macro, from Section 12.5.3, converts an irq number to the vector corresponding to that irq. Then `send_IPI_self()`, from Section 13.5.3.3, sends an interprocessor interrupt for that vector to the same CPU.

222　on a uniprocessor, this is a null function.

14

The input–output advanced programmable interrupt controller (the IO APIC)

In a multiprocessor configuration, as well as the local APIC on each computer processing unit (CPU) chip, there is also a separate IO APIC. The presence of such an APIC is determined by CONFIG_X86_IO_APIC. External hardware lines from physical devices are connected to pins on this APIC, and it can be programmed to generate a specific vector when one of these is asserted. The IO APIC takes the place of the 8259 programmable interrupt controller (PIC) in the system. It routes incoming irqs (interrupt requests) to the local APIC of the appropriate CPU. When it does, the interrupt is not received on a physical signal line but over the system bus. However, the effect in the local APIC is just the same.

In addition, the local APIC sends all interprocessor interrupts (IPIs) to this IO APIC in the first instance, which then sends them on either to all CPUs (broadcast) or to the specific CPU requested by the sender. It is also possible, on a larger system, to have more than one IO APIC, thus adding to the complexity of the software.

14.1 Interrupt configuration tables in Linux

Linux records a considerable amount of information about the configuration of any IO APICs installed in the system. The format of this information conforms to the Intel multiprocessor specification. The data structures containing this information are filled in during the initial stages of bootup; how that is done is not the concern of this book. This section first describes the static data structures themselves, then the functions that operate on these structures.

The Linux Process Manager. The Internals of Scheduling, Interrupts and Signals John O'Gorman
© 2003 John Wiley & Sons, Ltd ISBN: 0 470 84771 9

14.1.1 Data structures

There are a number of arrays, which will be examined first. Then the data types making up these arrays will be described.

14.1.1.1 Configuration table structures

A system may have more than one IO APIC, each containing many registers. There will also be many sources of interrupts in the system. The data structures that keep track of all of this information are shown in Figure 14.1, from `arch/i386/kernel/mpparse.c`.

```
38   int                    mp_bus_id_to_type [MAX_MP_BUSSES];

44   struct mpc_config_ioapic   mp_ioapics[MAX_IO_APICS];

47   struct mpc_config_intsrc   mp_irqs[MAX_IRQ_SOURCES];

50   int                    mp_irq_entries;
51
52   int                    nr_ioapics;
53
54   int                    pic_mode;

64   unsigned long          phys_cpu_present_map;
```

Figure 14.1 Configuration tables for IO APICs

38 there can be up to four different types of IO bus present in a PC, as enumerated in Section 14.1.1.2. Busses are physically numbered 0, 1, ..., and so on. This array serves to identify the `type` of any particular bus.

44 the `struct mpc_config_ioapic` describes how a particular IO APIC is actually configured into the system. This array has room for the maximum number of APICs. Each APIC is identified by its place in this array. The structure itself is described in Section 14.1.1.3.

47 the `struct mpc_config_intsrc` describes the properties of a particular interrupt source in the system. There is one of these structures for each interrupt source. The structure itself is described in Section 14.1.1.4.

50 this variable contains the actual number of entries in `mp_irqs[]`. It is used to prevent searches going into uninitialised data.

52 as the name implies, this variable maintains the number of IO APICs in the system. Its value is determined at boot time.

54 if this is set to 1, it means that there is a PIC physically present on the motherboard. This can be switched in to replace the APICs (see the function in Section 13.2.5).

64 this is a bitmap, with bits set corresponding to physically present CPUs.

14.1.1.2   Bus types

The four different bus types that can be found in a PC are detailed in the enumeration shown in Figure 14.2, from `<asm-i386/mpspec.h>`.

```
194  enum mp_bustype {
195       MP_BUS_ISA = 1,
196       MP_BUS_EISA,
197       MP_BUS_PCI,
198       MP_BUS_MCA
199  };
```

Figure 14.2   Bus types

195   this is the industry standard architecture (ISA) legacy bus on the PC, used for interfacing to slower peripherals.

196   this is the extended ISA (EISA) bus; it is not very common.

197   the peripheral component interconnect (PCI) is the standard internal bus in a modern PC.

198   the microchannel architecture (MCA) bus is used mainly on the PS/2. It is not common nowadays.

14.1.1.3   Data structure representing an IO APIC

Figure 14.3. from `<asm-i386/mpspec.h>`, shows the data structure describing an IO APIC to the system. There is one of these structures for each installed IO APIC.

```
109  struct mpc_config_ioapic
110  {
111       unsigned char mpc_type;
112       unsigned char mpc_apicid;
113       unsigned char mpc_apicver;
114       unsigned char mpc_flags;
115  #define MPC_APIC_USABLE      0x01
116       unsigned long  mpc_apicaddr;
117  };
```

Figure 14.3   Data structure describing an IO APIC

111   the `type` field identifies it as an APIC, processor, and so on. All entries in configuration tables have a similar format. A value of 2 identifies it as an IO APIC.

112   this is the identification (ID) number of the particular APIC.

113   this is the version number of the APIC. This value is also in bits 0–7 of the version register.

114–115   the only bit defined in the flags field at present is the MPC_APIC_USABLE bit. If 0, then this one is unusable.

116   this is the address of the APIC in the memory map.

14.1.1.4 Data structure representing an interrupt source

Figure 14.4, from <asm-i386/mpspec.h>, shows the data structure representing an external interrupt source. There is one of these structures set up at boot time for each irq line in the system.

```
119  struct mpc_config_intsrc
120  {
121          unsigned char        mpc_type;
122          unsigned char        mpc_irqtype;
123          unsigned short       mpc_irqflag;
124          unsigned char        mpc_srcbus;
125          unsigned char        mpc_srcbusirq;
126          unsigned char        mpc_dstapic;
127          unsigned char        mpc_dstirq;
128  };

150  #define MP_APIC_ALL      0xFF
```

Figure 14.4   Data structure describing an interrupt source

121   a value of 3 in the type field identifies it as an interrupt entry.

122   this is the type of the irq. The various possibilities are discussed in Section 14.1.1.5.

123   the flag field contains bits such as polarity and trigger mode.

124   this is the ID number of the bus that generates this irq (e.g. 0, 1, 2, etc.).

125   this is the identifier of that irq on the source bus, beginning at 0.

126   this is the number of the APIC to which it is physically connected.

127   this is the pin number on that APIC.

150   this value in the mpc_dstapic field means all IO APICs.

14.1.1.5 Types of interrupt

Linux recognises four different types of interrupt, even though it does not use them all. Figure 14.5, from <asm-i386/mpspec.h>, shows the enumeration listing the possibilities.

```
130  enum mp_irq_source_types {
131       mp_INT = 0 ,
132       mp_NMI = 1 ,
133       mp_SMI = 2 ,
134       mp_ExtINT = 3
135  };
```

Figure 14.5   Types of interrupt

131   this is a vectored interrupt with the vector supplied by the APIC redirection table.

132   this is a nonmaskable interrupt (nmi). Vector information is irrelevant in this case.

133   this is a system management interrupt, which sets the destination processor into a special system management mode. It is not used by Linux.

134   this is also a vectored interrupt, but with the vector supplied by the 8259A PIC.

14.1.1.6   *The* pirq_entries[] *array*

By default, interrupts 0–7 on the PCI bus are assigned irq numbers 16–23, but, if required, they can be redirected to one of the irq lines between 0–15. Such redirection is recorded in the pirq_entries[] array; see Figure 14.6, from arch/i386/kernel/io_apic.c.

```
171  #define MAX_PIRQS 8
174  int pirq_entries [MAX_PIRQS];
175  int pirqs_enabled;
```

Figure 14.6   Redirecting peripheral component interconnect (PCI) interrupts

173   there are only eight PCI interrupts, numbered 0–7.

174   this eight-element array of int will map PCI interrupts 0–7 onto irq numbers in the range 0–15.

175   this flag is set if any PCI interrupts are redirected.

14.1.2   Reading the interrupt configuration tables

Linux supplies a number of functions for reading the configuration tables described in the previous section; these will now be considered.

14.1.2.1   *Finding a specified entry in* mp_irqs[]

Figure 14.7, from arch/i386/kernel/io_apic.c, shows the function that finds the entry number in mp_irqs[] corresponding to a particular APIC/pin/type combination. This function goes through the whole mp_irqs[] array, checking for an entry that matches the parameters type, apic, and pin.

```
215  static int __init find_irq_entry(int apic, int pin, int type)
216  {
217      int i;
218
219      for (i = 0; i < mp_irq_entries; i++)
220          if (mp_irqs[i].mpc_irqtype == type &&
221      (mp_irqs[i].mpc_dstapic == mp_ioapics[apic].mpc_apicid ||
222                      mp_irqs[i].mpc_dstapic == MP_APIC_ALL) &&
223                          mp_irqs[i].mpc_dstirq == pin)
224              return i;
225
226      return -1;
227  }
```

Figure 14.7 Finding the irq (interrupt request) number of a given pin

219 the `mp_irq_entries` variable (Section 14.1.1.1) contains the actual number of entries in the `mp_irqs[]` array, so the search will never get into uninitialised data.

220–223 the rather complicated looking test breaks down into three parts, as follows.

220 the `type` parameter must match the `mpc_irqtype` field.

221–222 the test on the `apic` parameter is not so straightforward. The `apic` parameter identifies the IO APIC by its sequence number (i.e. APIC 0, APIC 1, etc.). The `mp_destapic` field identifies the APIC by its logical ID address, so the sequence number has to be converted to a logical ID before a comparison can be made. This is done by using the sequence number to index into the `mp_ioapics[]` array (Section 14.1.1.1) to find the corresponding logical ID. Another possibility is that the entry may not match this APIC directly, but the entry may have a wildcard value, meaning this irq source is connected to all APICs. The `MP_APIC_ALL` macro is defined in Section 14.1.1.4.

223 the `pin` must match the `mpc_dstirq` field.

224 if a match is found, the index is returned into the `mp_irqs[]` array corresponding to the matching entry.

226 if all the entries have been searched without finding a match, −1 is returned to indicate failure.

14.1.2.2 Converting an irq to a pin number

The function shown in 14.8, from `arch/i386/kernel/io_apic.c`, finds the pin to which a particular irq line on the ISA bus is connected. It does not work for PCI bus lines.

```
232  static int __init find_isa_irq_pin(int irq, int type)
233  {
234      int i;
235
236      for (i = 0; i < mp_irq_entries; i++) {
237          int lbus = mp_irqs[i].mpc_srcbus;
```

```
238
239              if ((mp_bus_id_to_type[lbus] == MP_BUS_ISA ||
240                   mp_bus_id_to_type[lbus] == MP_BUS_EISA ||
241                   mp_bus_id_to_type[lbus] == MP_BUS_MCA) &&
242                  (mp_irqs[i].mpc_irqtype == type) &&
243                  (mp_irqs[i].mpc_srcbusirq == irq))

245                      return mp_irqs[i].mpc_dstirq;
246      }
247      return -1;
248  }
```

Figure 14.8   Finding the pin to which a particular irq (interrupt request) line is connected

232   the parameters are the number of the irq line, and the bus type.

236–246   this loop goes through each entry in the mp_irqs[] array until the appropriate one is found.

237   the ID number of the source bus for the current entry is found.

243–245   this array converts between bus number and bus type (see Section 14.1.1.1). It is filled in at boot time, indexed on the ID number of the bus. Each entry contains an element of the enumeration from the code in Section 14.1.1.2, identifying the type of that bus. It must be an ISA, EISA, or MCA bus.

242–244   as well as that, the entry must match both the parameters.

245   if the foregoing three tests are passed, then we have a match, so we return the dstirq field, which identifies the pin. Otherwise, we try the next entry.

247   if no match found after the whole array has been examined, we return −1 to indicate failure.

14.1.2.3   Converting a pin number to an irq

Figure 14.9, from arch/i386/kernel/io_apic.c, returns the number of the irq line connected to a given pin on an IO APIC.

```
483  static int pin_2_irq(int idx, int apic, int pin)
484  {
485      int irq, i;
486      int bus = mp_irqs[idx].mpc_srcbus;

491      if (mp_irqs[idx].mpc_dstirq != pin)
492          printk(KERN_ERR "broken BIOS or MPTABLE parser,
                                                    ayiee!!\n");

494      switch (mp_bus_id_to_type[bus])
495      {
496              case MP_BUS_ISA:
497              case MP_BUS_EISA:
```

```
498                    case MP_BUS_MCA:
499                    {
500                        irq = mp_irqs[idx].mpc_srcbusirq;
501                        break;
502                    }
503                    case MP_BUS_PCI:
504                    {
508                        i = irq = 0;
509                        while (i < apic)
510                            irq += nr_ioapic_registers[i++];
511                        irq += pin;
512                        break;
513                    }
514                    default:
515                    {
516                        printk(KERN_ERR "unknown bus type %d.\n", bus);
517                        irq = 0;
518                        break;
519                    }
520            }

525            if ((pin >= 16) && (pin <= 23)) {
526                if (pirq_entries[pin-16] != -1) {
527                    if (!pirq_entries[pin-16]) {
528                    printk(KERN_DEBUG "disabling PIRQ%d\n", pin-16);
529                    } else {
530                        irq = pirq_entries[pin-16];
531                        printk(KERN_DEBUG "using PIRQ%d -> IRQ %d\n",
532            pin-16, irq);
533                    }
534                }
535            }
536        return irq;
537 }
```

Figure 14.9   Returning the irq corresponding to a given pin

483   the first parameter is an index into the `mp_irqs[]` array. This saves the work of searching the whole array. The second specifies the APIC, and the third is the pin on that APIC.

486   we use the supplied parameter to index into the `mp_irqs[]` array and get the ID number (e.g. 0, 1, ...) of the bus that generates this irq from the `mpc_srcbus` field.

491–492   this is a debugging check. If the value saved in the `mpc_dstirq` field is not the correct pin number, there is something seriously wrong.

494   this array converts between bus number and bus type (see Section 14.1.1.1). It is filled in at boot time, indexed on the ID number of the bus. Each entry contains an element of the enumeration from the code in Section 14.1.1.2, identifying the type of that bus.

496–502 if we have an ISA, EISA, or MCA bus, then the number to return is simply the `mpc_srcbusirq` field in the `mp_irqs[]` entry, which contains the irq number.

503–513 for a PCI bus interrupt, the `srcbusirq` field does not contain the irq number; rather, that field is faceted. Bits 0–1 identify the PCI interrupt signal, where `00` corresponds to `INTA#`, `01` to `INTB#`, `10` to `INTC#`, and `11` to `INTD#`. Bits 2–6 give the PCI device number where the interrupt originates, so another method has to be used to get the irq number.

508–510 a PCI bus will always be connected to the last IO APIC (typically, the second). The variable `i` is going to count its way through the IO APICs until it comes to the specified one; `irq` is going to accumulate the number of pins in each. After this loop, `irq` is the sequence number of the first pin on the last APIC (i.e. the first PCI pin).

511 now `irq` points to the specified pin on that IO APIC. An example of a typical configuration may help here. Suppose IO APIC 0 is connected to an ISA bus, and IO APIC 1 to a PCI bus. Then the `while` loop will be executed only once, setting `irq` to 16. Line 511 will then identify irq16 for pin 0, irq17 for pin 1, and so on.

514–519 all the bus types specified in Section 14.1.1.2 have now been checked. If an unknown bus type is encountered, the message is printed and an irq of 0 is returned.

525–535 the discussion of the PCI bus at lines 503–513 was the straightforward case, but the irq numbers assigned to PCI pins (between 16 and 23) can be redirected. The `pirq_entries[]` array is used for this (see Section 14.1.1.6). This block of code is checking to see if any such redirection has been set up. It is executed only if dealing with a pin number between 16 and 23.

526–534 this code is executed if the corresponding entry in `pirq_entries[]` is valid (i.e. if this PCI interrupt has been redirected). Otherwise, control transfers to the `return` at line 536.

527–528 if the irq number is recorded as redirected to irq 0, that means that it has in fact been disabled, so the message is printed, but the irq number is still returned.

530–531 otherwise, we change `irq` to be the number to which it has been redirected and print the message saying that PIRQx has been redirected to IRQ y.

536 the irq number is returned.

14.1.3   Getting the polarity and trigger type of an irq line

The polarity of an irq line indicates whether it is active high or low. Also, a line can be edge triggered or level triggered. This section will examine the standard definitions for the different busses, and various functions provided for determining the polarity and trigger type of a particular irq.

14.1.3.1   Default polarity and trigger type

The four different bus types have different values for polarity and trigger type, as defined in Figure 14.10, from `arch/i386/kernel/io_apic.c`.

```
299   static int __init EISA_ELCR(unsigned int irq)
300   {
301       if (irq < 16) {
302           unsigned int port = 0x4d0 + (irq >> 3);
303           return (inb(port) >> (irq & 7)) & 1;
304       }
305       printk(KERN_INFO "Broken MPtable reports ISA irq
                                                %d\n", irq);
306       return 0;
307   }


314   #define default_EISA_trigger(idx) (EISA_ELCR(mp_irqs[idx].
                                                mpc_srcbusirq))
315   #define default_EISA_polarity(idx)    (0)

320   #define default_ISA_trigger(idx)      (0)
321   #define default_ISA_polarity(idx)     (0)

326   #define default_PCI_trigger(idx)      (1)
327   #define default_PCI_polarity(idx)     (1)

332   #define default_MCA_trigger(idx)      (1)
333   #define default_MCA_polarity(idx)     (0)
```

Figure 14.10   Default polarity and trigger types

299–307   this function reads from the EISA edge/level control register (ELCR) to return the trigger type of a particular EISA irq line.

301–304   if it really is an EISA irq, then it should be between 0–15.

302   there is one bit per irq, so requiring two 8-bit ports. Shifting `irq` right 3 bits gives 0 or 1, thus selecting port $0x4D0$ (for irqs 0–7), or $0x4D1$ (for irqs 8–15).

303   this reads from the IO port, using the function from Section 12.9.1.2. The value is shifted right so that the bit corresponding to the irq number is in the rightmost position, and all other bits are masked out. This will result in either 0 (for edge triggered), or 1 (for level triggered).

314–333   in all cases the parameter is an index into the `mp_irqs[]` array.

314   EISA interrupts can be edge or level trigger, depending on the ELCR value. If an interrupt is listed as EISA conforming in the configuration table, that means its trigger type must be read in from the EISA ELCR (see line 299).

315   EISA interrupts are always polarity zero.

320–321   ISA interrupts are always polarity zero, edge triggered.

326–327   PCI interrupts are always polarity one, level triggered.

332–333   MCA interrupts are always polarity zero, level triggered.

14.1.3.2　*Wrapper functions to return polarity and trigger type*

Figure 14.11, from `arch/i386/kernel/io_apic.c`, shows two wrapper functions that return information from the configuration tables about polarity and trigger type. In both cases the parameter is an index into the `mp_irqs[]` array.

```
473  static inline int irq_polarity(int idx)
474  {
475        return MPBIOS_polarity(idx);
476  }
477
478  static inline int irq_trigger(int idx)
479  {
480        return MPBIOS_trigger(idx);
481  }
```

Figure 14.11　Returning polarity and trigger type of an irq (interrupt request)

475　this function is discussed in detail in Section 14.1.3.3.

480　this function is discussed in detail in Section 14.1.3.4.

14.1.3.3　*Getting the polarity of an irq line*

The function in Figure 14.12, from `arch/i386/kernel/io_apic.c`, is supplied with an index into the `mp_irqs[]` table, and it returns the polarity of the corresponding irq.

```
335  static int __init MPBIOS_polarity(int idx)
336  {
337       int bus = mp_irqs[idx].mpc_srcbus;
338       int polarity;

343       switch (mp_irqs[idx].mpc_irqflag & 3)
344       {
345            case 0:
346          {
347                 switch (mp_bus_id_to_type[bus])
348                 {
349                  case MP_BUS_ISA:
350                  {
351                       polarity = default_ISA_polarity(idx);
352                       break;
353                  }
354                  case MP_BUS_EISA:
355                  {
356                       polarity = default_EISA_polarity(idx);
357                       break;
358                  }
359                  case MP_BUS_PCI:
```

```
360                      {
361                          polarity = default_PCI_polarity(idx);
362                          break;
363                      }
364                      case MP_BUS_MCA:
365                      {
366                          polarity = default_MCA_polarity(idx);
367                          break;
368                      }
369                      default:
370                      {
371                          printk(KERN_WARNING "broken BIOS!!\n");
372                          polarity = 1;
373                          break;
374                      }
375                  }
376                  break;
377              }
378              case 1:
379              {
380                  polarity = 0;
381                  break;
382              }
383              case 2:
384              {
385                  printk(KERN_WARNING "broken BIOS!!\n");
386                  polarity = 1;
387                  break;
388              }
389              case 3:
390              {
391                  polarity = 1;
392                  break;
393              }
394              default:
395              {
396                  printk(KERN_WARNING "broken BIOS!!\n");
397                  polarity = 1;
398                  break;
399              }
400          }
401      return polarity;
402  }
```

Figure 14.12   Getting the polarity of an irq (interrupt request) line

337   this determines the ID number of the bus corresponding to this irq, using the array introduced in
Section 14.1.1.1.

343   bits 0–1 of the `mpc_irqflag` field has information about the polarity of the corresponding irq.

345–377   a value of 00 here means that the irq line has the default polarity for the particular type of bus.

347   this converts bus number to bus type, using the lookup table from Section 14.1.1.1.

349–368   if we have an ISA, EISA, PCI, or MCA bus, then we use the appropriate macro from Section 14.1.3.1. to get the default polarity.

369–374   if we do not have one of the recognised bus types then there is some inconsistency in the tables, so we print a warning message and assign the polarity as 1 (active low).

378–382   a value of 01 in the `mpc_irqflag` field means a polarity of 0 (active high).

383–388   a value of 10 in the `mpc_irqflag` field is illegal, so we print a warning message and assign the polarity as 1 (active low).

389–393   a value of 11 in the `mpc_irqflag` field means a polarity of 1 (active low).

394–399   this is genuine paranoia. A 2-bit field cannot produce more than four possibilities, but, in case it does produce more, we print the warning message and assign the polarity as 1 (active low).

14.1.3.4   *Getting the trigger type of an irq line*

The function shown in Figure 14.13, from `arch/i386/kernel/io_apic.c`, is supplied with an index into the `mp_irqs[]` array, and it returns the trigger type (edge or level sensitive) of the corresponding irq.

```
404  static int __init MPBIOS_trigger(int idx)
405  {
406      int bus = mp_irqs[idx].mpc_srcbus;
407      int trigger;

412      switch ((mp_irqs[idx].mpc_irqflag>>2) & 3)
413      {
414          case 0:
415          {
416              switch (mp_bus_id_to_type[bus])
417              {
418                  case MP_BUS_ISA:
419                  {
420                      trigger = default_ISA_trigger(idx);
421                      break;
422                  }
423                  case MP_BUS_EISA:
424                  {
425                      trigger = default_EISA_trigger(idx);
426                      break;
427                  }
428                  case MP_BUS_PCI:
```

```
429                              {
430                                      trigger = default_PCI_trigger(idx);
431                                      break;
432                              }
433                              case MP_BUS_MCA:
434                              {
435                                      trigger = default_MCA_trigger(idx);
436                                      break;
437                              }
438                              default:
439                              {
440                                      printk(KERN_WARNING
                                                      "broken BIOS!!\n");
441                                      trigger = 1;
442                                      break;
443                              }
444                      }
445                      break;
446              }
447              case 1:
448              {
449                      trigger = 0;
450                      break;
451              }
452              case 2:
453              {
454                      printk(KERN_WARNING "broken BIOS!!\n");
455                      trigger = 1;
456                      break;
457              }
458              case 3:
459              {
460                      trigger = 1;
461                      break;
462              }
463              default:
464              {
465                      printk(KERN_WARNING "broken BIOS!!\n");
466                      trigger = 0;
467                      break;
468              }
469      }
470      return trigger;
471 }
```

Figure 14.13   Getting the trigger type of an irq (interrupt request) line

406   this determines the ID number of the bus corresponding to this irq, using the array introduced in Section 14.1.1.1.

412   bits 2–3 of the `mpc_irqflag` field has information about the trigger type of the corresponding irq.

414–446   a value of 00 here means that the irq line has the default trigger type for the particular type of bus.

416   this converts bus number to bus type, using the lookup table from Section 14.1.1.1.

418–437   if we have an ISA, EISA, PCI, or MCA bus, then we use the appropriate macro from Section 14.1.3.1 to get the default trigger type.

438–443   if we do not have one of the recognised bus types, then there is some inconsistency in the tables, so we print a warning message and assign the trigger type as 1 (level).

447–451   a value of 01 in the `mpc_irqflag` field means that the irq line is edge triggered (0).

452–457   a value of 10 in the `mpc_irqflag` field is illegal, so we print a warning message and assign the trigger type as 1 (level).

458–462   a value of 11 in the `mpc_irqflag` field means that the irq is level triggered (1).

463–468   this is more paranoia. A 2-bit field cannot produce more than four possibilities, but, in case it does produce more, we print the warning message and assign a trigger type of 0 (edge).

14.1.3.5   Converting irq number to trigger type

The function shown in Figure 14.14, from `arch/i386/kernel/io_apic.c`, returns the trigger type for a particular irq. Unlike the function shown in Section 14.1.3.4, this one is given the irq number, not an index into the `mp_irqs[]` table.

```
539  static inline int IO_APIC_irq_trigger(int irq)
540  {
541      int apic, idx, pin;
542
543      for (apic = 0; apic < nr_ioapics; apic++) {
544          for (pin = 0; pin < nr_ioapic_registers[apic]; pin++) {
545              idx = find_irq_entry(apic, pin, mp_INT);
546              if ((idx != -1) && (irq == pin_2_irq(idx, apic, pin)))
547                  return irq_trigger(idx);
548          }
549      }

553      return 0;
554  }
```

Figure 14.14   Returning the trigger type of an irq (interrupt request)

543–549   this loop goes through each IO APIC in turn, using the number of APICs as defined in Section 14.1.1.1.

544–548   this loop goes through each pin on the APIC.

545   this function, described in Section 14.1.2.1, goes through each entry in the `mp_irqs[]` array until it finds one corresponding to these three parameters. It then returns the array index for that entry, or −1 if no entry was found. The third parameter is from the enumeration in Section 14.1.1.5, specifying a vectored interrupt, with the vector in the APIC redirection table.

546   if there is a valid entry for this combination, it must also match the irq supplied as a parameter. The `pin_2_irq()` function is described in Section 14.1.2.3; it returns the irq number corresponding to this entry.

547   there is no field in `mp_irqs[]` for trigger type. This has to be determined by the function described in Section 14.1.3.2. A value of 1 is level triggered; 0 is edge triggered.

553   if no match has been found, then a 0 (edge) is returned by default.

14.1.4 The `irq_2_pin[]` array

As seen in Section 14.1.2.2, there is a function that determines the pin to which a particular irq line is connected, but it works by searching through the whole `mp_irqs[]` array each time, which is very slow, so Linux provides a lookup table for mapping an irq number to a pin, the `irq_2_pin[]` array.

14.1.4.1 Mapping between irq and pin

There is an array that keeps track of which irq lines are physically connected to which pins on which APIC. For performance reasons the indexing order of this array favours 1:1 mappings between pins and irqs, but if the irq line from a particular device is connected to more than one IO APIC that situation has to be catered for. This array is shown in Figure 14.15, from `arch/i386/kernel/io_apic.c`.

```
51    #define MAX_PLUS_SHARED_IRQS NR_IRQS
52    #define PIN_MAP_SIZE (MAX_PLUS_SHARED_IRQS + NR_IRQS)

61    static struct irq_pin_list {
62        int apic, pin, next;
63    } irq_2_pin[PIN_MAP_SIZE];
```

Figure 14.15   Mapping between irq and pin

51   NR_IRQS has already been defined as 224 (Section 12.2.4); it is assumed that there will be as many again irq lines shared between APICs.

52   this is the total number of entries in the array – first, we have space for all possible irqs, then extra space for the shared ones. Currently, the number is twice NR_IRQS. It seems a very complicated way of specifying a constant.

61–63   this array maps between irqs and physical pins on all IO APICs. There are sufficient entries for all possible irqs – far more than the number of pins. Each entry contains the ID of the IO APIC, the number of the pin on that APIC, and (if relevant) the number of the entry mapping that irq to a pin on another APIC. The first half of the array is indexed on irq number; the second half is accessed by links from an entry in the first (see Figure 14.16). For any particular entry, the irq for which it is an entry is identified by the chain it is on, and the APIC–pin combination is identified by the entry in the array.

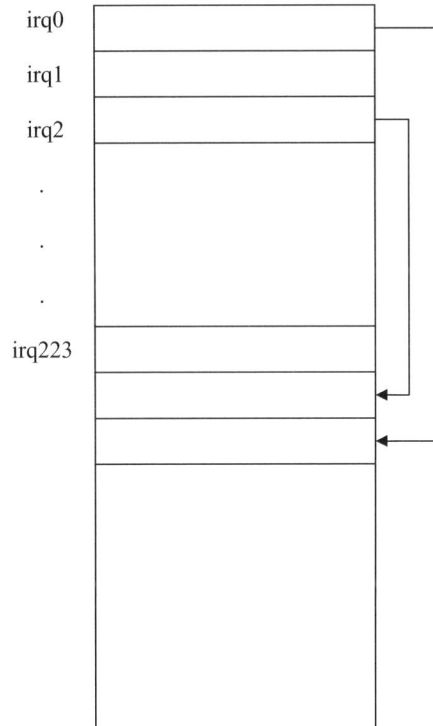

Figure 14.16 The `irq_2_pin[]` array

14.1.4.2 *Inserting an entry in the* `irq_2_pin[]` *array*

The interrupt manager provides a function to insert an entry into this array; see Figure 14.17, from `arch/i386/kernel/ioapic.c`. This is heavily used at boot time, but it is also available to the initialisation function in a driver.

```
70    static void add_pin_to_irq(unsigned int irq, int apic, int pin)
71    {
72            static int first_free_entry = NR_IRQS;
73            struct irq_pin_list *entry = irq_2_pin + irq;
74
75            while (entry->next)
76                    entry = irq_2_pin + entry->next;
77
78            if (entry->pin != -1) {
```

```
79                          entry->next = first_free_entry;
80                          entry = irq_2_pin + entry->next;
81                          if (++first_free_entry >= PIN_MAP_SIZE)
82                                  panic("io_apic.c: whoops");
83                  }
84          entry->apic = apic;
85          entry->pin = pin;
86      }
```

Figure 14.17   Inserting an entry in the `irq_2_pin[]` array

70   this function inserts an entry in the `irq_2_pin[]` array. The parameters specify the irq, the IO APIC, and the pin number. The common case is 1:1 mapping between irq and pin, but sometimes there are ISA irqs shared between APICs, and they have to be supported. Within the kernel, it is only ever called by `setup_IO_APIC_irqs()` (see Section 14.2.3.2).

72   the number of the first free entry is calculated as `NR_IRQS` (see Section 12.2.4); this is currently initialised halfway along the array, but note it is `static` and is incremented at line 81.

73   `irq_2_pin` is the address of the array; adding `irq` does pointer arithmetic on this and gives a pointer to the array element corresponding to this irq.

75–76   if this irq line is attached to more than one APIC pin there may be an entry already. This new one is to be added at the end, so we skip on to there. At this stage, `entry` is pointing to an entry whose `next` field is 0.

78–83   this code is executed only if the current entry (the last one in the chain) is in use. In other words, it is not used to insert a first entry for an irq.

79   this finds the next unused slot and links the current one to it.

80   the variable `entry` contains the index of the free slot that is going to be filled in.

81–82   this increments the static index to the next free entry. If this overflows, the operating system is shut down, with a rather unhelpful message.

84–85   at this stage, `entry` has its value either from line 73, line 76, or line 80. In any case, we fill in the fields in this entry.

14.2   IO APIC registers

We can now move on to examine the IO APIC itself. There are a number of data structures defined for manipulating the registers in an IO APIC, as well as functions for initialising, allocating, and deallocating these registers.

14.2.1   General APIC registers

The different internal formats for the first three registers are defined in Figure 14.18, from `<asm-i386/io_apic.h>`. These correspond to the ID register, version register, and arbitration priority register in a local APIC. Each of these registers is 32 bits wide.

```
17   #define IO_APIC_BASE(idx)                                          \
18       ((volatile int *)(__fix_to_virt(FIX_IO_APIC_BASE_0 + idx)      \
19           + (mp_ioapics[idx].mpc_apicaddr & ~PAGE_MASK)))
24   struct IO_APIC_reg_00 {
25       __u32 __reserved_2              : 24,
26            ID                         :  4,
27            __reserved_1               :  4;
28   } __attribute__ ((packed));
29
30   struct IO_APIC_reg_01 {
31       __u32 version                   :  8,
32            __reserved_2               :  7,
33            PRQ                        :  1,
34            entries                    :  8,
35            __reserved_1               :  8;
36   } __attribute__ ((packed));
37
38   struct IO_APIC_reg_02 {
39       __u32 __reserved_2              : 24,
40            arbitration                :  4,
41            __reserved_1               :  4;
42   } __attribute__ ((packed));
```

Figure 14.18   IO APIC register formats

17–19   each IO APIC is given a 4k space in the virtual address map. The first part of this macro calculates the base virtual address at which a particular IO APIC, identified by `idx`, is to be addressed. The second part of the macro adds an offset to that, from the `mp_ioapics[]` array. ANDing this offset with `~PAGE_MASK` strips off the low-order 12 bits and so aligns it on a page boundary. Finally, it is returned as a pointer to `int`.

24–28   this is internal format for IO APIC register 0. Only bits 24–27 are defined, and these contain the ID number of the APIC.

30–36   this is the internal format for IO APIC register 1. Bits 0–7 contain the version of the APIC. Bits 16–23 are the `entries` field, the number of irq routing registers in this APIC.

38–42   this is the internal format for IO APIC register 2. Only bits 24–27 are defined; these are used by the hardware to arbitrate between the different IO APICs in the system. This register is never manipulated by Linux. It is read at boot time.

14.2.2   Routing registers

The IO APIC has a dedicated internal register for each pin, which contains information about the irq corresponding to that pin. These are 64-bit registers, beginning at offset `0x10`. Typically, there are 16 of these in each APIC.

14.2.2.1   Number of routing registers

Some miscellaneous data structures used by Linux when dealing with IO APICs are shown in Figure 14.19, from `arch/i386/kernel/io_apic.c`.

```
40    static spinlock_t         ioapic_lock = SPIN_LOCK_UNLOCKED;

45    int                       nr_ioapic_registers[MAX_IO_APICS];
```

Figure 14.19   Miscellaneous IO APIC data structures

40   this spinlock is used to protect writes to the redirection registers of the IO APIC.

45   different IO APICs may have different numbers of irq routing registers. This array is set up at boot time, and contains the number of registers in each APIC. The constant MAX_IO_APICS is defined as 8 at line 110 of `<asm-i386/apicdef.h>`.

14.2.2.2   Routing entry for an IO APIC

All the information needed to control the routing of interrupts within an IO APIC is encapsulated in the `struct IO_APIC_route_entry`, as shown in Figure 14.20, from `<asm-i386/io_apic.h>`. This is in fact the internal format of an APIC routing register.

```
61    struct IO_APIC_route_entry {
62          __u32 vector            :  8,
63                delivery_mode     :  3,

67                dest_mode         :  1,
68                delivery_status   :  1,
69                polarity          :  1,
70                irr               :  1,
71                trigger           :  1,
72                mask              :  1,
73                __reserved_2      : 15;
74
75    union {    struct { __u32
76                           __reserved_1       : 24,
77                           physical_dest      :  4,
78                           __reserved_2       :  4;
79                } physical;
80
81               struct { __u32
82                           __reserved_1       : 24,
83                           logical_dest       :  8;
84                } logical;
85          } dest;
86
87    } __attribute__ ((packed));
```

Figure 14.20   Routing entry for an IO APIC

62 bits 0–7 contain the interrupt descriptor table (IDT) vector associated with this irq.

63 bits 8–10 contain information about how this interrupt is to be delivered. This may be fixed, lowest priority, or external interrupt, from the enumeration in Section 14.2.2.3.

67 bit 11 determines whether physical or logical addressing is to be used when sending this interrupt to the local APIC. This bit set means that the destination mode is logical; when clear, it is physical. The address at lines 75–85 is interpreted accordingly.

68 a 0 here means that this particular pin is idle; 1 means that the previous irq on this pin is still being processed.

69 this is the interrupt input pin polarity; 0 means active high, 1 means active low. This bit is meaningful only for level triggered interrupts (see line 71).

70 this is the interrupt request register bit. This is valid only for level triggered interrupts; it is not defined for edge triggered interrupts. It is set when the APIC accepts the irq; it is cleared when an end-of-interrupt (EOI) is received.

71 when bit 15 is set, the irq is level triggered; when clear, it is edge triggered.

72 bit 16 is the mask bit. As usual, 0 means the irq is enabled, 1 means it is disabled.

73 bits 17–31 are reserved for future use.

75–85 this union represents the high-order 32 bits of the routing register. It contains the ID of the local APIC to which the particular irq is to be sent. Bit 11 determined the destination mode, whether physical or logical addressing is to be used when sending interrupts to the local APIC. This union defines the two different address formats.

77 a physical address is in bits 24–27. This is the number of the CPU.

83 a logical address is in bits 24–31. A bit set in this signifies the corresponding CPU as a target.

14.2.2.3 Delivery modes for interrupts

The possible values for the `delivery_mode` field at line 63 of Figure 14.20 are shown in Figure 14.21, from `<asm-i386/io_apic.h>`.

```
50   enum ioapic_irq_destination_types {
51        dest_Fixed = 0,
52        dest_LowestPrio = 1,
53        dest_SMI = 2,
54        dest__reserved_1 = 3,
55        dest_NMI = 4,
56        dest_INIT = 5,
57        dest__reserved_2 = 6,
58        dest_ExtINT = 7
59   };
```

Figure 14.21 Possible values for the delivery mode

51 this is fixed delivery mode. The irq will be sent to the CPU specified by the destination field in the routing register, and none other.

52 an interrupt of this mode will be sent to the CPU running at the lowest priority.

53 this is the system management interrupt (SMI). This sets the target CPU into a special system management mode. It is not used by Linux.

54 this value is currently unused.

55 this irq is delivered to the target CPU as a nonmaskable interrupt. Again, it is not used by Linux.

56 this irq is delivered to the target CPU as an INIT interrupt and is not used by Linux.

57 this value is currently unused.

58 this irq is delivered to the local APIC as if it originated from an 8259A PIC. Vector information is supplied, and an INTA is expected. Such an irq is always level triggered.

14.2.2.4 Addressing modes

Figure 14.22, from <asm-i386/smp.h>, shows how the addresses of target CPUs for interrupt routing are set up, in the dest_mode and dest fields of Figure 14.20.

```
25    #ifdef CONFIG_SMP
26    # ifdef CONFIG_MULTIQUAD
27    #   define TARGET_CPUS 0xf
28    #   define INT_DELIVERY_MODE 0
29    # else
30    #   define TARGET_CPUS cpu_online_map
31    #   define INT_DELIVERY_MODE 1
32    # endif
33    #else
34    # define INT_DELIVERY_MODE 1
35    # define TARGET_CPUS 0x01
36    #endif
```

Figure 14.22 Target computer processing units (CPUs) for interrupts

25–32 these are the definitions for a multiprocessor kernel.

26–29 these are definitions for very high specification multiprocessors, with NUMA architectures.

27 this delivers interrupts to all CPUs.

28 this delivers using physical addressing. This value would be set in the dest_mode field.

30–31 these are definitions for standard multiprocessors

30 this delivers interrupts to those CPUs that are online (see Section 7.2.1.2 for cpu_online_map).

31   this uses logical addressing. This value would be set in the `dest_mode` field.

34–35   these are definitions for a uniprocessor machine.

34   this uses logical addressing. This value would be set in the `dest_mode` field.

35   this sends interrupts to CPU number 1 (the only one present).

14.2.3   Initialising the IO APIC

There are a number of steps involved in initialising an IO APIC. Some of the data structures described in Section 14.1.1.1 have to be set up, then values have to be written to each of the routing registers in the APIC itself, but, of course, the IDT table also has to be set up, to handle these interrupts when they arrive.

14.2.3.1   Initialising the IO APIC data structures

The function shown in Figure 14.23, from `arch/i386/kernel/io_apic.c`, is called at boot time to initialise the data structures representing any IO APICs in the system.

```
996   static void __init enable_IO_APIC(void)
997   {
998         struct IO_APIC_reg_01 reg_01;
999         int i;
1000        unsigned long flags;
1001
1002        for (i = 0; i < PIN_MAP_SIZE; i++) {
1003              irq_2_pin[i].pin = -1;
1004              irq_2_pin[i].next = 0;
1005        }
1006        if (!pirqs_enabled)
1007              for (i = 0; i < MAX_PIRQS; i++)
1008                    pirq_entries[i] = -1;

1013        for (i = 0; i < nr_ioapics; i++) {
1014              spin_lock_irqsave(&ioapic_lock, flags);
1015              *(int *)&reg_01 = io_apic_read(i, 1);
1016              spin_unlock_irqrestore(&ioapic_lock, flags);
1017              nr_ioapic_registers[i] = reg_01.entries+1;
1018        }

1023        clear_IO_APIC();
1024 }
```

Figure 14.23   Initialising an IO APIC

1002–1005   this code initialises the `irq_2_pin[]` array, which is described in detail in Section 14.1.4. The literal constant `PIN_MAP_SIZE` is defined in Section 14.1.4.1 as the size of this array. The `pin` field of each entry is set to −1, to signify that it is unused. The next field is set to 0, as there are no links.

1006–1008 if pirq_entries[] has not been set up already (see Section 14.1.1.6), each array entry is initialised to −1.

1013–1018 this loop goes through all the IO APICs present in the system.

1014–1016 the read from the APIC register is protected by the interrupt-safe spinlock declared in Section 14.2.2.1.

1015 this reads the full 32-bit value from register 1 in each IO APIC and writes it to the reg_01 structure, cast to an int. Register 1 in the APIC contains the (zero-based) number of redirection registers implemented. The io_apic_read() function is described in Section 14.4.5.1.

1017 this number (plus 1) is then written to the entry in nr_ioapic_registers[] corresponding to this IO APIC.

1023 we do not trust the IO APICs being empty at bootup, so we clear all registers (see Section 14.2.4.2).

14.2.3.2 Setting up routing table entries on an IO APIC

The function shown in Figure 14.24, from arch/i386/kernel/io_apic.c, is called at boot time. It sets up internal registers in the IO APIC to handle irqs arriving at the APIC pins. It is analogous to setting up irqs on a PIC.

```
613  void __init setup_IO_APIC_irqs(void)
614  {
615      struct IO_APIC_route_entry entry;
616      int apic, pin, idx, irq, first_notcon = 1, vector;
617      unsigned long flags;
618
619      printk(KERN_DEBUG "init IO_APIC IRQs\n");
620
621      for (apic = 0; apic < nr_ioapics; apic++) {
622          for (pin = 0; pin < nr_ioapic_registers[apic]; pin++) {

627              memset(&entry, 0, sizeof(entry));
628
629              entry.delivery_mode = dest_LowestPrio;
630              entry.dest_mode = INT_DELIVERY_MODE;
631              entry.mask = 0;
632              entry.dest.logical.logical_dest = TARGET_CPUS;
633
634              idx = find_irq_entry(apic, pin, mp_INT);
635              if (idx == -1) {
636                  if (first_notcon) {
```

```
637                           printk(KERN_DEBUG " IO-APIC (apicid-pin)
                                  %d-%d", mp_ioapics[apic].mpc_apicid, pin);
638                          first_notcon = 0;
639                      } else
640                          printk(", %d-%d", mp_ioapics[apic].mpc_apicid, pin);
641                      continue;
642                  }
643
644              entry.trigger = irq_trigger(idx);
645              entry.polarity = irq_polarity(idx);
646
647              if (irq_trigger(idx)) {
648                  entry.trigger = 1;
649                  entry.mask = 1;
650                  entry.dest.logical.logical_dest = TARGET_CPUS;
651              }
652
653              irq = pin_2_irq(idx, apic, pin);
654              add_pin_to_irq(irq, apic, pin);
655
656              if (!apic && !IO_APIC_IRQ(irq))
657                  continue;
658
659              if (IO_APIC_IRQ(irq)) {
660                  vector = assign_irq_vector(irq);
661                  entry.vector = vector;
662
663                  if (IO_APIC_irq_trigger(irq))
664                      irq_desc[irq].handler = &ioapic_level_irq_type;
665                  else
666                      irq_desc[irq].handler = &ioapic_edge_irq_type;
667
668                  set_intr_gate(vector, interrupt[irq]);
669
670                  if (!apic && (irq < 16))
671                      disable_8259A_irq(irq);
672              }
673              spin_lock_irqsave(&ioapic_lock, flags);
674              io_apic_write(apic, 0x11+2*pin, *(((int *)&entry)+1));
675              io_apic_write(apic, 0x10+2*pin, *(((int *)&entry)+0));
676              spin_unlock_irqrestore(&ioapic_lock, flags);
677      }
678      }
679
680      if (!first_notcon)
681          printk(" not connected.\n");
682  }
```

Figure 14.24 Setting up irqs (interrupt requests) on an IO APIC

616   the variable `first_notcon` is initialised to 1. If an unconnected pin is encountered, this value is cleared to 0. It is used in formatting the message output about unconnected pins.

619   this is part of the bootup information, announcing that irqs are being initialised on the IO APIC.

621–678   this code works through each IO APIC in turn. Most systems would have only one.

622–677   this code works through each pin on the current APIC. For each one it initialises the irq routing table register for that pin, as described in Section 14.2.2.2.

627   each time around the inner loop, the `memset()` macro fills the local `entry` variable with 0s. The remainder of the loop fills in the various fields of this variable, and at the end it is written to the appropriate routing register of the APIC.

629   the struct `IO_APIC_route_entry` has been described in Section 14.2.2.2. The value assigned to the `delivery_mode` field is an element of the enumeration given in Section 14.2.2.3. This assignment means that (by default) an irq arriving at this pin will be sent to the lowest-priority CPU.

630   the destination mode field is set to either logical or physical, as determined in the code in Section 14.2.2.4.

631   by setting the `mask` field to 0 we enable that irq,

632   the logical destination address is whatever `TARGET_CPUS` was set to (see Section 14.2.2.4).

634   the physical configuration of busses, irq lines, APICs, and pins is determined at boot time and written into a number of arrays, which have been described in Section 14.1.1.1. The most important of these is `mp_irqs[]`. It contains information about every potential source of a physical interrupt in the system. This function (see Section 14.1.2.1) checks through the `mp_irqs[]` array to find an entry that matches the three parameters. The third parameter is from the enumeration given in Section 14.1.1.5. It means that the vector for this irq will be supplied by the APIC. If found, the index of that entry in the array is returned; otherwise, -1 is returned.

635–642   this block of code is executed if no irq source is registered as being connected to that particular pin on the APIC currently being considered.

636–639   if this is the first time this has happened in the whole function, then we print a message at KERN_DEBUG priority, identifying the APIC and pin.

638   the flag `first_notcon`, initialised to 1 at line 616, is here cleared to 0, so that the foregoing message will not be printed again.

640   on all subsequent occasions, the message is printed as a continuation of the previous one.

641   this jumps to the end of the inner loop; there is no point doing any further work on this pin. If there are further pins, these will be handled next.

644   this function, from Section 14.1.3.2, returns the trigger type (edge or level) of the irq identified by index `idx` in the `mp_irqs[]` array.

645   this function, also from Section 14.1.3.2, returns the polarity (high or low) of the irq identified by index `idx` in the `mp_irqs[]` array.

648–651   this block of code is executed if the particular irq is level triggered; see Section 14.1.3.2 for the function.

648   this overwrites the entry at line 644 and sets it to be level triggered. This line seems to be redundant.

649   this overwrites the entry at line 631, masking this interrupt out.

650   this is just repeating the entry made at line 632. Again, it seems to be redundant.

653   this function is described in Section 14.1.2.3. It returns the irq number corresponding to a given pin on a specified IO APIC. Remember, the current function is dealing with pins.

654   there is a considerable amount of information in the `mpc_irqs[]` array that is rarely needed. Also, the information is stored in no particular order, and the whole array has to be searched linearly each time. To overcome this drawback, Linux maintains another array, `irq_2_pin[]`, which, as its name implies, is indexed on irq number and contains the APIC–pin combination corresponding to each irq. This array is described in detail in Section 14.1.4. The `add_pin_to_irq()` function, from Section 14.1.4.2, inserts a new entry in the `irq_2_pin[]` array.

656–657   these two lines deal with the very unusual situation where one of the original 16 irqs is not physically routed through the APIC. (It would presumably be connected directly to a pin on a local APIC.) The `IO_APIC_IRQ()` macro is defined in <asm-i386/hw_irq.h> as:

```
93    #define IO_APIC_IRQ(x) (((x) >= 16) || ((1<<(x)) & io_apic_irqs))
```

It returns TRUE if either the irq is not one of the original 16 or the bit corresponding to this irq is set in `io_apics_irqs` (i.e. the irq is routed through the IO APIC). In such a case, there is no entry in the redirection table for this pin. Also, entries in other software tables, such as `irq_desc[]` and the IDT, are set up elsewhere, not here. We jump to the end of the inner loop and go on to the next pin on this APIC.

659–672   this code is executed if the irq is not one of the original 16 or if the bit corresponding to this irq is set in `io_apic_irqs`. Any bit set in this mask means the corresponding irq is routed through the IO APIC. The mask is declared in Section 12.7.2.2, so the irq being dealt with *is* routed through the IO APIC and must be set up.

660   this function, described in Section 14.2.3.3, returns a vector number to assign to this irq.

661   this fills in the `vector` field.

663–666   depending on the trigger type (Section 14.1.3.5), the appropriate controller handler function is set for this irq, in `irq_desc[]`. These handler functions will be described in Sections 14.3.1.1 (edge) and 14.3.2.1 (level).

668   this sets up an entry in the interrupt descriptor table for this irq (see Section 10.2.1.2 for the function).

670–671 if this is IO APIC 0, and the irq in question is one of the first 16, then this code disables this irq on the 8259A. It is being handled by the IO APIC, and the PIC would only interfere. The function was described in Section 12.7.6. Normally, the whole PIC would be disabled by hardware, anyway. This is just making sure.

673–676 the write to the APIC register is protected by the interrupt-safe spinlock declared in the code in Section 14.2.2.1.

674 see Section 14.4.5.2 for the function. The first parameter specifies the APIC; the second specifies the register; the third is the value to be written. Thus, this line writes the second int of entry to the high-order part of the register corresponding to this irq. The second parameter needs some explanation. Redirection registers begin at 0x10. Even though they are 64-bit registers, they are numbered, and accessed, as 32-bit entities. So the low half of redirection register 0 is at 0x10; the high half is at 0x11. The high half of the register corresponding to any pin can be found by adding twice the pin number to this.

675 this writes the first int of entry to the low-order part of the register.

677 this is the end of the inner for loop, going through each of the pins.

678 this is the end of the outer for loop, going through each of the IO APICs.

680–681 this test is made after all pins on all APICs have been tested. If first_notcon is 0, that means that at least one unassigned pin has been found. This concludes the printed list of unconnected pins.

14.2.3.3 Assigning a vector to an irq

The function shown in Figure 14.25, from arch/i386/kernel/io_apic.c, assigns an IDT vector number to an irq line at boot time. It attempts to spread these evenly over the vector space. With the present IO APIC hardware, there is an advantage in not having more than two irqs on the same priority level.

```
589  int irq_vector[NR_IRQS] = { FIRST_DEVICE_VECTOR , 0 };
590
591  static int __init assign_irq_vector(int irq)
592  {
593        static int current_vector = FIRST_DEVICE_VECTOR, offset = 0;
594        if (IO_APIC_VECTOR(irq) > 0)
595            return IO_APIC_VECTOR(irq);
596  next:
597        current_vector += 8;
598        if (current_vector == SYSCALL_VECTOR)
599            goto next;
600
601        if (current_vector > FIRST_SYSTEM_VECTOR) {
602            offset++;
603            current_vector = FIRST_DEVICE_VECTOR + offset;
```

```
604        }
605
606        if (current_vector == FIRST_SYSTEM_VECTOR)
607                panic("ran out of interrupt sources!");
608
609        IO_APIC_VECTOR(irq) = current_vector;
610        return current_vector;
611 }
```

Figure 14.25   Assigning a vector to an irq

589   this array has 224 entries, each mapping between an irq number and an IDT vector. The first one is initialised to FIRST_DEVICE_VECTOR (0x31); all the other entries are initialised to 0.

593   note the declaration `static`. While it begins at FIRST_DEVICE_VECTOR, current_vector is incremented each time at line 597, so it always points to the next vector to assign. The offset variable is also `static`, incremented each time at line 602.

594–595   if a valid vector already exists for that irq then that value is returned; otherwise a value is assigned. The IO_APIC_VECTOR() macro is from Section 12.5.3.

597   incrementing by 8 means the irq assignment routine will try 0x39, 0x41, 0x49, etc., and hence it will not put more than 2 irqs at the same priority level.

598   if this happens to land on SYSCALL_VECTOR (0x80), which is reserved, skip over it to 0x88.

601–604   if it lands above FIRST_SYSTEM_VECTOR (0xEF), then this code increments the (`static`) offset and assigns a vector that distance above FIRST_DEVICE_VECTOR. This means trying 0x32, 0x3A, 0x42, and so on.

606–607   if it lands on FIRST_SYSTEM_VECTOR, then the system has run out of vectors and it shuts down. This would be very unusual.

609   this saves the vector number in the array entry corresponding to this irq.

14.2.4   Disabling an IO APIC before rebooting

Linux provides a number of functions for clearing one or more entries from the IO APIC registers as well as for disabling the whole APIC. These are typically used by the reboot code.

14.2.4.1   Disabling IO APICs

The function shown in Figure 14.26, from arch/i386/kernel/io_apic.c, is used by the reboot code. It clears all registers in all IO APICs before rebooting.

```
1029 void disable_IO_APIC(void)
1030 {

1034     clear_IO_APIC();
```

```
1035
1036      disconnect_bsp_APIC();
1037 }
```

Figure 14.26   Disabling IO APICs

1034   this clears all the registers in all IO APICs (see Section 14.2.4.2).

1036   this function reenables the PIC now that the APIC is disabled (see Section 14.2.4.4).

14.2.4.2   *Clearing the redirection registers of all IO APICs*

When disabling an IO APIC, it is necessary to clear all the redirection registers. The code to do this for all IO APICs is shown in Figure 14.27, from `arch/i386/kernel/io_apic.c`.

```
182  static void clear_IO_APIC (void)
183  {
184       int apic, pin;
185
186       for (apic = 0; apic < nr_ioapics; apic++)
187            for (pin = 0; pin < nr_ioapic_registers[apic]; pin++)
188                 clear_IO_APIC_pin(apic, pin);
189  }
```

Figure 14.27   Clearing the redirection registers of all IO APICs

186   this loop works its way through each IO APIC in the system.

187   this loop works through each pin on the APIC (and consequently each register). The number of pins in each is determined by the `nr_ioapic_registers[]` array, from Section 14.2.2.1.

188   this is the function that does the actual work; see Section 14.2.4.3.

14.2.4.3   *Removing an entry from an IO APIC redirection table*

The code shown in Figure 14.28, from `arch/i386/kernel/io_apic.c`, zeroes the entry in the redirection table corresponding to a particular pin of a specific IO APIC. It also masks (disables) that irq.

```
166  void clear_IO_APIC_pin(unsigned int apic, unsigned int pin)
167  {
168       struct IO_APIC_route_entry entry;
169       unsigned long flags;

174       memset(&entry, 0, sizeof(entry));
175       entry.mask = 1;
176       spin_lock_irqsave(&ioapic_lock, flags);
```

```
177         io_apic_write(apic, 0x10 + 2 * pin, *(((int *)&entry) + 0));
178         io_apic_write(apic, 0x11 + 2 * pin, *(((int *)&entry) + 1));
179         spin_unlock_irqrestore(&ioapic_lock, flags);
180 }
```

Figure 14.28   Removing an entry from the routing table

166   the parameters identify the particular IO APIC, and the pin on that APIC (this in turn identifies the register).

174   the local variable `entry`, declared at line 168, is cleared to all zeros.

175   setting the mask bit to 1 disables the irq.

176–179   the write to the APIC register is protected by the interrupt-safe spinlock declared in Section 14.2.2.1.

177–178   the double write copies the `struct entry` to the APIC register corresponding to this pin. The function is described in Section 14.2.2.1.

14.2.4.4   Returning to PIC mode

The function shown in Figure 14.29, from `arch/i386/kernel/apic.c`, puts the motherboard back into PIC mode. It has an effect only on certain older boards, designated by the `pic_mode` flag being set (see Section 14.1.1.1). PIC mode effectively bypasses all APIC components and forces the system to operate in single processor mode. Note that APIC interrupts, including IPIs, do not work after this.

```
116 void disconnect_bsp_APIC(void)
117 {
118       if (pic_mode) {

125             printk("disabling APIC mode, entering PIC mode.\n");
126             outb(0x70, 0x22);
127             outb(0x00, 0x23);
128       }
129 }
```

Figure 14.29   Putting the motherboard back into PIC mode

118   this was declared the code in Section 14.1.1.1. It is set at bootup time; 1 means the Intel multiprocessor specification; 0 means virtual wire mode.

126   ports `0x22` and `0x23` are for the interrupt mode configuration register (IMCR). Writing `0x70` to port `0x22` selects the IMCR.

127   writing a value of `0x00` to port `0x23` connects the `INTR` (from PIC) and nmi lines directly to the bootstrap processor, bypassing the IO and local APICs. A value of `0x01` here disconnects the PIC and connects the interrupt lines to the IO APIC.

14.3   Controller functions for an IO APIC

Section 12.1 of Chapter 12 introduced the `struct hw_interrupt_type`, which encapsulates all that needs to be known about the hardware of an interrupt controller. Because an irq line on the IO APIC can be either edge triggered or level triggered, two different versions of this `struct` are supplied. The one for edge triggered interrupts is discussed first; then, in the following section, the descriptor for level triggered interrupts will be discussed.

14.3.1   Edge triggered interrupts on an IO APIC

The discussion begins with the `struct hw_interrupt_type` and then we go on to look at the individual functions.

14.3.1.1   Controller functions for edge triggered interrupts

The `struct hw_interrupt_type` declared and initialised for an edge triggered irq is shown in Figure 14.30, from `arch/i386/kernel/io_apic.c`.

```
1334 static struct hw_interrupt_type ioapic_edge_irq_type = {
1335       "IO-APIC-edge",
1336       startup_edge_ioapic_irq,
1337       shutdown_edge_ioapic_irq,
1338       enable_edge_ioapic_irq,
1339       disable_edge_ioapic_irq,
1340       ack_edge_ioapic_irq,
1341       end_edge_ioapic_irq,
1342       set_ioapic_affinity,
1343 };
```

Figure 14.30   Controller functions for edge triggered interrupts

1336–1341   each of these functions will now be considered in detail, in Sections 14.3.1.2–14.3.1.4.

1342   as this is not really concerned with manipulating the APIC, there is no specific function supplied. Instead, the trigger-independent function `set_ioapic_affinity()` (see Section 14.4.4) is specified.

14.3.1.2   Startup and shutdown

The code for starting up and shutting down edge triggered interrupts on an IO APIC is shown in Figure 14.31, from `arch/i386/kernel/io_apic.c`.

```
1191 static unsigned int startup_edge_ioapic_irq(unsigned int irq)
1192 {
1193       int was_pending = 0;
1194       unsigned long flags;
1195
1196       spin_lock_irqsave(&ioapic_lock, flags);
1197       if (irq < 16) {
```

```
1198            disable_8259A_irq(irq);
1199            if(i8259A_irq_pending(irq))
1200                was_pending = 1;
1201        }
1202        __unmask_IO_APIC_irq(irq);
1203        spin_unlock_irqrestore(&ioapic_lock, flags);
1204
1205        return was_pending;
1206 }
1207
1208 #define shutdown_edge_ioapic_irq        disable_edge_ioapic_irq
```

Figure 14.31   Starting up an edge triggered interrupt

1191   with an edge triggered interrupt, it is only the change from one state to another that marks the occurrence of the interrupt. It is not possible to tell from the state of the irq line whether an interrupt is pending or not, so at startup the interrupt is necessary to check if the interrupt is already asserted or not. The integer returned indicates this; 1 for pending, 0 if not.

1193   this local variable, which will be returned to the caller, is initialised to a default value of 'not pending'.

1196–1203   because the IO APIC is a shared resource, these lines form a critical section. The lock is defined and initialised in Section 14.2.2.1. The interrupt-safe spinlock macros are from Section 12.8.1.

1197–1201   this code is executed only if the irq in question is one of the first 16.

1198   as this irq is about to be started up on the APIC, it is first disabled on the 8259A, using the PIC function (see Section 12.7.6). This is just to avoid any possibility of contention.

1199–1200   if the PIC records that there was an interrupt pending on that irq, a note is made of it and that information is returned. The test function was described in Section 12.7.9.

1202   this line is always executed. It is generic IO APIC code, independent of how the irq is triggered. As the name implies, it unmasks the specific irq (see Section 14.4.2).

1205   the return value is 1 if an interrupt was pending on the irq; otherwise (no irq pending, or not one of the original 16) the return value is 0.

1208   shutdown is trivial, as it is aliased onto disable (which actually does nothing); see Section 14.3.1.3.

14.3.1.3   Enable and disable

The trivial code that implements the enabling and disabling of edge triggered interrupts on an IO APIC is given in Figure 14.3.2.1, from `arch/i386/kernel/io_apic.c`.

```
1177 #define enable_edge_ioapic_irq unmask_IO_APIC_irq
1178
1179 static void disable_edge_ioapic_irq (unsigned int irq) {}
```

Figure 14.32   Enabling and disabling an edge triggered irq (interrupt request) on an APIC

1177 this is aliased onto `unmask_IO_APIC_irq()`, which is trigger-independent code (see Section 14.4.1).

1179 the disable function does nothing.

14.3.1.4 Acknowledge and end

The code for `acknowledge()`, and `end()`, is given in Figure 14.33, from `arch/i386/kernel/io_apic.c`.

```
1175 static void ack_edge_ioapic_irq(unsigned int irq)
1176 {
1177      if((irq_desc[irq].status & (IRQ_PENDING | IRQ_DISABLED))
1178      ==(IRQ_PENDING|IRQ_DISABLED)
1179          mask_IO_APIC_irq(irq);
1180      ack_APIC_irq();
1181 }
1182
1183 static void end_edge_ioapic_irq (unsigned int i) { }
1184
```

Figure 14.33 Acknowledging and ending an edge triggered irq (interrupt request) on an IO APIC

1177–1179 the condition will be TRUE if both the `IRQ_PENDING` and the `IRQ_DISABLED` bits are set in the `status` field corresponding to this irq. In that case, it should be masked out, using the trigger-independent function `mask_IO_APIC_irq()` (see Section 14.4.1). This prevents irq storms from unhandled devices.

1180 in all cases the local APIC function `ack_APIC_irq()` is called to send an EOI (see Section 13.3.2.4).

1183 there is no need to inform the IO APIC when a handler for an edge triggered irq has finished, so the end function does nothing.

14.3.2 Level triggered interrupts on an IO APIC

Level triggered interrupts are special because no IO APIC registers are touched while handling them. The APIC is acknowledged in the end handler, not in the start handler. Protection against re-entrance from the same interrupt is still provided, both by the generic irq layer and by the fact that an unacknowledged local APIC does not accept irqs.

14.3.2.1 Controller functions for level triggered interrupts

There is also a `struct hw_interrupt_type` declared and initialised for an IO APIC with level triggered interrupts, as shown in Figure 14.34, from `arch/i386/kernel/io_apic.c`.

```
1345 static struct hw_interrupt_type ioapic_level_irq_type = {
1346     "IO-APIC-level",
1347     startup_level_ioapic_irq,
1348     shutdown_level_ioapic_irq,
1349     enable_level_ioapic_irq,
1350     disable_level_ioapic_irq,
1351     mask_and_ack_level_ioapic_irq,
1352     end_level_ioapic_irq,
1353     set_ioapic_affinity,
1354 };
```

Figure 14.34   Controller functions for level triggered interrupts

1353   note that the final function in Figure 14.34 is not specific to level triggered APICs; it is the generic `set_ioapic_affinity()` function (see Section 14.4.4).

14.3.2.2   Manipulating a level triggered IO APIC

The implementation of the functions that startup, shutdown, enable, and disable a level triggered IO APIC are given in Figure 14.35, from `arch/i386/kernel/io_apic.c`.

```
1200 static unsigned int startup_level_ioapic_irq(unsigned int irq)
1201 {
1202     unmask_IO_APIC_irq(irq);
1203
1204     return 0;
1205 }
1206
1207 #define shutdown_level_ioapic_irq     mask_IO_APIC_irq
1208 #define enable_level_ioapic_irq       unmask_IO_APIC_irq
1209 #define disable_level_ioapic_irq      mask_IO_APIC_irq
```

Figure 14.35   Manipulating a level triggered IO APIC

1202   the startup function is aliased onto the trigger-independent function `unmask_IO_APIC_irq()` (see Section 14.4.1).

1204   we always return 0, a 'not pending' value.

1207–1209   these three functions are also aliased onto corresponding trigger-independent functions (see Section 14.4.1).

14.3.2.3   Ending a level triggered irq

What should be a relatively trivial function is complicated by a patch to solve a hardware problem in some IO APICs. Under certain conditions a level triggered interrupt is delivered as edge triggered, with the respective interrupt request register (IRR) bit set. So the APIC expects an EOI, which never arrives, and it locks up. The function that works around this problem is given in Figure 14.36, from `arch/i386/kernel/io_apic.c`.

```
1251 static void end_level_ioapic_irq (unsigned int irq)
1252 {
1253      unsigned long v;
1254      int i;

1275      i = IO_APIC_VECTOR(irq);
1276      v = apic_read(APIC_TMR + ((i & ~0x1f) >> 1));
1277
1278      ack_APIC_irq();
1279
1280      if (!(v & (1 << (i & 0x1f)))) {
1281 #ifdef APIC_LOCKUP_DEBUG
1282          struct irq_pin_list *entry;
1283 #endif
1284
1285 #ifdef APIC_MISMATCH_DEBUG
1286          atomic_inc(&irq_mis_count);
1287 #endif
1288          spin_lock(&ioapic_lock);
1289          __mask_and_edge_IO_APIC_irq(irq);
1290 #ifdef APIC_LOCKUP_DEBUG
1291          for (entry = irq_2_pin + irq; ;) {
1292              unsigned int reg;
1293
1294              if (entry->pin == -1)
1295                  break;
1296              reg = io_apic_read(entry->apic, 0x10 + entry->pin * 2);
1297              if (reg & 0x00004000)
1298                  printk(KERN_CRIT "Aieee!!!
1299              Remote IRR still set after unlock!\n");
1300              if (!entry->next)
1301                  break;
1302              entry = irq_2_pin + entry->next;
1303          }
1304 #endif
1305          __unmask_and_level_IO_APIC_irq(irq);
1306          spin_unlock(&ioapic_lock);
1307      }
1308 }
1309
1310 static void mask_and_ack_level_ioapic_irq (unsigned int i) {}
```

Figure 14.36   Ending a level triggered irq (interrupt request)

1275   this reads the vector number associated with this irq, using the macro from Section 12.5.3.

1276   this clears the low-order 5 bits of the vector number and shifts it right one bit. This identifies the long containing the bit corresponding to this vector. The appropriate part of the trigger mode register is read, using the function from Section 13.4.1.

1278	this acknowledges the irq to the local APIC, using the function from Section 13.4.2.4.
1280–1307	this block of code is executed only if the bit corresponding to this vector is clear in the trigger mode register (TMR), implying an edge triggered irq. Otherwise, the function does nothing more.
1281–1283	if this debugging mode is switched on, this pointer will be needed at lines 1290–1304.
1285–1287	if this debugging mode is switched on, then the count of mismatches encountered (Section 14.5.1.1) should be incremented atomically, using the function from Section 5.2.5.
1288–1306	this takes out the IO APIC lock, defined in Section 14.2.2.1.
1289	this sets the trigger mode to edge and disables the irq, using the function from Section 14.4.2.
1290–1304	code is compiled in only if this debugging mode is enabled.
1291–1303	this loop goes through each entry in the `irq_2_pin[]` array corresponding to this irq line (see Section 14.1.4). The `entry` control is advanced each time at line 1302.
1294–1295	if there is no pin corresponding to this entry, we just break out of the loop.
1296	this reads from the appropriate redirection register in the IO APIC for the pin currently being considered, using the function from Section 14.4.5.1.
1297–1299	bit 14 is the interrupt request bit (see Section 14.2.2.2). This bit is set when the APIC accepts a level triggered irq; it is cleared when an EOI is received from the local APIC. If it is set now, the warning message is printed.
1300–1301	if this is the last pin for this irq, we break out of the loop.
1302	otherwise, we move on to the next pin for this irq and go around the loop again.
1305	this line is always executed. It unmasks the irq and sets it back to be level triggered. The function is described in Section 14.4.2.
1310	this function does nothing.

14.4 Generic IO APIC code

Whether the irqs are level triggered or edge triggered, manipulation of the registers of the IO APIC is a standard procedure. The functions supplied for this will be considered in this section.

There are two principal manipulations on an IO APIC, to mask and unmask an irq. Then there is a function to program an APIC to associate a particular irq with a specified CPU. Finally, there is a group of worker functions, used by the foregoing, which actually read and write registers in the APIC.

14.4.1 Masking and unmasking irqs on an IO APIC

Figure 14.37, from `arch/i386/kernel/io_apic.c`, shows the two generic functions that mask and unmask an irq on an IO APIC. Both of these functions are just wrappers, which take out a spinlock from Section 14.2.2.1, using the interrupt-safe spinlock macros from Section 12.8.1. Each then calls the appropriate macro, as discussed in the next section.

```
148  static void mask_IO_APIC_irq (unsigned int irq)
149  {
150      unsigned long flags;
151
152      spin_lock_irqsave(&ioapic_lock, flags);
153      __mask_IO_APIC_irq(irq);
154      spin_unlock_irqrestore(&ioapic_lock, flags);
155  }
156
157  static void unmask_IO_APIC_irq (unsigned int irq)
158  {
159      unsigned long flags;
160
161      spin_lock_irqsave(&ioapic_lock, flags);
162      __unmask_IO_APIC_irq(irq);
163      spin_unlock_irqrestore(&ioapic_lock, flags);
164  }
```

Figure 14.37   Masking and unmasking an irq (interrupt request) on an IO APIC

14.4.2   Macros to generate masking and unmasking functions

The macros shown in Figure 14.38, from `arch/i386/kernel/io_apic.c`, generate generic masking and unmasking functions for an IO APIC.

```
134  #define DO_ACTION(name, R, ACTION, FINAL)                              \
135                                                                         \
136      static void name##_IO_APIC_irq (unsigned int irq)                 \
137      __DO_ACTION(R, ACTION, FINAL)
138
139  DO_ACTION(__mask, 0, |= 0x00010000, io_apic_sync(entry->apic))
140
141  DO_ACTION(__unmask, 0, &= 0xfffeffff, )
142
143  DO_ACTION(__mask_and_edge, 0, = (reg & 0xffff7fff) | 0x00010000, )
144
145  DO_ACTION(__unmask_and_level, 0, = (reg & 0xfffeffff) | 0x00008000, )
```

Figure 14.38   Macros to generate masking and unmasking functions

134–137   this macro actually generates a C function. The `name` parameter is the specific part of the name given to the generated function; R is the APIC register to manipulate; `ACTION` specifies the operation to perform on that register; `FINAL` can specify any required postprocessing.

136 this is the description; depending on the parameter passed, it will generate a function called
`__name_IO_APIC_irq()`, e.g. `__mask_IO_APIC_irq`.

137 this macro will be discussed in the following section. It does some modification specified by
`ACTION` to an APIC register specified by `R` and also performs any action specified by the
parameter `FINAL`.

139 this is one instantiation of the macro. It creates the function `__mask_IO_APIC_irq()`, which
sets bit 16 (the mask bit) in an APIC redirection register corresponding to this irq and then calls
the `io_apic_sync()` function (see Section 14.4.5.4).

141 this is the second instantiation of the macro. It creates the function
`__unmask_IO_APIC_irq()`, which clears bit 16 (the mask bit) in an APIC redirection register
corresponding to this irq. It does not call the `io_apic_sync()` function nor does it do any
other postprocessing.

143 this generates the function `__mask_and_edge()`, which sets bit 16 (the mask bit), so marking it
as disabled. But it also clears bit 15 (the trigger bit). Clearing this bit means that it is edge triggered.

145 this generates the function `__unmask_and_level()`, which clears bit 16 (the mask bit), so
enabling the irq. It also sets bit 15 (the trigger bit), for level triggered.

14.4.3 Macro to manipulate an IO APIC register

The macro shown in Figure 14.39, from `arch/i386/kernel/io_apic.c`, modifies an
IO APIC register specified by R. The particular modification is specified by `ACTION`. After
this, the operation specified by `FINAL` is carried out. It is used at line 112, in Section 14.4.2.

```
134  #define __DO_ACTION(R, ACTION, FINAL)                             \
135                                                                    \
136  {                                                                 \
137          int pin;                                                  \
138          struct irq_pin_list *entry = irq_2_pin + irq;             \
139                                                                    \
140          for (;;) {                                                 \
141               unsigned int reg;                                    \
142               pin = entry->pin;                                    \
143               if (pin == -1)                                       \
144                    break;                                          \
145               reg = io_apic_read(entry->apic, 0x10 + R + pin*2);   \
146               reg ACTION;                                          \
147               io_apic_modify(entry->apic, reg);                   \
148               if (!entry->next)                                    \
149                    break;                                          \
150               entry = irq_2_pin + entry->next;                     \
151          }                                                         \
152          FINAL;                                                    \
153      }
```

Figure 14.39 Macro to modify an APIC register

138   this sets up `entry` as a pointer to the entry in the `irq_2_pin[]` array corresponding to this irq (see Section 14.1.4.1).

140–151   this loop works its way along a linked list of entries registered for this irq, modifying the appropriate APIC register each time.

142   this takes a local copy of the number of the pin corresponding to this irq from the table.

143–144   if no pin is assigned to this irq, we break out of the loop.

145   the first parameter is an `int` identifying the APIC (from the table). The second parameter specifies which APIC redirection register is to be read. Redirection registers begin at offset `0x10`; `pin * 2` specifies the register; R, which can be 0 or 1, specifies the low or high half of the register [see Section 14.4.5.1 for the `io_apic_read()` function].

146   the value returned by the previous line is manipulated in some way specified by the parameter `ACTION` (e.g. bits will be set or cleared in it). For example, `__mask` sets bit 16, `__unmask` clears bit 16.

147   this writes the new value back to the APIC (see Section 14.4.5.3).

148–149   if the link field in the list is `NULL`, we break out of the loop.

150   otherwise, there is a second entry corresponding to this irq. This sets up an index to the entry in the `irq_2_pin[]` array, corresponding to the irq specified in the `next` field of the entry just dealt with. Then we go around the loop again and deal with that one.

152   this carries out any processing specified by the parameter `FINAL`.

14.4.4   Setting affinity for an IO APIC

The function shown in Figure 14.40 is from `arch/i386/kernel/io_apic.c`. It is used for both edge triggered and level triggered irqs.

```
1312 static void set_ioapic_affinity (unsigned int irq, unsigned long mask)
1313 {
1314      unsigned long flags;

1318      mask = mask << 24;
1319
1320      spin_lock_irqsave(&ioapic_lock, flags);
1321      __DO_ACTION(1, = mask, )
1322      spin_unlock_irqrestore(&ioapic_lock, flags);
1323 }
```

Figure 14.40   Setting affinity for a level triggered APIC

1312   this sets up an affinity between the interrupt specified by the `irq` parameter and the CPU specified by the `mask` parameter.

1318   only the high-order 8 bits are now valid – the other 24 are zeros. These bits represent the destination field in the redirection register.

1320–1322   this takes out the lock from Section 14.2.2.1, using the interrupt-safe spinlock macros from Section 12.8.1.

1321   the macro, discussed in Section 14.4.3, writes `mask` to the high-order 32 bits of the APIC redirection register (specified by the 1), so it is setting up the destination CPU(s) to which the irq is to be sent.

14.4.5   Reading and writing IO APICs

A number of functions are provided in `<asm-i386/io_apic.h>` for reading, writing, and modifying specific registers in an IO APIC. These will be considered in this section.

14.4.5.1   *Reading from an IO APIC register*

The function shown in Figure 14.41 reads from a specific IO APIC register.

```
105  static inline unsigned int io_apic_read(unsigned int apic,
                                             unsigned int reg)
106  {
107       *IO_APIC_BASE(apic) = reg;
108       return *(IO_APIC_BASE(apic)+4);
109  }
```

Figure 14.41   Reading from an IO APIC register

105   the first parameter identifies the APIC; the second identifies the register that is to be read.

107   the macro `IO_APIC_BASE()` returns a pointer to the virtual address corresponding to the first register in this particular IO APIC (see Section 14.2.1). The offset of the register to be read is written there. This causes the APIC to make the value in that internal register available 16 bytes farther on in the virtual address space.

108   this returns the value from the virtual memory location 16 bytes on from the base register, which is the value in the specified register `reg`.

14.4.5.2   *Writing to an IO APIC register*

The function shown in Figure 14.42 writes to a specific IO APIC register.

```
111  static inline void io_apic_write(unsigned int apic,
                                      unsigned int reg, unsigned int value)
112  {
113       *IO_APIC_BASE(apic) = reg;
114       *(IO_APIC_BASE(apic)+4) = value;
115  }
```

Figure 14.42   Writing to an IO APIC register

113   the macro IO_APIC_BASE() returns a pointer to the virtual address corresponding to the first register in this particular IO APIC (see Section 14.2.1). The offset of the register to be read is written there. This causes the APIC to make that internal register available 16 bytes further on in the virtual address space.

114   the value parameter is copied to the virtual memory location 16 bytes on from the previous value. This writes it to the register at an offset of reg from the IO APIC's index register.

14.4.5.3 Modifying an IO APIC register

The function shown in Figure 14.43 rewrites a value. It is used for read–modify–write cycles where the read has already been done and has set up the index register.

```
121  static inline void io_apic_modify(unsigned int apic,
                                         unsigned int value)
122  {
123      *(IO_APIC_BASE(apic)+4) = value;
124  }
```

Figure 14.43 Modifying an IO APIC register

123   the value parameter is copied to the location 16 bytes from the APIC's base address in virtual memory. This writes it to the previously selected register.

14.4.5.4 Synchronising the IO APIC and the central processing unit

This is achieved by doing a dummy read from the IO APIC; see Figure 14.44, from <asm-i386/io_apic.h>.

```
130  static inline void io_apic_sync(unsigned int apic)
131  {
132      (void) *(IO_APIC_BASE(apic)+4);
133  }
```

Figure 14.44 Synchronising the IO APIC and the computer processing unit

14.5 Global interrupts

In a multiprocessor environment, disabling interrupts on the local CPU does not guarantee mutual exclusion against interrupt handlers running on other CPUs, so a special lock, the global interrupt request lock, is introduced for this.

14.5.1 The global interrupt request lock

At times there may be a requirement to disable interrupts on all CPUs. This is forced by one of the CPUs acquiring and holding the global interrupt request lock, global_irq_lock; the ID of the CPU holding that lock is in global_irq_holder.

14.5.1.1 Definition of the global interrupt request lock

Figure 14.45, from `arch/i386/kernel/irq.c`, shows the definition of the variables involved in controlling interrupts globally.

```
123  atomic_t irq_err_count;
124  #ifdef CONFIG_X86_IO_APIC
125  #ifdef APIC_MISMATCH_DEBUG
126  atomic_t irq_mis_count;
127  #endif
128  #endif

192  unsigned char          global_irq_holder = NO_PROC_ID;
193  unsigned volatile long  global_irq_lock;
```

Figure 14.45 Global interrupt locks for SMP

123   this is a cumulative count of the number of spurious irqs that have accumulated since boot time.

126   this is a cumulative count of the number of trigger-type mismatches that have accumulated since boot time.

192   this is the logical identifier of the CPU holding the `global_irq_lock`. It is initialised so that 'nobody' is holding it.

193   this is the lock itself. It is declared as `long` for compatibility with the `test_and_set_bit()` macro, which is used to manipulate it.

14.5.1.2 Acquiring the global interrupt request lock

Figure 14.46, from `arch/i386/kernel/irq.c`, shows the function `get_irqlock()`, which acquires the global interrupt request lock and waits for any interrupt service routines running on other processors to terminate. To avoid the possibility of deadlock, a CPU should not call this function if local interrupts are already disabled or while it is running an interrupt service routine itself.

```
317  static inline void get_irqlock(int cpu)
318  {
319      if (test_and_set_bit(0,&global_irq_lock)) {
320
321          if ((unsigned char) cpu == global_irq_holder)
322              return;
323
324          do {
325              do {
326                  rep_nop();
327              } while (test_bit(0,&global_irq_lock));
328          } while (test_and_set_bit(0,&global_irq_lock));
```

```
329        }

334        wait_on_irq(cpu);

339        global_irq_holder = cpu;
340 }
```

Figure 14.46 Acquiring the global interrupt request lock

319 the function is from Section 5.1.4.1. If bit 0 was clear beforehand, the lock was free and we have acquired it now, by setting it to 1. The function returns FALSE in that case, so we go on to line 334.

320–328 this code is executed only if the lock was held beforehand.

321 this line checks if this process is the holder. The global_irq_holder always contains the ID of the CPU holding the lock.

322 if this process is already holding the lock, then there is no more to be done.

324–328 some other CPU has the lock, so this one must wait for it to become free and acquire it. When it does find the bit free, the function returns FALSE.

325–327 we spin in the inner loop, while the global_irq_lock is held. The test_bit() function, from Section 5.1.3, returns TRUE if the bit is set.

326 this function, from Section 9.4.2.2, merely puts a delay into the busy waiting loop.

328 if the process cannot acquire the lock after the lock has been released (some other process beats it to it) it goes around the outer loop again.

334 this process has now acquired the lock. It must also make sure that no other process is running in interrupt context. The function is described in Section 14.5.1.4.

339 the process announces that it is holding the lock.

14.5.1.3 *Releasing the global interrupt request lock*

Figure 14.47, from <asm-i386/hardirq.h>, shows the function that releases the global interrupt request lock. It is strange that this is in a different file from the code shown in Figure 14.46.

```
57   static inline void release_irqlock(int cpu)
58   {
59
60        if (global_irq_holder == (unsigned char) cpu) {
61             global_irq_holder = NO_PROC_ID;
62             clear_bit(0,&global_irq_lock);
63        }
64   }
```

Figure 14.47 Releasing the global interrupt request lock

60   if this process does not own the interrupt request-lock, then we do nothing, just return.

61   no process owns the lock now. The macro is defined in `<asm-i386/smp.h>` as:

```
123  #define NO_PROC_ID  0xFF
```

62   this clears the lock bit, using the function from Section 5.1.2. It is important that these two operations be done in this order. If the lock was released first, the current process could be interrupted. By the time it is resumed, another process could have claimed the lock. The assignment of NO_PROC_ID on this line would then overwrite the entry corresponding to that process, effectively taking the ownership of the lock from it.

14.5.1.4   *Waiting to acquire the global interrupt request lock*

The function shown in Figure 14.48, from `arch/i386/kernel/irq.c`, checks that no other CPU is running in interrupt context. If one is, the function waits until it finishes. It then acquires the global interrupt request lock.

```
263  static inline void wait_on_irq(int cpu)
264  {
265      int count = MAXCOUNT;
266
267      for (;;) {

274          if (!irqs_running())
275              if (local_bh_count(cpu) ||
                                !spin_is_locked(&global_bh_lock))
276                  break;

279          clear_bit(0,&global_irq_lock);
280
281          for (;;) {
282              if (!-count) {
283                  show("wait_on_irq");
284                  count = ~0;
285              }
286              __sti();
287              SYNC_OTHER_CORES(cpu);
288              __cli();
289              if (irqs_running())
290                  continue;
291              if (global_irq_lock)
292                  continue;
293              if (!local_bh_count(cpu) &&
                                spin_is_locked(&global_bh_lock))
294                  continue;
295              if (!test_and_set_bit(0,&global_irq_lock))
296                  break;
297          }
```

```
298       }
299  }
```

Figure 14.48   Waiting until interrupt handlers have terminated.

265   this value is defined in `arch/i386/kernel/irq.c` as:

```
234   #define MAXCOUNT 100000000
```

267   this infinite loop runs down to line 298. It continues looping and testing until no other CPU is running in interrupt context.

274   if there are any interrupt service routines running on any CPU, we skip on to line 279. The function is described in Section 14.5.1.5.

275–276   bottom halves are described in Section 16.3. If the `local_bh_count()` macro from Section 16.5.1.2 evaluates positive, there are bottom halves running on this CPU. This will happen only when there are no interrupts to be serviced on this CPU. The `global_bh_lock` is from Section 16.3.1.1. It is used to provide mutual exclusion for bottom halves running on different CPUs. This code checks whether it is held or not, using the macro from Section 5.3.1. So, if no interrupts are being handled anywhere, and no bottom halves are running (except possibly on the local CPU), then control breaks out of the outer loop. This is the only place where control breaks out of the outer loop.

279   the current thread is now going to wait until all interrupt service routines are finished. This has to be done in a loop, so the interrupt lock is released to avoid deadlocks. The function is from Section 5.1.2.

281   this loop runs down to line 297.

282–285   the `count` variable is decremented each time around the inner loop. When it gets to 0, we display a message and reinitialise it to all 1s again. The `show()` function is described in Section 22.6.1. Thus this message is displayed after the first $100\,000\,000$ times around this inner loop, and thereafter every 2^{32} times around the loop.

286   this enables local interrupts, using the macro from Section 12.8.2.

287   the macro is discussed in Section 14.5.3.3. It is basically a bugfix, which introduces a delay, so that all CPUs have a consistent view of memory.

288   this disables local interrupts, using the macro from Section 12.8.2.

289–290   if there are any interrupt service routines running on any CPU, we go around the inner loop again, without doing any further checking. We do not want even to try for the lock. The function is discussed in Section 14.5.1.5.

291–292   if the `global_irq_lock` is held, we go around the inner loop again, without doing any further checking. We do not want even to try for the lock.

293–294   if there are no local bottom halves being serviced on this CPU, *and* the global bottom half lock is held, we go around the inner loop again, as some other CPU is servicing a bottom half. If we are servicing a bottom half locally, then it is we who are holding the lock, so we just go on and try to acquire the global interrupt request lock.

295–296 here we try to acquire the global interrupt request lock. If we acquire it (it was not set beforehand, so the function returns 0) then we break out of the inner loop and go around the outer loop again. This is the only place where we break out of the inner loop.

297 otherwise, we go around the inner loop again.

14.5.1.5 Checking all computer processing units for active interrupt handlers

Figure 14.49, from `<asm/hardirq.h>`, shows the code that checks all CPUs for active interrupt handlers.

```
47   static inline int irqs_running (void)
48   {
49       int i;
50
51       for (i = 0; i < smp_num_cpus; i++)
52           if (local_irq_count(i))
53               return 1;
54       return 0;
55   }
```

Figure 14.49 Checking for active interrupt service routines

51–53 this checks all CPUs. If even one is found to be servicing an interrupt, we return 1 (TRUE) immediately.

52 this macro, from Section 16.5.1.2, evaluates to the nesting level of the interrupt service routines running on the specified CPU.

54 if none of them is servicing an interrupt, we return 0 (FALSE).

14.5.2 Enabling and disabling interrupts globally

On a multiprocessor, as well as the need to inhibit interrupts on all the CPUs there may be a requirement to save information about the state of the local CPU. This is so that when global interrupts are enabled at a later stage the interrupt handling state of the local CPU can be restored just as it was.

14.5.2.1 Disabling interrupts globally

The function shown in Figure 14.50, from `arch/i386/kernel/irq.c`, disables local interrupts. If the calling CPU is not currently servicing an interrupt it also takes out the global interrupt request lock, thus disabling interrupts globally.

```
342  #define EFLAGS_IF_SHIFT 9

356  void __global_cli(void)
```

```
357  {
358        unsigned int flags;
359
360        __save_flags(flags);
361        if (flags & (1 << EFLAGS_IF_SHIFT)) {
362              int cpu = smp_processor_id();
363              __cli();
364              if (!local_irq_count(cpu))
365                    get_irqlock(cpu);
366        }
367  }
```

Figure 14.50 Disabling interrupt processing on all computer processing units

342   the IF (interrupt enable) bit is in position 9 in the EFLAGS register.

360   this gets a copy of the EFLAGS register of the local CPU into the local flags variable. The macro was discussed in Section 12.8.2.

361   if the IF bit is cleared in flags (i.e. interrupts are already disabled), we do nothing. A process running in the kernel with interrupts disabled is very likely to be holding spinlocks. There is a significant possibility of deadlock when we get to line 365.

362–366   this block of code is executed only if interrupts are enabled locally.

362   this gets the ID of the processor on which we are running (see Section 12.8.2).

363   this disables interrupts on the local CPU. This macro was discussed in Section 12.8.2.

364–365   the local_irq_count() macro is defined in 16.5.1.2. If the local CPU is not currently servicing an interrupt, we take out the global interrupt request lock. This prevents any other CPU from servicing an interrupt. If it is currently servicing an interrupt, then there is a possibility of the function on the next line deadlocking. So we do nothing further, and __global_cli() is equivalent to a local __cli().

365   this function is discussed in Section 14.5.1.2. It waits for any interrupt handlers running on other processors to terminate and then takes out the global interrupt request lock.

14.5.2.2 Enabling interrupts globally

Figure 14.51, from arch/i386/kernel/irq.c, is the dual of Figure 14.50. The code here releases the interrupt request lock, so enabling other CPUs to service interrupts again.

```
369  void __global_sti(void)
370  {
371        int cpu = smp_processor_id();
372
373        if (!local_irq_count(cpu))
374              release_irqlock(cpu);
```

```
375          __sti();
376  }
```

Figure 14.51   Reenabling interrupt processing on all computer processing units

371   this gets the ID of the processor on which we are running (see Section 7.2.1.4).

373–374 only if the local CPU is not currently servicing an interrupt (i.e. all nested interrupts have been serviced), do we release the global interrupt request lock, which prevents any other CPU from servicing an interrupt. The `local_irq_count()` macro is described in Section 16.5.1.2; the `release_irqlock()` function is from Section 16.5.3.2.

375   this enables local interrupts, using the macro from Section 12.8.2. If the local CPU is actually servicing an interrupt, then `__global_sti()` becomes equivalent to a local `__sti()`.

14.5.3   Global flags

The SMP versions of saving and restoring flags deal with recording and restoring the state of interrupt handling for the whole system.

14.5.3.1   *Saving global interrupt handling information*

The `__global_save_flags()` function, from `arch/i386/kernel/irq.c` (see Figure 14.52) returns an integer that describes the state of the system, as follows:

- 0: the local CPU is not servicing an interrupt but is holding the global interrupt request lock. It may or may not have interrupts enabled locally, so no other CPU can service any interrupt. Interrupts are disabled globally.

- 1: the local CPU is not servicing an interrupt; it has interrupts enabled locally but is not holding the global interrupt request lock, so any CPU can service any interrupt, including this one. Interrupts are enabled globally.

- 2: the local CPU is servicing an interrupt, interrupts are disabled locally, and it may or may not be holding the global interrupt request lock.

- 3: the local CPU is servicing an interrupt, interrupts are enabled locally, and it may or may not be holding the global interrupt request lock.

The caller then saves this integer, which it eventually passes to `__global_restore_flags()`.

```
385  unsigned long __global_save_flags(void)
386  {
387      int retval;
388      int local_enabled;
389      unsigned long flags;
390      int cpu = smp_processor_id();
```

```
391
392          __save_flags(flags);
393          local_enabled = (flags >> EFLAGS_IF_SHIFT) & 1;
394
395          retval = 2 + local_enabled;

398          if (!local_irq_count(cpu)) {
399              if (local_enabled)
400                  retval = 1;
401              if (global_irq_holder == cpu)
402                  retval = 0;
403          }
404          return retval;
405  }
```

Figure 14.52   Saving global interrupt handling information

390   this gets the ID of the processor on which we are running (see Section 7.2.1.4).

392   this gets a copy of the EFLAGS register on the local CPU into the local variable flags. The macro was discussed in Section 12.8.2.

393   the right shift brings the IF bit into the least significant position. ANDing it with 1 sets local_enabled to 1 if interrupts are enabled on this CPU and sets it to 0 otherwise.

395   the default retval to be returned is either 2 if interrupts are disabled locally, or 3 if enabled.

398   if the local CPU is currently servicing an interrupt, then we do nothing further, but we return the value in retval, corresponding to whether interrupts are enabled or not on the local CPU. The macro is from Section 16.5.1.2.

399–403   this code is executed only if the local CPU is not servicing an interrupt. It checks for global flags. Remember, neither of these might be true, in which case the value of retval from line 395 is still valid.

399–400   we return 1 if interrupts are enabled on the local CPU.

401–402   if interrupts are not enabled, and this CPU is the global_irq_holder, we return 0.

14.5.3.2   Restoring global interrupt handling information

Figure 14.53, from arch/i386/kernel/irq.c, restores the global interrupt state. The parameter passed to it is the value previously returned by __global_save_flags(). Depending on this, the function restores local and/or global interrupts to the state they were in when __global_save_flags() was last called.

```
407  void __global_restore_flags(unsigned long flags)
408  {
409      switch (flags) {
410      case 0:
```

```
411                    __global_cli();
412               break;
413          case 1:
414               __global_sti();
415               break;
416          case 2:
417               __cli();
418               break;
419          case 3:
420               __sti();
421               break;
422          default:
423               printk("global_restore_flags: %08lx (%08lx)\n",
424                    flags, (&flags)[-1]);
425          }
426  }
427
428  #endif
```

Figure 14.53 Restoring global interrupt handling information

410–412 the local CPU was holding the global interrupt request lock, so we call __global_cli() (Section 14.5.2.1), which will disable interrupts locally, and attempt to take out that lock again.

413–415 the local CPU was not holding the global interrupt request lock, so we call __global_sti() (Section 14.5.2.2), which will enable interrupts locally, and give back the lock (as long as the local CPU is not in interrupt context).

416–418 the local CPU had interrupts disabled, so we disable them now, using the macro from Section 12.8.2.

419–421 the local CPU had interrupts enabled, so we enable them now, using the macro from Section 12.8.2.

423–424 if the flags value is out of range, we print an error message giving the parameter itself and the address of the location below the parameter flags on the stack. This is the return address, which identifies the caller.

14.5.3.3 Limiting memory update frequency

The macro defined in Figure 14.54, from arch/i386/kernel/irq.c, is basically a bug fix. It appears that on some multiprocessors a spin_unlock() followed tightly by a spin_lock() on the same processor locks out other processors. These other processors should have noticed the spin_unlock() but apparently the spin_unlock() information did not make it through to them. The problem is probably due to snooping latency between the caches; the delay introduced by SYNC_OTHER_CORES() solves the problem.

```
252  #define SUSPECTED_CPU_OR_CHIPSET_BUG_WORKAROUND 0
253
254  #if SUSPECTED_CPU_OR_CHIPSET_BUG_WORKAROUND
```

```
255  # define SYNC_OTHER_CORES(x) udelay(x+1)
256  #else

260  # define SYNC_OTHER_CORES(x) __asm__ __volatile__ ("nop")
261  #endif
```

Figure 14.54   Limiting memory update frequency

255   this introduces a delay of x+1 microseconds.

260   the macro is always wrapped in the calling function by __sti() and __cli(). In order to allow irqs to arrive between __sti and __cli, a NOP instruction is introduced.

15

The timer interrupt

Of all of the hardware interrupts examined in previous chapters, the timer interrupt is the one that is most the responsibility of the process manager. There is a sense in which this interrupt drives the whole operating system.

15.1 Timer interrupt handling

Timer interrupts are handled at two levels. First there is the absolutely necessary processing, which at the very least means making a note that the interrupt has occurred. Then there is the processing that can be delayed, as long as it is done eventually. This second-level processing is described in Section 15.1.4.

15.1.1 Variables used by timer interrupt handler

As has been the case in many previous sections, the first part of the code to consider is the declaration and initialisation of the variables used within the kernel. The first group, shown in Figure 15.1, from `kernel/timer.c`, is rather a mixed bag.

```
32    long tick = (1000000 + HZ/2) / HZ;

40    DECLARE_TASK_QUEUE(tq_timer);
41    DECLARE_TASK_QUEUE(tq_immediate);

68    unsigned long volatile jiffies;
```

Figure 15.1 Variables used by time functions

32   a `tick` is the timer interrupt period. The standard hardware clock interrupts every 10 ms, so the standard HZ is 100. At this rate, a tick is $1\,000\,050/100$ μs or $10\,000$ μs. So each `tick` is 10 ms. The extra `HZ/2` is to compensate for any rounding errors that may result in conversion from decimal to binary by the compiler.

The Linux Process Manager: The Internals of Scheduling, Interrupts and Signals   John O'Gorman
© 2003 John Wiley & Sons, Ltd   ISBN: 0 470 84771 9

40–41   these two lines are declaring (setting up) task queues. Task queues are dealt with in detail in Section 16.4. Essentially, the ones being set up here are queues of actions to be carried out at a later time, as described in Section 16.4.4. The DECLARE_TASK_QUEUE() macro is described in Section 16.4.1.

68   the jiffies variable records the time since the system was booted, in ticks. Recall from line 32 that a tick is 10 ms.

15.1.2 The timer interrupt handler

The function shown in Figure 15.2, from kernel/timer.c, is the root of all timer interrupt handling. It is called on every timer interrupt. It is short and to the point.

```
674  void do_timer(struct pt_regs * regs)
675  {
676       (*(unsigned long *)&jiffies)++;
677  #ifndef CONFIG_SMP

680       update_process_times(user_mode(regs));
681  #endif
682       mark_bh(TIMER_BH);
683       if (TQ_ACTIVE(tq_timer))
684            mark_bh(TQUEUE_BH);
685  }
```

Figure 15.2 High-priority timer handling

674   the struct pt_regs defines the way the registers are stored on the stack during interrupt handling. It has been described in detail in Section 10.3.1.1.

676   we begin by incrementing the count of jiffies (see Section 15.1.1). This guarantees that jiffies will be treated as an unsigned long and so will not overflow in any reasonable time.

677–681   this is how accounting is done on a uniprocessor. SMP process accounting uses the local APIC (advanced programmable interrupt controller) timer (see Section 13.6.2.2).

680   the user_mode() macro is described in Section 10.3.1.4. It checks whether the processor was in user mode (1) or kernel mode (0) when the interrupt occurred, so update_process_times() (Section 15.1.3.1) is called with either 1 or 0.

682   then the mark_bh() function, as described in Section 16.3.3, sets up the timer bottom-half handler to be called later, at lower priority.

683–684   finally, if there are entries on the tqueue_timer task queue, its bottom half is also set up to be called later. The TQ_ACTIVE() macro is from Section 16.4.1.

15.1.3 Subsidiary functions

The previous section considered the first-level function that services the timer interrupt. There is a whole chain of subsidiary functions called by that, which will be described in this section.

15.1.3.1   Updating computer processing unit statistics

On each timer tick, a range of system variables have to be updated. These include such things as the quantum of the current process and running totals of computer processing unit (CPU) usage. The function shown in Figure 15.3, from `kernel/timer.c`, which is called on each timer interrupt, takes care of all of that.

```
579  void update_process_times(int user_tick)
580  {
581      struct task_struct *p = current;
582      int cpu = smp_processor_id(), system = user_tick ^ 1;
583
584      update_one_process(p, user_tick, system, cpu);
585      if (p->pid) {
586          if (-p->counter <= 0) {
587              p->counter = 0;
588              p->need_resched = 1;
589          }
590          if (p->nice > 0)
591              kstat.per_cpu_nice[cpu] += user_tick;
592          else
593              kstat.per_cpu_user[cpu] += user_tick;
594          kstat.per_cpu_system[cpu] += system;
595      } else if (local_bh_count(cpu) || local_irq_count(cpu) > 1)
596          kstat.per_cpu_system[cpu] += system;
597  }
```

Figure 15.3   Timer interrupt handling for the current process

579   the parameter `user_tick` indicates whether it is a user mode (1) or kernel mode (0) tick that is being accounted for.

581   this takes a pointer to the `task_struct` of the current process.

582   this gets the identification (ID) number of the CPU on which this code is running. The `smp_processor_id()` macro was described in Section 7.2.1.4. The `system` variable is initialised to be the opposite of `user_tick`. If the CPU spent the previous tick in kernel mode, then `system` should be 1. If `user_tick` is 1, then it spent the last tick in user mode, so `system` should be 0.

584   this updates statistics for the current process, using the function from Section 15.1.3.2.

585   if dealing with process 0, the null process, then we skip down to line 595. The null process does not have a quantum, so there is no need to check it, nor can it lower its priority using `nice`.

586   this decrements the quantum for the current process.

587   in case it is negative (i.e. it was zero before the decrement), then we set it back to zero.

588   if it has expired, we set the `need_resched` flag for this process.

590–593 this updates per CPU statistics. This line adds one user tick either to `per_cpu_nice[]`, or `per_cpu_user[]`, depending on whether the priority of the process has been reduced below the default (by `nice`), or not. Of course, if it was a kernel tick, this adds nothing. The whole `kstat` structure is defined in Section 7.2.4.1.

594 in any case, one tick is added to `per_cpu_system[]`. If it was a user tick, nothing is added.

595–596 if the null process is running, and there are either bottom halves or local interrupts being handled by that CPU this code updates `per_cpu_system[]` if it was a system tick, so the null process is charged to the system, if it happens to be doing work for the system. The macros are described in Section 16.5.1.2.

15.1.3.2 Updating statistics for one process

The previous section dealt with updating systemwide statistics. The function shown in Figure 15.4, from `kernel/timer.c`, updates statistics for the current process, including the virtual and profiling timers.

```
566  void update_one_process(struct task_struct *p,
567       unsigned long user, unsigned long system, int cpu)
568  {
569       p->per_cpu_utime[cpu] += user;
570       p->per_cpu_stime[cpu] += system;
571       do_process_times(p, user, system);
572       do_it_virt(p, user);
573       do_it_prof(p);
574  }
```

Figure 15.4 Updating process statistics and times

567 either `user` will be 1 and `system` 0, or vice versa, depending on whether the timer interrupt occurred in user mode or kernel mode.

569–570 this code increments the running total of either user time or system time used on this CPU.

571 the `do_process_times()` function checks if CPU limits for this process have been exceeded (see Section 15.1.3.3).

572–573 finally, a check is made to see if any virtual or profiling timers have expired (see Sections 15.1.3.4 and 15.1.3.5, respectively, for these functions).

15.1.3.3 Checking limits

As well as its quantum, each process is given a maximum amount of CPU time (in seconds) that it can use during its lifetime. This is to prevent runaway processes monopolising the CPU. There are actually two limits to CPU use, a soft limit (`rlim_cur`) and a hard limit (`rlim_max`). When the first is exceeded, the process is sent the `SIGXCPU` signal. When the hard limit is exceeded, it is sent the `SIGKILL` signal. The function shown in Figure 15.5, from `kernel/timer.c`, checks if CPU limits for a process have been exceeded.

```
522    static inline void do_process_times(struct task_struct *p,
523            unsigned long user, unsigned long system)
524    {
525            unsigned long psecs;
526
527            psecs = (p->times.tms_utime += user);
528            psecs += (p->times.tms_stime += system);
529            if (psecs / HZ > p->rlim[RLIMIT_CPU].rlim_cur){
530
531                    if (!(psecs % HZ))
532                            send_sig(SIGXCPU, p, 1);
533
534                    if (psecs / HZ > p->rlim[RLIMIT_CPU].rlim_max)
535                            send_sig(SIGKILL, p, 1);
536            }
537    }
```

Figure 15.5 Checking limits on user and system times for a process

522–523   the first parameter is a pointer to the `task_struct` of the process in question. The other two, `user` and `system`, are the time spent in user or system mode, which are to be added in. One of these will be 1, the other 0.

527   this updates the `tms_utime` field of the process descriptor, if this is a user tick. In any case, we take the total of user time into `psecs`.

528   this updates the `tms_stime` field of the process descriptor, if this is a system tick. In any case, we add the total of system time into `psecs`, which is now the total time used so far, in ticks.

529–536   division of `ticks` by HZ gives seconds (HZ is the number of ticks per second, typically 100). This block of code is executed only if the soft limit has been exceeded.

531–532   send `SIGXCPU` is sent whenever a further second of CPU time is used. The value of `psecs % HZ` will be 0 once every second. The `send_sig()` function is described in Section 18.2.7. The process can catch this signal, for example printing a warning message.

534–535   when the hard limit is exceeded, the process is sent a `SIGKILL`, so it is killed off.

15.1.3.4   *Updating the virtual interrupt timer*

Linux provides a number of mechanisms by which a process can request that a signal be sent to it at specified intervals. One of these is the virtual interval timer, which only counts time spent by the process in user mode. It sends the `SIGVTALRM` signal. The `it_virt_incr` field in the `task_struct` contains the interval (measured in ticks) between signals from this timer; the corresponding `it_virt_value` field contains the current value of the timer. The function shown in Figure 15.6, from `kernel/timer.c`, updates and checks for the expiry of the virtual interrupt timer.

```
539  static inline void do_it_virt(struct task_struct * p,
                                               unsigned long ticks)
540  {
541          unsigned long it_virt = p->it_virt_value;
542
543          if (it_virt) {
544                  it_virt -= ticks;
545                  if (!it_virt) {
546                          it_virt = p->it_virt_incr;
547                          send_sig(SIGVTALRM, p, 1);
548                  }
549                  p->it_virt_value = it_virt;
550          }
551  }
```

Figure 15.6   Checking for expiry of a virtual interval timer

539   the `ticks` parameter specifies whether the last tick was spent in user mode (1) or system mode (0). The virtual interval timer only counts time spent in user mode. It could be argued that this test should be done by the caller [`update_one_process()`, Section 15.1.3.2].

541   this takes a local copy of the time remaining on the virtual timer.

543–550   this code is executed only if the `it_virt_value` field in the process descriptor is not zero (i.e. if a virtual timer is in use); otherwise it does nothing.

544   this decrements the virtual timer by the value of `ticks`. This will be 1 if the process spent the last tick in user mode, otherwise it is 0. This is the definition of a virtual timer – it only counts time spent in user mode.

545–548   if after this decrement the time remaining on it is 0 (i.e. if it has timed out), then we reset the local value to the value specified by the process and send the signal `SIGVTALRM` to the process [see Section 18.2.7 for the `send_sig()` function].

549   whether it has timed out or not, the last line resets the `it_virt_value` field in the process descriptor to be equal to the local `it_virt`. This is either its decremented value, or the new starting value specified in `it_virt_incr`, or (if it was a system tick) the value that was there beforehand. It seems that this could be optimised for system ticks.

15.1.3.5   Updating the profiling timer

There is also a so-called profiling interval timer, which counts all the time the process spends on the CPU, whether in user or kernel mode. It sends the `SIGPROF` signal. The `it_prof_incr` field in the `task_struct` contains the interval (measured in ticks) between signals from this timer; the corresponding `it_prof_value` field contains the current value of the timer. The function shown in Figure 15.7, from `kernel/timer.c`, updates and checks for the expiry of the profiling timer.

```
553  static inline void do_it_prof(struct task_struct *p)
554  {
555      unsigned long it_prof = p->it_prof_value;
556
557      if (it_prof) {
558          if (-it_prof == 0) {
559              it_prof = p->it_prof_incr;
560              send_sig(SIGPROF, p, 1);
561          }
562          p->it_prof_value = it_prof;
563      }
564  }
```

Figure 15.7   Checking for expiry of a profiling interval timer

553   the parameter is a pointer to the `task_struct` of the current process. There is no need to specify whether this is a user or kernel tick, as this function counts either of them.

555   this takes a local copy of the time remaining on the profiling timer.

557   if there is no profiling timer set (i.e. the `it_prof_value` field in the process descriptor is zero) then this code does nothing.

558–561   this block of code is executed only if, after decrementing the timer, the process has timed out.

559   this sets the local copy to the default starting value.

560   this sends the signal `SIGPROF` to the process [see Section 18.2.7 for the `send_sig()` function].

562   whether the process has timed out or not, the last line resets the `it_prof_value` field in the process descriptor to the value of the local `it_prof_incr`. This is either its decremented value or the new starting value specified in `it_virt_incr`.

15.1.4   Second-level timer interrupt handling

There is other, lower-priority, processing that has to be done periodically but not immediately the timer interrupt occurs nor as frequently as each timer tick. This is handled by the timer bottom half, as shown in Figure 15.8, from `kernel/timer.c`. Not surprisingly, this function is never called directly, but its address was passed to `init_bh()` (see Section 1.3.2). Then, each time software interrupts are processed, this function is executed. Basically, it handles all the second-level processing that needs to be done on a timer interrupt.

```
669  void timer_bh(void)
670  {
671      update_times();
672      run_timer_list();
673  }
```

Figure 15.8   Bottom half of the timer interrupt

671   this function, discussed in Section 15.2, handles all the processing related to the time-of-day clock and the calculating of statistics relative to system load.

672   this function, discussed in Section 15.3.4.1, checks for expired event timers, as described in Section 15.3.

15.2   Updating the time-of-day clock

When the timer bottom half is called, one of the things it has to do is update the time-of-day clock. This is one of the most complex parts of the whole kernel. The processing is organised as one root function, `update_times()`, which calls a whole chain of subfunctions. Each of these will be described in turn.

15.2.1   Delayed timer processing

The timer bottom half may not be run for some time after the first-level handler, depending on the load on the machine. In an extreme case, several timer ticks may occur before the bottom-half handler runs. So, first of all, it has to figure out how many timer interrupts have occurred since it last ran. The function to do this is shown in Figure 15.9, from `kernel/timer.c`.

```
642  unsigned long wall_jiffies;

647  rwlock_t xtime_lock = RW_LOCK_UNLOCKED;
648
649  static inline void update_times(void)
650  {
651      unsigned long ticks;

658      write_lock_irq(&xtime_lock);
659
660      ticks = jiffies - wall_jiffies;
661      if (ticks) {
662          wall_jiffies += ticks;
663          update_wall_time(ticks);
664      }
665      write_unlock_irq(&xtime_lock);
666      calc_load(ticks);
667  }
```

Figure 15.9   Handling lost ticks

642   the variable `wall_jiffies` is the value of `jiffies` at the most recent update of the time-of-day clock.

658–665   the function is going to update the global variable `xtime` (see Section 15.2.2.2). This read–write lock (defined at line 647) protects it from interference from other CPUs while doing so. The macros for manipulating interrupt safe read–write locks are from Section 12.8.1.

660 the global variable `jiffies` has been defined in Section 15.1.1. It maintains a count of ticks since the system was booted. The variable `wall_jiffies` is the value of `jiffies` at the most recent update of the time-of-day clock, so this line is calculating how many ticks have elapsed since the last update of wall time – it should be at least 1.

661 if no ticks have elapsed, then this code does nothing. This would be unusual, but a sound precaution.

662 this updates `wall_jiffies` to `jiffies`, as the time-of-day clock is about to be updated.

663 this calls `update_wall_time()` with the number of ticks that have elapsed since it was last called (see Section 15.2.2.2 for the function).

666 this calls `calc_load()` to update statistical information about the load on the system (see Section 15.2.5.1 for the function).

15.2.2 Maintaining the time of day

The time of day is maintained in seconds and microseconds in the variable `xtime` (see Section 15.2.2.2). This is known as wall time. This section will first examine the data structure used to maintain time in this format and then the function that actually updates it.

15.2.2.1 The `timeval` structure

Linux maintains time of day to a granularity of a microsecond. It is not stored in the usual year/month/day format but in the number of seconds that have elapsed since 1 January 1970. Figure 15.10, from `<linux/time.h>`, shows the data structure used to maintain time in this format.

```
88    struct timeval {
89        time_t        tv_sec;
90        suseconds_t   tv_usec;
91    };
```

Figure 15.10   The `timeval` structure

89 this is the seconds field.

90 this field contains a count of the number of microseconds into the last second.

15.2.2.2 Updating the time-of-day clock

The function shown in Figure 15.11, from `kernel/timer.c`, updates wall time one tick at a time. The parameter is a count of the number of timer interrupts that have occurred since it was last called, known as lost ticks. It is normally called with a value of 1, as it is not usual to lose more than one clock tick at a time.

```
35    volatile struct timeval xtime __attribute__ ((aligned (16)));

508   static void update_wall_time (unsigned long ticks)
509   {
510       do {
511           ticks-;
512           update_wall_time_one_tick();
513       } while (ticks);
514
515       if (xtime.tv_usec >= 1000000) {
516           xtime.tv_usec -= 1000000;
517           xtime.tv_sec++;
518           second_overflow();
519       }
520   }
```

Figure 15.11   Updating wall time

35   this variable xtime is used to maintain time of day for the system. The struct timeval has been defined in Section 15.2.2.1. It is aligned on a 16-byte boundary, so that the whole structure can be accessed in one read on a Pentium.

510–513   use of a loop looks inefficient; it might seem better to have a parameterised function, but ticks is usually just 1.

512   this function is described in Section 15.2.3.2. Its name describes what it does.

515–519   after updating the wall time, the microsecond counter is checked for overflow. If it has overflowed (after 1 000 000) then it is decremented by a million microseconds, and the seconds counter is incremented. This way, no microseconds are lost count of, even if the overflow is not noticed for some time after it has occurred.

518   the function second_overflow(), from Section 15.2.4.1, is called to handle leap seconds and speeding up and slowing down of the clock. Placed where it is in the code here, it is called once a second.

15.2.3   Updating the time-of-day clock by one tick

The timer interrupt is used, among other things, to update the computer's time-of-day clock. But, owing to small irregularities in the frequency of this interrupt, the clock may run fast or slow over a period of time. Sophisticated algorithms are used in an attempt to offset this.

Any attempt to correct a clock relies on access to an external time-source. This source updates kernel variables, which are then read by the functions described in this and the following sections. Before describing the function that updates the clock by the correct amount corresponding to one timer interrupt, we must first examine a number of literal constants used in that code.

15.2.3.1   Fixed-point values

In general, the various time quantities are stored as integer microseconds, but in some cases a greater precision is required, so time values are stored in fixed-point format. The high-order bits represent integer microseconds, the low-order bits represent binary fractions ($\frac{1}{2}$, $\frac{1}{4}$, etc.). It might seem more logical to store values in nanoseconds, but 32-bit fields are not big enough to store all the values involved.

Even with fixed point, it is not possible to have the fraction point in the same place for all values. Quite a lot of care was taken to ensure that variables never overflowed or under-flowed. This resulted in a number of different scaling factors being used. Figure 15.12, from <linux/timex.h>, shows the literal constants that control these fixed-point values.

```
92    #define SHIFT_KG 6

95    #define MAXTC 6

111   #define SHIFT_SCALE 22
112   #define SHIFT_UPDATE (SHIFT_KG + MAXTC)
113   #define SHIFT_USEC 16
114   #define FINEUSEC (1L << SHIFT_SCALE)
115
116   #define MAXPHASE 512000L
117   #define MAXFREQ (512L << SHIFT_USEC)
118   #define MAXTIME (200L << PPS_AVG)
119   #define MINSEC 16L

121   #define NTP_PHASE_LIMIT (MAXPHASE << 5)
```

Figure 15.12   Time constants and fraction points

92   this factor is used in damping the amount of adjustment made in the phase-lock loop shown in Section 15.2.4.4.

95   with SHIFT_KG from the previous line, MAXTC is used to establish the value of SHIFT_UPDATE on line 112.

111   this establishes the fraction point in the time_phase variable, used to accumulate the fractions of a microsecond by which the clock is ahead or behind. This is effectively an extension of the microsecond field of the clock. Its use is discussed in Section 15.2.3.2.

112   this establishes the fraction point in the time_offset variable (see Section 15.2.4.4), which represents the current amount that the clock is different from standard time. With the values currently hard coded into the kernel, SHIFT_UPDATE has a value of 12.

113   this establishes the fraction point in the time_freq and time_tolerance variables. The former is the current frequency of the particular oscillator (see Section 15.2.4.5), the latter is the maximum frequency tolerance see (Section 15.2.4.1).

114   this represents 1 microsecond in the scaled units used in time_phase (SHIFT_SCALE).

116   this is the maximum allowable discrepancy between the local clock and the external time source, in microseconds. It is initialised to 512 000 μs.

117   this is the maximum difference between the frequency of the local clock and that of the external source. It is initialised to 512, in SHIFT_USEC format.

118   this is the maximum error acceptable when a pulse-per-second signal is being received. PPS_AVG is an averaging constant (2).

119   this is the minimum interval between updates, in seconds.

121   if the NTP protocol is in use, this is the maximum discrepancy between NTP time and local time that can be handled. It is 32 times MAXPHASE, or 16 seconds.

15.2.3.2   *Advancing the time-of-day clock one tick*

The function shown in Figure 15.13, from kernel/timer.c, increments the microsecond field of the clock by one tick, taking into account any adjustment being implemented to slow down or speed up. It is called once for each timer interrupt.

```
38    int tickadj = 500/HZ ? : 1;

56    long time_phase;

59    long time_adj;                /* tick adjust (scaled 1/HZ) */

62    long time_adjust;
63    long time_adjust_step;

463   static void update_wall_time_one_tick(void)
464   {
465       if ( (time_adjust_step = time_adjust) != 0 ) {

475           if (time_adjust > tickadj)
476               time_adjust_step = tickadj;
477           else if (time_adjust < -tickadj)
478               time_adjust_step = -tickadj;

481           time_adjust -= time_adjust_step;
482       }
483       xtime.tv_usec += tick + time_adjust_step;

488       time_phase += time_adj;
489       if (time_phase <= -FINEUSEC) {
490           long ltemp = -time_phase >> SHIFT_SCALE;
491           time_phase += ltemp << SHIFT_SCALE;
492           xtime.tv_usec -= ltemp;
493       }
494       else if (time_phase >= FINEUSEC) {
```

```
495                    long ltemp = time_phase >> SHIFT_SCALE;
496                    time_phase -= ltemp << SHIFT_SCALE;
497                    xtime.tv_usec += ltemp;
498          }
499  }
```

Figure 15.13   Updating the clock by one tick

38   this is the maximum adjustment that can be made per tick when adjusting a clock that is running fast or slow. It is always measured in microseconds. If HZ is less than 500 (e.g. the standard HZ of 100), then 500/HZ is positive. In that case, the value of `tickadj` is 500/HZ, but, if HZ is greater than 500, then `tickadj` would be 0. In that case, it is set to a minimum of 1 microsecond.

56   this variable is used to accumulate the fractions of a microsecond by which the clock is ahead or behind, so it serves as an extension to the microsecond field of `xtime`. It is maintained in scaled microseconds, with `SHIFT_SCALE` (22 bits) establishing the fraction point.

59   this is the fraction of a microsecond by which the clock has to be advanced or retarded on each timer interrupt. Because it is a fraction, it is maintained in scaled format. It is updated by `second_overflow()` (see Sections 15.2.4.4 and 15.2.4.5).

62   this variable is only ever used if the timing system is connected to an external time source. In that case, the total adjustment (backward or forwards) in integer microseconds is written there at each synchronisation point. The `update_wall_time_one_tick()` function then reads this value, updates the clock by a certain amount, and reduces `time_adjust` by that amount.

63   this is the number of microseconds by which the time-of-day clock is to be adjusted on each tick, so it is a fraction of `time_adjust`. It used internally in the `update_wall_time_one_tick()` function.

465–482   if the clock is out of synchronisation with the external source, it is not updated all at once. Such large jumps (particularly backwards) could lead to inconsistencies in subsystems relying on time stamps (e.g. the file system). Instead, when updating the time-of-day clock on every tick, a very small adjustment is made to the number of microseconds to be added. This block of code calculates whether the clock needs such adjusting and, if so, by how much.

465   the `time_adjust` variable indicates whether the time needs adjusting and, if so, by how much. This is set by an external time source, so will be taken as a given here. If there is no external source, then it will still have its initialisation value of 0, and lines 475–482 are skipped. If `time_adjust` is not zero, this means that the clock is to be run faster (positive value) or slower (negative value). The `time_adjust_step` variable is the amount by which the microsecond field is to be incremented every tick.

475–478   any adjustment to the clock will not be made all at once but in a number of steps. The size of such a step is limited to be in the range -tickadj ... +tickadj. If the amount of the adjustment (`time_adjust`) is small enough, it can be done in one step. In any case, the size of the step will be in `time_adjust_step`.

475–476   if the amount of the increase (`time_adjust`) is greater than `tickadj`, then the step is reduced to `tickadj`, to limit the step to the range −tickadj ... +tickadj.

477–478   if the amount of the decrease if less than `-tickadj`, then the adjustment is limited to `-tickadj`.

481   the clock is going to be adjusted by one step at a time; this reduces the total adjustment required by the size of the step. The remaining adjustment (if any) will be handled next time.

483   the microsecond field of the time-of-day clock is incremented by a tick and adjusted one step (if necessary), so each update is 10 000 μs, with a possible adjustment of ± 5.

488–498   the addition of an integer number of microseconds to the time-of-day clock on each timer interrupt may not be absolutely accurate, and such inaccuracies can accumulate over time, so a further adjustment value, `time_adj` (in fractions of a microsecond), is calculated for each specific hardware timer. How this is done is described in Sections 15.2.4.4 and 15.2.4.5. Because the value in `time_adj` will be very small, it is maintained in a scaled format, shifted left 22 bits. Lines 488–498 are concerned with making these very fine adjustments to the microsecond field of the time-of-day clock. Each time the function is called, the `time_phase` variable is adjusted up or down by this small quantity `time_adj`. When `time_phase` eventually reaches 1 μs, the adjustment is transferred to the time-of-day clock.

489–493   this is for the case when the phase is negative (the clock needs to be slowed down), and its absolute value has become greater than one microsecond. FINEUSEC is 1 μs in scaled format, with the fraction point determined by SHIFT_SCALE.

490   this code is executed only if `time_phase` was negative, so `ltemp` is now `time_phase` shifted right 22 bits. This shifts out the fractional part, leaving only the integer part.

491   the integer part of `ltemp` is moved back to its correct position (filling the least significant 22 bits with 0). The whole line adds the (positive) integer part to the (negative) `time_phase`, so resulting in the (negative) fractional part in `time_phase`.

492   the microsecond field of the time-of-day clock is decremented by the value in `ltemp`, typically 1 μs.

494–497   this is for the case when the phase is positive, the clock is falling behind and has to be advanced slightly. The code is almost identical to that in lines 489–493.

15.2.4   Refining the accuracy of the clock

As described in Section 15.2.2.2, the time-of-day clock is updated on every timer tick, but if the system is connected to an external time-source, such as NTP, then there is further processing to be done. The external source writes values into variables; the `second_overflow()` function considered in this section, from `kernel/timer.c`, takes the values from these variables and feeds them into the normal timer processing. The function is called once per second, from `update_wall_time()`, given in Section 15.2.2.2.

Not only is the clock brought into line with the external source, but also an attempt is made to calculate the amount by which the clock is drifting (the 'phase') and compensate for that internally. The function also recognises when 'leap seconds' are signalled by the external source, and adjusts the clock accordingly.

15.2.4.1   Handling leap seconds

The first part of the second_overflow() function, shown in Figure 15.14, handles the
insertion or deletion of leap seconds, as directed by an external time-source.

```
48    int time_state = TIME_OK;
49    int time_status = STA_UNSYNC;

52    long time_tolerance = MAXFREQ;

54    long time_maxerror = NTP_PHASE_LIMIT;

348   static void second_overflow(void)
349   {
350        long ltemp;

353        time_maxerror += time_tolerance >> SHIFT_USEC;
354        if ( time_maxerror > NTP_PHASE_LIMIT) {
355             time_maxerror = NTP_PHASE_LIMIT;
356             time_status |= STA_UNSYNC;
357        }

368        switch (time_state) {
369
370        case TIME_OK:
371             if (time_status & STA_INS)
372                  time_state = TIME_INS;
373             else if (time_status & STA_DEL)
374                  time_state = TIME_DEL;
375             break;
376
377        case TIME_INS:
378             if (xtime.tv_sec % 86400 == 0) {
379                  xtime.tv_sec - ;
380                  time_state = TIME_OOP;
381                  printk(KERN_NOTICE "Clock: inserting leap
                                              second 23:59:60 UTC\n");
382             }
383             break;
384
385        case TIME_DEL:
386             if ((xtime.tv_sec + 1) % 86400 == 0) {
387                  xtime.tv_sec++;
388                  time_state = TIME_WAIT;
389                  printk(kern_notice "Clock: deleting leap
                                              second 23:59:59 UTC\n");
390             }
391             break;
392
```

```
393        case TIME_OOP:
394             time_state = TIME_WAIT;
395             break;
396
397        case TIME_WAIT:
398             if (!(time_status & (STA_INS | STA_DEL)))
399                  time_state = TIME_OK;
400        }
```

Figure 15.14   Code to handle leap seconds

48   this variable controls the leap-second management in this part of the function. It is initialised to TIME_OK. If an external time-source signals that a leap-second adjustment is to be made, that information is recorded in time_state until midnight arrives, at which time the change is made. All the possible states are described in Section 15.2.4.2.

49   the time_status variable is actually a bit field that controls the state machine used to insert or delete leap seconds and shows the status of the time-keeping system. The meaning of the different bits in this variable are described in Section 15.2.4.3.

52   the integer part of time_tolerance is in the high-order 16 bits, and the fraction in the low-order 16 bits. This variable represents the maximum frequency error that can be expected from the particular hardware timer and so is a property of the hardware. The initial value is MAXFREQ (512).

54   time_maxerror is the maximum allowable difference between the time indicated by the time-of-day clock and the external time-source, in microseconds. It is initialised to the maximum and reset at each synchronisation point. From Section 15.2.3.1, the NTP_PHASE_LIMIT is 16 s.

353–357 this first block of code is a sort of watchdog timer. Every time it is called it bumps up the time_maxerror field by the integer part of time_tolerance. This is assuming that the hardware clock is drifting off at its maximum rate. When eventually this causes it to overflow its limit of NTP_PHASE_LIMIT, it sets the STA_UNSYNC bit. This signals to other parts of the kernel that the clock is no longer guaranteed to be in synchronisation with the external time-source.

353   the time_maxerror variable was initialised to NTP_PHASE_LIMIT. On a standalone machine it retains that value. An external time-source would reset it at every update. The value of time_tolerance represents the maximum frequency error that can be expected from the particular hardware timer. The initial value of time_tolerance is 512. It is maintained in microseconds as a 16-bit integer, 16-bit fraction. Shifting it right converts it to integer microseconds, so that it can be added to time_maxerror, which is maintained in integer microseconds.

355–356 these two assignments are the initial values. The STA_UNSYNC bit at least is set, to indicate that the clock is out of synchronisation with the external time-source, so its accuracy cannot be relied on.

368–400 this block of code does leap-second processing, depending on the value in time_state (clock synchronisation status).

370–375 the value in `time_state` was `TIME_OK` after the last run of this function. That means that there is an external source and it is working. Now the function checks if the `time_status` variable has changed in the meantime.

371–374 if the `STA_INS` or `STA_DEL` flags have been set in `time_status` by the external source, this then changes `time_state` to `TIME_INS` or `TIME_DEL`, respectively. This will only be seen the next time around. If either of these bits are set at the end of the day, the system clock is adjusted one second.

377–382 if the value of `time_state` is `TIME_INS`, and it is midnight, then this decrements the seconds counter in `xtime` (i.e. inserts a leap second); `time_state` is set to be `TIME_OOP` (i.e. a leap second is being inserted). This will be seen the next time around.

385–390 if the value of `time_state` is `TIME_DEL`, and it is a second before midnight, then this increments the seconds counter in `xtime` (i.e. deletes a leap second); `time_state` is set to `TIME_WAIT` (i.e. leap-second processing has finished). This will be seen the next time around. Note that the printed message is timed a second before midnight. The system remains in the `TIME_WAIT` state until the `STA_INS` or `STA_DEL` bit is cleared by the external time source.

393–395 if the value is `TIME_OOP` (i.e. a leap second was inserted the last time), then `time_state` is set to `TIME_WAIT`. That leap second is now over, and leap-second processing has finished. The system remains in the `TIME_WAIT` state until the `STA_INS` or `STA_DEL` bit is cleared by the external time-source.

397–399 if the value is `TIME_WAIT` (i.e. a leap second was deleted or inserted at the previous midnight), then `time_state` is set to `TIME_OK`, unless, of course, either the `STA_INS` or `STA_DEL` flag is set in `time_status`, in which case the system remains in the `TIME_WAIT` state until this bit is cleared by the external time-source.

15.2.4.2 Possible clock states

The symbolic constants representing all the different possible values in the `time_state` variable introduced in Section 15.2.4.1 are shown in Figure 15.15, from `<linux/timex.h>`. These represent possible states of the leap-second mechanism.

```
239  #define TIME_OK     0
240  #define TIME_INS    1
241  #define TIME_DEL    2
242  #define TIME_OOP    3
243  #define TIME_WAIT   4
244  #define TIME_ERROR  5
245  #define TIME_BAD    TIME_ERROR
```

Figure 15.15   Possible clock states

239 here the clock is synchronised; there is no leap second being processed. This in the initial, and normal, state. For a standalone system, this is the only state.

240 when an external source signals that a leap second is to be inserted, `time_state` is changed to this value. The actual insertion is always done at the next midnight.

241   this is used if a leap second were to be deleted. This has never happened so far, nor is it likely to be used.

242   this is the value in `time_state` while the insertion of a leap second is actually in progress.

243   this is the value in `time_state` after the insertion or deletion of a leap second, until the external source removes the indication.

244   the clock is not synchronised, for whatever reason.

245   this alias for TIME_ERROR is not used on i386 systems.

15.2.4.3   Status codes

The `time_status` variable introduced in Section 15.2.4.1 is actually a bit field, with individual bits used to signify the status of different aspects of the time-of-day clock. The literal constants representing these status bits are shown in Figure 15.16, from `<linux/timex.h>`.

```
219  #define STA_FLL          0x0008
220
221  #define STA_INS          0x0010
222  #define STA_DEL          0x0020
223  #define STA_UNSYNC       0x0040

226  #define STA_PPSJITTER    0x0200
228  #define STA_PPSWANDER    0x0400
229  #define STA_PPSERROR     0x0800
```

Figure 15.16   Status codes

219   when set, bit 3 indicates that frequency-lock loop mode is selected; otherwise, the clock is to run in phase-lock loop mode. This is set by an external agency and is read by the code given in Section 15.2.4.4.

221–222   a leap second is to be inserted or deleted at the next midnight. These bits are set the previous day by an external source and cleared by it the day after.

223   the clock is out of synchronisation with the external source, so its accuracy cannot be relied on.

226–229   these bits are relevant only when a pulse per second (PPS) external source is connected.

226   when this is set, it indicates that this signal is being received.

227   when this is set, it indicates that the jitter limit on the PPS signal has been exceeded. Jitter describes short-term variations in the frequency of the signal.

228   when this is set, the wander limit on the PPS signal has been exceeded. Wander describes long-term variations in frequency.

229   this bit set indicates that some calibration error has been detected in the PPS signal.

15.2.4.4 Computing the phase adjustment

When we looked at updating the time-of-day clock on each tick (Section 15.2.3.2) we saw there were three components to the adjustment. First, there was the number of microseconds in a tick, typically 10 000. Then there was the adjustment to bring the local clock into line with universal time. This varies from 5 μs (maximum) to 0 μs (if not connected to an external source). The third element of the adjustment was `time_adj`. This is to compensate for the inherent inaccuracy of the local timer interrupt, which does not have an exact frequency of HZ.

The remainder of the `second_overflow()` function is concerned with determining the value of `time_adj`. There are two parts to this. The first, considered in this section, calculates the size of this `time_adj`, or how much to advance or retard the clock each tick. As the current function is run once per second, this computes the adjustment for the next second. The second adjustment is described in Section 15.2.4.5. It refines the previously calculated value, based on the frequency error of the local clock, as compared with a PPS signal.

Figure 15.17 shows how the initial estimate for the value of `time_adj` (in fractions of a microsecond) is calculated from the phase variable (`time_offset`) previously supplied by the external source.

```
50     long time_offset;
51     long time_constant = 2;

411        if (time_offset < 0) {
412            ltemp = -time_offset;
413            if (!(time_status & STA_FLL))
414                ltemp >>= SHIFT_KG + time_constant;
415            if (ltemp > (MAXPHASE /MINSEC) << SHIFT_UPDATE)
416                ltemp = (MAXPHASE /MINSEC) << SHIFT_UPDATE;
417            time_offset += ltemp;
418            time_adj = -ltemp <<
                        (SHIFT_SCALE - SHIFT_HZ - SHIFT_UPDATE);
419        } else {
420            ltemp = time_offset;
421            if (!(time_status & STA_FLL))
422                ltemp >>= SHIFT_KG + time_constant;
423            if (ltemp > (MAXPHASE /MINSEC) << SHIFT_UPDATE)
424                ltemp = (MAXPHASE /MINSEC) << SHIFT_UPDATE;
425            time_offset -= ltemp;
426            time_adj = ltemp << (SHIFT_SCALE - SHIFT_HZ -
                        SHIFT_UPDATE);
427        }
```

Figure 15.17 Computing the phase adjustment

50 sometimes a system is connected to an external time source that periodically supplies a very accurate time of day. If the value in the local `xtime` differs from this, the total amount of the adjustment needed is saved in `time_offset`. This value is then used to calculate an appropriate adjustment to the amount the clock is to be advanced each tick. SHIFT_UPDATE establishes the fraction point within this.

51   this time_constant is one factor in determining the damping of the phase-lock loop, at line 414.

411   there are two different possibilities, depending on whether time_offset is negative or positive.

412   this takes the absolute value of the total adjustment still to be made into the local temporary variable ltemp.

413–414 if the STA_FLL bit is not set in time_status, then the system is in phase-lock loop mode. In that case, the adjustment is reduced (divided) by a fixed factor of 8. This enforces small changes at a time, so it prevents the system oscillating between large positive and negative adjustments. With a value of 8, 1/256 of the time_offset value is taken. If the STA_FLL bit is set, then the system is in frequency-lock mode. In that case ltemp is not shifted at all, it is just the absolute value of time_offset. This is the effective difference between the two modes.

415–416 in either mode, the maximum phase adjustment for each second is limited so as not to make noticeably large adjustments all at once.

- MAXPHASE is the maximum phase error, defined as 512000 μs. This is the largest discrepancy between the system clock and the external source that can be handled.

- MINSEC is the minimum interval between updates from the external source, defined as 16 s.

- MAXPHASE/MINSEC is $32\,000$. This is the maximum phase adjustment that could be required per second, in microseconds.

- SHIFT_UPDATE is the time offset scale, defined as 12. This adjusts the fraction point, as required after the division.

417   this is effectively subtracting the newly calculated adjustment from time_offset. That is how much of the adjustment will be taken into account in the next second. It may leave a remainder to be dealt with on the next call to second_overflow(), a second later.

418   this line is converting from adjustment per second to adjustment per tick. The adjustment per second was in SHIFT_UPDATE format. The result is required in SHIFT_SCALE format. What is being done on the right-hand side here is:

```
ltemp = ltemp >> SHIFT_UPDATE;
ltemp = ltemp << SHIFT_SCALE;
ltemp = ltemp >> SHIFT_HZ;
```

but because the first operation would cause underflow, the three are amalgamated into one shift.

419–427 these lines deal with the case where the adjustment to be made is positive. The comments on lines 412–418 apply here.

15.2.4.5 Refining the phase adjustment

The final part of the `second_overflow()` function, shown in Figure 15.18, further refines the phase adjustment `time_adj`, this time based on frequency error.

```
57    long time_freq = ((1000000 + HZ/2) % HZ – HZ/2) << SHIFT_USEC;
```

```
436         pps_valid++;
437         if (pps_valid == PPS_VALID) { /* PPS signal lost */
438             pps_jitter = MAXTIME;
439             pps_stabil = MAXFREQ;
440             time_status &= ~(STA_PPSSIGNAL | STA_PPSJITTER|
441     STA_PPSWANDER | STA_PPSERROR);
442         }
443         ltemp = time_freq + pps_freq;
444         if (ltemp < 0)
445             time_adj -= -ltemp >>
446                 (SHIFT_USEC + SHIFT_HZ – SHIFT_SCALE);
447         else
448             time_adj += ltemp >>
449     (SHIFT_USEC + SHIFT_HZ – SHIFT_SCALE);
450
451 #if HZ == 100

455         if (time_adj < 0)
456             time_adj -= -time_adj >> 2 + (-time_adj >> 5);
457         else
458             time_adj += time_adj >> 2 + (time_adj >> 5);
459 #endif
460 }
```

Figure 15.18   Refining the phase adjustment

57   the current frequency of the particular CPU clock oscillator is in `time_freq`. The integer part in the high-order 16 bits and the fraction in the low-order 16 bits. On a standalone system, this remains fixed at its initial value. The standard hardware clock interrupts every 10 ms, so the standard HZ is 100. At this rate, `time_freq` is 1000050 MOD 100, or 10 000 μs. The extra HZ/2 is to compensate for any rounding errors that may result in conversion from decimal to binary by the compiler.

436–442   this block of code deals with the PPS external synchronisation signal.

436   this variable is declared and initialised in the code given in Section 15.2.4.6 as PPS_VALID. This is defined in <linux/timex.h> as

```
146 #define PPS_VALID 120 .
```

PPS_VALID is the maximum interval (in seconds) after which the PPS signal is considered invalid. Each time a PPS signal is received, it is reset to 0. On a standalone system it is irrelevant.

437 if after the increment the variable has reached PPS_VALID, this implies the PPS signal was lost so a number of fields connected with this are reset to their default values.

438 the jitter on the PPS signal is set to MAXTIME (800 μs; see Section 15.2.3.1).

439 the stability on the pulse per second signal is set to MAXFREQ (512; see Section 15.2.3.1).

440–441 various status bits are turned off in the time_status field, to indicate that the PPS signal has been lost. These bits have been defined in Section 15.2.4.3.

443–449 this is where the value of time_adj for the next second, which has just been calculated in Section 15.2.4.4, is further refined, based on the frequency error.

443 this is an estimate of the frequency. The standard frequency is in time_freq. An estimate of how much the clock is going off from the PPS signal each second has been written to pps_freq (see Section 15.2.4.6) by the PPS driver.

445–446 the absolute value of the estimate is shifted right SHIFT_USEC, which converts it to integer microseconds. It is then shifted right by SHIFT_HZ (see Section 15.2.4.7) to convert it from a 'per second' to a 'per tick' figure. Finally, it is shifted left SHIFT_SCALE, to bring the fraction point back to where it is in time_adj. Then time_adj is advanced or retarded by that amount.

448–449 these lines are for positive adjustments.

451–459 this block of code is for the very common (PC) case where HZ is 100, and not 128 as specified by SHIFT_HZ. In that case, adjusts by $\frac{1}{4}$ of time_adj (25%) and 1/32 of time_adj (3%) to compensate. It might seem that this adjustment should only have been made to ltemp, but time_adj was calculated in the code in Section 15.2.4.4 using the value of 128 for HZ, so the whole time_adj is correctly adjusted here.

15.2.4.6   *The pulse-per-second signal*

The variables shown in Figure 15.19, from kernel/time.c, are used in the implementation of the PPS signal.

```
188  long pps_jitter = MAXTIME;
189
190  long pps_freq;
191  long pps_stabil = MAXFREQ;
192
193  long pps_valid = PPS_VALID;
```

Figure 15.19   Pulse-per-second variables

188 this is the average discrepancy in the PPS signal, measured in microseconds. It is initialised to MAXTIME (800 μs; see Section 15.2.3.1). It is only ever changed by the PPS driver.

190 this is an estimate of the difference between the CPU clock frequency and the PPS frequency. It is maintained in SHIFT_USEC format, by the PPS driver. If there is no PPS signal, this would be 0.

191 this is the average frequency error in the PPS signal itself. It is maintained by the PPS driver in SHIFT_USEC format.

193 this is the PPS signal watchdog counter, to check for loss of PPS signal. It is incremented each second and when it reaches PPS_VALID the signal is presumed lost.

15.2.4.7 Macros for dividing by HZ

In several places in the calculations for updating time there is a requirement to divide by HZ (to get a 'per tick' figure). In order to optimise this division, it is in fact implemented by a right shift that divides by a power of two. The macros in Figure 15.20, from <linux/timex.h>, show how the literal constant SHIFT_HZ is defined for a range of HZ from 12 to 1536. This is accurate only for those values of HZ that are an even power of two.

```
63   #if HZ >= 12 && HZ < 24
64   # define SHIFT_HZ      4
65   #elif HZ >= 24 && HZ < 48
66   # define SHIFT_HZ      5
67   #elif HZ >= 48 && HZ < 96
68   # define SHIFT_HZ      6
69   #elif HZ >= 96 && HZ < 192
70   # define SHIFT_HZ      7
71   #elif HZ >= 192 && HZ < 384
72   # define SHIFT_HZ      8
73   #elif HZ >= 384 && HZ < 768
74   # define SHIFT_HZ      9
75   #elif HZ >= 768 && HZ < 1536
76   # define SHIFT_HZ      10
77   #else
78   # error You lose.
79   #endif
```

Figure 15.20 Macros for dividing by HZ

15.2.5 Generating load statistics

Another aspect of the processing done by the timer bottom half is to generate load statistics. The discussion here will consider: the main function called to do that, calc_load(); a subsidiary function called to determine the number of processes currently active; and some miscellaneous macros used in the calculations.

15.2.4.8 Calculating load

The function shown in Figure 15.21, from kernel/timer.c, records load averages at fixed intervals. It is called every time the timer bottom half runs. The parameter ticks is the number of ticks that have not been serviced since it was last called.

```
624  unsigned long avenrun[3];
```

```
625
626   static inline void calc_load(unsigned long ticks)
627   {
628         unsigned long          active_tasks;
629         static int      count = LOAD_FREQ;
630
631         count -= ticks;
632         if (count < 0) {
633             count += LOAD_FREQ;
634             active_tasks = count_active_tasks();
635             CALC_LOAD(avenrun[0], EXP_1, active_tasks);
636             CALC_LOAD(avenrun[1], EXP_5, active_tasks);
637             CALC_LOAD(avenrun[2], EXP_15, active_tasks);
638         }
639   }
```

Figure 15.21   Calculating load

624   this array contains the average number running (avenrun) over the last 1, 5, and 15 minutes. It is maintained by this function, and is available to other parts of the kernel.

628   this `unsigned long` will be used to hold the number of active processes, in fixed-point format.

629   this `static` variable controls the frequency (in ticks) at which the load is calculated. It is initialised as 5 s (see Section 15.2.5.3).

631–632   if 5 s of ticks have not expired, the function just returns. Note that `count` is `static`.

633   this adds another 5 s of ticks.

634   the `count_active_tasks()` function, from Section 15.2.5.2, returns the number of active tasks on the process list, in fixed-point format.

635–637   the macro `CALC_LOAD()` and its parameters are discussed in Section 15.2.5.3. Basically, it maintains a running average of the load. It writes values into `avenrun[]` but does not return a value itself. The `avenrun[]` array is used in various places outside the kernel, to report status. The different instantiations of the macro, on lines 635, 636, and 637, update statistics for the last 1, 5, and 15 minutes, respectively.

15.2.5.2   *Counting the number of active processes*

In this context, an active process is one in the TASK_RUNNING or TASK_UNINTERRUPTIBLE state. The function shown in Figure 15.22, from `kernel/timer.c`, returns the number of such active processes, in fixed-point format.

```
603   static unsigned long count_active_tasks(void)
604   {
605         struct task_struct *p;
606         unsigned long nr = 0;
607
```

```
608        read_lock(&tasklist_lock);
609        for_each_task(p) {
610        if ((p->state == TASK_RUNNING ||
611  p->state == TASK_UNINTERRUPTIBLE))))
612              nr += FIXED_1;
613        }
614        read_unlock(&tasklist_lock);
615        return nr;
616  }
```

Figure 15.22 Counting the number of active tasks

608–614 the process takes out a readlock on the process list, so that no other process can change that list while this process is reading it. The `read_lock()` macro is described in Section 5.6 for the uniprocessor case and in Section 5.7.2.1 for the multiprocessor case; the lock itself is defined in Section 7.2.2.

609–613 then, each entry in the process list is checked. The `for_each task()` macro is described in Section 3.1.3.

610–611 however, only those processes in the running or uninterruptible state are counted. A process on a long-term wait is not considered.

612 the running count is incremented by FIXED_1, as defined in Section 15.2.5.3. It represents 1.0 in fixed-point format, with 11 bits of precision.

614 see Section 5.7.2.4 for the `read_unlock()` macro.

15.2.5.3   Updating the running average of load

There are a number of constants and macros used in the calculation of load average, which are shown in Figure 15.23, from `<linux/sched.h>`.

```
60   #define FSHIFT       11
61   #define FIXED_1      (1<<FSHIFT)
62   #define LOAD_FREQ    (5*HZ)
63   #define EXP_1        1884
64   #define EXP_5        2014
65   #define EXP_15       2037
66
67   #define CALC_LOAD(load,exp,n)      \
68         load *= exp;                 \
69         load += n*(FIXED_1-exp);     \
70         load >>= FSHIFT;
71
72   #define CT_TO_SECS(x)    ((x) / HZ)
73   #define CT_TO_USECS(x)   (((x) % HZ) * 1000000/HZ)
```

Figure 15.23 Updating the running average of load

60   this is the number of bits of precision – it fixes the fraction point.

61   this represents 1.0 in fixed-point format, scaled by `FSHIFT`.

62   this controls the frequency (in ticks) at which the load is calculated. For `HZ` of 100, this is 500 ticks, or 5 s, so the load is only calculated every 5 s.

63   this factor is used when calculating averages over 1 minute. It represents the fraction 55/60 in `FSHIFT` format.

64   this factor is used when calculating averages over 5 minutes. It represents the fraction 295/300 in `FSHIFT` format.

65   this factor is used when calculating averages over 15 minutes. It represents the fraction 895/900 in `FSHIFT` format.

67   this macro calculates a running average. The first parameter is the field to be updated. It is usually an element of the array `avenrun[]`. The second parameter specifies the time scale over which the average is to be calculated – either 1, 5, or 15 minutes. It is actually the fraction of the time scale represented by previous updates: either 55/60 [(5 s)/(60 s)], 295/300 [(5 s)/(300 s)], or 895/900 [(5 s)/(900 s)]. The third parameter is the current number of active processes.

68   this takes the previous value for `load` and scales it down appropriately. For example, if the load is to be calculated over 12 samples, then 11/12 of the previous value is taken. Note that as a result of the multiplication, the fraction point is now at 22. This leaves only 10 bits for the integer value.

69   `FIXED_1` is 1.0 in fixed point; so, continuing the example, `FIXED_1` – exp is 1/12. n * (`FIXED_1` – exp) is 1/12 of the current load. This is added to the 11/12 of the previous value, to give the new load average. The fraction points on both sides of the assignment are at 22, so they are compatible.

70   the new value is shifted right `FSHIFT` (11) bits, to normalise it.

72   this macro converts ticks to integer seconds, discarding any remainder.

73   this macro converts ticks to microseconds, discarding any integer seconds. The `MOD` operation (x) % HZ gives the remainder, in ticks. 1000000/HZ is the number of microseconds in a tick.

15.3   Event timers

Linux provides a facility, known as event timers, that makes it possible to specify that a particular function is to be run at some predetermined time in the future. There are three aspects to the management of such event timers. First, there are the data structures that keep track of the functions and the time at which to run them. Second, there are the group of functions for maintaining these data structures. Last, there is a routine called periodically to check these lists and run any function whose time has come.

15.3.1   Event timer data structures

Each timer is represented by a `struct timer_list` which specifies the function and when it is to be run. Then Linux uses what at first sight might seem an unusual data structure to keep track of these structures. It has headers for 512 different lists, sorted on the order in which the timer is to expire. These are divided into five different groups, known as vectors. The first one, the root vector, contains headers for 256 different lists. This is the 'ready-use' vector; it maintains timers with a granularity of one tick and is replenished every 256 ticks. The other four, for successively longer expiry times, each has headers for 64 lists. These maintain timers with increasingly coarser granularity. Timers percolate down through these lists. As they do, they are sorted by increasingly finer granularity; by the time they have reached list 1 (the root vector) they are maintained with a granularity of one tick. The various data structures making up this complex will be examined first (Sections 15.3.1.1 and 15.3.1.2); then the function that initialises the whole structure will be discussed (Section 15.3.1.3).

15.3.1.1   *The* `timer_list` *structure*

Each request to execute a function in the future, known as a timer, is encapsulated in a `struct timer_list`, as shown in Figure 15.24, from `<linux/timer.h>`. These are created dynamically, as required, and destroyed after they have expired.

```
16    struct timer_list {
17        struct list_head list;
18        unsigned long expires;
19        unsigned long data;
20        void (*function)(unsigned long);
21    };
```

Figure 15.24   The `timer_list` structure

17   timers are maintained by using the standard Linux list-handling functions (see Section 4.3). This field contains the backward and forward links.

18   this is the time (in `jiffies`) at which the timer is to expire.

19   this field contains (optional) data which will be passed to the function when it is called. By parameterising the function in this way, a common timeout function can be used in different situations. This field distinguishes between them.

20   this is a pointer to the function to be run when the timer expires. Note that it must take an `unsigned long` as parameter, in accordance with the declaration of `data` on the previous line. The pointer is declared as `void`, as the type of the function cannot be known in advance.

15.3.1.2   *The timer lists*

Figure 15.25, from `kernel/timer.c`, shows the various definitions and declarations that underlie the timer list in Linux.

```
78    #define TVN_BITS 6
79    #define TVR_BITS 8
80    #define TVN_SIZE (1 << TVN_BITS)
81    #define TVR_SIZE (1 << TVR_BITS)
82    #define TVN_MASK (TVN_SIZE - 1)
83    #define TVR_MASK (TVR_SIZE - 1)
84
85    struct timer_vec {
86        int index;
87        struct list_head vec[TVN_SIZE];
88    };
89
90    struct timer_vec_root {
91        int index;
92        struct list_head vec[TVR_SIZE];
93    };
94
95    static struct timer_vec tv5;
96    static struct timer_vec tv4;
97    static struct timer_vec tv3;
98    static struct timer_vec tv2;
99    static struct timer_vec_root tv1;
100
101   static struct timer_vec * const tvecs[] = {
102       (struct timer_vec *)&tv1, &tv2, &tv3, &tv4, &tv5
103   };
104
105   #define NOOF_TVECS (sizeof(tvecs) / sizeof(tvecs[0]))
```

Figure 15.25   Timer data structures

78–83   in these lines, TVR denotes the root timer vector; TVN denotes one of the four normal vectors.

78   the number of headers in a normal timer vector is 64; each of these can be identified with 6 bits.

79   the number of headers in the root timer vector is 256; each of these can be identified with 8 bits.

80   bits vacated by the shift are zero-filled, so TVN_SIZE is 0100 0000, or 64 decimal.

81   similarly, TVR_SIZE is 1 0000, or 256 decimal.

82   this literal constant is 0011 1111. It will be used to mask off the TVN bits.

83   this literal constant is 1111 1111. It will be used to mask off the TVR bits.

85–88   this is the data structure representing a normal timer vector.

86   at any given time the `index` field indicates the `list_head` in the array that is to be processed next.

87   there are headers for 64 lists in this array.

90–93   this is the data structure representing the root timer vector.

92   there are headers for 256 lists in this array. Figure 15.26 attempts to illustrate such a vector, with its dependent lists of struct timer_struct.

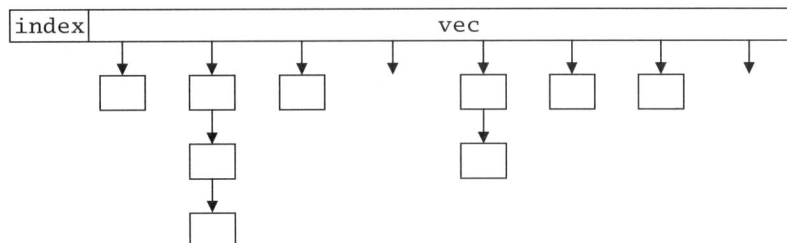

Figure 15.26   A timer_vec structure

95–99   this declares timer vectors 1 to 5. The root timer vector tv1 has a 256-element array of struct list_head; the other four each have a 64-element array.

101–103   the root of all of this is tvecs[], which is statically initialised to point to the five structures just declared in the previous lines. Figure 15.27 attempts to illustrate the situation at this stage.

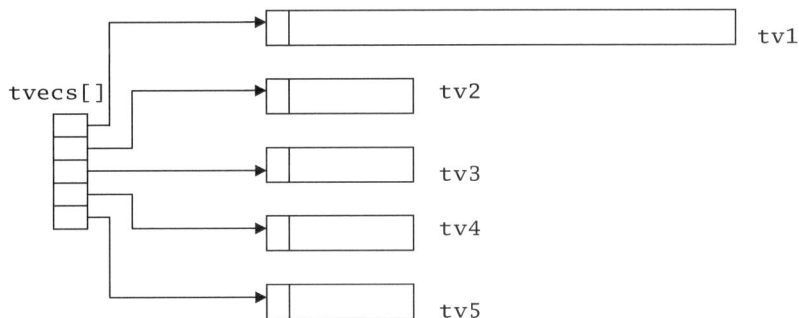

Figure 15.27   Timer lists

105   this macro dynamically calculates the number of different types of timer lists available. Dividing the size of the whole array by the size of one entry should give the number of entries (normally 5).

15.3.1.3   Initialising the timer lists

The previous section showed how the static arrangement of list heads is declared. The function shown in Figure 15.28, from kernel/timer.c, initialises each element in all the vectors. It is called from sched_init() (see Section 1.3.2).

```
107  void init_timervecs (void)
108  {
109       int i;
110
111       for (i = 0; i < TVN_SIZE; i++) {
112            INIT_LIST_HEAD(tv5.vec + i);
113            INIT_LIST_HEAD(tv4.vec + i);
114            INIT_LIST_HEAD(tv3.vec + i);
115            INIT_LIST_HEAD(tv2.vec + i);
116       }
117       for (i = 0; i < TVR_SIZE; i++)
118            INIT_LIST_HEAD(tv1.vec + i);
119  }
```

Figure 15.28   Initialising the timer vectors

111–116   the `tv2` to `tv5` timer vectors each have `TVN_SIZE` (64) elements. These are initialised together.

112   the `INIT_LIST_HEAD()` macro is from Section 4.3.1.

117–118   the `tv1` structure has `TVR_SIZE` (256) elements; it is initialised separately.

15.3.2   Timer management

The functions described in this section insert, modify, and delete elements in these timer lists. They are used heavily by all sorts of drivers.

15.3.2.1   *Initialising a* `timer_list` *structure*

In order to indicate when a particular `timer_list` structure is not inserted into the tree, its pointer fields are set to NULL. The function to do this, from `<linux/timer.h>`, is shown in Figure 15.29.

```
46   static inline void init_timer(struct timer_list * timer)
47   {
48        timer->list.next = timer->list.prev = NULL;
49   }
```

Figure 15.29   Initialising a `timer_list` structure

15.3.2.2   *Adding a timer to the list*

All functions that use timers have a requirement to insert structures on the timer list. The function shown in Figure 15.30, from `kernel/timer.c`, is a wrapper that takes out mutual exclusion, before putting a `timer_list` structure on the appropriate timer list.

```
164  spinlock_t timerlist_lock = SPIN_LOCK_UNLOCKED;

177  void add_timer(struct timer_list *timer)
```

```
178  {
179        unsigned long flags;
180
181        spin_lock_irqsave(&timerlist_lock, flags);
182        if (timer_pending(timer))
183            goto bug;
184        internal_add_timer(timer);
185        spin_unlock_irqrestore(&timerlist_lock, flags);
186        return;
187  bug:
188        spin_unlock_irqrestore(&timerlist_lock, flags);
189        printk("bug: kernel timer added twice at %p.\n",
190        __builtin_return_address(0));
191  }
```

Figure 15.30   Adding a timer to the list

181–185   the function does all its work under the protection of the `timerlist_lock` spinlock, declared on line 164. The interrupt-safe spinlock macros are from Section 12.8.1.

182–183   the function checks that the timer has not been inserted already. The `timer_pending()` function is from Section 15.3.2.7. If it is already on the list, then there is something wrong.

184   it is not already on the list, then it is inserted (see Section 15.3.2.4 for the function).

187   if the `timer_list` structure supplied as a parameter is already on a list, then this error-handling code is executed.

188   this gives back the spinlock.

189   an error message is printed, giving the return address on the stack, that is, the address of the function that called this, with an erroneous parameter.

15.3.2.3   *Changing the value of a timer*

Sometimes, after a timer has been entered on a list, it becomes necessary to change its expiry time. The function shown in Figure 15.31, from `kernel/timer.c`, changes the value of a timer specified by the `timer` parameter to be the value specified by the parameter `expires`. It removes the timer from its present location in the list and inserts it at the place appropriate to its new value.

```
201  int mod_timer(struct timer_list *timer, unsigned long expires)
202  {
203        int ret;
204        unsigned long flags;
205
206        spin_lock_irqsave(&timerlist_lock, flags);
207        timer->expires = expires;
208        ret = detach_timer(timer);
```

```
209        internal_add_timer(timer);
210        spin_unlock_irqrestore(&timerlist_lock, flags);
211        return ret;
212  }
```

Figure 15.31   Changing the value of a timer

206–210   all operations on the timer list are carried out under the protection of the `timerlist_lock` spinlock.

207   this it changes the appropriate field in the `timer_list` structure to reflect the new expiry time.

208   this detaches the timer from the list (see Section 15.3.2.6). The return value (1 for success, 0 for failure) is not checked here.

209   the time is then added at the new (appropriate) place in the list (see Section 15.3.2.4). This is done even if it was not possible to detach the timer on the previous line.

210   this releases the spinlock.

211   the function returns the value it got from `detach_timer()`, which should have been 1 for success, 0 for failure (if there was no such structure on the list).

15.3.2.4 *Worker function to add a timer to the appropriate list*

A timer is put on one of five different lists, depending on the timeout requested. The function shown in Figure 15.32, from `kernel/timer.c`, determines which list is appropriate and inserts the structure on that list. It is called from three different functions – `add_timer()`, `mod_timer()`, and `cascade_timers()` – all described in this section. In each case the `timerlist_lock` spinlock is held by the caller.

```
121  static unsigned long timer_jiffies;
122
123  static inline void internal_add_timer(struct timer_list *timer)
124  {

128        unsigned long expires = timer->expires;
129        unsigned long idx = expires - timer_jiffies;
130        struct list_head * vec
131
132        if (idx < TVR_SIZE) {
133             int i = expires & TVR_MASK;
134             vec = tv1.vec + i;
135        } else if (idx < 1 << (TVR_BITS + TVN_BITS)) {
136             int i = (expires >> TVR_BITS) & TVN_MASK;
137             vec = tv2.vec + i;
138        } else if (idx < 1 << (TVR_BITS + 2 * TVN_BITS)) {
139             int i = (expires >> (TVR_BITS + TVN_BITS)) & TVN_MASK;
140             vec = tv3.vec + i;
```

```
141          } else if (idx < 1 << (TVR_BITS + 3 * TVN_BITS)) {
142               int i = (expires >> (TVR_BITS + 2 * TVN_BITS)) & TVN_MASK;
143               vec = tv4.vec + i;
144          } else if ((signed long) idx < 0) {

148               vec = tv1.vec + tv1.index;
149          } else if (idx <= 0xffffffffUL) {
150               int i = (expires >> (TVR_BITS + 3 * TVN_BITS)) & TVN_MASK;
151               vec = tv5.vec + i;
152          } else {

154               INIT_LIST_HEAD(&timer->list);
155               return;
156          }
160          list_add(&timer->list, vec->prev);
161 }
```

Figure 15.32   Selecting the appropriate list for the timer request

121   the `timer_jiffies` variable is a copy of the current time (jiffies) when `run_timer_list()` last ran.

128   this line takes a local copy of the time at which this timer is to expire.

129   the `timer_jiffies` variable was declared on line 121. It is a copy of the current time (jiffies) when `run_timer_list()` last ran. When it next runs, it will begin checking for expired timers from that time, so the interval left on this new timer which is being inserted (`idx`) is calculated from then.

132   `TVR_SIZE` is defined as 256 (see Section 15.3.1.2). If there are less than that many ticks in the interval, then it is inserted on timer list 1.

133   `TVR_MASK` is 1111 1111 (see Section 15.3.1.2) so this is masking out all but the low-order 8 bits of `expires`. These are sufficient to identify uniquely which of the 256 lists in `tv1` on which to insert the timer.

134   the list chosen for this particular `timer_list` structure is headed from entry i in `tv1`; we then go to line 160.

135   TVR_BITS + TVN_BITS = 8 + 6, so 1 << 14 is 100 0000 0000 0000 or 0x4000, or 16k. If the interval is greater than 256 but still less than 16k ticks then timer list 2 is selected.

136   TVR_BITS is 8, so this divides `expires` by 256. This vector does not have a list for every tick, as `tv1` does. Rather, each list groups together timers that will expire over a range of 256 ticks then masks out all but the low-order 6 bits. These are sufficient to identify uniquely which of the 64 lists in `tv2` on which to insert the timer.

137   this selects the list headed from i in `tv2`. Each list in `tv2` has timers with a range of 256 ticks in their `expires` field; we then go to line 160.

138 shifting 1 left 20 bits gives 0x 100 000 or 1M. If the interval is between 16k and 1M ticks, then the timer is inserted on tv2.

139 this divides expires by 16k and masks off all but the low-order 6 bits. Each list in this vector groups together timers that will expire over a range of 16k ticks.

140 this selects the list headed from i in tv3; we then go to line 160.

141–143 if the interval is between 1M and 64M ticks, then this divides expires by 1M and selects the list headed by i in tv4; we then go to line 160.

144 this condition can happen if a timer is set to go off in the past. In such a case, vec will have been assigned successive values all the way down, and this is the definitive value. It seems that this test should have come first.

148 the list selected is the next one to expire, the list in tv1 pointed to by index; we then go to line 160.

149 if the interval fits in 32 bits, then this divides expires by 64M and selects the list headed by i in tv5; we then go to 160.

152 this can happen only on architectures with 64-bit jiffies, and so is not relevant to a PC. INIT_LIST_HEAD() is in Section 4.3.1. It initialises the struct timer_list pointing to itself, and returns.

160 finally, this inserts the timer at the end of the selected list; vec->prev points to the end of the list. The list_add() function is given in Section 4.3.2.

15.3.2.5 Deleting a timer from the list

When a timer expires, the kernel removes it from the list, but it can also be removed before it expires. The function shown in Figure 15.33, from kernel/timer.c, is used in both cases.

```
214  int del_timer(struct timer_list * timer)
215  {
216      int ret;
217      unsigned long flags;
218
219      spin_lock_irqsave(&timerlist_lock, flags);
220      ret = detach_timer(timer);
221      timer->list.next = timer->list.prev = NULL;
222      spin_unlock_irqrestore(&timerlist_lock, flags);
223      return ret;
224  }
```

Figure 15.33 Deleting a timer from the list

219–222 as with all functions that operate on the timer list, this takes out a spinlock for mutual exclusion.

220   it detaches the timer from the list (see Section 15.3.2.6). The return value is not checked at this
       stage but is passed back to the caller at line 223.

221   this sets the links in the timer_list structure to NULL, to indicate that the timer is no longer
       on any list. The data structure itself was allocated by the caller, and the caller should deallocate it
       after this function returns.

223   this returns the success or failure from detach_timer(), which should have been 1 for
       success, 0 for failure (if there were no such structure on the list).

15.3.2.6 Worker function to remove a timer from a list

The function shown in Figure 15.34, from kernel/timer.c, actually unlinks a timer
from a list. It is called from mod_timer() and del_timer() (see Sections 15.3.2.3 and
15.3.2.5). In both cases the caller is holding a spinlock on the timer list.

```
193  static inline int detach_timer(struct timer_list *timer)
194  {
195      if (!timer_pending(timer))
196          return 0;
197      list_del(&timer->list);
198      return 1;
199  }
```

Figure 15.34   Removing a timer from a list

195–196   if the timer_list structure it is passed is not linked onto some list then the function returns 0.
          The function is discussed in Section 15.3.2.7.

197   otherwise, it removes the entry, using list_del() from Section 4.3.3.

198   the function returns 1 to indicate a successful detachment.

15.3.2.7 Checking if a timer is on a list

In order to check whether a particular timer_list structure is inserted into the tvecs[]
tree or not, the function shown in Figure 15.35, from kernel/timer.c, is supplied. It
relies on the fact that, at initialisation, and when it is removed from the tree, the pointer
fields in a struct timer_list are set to NULL. This property is then used to decide
whether it is on a list or not.

```
51  static inline int timer_pending (const struct timer_list *timer)
52  {
53      return timer->list.next != NULL;
54  }
```

Figure 15.35   Checking if a timer is on a list

15.3.3   Sleeping for a fixed length of time

Sometimes a process may want to put itself to sleep for a fixed length of time. Linux uses a standard timer for that and also provides a skeleton function for the timer to run, which merely wakes up the process.

15.3.3.1   *Scheduling a timeout*

The function shown in Figure 15.36, from `kernel/sched.h`, puts a process to sleep for the number of ticks specified by the parameter `timeout`. It is called from many places in the kernel, mostly from drivers.

```
410  signed long schedule_timeout(signed long timeout)
411  {
412       struct timer_list timer;
413       unsigned long expire;
414
415       switch (timeout)
416       {
417       case MAX_SCHEDULE_TIMEOUT:

425           schedule();
426           goto out;
427       default:

435           if (timeout < 0)
436           {
437               printk(KERN_ERR "schedule_timeout: wrong timeout "
438       "value %lx from %p\n", timeout,
439       __builtin_return_address(0));
440               current->state = TASK_RUNNING;
441               goto out;
442           }
443       }
444
445       expire = timeout + jiffies;
446
447       init_timer(&timer);
448       timer.expires = expire;
449       timer.data = (unsigned long) current;
450       timer.function = process_timeout;
451
452       add_timer(&timer);
453       schedule();
454       del_timer_sync(&timer);
455
456       timeout = expire - jiffies;
457
458  out:
```

```
459        return timeout < 0 ? 0 : timeout;
460  }
```

Figure 15.36   Scheduling a timeout

415–443   this switch statement is meant to filter out invalid values.

417–426   if the timeout is MAX_SCHEDULE_TIMEOUT, then the process wants to sleep for an indefinite period of time. The symbolic constant is defined in <linux/sched.h> as

```
154  #define MAX_SCHEDULE_TIMEOUT LONG_MAX .
```

This, in turn, is defined in <linux/kernel.h> as

```
22   #define LONG_MAX ((long)(~0UL >> 1)) .
```

Because unsigned, the shifted value is zero-filled on the left. The actual value is unimportant, however; it is merely a sentinel value. No attempt will be made to enter this request on any timer queue. Normally, a process would put itself into one of the wait states before calling schedule_timeout() with this parameter.

426   the process is not woken up at any specified time but by some other agent changing its state and putting it on the runqueue. When it is next scheduled to run it returns the timeout as specified by the caller (MAX_SCHEDULE_TIMEOUT).

427–442   the only other problem could be a negative timeout, which is invalid.

437–439   the printk() tells that something has gone wrong, giving the value and the address of the caller.

440   the process is not going to be put to sleep in this case; it continues to run and handle the error.

441   line 459 arranges to return a 0 retval in this case.

445   after the initial paranoia, the function really begins here. It calculates when the timeout should occur by adding the length of the timeout to the current time (both in ticks). The jiffies counter was described in Section 15.1.1.

447   then it initialises the timer_list structure declared at line 412. The init_timer() function is from Section 15.3.2.1.

448–450   these lines populate the timer_list structure. The data field is the address of the task_struct of the current process, cast to be unsigned long. The process_timeout() function is described in Section 15.3.3.2.

452   this adds the timer at the appropriate place in the list. The add_timer() function is described in Section 15.3.2.2.

453   this calls the scheduler to give up control of the CPU.

454   after waking up the process, the function removes the `timer_list` structure from the list. The function is described in Section 15.3.2.5.

456   this line calculates any time left on the timer after it has woken up. This could happen if the process woke up for some other reason, before the timer expired.

459   if the value is less than 0, it returns 0 instead. Positive values are returned unchanged.

15.3.3.2 Waking up after a timeout

Because Linux uses its standard timers to put a process to sleep for a fixed time, it must provide a function to be executed when that timer expires. This function, from `kernel/sched.c`, is shown in Figure 15.37.

```
377  static void process_timeout(unsigned long __data)
378  {
379        struct task_struct * p = (struct task_struct *) __data;
380
381        wake_up_process(p);
382  }
```

Figure 15.37   Waking up after a timeout

379   the function is only a wrapper, supplying this line to convert the parameter from `unsigned long` to a pointer to a `struct task_struct`.

381   this function was described in Section 4.7.5.

15.3.3.3 Handling and resetting the interval timer

A process can set up an interval timer, which will send it a `SIGALRM` signal at fixed intervals. The data structures for this are actually part of the `task_struct` of the process (see Section 2.3). It is implemented as an entry on the standard timer list. The function executed when that timer expires is shown in Figure 15.38, from `kernel/itimer.c`.

```
93   void it_real_fn(unsigned long __data)
94   {
95         struct task_struct * p = (struct task_struct *) __data;
96         unsigned long interval;
97
98         send_sig(SIGALRM, p, 1);
99         interval = p->it_real_incr;
100        if (interval) {
101             if (interval > (unsigned long) LONG_MAX)
102                   interval = LONG_MAX;
103             p->real_timer.expires = jiffies + interval;
104             add_timer(&p->real_timer);
```

```
105        }
106  }
```

Figure 15.38 Handling and resetting the interval timer

93 the parameter is a pointer to the `task_struct` of the process to which this interval timer belongs.

98 this sends a `SIGALRM` to the process, using the function from Section 18.2.7.

99 this gets, from the `task_struct` of the relevant process, the interval after which the timer should expire again.

100–105 if the interval is 0, nothing further is done.

101–102 a ceiling is put on the interval, defined in <`linux/kernel.h`> as

```
22   #define LONG_MAX ((long)(~0UL >> 1)).
```

The shifted value is zero-filled on the left.

103 this sets the `expires` field of the `struct timer_list` in the `task_struct` (see Section 2.3) to the time at which the timer should expire.

104 this inserts it into the timer structure, using the function from Section 15.3.2.2.

15.3.4 Handling expired timers

The previous section examined the functions that maintain the timer lists; this section goes on to consider how timers are taken off the list at the appropriate time and executed. There are two parts to this. First, all the timers on the list corresponding to the current jiffie must be executed. But every so often, when one of the four lower groups of timer lists is empty, a list must be moved down from the next highest group and partitioned over the empty spaces.

15.3.4.1 Executing expired timers

The function shown in Figure 15.39, from `kernel/timer.c`, checks the list of timers for any that have expired – for which the time is less than `jiffies` – and executes the appropriate function. It is called by the timer bottom half (see Section 15.1.4).

```
289  static inline void run_timer_list(void)
290  {
291      spin_lock_irq(&timerlist_lock);
292      while ((long)(jiffies - timer_jiffies) >= 0) {
293          struct list_head *head, *curr;
294          if (!tv1.index) {
```

```
295                     int n = 1;
296                     do {
297                     cascade_timers(tvecs[n]);
298                     } while (tvecs[n]->index == 1 && ++n < NOOF_TVECS);
299             }
300   repeat:
301             head = tv1.vec + tv1.index;
302             curr = head->next;
303             if (curr != head) {
304                 struct timer_list *timer;
305                 void (*fn)(unsigned long);
306                 unsigned long data;
307
308                 timer = list_entry(curr, struct timer_list, list);
309                 fn = timer->function;
310                 data = timer->data;
311
312                 detach_timer(timer);
313                 timer->list.next = timer->list.prev = NULL;
314                 timer_enter(timer);
315                 spin_unlock_irq(&timerlist_lock);
316                 fn(data);
317                 spin_lock_irq(&timerlist_lock);
318                 timer_exit()
319                 goto repeat;
320             }
321             ++timer_jiffies;
322             tv1.index = (tv1.index + 1) & TVR_MASK;
323         }
324     spin_unlock_irq(&timerlist_lock);
325  }
```

Figure 15.39 Executing expired timers

291–324 this spinlock on the timer list guarantees mutual exclusion. Another process should not be able to change the list while this function is manipulating it. The lock is, however, released and reacquired between lines 315–317, while the function specified by an expired timer is actually being executed.

292–323 it is possible that more than one jiffie could have elapsed since this function last ran, so this loop is executed once per jiffie. To implement this, the kernel maintains the time in jiffies when the function last ran, in timer_jiffies. Over the interval since it last ran, this loop checks each jiffie for an expired timer.

294–299 this code is executed only if the tv1.index field is 0; that is, all the lists headed from tv1 have already been executed and are empty.

297 the function calls cascade_timers() (Section 15.3.4.2) for the next group up. Note that, owing to zero-based arrays in C, `tvecs[1]` is pointing to `tv2`. This moves the next list from `tv2` and distributes it over the 256 lists of `tv1`.

298 this has exhausted the higher group, its `index` field will be back to 1. The NOOF_TVECS macro was described in Section 15.3.1.2. It evaluates to the number of groups of timer lists in the system, so this loop will move timers down the lists to fill any empty (expired) lower lists.

301 at this stage the `tv1` group is certainly valid. This line sets up a pointer to the head of the next list to be processed within that group.

302 this gets a pointer to the next entry on that next list. The first time around, this next entry will be the first entry, but this loop may be executed several times if more than one timer is set to expire at the same time.

303–320 this block of code is executed if there is a valid entry on that next list. Because it is a circular list, `curr` will be equal to `head` if the list is empty, or when the last entry has been processed.

308–310 this gets pointers to the next timer on the list, to its function, and to its data. The `list_entry()` macro was described in Section 4.3.4.3. It converts a pointer to the `list_head` link, to a pointer to the actual structure of which it is a linked list (e.g. `timer_list`).

312 this detaches the timer from the list (see Section 15.3.2.6 for the function).

313 this marks the timer's pointer fields as NULL, to indicate that the timer is no longer active.

314–318 this block of code executes the function specified for this timer. The timer list lock is released while doing this and is reacquired afterwards before the function continues to process the list. There is no problem with other timers being manipulated while this function is running. The bracketing `timer_enter()` and `timer_exit()` let other processes know that the function is running. This is really only relevant in SMP mode. The macros are described in Section 15.3.4.3.

319 we go back and do this for all timers expiring at this time.

321 this line is executed when there are no further entries on the particular list. All the timers scheduled for that particular value of `timer_jiffies` have been processed.

322 this increments the `index` field in `tv1`. The bitwise AND with TVR_MASK (255) makes it roll over.

323 this is the end of the 'while' loop (line 292). We around this loop again until `timer_jiffies` is up to `jiffies`.

15.3.4.2 Cascading timers down one level

When all the timer lists headed from any particular group have been processed it is necessary to move one list down from the next group. This is known as cascading the timers. The function shown in Figure 15.40, from `kernel/timers.c`, does this. It is passed a pointer to the group on which it is to operate. It cascades the current timer list in the vector denoted by `tv` down one level

```
265   static inline void cascade_timers(struct timer_vec *tv)
266   {
267
268         struct list_head *head, *curr, *next;
269
270         head = tv->vec + tv->index;
271         curr = head->next;

276         while (curr != head) {
277               struct timer_list *tmp;
278
279               tmp = list_entry(curr, struct timer_list, list);
280               next = curr->next;
281               list_del(curr); /* not needed */
282               internal_add_timer(tmp);
283               curr = next;
284         }
285         INIT_LIST_HEAD(head);
286         tv->index = (tv->index + 1) & TVN_MASK;
287   }
```

Figure 15.40   *Cascading timers down one level*

270   this sets up a pointer (head) to the head of the next list of timers to be processed in the vector tv.

271   this sets up a pointer to the first entry on that list.

276–284   this loop goes through all the timers on the list.

279   this gets a pointer to the first entry into the tmp variable. The list_entry() macro was described in Section 4.3.4.3. It converts a pointer to the list_head link to a pointer to the actual structure of which it is a linked list (e.g. timer_list). The parameters are a pointer to the entry, the type of the list, and the type of a member.

280   before removing the timer we must remember its successor on the list.

281   the timer is removed from the list (see Section 4.3.3). The comment says this is not needed.

282   this inserts the time just removed at its correct place, which is implicitly specified by its expires field. The function, described in Section 15.3.2.4, will insert each timer in its appropriate place on the next group down.

283   we move on to the next timer on the next list.

285   this code is why line 281 is not necessary. The list is reinitialised afterwards, so there is no need to detach timers individually. The macro is in Section 4.3.1.

286   this increments the index of this level, mod 64, so that it rolls over.

15.3.4.3 Synchronising with running timer functions

In SMP mode, a process running on another CPU may need to know whether a particular timer function is actually running or not, so a set of macros are supplied for announcing and checking this, as shown in Figure 15.41, from `kernel/timer.c`.

```
165  #ifdef CONFIG_SMP
166  volatile struct timer_list * volatile running_timer;
167  #define timer_enter(t) do { running_timer = t; mb(); } while (0)
168  #define timer_exit() do { running_timer = NULL; } while (0)
169  #define timer_is_running(t) (running_timer == t)
170  #define timer_synchronize(t) while (timer_is_running(t)) barrier()
171  #else
172  #define timer_enter(t)   do { } while (0)
173  #define timer_exit()     do { } while (0)
174  #endif
```

Figure 15.41 Synchronising with running timer functions

166–170 these functions are really only relevant in the SMP case.

166 this variable is used to record the address of the running timer function.

167 this saves the address of the `timer_list` and waits until that write has been propagated to memory.

168 this undoes the previous assignment.

169 this macro returns TRUE if there is a pointer to the specified timer in `running_timer`, otherwise it returns FALSE.

170 this is a busy waiting loop, until some other process calls `timer_exit()` on that timer.

172–173 the uniprocessor versions of these macros do nothing, and the compiler will optimise them away.

16

Software interrupts

All operating systems divide the handling of interrupts into two phases. These are generally referred to as hardware and software interrupts. The hardware interrupt is just what its name implies. Some hardware device interrupts the computer processing unit (CPU), which stops running the current process and turns its attention instead to a service routine for that particular interrupt. Typically, other interrupts (at least at the same priority level) are masked while this interrupt service routine is running, so it is very important to keep such routines as short as possible. This is where software interrupts come in. The handling required for an interrupt can almost always be divided in two: processing that is very urgent, and processing that is not so urgent. For example, with a keyboard interrupt, information must be moved immediately from the data register of the keyboard interface into memory, to avoid these data being overwritten by the next keystroke. Once these data are safe in memory there is no immediate urgency in interpreting them, as long as this is done in a reasonable time, say several hundred milliseconds, so the interrupt service routine does the absolute minimum processing and then arranges for another routine to be called at a later stage to do the less urgent processing. Note that this 'later stage' may be immediately if there are no further hardware interrupts pending. The critical requirement is that all hardware interrupts must be serviced before attending to software interrupts.

Linux has always had this concept of two-part interrupt handling, but it was one of the less-well-inspired aspects of the original design. It has been radically redesigned not once, but twice, and, because legacy software may continue to use the old designs, the new improved system also has to be backward compatible, which makes it more complicated than it need be.

In the beginning there were bottom halves. When an interrupt service routine finished, as long as there were no other hardware interrupts pending, the kernel scanned a table of bottom halves. Each entry in this could be marked active or inactive. If active, then it was carried out once and marked inactive. As only one such bottom half could be running at any one time, there was no need to worry about mutual exclusion. In version 2.0 of Linux, bottom halves were extended to task queues. This mechanism links 'tasks' together on a queue rather than on an array. This overcomes the limitation of a fixed size array. Now version 2.4 has gone a step further. First, there is a generic software interrupt mechanism, which embraces all the earlier ones, and there is a new feature added, a tasklet. The bottom-half mechanism was developed for uniprocessors; only one bottom half could be running at

The Linux Process Manager. The Internals of Scheduling, Interrupts and Signals   John O'Gorman
© 2003 John Wiley & Sons, Ltd   ISBN: 0 470 84771 9

any one time. With the advent of multiprocessors, this was unnecessarily restrictive. Now different tasklets may be running simultaneously on different CPUs.

16.1 The software interrupt mechanism

We will begin by examining the data structures used by the system to keep track of software interrupts. Two particular software interrupts are set up at boot time, and these will be described next. Then we look at when and how these software interrupts are actually executed. Finally, the functions used (typically by a driver) to mark a software interrupt for execution are described.

16.1.1 Data structures

The mechanism for keeping track of software interrupts is relatively simple, a 32-element array, with some predefined entries.

16.1.1.1 Recording software interrupts

The root of all the information maintained about software interrupts is the following array, as declared in `kernel/softirq.c`:

```
45    static struct softirq_action softirq_vec[32] __cacheline_aligned;
```

So, there can be a maximum of 32 software interrupts registered on a system. Each element in this array is a `struct softirq_action`, as shown in Figure 16.1, from `<linux/interrupt.h>`.

```
68    struct softirq_action
69    {
70        void (*action)(struct softirq_action *);
71        void *data;
72    };
```

Figure 16.1 Structure representing a software interrupt

70 this is a pointer to a function `action` (which is to be executed when the software interrupt is run). This function takes a pointer to such a `softirq_action` structure as a parameter.

71 this is a pointer to data that may be used by that function.

16.1.1.2 Pre-allocated software interrupts

The first four of these software interrupts are preallocated; see Figure 16.2, from `<linux/interrupt.h>`. This is the order in which they will be serviced. Only `HI_SOFTIRQ` and `TASKLET_SOFTIRQ` are installed by default (see Section 16.1.2.1). The other two are installed if networking is enabled. Others may be installed by the user, although they should only be used if *really* urgent and high-frequency servicing is required. For almost all purposes, tasklets (see Section 16.2) are more than enough.

```
56    enum
57    {
58          HI_SOFTIRQ=0,
59          NET_TX_SOFTIRQ,
60          NET_RX_SOFTIRQ,
61          TASKLET_SOFTIRQ
62    };
```

Figure 16.2   Predefined software interrupts

16.1.2   Initialising software interrupts

Some software interrupts are initialised at boot time, but it is also possible to set them up while the system is running. This section considers both possibilities.

16.1.2.1   *Boot-time initialisation of the software interrupt mechanism*

The function shown in Figure 16.3 is from `kernel/softirq.c`. As its name implies, it initialises the software interrupt mechanism. It is called from `start_kernel()` at boot time (see Section 1.3.1).

```
324  void __init softirq_init()
325  {
326       int i;
327
328       for (i=0; i<32; i++)
329            tasklet_init(bh_task_vec+i, bh_action, i);
330
331       open_softirq(TASKLET_SOFTIRQ, tasklet_action, NULL);
332       open_softirq(HI_SOFTIRQ, tasklet_hi_action, NULL);
333  }
```

Figure 16.3   Initialising the software interrupt mechanism

328–329   basically, this function does two different things. First, it initialises the tasklet subsystem. What is going on here can only be fully understood after we have examined the tasklet subsystem in Section 16.2, but, essentially, it is initialising each entry in an array of tasklet handlers to point to the function `bh_action()`. We will consider this function in Section 16.3.2. The function used to populate the array, `tasklet_init()`, will be discussed in Section 16.2.1.2.

331–332   next, it sets up two software interrupts. The function called to do this, `open_softirq()`, will be examined in Section 16.1.2.2.

331   `TASKLET_SOFTIRQ` is number 3 in the enumeration in Figure 16.2. The function `tasklet _action()` will be discussed in Section 16.2.6. The third parameter is NULL; no data are supplied for this function. When called, this will execute all standard priority tasklets that are pending.

332   HI_SOFTIRQ is number 0 in the enumeration in 16.2, so it is always the first to be executed. The function `tasklet_hi_action()` will be discussed in Section 16.2.7. The third parameter is NULL; no data are supplied for this function. When called, this will execute all high-priority tasklets that are pending.

16.1.2.2   *Setting up a software interrupt*

The trivial function shown in Figure 16.4 is from `kernel/softirq.c`. It sets up an entry in the `softirq_vec[]` array. It is passed the number of the entry to set up, a pointer to the function that handles that software interrupt, and a pointer to the data required by that function. There does not appear to be a function to remove a software interrupt from the list. Presumably, it could be overwritten with a NULL entry.

```
140  void open_softirq(int nr, void (*action)(struct
                                      softirq_action*), void *data)
141  {
142      softirq_vec[nr].data = data;
143      softirq_vec[nr].action = action;
144  }
```

Figure 16.4   Installing a software interrupt

142 –143   this is the table of software interrupts, which we have just seen. These lines are filling in the `data` and the `action` field for this particular interrupt.

16.1.3   Running a software interrupt

The function shown in Figure 16.5, from `kernel/softirq.c`, is called by the first-level interrupt handler, `do_IRQ()` (Section 12.4.1), each time it runs. It goes through the `softirq_vec[]` array and runs the appropriate handler for any software interrupt that is installed.

```
61  asmlinkage void do_softirq()
62  {
63      int      cpu = smp_processor_id();
64      __u32    pending;
65      long     flags;
66      __32     mask;
67
68      if (in_interrupt())
69          return;
70
71      local_irq_save(flags);
72
73      pending = softirq_pending(cpu);
```

```
74
75        if (pending) {
76             struct softirq_action *h;
77
78             mask = ~pending;
79             local_bh_disable();
80  restart:
81
82             softirq_pending(cpu) = 0;
83
84             local_irq_enable();
85
86             h = softirq_vec;
87
88             do {
89                 if (pending & 1)
90                     h->action(h);
91                 h++;
92                 pending >>= 1;
93             } while (pending);
94
95             local_irq_disable();
96
97             pending = softirq_pending(cpu);
98             if (pending & mask) {
99                 mask &= ~pending;
100                goto restart;
101            }
102            __local_bh_enable();
103
104            if (pending)
105                wakeup_softirqd(cpu);
106        }
107
108        local_irq_restore(flags);
109 }
```

Figure 16.5 Handling software interrupts

63 this finds the identification (ID) number of the CPU on which we are running (see Section 7.2.1.4).

68–69 if this function has been called while in interrupt context, it just returns without doing anything. Any hardware interrupts should be serviced first. The first-level interrupt handler do_IRQ() only calls do_softirq() after it has serviced the hardware interrupt. The macro in_interrupt() is from Section 16.5.3.1.

71 this macro, from Section 12.8.2, saves the value of the EFLAGS register and disables hardware interrupts on the local CPU. This ensures mutual exclusion on the bitmap of pending software interrupts for this CPU.

73 this takes a local copy of the bitmap of pending software interrupts, using the macro from Section 16.5.1.2.

75–106 this block of code is executed only if there is at least one software interrupt pending. Otherwise, control skips on to line 108.

78 the `mask` bitmap now contains the inverse of `pending`.

79 the macro, from Section 16.5.2, increments the nesting level of software interrupts in progress on the local CPU.

82 as the local `pending` now has all the information about pending software interrupts, the global bitmap can be zeroed, using the macro from Section 16.5.1.2.

84 we can enable hardware interrupts on the local CPU from here on, as we are finished with the public mask. The macro is in Section 12.8.2. Interrupt handlers can now run and set bits in the public mask.

86 this is the array of `struct softirq_action` (see Section 16.1.1.1). Here, we take a pointer to the first element in that array. This pointer variable was declared on line 76.

88–93 this loop is executed as long as there are still bits set in `pending`. For each one set, we are going to execute the appropriate software interrupt handler. If there was not at least one set, we would not have entered the scope at line 75 or entered it at the label on line 80, so the loop is executed at least once.

89–90 if the least significant bit of `pending` is set, the action is carried out for the appropriate software interrupt. Remember that `h` is a pointer to an element in `softirq_vec[]`, a `struct softirq_action`. The action field of that structure is a pointer to a handler. Note that the function is passed a pointer to the `struct softirq_action` as parameter.

91–92 this advances h to the next entry in the array and shifts the next bit in `pending` right, ready for comparison.

95 we are now going to check the `__softirq_pending` mask again, so we disable hardware interrupts on the local CPU, using the macro from Section 12.8.2.

97 we refresh the local copy of the bitmap of pending software interrupts, using the macro given in Section 16.5.1.2. This picks up any software interrupts that have been scheduled to run since line 73.

98–101 this block of code is executed only if there is at least one bit set now that was not set the last time this bitmap was checked, so only *new* software interrupts will be handled.

99 the `mask` bitmap is updated to reflect all software interrupts that have been accepted for handling since this function began to run.

100 from here, we go and handle the new batch of software interrupts.

102   when there are no further software interrupts to be serviced, we decrement the count of software interrupts being handled by the local CPU, using the macro from Section 16.5.2.

104–105   if even one of the software interrupts just handled is pending again, then the load of software interrupts is becoming too great to handle in interrupt context, so the function from Section 16.1.4.3 is called, to wake up the `softirqd` kernel thread on this CPU.

108   this macro, from Section 12.8.2, restores the interrupt state as it was on entry to `do_softirq()`.

16.1.4   The software interrupt kernel thread

The previous section has described how software interrupts are handled in interrupt context on the return path from hardware interrupt handling, but there is also a kernel thread (in fact, one per CPU) dedicated to handling software interrupts. This thread is woken up when the load of software interrupts becomes too great to handle in interrupt context (it would take too many machine cycles from the current process).

16.1.4.1   Spawning kernel threads to handle software interrupts

At boot time, one kernel thread running `ksoftirqd` is spawned for each CPU, by the function shown in Figure 16.6, from `kernel/softirq.c`.

```
399  static __init int spawn_ksoftirqd(void)
400  {
401      int cpu;
402
403      for (cpu = 0; cpu < smp_num_cpus; cpu++) {
404          if (kernel_thread(ksoftirqd, (void *) (long) cpu,
405              CLONE_FS | CLONE_FILES | CLONE_SIGNAL) < 0)
406          printk("spawn_ksoftirqd() failed for cpu %d\n", cpu);
407          else {
408          while (!ksoftirqd_task(cpu_logical_map(cpu))) {
409              current->policy |= SCHED_YIELD;
410              schedule();
411          }
412          }
413      }
414
415      return 0;
416  }
```

Figure 16.6   Spawning kernel threads for software interrupts

403–413   we go through each CPU, using the count of CPUs defined in Section 7.2.1.1.

404–406   we create a kernel thread; if we are unable to do this an informational message is printed.

404   the `kernel_thread()` function was described in Section 8.5. Its parameters are a pointer to

the function to run (see Section 16.1.4.2), a pointer to the argument to that function (the number of the CPU on which it is to run, cast as a pointer to void), and the clone flags that govern its creation.

405 the function is to share file systems, open files, and signal handlers with its parent (see Section 8.3.1 for these flags).

408–412 this block of code is executed if the thread was created successfully.

408 this converts a sequence number to a CPU ID, using the function given in Section 7.2.1.2. Then, if the newly cloned thread has not yet completed its initialisation (by announcing itself in the array in Section 16.5.1.1), the parent does not go on to create the next thread until this one is fully set up.

409–410 this yields the CPU for one pass through the scheduler.

16.1.4.2 The ksoftirq kernel thread

The function executed by the ksoftirq kernel thread is shown in Figure 16.7, from kernel/softirq.c.

```
362    static int ksoftirqd(void * __bind_cpu)
363    {
364        int bind_cpu = (int) (long) __bind_cpu;
365        int cpu = cpu_logical_map(bind_cpu);
366
367        demonise();
368        current->nice = 19;
369        sigfillset(&current->blocked);

372        current->cpus_allowed = 1UL << cpu;
373        while (smp_processor_id() != cpu)
374            schedule();
375
376        sprintf(current->comm, "ksoftirqd_CPU%d", bind_cpu);
377
378        __set_current_state(TASK_INTERRUPTIBLE);
379        mb();
380
381        ksoftirqd_task(cpu) = current;
382
383        for (;;) {
384            if (!softirq_pending(cpu))
385                schedule();
386
387            __set_current_state(TASK_RUNNING);
388
389            while (softirq_pending(cpu)) {
390                do_softirq();
```

```
391                        if (current->need_resched)
392                             schedule();
393               }
394
395               __set_current_state(TASK_INTERRUPTIBLE);
396          }
397 }
```

Figure 16.7   The ksoftirqd kernel thread

362   the parameter is an int, containing the sequence number of the CPU for which it is created, cast as a pointer to void.

364   this casts the void pointer to long, and then to int.

365   this converts the sequence number to a logical ID, using the function from Section 7.2.1.2.

367   this function deallocates memory and file-system resources, not needed by a kernel thread.

368   the priority is set very low.

369   this marks all signals blocked to this thread, using the function from Section 17.2.2.5.

372   setting the bit corresponding to cpu in this bitmap limits it to running on that CPU only.

373–374   if the process is not currently running on its home processor, then the scheduler is called, and the CPU is given up. When the process runs again, it will be on its home processor.

376   in the comm field of the task_struct of this thread, we set up the name of the program it is running as ksoftirqd_CPU**x**, where **x** is the sequence number of the CPU.

378   here, the process is set it up for sleeping interruptibly (long term), using the macro from Section 4.6.1.3.

379   this macro forces strict CPU ordering, so that all CPUs see the foregoing assignments.

381   this puts a pointer to its task_struct into the appropriate element of the array described in Section 16.5.1.1, using the macro from Section 16.5.1.2.

383–396   now that the initialisation has been done, the program goes into its infinite loop.

384–385   if no software interrupts are pending, then the CPU is yielded. The state of the process will be TASK_INTERRUPTIBLE, from line 378 or 395.

387   when the process wakes up again, it is set to be runable.

389–393   this loop is executed as long as there are any software interrupts pending.

390   they are executed, using the function from Section 16.1.3.

391–392   if the process is marked as needing to be rescheduled, the CPU is yielded.

395 control comes here only when there are no further software interrupts to run. The process is set up for sleeping interruptibly (long term), using the macro from Section 4.6.1.3.

16.1.4.3 *Waking up the software interrupt kernel thread*

When the load of software interrupts becomes too great to handle in interrupt context, do_softirq() wakes up the softirqd kernel thread to handle them. The function to do this is shown in Figure 16.8, from kernel/softirq.c.

```
53   static inline void wakeup_softirqd(unsigned cpu)
54   {
55       struct task_struct * tsk = ksoftirqd_task(cpu);
56
57       if (tsk && tsk->state != TASK_RUNNING)
58           wake_up_process(tsk);
59   }
```

Figure 16.8 Waking up the softirqd kernel thread

55 this macro, from Section 16.5.1.2, returns a pointer to the task_struct of the softirqd kernel thread corresponding to cpu.

57–58 if there is such a thread, and it is not currently runable, it is woken up, using the function from Section 4.7.5.

16.1.5 Raising a software interrupt

Raising a software interrupt is done by setting the appropriate bit in the bitmap of pending software interrupts. This may seem trivial, but Linux provides two functions and a macro to implement various options.

16.1.5.1 *Raising a software interrupt on the local computer processing unit*

The function shown in Figure 16.9, from <linux/interrupt.h>, raises a particular software interrupt on the local CPU.

```
131  static inline void raise_softirq(int nr)
132  {
133      unsigned long flags;
134
135      local_irq_save(flags);
136      cpu_raise_softirq(smp_processor_id(), nr);
137      local_irq_restore(flags);
138  }
```

Figure 16.9 Raising a software interrupt

131–138 this function is only a wrapper, that turns off hardware interrupts on the local CPU, raises a software interrupt on that CPU, and then enables interrupts again.

136 the `smp_processor_id()` macro is described in Section 7.2.1.4. For the `cpu_raise_softirq()` function, see Section 16.1.5.2.

16.1.5.2 *Raising a software interrupt on a specified computer processing unit*

The generic function to raise a software interrupt on a particular CPU is shown in Figure 16.10, from `kernel/softirq.c`. This function must run with interrupt requests (irqs) disabled.

```
114  inline void cpu_raise_softirq(unsigned int cpu, unsigned int nr)
115  {
116      __cpu_raise_softirq(cpu, nr);

127      if (!(local_irq_count(cpu) | local_bh_count(cpu)))
128          wakeup_softirqd(cpu);
129  }
```

Figure 16.10 Raising a software interrupt on a specified computer processing unit (CPU)

114 the parameters are the ID of the CPU and the number of the software interrupt.

116 this macro, from Section 16.1.5.3, actually sets the bit in the appropriate bitmap.

127 if the function is called while servicing either a hardware or a software interrupt, then nothing further is done. The software interrupt just raised will run when we return from processing either.

128 otherwise, no software interrupt handling will be done for an indeterminate time in the future, so we wake up the software interrupt kernel thread to handle it. The function is from Section 16.1.4.3.

16.1.5.3 *Setting the bit in the appropriate software interrupt bitmap*

The macro in Figure 16.11 , from `<linux/interrupt.h>`, sets the bit corresponding to nr in the __softirq_pending field corresponding to cpu.

```
77   #define __cpu_raise_softirq(cpu, nr)
                         do { softirq_pending(cpu) |= 1UL << (nr); } while (0)
```

Figure 16.11 Setting the bit in the appropriate software interrupt bitmap

77 this sets the bit corresponding to the software interrupt (nr) in the `softirq_active` mask of the specified CPU, whether already set or not [see Section 16.5.1.2 for the `softirq_pending()` macro].

16.2   Tasklets

From the previous section, there are 32 software interrupts, some of which are preallocated. Although programmers can dedicate a software interrupt directly to their own use, this is not recommended. Instead, Linux supplies tasklets, which are an attempt to multiplex groups of tasks over two software interrupts, numbers 0 and 3. Tasklets can be assigned either a normal or a high priority.

Tasklets are installed and maintained on a systemwide basis, but, when it is needed, a tasklet is marked to run on a specific CPU. This makes better use of a multiprocessor system. This is one of the big improvements that tasklets bring over the older bottom halves (see Section 16.5.1.2). Only one bottom half can be executing at any given time, no matter how many CPUs there are in the system. Different tasklets can run simultaneously on different CPUs.

16.2.1   Data structures

The root of the tasklet subsystem is the array `bh_task_vec[]`, which is defined in `kernel/softirq.c` as:

```
276   struct tasklet_struct bh_task_vec[32];
```

This is a 32-element array of `tasklet_struct`. Each of these identifies a tasklet, so there can be at most 32 tasklets defined in the system. Note that all these structures are allocated at compile time; all manipulations are done within this array.

16.2.1.1   The tasklet structure

The tasklet structure itself is given in Figure 16.12, from `<linux/interrupt.h>`, along with some associated data structures.

```
103   struct tasklet_struct
104   {
105       struct tasklet_struct *next;
106       unsigned long state;
107       atomic_t count;
108       void (*func)(unsigned long);
109       unsigned long data;
110   };
111
112   #define DECLARE_TASKLET(name, func, data)                \
113   struct tasklet_struct name = { NULL, 0, ATOMIC_INIT(0), func, data }
114
115   #define DECLARE_TASKLET_DISABLED(name, func, data)   \
116   struct tasklet_struct name = { NULL, 0, ATOMIC_INIT(1), func, data }

119   enum
120   {
```

```
121        TASKLET_STATE_SCHED,
122        TASKLET_STATE_RUN
123  };
```

Figure 16.12   Tasklet data structures and definitions

105   when they are queued for execution, tasklets are linked through this field.

106   the `state` field contains an element of the enumeration from lines 119–123.

107   the `count` field determines whether the particular tasklet is enabled (0) or disabled (positive).

108   this is a pointer to the function that executes the tasklet.

109   these are data to be passed to the function.

112–113   this is a macro that declares and initialises a `tasklet_struct` in the enabled state. The link field is NULL, all bits are cleared in the `state` field, and the `count` field is atomically initialised to zero. The supplied function pointer and data are assigned to the `func` and `data` fields, respectively.

115–116   this is a macro that declares and initialises a `tasklet_struct` in the disabled state. Note that the third field (`count`) is atomically initialised to 1.

119–123   this is an enumeration of tasklet state.

121   bit 0 is set when a tasklet is actually scheduled for execution.

122   bit 1 is set while a tasklet is actually running. It is used as a lock bit, to prevent a tasklet being run simultaneously on more than one CPU (see Section 16.2.8).

16.2.1.2   Initialising a tasklet structure

The function shown in Figure 16.13 is from `kernel/softirq.c`. It initialises an existing `tasklet_struct` to the supplied values.

```
245  void tasklet_init(struct tasklet_struct *t,
246        void (*func)(unsigned long), unsigned long data)
247  {
248        t->next = NULL;
249        t->state = 0;
250        atomic_set(&t->count, 0);
251        t->func = func;
252        t->data = data;
253  }
```

Figure 16.13   Inserting values in a `tasklet_struct`

245–246   it is passed a pointer to a `struct tasklet_struct` which is to be initialised, a pointer to the function to be executed when called, and data to be passed to that function.

248   the link field `next` is set to NULL.

249–252   the fields of the `tasklet_struct` are populated with the supplied values.

249   its `state` field is set to 0, so it is neither scheduled for execution nor running.

250   the `count` field is set to 0, atomically, so it is marked as enabled.

We can now understand the loop at lines 328–329 of Figure 16.3 a little better. It is initialising 32 entries in the `bh_task_vec[]`. Each is initialised to the `bh_action` function (see Section 16.3.2) and is passed its offset in the array as parameter.

16.2.2   The per-CPU tasklet lists

We have just seen that the information about all tasklets installed in the system is maintained in the `bh_task_vec[]` array. When a tasklet is actually scheduled to be run, the element of the array corresponding to that tasklet is linked onto a CPU-specific list, using the `next` field in the `tasklet_struct`.

16.2.2.1   Tasklet lists

There are two of these tasklet lists per CPU; see Figure 16.14, from `kernel/softirq.c`.

```
149  struct tasklet_head tasklet_vec[NR_CPUS] __cacheline_aligned;
150  struct tasklet_head tasklet_hi_vec[NR_CPUS] __cacheline_aligned;
```

Figure 16.14   The per-CPU tasklet lists

149   normal priority tasklets are linked from this.

150   high-priority tasklets are linked from this.

16.2.2.2   Tasklet list headers

Figure 16.15, from `<linux/interrupt.h>`, shows the head of a tasklet list. It is merely a pointer to the first `struct tasklet_struct` on the list.

```
125  struct tasklet_head
126  {
127        struct tasklet_struct *list;
128  } __attribute__ ((__aligned__(SMP_CACHE_BYTES)));
```

Figure 16.15   The head of a tasklet list

16.2.3   Scheduling standard-priority tasklets

Two functions are provided for this. One checks that the particular tasklet is not already scheduled to run (on any list) and then calls the second function, which inserts it on the standard priority list for the current CPU.

16.2.3.1 Checking that the tasklet is not already scheduled

The code in Figure 16.16, from <linux/interrupt.h>, sets bit 0 of the state field in the tasklet_struct. If it was clear (0) beforehand, then it is not on any list and so can be scheduled.

```
157  static inline void tasklet_schedule(struct tasklet_struct *t)
158  {
159      if (!test_and_set_bit(TASKLET_STATE_SCHED, &t->state)) {
160          __tasklet_schedule(t);
169  }
```

Figure 16.16 Checking that the tasklet is not already scheduled

159 the test_and_set_bit() function has been described in Section 5.1.4.1. If the bit was set, then this tasklet is already installed on a list, to be executed. We do nothing, and just return. If the bit was not set beforehand, then this line sets it.

160 the function to insert a tasklet into a list is described in Section 16.2.3.2.

16.2.3.2 Inserting a tasklet onto the standard list

The code shown in Figure 16.17, from kernel/softirq.c, inserts a tasklet_struct into the standard tasklet list for the current CPU. The tasklet is guaranteed to be executed at least once after this.

```
152  void __tasklet_schedule(struct tasklet_struct *t)
153  {
154      int cpu = smp_processor_id();
155      unsigned long flags;
156
157      local_irq_save(flags);
158      t->next = tasklet_vec[cpu].list;
159      tasklet_vec[cpu].list = t;
160      cpu_raise_softirq(cpu, TASKLET_SOFTIRQ);
161      local_irq_restore(flags);
162  }
```

Figure 16.17 Insert a tasklet onto the standard list for this cpu

154 this gets the ID of the CPU on which we are running (see Section 7.2.1.4).

157–161 this disables hardware interrupt requests on this processor and saves EFLAGS while this block of code is being executed, using the macro from Section 12.8.2. We do not want another interrupt handler to be able to access this list while we are putting an entry onto it.

158 this makes our tasklet point to the first element in the list for this CPU.

159   this points the list head to our `tasklet_struct`. These two assignments (lines 158 and 159) together have the effect of inserting this tasklet at the head of the list.

160   this function, from Section 16.1.5.2, sets the bit representing a standard tasklet software interrupt (3) in the `__softirq_active` bitmap for this CPU, whether it is already set or not. This signifies to the CPU that there is at least one tasklet pending.

16.2.4   Scheduling high-priority tasklets

Two functions are also provided for this. One checks that the particular tasklet is not already scheduled to run (on any list), and then calls the second function, which inserts it on the high-priority list for this CPU.

16.2.4.1   *Checking that the tasklet is not already scheduled*

The code in Figure 16.18, from `<linux/interrupt.h>`, sets bit 0 of the `state` field in the `tasklet_struct`. If it was clear (0) beforehand, then it is not on any list and can be scheduled onto this one.

```
165   static inline void tasklet_hi_schedule(struct tasklet_struct *t)
166   {
167        if (!test_and_set_bit(TASKLET_STATE_SCHED, &t->state))
168             __tasklet_hi_schedule(t);
169   }
```

Figure 16.18   Checking that the tasklet is not already scheduled

167–168   the comments on Figure 16.16 are relevant here. The `__tasklet_hi_schedule()` function is described in Section 16.2.4.2.

16.2.4.2   *Inserting a tasklet onto the high-priority list*

The actual function that inserts a tasklet onto the high-priority list is shown in Figure 16.19, from `kernel/softirq.c`.

```
164   void __tasklet_hi_schedule(struct tasklet_struct *t)
165   {
166        int cpu = smp_processor_id();
167        unsigned long flags;
168
169        local_irq_save(flags);
170        t->next = tasklet_hi_vec[cpu].list;
171        tasklet_hi_vec[cpu].list = t;
172        cpu_raise_softirq(cpu, HI_SOFTIRQ);
173        local_irq_restore(flags);
174   }
```

Figure 16.19   Inserting a tasklet onto the high-priority list

166–172   the comments on Figure 16.17 are all relevant here. The only difference is in lines 170 and 171, which deal with the `tasklet_hi_vec[]` array, and line 172, which specifies `HI_SOFTIRQ`.

16.2.5   Enabling and disabling tasklets

It is also possible to mark a tasklet as disabled. Although a tasklet can always be scheduled to run, it will not actually be run until it is in the enabled state. This is indicated by its `count` field having a value of 0.

16.2.5.1   Disabling tasklets

Two functions are provided for disabling tasklets; see Figure 16.20, from `<linux/interrupt.h>`. Although disabled, a tasklet may still be scheduled to run, using the functions from Section 16.2.3 or Section 16.2.4, but it will not run until enabled again, by one of the functions from Section 16.2.5.2.

```
172  static inline void tasklet_disable_nosync(struct tasklet_struct *t)
173  {
174        atomic_inc(&t->count);
175        smp_mb__after_atomic_inc();
176  }
177
178  static inline void tasklet_disable(struct tasklet_struct *t)
179  {
180        tasklet_disable_nosync(t);
181        tasklet_unlock_wait(t);
182        smp_mb();
183  }
```

Figure 16.20   Disabling tasklets

172–176   this function disables a tasklet and returns immediately, whether the tasklet is actually running or not.

174   by writing a nonzero value to the `count` field of the `tasklet_struct`, we mark the tasklet as disabled. The function is from Section 5.2.5.

175   this is an alias for the `barrier()` macro and makes sure that all other CPUs see this write.

178–183   this function also disables a tasklet, but if the tasklet is running (on another CPU) it waits until it is finished before returning.

180   this uses the function at line 172 to mark the tasklet as disabled.

181   this function, from Section 16.2.8, busy waits until the TASKLET_STATE_RUN bit is clear in the `state` field of the `tasklet_struct`.

182   this is an alias for the `mb()` macro, to force strict CPU ordering.

16.2.5.2   Enabling tasklets

There are also two functions provided for enabling tasklets, bur for a different reason. There is one for each of the two tasklet lists. However, for the current implementation, these are identical; see Figure 16.21, from <linux/interrupt.h>.

```
185   static inline void tasklet_enable(struct tasklet_struct *t)
186   {
187         smp_mb__before_atomic_dec();
188         atomic_dec(&t->count);
189   }
190
191   static inline void tasklet_hi_enable(struct tasklet_struct *t)
192   {
193         smp_mb__before_atomic_dec();
194         atomic_dec(&t->count);
195   }
```

Figure 16.21   Enabling tasklets

187   this is an alias for the barrier() macro and makes sure that all CPUs have a consistent view of memory.

188   this atomically decrements the count field of the tasklet_struct. When the value gets to 0, the tasklet is enabled again.

191–195   this is identical to the function at lines 185–189.

16.2.5.3   Killing a tasklet

If a tasklet is rescheduling itself continuously then a special function is needed to break in and stop this. The function shown in Figure 16.22, from <linux/interrupt.h>, is given a pointer to a tasklet in the bh_task_vec[] array. It waits until that tasklet is inactive and then clears the TASKLET_STATE_SCHED bit so that it will not be executed any further.

```
255   void tasklet_kill(struct tasklet_struct *t)
256   {
257         if (in_interrupt())
258             printk("Attempt to kill tasklet from interrupt\n");
259
260         while (test_and_set_bit(TASKLET_STATE_SCHED,&t->state)){
261             current->state = TASK_RUNNING;
262             do {
263                 current->policy |= SCHED_YIELD;
264                 schedule();
265             } while (test_bit(TASKLET_STATE_SCHED, &t->state));
266         }
267         tasklet_unlock_wait(t);
```

```
268        clear_bit(TASKLET_STATE_SCHED, &t->state);
269 }
```

Figure 16.22   Killing a tasklet

257–258   it is illegal for an interrupt handler to call this function. The macro is from Section 16.5.3.1.

260–266   the `test_and_set_bit()` function, from Section 5.1.4.1, always sets the bit. It returns TRUE if clear beforehand, FALSE if set beforehand. Thus, if the TASKLET_STATE_SCHED bit was clear in the `state` field of the tasklet, implying that this tasklet is not currently scheduled to be run, this loop is executed. Otherwise, if the bit was set, implying that this tasklet is scheduled to be run on any CPU, we skip on to line 267.

261   this sets the current process to the TASK_RUNNING state. This line is not needed first time around the loop, as this function would always run in the context of the current process, which must be in the TASK_RUNNING state anyway, but it is needed for the second and subsequent iterations of the loop.

262–265   this loop is executed, as long as the TASKLET_STATE_SCHED bit is set (i.e. until the tasklet has been executed).

263   this sets the SCHED_YIELD bit in the `policy` field of the `task_struct` of the current (calling) process, so the current process is yielding the CPU but is leaving itself on the runqueue. It will be rescheduled very soon, maybe next.

264   we have yielded the CPU for one pass, so we call the scheduler (Section 7.3).

265   if when we run again the TASKLET_STATE_SCHED bit is still set (the tasklet has not run in the meantime), we yield again. For the `test_bit()` function, see Section 5.1.3.

267   we always come here from line 260, with the TASKLET_STATE_SCHED bit set. The tasklet we are concerned with has run, or is maybe actually running. This function, which is discussed in Section 16.2.8, waits until the TASKLET_STATE_RUN bit is cleared (i.e. until it has finished running).

268   this clears the TASKLET_STATE_SCHED bit. For the inline function, see Section 5.1.2. This finally unschedules the tasklet.

16.2.6   The standard priority tasklet software interrupt

The function shown in Figure 16.23, from `kernel/softirq.c`, is set up at boot time as the handler for software interrupt number 3 (see Section 16.1.2). When called, it runs all the standard priority tasklets queued for the CPU on which it is running.

```
176 static void tasklet_action(struct softirq_action *a)
177 {
178        int cpu = smp_processor_id();
179        struct tasklet_struct *list;
180
181        local_irq_disable();
```

```
182        list = tasklet_vec[cpu].list;
183        tasklet_vec[cpu].list = NULL;
184        local_irq_enable();
185
186        while (list) {
187            struct tasklet_struct *t = list;
188
189            list = list->next;
190
191            if (tasklet_trylock(t)) {
192                if (!atomic_read(&t->count)) {
193                    if (!test_and_clear_bit (TASKLET_STATE_SCHED,
                                                            &t->state))
194                        BUG();
195                    t->func(t->data);
196                    tasklet_unlock(t);
197                    continue;
198                }
199                tasklet_unlock(t);
200            }
201
202            local_irq_disable();
203            t->next = tasklet_vec[cpu].list;
204            tasklet_vec[cpu].list = t;
205            __cpu_raise_softirq(cpu, TASKLET_SOFTIRQ);
206            local_irq_enable();
207        }
208 }
```

Figure 16.23 Handler for the standard tasklet software interrupt

176   although the function is passed a pointer to a `struct softirq_action` as a parameter it is never used, but other software interrupts could use this pointer, so it is part of the prototype.

178   this finds the CPU on which we are running (see Section 7.2.1.4).

181–184   we are going to take the whole list of scheduled tasklets, but an interrupt handler could attempt to put a new tasklet onto the list while we are manipulating it, so, to guarantee mutual exclusion for this block of code, hardware interrupts are disabled on the local CPU, as the list is CPU-specific.

181   the macro is given in Section 12.8.2. It disables interrupts on the local CPU.

182   as we have seen in Section 16.2.2.1, `tasklet_vec[]` is an array of `struct tasklet_head`, one per CPU. Each of these heads a linked list of `tasklet_struct`. We take a local copy of the head pointer, the `list` field of the entry in `tasklet_vec[]` corresponding to this CPU.

183   this sets that field NULL behind us. We have taken the list and do not want to take it again. There is no need for a lock on the list as it is CPU-specific and local interrupts are disabled.

184   the macro is in Section 12.8.2; it enables interrupts on the local CPU.

186–207 this loop is repeated until all the tasklets in the list have been executed. If the list was empty in the first place, then the function terminates immediately.

187 for the remainder of the loop, t now points to the current tasklet we are considering.

189 from here on, list points to the next tasklet, in preparation for the next iteration of the loop.

191–200 this code is executed only if the tasklet is not locked (running) beforehand (see Section 16.2.8 for a discussion of tasklet locks). A locked tasklet indicates that it is running on some other CPU. In that case, it is not executed but is back at the head of the list for the current CPU (see lines 202–206).

192–198 this code is executed only if the count field of the tasklet is zero, implying that the tasklet is enabled. Otherwise (disabled) it just unlocks it and continues. A disabled tasklet can be scheduled for execution but it will not run until it is enabled.

193 this clears the TASKLET_STATE_SCHED bit in the state field of the tasklet_struct. When set, this bit means that the tasklet is scheduled for execution. As we are about to execute it, we do not want to execute it again. If it was clear beforehand, there is some inconsistency, so we call the BUG() macro from Section 4.1.3.3. The test_and_clear_bit() function was described in Section 5.1.5.

195 this executes the function assigned to that particular tasklet, using the appropriate data.

196 now that we are finished with the tasklet, we unlock it, using the function from Section 16.2.8. This lock was held all the time the tasklet was running, so no interrupt, or other CPU, could get at it.

197 this causes the next iteration of the while at line 186 to begin (i.e. the next tasklet on the list is dealt with).

199 this line of code is executed only if the tasklet was found to be disabled at line 192. We unlock the tasklet and fall through to line 202.

202–206 this block of code is executed only if the tasklet was found to be running or disabled. We are going to put it back on the list for this CPU, to be handled later. We disable local interrupts while manipulating the list to lock out interrupt handlers, using the macro from Section 12.8.2.

203 a new list may have grown up since we took the list at line 182. This links the new list from this tasklet.

204 in any case, this tasklet is made the head of the list for this CPU.

205 this sets the TASKLET_SOFTIRQ bit in the softirq_active mask of the current CPU, whether it was already set or not (see Section 16.1.5.3). A tasklet has just been put on the list; we want it to be dealt with. Note that software interrupt number 3 is specified.

207 this is the end of the while loop, begun at line 186. We go back and process the next tasklet on the list.

16.2.7 The high-priority tasklet software interrupt

The function shown in Figure 16.24, from softirq.c, is set up at boot time as the handler for software interrupt number 0. When called, it runs all the high-priority tasklets queued for the CPU on which it is running. It is almost identical to the earlier function (Section 16.2.6), so the same comments apply.

```
210   static void tasklet_hi_action(struct softirq_action *a)
211   {
212         int cpu = smp_processor_id();
213         struct tasklet_struct *list;
214
215         local_irq_disable();
216         list = tasklet_hi_vec[cpu].list;
217         tasklet_hi_vec[cpu].list = NULL;
218         local_irq_enable();
219
220         while (list) {
221               struct tasklet_struct *t = list;
222
223               list = list->next;
224
225               if (tasklet_trylock(t)) {
226                     if (!atomic_read(&t->count)) {
227                           if (!test_and_clear_bit(TASKLET_STATE_SCHED,
                                                                  &t->state))
228                                 BUG();
229                           t->func(t->data);
230                           tasklet_unlock(t);
231                           continue;
232                     }
233                     tasklet_unlock(t);
234               }
235
236               local_irq_disable();
237               t->next = tasklet_hi_vec[cpu].list;
238               tasklet_hi_vec[cpu].list = t;
239               __cpu_raise_softirq(cpu, HI_SOFTIRQ);
240               local_irq_enable();
241         }
242   }
```

Figure 16.24   Handler for the high-priority tasklet software interrupt

216–217   this time we are dealing with a different list, headed from `tasklet_hi_vec[]`.

237–238   again, we are dealing with a different list.

239   this time the macro sets the `HI_SOFTIRQ` bit in the CPU-specific mask.

16.2.8 Tasklet locking

The TASKLET_STATE_RUN bit in the state field of the tasklet_struct is used as a lock bit in the tasklet subsystem. A number of macros are declared for manipulating this bit in <linux/interrupt.h> (see Figure 16.25).

```
133  #ifdef CONFIG_SMP
134  static inline int tasklet_trylock(struct tasklet_struct *t)
135  {
136      return !test_and_set_bit(TASKLET_STATE_RUN, &(t)->state);
137  }
138
139  static inline void tasklet_unlock(struct tasklet_struct *t)
140  {
141      smp_mb__before_clear_bit();
142      clear_bit(TASKLET_STATE_RUN, &(t)->state);
143  }
144
145  static inline void tasklet_unlock_wait(struct tasklet_struct *t)
146  {
147      while (test_bit(TASKLET_STATE_RUN, &(t)->state)) { barrier(); }
148  }
149  #else
150  #define tasklet_trylock(t) 1
151  #define tasklet_unlock_wait(t) do { } while (0)
152  #define tasklet_unlock(t) do { } while (0)
153  #endif
```

Figure 16.25 Tasklet locking macros

133–148 these are functions for the SMP case.

136 the test_and_set_bit() function, which here sets the TASKLET_STATE_RUN bit in the state field of the specified tasklet_struct, was described in Section 5.1.4.1. If the bit was set beforehand, it returns FALSE (we did not acquire the lock). If the bit was clear beforehand, it returns TRUE (we did acquire the lock). Thus, if the bit was set beforehand (the tasklet was running), the tasklet_trylock() function returns TRUE; otherwise, it returns FALSE. In all cases, the bit is set when this function returns.

141 this macro is an alias for the barrier() instruction, which guarantees that all CPUs have a consistent view of memory.

142 this clears the TASKLET_STATE_RUN bit in the state field of the specified tasklet_struct [see Section 5.1.2 for the clear_bit() function].

145–148 this function busy waits until the bit is clear.

147 for the test_bit() function, see Section 5.1.3.

150–152 this is the uniprocessor case. There is no actual setting or testing of any bit in the `state` field, as there can be only one tasklet running at a time.

150 this macro always evaluates to TRUE, as there can be only one tasklet at a time, so anytime it wants the lock it can have it.

151 it does not wait, as there can be nothing to wait for.

152 it does nothing, as there is no lock.

16.3 Bottom halves

Bottom halves were the earliest implementation of software interrupts in Linux. When an interrupt service routine finished, as long as there were no other hardware interrupts pending, the kernel scanned a table of bottom halves. Each entry in this could be marked active or inactive. If active, then it was carried out once, and marked inactive.

16.3.1 Data structures

Bottom halves are still supported in version 2.4 of Linux. This section will examine the data structures underlying the present implementation of bottom halves.

16.3.1.1 The bottom-half array

Bottom halves are tracked by the array `bh_base[]`, which contains pointers to the bottom-half handlers; see Figure 16.26, from `kernel/softirq.c`.

```
232   static void (*bh_base[32])(void);

287   spinlock_t global_bh_lock = SPIN_LOCK_UNLOCKED;
```

Figure 16.26   Bottom-half data structures

232 this array is never initialised, but insertions and deletions are done by `init_bh()` and `remove_bh()` (see Section 16.3.1.3).

287 mutual exclusion is guaranteed by taking out the `global_bh_lock` spinlock while running a bottom half.

16.3.1.2 Predefined bottom halves

The first 15 or so bottom halves are assigned fixed numbers. The enumeration shown in Figure 16.27, from `<linux/interrupt.h>`, decides 'who' gets which entry in `bh_base[]`. It seems reasonable that things that will occur most often should come first. The only ones we will come across again are TIMER_BH (0), TQUEUE_BH (1) and IMMEDIATE_BH (9).

```
27   enum {
28         TIMER_BH = 0,
29         TQUEUE_BH,
30         DIGI_BH,
31         SERIAL_BH,
32         RISCOM8_BH,
33         SPECIALIX_BH,
34         AURORA_BH,
35         ESP_BH,
36         SCSI_BH,
37         IMMEDIATE_BH,
38         CYCLADES_BH,
39         CM206_BH,
40         JS_BH,
41         MACSERIAL_BH,
42         ISICOM_BH
43   };
```

Figure 16.27   Some predefined bottom halves

16.3.1.3   Inserting and removing bottom halves

Bottom-half handlers are installed by inserting a pointer to the handler into the appropriate element of the bh_base[] array. The two functions shown in Figure 16.28 are from kernel/softirq.c.

```
312  void init_bh(int nr, void (*routine)(void))
313  {
314        bh_base[nr] = routine;
315        mb();
316  }
317
318  void remove_bh(int nr)
319  {
320        tasklet_kill(bh_task_vec+nr);
321        bh_base[nr] = NULL;
322  }
```

Figure 16.28   Inserting and removing bottom halves

312–316   this function sets up a bottom-half handler. It merely inserts the supplied pointer into the specified element in the bh_base[] array. The mb() is required to guarantee that the update is written to memory before returning.

318–322   this function removes a bottom-half handler from the array.

320   the next section will explain that bottom halves are actually executed using the tasklet mechanism. So, first of all, we check if the tasklet corresponding to this bottom half is currently running or scheduled to run and, if so, we wait [see Section 16.2.5.3 for the `tasklet_kill()` function].

321   we then put a NULL in the appropriate element of the `bh_base[]` array.

16.3.2   Executing bottom halves

It is envisaged that eventually bottom halves will disappear and be replaced by tasklets. Even in Linux 2.4, although bottom halves are still registered using their own array, as we have just seen, they are executed using the tasklet mechanism. This is done by setting up a one-to-one correspondence between tasklets and bottom halves.

As we have seen in Section 16.1.2.1, the default initialisation of the tasklet array, `bh_task_vec[]`, is that each element is pointed to the same function, `bh_action()`, shown in Figure 16.29, from `kernel/softirq.c`. This function runs the bottom-half handler installed in the corresponding position in the `bh_base[]` array.

```
289   static void bh_action(unsigned long nr)
290   {
291       int cpu = smp_processor_id();
292
293       if (!spin_trylock(&global_bh_lock))
294           goto resched;
295
296       if (!hardirq_trylock(cpu))
297           goto resched_unlock;
298
299       if (bh_base[nr])
300           bh_base[nr]();
301
302       hardirq_endlock(cpu);
303       spin_unlock(&global_bh_lock);
304       return;
305
306   resched_unlock:
307       spin_unlock(&global_bh_lock);
308   resched:
309       mark_bh(nr);
310   }
```

Figure 16.29   Default tasklet handler

289   the parameter `nr` is the number of the bottom half to run.

291   this finds the ID of the CPU on which we are running (see Section 7.2.1.4).

293–294   the `spin_trylock()` function is in Section 5.4.3.1. It returns TRUE if it acquires the lock, otherwise FALSE. It does not wait. If the global bottom-half lock (defined in Section 16.3.1.1) is not free, that means some other bottom half is currently running, so we go to line 308, which merely marks this bottom half for processing later and returns.

296–297   the `hardirq_trylock()` is defined as a macro in Section 16.5.3.1 (the uniprocessor case) and as a function in Section 16.5.3.2 (for the multiprocessor case). It evaluates to TRUE if no hardware interrupt handlers are running, otherwise FALSE. It does not wait. If we have acquired the global bottom-half lock, but the hardirq lock is not free, we go to line 306. This gives back the global bottom-half lock, marks this bottom half for processing later, and returns.

299–300   if there is a valid function pointer in the element of the `bh_base[]` array corresponding to the number supplied, then that function is called; otherwise, this line does nothing.

302–304   in either case, we give back both of the locks and return. The `hardirq_endlock()` macro is in Section 16.5.3.1. The `spin_unlock()` macro is from Section 5.3.1.

309   this function schedules a bottom half for processing later. It is dealt with in Section 16.3.3.

16.3.3 Marking a bottom half for execution

Figure 16.30, from `<linux/interrupt.h>`, shows the function that marks a bottom half for execution as soon as possible. Effectively, it converts the old `mark_bh()` into a call to `tasklet_hi_schedule()`, with a converted parameter. This schedules the tasklet corresponding to that bottom half, for execution on the high-priority tasklet queue of the current CPU (see Section 16.2.4.1).

```
227   static inline void mark_bh(int nr)
228   {
229        tasklet_hi_schedule(bh_task_vec+nr);
230   }
```

Figure 16.30   Marking a bottom half for execution later

229   the parameter `bh_task_vec + nr` is a pointer to the `tasklet_struct` corresponding to `nr` in the `bh_task_vec[]` array.

16.4 Task queues

Version 2.0 of Linux introduced task queues as an extension to and intended eventual replacement for bottom halves. This mechanism uses a queue of `tq_struct` rather than an array. You can have as many of them as you want.

The task queue mechanism is still there in Linux 2.4 and will be described in this section, but it should be noted that it is completely separate from the generic software interrupts and tasklets described in previous sections. Task queues are run by calls to the `run_task_queue()` function. This is passed a pointer to a particular task queue and processes all the elements in it in order.

There are three queues defined:

- `tq_timer`: run as soon as possible after each timer interrupt.

- `tq_immediate`: run as soon as possible after a `mark_bh()`, so this is effectively the old bottom-half handler.

- `tq_disk`: called by the input−output (IO) subsystem.

16.4.1 Task queue entries

Figure 16.31, from `<linux/tqueue.h>`, shows some data definitions and macros used in manipulating task queues.

```
38    struct tq_struct {
39        struct list_head list;
40        unsigned long sync;
41        void (*routine)(void *);
42        void *data;
43    };
64    typedef struct list_head task_queue;
65
66    #define DECLARE_TASK_QUEUE(q)       LIST_HEAD(q)
67    #define TQ_ACTIVE(q)                (!list_empty(&q))
```

Figure 16.31   Task queue data structures

38−43   this is the structure that is used to represent an entry in a task queue.

39   the task queue is maintained as a linked list, using the generic Linux list-handling mechanism. The `struct list_head` consists of forward and backward pointers (see Section 4.3.1).

40   the `sync` field must be initialised to 0. It is set to 1 when this entry is inserted on a queue. This feature prevents a `tq_struct` from being inserted on two lists at the same time. Before calling the function specified on the next line, the `sync` flag is cleared to 0, so the function could insert this in another queue, as part of its processing.

41   this is a pointer to the function that actually carries out the task.

42   this is a pointer to the value to pass to the handler function.

64   each queue is headed by a `task_queue`, which is merely a generic `list_head` (see Section 4.3.1).

66   this macro creates a header for a task queue. It is used in the code in Section 15.1.1. The `LIST_HEAD()` macro is described in Section 4.3.1.

67   this macro checks whether a particular queue is empty or not. The `list_empty()` function is described in Section 4.3.4.1. If there are entries on the queue, this macro evaluates to TRUE; otherwise, FALSE.

16.4.2 Inserting a task on a queue

The function shown in Figure 16.32, from `<linux/tqueue.h>`, is used to queue an entry on a task queue. It returns 1 if it was successfully added, otherwise it returns 0.

```
100  static inline int queue_task(struct tq_struct *bh_pointer,
                                              task_queue *bh_list)
101  {
102      int ret = 0;
103      if (!test_and_set_bit(0,&bh_pointer->sync)) {
104          unsigned long flags;
105          spin_lock_irqsave(&tqueue_lock, flags);
106          list_add_tail(&bh_pointer->list, bh_list);
107          spin_unlock_irqrestore(&tqueue_lock, flags);
108          ret = 1;
109      }
110      return ret;
111  }
```

Figure 16.32   Inserting an entry into a task queue

100   the function is passed a pointer to a `struct tq_struct` and a pointer to the head of the task queue on which it is to be inserted.

102   this sets up a default return value of 0 (failure).

103   bit 0 of the `sync` field in the `tq_struct` indicates whether the particular structure is currently on a list or not and is used to prevent it being inserted on more than one queue at the same time. At this stage, the bit should be clear, so we atomically set it, using the function from Section 5.1.4.1. If it was clear beforehand, then `test_and_set_bit()` returns FALSE. The `if` condition is now TRUE, so we go into the scope from 103–109. If the bit was set beforehand, the `test_and_set_bit()` returns TRUE. The `if` condition is now FALSE, so we skip on to line 110 and return 0.

105   this takes out the `tqueue_lock` spinlock and saves the value of the EFLAGS register. This global spinlock on all task queues is defined and initialised to the unlocked state in Section 16.4.4.1.

106   this adds the `tq_struct` to the tail of the list (before the head in a circular list), using the `list` field in the structure, which is the link field. The function has been discussed in Section 4.3.2.

107   this gives back the spinlock and restores EFLAGS.

108   the entry has been successfully added to the list, so we return 1 (success).

16.4.3   Run queued tasks

Linux provides two functions for executing tasks on a task queue. One checks for entries on the queue, the other runs them.

16.4.3.1   Checking for entries on a task queue

The function shown in Figure 16.33, from `<linux/tqueue.h>`, checks if there are any tasks on the specified queue. If there are, it calls `__run_task_queue()` (see Section 16.4.3.2) to run all the tasks.

```
119  static inline void run_task_queue(task_queue *list)
120  {
121      if (TQ_ACTIVE(*list))
122          __run_task_queue(list);
123  }
```

Figure 16.33   Checking for an empty queue before running tasks

121   the macro was defined in Section 16.4.1. If there are entries on the queue it evaluates to TRUE; otherwise, FALSE.

122   this function is considered next, in Section 16.4.3.2.

16.4.3.2   Executing the tasks on a specified queue

Figure 16.34 is from `kernel/softirq.c`. The function is passed a pointer to a task queue and actually runs the tasks on that queue.

```
335  void __run_task_queue(task_queue *list)
336  {
337      struct list_head head, *next;
338      unsigned long flags;
339
340      spin_lock_irqsave(&tqueue_lock, flags);
341      list_add(&head, list);
342      list_del_init(list);
343      spin_unlock_irqrestore(&tqueue_lock, flags);
344
345      next = head.next;
346      while (next != &head) {
347          void (*f)(void *);
348          struct tq_struct *p;
349          void *data;
350
351          p = list_entry(next, struct tq_struct, list);
352          next = next->next;
353          f = p->routine;
354          data = p->data;
355          wmb();
356          p->sync = 0;
357          if (f)
358              f(data);
359      }
360  }
```

Figure 16.34   Running the tasks on a specified task queue

340   the present function will unlink the entries from the list and set them up as a private list, headed from head. This means that interrupt handlers can be putting new tasks on the list while these ones are being handled. So, the global list need only be locked while entries are actually being unlinked from it, not all the time that entries are being processed. We take out a lock and save the contents of EFLAGS. The lock is defined and initialised in Section 16.4.4.1. The macros for manipulating interrupt-safe spinlocks were described in Section 12.8.1.

341 this function, from Section 4.3.2, adds a struct list_head at the beginning of the task queue list. All task queues are headed by a struct list_head, aliased as task_queue.

342 see Section 4.3.3. This initialises the first entry in the global list to NULL, so now the global list is empty and we have our local list headed from head.

343 at this stage we are finished with the global list so we can give back the lock.

345 from here on, next is pointing to the list entry that is currently being processed. It is advanced each time around the loop, at line 352.

346–359 this loop works its way along the queue until it gets back to the head again.

351 the list_entry() macro was described in Section 4.3.4.3. It converts a pointer to the list_head link (next) to a pointer to the actual structure of which it is a linked list (e.g. tq_struct).

352 this advances the next pointer to the following entry in the queue.

353–354 these get local pointers to the routine to be executed and the data to be passed to it.

355 this is a write memory barrier. It makes sure that all the previous assignments have actually been written to memory before going on. The wmb() macro is architecture-specific. On the 386 it does not do anything, as Intel CPUs guarantee that all writes are seen in program order.

356 the sync field is cleared to signify that it has been run. This is done before it is run rather than immediately after so that the handler can insert this tq_struct back on this or another list if it wants to.

357–358 if the function pointer is valid, the task is executed.

359 we go around the while loop again and execute the next task.

16.4.4 Predefined task queues

There are currently three task queues defined, but only two of these are relevant to the process manager.

16.4.4.1 The timer bottom half

The timer mechanism described in the previous chapter is now the standard timer mechanism in Linux. Some other, older, interfaces using task queues are still supported. The function shown in Figure 16.35, from kernel/timer.c, is the timer bottom half.

```
326  spinlock_t tqueue_lock = SPIN_LOCK_UNLOCKED;
327
```

```
328  void tqueue_bh(void)
329  {
330        run_task_queue(&tq_timer);
331  }
```

Figure 16.35   Function to process a task queue

330   this merely calls `run_task_queue()`, from Section 16.4.3.1, which processes a task queue. Its parameter is a pointer to a particular task queue, in this case the timer task queue, `tq_timer`. This timer queue is serviced at each timer interrupt or as soon as possible afterwards [see the call to `mark_bh(TIMER_BH)` in Section 15.1.2].

16.4.4.2 *The immediate bottom half*

The timer bottom half, examined in Section 16.4.4.1, is periodically marked for execution by the timer interrupt handler, but there may be routines requiring to be run not periodically but as and when required. The immediate task queue is used for that. This queue is serviced as soon as possible after a driver calls the function `mark_bh(IMMEDIATE_BH)` and thus corresponds to a driver bottom half in earlier versions of Linux.

The function shown in Figure 16.36, from `kernel/softirq.c`, processes the immediate task queue.

```
333  void immediate_bh(void)
334  {
335        run_task_queue(&tq_immediate);
336  }
```

Figure 16.36   Function to process an immediate task queue

335   the function `run_task_queue()` is from Section 16.4.3.1. Its parameter is a pointer to the immediate task queue. It processes all the `tq_struct` structures on that queue by calling their associated functions.

16.5   Interrupt request statistics

The process manager maintains statistics about any 'interruptions' that it is in the course of handling. These include such events as software and hardware interrupts, system calls, and nonmaskable interrupts. Now that software interrupts have been considered, these facilities can be introduced.

16.5.1 Data structures and macros

This section examines the basic data structures provided for maintaining this information and some low-level macros that manipulate them.

16.5.1.1 The `irq_stat[]` array

The basic data structure for this information is shown in Figure 16.37, from
`<asm/hardirq.h>`. There is a warning comment in the code that assembly language
routines in `entry.S` reference these fields by offset rather than by name so their relative
positions are important. There is an example of such use in Section 16.5.2.

```
9     typedef struct {
10          unsigned int              __softirq_pending;
11          unsigned int              __local_irq_count;
12          unsigned int              __local_bh_count;
13          unsigned int              __syscall_count;
14          struct task_struct *      __ksoftirqd_task;
15          unsigned int              __nmi_count;
16    } ____cacheline_aligned irq_cpustat_t;
```

Figure 16.37 Computer processing unit interrupt statistics

10 this field has a bit for each of the 32 possible software interrupts. If a particular one is pending,
the corresponding bit is set.

11 this is the nesting level of hardware interrupts currently being serviced on this CPU.

12 despite its name, this is the nesting level of software interrupts currently being serviced on this CPU.

13 this is the cumulative number of system calls handled to date on this CPU.

14 this is a pointer to the `task_struct` of the kernel thread spawned to handle software interrupts
on this CPU.

15 this is the cumulative number of nonmaskable interrupts currently handled on this CPU. This
field is architecture-dependent, for i386 and IA64. This information is maintained on a per CPU
basis, so there is an array `irq_stat[]` defined in `kernel/softirq.c`, as

```
43    irq_cpustat_t irq_stat[NR_CPUS];
```

16.5.1.2 Accessing fields in `irq_stat_t`

Linux provides an individual macro to facilitate access to each field in the `irq_stat[]`
array, introduced in the previous section; see Figure 16.38, from
`<linux/irq_cpustat.h>`.

```
29    #define softirq_pending(cpu)
                          __IRQ_STAT((cpu), __softirq_pending)
30    #define local_irq_count(cpu)
                          __IRQ_STAT((cpu), __local_irq_count)
31    #define local_bh_count(cpu)
                          __IRQ_STAT((cpu), __local_bh_count)
32    #define syscall_count(cpu)
                          __IRQ_STAT((cpu), __syscall_count)
```

```
33    #define ksoftirqd_task(cpu)                                    \
                          __IRQ_STAT((cpu), __ksoftirqd_task)
34
35    #define nmi_count(cpu)    __IRQ_STAT((cpu), __nmi_count)
```

Figure 16.38　Macros to access fields in the `irq_cpustat_t`

All these in turn use the `__IRQ_STAT()` macro (see Section 16.5.1.3), passing it the ID of the particular CPU and the name of the field to reference.

16.5.1.3 Extracting information from the `irq_stat_t`

The `__IRQ_STAT()` macro, as used in the previous subsection, is shown in Figure 16.39, from `<linux/irq_cpustat.h>`.

```
22    #ifdef CONFIG_SMP
23    #define __IRQ_STAT(cpu, member)    (irq_stat[cpu].member)
24    #else
25    #define __IRQ_STAT(cpu, member)((void)(cpu), irq_stat[0].member)
26    #endif
```

Figure 16.39　Macro to extract information from `irq_stat[]`

23　in the SMP case, the macro merely evaluates to the appropriate member of the array element corresponding to the specified CPU.

25　in the uniprocessor case, it reduces to the appropriate member of element 0 of the array.

16.5.2 Nesting software interrupts

Figure 16.40, from `<asm-i386/softirq.h>`, shows a number of higher-level macros that keep track of how deeply nested we are into software interrupts.

```
8     #define __cpu_bh_enable(cpu)                                   \
9         do { barrier(); local_bh_count(cpu)-; } while (0)
10    #define cpu_bh_disable(cpu)                                    \
11        do { local_bh_count(cpu)++; barrier(); } while (0)
12
13    #define local_bh_disable() (cpu_bh_disable(smp_processor_id()))
14    #define local_bh_enable() cpu_bh_enable(smp_processor_id())
15    #define in_softirq()(local_bh_count(smp_processor_id()) !=0)

26    #define local_bh_enable()                                      \
27    do {                                                           \
28        unsigned int *ptr = &local_bh_count(smp_processor_id());   \
29                                                                   \
30            barrier();                                             \
31            if (!-*ptr)                                            \
32                __asm____volatile__ (                              \
```

```
33          "cmpl $0, -8(%0);"                                               \
34          "jnz 2f;"                                                        \
35          "1:;"                                                            \
36                                                                           \
37          ".subsection 1;"                                                 \
38          ".ifndef _text_lock_" __stringify(KBUILD_BASENAME) "\n"          \
39          "_text_lock_" __stringify(KBUILD_BASENAME) ":\n"                 \
40          ".endif\n"                                                       \
41          "2: pushl %%eax; pushl %%ecx; pushl %%edx;"                      \
42          "call %c1;"                                                      \
43          "popl %%edx; popl %%ecx; popl %%eax;"                            \
44          "jmp 1b;"                                                        \
45          ".subsection 0;"                                                 \
46                                                                           \
47          : /* no output */                                                \
48          : "r" (ptr), "i" (do_softirq)                                    \
49          /* no registers clobbered */);                                   \
50   } while (0)
```

Figure 16.40   Nesting level of software interrupts

8–9   this macro does not actually enable anything. It calls the `barrier()` macro to ensure that any changes made to `__local_bh_count` have been propagated to memory, then it uses the macro from Section 16.5.1.2 to decrement the nesting level of software interrupts running on the specified CPU.

10–11   the name of this macro is also rather misleading in that it does not disable anything. It merely increments the `__local_bh_count` field in the `irq_stat_t` corresponding to the specified CPU (see Section 16.5.1.2). It then calls the `barrier()` macro to ensure that this write has been flushed to memory, before continuing.

13–14   each of these macros first identifies the processor on which it is running, using the macro from Section 7.2.1.4.

13   it then calls the `cpu_bh_disable()` macro from line 10.

14   it then calls the `__cpu_bh_enable()` macro from line 8.

15   if the `__local_bh_count` for the CPU on which we are running is not zero, then we must be servicing a software interrupt; so we evaluate to TRUE.

26–50   this macro decrements the nesting level of software interrupts running on the current CPU, but it also checks for pending software interrupts and calls `do_softirq()` if necessary.

28   the `local_bh_count()` macro from Section 16.5.1.2 evaluates to the `__local_bh_count` value for the current CPU. This line takes a pointer to the appropriate element of the array.

30   this ensures that any changes made to `__local_bh_count` have been propagated to memory (and not just in cache).

31   the software interrupt nesting level on this CPU is decremented. If it is still positive after this, nothing further is done. Note that lines 32–49 are one C instruction.

32–49 this assembler code is executed if there are now no software interrupts running on the CPU.

33 parameter 0 is a pointer to `__local_bh_count`. The location 8 bytes before that in memory is `__softirq_pending` (see Section 16.5.1.1). We check if that is 0.

34 if there are software interrupts pending, we jump on to line 41.

35 if not, we do nothing further, because lines 37–44 are in a different section, so execution falls through to line 50.

37–44 this code is compiled into a different subsection.

38–40 these lines are for the assembler. The `__stringify()` macro converts the kernel build number (e.g. 2.4.18) to a string. Then, if a label of the form `_text_lock_buildnumber` does not already exist, it is placed here in the code for the assembler. Note the colon at the end of line 39, indicating a label definition. This label is inserted merely to help with debugging kernel code.

41 the EAX, ECX, and EDX registers are saved on the stack; these will be used by the function called at line 42.

42 parameter 1 is a pointer to the function `do_softirq()`, described in Section 16.1.3.

43 after `do_softirq()` returns, we restore the values saved at line 41.

44 this jumps back to the main section and exits the macro.

48 parameter 0 is read only, in a register (`"r"`), the pointer to `__local_bh_count`; parameter 1 is an immediate (`"i"`) pointer to the function `do_softirq()`.

16.5.3 Manipulating interrupt counters

Finally, there are a number of miscellaneous routines that manipulate the counter fields introduced in Section 16.5.1.1. The uniprocessor versions of these routines are implemented as macros; the multiprocessor versions are full-blown functions.

16.5.3.1 Macros for the uniprocessor case

Figure 16.41, from `<asm-i386/hardirq.h>`, shows a number of macros that manipulate the interrupt counter fields. These are used in uniprocessor systems.

```
24   #define in_interrupt() ({ int __cpu = smp_processor_id();          \
25        (local_irq_count(__cpu) + local_bh_count(__cpu) != 0);})
26
27   #define in_irq() (local_irq_count(smp_processor_id()) != 0)
28
29   #ifndef CONFIG_SMP
30
31   #define hardirq_trylock(cpu)      (local_irq_count(cpu) == 0)
32   #define hardirq_endlock(cpu)      do { } while (0)
33
```

```
34    #define irq_enter(cpu, irq)        (local_irq_count(cpu)++)
35    #define irq_exit(cpu, irq)         (local_irq_count(cpu)-)
36
37    #define synchronize_irq()          barrier()
```

Figure 16.41 Uniprocessor version of interrupt macros

24 this finds the ID number of the CPU on which we are running. The `smp_processor_id()` macro has been described in Section 7.2.1.4.

25 both `local_irq_count()` and `local_bh_count()` were described in Section 16.5.1.2. They return values from CPU-specific counters that are incremented each time a hardware or software interrupt handler is entered. If either or both of these counters is not zero, then it returns TRUE. Only if both are zero does it return FALSE.

27 this is a cut-down version of the foregoing macro. It checks only for hardware interrupts.

31 if there are no hardware interrupts in progress on the local CPU, this macro evaluates to TRUE; otherwise, FALSE, so it does not actually take out any lock.

32 the uniprocessor version of this macro does nothing.

34–35 these macros bracket the handling of hardware interrupts. They merely increment and decrement the nesting level of hardware interrupts in progress on the specified CPU.

37 the `barrier()` macro guarantees that any writes by other CPUs have been flushed to main memory and so are visible to this CPU.

16.5.3.2 Functions for the multiprocessor case

In a multiprocessor system, the macros discussed in the previous subsection are implemented as functions, as shown in Figure 16.42, from `<asm-i386/hardirq.h>`.

```
47    static inline int irqs_running (void)
48    {
49        int i;
50
51        for (i = 0; i < smp_num_cpus; i++)
52            if (local_irq_count(i))
53                return 1;
54        return 0;
55    }
56
57    static inline void release_irqlock(int cpu)
58    {
59
60        if (global_irq_holder == (unsigned char) cpu) {
61            global_irq_holder = NO_PROC_ID;
62            clear_bit(0, &global_irq_lock);
63        }
```

```
64   }
65
66   static inline void irq_enter(int cpu, int irq)
67   {
68        ++local_irq_count(cpu);
69
70        while (test_bit(0,&global_irq_lock)) {
71             cpu_relax();
72        }
73   }
74
75   static inline void irq_exit(int cpu, int irq)
76   {
77        -local_irq_count(cpu);
78   }
79
80   static inline int hardirq_trylock(int cpu)
81   {
82        return !local_irq_count(cpu) && !test_bit(0,&global_irq_lock);
83   }
```

Figure 16.42 Multiprocessor version of interrupt related macros

51–53	we go through each of the CPUs and if there is at least one hardware interrupt handler running on any of them we return TRUE.
51	the smp_num_cpus variable was defined in Section 7.2.1.1.
52	the local_irq_count() macro is from Section 16.5.1.2.
54	otherwise, we return 0.
60–62	if the current CPU owns the global_irq_lock, then we give it back; otherwise, we do nothing. Both the lock field itself and the global_irq_holder variable were defined in Section 14.5.1.1.
61	no CPU now owns the lock.
62	this clears the lock bit to signify that, using the function from Section 5.1.2.
68	this is the uniprocessor part, using the macro from Section 16.5.1.2.
70–71	we loop if some other CPU is holding the global interrupt lock, until that lock is released. The cpu_relax() macro, from Section 9.4.2.2, introduces a delay into the busy waiting loop.
75–78	this is equivalent to the uniprocessor version. It merely decrements the count of hardware interrupts in progress on the local CPU.
82	if no hardware interrupts are being processed on this CPU, and the global interrupt lock is free, then we return TRUE; otherwise, FALSE.

17

The signal mechanism

The foregoing chapters have dealt with interruptions to the normal running of the operating system. Now we go on, in the next three chapters, to consider the signal mechanism. This is another form of interruption. This time it is a user process that is being interrupted, either by the operating system or by another process.

The signal mechanism in Unix allows one process to notify another that a particular event has occurred, and it arranges for a user-defined function to be called. There is a system-defined set of signals, each corresponding to a different event. These are identified by integers, defined as symbolic constants, beginning with SIG, and some mnemonic hint of a particular event; for example, SIGCHLD is the signal sent to a parent when a child process dies.

There are an unexpectedly large number of data structures involved in the kernel implementation of signals. These, and the functions that manipulate them, are the subject of the present chapter. With this background in place, Chapter 18 will then go on to examine how signals are posted by the source process and actually delivered to the target process. Signals are delivered to a process in kernel mode; but the handler must run in user mode. The mechanism used to implement this is described in Chapter 19.

17.1 Data structures used to implement signals

The basic data structures involved in the kernel implementation of signals will be examined in this first section so that they will be available for all that follows. Most of these data structures, including the list of signals itself, are architecture-specific.

17.1.1 Basic definitions

The set of signals is frequently represented by a bitmap. A number of basic definitions for the implementation of signals on the i386 architecture are given in Figure 17.1, from `<asm-i386/signal.h>`.

The Linux Process Manager. The Internals of Scheduling, Interrupts and Signals   John O'Gorman
© 2003 John Wiley & Sons, Ltd   ISBN: 0 470 84771 9

```
13    #define _NSIG              64
14    #define _NSIG_BPW          32
15    #define _NSIG_WORDS        (_NSIG / _NSIG_BPW)

19    typedef struct {
20        unsigned long sig[_NSIG_WORDS];
21    } sigset_t;
```

Figure 17.1   Basic signal definitions

13   there are 64 possible signals available in the i386 architecture.

14   this is the number of bits in the basic processor word [bits per word (BPW)].

15   this is the number of words in a bitmap representing all possible signals (2).

19–21   the basic bitmap representing signals (sigset_t) is implemented as an array of unsigned long. On the i386, this has two elements.

17.1.2   Signal definitions

The definitions of the standard signals used on the i386 are shown in Figure 17.2, from <asm-i386/signal.h>. It is not necessary to understand the uses to which each signal is put in order to appreciate how the mechanism works, but a brief description is given of each.

```
31    #define SIGHUP       1
32    #define SIGINT       2
33    #define SIGQUIT      3
34    #define SIGILL       4
35    #define SIGTRAP      5
36    #define SIGABRT      6
37    #define SIGIOT       6
38    #define SIGBUS       7
39    #define SIGFPE       8
40    #define SIGKILL      9
41    #define SIGUSR1      10
42    #define SIGSEGV      11
43    #define SIGUSR2      12
44    #define SIGPIPE      13
45    #define SIGALRM      14
46    #define SIGTERM      15
47    #define SIGSTKFLT    16
48    #define SIGCHLD      17
49    #define SIGCONT      18
50    #define SIGSTOP      19
51    #define SIGTSTP      20
52    #define SIGTTIN      21
53    #define SIGTTOU      22
```

```
54    #define SIGURG       23
55    #define SIGXCPU      24
56    #define SIGXFSZ      25
57    #define SIGVTALRM    26
58    #define SIGPROF      27
59    #define SIGWINCH     28
60    #define SIGIO        29
61    #define SIGPOLL      SIGIO

65    #define SIGPWR       30
66    #define SIGSYS       31
67    #define SIGUNUSED    31

70    #define SIGRTMIN     32
71    #define SIGRTMAX     (_NSIG-1)
```

Figure 17.2   Signal definitions

31   the hangup signal is sent by the kernel to all processes attached to a controlling terminal when that terminal is disconnected. It is also sent to each process in the foreground process group when the session leader terminates. A secondary use for it is to tell daemon processes to reread their configuration files. Normally, a daemon would not have a controlling terminal so there is no confusion.

32   when the interrupt key (CTRL-C) is pressed, the terminal driver sends this signal to all processes in the foreground process group. It is the conventional way of stopping a running program.

33   when the quit key (CTRL-\) is pressed, the terminal driver sends this signal to all processes in the foreground process group. It is similar to SIGINT but has the extra effect of generating a core file.

34   the kernel sends this signal to a process that has attempted to execute an illegal computer processing unit (CPU) instruction.

35   this is a signal used by debuggers. It is sent by the kernel when the hardware detects a breakpoint.

36   the abort() function generates this signal.

37   some specific hardware faults cause this signal to be sent to the current process. It is normally sent by a driver, and never by the kernel. Note that the system makes no distinction between this and SIGABRT.

38   a hardware bus fault causes this signal to be sent to the current process. It is normally sent by a driver, and never by the kernel.

39   this is sent at an error in an arithmetic operation, such as division by 0.

40   this is a sure way to kill a process. This signal cannot be caught or ignored.

41   the user can define the meaning of this signal. It is never sent by the kernel.

42 this signal is sent on an invalid memory reference.

43 the user can also define the meaning of this signal. It is never sent by the kernel.

44 this is the signal generated when a process writes to a pipe or socket and the process at the other end has disconnected, or even terminated.

45 this is generated when a timer expires.

46 this is an instruction to terminate. It is the default signal sent by the `kill(1)` command from the terminal, but this signal can be caught and handled, unlike `SIGKILL`.

47 the kernel sends this signal to the current process when there is an error on the floating point unit's (FPU's) internal stack.

48 this signal is sent to the parent when a child process stops or terminates.

49 this signal is sent to a stopped process when that process is to continue.

50 this signal stops a process (i.e. it moves it to the `TASK_STOPPED` state). It cannot be caught or ignored.

51 when the suspend key (`CTRL-Z`) is pressed, the terminal driver sends this signal to all processes in the foreground process group. Its effect is to move them to the `TASK_STOPPED` state.

52 when a process in a background process group tries to read from its terminal, the terminal driver sends this signal to the process.

53 when a process in a background process group tries to write to its terminal, the terminal driver sends this signal to the process.

54 this signal notifies a process that an urgent condition has occurred (e.g. urgent or out-of-band data on a network connection).

55 this is sent to a process when it exceeds its soft CPU limit.

56 this is sent to a process when it exceeds its soft file size limit.

57 this signal is sent when a virtual interval timer expires.

58 this signal is sent when a profiling interval timer expires.

59 this signal is sent to the foreground process group when the size of a screen window is changed.

60 this signal is sent to indicate that an asynchronous input–output (IO) event has occurred.

61 this signal is generated when a specific event occurs on a device being monitored by `poll()`. Note that in Linux it is not distinguished from `SIGIO`.

65 this signal is sent on a power supply failure.

66 this indicates an invalid system call.

67 this is not really a signal definition, it is only a marker.

70 this is the first (lowest-numbered) real time signal.

71 this is the highest numbered real time signal.

17.1.3 Process-specific signal handling information

One fundamental facility required when handling signals is the ability to keep track of what action to take when a particular signal is raised. The various data structures considered in this section are part of the infrastructure underlying this.

17.1.3.1 The signal_struct structure

Each process is allocated a data structure to record the action it is to take when any particular signal is raised. This is shown in Figure 17.3, from <linux/sched.h>. It is linked from the sig field in the task_struct of the process (see Section 2.8).

```
247  struct signal_struct {
248  atomic_t                  count;
249  struct k_sigaction        action[_NSIG];
250  spinlock_t                siglock;
251  };
```

Figure 17.3   The signal_struct structure

248 these structures can be shared by processes, if the appropriate flags are passed to clone(). This field tracks the number of users sharing a structure. Only when the use count drops to 0 will it be deallocated.

249 there is one element in this array for each signal. Each entry is a struct k_sigaction, discussed in Section 17.1.3.3

250 this spinlock is used to guarantee mutual exclusion on the whole structure.

17.1.3.2 Initialising the signal_struct

When a new signal_struct is allocated it is initialised to the values shown in Figure 17.4, from <linux/sched.h>.

```
254  #define INIT_SIGNALS {                             \
255  count:                    ATOMIC_INIT(1),          \
256  action:                   { {{0,}}, },             \
257  siglock:                  SPIN_LOCK_UNLOCKED       \
258  }
```

Figure 17.4   Initialising the signal_struct

255 there is this one (initial) user. The ATOMIC_INIT() macro has been described in Section 5.2.1.

256 the outermost braces indicate that each element in the array is to be initialised as indicated. The next pair of braces refer to the `struct k_sigaction`, so each `struct sigaction` is initialised as `{0, }`. That is, the first field is set to 0, or `SIG_DFL` (see Section 17.1.3.3).

257 the spinlock is initialised to the unlocked state.

17.1.3.3 The `sigaction` structure

The definition of the `struct k_sigaction` (the kernel version of the `struct sigaction`) is shown in Figure 17.5, from `<asm-i386/signal.h>`.

```
129  typedef void (*__sighandler_t)(int);
130
131  #define SIG_DFL ((__sighandler_t)0)
132  #define SIG_IGN ((__sighandler_t)1)

143  struct sigaction {
144        __sighandler_t sa_handler;
145        unsigned long sa_flags;
146        void (*sa_restorer)(void);
147        sigset_t sa_mask;
148  };
149
150  struct k_sigaction {
151        struct sigaction sa;
152  };
```

Figure 17.5 The `sigaction` structure

129 this is the prototype for a signal handler function. They all take a single `int` parameter (usually the number of the signal) and do not return any value.

131–132 there are two system-defined handling routines. These are identified by small integers, whereas all other handlers are identified by pointers to their functions.

131 if this value is set in the `sa_handler` field (see line 144) then the system is to take the default handling for that signal.

132 if this value is set in the `sa_handler` field, then the system is to ignore that signal.

143–148 this data structure represents the action to be taken for a particular signal.

144 this field specifies the handler function. It contains either a pointer to the function or one of the values from lines 131–132.

145 this provides further information about how the signal is to be handled, which modifies the behaviour of the signal handling process (see Section 17.1.3.4 for the possible values).

146 this field is obsolete and should not be used. It is not specified by POSIX.

147 this is a bitmap specifying those signals that are to be blocked while this handler is running. In addition, the signal that triggered the handler will also be blocked unless either the SA_DEFER or the SA_NOMASK bit is set in the sa_flags field.

150–152 for compatibility reasons, the foregoing structure is also defined like this. Each process has an array of these, one per signal, as seen in Section 17.1.3.1.

17.1.3.4 Signal types

When a handler is being set up for a signal it can be given a number of different properties, in the sa_flags field. These are defined in Figure 17.6, from `<asm-i386/signal.h>`.

```
87   #define SA_NOCLDSTOP        0x00000001
88   #define SA_NOCLDWAIT        0x00000002
89   #define SA_SIGINFO          0x00000004
90   #define SA_ONSTACK          0x08000000
91   #define SA_RESTART          0x10000000
92   #define SA_NODEFER          0x40000000
93   #define SA_RESETHAND        0x80000000
94
95   #define SA_NOMASK           SA_NODEFER
96   #define SA_ONESHOT          SA_RESETHAND
97   #define SA_INTERRUPT        0x20000000
98
99   #define SA_RESTORER 0       x04000000

119  #define SA_PROBE            SA_ONESHOT
120  #define SA_SAMPLE_RANDOM    SA_RESTART
121  #define SA_SHIRQ            0x04000000
```

Figure 17.6   Signal handler types

87 this flag is valid only for SIGGHLD. When children stop, as a result of SIGSTOP, SIGTSTP, SIGTTIN, or SIGTTOU, the parent is normally sent a SIGCHLD signal. If this bit is set in the sa_flags field of the struct k_sigaction representing SIGCHLD it inhibits the parent from receiving any notification.

88 this flag on SIGCHLD inhibits zombie processes, that is, the child does not wait for the parent to reap it. It is not supported yet in Linux.

89 this bit indicates that additional information is available to the signal handler, in a struct siginfo (see Section 17.1.5.1).

90 an alternate stack is used while executing this handler (see Section 17.6).

91 a system call interrupted by this signal is automatically restarted.

92 this bit prevents the signal from being masked in its own handler.

93   when this bit is set, the handler is cleared after the signal is delivered and set to SIG_DFL for future occurrences of this signal.

97   the handler must execute with interrupts disabled.

99   this is a dummy, still there for historical reasons. It should not be used for new handlers.

121 this bit is used only by interrupt handlers for PCI and EISA devices. It means that the handler supports sharing of interrupt lines.

17.1.4 Queue of pending signals

The previous section examined how the process keeps track of the handlers for each different signal, but the task_struct has another pointer field, pending. This points to the head of a linked list of data structures, each representing one pending signal.

17.1.4.1 Data structures representing the pending queue

The data structures used to implement these queues of pending signals are shown in Figure 17.7, from <linux/signal.h>.

```
12   struct sigqueue {
13        struct sigqueue *next;
14        siginfo_t info;
15   };
16
17   struct sigpending {
18        struct sigqueue *head, **tail;
19        sigset_t signal;
20   };
```

Figure 17.7   Data structures for queuing signals

12–15   this structure represents one instance of a queued signal.

13   this is the link for the (singly linked) queue.

14   this field contains the information about the signal. It is a struct siginfo (see Section 17.1.5.1).

17–20   this is the header of the queue. It is linked from the pending field in the task_struct of the process to which these signals are queued.

18   this is the head pointer, to the first element in the queue. The tail pointer is always set to the next field of the last entry.

19   this is a bitmap (see Section 17.1.1). Each bit represents one signal and is set if that signal is pending. It is used to look up which signals (if any) are pending before searching the whole queue.

17.1.4.2   Initialising the `sigpending` structure for a process

Each process has a pending field in its `task_struct`. This is a `struct sigpending` (see Section 2.8). That structure is then initialised by the function shown in Figure 17.8, from `<linux/signal.h>`.

```
214  static inline void init_sigpending (struct sigpending *sig)
215  {
216      sigemptyset(&sig->signal);
217      sig->head = NULL;
218      sig->tail = &sig->head;
219  }
```

Figure 17.8   Initialising the `sigpending` structure for a process

216   we pass a pointer to the `signal` field in the `struct sigpending` to this function (from Section 17.2.2.4) which clears all bits in it.

217   the `head` pointer is set to NULL.

218   the `tail` pointer is set to the `head` field in the `struct sigpending`.

17.1.5   Extended information about a signal

Primitive implementations of the signal mechanism merely recorded the fact that a signal was pending. Modern versions of Unix, including Linux, pass quite an amount of information about the signal from the sender to the target process. This section examines how that information is encapsulated.

17.1.5.1   The `siginfo` structure

This extended information about a signal is recorded in a `struct siginfo`, or `siginfo_t`, as shown in Figure 17.9, from `<asm-i386/siginfo.h>`. Because different information is needed about different signals, the body of this structure is a large `union`, with options for different types of signal. This makes it look more complicated than it really is.

```
8       typedef union sigval {
9           int sival_int;
10          void *sival_ptr;
11      } sigval_t;
12
13  #define SI_MAX_SIZE        128
14  #define SI_PAD_SIZE        ((SI_MAX_SIZE/sizeof(int)) - 3)
15
16  typedef struct siginfo {
17          int si_signo;
18          int si_errno;
19          int si_code;
20
```

```
21          union {
22                  int _pad[SI_PAD_SIZE];

25                  struct {
26                          pid_t _pid;
27                          uid_t _uid;
28                  } _kill;

31                  struct {
32                          unsigned int _timer1;
33                          unsigned int _timer2;
34                  } _timer;

37                  struct {
38                          pid_t _pid;
39                          uid_t _uid;
40                          sigval_t _sigval;
41                  } _rt;
44                  struct {
45                          pid_t _pid;
46                          uid_t _uid;
47                          int _status;
48                          clock_t _utime;
49                          clock_t _stime;
50                  } _sigchld;

53                  struct {
54                          void * _addr;
55                  } _sigfault;

58                  struct {
59                          int _band;
60                          int _fd;
61                          } _sigpoll;
62          } _sifields;
63  } siginfo_t;
```

Figure 17.9 The `siginfo` structure

8–11 this is required by POSIX real-time signals. It is a device to allow extra information to be passed to the handler. The `union` allows either an `int` value, or a pointer, to be passed. This should cater for all possible data types. It is used at line 40.

13 this is the maximum size of a `struct siginfo`, measured in bytes.

14 this field is measured in `int`. At the very least, there are three `int` fields in the structure. In that case, it needs to be padded out to the maximum of 128 bytes. On the i386, with an `int` being 4 bytes, this padding would be 29 `int`.

17 this is the number of the signal, as defined in Section 17.1.2.

18 the error number is application-specific.

19 this field identifies the sender of the signal. Possible values are discussed in Sections 17.1.5.4–17.1.5.7.

22 if no further information is provided, this field pads the structure out to its full length (see line 14).

25–28 this information is sent with SIGKILL; it merely includes the pid and uid of the sender.

31–34 this information is for POSIX 1b timer signals. It merely includes the values of both timers.

37–41 this information is required by POSIX real-time signals. As well as the sender's pid and uid, it includes a union sigval, as defined in lines 8–11.

44–50 this gives special information for a SIGCHLD signal.

45–46 these are the pid and uid of the sender (to identify which child).

47 this is the exit code from the child, giving the reason for the signal (e.g. has it terminated or just stopped).

48–49 these lines give the cumulative time the child has spent running in user and kernel mode, respectively.

53–55 these provide extra information sent with the SIGILL, SIGFPE, SIGSEGV, or SIGBUS signals. Each of these indicates some hardware problem.

54 this is a pointer to the instruction (in the code) that caused the problem.

58–61 these give extra information to accompany the SIGPOLL signal.

59 this identifies the reason for the signal.

60 this identifies the stream for which it is a notification.

17.1.5.2 Shortcuts for accessing siginfo fields

The struct siginfo examined in the previous section consists of structures within structures within a union. Referencing individual fields in this can become quite complicated, so shortcuts are defined for some of them, as seen in Figure 17.10, from <asm-i386/signal.h>. They are self-explanatory.

```
68   #define si_pid      _sifields._kill._pid
69   #define si_uid      _sifields._kill._uid
70   #define si_status   _sifields._sigchld._status
71   #define si_utime    _sifields._sigchld._utime
72   #define si_stime    _sifields._sigchld._stime
73   #define si_value    _sifields._rt._sigval
74   #define si_int      _sifields._rt._sigval.sival_int
```

```
75    #define si_ptr       _sifields._rt._sigval.sival_ptr
76    #define si_addr      _sifields._sigfault._addr
77    #define si_band      _sifields._sigpoll._band
78    #define si_fd        _sifields._sigpoll._fd
```

Figure 17.10   Shortcuts for accessing `siginfo` fields

17.1.5.3   Codes indicating the signal group

The `si_code` field in the `struct siginfo` contains information about the source of the signal. This field is faceted, with the high-order 16 bits indicating which element of the union is valid, and the low-order bits indicating the source. The macros shown in Figure 17.11, from `<asm-i386/siginfo.h>`, set up the high-order field. These are never used directly; low-order values are appended before they are inserted in the `si_code` field.

```
81    #define __SI_MASK         0xffff0000
82    #define __SI_KILL         (0 << 16)
83    #define __SI_TIMER        (1 << 16)
84    #define __SI_POLL         (2 << 16)
85    #define __SI_FAULT        (3 << 16)
86    #define __SI_CHLD         (4 << 16)
87    #define __SI_RT           (5 << 16)
88    #define __SI_CODE(T,N)    ((T) << 16 | ((N) & 0xffff))
```

Figure 17.11   Generic `si_code` values

81   this mask is used to zero the low-order 16 bits.

82   this macro indicates that the `_kill` field of the `union` is valid.

83   this macro indicates that the `_timer` field of the `union` is valid.

84   this macro indicates that the `_sigpoll` field of the `union` is valid.

85   this macro indicates that the `_sigfault` field of the `union` is valid.

86   this macro indicates that the `_sigchld` field of the `union` is valid.

87   this macro indicates that the `_rt` field of the `union` is valid.

88   this macro constructs a 32-bit code. The T parameter is in the high-order 16 bits, whereas the N parameter is in the low-order bits. The N parameter is prevented from overlapping into the T space by ANDing it with `0xffff`.

17.1.5.4   Codes indicating the source of a signal

The low-order 16 bits of the `si_code` field indicate the sender of the signal. Figure 17.12, from `<asm-i386/siginfo.h>`, indicates the predefined sources. Note that negative values indicate POSIX real-time signals, a zero value indicates a user mode signal, and a positive value indicates that the signal originated in the kernel.

```
103  #define SI_USER      0
104  #define SI_KERNEL    0x80
105  #define SI_QUEUE     -1
106  #define SI_TIMER     __SI_CODE(__SI_TIMER,-2)
107  #define SI_MESGQ     -3
108  #define SI_ASYNCIO   -4
109  #define SI_SIGIO     -5
110
111  #define SI_FROMUSER(siptr)   ((siptr)->si_code <= 0)
112  #define SI_FROMKERNEL(siptr) ((siptr)->si_code > 0)
```

Figure 17.12 Codes indicating the source of the signal

103 this indicates that the signal was sent from user mode, using for example the kill() or raise() system services.

104 this indicates that the signal was sent from somewhere in the kernel. In most cases, one of the more specific values defined in Sections 17.1.5.5–17.1.5.7 will be used.

105 the signal was sent by sigqueue(). This is part of the POSIX extension to the signal mechanism, not yet fully implemented in Linux.

106 the signal was sent by an expiring timer. The high-order 16 bits contain __SI_TIMER, the low-order bits −2. The __SI_CODE() macro was described in Section 17.1.5.3.

107 this identifies a signal sent to a waiting process when a message has arrived for an empty POSIX message queue.

108 the signal was sent on completion of an asynchronous IO request, such as aio_read().

109 an IO stream can be set up in such a way that it will post a signal to a process when IO is possible. It usually sends the SIGIO signal. This value indicates that such a stream was the source of the signal.

111 the parameter siptr is a pointer to a struct siginfo. The macro evaluates to TRUE if the value in the si_code field is 0 or negative, evaluating to FALSE otherwise.

112 this macro evaluates to TRUE if the signal was sent by the kernel, FALSE otherwise.

17.1.5.5 Special si_code values for CPU-generated faults

When the CPU runs into some problem while executing a program it raises an exception. The exception handlers examined in Chapter 11 send a signal to the current process. The si_code field attempts to further refine the cause of this signal, using one of the codes defined in Figure 17.13, from <asm/siginfo.h>. In all cases the high-order 16 bits contain __SI_FAULT.

```
117  #define ILL_ILLOPC  (__SI_FAULT|1)
118  #define ILL_ILLOPN  (__SI_FAULT|2)
119  #define ILL_ILLADR  (__SI_FAULT|3)
```

```
120  #define ILL_ILLTRP  (__SI_FAULT|4)
121  #define ILL_PRVOPC  (__SI_FAULT|5)
122  #define ILL_PRVREG  (__SI_FAULT|6)
123  #define ILL_COPROC  (__SI_FAULT|7)
124  #define ILL_BADSTK  (__SI_FAULT|8)

130  #define FPE_INTDIV  (__SI_FAULT|1)
131  #define FPE_INTOVF  (__SI_FAULT|2)
132  #define FPE_FLTDIV  (__SI_FAULT|3)
133  #define FPE_FLTOVF  (__SI_FAULT|4)
134  #define FPE_FLTUND  (__SI_FAULT|5)
135  #define FPE_FLTRES  (__SI_FAULT|6)
136  #define FPE_FLTINV  (__SI_FAULT|7)
137  #define FPE_FLTSUB  (__SI_FAULT|8)

143  #define SEGV_MAPERR (__SI_FAULT|1)
144  #define SEGV_ACCERR (__SI_FAULT|2)

150  #define BUS_ADRALN  (__SI_FAULT|1)
151  #define BUS_ADRERR  (__SI_FAULT|2)
152  #define BUS_OBJERR  (__SI_FAULT|3)

158  #define TRAP_BRKPT  (__SI_FAULT|1)
159  #define TRAP_TRACE  (__SI_FAULT|2)
```

Figure 17.13   Special si_code values for CPU-generated faults

117–124   when a process attempts to execute an invalid opcode, the kernel sends it a SIGILL signal, and the si_code field contains one of these values.

117   the opcode itself was invalid.

118   one of the operands was invalid.

119   the addressing mode used was illegal.

120   the instruction was an illegal trap. This is not actually used by the kernel.

121   the opcode was privileged and so could not be executed in user mode.

122   the instruction attempted to access a privileged register.

123   some error in the FPU.

124   the internal FPU stack caused the problem.

130–137   when an exception is raised by the FPU, the kernel sends a SIGFPE signal to the current process, and the si_code field contains one of these codes. Note that they have the same values as the previous eight, but the combination of signal number and si_code value is unique.

130   integer divide by zero.

131   integer overflow.

132   floating point divide by zero.

133   floating point overflow.

134   floating point underflow.

135   floating point inexact result.

136   floating point invalid operation.

137   floating point subscript out of range.

143–144   when the hardware memory management unit detects an invalid memory access, the kernel sends a SIGSEGV signal to the current process, and the si_code field contains one of these values. This is really the province of the memory manager; they are included here for completeness.

143   the virtual address provided is not actually mapped into the address space.

144   the address is valid but the process does not have permission for the specified access (e.g. read, write, execute).

150–152   when the hardware memory management unit detects some problem with physical memory, the kernel sends a SIGBUS signal to the current process and the si_code field contains one of these values. This is really the province of the memory manager; they are also included for completeness.

150   the address is not properly aligned (e.g. an attempt to read a long with an address not aligned on a 4 byte boundary).

151   the physical address specified does not exist.

152   this indicates some hardware error on the object backing this area of memory.

158–159   when the CPU raises a trap exception, the kernel sends a SIGTRAP signal to the current process, and the si_code field contains one of these values.

158   execution has arrived at a previously set breakpoint in the code.

159   the process is being traced, and the tracer wants to interrupt.

17.1.5.6   *Special* si_code *values for the* SIGCHLD *signal*

When the state of a child process changes, the kernel sends a SIGCHLD signal to the parent process. The si_code field attempts to further refine the cause of this signal, using one of the codes defined in Figure 17.14, from <asm-i386/siginfo.h>. In all cases the high-order 16 bits contain __SI_CHLD.

```
165   #define CLD_EXITED        (__SI_CHLD|1)
166   #define CLD_KILLED        (__SI_CHLD|2)
167   #define CLD_DUMPED        (__SI_CHLD|3)
```

```
168  #define CLD_TRAPPED      (__SI_CHLD|4)
169  #define CLD_STOPPED      (__SI_CHLD|5)
170  #define CLD_CONTINUED    (__SI_CHLD|6)
```

Figure 17.14   Special si_code values for the SIGCHLD signal

165   the child has called exit().

166   the child was killed by a SIGKILL.

167   the child terminated abnormally.

168   a traced child has trapped.

169   a child has stopped.

170   a stopped child has continued.

17.1.5.7   *Special* si_code *values for the* SIGPOLL *signal*

When a specific event occurs on a device being monitored by poll(), the driver sends a SIGPOLL signal to the specified process. The si_code field attempts to further refine the cause of this signal, using one of the codes defined in Figure 17.15, from <asm/siginfo.h>. In all cases the high-order 16 bits contain __SI_POLL. This is really the province of the IO manager; they are included here for completeness.

```
176  #define POLL_IN      (__SI_POLL|1)
177  #define POLL_OUT     (__SI_POLL|2)
178  #define POLL_MSG     (__SI_POLL|3)
179  #define POLL_ERR     (__SI_POLL|4)
180  #define POLL_PRI     (__SI_POLL|5)
181  #define POLL_HUP     (__SI_POLL|6)
```

Figure 17.15   Special si_code values for the SIGPOLL signal

176   input data are available, so they may be read without blocking.

177   output buffers are available, so data may be written without blocking.

178   an input message is available.

179   an IO error has occurred.

180   high-priority input may be received without blocking.

181   the device is disconnected.

17.2 Bitmap handlers

Bitmaps representing sets of signals were defined as type `sigset_t` in Section 17.1.1. There are a number of functions that manipulate such bitmaps, discussed in this section.

17.2.1 Manipulating a specific bit in a bitmap

First of all we will examine a number of worker functions that set, clear, and test a specific bit in a signal bitmap and that are called from many of the mainstream signal handling functions.

17.2.1.1 Setting or clearing a specific bit

The two functions shown in Figure 17.16, from `<asm-i386/signal.h>`, set or clear individual bits in a `sigset_t` bitmap. These are i386-specific; there are also generic versions of these functions, that are compiled in only if __HAVE_ARCH_SIG_BITOPS is not defined.

```
180  #define __HAVE_ARCH_SIG_BITOPS
181
182  extern __inline__ void sigaddset(sigset_t *set, int _sig)
183  {
184    __asm__("btsl %1,%0" : "=m"(*set) : "Ir"(_sig - 1) : "cc");
185  }
186
187  extern __inline__ void sigdelset(sigset_t *set, int _sig)
188  {
189    __asm__("btrl %1,%0" : "=m"(*set) : "Ir"(_sig - 1) : "cc");
190  }
```

Figure 17.16   Signal bitmap handlers

180   this macro is defined if there are architecture-specific bitmap handlers available. On some architectures (such as i386) there are machine instructions available for bit handling. In that case we use them, rather than writing it all in C. On the i386 these work only on the first 32 bits.

184   this sets the bit corresponding to parameter 1 (`_sig - 1`) in the signal set pointed to by parameter 0 (`set`). The output parameter `*set` is write only, and may be in memory (`"=m"`). For the input parameter, `"I"` specifies an integer value in the range 0 to 31. Signals are numbered 1, ..., 32, and the bitmap is zero-based. So bit n - 1 corresponds to signal n, `"r"` means that the value may be in a register. This function can operate only on the first 32 bits. `"cc"` warns the compiler that the condition code register EFLAGS is altered by this instruction.

189   this resets or clears the bit corresponding to `_sig - 1` in the signal set pointed to by `set`. The operand constraints are as in line 184.

17.2.1.2   Bit-testing functions

The kernel provides a number of functions for checking whether a particular bit in a given signal bitmap is set or not. These are shown in Figure 17.17, from `<asm-i386/signal.h>`.

```
192  static __inline__ int __const_sigismember(sigset_t *set, int _sig)
193  {
194        unsigned long sig = _sig - 1;
195        return 1 & (set->sig[sig / _NSIG_BPW] >> (sig % _NSIG_BPW));
196  }
197
198  static __inline__ int __gen_sigismember(sigset_t *set, int _sig)
199  {
200        int ret;
201        __asm__("btl %2,%1\n\tsbbl %0,%0"
202                              : "=r"(ret) : "m"(*set), "Ir"(_sig-1) : "cc");
203        return ret;
204  }
205
206  #define sigismember(set,sig)                    \
207        (__builtin_constant_p(sig) ?            \
208        __const_sigismember((set),(sig)) :     \
209        __gen_sigismember((set),(sig)))
210
211  #define sigmask(sig) (1UL << ((sig) - 1))
```

Figure 17.17   Bit-testing functions

192–196   this function works on bitmaps of any length.

194   bitmaps are zero-based; signals begin at 1. Hence we need this conversion.

195   this takes the word in the signal mask and shifts it right by the index of that signal in the word. This brings the bit corresponding to `sig` into the least significant bit position. ANDing with 1 will return TRUE if this bit is set; otherwise, FALSE is returned.

198–204   this function works only on the first 32 bits of the bitmap.

201   the `btl` instruction tests for bit `_sig - 1` in the `long` pointed to by `set`. The value of that bit is written to the carry flag. The `sbbl` (subtract with borrow) instruction subtracts `ret + carry` flag from `ret`. If the bit was clear, this is 0. If the bit was set, this is −1; so `ret` is all 1s.

202   the output parameter `ret` is write only and is expected to be in a register. For the input parameters, `*set` is expected to be in memory. `"I"` specifies an integer value in the range 0 to 31. Signals are numbered 1, ..., 32, while the bitmap is zero-based. So bit n − 1 corresponds to signal n. `"r"` means that the value may be in a register. This function can operate only on the first 32 bits. `"cc"` warns the compiler that the condition code register EFLAGS is altered by this instruction.

206–209 the gcc built-in function evaluates to TRUE if the argument is a compile time constant, FALSE otherwise, so it determines from the value of `sig` whether it can call the more efficient `__const_sigismember()` function or whether it needs to call the `__gen_sigismember()` function.

211 this generates a bit map, with one bit set, corresponding to `sig`.

17.2.2 Manipulating whole bitmaps

There are another group of functions that clear, set, or do logical operations on whole bitmaps. Some of these are generated by parameterised macros; others are straightforward functions.

17.2.2.1 *Macro to generate bit-manipulating functions*

The macro shown in Figure 17.18, from `<linux/signal.h>`, generates a function called *name*, that performs the bitwise (binary) operation specified by *op* on two input signal masks pointed to by a and b and writes the result to the signal mask pointed to by r. In practice, it is used to generate the three functions `sigorsets()`, `sigandsets()`, and `signandsets()` (see Section 17.2.2.2).

```
70    #define _SIG_SET_BINOP(name, op)                                          \
71    static inline void name(sigset_t *r, const sigset_t *a,
                                                     const sigset_t *b) \
72    {                                                                         \
73        unsigned long a0, a1, a2, a3, b0, b1, b2, b3;                         \
74        unsigned long i;                                                      \
75                                                                              \
76        for (i = 0; i < _NSIG_WORDS/4; ++i) {                                 \
77                a0 = a->sig[4*i+0]; a1 = a->sig[4*i+1];                       \
78                a2 = a->sig[4*i+2]; a3 = a->sig[4*i+3];                       \
79                b0 = b->sig[4*i+0]; b1 = b->sig[4*i+1];                       \
80                b2 = b->sig[4*i+2]; b3 = b->sig[4*i+3];                       \
81                r->sig[4*i+0] = op(a0, b0);                                   \
82                r->sig[4*i+1] = op(a1, b1);                                   \
83                r->sig[4*i+2] = op(a2, b2);                                   \
84                r->sig[4*i+3] = op(a3, b3);                                   \
85        }                                                                     \
86        switch (_NSIG_WORDS % 4) {                                            \
87            case 3:                                                           \
88                a0 = a->sig[4*i+0]; a1 = a->sig[4*i+1];
                                            a2 = a->sig[4*i+2]; \
89                b0 = b->sig[4*i+0]; b1 = b->sig[4*i+1];
                                            b2 = b->sig[4*i+2]; \
90                r->sig[4*i+0] = op(a0, b0);                                   \
91                r->sig[4*i+1] = op(a1, b1);                                   \
92                r->sig[4*i+2] = op(a2, b2);                                   \
93                break;                                                        \
```

```
94                  case 2:                                               \
95                      a0 = a->sig[4*i+0]; a1 = a->sig[4*i+1];          \
96                      b0 = b->sig[4*i+0]; b1 = b->sig[4*i+1];          \
97                      r->sig[4*i+0] = op(a0, b0);                       \
98                      r->sig[4*i+1] = op(a1, b1);                       \
99                      break;                                            \
100                 case 1:                                               \
101                     a0 = a->sig[4*i+0]; b0 = b->sig[4*i+0];          \
102                     r->sig[4*i+0] = op(a0, b0);                       \
103                     break;                                            \
104         }                                                             \
105 }
```

Figure 17.18   Generate bit manipulation functions

76–85   the _NSIG_WORDS macro is 2 in i386 systems (see Section 17.1.1), so this loop is never entered. It works by breaking the bitmap down into successive groups of four unsigned long and performing the specified operation on one group each time around the loop.

77–78   these four assignments copy the next four elements of the sig[] array from the sigset_t identified by a to the four variables a0, a1, a2, and a3.

79–80   these assignments break up the next four elements from *b into four independent variables.

81–84   these four lines perform the specified operation on the four pairs of variables, writing the results to the appropriate element of the sig[] array from the sigset_t identified by r.

86–104   the previous block of code dealt with successive groups of four words. This switch statement deals with any remaining words, less than four. In the i386 case, _NSIG_WORDS % 4 is 2.

87–93   this is similar to one iteration of the previous loop, but only three operations are done. Note that i will have a value from the foregoing loop, so this case will always be dealing with the last three words in the bit string.

94–99   this is for the case where there are two words left over after the loop. This is always the case on the i386 architecture, with i having a value of 0 from line 76.

95   the two unsigned long that make up the end of the signal mask identified by a are broken into a0 and a1.

96   likewise, the two unsigned long that make up the end of the signal mask identified by b are broken into b0 and b1.

97   the result of operating on the first two unsigned long is written to the first unsigned long of the result mask, identified by r.

98   likewise, the result of operating on the second two unsigned long is written to the second unsigned long of the result mask, identified by r.

100–103   this is for the case where there is only one unsigned long left over after the loop at lines 76–85.

17.2.2.2 Instantiating generating macros for bit-manipulating functions

The previous subsection examined a macro that generates different functions depending on its input parameter. This section shows three different instantiations of that macro, to generate the three functions `sigorsets()`, `sigandsets()`, and `signandsets()`; see Figure 17.19, from `<linux/signal.h>`.

```
107  #define _sig_or(x,y)    ((x) | (y))
108  _SIG_SET_BINOP(sigorsets, _sig_or)
109
110  #define _sig_and(x,y)    ((x) & (y))
111  _SIG_SET_BINOP(sigandsets, _sig_and)
112
113  #define _sig_nand(x,y)   ((x) & ~(y))
114  _SIG_SET_BINOP(signandsets, _sig_nand)
115
116  #undef _SIG_SET_BINOP
117  #undef _sig_or
118  #undef _sig_and
119  #undef _sig_nand
```

Figure 17.19   Instantiating generating macros for bit-manipulating functions

107–108   the macro from Section 17.2.2.1 is instantiated to define a function named `sigorsets()`, which performs a bitwise OR on its parameters.

110–111   the macro is instantiated, to define the function `sigandsets()`, which performs a bitwise AND on its parameters.

113–114   the macro is instantiated, to define the function `signandsets()`, which performs a bitwise NAND on its parameters.

116–119   now that the preprocessor has expanded the function code, and it is available for the compiler, these macros are no longer needed.

17.2.2.3 Macro to generate a bit-setting function

The macro shown in 17.20, from `<linux/signal.h>`, generates a function that operates on the bits in the signal mask pointed to by `set`. The (unary) operation performed is specified by the parameter `op`.

```
121  #define _SIG_SET_OP(name, op)                              \
122  static inline void name(sigset_t *set)                     \
123  {                                                          \
124      unsigned long i;                                       \
125                                                             \
126      for (i = 0; i < _NSIG_WORDS/4; ++i) {                  \
127          set->sig[4*i+0] = op(set->sig[4*i+0]);             \
128          set->sig[4*i+1] = op(set->sig[4*i+1]);             \
```

```
129                    set->sig[4*i+2] = op(set->sig[4*i+2]);          \
130                    set->sig[4*i+3] = op(set->sig[4*i+3]);          \
131            }                                                        \
132        switch (_NSIG_WORDS % 4) {                                   \
133                case 3: set->sig[4*i+2] = op(set->sig[4*i+2]);  \
134                case 2: set->sig[4*i+1] = op(set->sig[4*i+1]);  \
135                case 1: set->sig[4*i+0] = op(set->sig[4*i+0]);  \
136            }                                                        \
137    }
138
139    #define _sig_not(x) (~(x))
140    _SIG_SET_OP(signotset, _sig_not)
141
142    #undef _SIG_SET_OP
143    #undef _sig_not
```

Figure 17.20   Macro to generate bit-setting functions

126–131   each time around the loop, we perform the specified operation on four elements of the `sig[]` array from the `sigset_t` pointed to by `set`. The `_NSIG_WORDS` macro is 2 in i386 systems, so this loop is never entered.

132–136   the previous block of code dealt with groups of four words. This `switch` statement deals with any remaining words, less than four. Note that there are no `break` statements in the `switch`.

133   this performs the operation on the third remaining word.

134   in the i386 case, `_NSIG_WORDS % 4` is 2. Remember that `i` has a value of 0 from line 126. This line performs the operation on `sig[1]`.

135   execution falls through to here to perform the operation on `sig[0]`.

139–140   the macro is instantiated, to define a function named `signotset()` which inverts all of the bits in its parameter. This is the only use made of the foregoing macro. It might have been simpler to write a straightforward function.

142–143   now that the preprocessor has expanded the function code, and it is available for the compiler, these macros are no longer needed.

17.2.2.4   Clearing a signal mask

Another common requirement is to clear all the bits in a specified signal mask to 0. The function shown in Figure 17.21, from `<linux/signal.h>`, does just that. For short signal masks it uses assignment; for longer ones it calls on the memory manager.

```
145    static inline void sigemptyset(sigset_t *set)
146    {
147        switch (_NSIG_WORDS) {
148        default:
149                memset(set, 0, sizeof(sigset_t));
```

```
150                break;
151         case 2: set->sig[1] = 0;
152         case 1: set->sig[0] = 0;
153                break;
154        }
155   }
```

Figure 17.21   Clearing a signal mask

148–150   this is for systems with more than 2 words in a `sigset_t`.

149   this function, supplied by the memory manager, writes 0 to each byte of the structure pointed to by `set`.

151   this writes a 0 to the second word of the `sig[]` array.

152   this writes a 0 to the first word of the `sig[]` array. Note that the previous case falls through into this line, so dealing with the first word of a two-word `sigset_t`.

17.2.2.5   Setting all bits in a signal mask

The function shown in Figure 17.22, from `<linux/signal.h>`, sets all the bits in a specified signal mask to 1. It handles smaller signal sets by direct assignment; for larger ones it calls on the memory manager. Its operation is identical to the function in Section 17.2.2.4. Note that the binary representation of -1 is all 1s.

```
157   static inline void sigfillset(sigset_t *set)
158   {
159         switch (_NSIG_WORDS) {
160         default:
161               memset(set, -1, sizeof(sigset_t));
162               break;
163         case 2: set->sig[1] = -1;
164         case 1: set->sig[0] = -1;
165               break;
166        }
167   }
```

Figure 17.22   Setting all bits in a signal mask

17.2.3   Manipulating subsets of a bitmap

Sometimes there is a requirement to manipulate the bits representing the first 32 signals in particular, and special simple functions are supplied for that.

17.2.3.1   Setting or clearing specified bits

The two functions shown in Figure 17.23, from `<linux/signal.h>`, add or remove the bits specified by `mask` from the first word of the specified signal set.

```
173   static inline void sigaddsetmask(sigset_t *set, unsigned long mask)
174   {
175         set->sig[0] |= mask;
176   }
177
178   static inline void sigdelsetmask(sigset_t *set, unsigned long mask)
179   {
180         set->sig[0] &= ~mask;
181   }
182
183   static inline int sigtestsetmask(sigset_t *set, unsigned long mask)
184   {
185         return (set->sig[0] & mask) != 0;
186   }
```

Figure 17.23   Masking a signal set

175   any bits set in mask are set in the first word of the sig[] array in the sigset_t pointed to by set, whether or not they were set beforehand.

180   any bits set in mask are cleared in the first word of the sig[] array, whether or not they were clear beforehand.

185   if any of the bits set in mask are set in the first word of the sig[] array, this function returns TRUE; otherwise, it returns FALSE.

17.2.3.2   *Initialising a* sig[] *array to specified values*

It is a common requirement to set only a few bits in a bitmap, with all the others clear. The function shown in Figure 17.24, from <linux/signal.h>, sets up the first 32 bits as specified by mask while clearing all subsequent bits.

```
188   static inline void siginitset(sigset_t *set, unsigned long mask)
189   {
190         set->sig[0] = mask;
191         switch (_NSIG_WORDS) {
192             default:
193                 memset(&set->sig[1],0,sizeof(long)*(_NSIG_WORDS-1));
194                 break;
195             case 2: set->sig[1] = 0;
196             case 1: ;
197         }
198   }
```

Figure 17.24   Initialising the sig[] array to 0

190   this sets the first word in sig[] to the value of the mask supplied as a parameter. The remainder will then be initialised to 0.

192–194   for bitmaps greater than two words, the memory manager is used. Starting at `sig[1]`, it zeroes the following `_NSIG_WORDS – 1` entries in the array.

193   note that the * here denotes multiplication.

195   for a bitmap of two words, this zeroes the second one.

196   the first word has already been dealt with at line 190, so nothing needs doing here; this `case` is necessary to prevent one-word bitmaps being treated under `default`.

17.2.3.3   Initialising a `sig[]` array to inverse values

If almost all bits in a bitmap are to be set it is easier to specify those that are to be cleared. A function is supplied for this that initialises a `sig[]` array to the inverse of the `mask`; see Figure 17.25, from `<linux/signal.h>`.

```
200  static inline void siginitsetinv(sigset_t *set, unsigned long mask)
201  {
202  set->sig[0] = ~mask;
203  switch (_NSIG_WORDS) {
204      default:
205          memset(&set->sig[1], -1, sizeof(long)*(_NSIG_WORDS-1));
206          break;
207      case 2: set->sig[1] = -1;
208      case 1: ;
209  }
210  }
```

Figure 17.25   Initialising the `sig[]` array to 1

202   the first word of `sig[]` is set to the inverse of the `mask` supplied as a parameter.

203–209   the logic of this is identical to that of lines 191–197 of Figure 17.24. The only difference is that the fill value is -1. This is represented in binary as all 1s.

17.3   Installing a signal handler

Section 17.1.3 examined the data structures that record the handlers to be used for each signal. This section considers how these are set up. A user-specified signal handler can be installed for most signals. The function shown in Figure 17.26, from `kernel/signal.c`, is supplied to do just that.

```
1009 int
1010 do_sigaction(int sig, const struct k_sigaction *act, struct
                                                      k_sigaction *oact)
1011 {
1012      struct k_sigaction *k;
1013
1014      if (sig < 1 || sig > _NSIG ||
```

```
1015        (act && (sig == SIGKILL || sig == SIGSTOP)))
1016            return -EINVAL;
1017
1018        k = &current->sig->action[sig-1];
1019
1020        spin_lock(&current->sig->siglock);
1021
1022        if (oact)
1023            *oact = *k;
1024
1025        if (act) {
1026            *k = *act;
1027            sigdelsetmask(&k->sa.sa_mask, sigmask(SIGKILL) |
                                              sigmask(SIGSTOP));

1046            if (k->sa.sa_handler == SIG_IGN
1047                    || (k->sa.sa_handler == SIG_DFL
1048                        && (sig == SIGCONT ||
1049                            sig == SIGCHLD ||
1050                            sig == SIGWINCH))) {
1051                spin_lock_irq(&current->sigmask_lock);
                    if (rm_sig_from_queue(sig, current))
1053                    recalc_sigpending(current);
1054                spin_unlock_irq(&current->sigmask_lock);
1055            }
1056        }
1057
1058        spin_unlock(&current->sig->siglock);
1059        return 0;
1060 }
```

Figure 17.26 Installing a signal handler

1010   the parameters are the number of the signal, a pointer to a struct k_sigaction representing the new handler, and a similar pointer to an area of memory into which the
struct k_sigaction representing the old handler will be written.

1014–1016   there are three conditions here. The first two are only checking for an out-of-range signal number.
The third condition checks that a handler is not being supplied for either SIGKILL or SIGSTOP.
User-defined handlers cannot be set up for these two. Any of these cases is classed as an invalid
parameter, so EINVAL is returned.

1018   this takes a local pointer to the current struct k_sigaction specified for this signal.

1020–1058   the data structures representing signal handlers may be shared with other processes (parent
and/or children), so this spinlock is taken out to guarantee that only one can change them at a
time. Do not confuse this spinlock, which covers handlers, with the sigmask_lock, which
protects signal bitmaps.

1022–1023	if a valid pointer has been supplied, we copy the old struct k_sigaction to the area it is pointing to.
1025–1056	if a NULL pointer has been supplied for the new action, then the caller does not want to change the current one, it is only enquiring about the old one. This has already been done, so the function can skip down to line 1058 and return with a success value.
1026	this copies the new value into the appropriate element of the action[] array.
1027	this clears both the SIGKILL and SIGSTOP bits in the sa_mask field of this new entry, just in case the user had tried to specify that they should be masked. This is not allowed! The function was described in Section 17.2.3.1.
1046–1050	the condition is checking if this is an attempt to set SIG_IGN for any signal, or SIG_DFL for SIGCONT, SIGCHLD or SIGWINCH. POSIX (3.3.1.3) requires that, in any of these cases, if such a signal is actually pending then it is to be discarded, whether or not it is blocked. In any of these cases, lines 1051–1054 are executed and if there is a signal pending it is discarded.
1051–1054	the function now takes out the sigmask_lock for the process as well as the siglock it is already holding. The sigmask_lock protects the blocked and pending bitmaps in the task_struct, whereas siglock protects the array of handlers in the signal_struct.
1052–1053	if we find a signal of that type already queued, then we attempt to remove it, using the function described in Section 18.1.2.3.
1053	if this is successful, then there was such a signal pending so we update the signal status of the process, using the function from Section 18.3.2.

17.4 Deallocating signal-handling structures

When a process terminates, it gives back to the memory manager the data structures used to keep track of signals. These are the struct signal_struct, which keeps track of handlers, and the struct sigqueue, which heads the list of queued signals. There are a number of functions that collaborate in that.

17.4.1 Deallocating handler and queue head structures

When a process terminates it needs to deallocate the memory used to keep track of signal handlers. The function shown in Figure 17.27, from kernel/signal.c, is used for this. It deallocates the data structures controlling signal handlers and queues.

```
112  void exit_sighand(struct task_struct *tsk)
113  {
114      struct signal_struct * sig = tsk->sig;
115
116      spin_lock_irq(&tsk->sigmask_lock);
117      if (sig) {
118          tsk->sig = NULL;
119          if (atomic_dec_and_test(&sig->count))
```

```
120        kmem_cache_free(sigact_cachep, sig);
121     }
122     tsk->sigpending = 0;
123     flush_sigqueue(&tsk->pending);
124     spin_unlock_irq(&tsk->sigmask_lock);
125  }
```

Figure 17.27   Deallocating signal handling structures

112   the parameter is a pointer to the `task_struct` of the exiting process.

114   this gets a pointer to the `struct signal_struct`, which contains the handlers, from the `task_struct` of the process.

116–124   the spinlock prevents other processes from manipulating this structure (e.g. posting signals) while it is being removed. The lock and unlock functions were described in Section 12.8.1.

117–121   this is a sanity check. This block of code is executed only if the `struct signal_struct` actually exists. It is hard to see how this could happen, but it is a wise precaution.

118   this lets the system know that the `signal_struct` has been deallocated. As far as the signal manager is concerned, this process is now a zombie.

119–120   because these structures can be shared, we decrement the use count, using the function from Section 5.2.7. Only if no other process is using this structure do we return it to the memory manager.

120   the `kmem_cache_free()` function is part of the memory manager. It returns the memory to the slab cache. It is not described in this book.

122–123   even if the `signal_struct` does not exist, these lines are executed anyway. They can do no harm, and it is better to be safe. They are equivalent to calling `flush_signals()` (Section 17.4.3).

122   the new value indicates that there are no pending signals. The process is exiting so even if there are signals pending they are not going to be handled.

123   the function is discussed in Section 17.4.2. It flushes all pending signals from the queue associated with the process and deallocates the entries one by one.

17.4.2   Deallocating all queued signals

When the process manager needs to flush all queued signals it uses the function in Figure 17.28, from `kernel/signal.c`. This unlinks entries on the queue one by one and returns them to the memory manager. It leaves the queue head in its initialised state. The caller of this function is always holding the `sigmask_lock` of the process.

```
84   static void flush_sigqueue(struct sigpending *queue)
85   {
```

```
86          struct sigqueue *q, *n;
87
88          sigemptyset(&queue->signal);
89          q = queue->head;
90          queue->head = NULL;
91          queue->tail = &queue->head;
92
93          while (q) {
94              n = q->next;
95              kmem_cache_free(sigqueue_cachep, q);
96              atomic_dec(&nr_queued_signals);
97              q = n;
98          }
99      }
```

Figure 17.28   Flushing the signal queue

84   the parameter is a pointer to the queue of signals pending to the calling process.

88   this zeroes the `signal` bitmap, so indicating that there are no signals queued. The function was discussed in Section 17.2.2.4.

89   this takes a local copy of the `head` pointer, which is going to be set to NULL in the next line. This copy will be used later to work down the queue.

90–91   these lines set the `struct sigpending` back to its initialised state, with the `head` pointer NULL and the `tail` pointer set to the `head` field. This structure is part of the `task_struct` and remains until the `task_struct` is deallocated (see Section 9.4.2).

93–98   this loop works its way down the queue, returning entries one by one to the memory manager. The `next` pointer in the last entry will be pointing back to the `head` field in the `struct sigpending`. This has already been set to NULL, so the loop will terminate.

94   this gets a pointer to the next signal, before this one is deallocated.

95   this gives the memory back to the memory manager.

96   this atomically decrements the global count of queued signals (see Section 5.2.6 for the function).

97   the next entry becomes the current one, and we go around again.

17.4.3   Flushing all pending signals for a process

There are times when a process needs to discard all waiting signals that are on its queue. A function is supplied for that; see Figure 17.29, from `kernel/signal.c`. It is used only by drivers.

```
105  void
106  flush_signals(struct task_struct *t)
```

```
107  {
108       t->sigpending = 0;
109       flush_sigqueue(&t->pending);
110  }
```

Figure 17.29   Flushing all pending signals for a process

108   the new value indicates that there are no pending signals.

109   the function was discussed in Section 17.4.2. It flushes all signals from the queue associated with the process and returns the data structures to the memory manager.

17.4.4   Flushing all handlers for a process

At times a driver may need to remove all user-installed signal handlers. A function is provided for this, as shown in Figure 17.30, from `kernel/signal.c`. It replaces user-installed handlers with `SIG_DFL`.

```
131  void
132  flush_signal_handlers(struct task_struct *t)
133  {
134       int i;
135       struct k_sigaction *ka = &t->sig->action[0];
136       for (i = _NSIG ; i != 0 ; i-) {
137            if (ka->sa.sa_handler != SIG_IGN)
138                 ka->sa.sa_handler = SIG_DFL;
139            ka->sa.sa_flags = 0;
140            sigemptyset(&ka->sa.sa_mask);
141            ka++;
142       }
143  }
```

Figure 17.30   Flushing signal handlers

135   this sets up a pointer to the first entry in the `action[]` array. Each entry in this is a `struct k_sigaction`, as described in Section 17.1.3.3.

136–142   this loop works its way through all the entries in the `action[]` array (see Section 17.1.1 for the definition of _NSIG). Note that the loop counts down from the highest numbered signal to 1, but the loop counter `i` is never used inside the loop. In fact, entries are dealt with in ascending order, by incrementing the pointer `ka`.

137–138   unless currently set to `SIG_IGN`, we set the `sa_handler` field to `SIG_DFL`.

139   this zeroes the `flags` field.

140   this clears the `mask` field as well, using the function from Section 17.2.2.4. No signals are to be blocked while this one is being handled.

141   this points to the next entry in the array, in anticipation of the next iteration of the loop.

17.5   Notifying a user before handling signals

Sometimes a driver needs to be able to interfere in the signal mechanism, at a very fine granularity. It can always block signals, but the handler for these will run just as soon as they are unblocked. Linux provides a facility whereby a driver can specify a set of signals for which its permission is needed before they can be handled. The driver can then decide whether the signal should be ignored completely or be run as normal.

17.5.1   Setting up a callback function for signal handling

The function to set up such a callback is shown in Figure 17.31, from `kernel/signal.c`. Once this function has been run, every time `dequeue_signal()` is called to handle a pending signal it checks the bit corresponding to that signal in the `notifier_mask` of the process. If set, it calls the callback function. If the callback function returns nonzero, then the signal will be acted upon after all. If the notifier routine returns 0, then the signal will be left on the queue. A process can only set up one such callback at a time.

```
153  void
154  block_all_signals(int (*notifier)(void *priv), void *priv,
                                               sigset_t *mask)
155  {
156      unsigned long flags;
157
158      spin_lock_irqsave(&current->sigmask_lock, flags);
159      current->notifier_mask = mask;
160      current->notifier_data = priv;
161      current->notifier = notifier;
162      spin_unlock_irqrestore(&current->sigmask_lock, flags);
163  }
```

Figure 17.31   Blocking all signals

154   the first parameter is a pointer to the callback function `notifier()`. The second parameter `priv` is a pointer to private data that the notifier routine can use to determine if the signal should be blocked or not. The third parameter `mask` is the set of signals for which the function wants to be notified.

158–162   the changes to these three fields in the `task_struct` constitute a critical section, so an interrupt-safe spinlock is taken out. The spinlock is also declared in the `task_struct` (see Section 2.8).

159–161   the three parameters are written to the appropriate fields in the `task_struct` (see Section 2.8).

17.5.2   Deactivating the callback function

When a driver wants to reverse the effect of a call to `block_all_signals()` and notify the system to cancel a callback it uses the function in Figure 17.32, from `kernel/signal.c`.

```
167 void
168 unblock_all_signals(void)
169 {
170       unsigned long flags;
171
172       spin_lock_irqsave(&current->sigmask_lock, flags);
173       current->notifier = NULL;
174       current->notifier_data = NULL;
175       recalc_sigpending(current);
176       spin_unlock_irqrestore(&current->sigmask_lock, flags);
177 }
```

Figure 17.32   Unblocking all signals

172–176   the changes to these three fields in the task_struct constitute a critical section, so an interrupt-safe spinlock is taken out.

173–174   setting NULL pointers in these fields lets the system know that there is no callback in effect. Note that the mask field is not changed but it will never be checked on its own and is always overwritten the next time a callback is set up.

175   as the signal environment is back to normal again, we check to see if any signals are pending to the current process (see Section 18.3.2).

17.6   The alternate stack for signal handlers

By default, a signal is handled on the user mode stack of the target process. But if, for example, that does not expand automatically, it is useful to have the handler run on another stack. Linux provides a facility for this. The data structures that support this are examined first. The main function will be considered in Section 17.6.2, and some worker functions used by it will be examined in Section 17.6.3.

17.6.1   Alternate signal stack

Some definitions used in controlling this alternate stack, on which specified signal handlers run, are shown in Figure 17.33, from <asm-i386/signal.h>.

```
104 #define SS_ONSTACK   1
105 #define SS_DISABLE   2
106
107 #define MINSIGSTKSZ 2048
108 #define SIGSTKSZ       8192

171 typedef struct sigaltstack {
172       void       *ss_sp;
173       int        ss_flags;
174       size_t     ss_size;
175 } stack_t;
```

Figure 17.33   Controls for the alternate stack

104	the handler is running on the alternate stack.
105	the alternate stack is disabled.
107	this is the minimum size for an alternate stack.
108	this is the recommended default size for an alternate stack.
171–175	this is the data structure that represents an alternate stack to the system.
172	this is a pointer to the base of the stack area.
173	this contains flags specifying valid or not, from lines 104–105.
174	this is the length of the alternate stack.

17.6.2 Setting or getting an alternate stack context

The function shown in Figure 17.34, from `kernel/signal.c`, sets up an alternate stack for handling those signals that specify it. It implements the `sigaltstack()` system call.

```
1062 int
1063 do_sigaltstack (const stack_t *uss, stack_t *uoss, unsigned long sp)
1064 {
1065     stack_t oss;
1066     int error;
1067
1068     if (uoss) {
1069         oss.ss_sp = (void *) current->sas_ss_sp;
1070         oss.ss_size = current->sas_ss_size;
1071         oss.ss_flags = sas_ss_flags(sp);
1072     }
1073
1074     if (uss) {
1075         void *ss_sp;
1076         size_t ss_size;
1077         int ss_flags;
1078
1079         error = -EFAULT;
1080         if (verify_area(VERIFY_READ, uss, sizeof(*uss))
1081                 || __get_user(ss_sp, &uss->ss_sp)
1082                 || __get_user(ss_flags, &uss->ss_flags)
1083                 || __get_user(ss_size, &uss->ss_size))
1084             goto out;
1085
1086         error = -EPERM;
1087         if (on_sig_stack(sp))
```

```
1088                     goto out;
1089
1090              error = -EINVAL;

1099              if (ss_flags != SS_DISABLE
                                    && ss_flags != SS_ONSTACK && ss_flags != 0)
1100                     goto out;
1101
1102              if (ss_flags == SS_DISABLE) {
1103                  ss_size = 0;
1104                  ss_sp = NULL;
1105              } else {
1106                  error = -ENOMEM;
1107                  if (ss_size < MINSIGSTKSZ)
1108                      goto out;
1109              }
1110
1111              current->sas_ss_sp = (unsigned long) ss_sp;
1112              current->sas_ss_size = ss_size;
1113          }
1114
1115      if (uoss) {
1116          error = -EFAULT;
1117          if (copy_to_user(uoss, &oss, sizeof(oss)))
1118              goto out;
1119      }
1120
1121      error = 0;
1122 out:
1123      return error;
1124 }
```

Figure 17.34   Switching to an alternate signal-handling stack

1063   the first parameter, if not NULL, is a pointer to a `sigaltstack` structure specifying an area of memory in user space to be used as a stack while executing handlers for specified signals. The second parameter, if not NULL, points to a `sigaltstack` structure into which information about any alternate stack in use before the call will be written. The third is a copy of the SP value saved on the kernel stack.

1068–1072   if the caller has specified (by passing a valid pointer) that information about the previous state is to be returned, then this block of code is executed. The first two values are copied directly from the `task_struct` of the process. They are saved in a local temporary `struct sigaltstack`, as the value in the `task_struct` may be overwritten before they are copied back to user space.

1069   if not NULL, this is a pointer to any alternate stack previously set up.

1070   if not 0, this is the size of any alternate stack previously set up.

1071   this function is described in Section 17.6.3. It returns status information about any alternate stack previously set up. This will be either SS_DISABLE, if one has not been set up, or SS_ONSTACK, if the process is executing on an alternate stack; it will be 0 if an alternate stack is set up but not currently in use.

1074–1113 this block of code is executed if the caller supplied a valid pointer to a struct sigaltstack for the new alternate stack. This is the heart of the function.

1079–1084 if there is a problem with reading from user space, we return with EFAULT.

1080 this checks if it is possible to read from the struct sigaltstack in user space. The function is part of the memory manager; it returns 0 on success.

1081–1083 this copies each of the three fields of the new struct sigaltstack from user space into local kernel variables. The __get_user() function is part of the memory manager; it returns 0 on success.

1084 if even one of these four functions returns failure, the condition is TRUE, and control skips down to line 1122, where the function returns with EFAULT.

1086–1088 if the process is already working on an alternate stack, we return with EPERM. The function is described in Section 17.6.3. This test might have come before copying the information from user space.

1090 this sets up a default return value of EINVAL for the next section of code, which is checking the validity of the ss_flags field.

1099–1100 this condition filters out these three values for user supplied ss_flags. These are the only valid ones; any others and the function returns EINVAL.

1102–1104 if SS_DISABLE is set (i.e. if this is a request to cancel a previously requested alternate stack) then we zero the other two local fields, no matter what values the user may have provided.

1105–1109 because of the filter at lines 1099–1100, at this stage ss_flags must have a value of SS_ONSTACK or 0. The comment in the code says that for backward compatibility it should not try to distinguish between 0 and SS_ONSTACK. This is checking that the caller has allocated an alternate stack of at least the minimum size defined in Section 17.6.1. If not, it returns ENOMEM.

1111–1112 this sets up new values for the base and length of the alternate stack in the task_struct of the process. Note that ss_sp has to be cast to unsigned long because of the way the task_struct field is declared.

1115–1119 this block of code is executed if the caller supplied a valid pointer to a struct sigaltstruct, specifying where to write the old information. The temporary copy set up at lines 1068–1072 is copied to user space.

1116–1118 if we are unable to copy the information to user space, we return with EFAULT. The copy_to_user() function is part of the memory manager and will not be considered further here.

1121 this is the success value.

17.6.3 Checking for an alternate signal stack

The kernel supplies two functions that check whether an alternate signal stack has been set up or not. These are shown in Figure 17.35, from `<linux/sched.h>`.

```
678  static inline int on_sig_stack(unsigned long sp)
679  {
680      return (sp - current->sas_ss_sp < current->sas_ss_size);
681  }
682
683  static inline int sas_ss_flags(unsigned long sp)
684  {
685      return (current->sas_ss_size == 0 ? SS_DISABLE
686                          : on_sig_stack(sp) ? SS_ONSTACK : 0);
687  }
```

Figure 17.35   Checking for an alternate signal stack

678   the parameter is the saved value of the stack pointer. The function checks if the value of the stack pointer when the interrupt occurred falls within the area of the alternate stack or not.

680   subtraction of the base address of the alternate stack from the current stack pointer gives the offset of the stack pointer from the base of the alternate stack. If this is less than the declared size of the alternate stack, then the process is operating on this alternate stack and the function returns TRUE; otherwise, it is working on the main stack.

683   the parameter is the saved value of the stack pointer. This is checking the status of the alternate stack.

685–686   if the alternate stack is declared as size 0 then it is not set up so we return SS_DISABLE. If it is set up then, if the process is operating on the alternate stack, we return SS_ONSTACK; otherwise, we return 0.

18

Posting and delivering signals

The processing of signals falls neatly into two parts. First, there is the posting of a signal. This includes all the checking and processing involved on the sender side. The end result of this is that certain data structures are altered in the target process, indicating that the signal is 'pending'. No action is taken at this stage. Second, there is the delivery of the signal. This happens when the target process is made aware of the pending signal and takes the appropriate action. Both these aspects of the signal mechanism are considered in this chapter.

18.1 Posting signals

There are quite a number of functions involved in the sending of a signal, in one way or another. There is the fundamental function, `send_sig_info()`, which will be considered first. This calls a number of subsidiary functions, which will then be described. Finally, there are specialised functions supplied for sending signals, either to specified groups of processes or using other interfaces. All these ultimately call `send_sig_info()`.

18.1.1 Sending a signal, with extra information

The basic function that generates a signal is shown in Figure 18.1, from `kernel/signal.c`.

```
503 int
504 send_sig_info(int sig, struct siginfo *info, struct task_struct *t)
505 {
506     unsigned long flags;
507     int ret;

513
514     ret = -EINVAL;
```

The Linux Process Manager. The Internals of Scheduling, Interrupts and Signals John O'Gorman
© 2003 John Wiley & Sons, Ltd   ISBN: 0 470 84771 9

```
515        if (sig < 0 || sig > _NSIG)
516            goto out_nolock;
517
518        ret = -EPERM;
519        if (bad_signal(sig, info, t))
520            goto out_nolock;

524        ret = 0;
525        if (!sig || !t->sig)
526            goto out_nolock;
527
528        spin_lock_irqsave(&t->sigmask_lock, flags);
529        handle_stop_signal(sig, t);

535        if (ignored_signal(sig, t))
536            goto out;

541        if (sig < SIGRTMIN && sigismember(&t->pending.signal, sig))
542            goto out;
543
544        ret = deliver_signal(sig, info, t);
545 out:
546        spin_unlock_irqrestore(&t->sigmask_lock, flags);
547 out_nolock:
548 #if DEBUG_SIG
549        printk(" %d -> %d\n", signal_pending(t), ret);
550 #endif
551
552        return ret;
553 }
```

Figure 18.1   Sending a signal, with extra information

504   the three parameters are the number of the signal, a pointer to the extended information, and a pointer to the `task_struct` of the process to which the signal is to be sent.

510–512   in debugging mode, this would print a message identifying the program that is running, the `pid` of the process, and the number of the signal.

514–516   this checks the validity of the signal number; if invalid it return `EINVAL`. Note that a signal 0 is accepted (see lines 524–526). The `_NSIG` constant is the highest valid signal number (see Section 17.1.1).

516   no lock has been taken out yet, so this jumps beyond the code that releases the lock.

518–520   this checks that the caller has permission to send this signal to the specified process. The function is discussed in Section 18.1.2.1. If it returns TRUE (a bad signal), it returns with EPERM.

524–526   an attempt to send a signal numbered 0 or to send a signal to a process without a `sig` structure (this must be a zombie) still returns success (0), but no signal is actually delivered. This could be used to check for permissions or for the existence of the target process.

528–546 this is where the signal is going to be delivered; that is, the bitmap in the `task_struct` of the target process will be written too. Mutual exclusion is guaranteed by taking out the `sigmask_lock` specific to that process. The interrupt-safe spinlock macros are described in Section 12.8.1.

529 some signals have side-effects such as stopping or restarting processes. The `handle_stop_signal()` function, described in Section 18.1.2.2, deals with these side-effects immediately.

535–536 this is an optimisation. If the signal is ignored (either explicitly or by default) there is no point recording it, so we give back the spinlock and return with 0 in `retval`. The `ignored_signal()` function is described in Section 18.1.2.5.

541–542 if dealing with a nonreal-time signal (one of the ordinary ones), and there is already an instance of that signal marked as pending in the `signal` bitmap of the target process, there is nothing to be done. Only one instance of such a signal is recorded at a time, so we give back the spinlock and return with 0 in `retval`.

544 now that all the checking has been done, the function described in Section 18.1.3.1 actually delivers the signal. We pass back whatever value it supplies.

548–550 in debugging mode, this continues the message begun at line 511. It prints the result from `signal_pending()` (see Section 18.3.1) and the result from this function.

18.1.2 Subsidiary functions

The function to send a signal, discussed in the previous section, used a number of subsidiary functions; there will now be considered.

18.1.2.1 Checking permission to send a signal

The function shown in Figure 18.2, from `kernel/signal.c`, checks all the reasons why a process is prohibited from sending a signal to a particular target. The comment in the code describes this as being 'somewhat baroque'.

```
308  int bad_signal(int sig, struct siginfo *info, struct task_struct *t)
309  {
310  return (!info || ((unsigned long)info != 1
     && SI_FROMUSER(info)))
311     && ((sig != SIGCONT) || (current->session != t->session))
312  && (current->euid ^ t->suid) && (current->euid ^ t->uid)
313  && (current->uid ^ t->suid) && (current->uid ^ t->uid)
314  && !capable(CAP_KILL);
315  }
```

Figure 18.2 Checking permission to send a signal

310–314   the function returns TRUE only if each of these seven conditions is TRUE; that means the process cannot send the signal. Otherwise, it returns FALSE.

310   there are two halves to the OR. For this line to be TRUE, either `info` is a NULL pointer, or the pointer is valid but the `si_code` field indicates it is from user mode (see Section 17.1.5.4 for the macro). The kernel *must* supply a `struct siginfo`.

311   for a SIGCONT, the target must be in the same session as the sender.

312   There are two conditions on this line:

- the effective `uid` of the sender is different from the saved `uid` of the target;

- the effective `uid` of the sender is different from the real `uid` of the target.

If one of these matches, the signal can be sent.

313   there are two more conditions here:

- the real `uid` of the sender is different from the saved `uid` of the target;

- the real `uid` of the sender is different from the real `uid` of the target.

If one of these matches, the signal can be sent.

314   finally, it does not have the CAP_KILL capability (i.e. permission to override the restrictions on lines 312–313). The `capable()` function is described in Section 20.4.1.

18.1.2.2   *Special handling for some signals*

Some signals have implications of their own, apart from whatever the registered handler does. The function shown in Figure 18.3, from `kernel/signal.c`, checks for these signals and alters the state of the target process accordingly.

```
380  static void handle_stop_signal(int sig, struct task_struct *t)
381  {
382      switch (sig) {
383      case SIGKILL: case SIGCONT:
384
385          if (t->state == TASK_STOPPED)
386              wake_up_process(t);
387          t->exit_code = 0;
388          rm_sig_from_queue(SIGSTOP, t);
389          rm_sig_from_queue(SIGTSTP, t);
390          rm_sig_from_queue(SIGTTOU, t);
391          rm_sig_from_queue(SIGTTIN, t);
392          break;
393
394      case SIGSTOP: case SIGTSTP:
395      case SIGTTIN: case SIGTTOU:
```

```
396
397                rm_sig_from_queue(SIGCONT, t);
398                break;
399        }
400  }
```

Figure 18.3 Special handling for some signals

383–392 the SIGKILL and SIGCONT signals both have to wake up the target process if it is in the TASK_STOPPED state.

386 this function was described in Section 4.7.5. It changes the state of the process to TASK_RUNNING and moves it to the run queue, where the scheduler will find it. It will then run and execute the handler for this signal.

387 an exit code of 0 indicates that the process did not terminate voluntarily [e.g. by calling exit()].

388–391 either a SIGKILL (terminate) or a SIGCONT (run) makes these stop signals irrelevant. Just in case any of these signals are queued for the process, we remove them. The function is in Section 18.1.2.3.

394–398 any of these signals will cause the process to move to the TASK_STOPPED state, so we cancel any SIGCONT that might happen to be queued.

399 for any other signal, the function returns without doing anything.

18.1.2.3 Removing a queued signal

The function shown in Figure 18.4, from kernel/signal.c, is only a wrapper. It is passed a pointer to the task_struct of the target process and converts it to a pointer to the pending field. It returns TRUE if sig was found to be pending, in which case it has removed it from the queue. It expects its callers to be holding the sigmask_lock of the target process. The rm_from_queue() function is described in Section 18.1.2.4.

```
300  static int rm_sig_from_queue(int sig, struct task_struct *t)
301  {
302        return rm_from_queue(sig, &t->pending);
303  }
```

Figure 18.4 Removing a queued signal

18.1.2.4 Worker function to remove a signal from a queue

The mechanics of de-queueing a signal and deallocating the memory used is encapsulated in the function shown in Figure 18.5, from kernel/signal.c.

```
270  static int rm_from_queue(int sig, struct sigpending *s)
271  {
272        struct sigqueue *q, **pp;
```

```
273
274        if (!sigismember(&s->signal, sig))
275             return 0;
276
277        sigdelset(&s->signal, sig);
278
279        pp = &s->head;
280
281        while ((q = *pp) != NULL) {
282             if (q->info.si_signo == sig) {
283                  if ((*pp = q->next) == NULL)
284                       s->tail = pp;
285                  kmem_cache_free(sigqueue_cachep,q);
286                  atomic_dec(&nr_queued_signals);
287                  continue;
288             }
289             pp = &q->next;
290        }
291        return 1;
292   }
```

Figure 18.5   Worker function to de-queue a signal

274–275   if the specified signal is not on the queue, we return 0 for failure. The sigismember() macro was described in Section 17.2.1.2.

277   this clears the bit corresponding to this signal in the signal mask of the struct sigpending. The function was described in Section 17.2.1.1.

279   this takes an indirect pointer to the first entry on the queue.

281–290   this checks through the queue, looking for any entries corresponding to this signal. There may be more than one.

282–288   when an appropriate entry is found, it is de-queued.

283–284   if it happened to be the last one in the queue, we set the queue tail pointer to point to its predecessor.

285   this returns the struct sigqueue to the memory manager.

286   this atomically decrements the global count of queued signals, described in Section 18.1.3.2. The atomic_dec() function was described in Section 5.2.6.

287   we go around the loop again. The pp pointer was advanced at line 283.

289   if this was not an appropriate entry, we advance the pointer to the next one and go around the loop again.

291   this returns success. This is possible even if no entry was found on the queue, as long as a bit was found at line 274.

18.1.2.5 Checking for ignored signals

Signals with SIG_IGN handling can be ignored, except for the special case of a SIGCHLD. Some signals with SIG_DFL default to a nonaction and they can be ignored as well. The function shown in Figure 18.6, from kernel/signal.c, checks if a given signal should actually be posted or not. It is called by send_sig_info() at line 535.

```
365  static int ignored_signal(int sig, struct task_struct *t)
366  {
367
368  if ((t->ptrace & PT_PTRACED) || sigismember(&t->blocked, sig))
369      return 0;
370
371  return signal_type(sig, t->sig) == 0;
372  }
```

Figure 18.6   Checking for ignored signals

365   the parameters are the number of the signal and a pointer to the task_struct of the target process.

368–369   if the target process is being traced, or the particular signal is blocked, then it should not be ignored, so we return 0 (do not ignore). The sigismember() macro was described in Section 17.2.1.2.

371   otherwise, we call the subsidiary function (Section 18.1.2.6) to determine whether this particular signal should be ignored (0) or not (1). If the return value is 0, then the present function returns TRUE (ignore). With any other return value, the present function returns FALSE (do not ignore).

18.1.2.6 Determining the type of a signal

When checking for ignored signals, the set of all signals is partitioned into three subsets; those for which action should be spread to all threads, those that are ignored, and those that cause a process to wake up. Figure 18.7, from kernel/signal.c, shows the function that checks these properties and returns an appropriate value.

```
323  static int signal_type(int sig, struct signal_struct *signals)
324  {
325      unsigned long handler;
326
327      if (!signals)
328          return 0;
329
330      handler = (unsigned long) signals->action
                                              [sig-1].sa.sa_handler;
331      if (handler > 1)
332          return 1;

335      if (handler == 1)
```

```
336                    return sig == SIGCHLD;

339          switch (sig) {

342              case SIGCONT: case SIGWINCH:
343              case SIGCHLD: case SIGURG:
344                  return 0;
347              case SIGTSTP: case SIGTTIN: case SIGTTOU:
348                  return 1;

351              default:
352                  return -1;
353          }
354  }
```

Figure 18.7   Determining the type of a signal

323 the parameters are the number of the signal and a pointer to the `signal_struct` of the target process.

327–328 if the pointer to the `signal_struct` of the target process is NULL, this would imply a zombie. That signal can be ignored, so we return 0.

330 this takes a local copy of the pointer to the handler installed for the specified signal.

331–332 if the value of the pointer is greater than 1, then a valid handler is installed, it should not be ignored. We return 1.

335–336 if the value of the pointer is 1, then it has been set to `SIG_IGN`. However, there is one exception: a `SIGCHLD` signal cannot be ignored. If the signal is `SIGCHLD`, then we return 1; otherwise, 0. Note that `SIGCHLD` is a very unusual signal; if set to `SIG_IGN` it is not actually ignored but does automatic child reaping; if set to `SIG_DFL`, POSIX explicitly forces it to be ignored.

339–353 this block of code is executed only if the value of the pointer is less than 1. That means it has been set to `SIG_DFL`.

342–344 the default action for these four signals is to ignore them, so we return 0, which means ignored.

347–348 for these three signals, we return 1, which means they are not to be ignored, they must be posted. They have some implicit default behaviour.

351–352 for all others, we return −1. This value is never in fact used by the caller (Section 18.1.2.5), which distinguishes only between zero and nonzero.

18.1.3   Posting a signal to the target process

As part of the procedure of sending a signal, as discussed in Section 18.1.1, the signal has to be posted to the target process. This is the subject of the current section. There is one basic function, and a series of subfunctions called by this.

18.1.3.1 Delivering a signal

The root of all this processing is the function shown in Figure 18.8, from `kernel/signal.c`. It is called by `send_sig_info()` every time a signal is to be sent.

```
493  static int deliver_signal(int sig, struct siginfo *info,
                                              struct task_struct *t)
494  {
495      int retval = send_signal(sig, info, &t->pending);
496
497      if (!retval && !sigismember(&t->blocked, sig))
498          signal_wake_up(t);
499
500      return retval;
501  }
```

Figure 18.8 Delivering a signal

493   the parameters are the number of the signal to be sent, a pointer to the extra information, and a pointer to the `task_struct` of the target process.

495   this low-level function for sending a signal is described in Section 18.1.3.2. The third parameter is a pointer to the `pending` field in the `task_struct` of the target process. This is the only field that will be affected. It returns 0 if it succeeded in posting the signal, otherwise it returns an error code indicating why not.

497–498   if the call to `send_signal()` was successful (0), and the signal is not currently blocked, then we wake up the process to handle this signal, just in case it was sleeping. The `sigismember()` macro was described in Section 17.2.1.2.

498   the `signal_wake_up()` function will be discussed in Section 18.1.3.4.

500   this is the success or failure returned by `send_signal()` at line 495. This value is passed back to the sender of the signal.

18.1.3.2 Sending a signal

The low-level function that actually posts a signal to another process (i.e. the first one that actually manipulates the `task_struct` of the target process) is shown in Figure 18.9, from `kernel/signal.c`.

```
33   atomic_t      nr_queued_signals;
34   int           max_queued_signals = 1024;

402  static int send_signal(int sig, struct siginfo *info,
                                              struct sigpending *signals)
403  {
404      struct sigqueue * q = NULL;
414      if (atomic_read(&nr_queued_signals) < max_queued_signals){
415          q = kmem_cache_alloc(sigqueue_cachep, GFP_ATOMIC);
```

```
416         }
417
418         if (q) {
419             atomic_inc(&nr_queued_signals);
420             q->next = NULL;
421             *signals->tail = q;
422             signals->tail = &q->next;
423             switch ((unsigned long) info) {
424                 case 0:
425                     q->info.si_signo = sig;
426                     q->info.si_errno = 0;
427                     q->info.si_code = SI_USER;
428                     q->info.si_pid = current->pid;
429                     q->info.si_uid = current->uid;
430                     break;
431                 case 1:
432                     q->info.si_signo = sig;
433                     q->info.si_errno = 0;
434                     q->info.si_code = SI_KERNEL;
435                     q->info.si_pid = 0;
436                     q->info.si_uid = 0;
437                     break;
438                 default:
439                     copy_siginfo(&q->info, info);
440                     break;
441             }
442         } else if (sig >= SIGRTMIN && info &&
443         (unsigned long)info != 1 && info->si_code != SI_USER) {

448             return -EAGAIN;
449         }
450
451         sigaddset(&signals->signal, sig);
452         return 0;
453 }
```

Figure 18.9 Sending a signal

33 this is the systemwide count of signals queued to all processes.

34 there is a systemwide limit to the total number of signals that can be queued at any one time, in `max_queued_signals`, initialised to 1024.

402 the parameters are the number of the signal to be sent, a pointer to the extra information, and a pointer to the `struct sigpending` in the target process.

404 this pointer needs to be initialised to NULL. If the condition at line 414 is FALSE, then no queue entry is allocated. If the pointer is still NULL at line 418, this will be recognised.

414–416 only if the systemwide limit on the total number of signals that can be queued at any one time has not been exceeded is an attempt made to allocate memory for the queue entry [see Section 5.2.1 for the `atomic_read()` macro].

418–441 this block of code is executed only if the memory manager was able to allocate enough space for another `struct sigqueue`.

419 this increments the global count of queued signals (see Section 5.2.5 for the function).

420 as this is going to be the last entry on the queue, we set its forward pointer to NULL.

421 the `tail` pointer of the signal queue for this process was pointing to the `next` field of the previously last entry (which was NULL). This assignment changes the previously last entry, to point to this new one.

422 the `tail` pointer of the signal queue is set to the `next` field of this new entry.

423 this checks the meaning of the pointer `info`, passed in as a parameter. There are three possibilities.

424–430 if it was a NULL pointer, then the signal was sent by a user process and the caller had no extra information to pass to the target process. We fill in the appropriate fields of the newly allocated `struct sigqueue` with default values.

425 this is the number of the signal being sent.

426 there is no error number supplied, so default to 0.

427 this identifies the signal as being sent by a user process, using a system service (see Section 17.1.5.4 for these `si_code` values).

428–429 these supply the `pid` and `uid` of the current (sending) process.

431–437 if the value of the parameter `info` was 1, then it was an informationless signal sent by the kernel. The fields are all given the same default values, except for `si_code`, which indicates that the signal was sent from somewhere in the kernel (see Section 17.1.5.4 for these `si_code` values).

438–440 a valid pointer to a `struct siginfo` was supplied.

439 this copies the information from the `struct siginfo` to the `struct sigqueue`. The function is described in Section 18.1.3.3.

442–443 this test is performed only when the system is low on memory and was unable to allocate space for a `struct sigqueue` at line 415. If the following are all TRUE then no attempt is made to deliver it without its information and the function returns EAGAIN:

- it is a real-time signal (first condition);

- there is a valid `struct siginfo` supplied (second and third condition);

- it was not sent from user mode (fourth condition).

451 this line is executed in all other cases. It sets the corresponding bit in the signal mask of the target process and returns [see Section 17.2.1.1 for the `sigaddset()` function].

18.1.3.3   Copying the `siginfo` data

When a signal is queued to a process the data supplied in the `struct siginfo` are copied into the `info` field of the `struct sigqueue`. The function to do this is shown in Figure 18.10, from `<asm-i386/siginfo.h>`.

```
219  static inline void copy_siginfo(siginfo_t *to, siginfo_t *from)
220  {
221       if (from->si_code < 0)
222            memcpy(to, from, sizeof(siginfo_t));
223       else

225            memcpy(to, from,
                   3*sizeof(int) + sizeof(from >_sifields._sigchld));
226  }
```

Figure 18.10   Copy the `siginfo` data

219   the `to` parameter is the queue entry; the `from` parameter is the `struct siginfo` supplied by the sender.

221–222   if the `si_code` field is negative then it is a standard `siginfo_t` (Section 17.1.5.1) and a straight `memcpy()` is sufficient.

225   otherwise, we copy the currently largest known member of the `union`.

18.1.3.4   Announcing the arrival of a signal

When an unblocked signal is posted to a process then if that process is sleeping interruptibly it should be woken up and moved to the runqueue. The function to implement that is shown in Figure 18.11, from `kernel/signal.c`. The function expects the caller to be holding the `sigmask_lock`, and local interrupts must have been disabled when that was acquired.

```
466  static inline void signal_wake_up(struct task_struct *t)
467  {
468       t->sigpending = 1;
469
470  #ifdef CONFIG_SMP

481       spin_lock(&runqueue_lock);
482       if (t->has_cpu && t->processor != smp_processor_id())
483            smp_send_reschedule(t->processor);
484       spin_unlock(&runqueue_lock);
485  #endif
486
487       if (t->state & TASK_INTERRUPTIBLE) {
488            wake_up_process(t);
```

```
489                return;
490       }
491  }
```

Figure 18.11 Announcing the arrival of a signal

468 this sets a marker in the `task_struct` of the process to indicate that there is a signal pending.

470–485 this code is relevant only in the SMP case; the target process may actually be running [on another computer processing unit (CPU)].

481–484 this takes out the runqueue lock, so that the target process cannot change information while this one is reading it. The comment in the code accepts that this might occasionally kick the wrong CPU if the process is actually in the middle of changing – but no harm is done by that, other than doing an extra (lightweight) interprocessor interrupt.

482 this condition is TRUE if the target process is actually running, and on a processor different from the one on which this process is running. This rules out the case of a process sending a signal to itself. The `smp_processor_id()` is from Section 7.2.1.4.

483 this forces a reschedule on the other CPU to make it notice the new signal quickly (see Section 13.5.1 for the function).

487–490 if the target process is sleeping interruptibly, then we wake it up, using the function from Section 4.7.5, which changes its state to TASK_RUNNING and moves it to the runqueue. When the scheduler eventually gives it the CPU, it will handle this signal.

18.2 Other signal-sending functions

This section considers a number of functions, all of which send signals, after some preliminary processing. They all end up calling `send_sig_info()` to send the signal or signals.

18.2.1 Forcing the delivery of a signal

Sometimes it is necessary to force a process to receive a signal that it may have advertised as ignored or blocked. The function in Figure 18.12, from `kernel/signal.c`, does just that.

```
560  int
561  force_sig_info(int sig, struct siginfo *info, struct task_struct *t)
562  {
563      unsigned long int flags;
564
565      spin_lock_irqsave(&t->sigmask_lock, flags);
566      if (t->sig == NULL) {
567          spin_unlock_irqrestore(&t->sigmask_lock, flags);
568          return -ESRCH;
569      }
```

```
570
571        if (t->sig->action[sig-1].sa.sa_handler == SIG_IGN)
572            t->sig->action[sig-1].sa.sa_handler = SIG_DFL;
573        sigdelset(&t->blocked, sig);
574        recalc_sigpending(t);
575        spin_unlock_irqrestore(&t->sigmask_lock, flags);
576
577        return send_sig_info(sig, info, t);
578  }
```

Figure 18.12   Forcing the delivery of a signal

561   the parameters are the number of the signal, a pointer to the `struct siginfo`, and a pointer to the `task_struct` of the target process.

565–575   as the function will be writing to the `blocked` mask of the target process, it takes out a spinlock on it to prevent any other process manipulating it at the same time. The interrupt-safe spinlock macros were described in Section 12.8.1.

566–569   if the target process is a zombie, we give back the lock and restore the interrupt state. Then we return ESRCH (no such process).

571–572   if the process has set up `SIG_IGN` as the handler for the signal, we change it to `SIG_DFL` so that it will take the default action.

573   we mark this particular signal as unblocked, just in case it was blocked. The function was described in Section 17.2.1.1.

574   this function, from Section 18.3.2, updates the `sigpending` field of the `task_struct`, so that this signal will be noticed.

577   now we call the normal function for sending signals, as described in Section 18.1.1, and return whatever status value it supplies.

18.2.2   Sending a signal to all processes in a group

A special function is supplied that sends a signal to all processes in a group. This is used, for example, by keyboard control characters such as CTRL-C and CTRL-Z; see figure 18.13, from `kernel/signal.c`.

```
585  int
586  kill_pg_info(int sig, struct siginfo *info, pid_t pgrp)
587  {
588        int retval = -EINVAL;
589        if (pgrp > 0) {
590            struct task_struct *p;
591
592            retval = -ESRCH;
593            read_lock(&tasklist_lock);
594            for_each_task(p) {
```

```
595                    if (p->pgrp == pgrp) {
596                        int err = send_sig_info(sig, info, p);
597                        if (retval)
598                            retval = err;
599                    }
600                }
601                read_unlock(&tasklist_lock);
602            }
603            return retval;
604    }
```

Figure 18.13　Sending a signal to all processes in a group

586　the parameters are the number of the signal to be sent, a pointer to a `struct_siginfo`, and the number of the process group.

588　this sets up a default return value of EINVAL for an invalid process group number (0 or negative).

589–602　the body of the function is executed only if a legitimate process group number has been passed as a parameter.

592　this sets up a new default return value of ESRCH for a nonexistent group.

593–601　this lock establishes mutual exclusion on the process list so that no other process can change it while this one is traversing it [see Section 5.7.2.1 for the `read_lock()` function].

594–600　this loop goes through each process in the list, using the `for_each task()` macro from Section 3.1.3.

595–599　this block of code is executed only if the process currently being examined is in the specified process group.

596　we send it the specified signal, using the function described in Section 18.1.1.

597–598　if even one of the calls to `send_sig_info()` returns success (0), this will put a 0 into `retval`; otherwise `retval` will have the value returned by the last unsuccessful call. If there were no processes found in that (valid) group, it will be ESRCH.

601　see Section 5.7.2.4 for the `read_unlock()` macro.

18.2.3　Sending a signal to a session leader

The function shown in Figure 18.14, from `kernel/signal.c`, sends a signal to the leader of the current session; this is typically used to send SIGHUP to the controlling process of a terminal when the connection is lost. The code is almost identical to that described in Section 18.2.2, and only the differences will be noted.

```
612    int
613    kill_sl_info(int sig, struct siginfo *info, pid_t sess)
614    {
```

```
615        int retval = -EINVAL;
616        if (sess > 0) {
617            struct task_struct *p;
618
619            retval = -ESRCH;
620            read_lock(&tasklist_lock);
621            for_each_task(p) {
622                if (p->leader && p->session == sess) {
623                    int err = send_sig_info(sig, info, p);
624                    if (retval)
625                        retval = err;
626                }
627            }
628            read_unlock(&tasklist_lock);
629        }
630        return retval;
631  }
```

Figure 18.14   Sending a signal to a session leader

622–626   this block of code is executed only if the process currently being examined is a session leader and is a member of the specified session.

624–625   this code implies there can be more than one call to `send_sig_info()`. If even one of these returns success (0), this will put a 0 into `retval`; otherwise, `retval` will have the value returned by the last unsuccessful call, or ESRCH.

626   as a session should only have one leader, a `break` would have been expected here. Why examine the remainder of the list?

18.2.4   Sending a signal to a specific process identification number

The normal function for sending a signal, `send_sig_info()`, expects a pointer to the `task_struct` of the target process. A parallel function is supplied that allows the destination process to be identified by number [the process identification number (pid)]; see Figure 18.15, from `kernel/signal.c`.

```
633  inline int
634  kill_proc_info(int sig, struct siginfo *info, pid_t pid)
635  {
636      int error;
637      struct task_struct *p;
638
639      read_lock(&tasklist_lock);
640      p = find_task_by_pid(pid);
641      error = -ESRCH;
642      if (p)
643          error = send_sig_info(sig, info, p);
644      read_unlock(&tasklist_lock);
```

```
645       return error;
646  }
```

Figure 18.15   Send a signal to a specific process identification number (pid)

634   the parameters are the number of the signal to be sent, a pointer to a `struct_siginfo`, and the `pid` of the destination process.

639–644   this lock establishes mutual exclusion on the process list so that no other process can change it while this one is traversing it [see Section 5.7.2.1 for the `read_lock()` function].

640   this function, from Section 3.2.5, converts a `pid` to a `task_struct` pointer. It returns NULL if the `pid` supplied is invalid.

641   this sets up a default return value for the case where the `pid` number was invalid.

642–643   if there is such a process, then the signal can be sent in the normal way, using the function from Section 18.1.1. In that case the return value is whatever was sent back by `send_sig_info()`.

644   see Section 5.7.2.4 for the `read_unlock()` macro.

18.2.5   Sending a signal to a range of processes

By using zero-valued or negative pids, different ranges of processes can be specified as the target for a signal. The function shown in Figure 18.16, from `kernel/signal.c`, accepts such pids, and differentiates between them:

- 0 means the signal is sent to every process in the same group as the sender.

- A parameter of −1 means send the signal to any process for which it is permissible.

- If the parameter is less than −1, then the signal is sent to every process in the process group identified by the absolute value of the parameter.

- If the parameter is positive, then the signal is sent to the process identified by the parameter.

- If the signal number is 0, then no signal is sent, but error checking is still performed.

```
656  static int kill_something_info(int sig, struct siginfo *info, int pid)
657  {
658       if (!pid) {
659            return kill_pg_info(sig, info, current->pgrp);
660       } else if (pid == -1) {
661            int retval = 0, count = 0;
662            struct task_struct * p;
663
664            read_lock(&tasklist_lock);
```

```
665                 for_each_task(p) {
666                     if (p->pid > 1 && p != current) {
667                         int err = send_sig_info(sig, info, p);
668                         ++count;
669                             if (err != -EPERM)
670                                 retval = err;
671                     }
672                 }
673                 read_unlock(&tasklist_lock);
674                 return count ? retval : -ESRCH;
675         } else if (pid < 0) {
676             return kill_pg_info(sig, info, -pid);
677         } else {
678             return kill_proc_info(sig, info, pid);
679         }
680  }
```

Figure 18.16   Sending a signal to a range of processes

656   the parameters are the number of the signal to be sent, a pointer to a `struct_siginfo`, and the number specifying the range of target processes.

658–659   the pid supplied was 0, so we send the signal to all processes in the same group as the caller. The return value is whatever the `kill_pg_info()` function (Section 18.2.2) returns.

660–674   the `pid` supplied was −1, so we attempt to send the signal to all processes in the system.

661   this sets up a default success return value.

664–673   this takes out mutual exclusion on the process list so that it cannot be changed while this one is accessing it [see Section 5.7.2.1 for the `read_lock()` function].

665–672   we go through each process on the process list, using the `for_each_task()` macro from Section 3.1.3.

666–671   the only processes that we do not attempt to signal are `init` (pid 1) and the current process.

667   this sends the specified signal, using the function from Section 18.1.1.

668   this keeps track of how many signals have been sent.

669–670   a return value of EPERM means that the current process does not have permission to send the signal to this one. For a process to have permission to send a signal it must either have root privileges, or the real or effective user identification (uid) number of the sending process must equal the real or saved uid of the receiving process. If the result of attempting to send the signal was not the error EPERM, then we change `retval` to whatever `send_sig_info()` returned. If successful, `retval` will have success; if unsuccessful, for some reason other the EPERM, `retval` will have that reason. At the end of the loop, `retval` will have success or error, depending on what happened last.

673   see Section 5.7.2.4 for the `read_unlock()` macro.

674   if even one signal was sent, we return `retval`. If no signals were sent (because there were no processes to send them to), the return value is ESRCH (no such process).

675–676   the `pid` supplied was less than -1. Note that the -1 case has already been handled at line 660. Signals are to be sent to all processes in the group specified by the absolute value of `pid`. The return value is whatever the `kill_pg_info()` function (Section 18.2.2) returns.

677–678   the only possibility left is a `pid` greater than 1. The signal is sent to that specific process. The return value is whatever the `kill_proc_info()` function (Section 18.2.2) returns.

18.2.6 Sending signals to a parent

A pair of functions are provided for sending signals to a parent or to a parent's thread group. Although these can send any specified signal, they are most frequently used for sending SIGCHLD.

18.2.6.1 Notifying a child's change of status to its parent

When a child process changes its status (e.g. it stops or terminates), it is necessary to let its parent know about this status change. The function shown in Figure 18.17, from `kernel/signal.c`, fills in a `struct siginfo` with the relevant information and sends the specified signal to the parent.

```
734  void do_notify_parent(struct task_struct *tsk, int sig)
735  {
736      struct siginfo info;
737      int why, status;
738
739      info.si_signo = sig;
740      info.si_errno = 0;
741      info.si_pid = tsk->pid;
742      info.si_uid = tsk->uid;

745      info.si_utime = tsk->times.tms_utime;
746      info.si_stime = tsk->times.tms_stime;
747
748      status = tsk->exit_code & 0x7f;
749      why = SI_KERNEL;
750      switch (tsk->state) {
751          case TASK_STOPPED:
752
753              if (tsk->ptrace & PT_PTRACED)
754                  why = CLD_TRAPPED;
755              else
756                  why = CLD_STOPPED;
757              break;
758
759          default:
```

```
760                        if (tsk->exit_code & 0x80)
761                              why = CLD_DUMPED;
762                        else if (tsk->exit_code & 0x7f)
763                              why = CLD_KILLED;
764                        else {
765                              why = CLD_EXITED;
766                              status = tsk->exit_code >> 8;
767                        }
768                        break;
769                  }
770            info.si_code = why;
771            info.si_status = status;
772
773            send_sig_info(sig, &info, tsk->p_pptr);
774            wake_up_parent(tsk->p_pptr);
775  }
```

Figure 18.17   Notifying a parent about a child's change of status

734 the function is passed a pointer to the process whose status has changed and the number of the signal to send to its parent.

739–771 the body of this function populates the `struct siginfo` with extra information for the use of the signal handler in the parent. This structure was described in detail in Section 17.1.5.1.

739 this is the number of the signal to be sent to the parent; it was passed in as a parameter.

740 there is no relevant error number, so this field is set to 0.

741–742 the pid and uid of the child process doing the notifying are recorded.

745–746 the cumulative times of the child process, both in user and system mode, are recorded.

748 this masks off all but the low-order 7 bits of the `exit_code` field of the child in the default `status` value being made available to the parent, but this may be changed at line 766.

749 the reason for the notification is set up in the why variable. This line sets up a default reason of SI_KERNEL. This merely means that the signal was sent from somewhere in the kernel. This value should always be overwritten later in the function.

750–769 different information will be supplied, depending on whether the child process is in the TASK_STOPPED state or not.

753–754 if stopped because it is being traced, then the reason is CLD_TRAPPED (a traced child has trapped). The literal constants written to why have been defined in Section 17.1.5.6.

756 otherwise, the child has stopped, and no further reason is available.

759–768 this is the generic processing for a child in any state other than TASK_STOPPED.

760–761 if bit 7 of `exit_code` in the child is set, then the child terminated abnormally and produced a core dump.

762–763   if any of bits 0–6 of exit_code in the child is set then the child process was killed by a signal.

765–766   otherwise, the child has exited itself; in this case, the byte it wants to send back to its parent (in bits 8–15 of exit_code) is moved to the low-order byte of status.

770   the si_code field is set to the reason determined in the switch.

771   the si_status field is set to the status value determined in the switch. When the child exited voluntarily, this is the value of the status information it wants to pass back to its parent. In all other cases, it is the low-order 7 bits of the exit_code field in the child's task_struct.

773   this sends the specified signal to the parent process. The function is described in Section 18.1.1. The information in the struct siginfo is now available to the signal handler running in user mode.

774   this wakes all sleeping threads in the parent's group so that they will receive and process the signal. The function is described in Section 18.2.6.2.

18.2.6.2   Waking up all threads in the parent group

The function do_notify_parent() (Section 18.2.6.1) needs to wake up all sleeping threads in the thread group to which a process belongs. The function shown in Figure 18.18, from kernel/signal.c, does this by working its way along the linked list of threads, beginning from the parent process and waking up any of them that are waiting interruptibly for a child to exit.

```
720  static void wake_up_parent(struct task_struct *parent)
721  {
722        struct task_struct *tsk = parent;
723
724        do {
725              wake_up_interruptible(&tsk->wait_chldexit);
726              tsk = next_thread(tsk);
727        } while (tsk != parent);
728  }
```

Figure 18.18   Waking up all threads in parent's group

724–727   the thread list is a circular linked list, with the last entry pointing back to the parent, so this loop will traverse all entries on the list and then terminate.

725   this macro, which wakes up any process in the TASK_INTERRUPTIBLE state on the wait queue headed from wait_chldexit, has been described in Section 4.7.1. Its parameter is a pointer to the wait queue header in the task_struct of the particular thread.

726   this macro returns a pointer to the next task_struct on the thread group list. It has been described in Section 9.4.1.

18.2.6.3   Notifing a parent without a lock

The wrapper function shown in Figure 18.19, from `kernel/signal.c`, sends a specific signal to the parent of the current process. It takes out the tasklist lock before calling `do_notify_parent()`. This is necessary to prevent the possibility of the parent disappearing in the meantime.

```
785  void
786  notify_parent(struct task_struct *tsk, int sig)
787  {
788          read_lock(&tasklist_lock);
789          do_notify_parent(tsk, sig);
790          read_unlock(&tasklist_lock);
791  }
```

Figure 18.19   Notifying a parent without a lock

788   the lock and unlock macros are from Sections 5.6 (uniprocessor) and 5.7 (multiprocessor).

789   the function has been described in Section 18.2.6.1. It sends `sig` to the parent of `tsk`.

790   see Section 5.7.2.4 for the `read_unlock()` macro.

18.2.7   Backward compatibility functions for sending signals

A number of functions are provided for backward compatibility with the rest of the kernel source. They upgrade the older style functions to call extended `info` functions, making the required changes to the parameters; see Figure 18.20, from `kernel/signal.c`.

```
686  int
687  send_sig(int sig, struct task_struct *p, int priv)
688  {
689          return send_sig_info(sig, (void*)(long)(priv != 0), p);
690  }
691
692  void
693  force_sig(int sig, struct task_struct *p)
694  {
695          force_sig_info(sig, (void*)1L, p);
696
697
698  int
699  kill_pg(pid_t pgrp, int sig, int priv)
700  {
701          return kill_pg_info(sig, (void*)(long)(priv != 0), pgrp);
702  }
703
704  int
705  kill_sl(pid_t sess, int sig, int priv)
```

```
706 {
707         return kill_sl_info(sig, (void *)(long)(priv != 0), sess);
708 }
709
710 int
711 kill_proc(pid_t pid, int sig, int priv)
712 {
713         return kill_proc_info(sig, (void *)(long)(priv != 0), pid);
714 }
```

Figure 18.20   Backward compatibility functions

689   this function upgrades a send_sig() to a send_sig_info() by changing the order of the parameters and the type of priv, from int to void *. If priv is 0, meaning the signal is being sent from user mode, then (priv != 0) evaluates to FALSE (0), and this is returned as a pointer to void. For any other value of priv, kernel mode, it evaluates to 1. The send_sig_info() function was described in Section 18.1.1.

695   a new second parameter is generated, with 1 cast as a pointer to void. This means that the signal was sent from somewhere in the kernel. The force_sig_info() function was described in Section 18.2.1.

701   the priv parameter is converted from an int to a pointer to void, as discussed in line 689. The kill_pg_info() function was described in Section 18.2.2.

705   the sess parameter identifies a session. The signal sig is to be sent to the leader of that session.

707   this changes the order of the parameters and converts priv, as discussed for line 689. The kill_sl_info() function was described in Section 18.2.3.

713   this changes the order of the parameters and converts priv, as discussed for line 689. The kill_proc_info() function was described in Section 18.2.4.

18.3   Pending signals

The previous sections examined how signals are posted to a process. After the send_sig_info() function has run, the data structures representing the target process reflect the fact that a signal had been sent to that process. The kernel checks these data structures at one specific point – on the return path from a system call. At that stage it arranges for the process to take any appropriate action. This side of the mechanism is the subject matter of the remainder of this chapter. We begin by examining a number of functions that check whether or not a signal is pending to a process.

18.3.1   Checking the sigpending field

When a signal is pending to a process the sigpending field in its task_struct is set to 1. See Section 18.3.2. The trivial function shown in Figure 18.21, from <linux/sched.h>, checks this field for a specified process and returns TRUE or FALSE.

```
632  static inline int signal_pending(struct task_struct *p)
633  {
634        return (p->sigpending != 0);
635  }
```

Figure 18.21 Checking the `sigpending` field

18.3.2   Settin the `sigpending` field

The function shown in Figure 18.22, from `<linux/sched.h>`, sets the value of the
`sigpending` field. This needs to be reevaluated every time the `blocked` bitmap changes.
All callers should be holding the `sigmask_lock`.

```
671  static inline void recalc_sigpending(struct task_struct *t)
672  {
673        t->sigpending =
              has_pending_signals(&t->pending.signal, &t->blocked);
674  }
```

Figure 18.22 Evaluate the signal state of a process

673   thus it merely picks out the `signal` and `blocked` fields and passes them on to
`has_pending_signals()` (see Section 18.3.3). The `sigpending` field is set according to
the value (TRUE or FALSE) returned by this function.

18.3.3   Recalculating the signal state

The function shown in Figure 18.23, from `<linux/sched.h>`, recalculates the signal
state of a process from the set of pending and blocked signals.

```
641  static inline int has_pending_signals(sigset_t *signal,
                                                   sigset_t *blocked)
642  {
643        unsigned long ready;
644        long i;
645
646        switch (_NSIG_WORDS) {
647        default:
648            for (i = _NSIG_WORDS, ready = 0; --i >= 0 ;)
649                ready |= signal->sig[i] &~ blocked->sig[i];
650            break;
651
652        case 4: ready = signal->sig[3] &~ blocked->sig[3];
653                ready |= signal->sig[2] &~ blocked->sig[2];
654                ready |= signal->sig[1] &~ blocked->sig[1];
655                ready |= signal->sig[0] &~ blocked->sig[0];
656            break;
657
```

```
658                    case 2: ready = signal->sig[1] &~ blocked->sig[1];
659                            ready |= signal->sig[0] &~ blocked->sig[0];
660                            break;
661
662            case 1: ready = signal->sig[0] &~ blocked->sig[0];
663            }
664            return ready != 0;
665    }
```

Figure 18.23   Recalculating the pending state

641   the first parameter is a pointer to the bitmap of pending signals; the second is a pointer to the bitmap of blocked signals (both in the `task_struct` of the process).

646–663   because these bitmaps can be of different lengths on different architectures, there is separate handling for one, two, four, or more words.

647–650   this is for very long signal masks, greater than four words.

648   each iteration of the loop checks one `unsigned long` in the bitmap. Note that the initialisation of `ready` is done only once; it is part of the initialisation of the `for` loop.

649   any bits set in the current element of `signal` and cleared in the corresponding element of `blocked` are set in `ready`. It is possible that on successive iterations of the loop the same bit may be set in `ready`, but this does not matter – the function is checking only if at least one unmasked bit is set in `signal`.

652–656   for a four-word signal mask, this code is faster than using the loop in the previous case. Each line checks one word in the bitmap and sets any relevant bits in `ready`. As before, this may mean that some bit is set multiple times.

658–659   this is optimised for the two-word case, as with the i386 architecture.

662   this is for architectures that use only an `unsigned long` bitmap.

664   if even one bit is set in `ready`, we return TRUE; otherwise, we return FALSE.

18.4   Delivering a pending signal

Pending signals are actually handled on the return path from a system service call (see Section 10.6.3), that transfers control to the `do_signal()` function from `arch/i386/kernel/signal.c`. This routine does some preliminary checking and discarding. When it has found a signal that needs handling, it passes it on to `handle_signal()`, discussed in Section 19.1. All of this is architecture-specific code. This section describes `do_signal()`. As it is a long function, the discussion will be broken down into a number of functional parts.

18.4.1   Identifing the pending signal

The beginning of the do_signal() function is shown in Figure 18.24. Basically, all it does is to take the first signal off the queue.

```
584  int do_signal(struct pt_regs *regs, sigset_t *oldset)
585  {
586      siginfo_t info;
587      struct k_sigaction *ka;

595      if ((regs->xcs & 3) != 3)
596          return 1;

598      if (!oldset)
599          oldset = &current->blocked;

601      for (;;) {
602          unsigned long signr;

604          spin_lock_irq(&current->sigmask_lock);
605          signr = dequeue_signal(&current->blocked, &info);
606          spin_unlock_irq(&current->sigmask_lock);

608          if (!signr)
609              break;
```

Figure 18.24   Identifying the pending signal

584   the parameters are a pointer to the register values saved on the stack on entry to the kernel and a pointer to the blocked signal set of the current process.

595   this routine is normally called from the interrupt return path. This is checking whether the interrupt occurred while the process was running in user mode. The two least-significant bits in the xcs field (code segment) of the struct pt_regs passed in as a parameter represent the privilege level of the segment. If both of these are set, then the process was running in user mode when the interrupt occurred.

596   if the process was running in kernel mode when the interrupt occurred, signals are not handled at his stage, so we just return without doing anything. A return value of 1 from this function indicates successful operation (no errors were encountered).

598–599   if a NULL pointer was passed for the second parameter oldset, then the blocked bitmap of the current process is used instead. This is what should have been used anyway.

601   this begins an infinite loop, which goes on to line 706 (see Figures 18.24 to 18.28). Each time around the loop, one signal is processed. Sometimes, that signal can be ignored for one reason or another so the loop is short-circuited, using continue. If there are no further signals queued, then we break out of the loop at line 609. If a signal is found that needs to be handled, we do so and return from the whole function.

604–606 under the protection of the `sigmask_lock` spinlock of the current process, we find the number of the first signal on the queue. The interrupt-safe spinlock macros were described in Section 12.8.1.

605 the function `dequeue_signal()` will be described in Section 18.5. It returns the number of the next signal in `signr` and information about the signal in `info`.

608–609 if there is no signal on the queue, then we break out of the loop and fall through to line 709 (see Figure 18.29). This would not normally happen the first time around.

18.4.2 Signal pending to a traced process

The code shown in Figure 18.25, from `arch/i386/kernel/signal.c`, is executed only if the process is being traced and the signal being handled is something other than `SIGKILL`. Even if a process is being traced, `SIGKILL` still kills it off, without reference to its parent.

```
611          if ((current->ptrace & PT_PTRACED) && signr != SIGKILL){
612
613              current->exit_code = signr;
614              current->state = TASK_STOPPED;
615              notify_parent(current, SIGCHLD);
616              schedule();

619              if (!(signr = current->exit_code))
620                  continue;
621              current->exit_code = 0;

624              if (signr == SIGSTOP)
625                  continue;

628              if (signr != info.si_signo) {
629                  info.si_signo = signr;
630                  info.si_errno = 0;
631                  info.si_code = SI_USER;
632                  info.si_pid = current->p_pptr->pid;
633                  info.si_uid = current->p_pptr->uid;
634              }

637              if (sigismember(&current->blocked, signr)) {
638                  send_sig_info(signr, &info, current);
639                  continue;
640              }
641          }
```

Figure 18.25 Signal pending to a traced process

613–616 this is handing over control to the tracing process.

613 the number of the signal being handled is put in the `exit_code` field of the current process. This is how it lets the tracing process know which signal is pending.

614   its state is changed to TASK_STOPPED.

615   then its parent, the debugging process, is notified. The function notify_parent() has been examined in Section 18.2.6.3. It lets the parent know that the status of the child has changed, by sending it SIGCHLD.

616   finally the scheduler is called. This will remove the current process from the runqueue. Although the scheduler may not run the tracing process immediately it will run it eventually and certainly before this one runs again as its state is TASK_STOPPED.

619–620   when this process is context switched back in, after the tracing process has run, and has changed its state back to TASK_RUNNING, it takes up here. Taking a copy of exit_code into signr allows for the possibility of the tracing process changing the signal to be handled. If the tracing process cancelled the signal it will have put a zero in exit_code. In that case this signal can be forgotten. We then go around the loop again and check if another signal is pending.

621   otherwise, the debugger wants this process to handle the signal. Using exit_code to pass information back from the debugger is a little unorthodox. We clear it so that it will not cause confusion later.

624–625   if the signal being handled is SIGSTOP we just ignore it. After all, the process has just stopped and restarted. We go around the loop again to check if another signal is pending.

628   the variable info is a struct siginfo, declared in Section 17.1.5.1. This structure is used to provide processes with information on why a signal was generated. If the tracing process changed the number of the signal it wants this one to handle, then info will be stale.

629–633   these lines update the siginfo structure. We change the si_signo field. There is no error (yet). The signal was generated by a user process and the next two fields contain the pid and uid of the process that sent the signal. In this case, that is the tracing process, its parent.

637   this checks if the signal now being handled is blocked; the sigismember() macro was discussed in Section 17.2.1.2.

638–639   if so, we requeue it and go around again. The send_sig_info() function has been discussed in Section 18.1.1.

18.4.3   Ignoring a signal

By the time the code shown in Figure 18.26 is reached, there is a signal that needs handling, from whatever source. Now the checking is over, the emphasis is on determining how to handle it. This code deals with signals that are ignored by default.

```
643             ka = &current->sig->action[signr-1];
644             if (ka->sa.sa_handler == SIG_IGN) {
645                 if (signr != SIGCHLD)
646                     continue;
647
648                 while (sys_wait4(-1, NULL, WNOHANG, NULL) > 0)
649                     /* nothing */;
```

```
650                    continue;
651            }
```

Figure 18.26 Signal with handler set to SIG_IGN

643   this sets up a local pointer to the `struct k_sigaction` for the signal we are handling. This contains information on how to handle it.

645–650   this code is executed only if the handler is SIG_IGN.

645–646   for any signal other than SIGCHLD, we go around the loop again. The handler is SIG_IGN, so we do just that.

648   if it is SIGCHLD, then it means that a child process of this one has exited. In order to clean up after it, we call `sys_wait4()` (see Section 9.3). The first parameter specifies synchronisation with any child process. The second parameter is a pointer to an `int` into which status information about the child will be written. In this case, the present process is interested only in getting rid of the zombie, so it just puts a NULL here. The third specifies not to wait for a child that has not exited. The fourth is a pointer to a `struct rusage`, not required in this case either. On success, this function returns the child `pid`, so, if there is a child process waiting, this will pick up its zombie and allow it to die in peace. The `while` loop caters for the possibility that more than one child may have exited; it will clean up one each time around. When there is no (further) zombie, then `sys_wait4()` returns 0, and the loop terminates.

650   in any case, we go around the main loop again and check for the next signal.

18.4.4   Default handling for a signal

The code shown in Figure 18.27 is executed only if the handler is SIG_DFL.

```
653        if (ka->sa.sa_handler == SIG_DFL) {
654            int exit_code = signr;
657            if (current->pid == 1)
658                continue;
659
660        switch (signr) {
661        case SIGCONT: case SIGCHLD: case SIGWINCH:
662                continue;
663
664            case SIGTSTP: case SIGTTIN: case SIGTTOU:
665                if (is_orphaned_pgrp(current->pgrp))
666                    continue;
669            case SIGSTOP: {
670                struct signal_struct *sig;
671                current->state = TASK_STOPPED;
672                current->exit_code = signr;
673                sig = current->p_pptr->sig;
674                if (sig &&
            (sig-t;action[SIGCHLD-1].sa.sa_flags & SA_NOCLDSTOP))
```

```
675                          notify_parent(current, SIGCHLD);
676                    schedule();
677                    continue;
678               }
680          case SIGQUIT: case SIGILL: case SIGTRAP:
681          case SIGABRT: case SIGFPE: case SIGSEGV:
682          case SIGBUS: case SIGSYS: case SIGXCPU: case SIGXFSZ:
683               if (do_coredump(signr, regs))
684                    exit_code |= 0x80;
687          default:
688               sigaddset(&current->pending.signal, signr);
689               recalc_sigpending(current);
690               current->flags |= PF_SIGNALED;
691               do_exit(exit_code);
692
693          }
694     }
```

Figure 18.27   Signal with handler set to SIG_DFL

654   this sets a local variable `exit_code` to hold the number of the signal being processed. This may be updated at line 684 and used at line 691.

657–658   note that `init` (process 1) is a special process: it does not get signals it does not want to handle. Its default is to ignore signals. Thus you cannot kill `init` even with a `SIGKILL`, whether accidentally or on purpose. We go around the loop again and check the next signal.

660–693   different signals or groups of signals are given different default handling, using this switch statement.

661–662   the default handling for these is just to ignore them. We go around again and check the next signal.

664–666   these are terminal control signals. If the process group to which this process belongs is orphaned (i.e. has no controlling terminal), then we ignore the signal and go around the loop again. The function `is_orphaned_pgrp()` has been described in Section 9.2.3.3.2. Otherwise, we fall through into the next case. Note there is no `break` statement.

669   back at lines 624–625 of Figure 18.25 `SIGSTOP` was ignored, but that was in the debug case. Here we are dealing with the general case, and `SIGSTOP` must be handled. The difference between `SIGSTOP` and the previous three signals is that `SIGSTOP` always stops the process; the others only do so if their process group is not orphaned.

671–672   this sets the state of this process to be `TASK_STOPPED` and its `exit_code` to be the number of the signal being processed.

673   this takes a local pointer to the `signal_stuct` of the parent process.

674–675   unless the parent has specified that it is not to be bothered when one of its children stops, by clearing the `SA_NOCLDSTOP` flag in the `struct sigaction` corresponding to this signal, then we notify the parent that the child is stopping. Otherwise, we do nothing. This flag determines whether `SIGCHLD` is to be generated or not by a child process when it stops. It is always generated when a child process terminates. The `notify_parent()` function finds the parent process and notifies it of a status change in the child (see Section 18.2.6.3).

676 this calls the scheduler, which will remove this process from the runqueue and context switch in some other one.

677 when this process next runs, it will pick up here. The most likely reason it woke up is because a SIGCONT has been posted to it, so it will go around the loop again and check for further queued signals.

680–684 the default handling for this group of signals is to terminate the process and produce a core dump.

683–684 the actual writing of a core image to disk is done by the function `do_coredump()`. This is file-system-specific and is not considered in this book. Some file systems may not be able to produce a core dump; in that case, the function returns 0. If a core dump has been produced, then bit seven of the local `exit_code` is set to alert the parent to this. Whether a core dump is to be produced or not, it always falls through to the default case. Notice there is no `break` statement.

687–691 this is the default handler for the previous group and all other signals. It terminates the process.

688 this sets the bit corresponding to the signal being handled in the `pending` bitmap of the current process. The `sigaddset()` function has been described in Section 17.2.1.1.

689 the `recalc_sigpending()` function has been discussed in Section 18.3.2.

690 this sets the `PF_SIGNALLED` flag in the current process to indicate that it has been terminated by the arrival of a signal.

691 this terminates the current process and does not return. Remember these are signals whose default handling is to terminate the process. The function `do_exit()` has been discussed in Section 9.1.

693 note that this is the end of the `switch` statement begun on line 660.

694 this is the end of the `if` statement begun on line 653.

18.4.5 Signal with a user-defined handler

The code shown in Figure 18.28 is executed if the signal is actually going to be delivered, that is, if its handler is neither SIG_IGN or SIG_DFL.

```
701                 __asm__("movl %0,%%db7" : :
                                "r" (current->thread.debugreg[7]));

704                 handle_signal(signr, ka, &info, oldset, regs);
705                 ;return 1;
706         }
```

Figure 18.28   Re-enabling breakpoints and delivering signal

701 the debug registers on the i386 are used to control breakpoints in a program. DR7 is the debug control register, it enables or disables all the others. As this may have been cleared when the breakpoint occurred it is reset here from the value stored in the thread structure of the current process. The value is copied from current->thread.debugreg[7] to the hardware DR7.

704 this function (discussed in Section 19.1) arranges for the user-defined signal handler to be run (once the process is back in the user mode). It does this by altering saved values on both the kernel and the user mode stacks. When the handler is finished, and returns, the values it finds on its (user mode) stack cause it to return to kernel mode (discussed in Section 19.5) where it will attempt to handle any further signals pending to the process.

705 after that, we return from the whole do_signal() function, back to system call handling in Section 10.6.3. This returns the process to user mode, in the usual way, but it does not take up where it left off (at the next line after the system call) but rather at the beginning of the signal handler.

706 this is the end of the infinite for loop begun at line 601.

18.4.6   Restarting an interrupted system call

The only way control can transfer to the code shown in Figure 18.29 is by breaking out of the infinite loop at line 609 (Figure 18.24) because there were no further signals queued. One final possibility must be considered. When a process calls a system service that blocks, it is put into the TASK_INTERRUPTIBLE or TASK_UNINTERRUPTIBLE state. When a signal is posted to a process in the TASK_INTERRUPTIBLE state it is woken up and moved to the runqueue, even though the system service has not completed. In this case, when the system service handler resumes it detects that it has been woken up prematurely, so it puts an error value in the copy of EAX on the stack. This will be one of ERESTARTNOHAND, ERESTARTSYS, or ERESTARTNOINTR. These are used internally by system call handlers to specify whether the system call can be restarted or not. The system service handler than takes the normal exit path, in the course of which it checks if a signal is pending to the process, as usual. If so, and a user-defined handler is installed, then handle_signal() arranges for the system service itself to be restarted. However, it is possible that the signal was ignored or given default handling. The code in this section is checking for that. If the current process is on the return path from a system call and the value in the saved copy of EAX on the stack is one of these three, then the system call is to be restarted.

```
709          if (regs->orig_eax >= 0) {
710
711              if (regs->eax == -ERESTARTNOHAND ||
712                  regs->eax == -ERESTARTSYS ||
713                  regs->eax == -ERESTARTNOINTR) {
714                  regs->eax = regs->orig_eax;
715                  regs->eip -= 2;
716              }
717          }
718      return 0;
719  }
```

Figure 18.29   Restarting an interrupted system call

709 if there is a valid system call number in `orig_eax` on the stack, that means the process is on the return path from a system call. Note that 0 is a valid system call number.

711–713 this checks if it should be restarted. The `eax` field on the stack will have been loaded with a return value. Only if the return value planted by the system call in the copy of EAX on the stack is one of these should it be restarted. Any other value means the system call terminated normally (with either error or success).

714 this restores the system call number to `eax`, from `orig_eax`. The system call is going to be restarted, so the system will expect its number here.

715 this rewinds the saved copy of the instruction pointer by two bytes. In order to have called a system service, the last instruction executed in user mode must have been INT 0x80 or, in machine code, 0x CD 80. This left the EIP register pointing to the next instruction after the 0x80, and this is the value that was saved on the stack. Decrementing this value by 2 means that it is now pointing to the 0x CD instruction. When control returns to user mode, these values from the (kernel) stack will be restored to the hardware registers, so the next instruction executed after returning to user mode will be 0x CD 80, or INT 0x80, so repeating the request for the system service.

18.5 Removing a signal from a queue

Removing a signal from the queue of pending signals involves a number of functions. The main one, `dequeue_signal()`, is described in Section 18.5.1. A number of subsidiary functions are discussed after that.

18.5.1 Dequeue a signal

The function shown in Figure 18.30, from `kernel/signal.c`, takes a signal off the queue and returns the information about it to the caller, which is expected to be holding the `sigmask_lock`.

```
234        int
235        dequeue_signal(sigset_t *mask, siginfo_t *info)
236        {
237            int sig = 0;
238

243
244            sig = next_signal(current, mask);
245            if (sig) {
246                if (current->notifier) {
247                    if (sigismember(current->notifier_mask, sig)) {
248                        if (!(current->notifier)(current->
                                                   notifier_data)){
249                            current->sigpending = 0;
250                            return 0;
251                        }
```

```
252                              }
253                    }
254
255                    if (!collect_signal(sig, &current->pending, info))
256                         sig = 0;
260               }
261          recalc_sigpending(current);
262
263  #if DEBUG_SIG
264     printk("%d -> %d\n", signal_pending(current), sig);
265  #endif
266
267          return sig;
268     }
```

Figure 18.30   Dequeuing a signal

235   the parameters are a pointer to the `blocked` mask of the current process and a `struct siginfo` into which the extra information about the signal being dequeued will be written.

239–242   if debugging is enabled, this prints a message giving the name of the program, the `pid` of the process, and a 1 or 0, depending on whether a signal is pending to the current process or not [see Section 18.3.1 for the `signal_pending()` function].

244   this gets the number of the first pending, nonblocked, signal. The function is described in Section 18.5.2.1.

245–260   this block of code can be skipped if there is no signal on the queue.

248–251   for this block of code to be executed, the following three conditions must all be TRUE.

- there was at least one signal on the queue,

- there is a valid pointer in the `notifier` field of the `task_struct`,

- the bit corresponding to the signal is set in the `notifier_mask` of the process.

This means that the user wants to be consulted each time this signal is raised and has set up a callback function for that purpose (see Section 17.5).

248   this calls the notifier function, passing it `notifier_data` as a parameter. If it returns 0 then the user does not want the signal to be handled at this stage, so we clear the `sigpending` field in the `task_struct` and return 0. Note that by returning at this point the signal remains on the queue.

255–256   if no notifier function is registered, or the corresponding bit is not set in `notifier_mask`, or the notifier function returns 1, then we call `collect_signal()` (see Section 18.5.2.2). This function removes the queue entry, copies the relevant information from it, and deallocates the memory. It returns 1 for failure, and 0 for success, in which case `sig` is set to 0, in preparation for the `return` at line 267.

261   the signal state of the process has changed, so we check if there are still signals pending (see Section 18.3.2).

263–265   if debugging is enabled, this continues the message from lines 240–241, giving either 1 or 0, depending on whether there are still signals pending to the current process (see Section 18.3.1). It also prints the number of the signal that has just been dequeued.

267   this will be the number of the signal dequeued. A return value of 0 means no signal was dequeued, for whatever reason.

18.5.2   Subsidiary functions

There are two worker functions used by `dequeue_signal()`, which are considered in this section.

18.5.2.1   *Finding a signal to service*

Although there may be a number of signals pending, they can be handled only one at a time. The function shown in Figure 18.31, from `kernel/signal.c`, returns the number of the first pending signal that is not blocked.

```
50    static int
51    next_signal(struct task_struct *tsk, sigset_t *mask)
52    {
53         unsigned long i, *s, *m, x;
54         int sig = 0;
55
56         s = tsk->pending.signal.sig;
57         m = mask->sig;
58         switch (_NSIG_WORDS) {
59         default:
60              for (i = 0; i < _NSIG_WORDS; ++i, ++s, ++m)
61                   if ((x = *s & ~*m) != 0) {
62                        sig = ffz(~x) + i*_NSIG_BPW + 1;
63                        break;
64                   }
65              break;
66
67         case 2: if ((x = s[0] & ~m[0]) != 0)
68                   sig = 1;
69              else if ((x = s[1] & ~m[1]) != 0)
70                   sig = _NSIG_BPW + 1;
71              else
72                   break;
73              sig += ffz(~x);
74              break;
75
76         case 1: if ((x = *s & ~*m) != 0)
```

```
77                              sig = ffz(~x) + 1;
78                        break;
79              }
80
81              return sig;
82      }
```

Figure 18.31   Finding a signal to service

51   the first parameter is a pointer to the `task_struct` of the process; the second points to the `blocked` bitmap of the process.

56   this points s to the first element of the `sig[]` array representing signals pending to the process.

57   this points m to the first element of the `sig[]` array representing signals blocked in this process.

58–79   there are three different system configurations, depending on _NSIG_WORDS, or the number of elements in a `sig[]` array (see Section 17.1.1).

59–65   this is for an architecture with _NSIG_WORDS greater than 2.

60–64   the loop is executed once for each element in a `sig[]` array, advancing the pointers s and m each time.

61–62   the condition is TRUE if there is at least one bit set in the mask of signals pending to the process, with the corresponding bit clear in the `blocked` mask. In that case the value of the current element of the `pending` bitmap is in x.

62   the `ffz()` function from Section 5.1.6 finds the position of the first clear bit in (~x), (i.e. the first bit set in x). To convert that from an offset within the particular element to an offset from the beginning, we add _NSIG_BPW (bits per word) for each element already traversed. Finally, we add 1, as signals are not zero-based.

63   once the first match has been found, this breaks out of the `for` loop (and subsequently out of the `switch`).

67–72   this is an optimised version for the special case when _NSIG_WORDS is 2. This is the i386 case.

67–68   the variable x now contains the first element of the mask of signals pending to the process; m contains the first element in the `blocked` mask. The condition is TRUE if there is at least one bit set in x, with the corresponding bit clear in m.

68   in that case `sig` is an index to the first bit in the first element.

69–70   if there are no corresponding bits in the first element, we try the same test on the second element.

70   in that case, `sig` is an index to the first bit in the second element.

71–72   if no bits are set in either element, we break out of the switch statement and return the default value of `sig` (0 from line 54).

73   this line is executed if either of the tests at line 67 or 69 was TRUE. At this stage x will contain the value of either the first or the second element of the mask of pending signals. The `ffz()` function finds the offset of the first clear bit in (~x) (i.e. the first bit set in x). Adding this to the previously calculated value of `sig` gives the index of the bit representing the pending signal.

76–78 this is the case when _NSIG_WORDS is 1.

76–77 the test described in line 61 is done on this element. If there is at least one bit set in x, with the corresponding bit clear in m, then the `ffz()` function finds the position of the first clear bit in (~x) (i.e. the first bit set in x).

81 this is the index of the bit corresponding to the first pending, nonmasked signal.

18.5.2.2 Removing an entry from the signal queue

When it has been established that there is a pending signal on the queue, the next step is to gather the relevant information from it and remove the structure representing it. This is done by the function shown in Figure 18.32, from `kernel/signal.c`.

```
179  static int collect_signal(int sig, struct sigpending *list,
                                            siginfo_t *info)
180  {
181        if (sigismember(&list->signal, sig)) {
182
183              struct sigqueue *q, **pp;
184              pp = &list->head;
185              while ((q = *pp) != NULL) {
186                    if (q->info.si_signo == sig)
187                          goto found_it;
188                    pp = &q->next;
189              }
194              sigdelset(&list->signal, sig);
195              info->si_signo = sig;
196              info->si_errno = 0;
197              info->si_code = 0;
198              info->si_pid = 0;
199              info->si_uid = 0;
200              return 1;
201
202  found_it:
203              if ((*pp = q->next) == NULL)
204                    list->tail = pp;
207              copy_siginfo(info, &q->info);
208              kmem_cache_free(sigqueue_cachep, q);
209              atomic_dec(&nr_queued_signals);
212              if (sig >= SIGRTMIN) {
213                    while ((q = *pp) != NULL) {
214                          if (q->info.si_signo == sig)
215                                goto found_another;
```

```
216                          pp = &q->next;
217                      }
218                  }
219
220              sigdelset(&list->signal, sig);
221  found_another:
222              return 1;
223          }
224      return 0;
225  }
```

Figure 18.32   Removing an entry from the signal queue

179   the parameters are the signal number, a pointer to the head of the list of signals queued to that process, and a pointer to a `struct siginfo` into which information about the particular signal will be copied.

181   the main body of the function is executed only if the bit corresponding to this signal is set (i.e. there is an instance of this signal on the queue). This is a sanity check; if FALSE, something is wrong, so it returns failure at line 224. See Section 17.2.1.2 for the `sigismember()` macro.

184   this takes an indirect pointer to the first entry in the queue.

185–189   this searches through the queue until the appropriate entry is found or until the NULL pointer at the end is reached.

186–187   if this entry matches the supplied signal number, then we stop searching.

188   otherwise, we advance the pointer and try the next entry.

194–200   this is for the case when the whole queue has been searched and no corresponding entry has been found. This can happen if the memory manager ran out of queue space when the signal was being queued. The bit would have been set in the `list->signal` field at least to record the existence of the signal, but no further information would have been recorded.

194   this clears the bit in the bitmap indicating a queue entry for this signal. The function was described in Section 17.2.1.1.

195–199   this puts default values in the fields in the `siginfo` in which the caller is expecting to receive information about this signal.

195   this is the only line with any valid information, the number of the signal searched for.

200   we return success. There was such a signal posted, even if information about it cannot be supplied. Because there was no queue entry, the memory deallocation code is rightly skipped over.

202–222   this code is executed if the `struct sigqueue` has been found. It is concerned with unlinking and deallocating it.

203–204   if it was the last one on the list, we set the `tail` pointer to its predecessor.

207 this copies the information from the `struct sigqueue` to the `siginfo_t` supplied by the caller. The function has already been described in Section 18.1.3.3.

208 this frees the queue entry. The function is part of the memory manager and will not be considered here.

209 we atomically decrement the global count of queued signals (see Section 5.2.6 for the function).

212–218 this block of code is executed only if the entry just dequeued represented a real time signal.

213–217 we continue on through the queue looking for a second instance of the same signal.

214–215 if this entry matches the supplied signal number, then we stop searching. There is at least a second instance of the real time signal, so the bit corresponding to this signal should not be cleared. The `goto` skips the instruction to do that, at line 220.

216 we advance the pointer and try the next entry.

220 if not a real time signal, or no second instance of a real time signal was found, we clear the bit in the bitmap, indicating a queue entry for this signal (see Section 17.2.1.1 for the function).

221 if there was a second instance of the same real time signal pending, we leave the bit set in the mask. There is only one bit per signal here.

222 this is the success return value.

224 this returns error, because, according to the bitmap (tested at line 181), there is no entry corresponding to this signal on the queue

19

Executing a signal handler

When a user-defined handler is found to be registered for a particular signal, the kernel has to arrange for it to run. Such handlers run in user mode, so the machine must be temporarily switched into user mode to run the handler and then back to kernel mode when it is finished.

The discussion in this chapter is broken down into three parts. First, we consider the main function, `handle_signal()`. Then we look at functions that manipulate the user mode stack to ensure that, on return to user mode, the signal handler will run and not the mainstream program. Finally, we examine the function that arranges for control to return to the kernel after the handler has finished.

19.1 Handling a signal

Figure 19.1, from `arch/i386/kernel/signal.c`, shows the code that invokes a signal handler. It is called only if a user-defined handler is registered; it is never called in the `SIG_IGN` or `SIG_DFL` cases.

```
537  static void
538  handle_signal(unsigned long sig, struct k_sigaction *ka,
539  siginfo_t *info, sigset_t *oldset, struct pt_regs *regs)
540  {
541
542      if (regs->orig_eax >= 0) {
543
544          switch (regs->eax) {
545              case -ERESTARTNOHAND:
546                  regs->eax = -EINTR;
547                  break;
548
549              case -ERESTARTSYS:
```

The Linux Process Manager. The Internals of Scheduling, Interrupts and Signals   John O'Gorman
© 2003 John Wiley & Sons, Ltd   ISBN: 0 470 84771 9

```
550                          if (!(ka->sa.sa_flags & SA_RESTART)) {
551                              regs->eax = -EINTR;
552                              break;
553                          }
554                      /* fallthrough */
555                      case -ERESTARTNOINTR:
556                          regs->eax = regs->orig_eax;
557                          regs->eip -= 2;
558                  }
559          }

562          if (ka->sa.sa_flags & SA_SIGINFO)
563              setup_rt_frame(sig, ka, info, oldset, regs);
564          else
565              setup_frame(sig, ka, oldset, regs);

567          if (ka->sa.sa_flags & SA_ONESHOT)
568              ka->sa.sa_handler = SIG_DFL;

570          if (!(ka->sa.sa_flags & SA_NODEFER)) {
571              spin_lock_irq(&current->sigmask_lock);
572              sigorsets(&current->blocked,&current-
                                        >blocked,&ka->sa.sa_mask);
573              sigaddset(&current->blocked,sig);
574              recalc_sigpending(current);
575              spin_unlock_irq(&current->sigmask_lock);
576          }
577  }
```

Figure 19.1   Invoking a signal handler

538–539   the code is passed the number of the signal, a pointer to a `struct k_sigaction` specifying the handler for this signal, a pointer to a `struct siginfo` containing further information about this signal, a pointer to the `blocked` bitmap of the process, and a pointer to a `struct pt_regs`, containing the saved values of the registers on the stack.

542–559   this code is executed only if there is a valid system call number in the `orig_eax` field in `pt_regs`. This means the process was interrupted in the middle of a system call by the arrival of a signal.

544   when a process calls a system service that blocks, it is put into the TASK_INTERRUPTIBLE or TASK_UNINTERRUPTIBLE state. If a signal is sent to a process in the TASK_INTERRUPTIBLE state it is woken up and moved to the runqueue, even though the system service has not completed. In this case, when the system service runs again, it recognises that it has been woken by a signal even though it has not completed, so it puts an error value in the copy of EAX on the stack. This will be one of ERESTARTNOHAND, ERESTARTSYS, or ERESTARTNOINTR. These are used internally by system call handlers to specify that a system call is to be restarted after the signal is handled. The signal is now in the process of being handled.

545–547   if the internal code was ERESTARTNOHAND, then the return value is changed to EINTR. The system call will not be restarted.

549–553   if it was ERESTARTSYS, then whether or not the system call is restarted depends on the value of the SA_RESTART flag in the struct k_sigaction. If that bit was set, we leave the return value at ERESTARTSYS and fall through to the next case. The system call will be restarted later. Note that the break statement is within the if. Otherwise, we change the return value to EINTR and break out of the switch statement; the system call will not be restarted.

555–557   the system call is going to be restarted, so we restore the system call number to the saved EAX, from orig_eax, and rewind the saved copy of the instruction pointer by two bytes. In order to have called a system service, the last instruction executed in user mode must have been INT 0x80 or, in machine code, 0x CD 80. This left the EIP register pointing to the next instruction after the 0x80, and this is the value of EIP that was saved on the kernel stack. Decrementing this value by 2 means that it is now pointing to the 0x CD instruction. When control returns to user mode, after all pending signals have been handled, these values from the (kernel) stack will be restored to the hardware registers, so the next instruction executed after returning to user mode will be 0x CD 80, or INT 0x80, with the system call number in EAX, so repeating the request for the system service.

562–565   this sets up a stack frame for the user's signal handler. If the SA_SIGINFO flag is set, that means the user is willing to use any extra information that may be available about this signal, in the siginfo_t structure. Although different functions are called to set up the stack in each case, both arrange that after the handler has run in user mode control returns to the kernel. This is probably the single most complicated part of signal handling. Remember that at this stage the process is running in kernel mode. A signal handler is a user-defined function that must run in user mode, so the process must switch to user mode, run the handler, and then switch back to kernel mode. This is a sort of mirror image of a system call switching to kernel mode while it is executing. There is no clean way of doing this. When the signal handler finishes it must be tricked into returning to the kernel and not to the user program in which it is defined. This means altering values on the user mode stack, particularly the return address. The setup_frame() function (see Section 19.3.1) does just that, setting up a stack frame on the user stack. The setup_rt_frame() function builds an even more complicated stack frame, for handling extra information in a struct siginfo (see Section 19.3.2).

567–568   if the SA_ONESHOT flag was set by the user when registering the signal, then we change the handler to be SIG_DFL for future occurrences of this signal.

570–576   the SA_NODEFER flag means that no extra signals should be blocked while running the handler for this one, nor should it be masked itself, so we only go into the present block of code if that bit is clear and there are some extra signals to be blocked. The blocked bitmap of the current process is manipulated under the protection of its sigmask_lock spinlock.

572   the sa_mask field is a bitmap, specifying any extra signals that should be blocked while this one is being handled. The sigorsets() macro, described in Section 17.2.2.2, does a bitwise OR between blocked and the sa_mask field and puts the result into blocked. Effectively, this means that any bits set in sa_mask are also set in blocked, whether they were set beforehand or not.

573 the bit corresponding to the signal being handled is set in `blocked`. The function has been described in Section 17.2.1.1. A signal is always blocked while it is being handled.

574 this function has been described in Section 18.3.2. The `blocked` bitmap has just been altered, so the signal state of the process needs to be reevaluated.

19.2 The stack frame for signal handling

As discussed in Chapter 17, a signal handler has to run in user mode but return to kernel mode when it terminates. This irregular transfer of control is achieved by setting up special values on the user mode stack beforehand. The structure of this stack frame is the subject of this section. How such a structure is actually built will be described in Sections 19.3 and 19.4.

19.2.1 Structure of a stack frame

The structure of the frame that is built on the user's stack is shown in Figure 19.2, from `arch/i386/kernel/signal.c`. This may be built either on the normal user mode stack or on the alternate stack, as discussed in Section 17.6.

```
166  struct sigframe
167  {
168          char *pretcode;
169          int sig;
170          struct sigcontext sc;
171          struct _fpstate fpstate;
172          unsigned long extramask[_NSIG_WORDS-1];
173          char retcode[8];
174  };
175
176  struct rt_sigframe
177  {
178          char *pretcode;
179          int sig;
180          struct siginfo *pinfo;
181          void *puc;
182          struct siginfo info;
183          struct ucontext uc;
184          struct _fpstate fpstate;
185          char retcode[8];
186  };
```

Figure 19.2   Structure of a stack frame

166–174 this is the old-style, legacy, frame.

168 this field holds the address of the stub code that will force a return to kernel mode once the handler has terminated. It is at the bottom of the stack, so the hardware will pop it to `EIP`. It normally points to the `retcode[]` field later on in the frame (line 173), but it can be pointed to a user-supplied stub.

169   this is the number of the signal being handled.

170   a large amount of context information is made available (here on the stack) to the signal handler. The structure is discussed in Section 19.2.2.

171   if the process has used the computer processing unit (CPU) then the floating point state is also made available to the handler. The structure used for this is described in Section 19.2.4.

172   this is space for the remainder of the `blocked` bitmap, if longer than one word. The first word is saved in the `oldmask` field of the `struct sigcontext` (see Section 19.2.2).

173   this is space for the code stub that will return control to kernel mode when the handler terminates.

176–186   this is the new-style frame, with room for a `struct siginfo`.

178–179   see lines 168–169.

180   this is a pointer to the `struct siginfo` containing further information about this signal. This normally points to the `info` field at line 182; but this arrangement allows the `struct siginfo` to be elsewhere.

181   this is a pointer to a `struct ucontext`, an extension of the `struct sigcontext`. This is normally the `uc` field at line 183, but it could be elsewhere.

182   this is a `struct siginfo`, containing extra information about the signal. This structure has been described in Section 17.1.5.1.

183   this is an extension of the `struct sigcontext` (see Section 19.2.3).

184   see the description of line 171.

185   see the description of line 173.

19.2.2   Registering context for handling a signal

As part of the stack frame built on the user mode stack, the kernel makes a large amount of context information available to the handler. This consists mainly of the values in the CPU registers when the process last switched to kernel mode, along with some extra items of information. All this information is encapsulated in a `struct sigcontext`; see Figure 19.3, from `<asm-i386/sigcontext.h>`. Note that the order of the fields is completely different from that of a `struct pt_regs`.

```
57    struct sigcontext {
58        unsigned short    gs, __gsh;
59        unsigned short    fs, __fsh;
60        unsigned short    es, __esh;
61        unsigned short    ds, __dsh;
```

```
62       unsigned long       edi;
63       unsigned long       esi;
64       unsigned long       ebp;
65       unsigned long       esp;
66       unsigned long       ebx;
67       unsigned long       edx;
68       unsigned long       ecx;
69       unsigned long       eax;
70       unsigned long       trapno;
71       unsigned long       err;
72       unsigned long       eip;
73       unsigned short      cs, __csh;
74       unsigned long       eflags;
75       unsigned long       esp_at_signal;
76       unsigned short      ss, __ssh;
77       struct _fpstate     * fpstate;
78       unsigned long       oldmask;
79       unsigned long       cr2;
80   };
```

Figure 19.3   Registering context for handling a signal

58–69   these are standard CPU registers. Note that each of the 16-bit segment register values are padded out with dummy variables, to keep the stack aligned.

70–71   this information is supplied for a signal sent by the kernel. The number of the trap that caused the signal to be sent is in `trapno`, and any error number supplied by the hardware is in `err`.

72–74   there are standard CPU registers. Note that the 16-bit CS register value is padded out with a dummy variable, to keep the stack aligned.

75   a second copy of the stack pointer is saved here.

76   this is the saved SS value, padded out to 32 bits.

77   this is a pointer to a copy of the floating point register values (see Section 19.2.4 for the structure). This field normally points to the `fpstate` field in the `sigframe` structure on the stack (see Section 19.2.1), but it could point elsewhere.

78   the first `long` of the `blocked` bitmap is made available here.

79   the value of the CR2 register is saved here. This register is used by the CPU to save error information when a page exception is raised.

19.2.3   Extended context information for a signal handler

When using the POSIX extensions to signal handling, even more information is made available on the user stack. The `struct sigcontext` of Section 19.2.2 is replaced by a `struct ucontext`; see Figure 19.4, from `<asm-i386/ucontext.h>`.

```
4    struct ucontext {
5          unsigned long      uc_flags;
6          struct ucontext    *uc_link;
7          stack_t            uc_stack;
8          struct sigcontext  uc_mcontext;
9          sigset_t           uc_sigmask;
10   };
```

Figure 19.4   Extended context information for a signal handler

5   this field is currently unused. It is set to 0 by the function that creates an extended stack frame, `setup_rt_frame()` (see Section 19.3.2).

6   this field also is currently unused. It is set to 0 (NULL) by `setup_rt_frame()` (see Section 19.3.2).

7   the `stack t` has been defined in Section 17.6.1. It is filled in with information about the stack in use, such as a pointer to it, flags, and its size.

8   this is the old-style `sigcontext` structure (see Section 19.2.2).

9   this field contains the `blocked` bitmap of the current process. It is a full `sigset_t` (Section 17.1.1), not just an `unsigned long`.

19.2.4   Floating point state

If the process has used the floating point unit (FPU), then the state of the FPU registers is also made available to the signal handler. The structures used for this are shown in Figure 19.5, from `<asm-i386/sigcontext.h>`.

```
18   struct _fpreg {
19         unsigned short significand[4];
20         unsigned short exponent;
21   };
22
23   struct _fpxreg {
24         unsigned short significand[4];
25         unsigned short exponent;
26         unsigned short padding[3];
27   };
28
29   struct _xmmreg {
30         unsigned long element[4];
31   };
32
33   struct _fpstate {
34
35         unsigned long      cw;
```

```
36          unsigned long      sw;
37          unsigned long      tag;
38          unsigned long      ipoff;
39          unsigned long      cssel;
40          unsigned long      dataoff;
41          unsigned long      datasel;
42          struct _fpreg      _st[8];
43          unsigned short     status;
44          unsigned short     magic;

47          unsigned long      _fxsr_env[6];
48          unsigned long      mxcsr;
49          unsigned long      reserved;
50          struct _fpxreg     _fxsr_st[8];
51          struct _xmmreg     _xmm[8];
52          unsigned long      padding[56];
53     };
```

Figure 19.5   Floating point state

18–21   this is the structure of an internal FPU register.

19   there are 64 bits of significant information (including sign).

20   there are 16 bits for the exponent.

23–27   this is the structure of an extended-format FPU register. It has an extra 48 bits, to bring it up to 128.

29–31   for a CPU with XMM extensions, the registers are treated as an undifferentiated 128 bits.

33–53   this is the structure used to hold the whole state of the FPU. Lines 35–42 contain the normal i387 hardware registers.

42   this is for the eight FPU registers, see lines 18–21 for the `struct`.

43   the CSW register is copied here before entering the signal handler.

44   this field indicates whether the remainder of the `struct` is valid or not. `0xffff` means regular FPU data only have been provided. Otherwise, the remaining fields are valid.

47–51   these fields save FXSR register values. The FPU state data structure has had to grow to accommodate the extended state required by the streaming SIMD extensions (SSEs).

47   this space is for the FXSR FPU environment. It is similar to the information stored at lines 35–42, but in a different format.

48   this is the control and status register.

49   this field is reserved for future use.

50   this space is for the FXSR FPU register data.

51   this is for the eight XMM registers; see lines 29–31 for the structure.

52   this is really space for future extensions.

19.3   Setting up a stack frame for signal handling

Now that the structure of a signal-handling stack frame has been described, the next thing to consider is how such a frame is set up on the user stack. There are two functions provided for this. One sets up a standard stack frame, for old-style signal handling. The other is for the case when a `struct siginfo` has been supplied and this has to be put on the stack as well.

19.3.1   Setting up a standard stack frame

The function shown in Figure 19.6, from `arch/i386/kernel/signal.c`, sets up a standard stack frame. The comments should be read in conjunction with a copy of the `struct sigframe`, from Section 19.2.1.

```
388   static void setup_frame(int sig, struct k_sigaction *ka,
389        sigset_t *set, struct pt_regs *regs)
390   {
391        struct sigframe *frame;
392        int err = 0;
393
394        frame = get_sigframe(ka, regs, sizeof(*frame));
395
396        if (!access_ok(VERIFY_WRITE, frame, sizeof(*frame)))
397            goto give_sigsegv;
398
399        err |= __put_user((current->exec_domain
400            && current->exec_domain->signal_invmap
401            && sig < 32
402            ? current->exec_domain->signal_invmap[sig]
403                : sig),
404                &frame->sig);
405        if (err)
406            goto give_sigsegv;
407
408        err |= setup_sigcontext(&frame->sc, &frame->fpstate,
409                                                 regs, set->sig[0]);
409        if (err)
410            goto give_sigsegv;
411
412        if (_NSIG_WORDS > 1) {
413            err |= __copy_to_user(frame->extramask,
414            &set->sig[1], (frame->extramask));
415        }
416        if (err)
```

```
417                goto give_sigsegv;

421        if (ka->sa.sa_flags & SA_RESTORER) {
422                err |= __put_user(ka->sa.sa_restorer,&frame->pretcode);
423        } else {
424                err |= __put_user(frame->retcode, &frame->pretcode);
425
426                err |= __put_user(0xb858,(short *)(frame->retcode+0));
427                err |= __put_user(__NR_sigreturn,
                                        (int *)(frame->retcode+2));
428                err |= __put_user(0x80cd,(short *)(frame->retcode+6));
429        }
430
431        if (err)
432                goto give_sigsegv;

435        regs->esp = (unsigned long) frame;
436        regs->eip = (unsigned long) ka->sa.sa_handler;
437
438        set_fs(USER_DS);
439        regs->xds = __USER_DS;
440        regs->xes = __USER_DS;
441        regs->xss = __USER_DS;
442        regs->xcs = __USER_CS;
443        regs->eflags &= ~TF_MASK;
444
445 #if DEBUG_SIG
446        printk("SIG deliver (%s:%d): sp=%p pc=%p ra=%p\n",
447                current->comm, current->pid, frame, regs->eip,
                                        frame->pretcode);
448 #endif
449
450        return;
451
452 give_sigsegv:
453        if (sig == SIGSEGV)
454                ka->sa.sa_handler = SIG_DFL;
455        force_sig(SIGSEGV, current);
456 }
```

Figure 19.6   Setting up a stack frame for signal handling

388–389   the parameters are: the number of the signal being handled; a pointer to the struct k_
sigaction specifying the handler; a pointer to the blocked bitmap of the process (before any
temporary changes were made to it); and a pointer to the saved (user mode) register values on the
(kernel) stack.

394   this function (see Section 19.3.3) determines whether to use the normal user mode stack or an

alternative one. In either case, it returns a pointer to a stack area, which is treated as a `struct sigframe`.

396–397   if, for some reason, it is not possible to write to this structure, then we force a `SIGSEGV` signal on the process. The `access_ok()` function is part of the memory manager.

399–404   the `__put_user()` macro writes an integer value to user space, without checking the validity of the address. This is safe, as the address has been checked at line 396. It writes its first parameter into the address space specified by the second. In the present case, it converts the signal number, using execution domain information (if relevant) and writes it to the `sig` field of the `struct sigframe`.

405–406   if unable to do that, we force a `SIGSEGV` signal on the process.

408–410   this is the function that sets up the context information in the stack frame (see Section 19.4.2). The parameters are pointers to a `struct sigcontext` and a `struct _fpstate` (both fields of the `struct sigframe`) and to the saved registers on the stack as well as the contents of the first `long` of the blocked bitmap.

409–410   if unable to do so, we force a `SIGSEGV` on the process.

412–415   as this is i386-specific code, `_NSIG_WORDS` is 2, so this block of code is always executed. The remaining words of the bitmap of blocked signals are copied to the `extramask` field of the `struct sigframe`. In the i386 case, this is only the second word.

416–417   if unable to do so, we force a `SIGSEGV` on the process.

421–429   this block of code sets things up to return from user space to the kernel when the handler has finished.

421–422   if provided, we use a stub already in user space. If the SA_RESTORER bit is set in the `sa_flags` field of the `k_sigaction`, then we just copy the address of the user-supplied stub from `sa_restorer` into the appropriate field of the `struct sigframe`. The use of this is deprecated; it is here only for backward compatibility with older code.

423–429   otherwise, the kernel has to provide its own stub. This would be the most common case.

424   we write the address of the `retcode` field in `frame` to the `pretcode` field. This lets the system know that the stub code is in `retcode[]`.

426   this copies `0x b8 58` into the first two bytes of `retcode[]`. Because the i386 is little endian, this will go in as `58b8`.

- `0x 58` is POPL EAX. When executed, this instruction will pop the value from the bottom of the stack (the signal number), and effectively discard it.

- `0x B8` is move immediate into EAX. The immediate value will be in the next four bytes.

427   `__NR_sigreturn` is the number of the `sigreturn()` system service. This is a special system service in Linux, used only to return to kernel mode after a signal handler has executed. It is described in Section 19.5.1.

428   this copies 0x 80 cd to the last two bytes of `retcode[]`. Because the i386 is little endian, this will go in as 0x cd 80, or INT 80. This code now executes an INT 80, for `sigreturn()`.

431–432   if any one of these foregoing writes fails, we force a SIGSEGV on the process.

435–443   the saved copies of (user mode) registers are now changed, so that on return to user mode the program will run the handler, not continue on from where it was.

435   the copy of the ESP register on the kernel stack now points to the beginning of the new stack frame just set up in user space (i.e. to the `pretcode` field). This will be the return address popped when the handler terminates. It in turn points to the stub in `retcode[]`.

436   the copy of the IP register points to the user-defined handler. So the first instruction executed in user mode will be the beginning of the handler.

438–442   this is memory manager code, setting up default values in the segment registers, just in case any of these were changed since the kernel was entered.

438   this macro sets the default value for the end of the user segment.

439–441   the data, extra, and stack segment registers (`xds`, `xes`, and `xss`, respectively) are loaded with selectors for the user data segment.

442   the code segment register (`xcs`) is loaded with a selector for the user code segment.

443   the TF_MASK bit is cleared in the saved copy of the EFLAGS register. Signal handlers are not single stepped, by default.

445–448   if debugging is turned on, a message is printed giving the name of the program, the `pid` of the process, the address of the newly built stack frame, the address of the handler, and the address of the beginning of the return code (stub) just built on the stack.

450   everything is set up at this stage; this is the normal termination of this function. It returns to `handle_signal()` (see Section 19.1).

452–455   this is the error exit if at any stage it was not possible to write to user space.

453–454   if the signal that could not be handled was SIGSEGV itself, then we change the handling for that signal to SIG_DFL. There is no point in getting into an infinite loop.

455   in any case, we force a SIGSEGV on the current process. The function was described in Section 18.2.7.

19.3.2   Setting up an extended stack frame

When extra information is available about a signal in a `struct siginfo`, then the stack frame created in user space is a little more complicated. The function to set this up is shown in Figure 19.7, from `arch/i386/kernel/signal.c`. Much of it is similar to the code described in Section 19.3.1, and the explanation will not be repeated. It should be read in conjunction with a copy of the `struct rt_sigframe`, from Section 19.2.1.

```
458    static void setup_rt_frame(int sig, struct k_sigaction *ka,
459        siginfo_t *info, sigset_t *set, struct pt_regs *regs)
460    {
461        struct rt_sigframe *frame;
462        int err = 0;
463
464        frame = get_sigframe(ka, regs, sizeof(*frame));
465
466        if (!access_ok(VERIFY_WRITE, frame, sizeof(*frame)))
467            goto give_sigsegv;
468
469        err |= __put_user((current->exec_domain
470            && current->exec_domain->signal_invmap
471            && sig < 32
472            ? current->exec_domain->signal_invmap[sig]
473                : sig),
474                &frame->sig);
475        err |= __put_user(&frame->info, &frame->pinfo);
476        err |= __put_user(&frame->uc, &frame->puc);
477        err |= copy_siginfo_to_user(&frame->info, info);
478        if (err)
479            goto give_sigsegv;
480
482        err |= __put_user(0, &frame->uc.uc_flags);
483        err |= __put_user(0, &frame->uc.uc_link);
484        err |= __put_user(current->sas_ss_sp,
                                        &frame->uc.uc_stack.ss_sp);
485        err |= __put_user(sas_ss_flags(regs->esp),
486            &frame->uc.uc_stack.ss_flags);
487        err |= __put_user(current->sas_ss_size,
                                        &frame->uc.uc_stack.ss_size);
488        err |= setup_sigcontext(&frame->uc.uc_mcontext,
489            &frame->fpstate, regs, set->sig[0]);
490        err |= __copy_to_user(&frame->uc.uc_sigmask, set,
                                            sizeof(*set));
491        if (err)
492            goto give_sigsegv;
493
496        if (ka->sa.sa_flags & SA_RESTORER) {
497            err |= __put_user(ka->sa.sa_restorer, &frame->pretcode);
498        } else {
499            err |= __put_user(frame->retcode, &frame->pretcode);
500
501            err |= __put_user(0xb8, (char *)(frame->retcode+0));
502            err |= __put_user(__NR_rt_sigreturn,
                                        (int *)(frame->retcode+1));
503            err |= __put_user(0x80cd, (short *)(frame->retcode+5));
504        }
505
```

```
506        if (err)
507             goto give_sigsegv;

510        regs->esp = (unsigned long) frame;
511        regs->eip = (unsigned long) ka->sa.sa_handler;
512
513        set_fs(USER_DS);
514        regs->xds = __USER_DS;
515        regs->xes = __USER_DS;
516        regs->xss = __USER_DS;
517        regs->xcs = __USER_CS;
518        regs->eflags &= ~TF_MASK;
519
520 #if DEBUG_SIG
521        printk("SIG deliver (%s:%d): sp=%p pc=%p ra=%p\n",
522             current->comm, current->pid, frame, regs->eip,
                                                 frame->pretcode);
523 #endif
524
525        return;
526
527 give_sigsegv:
528        if (sig == SIGSEGV)
529             ka->sa.sa_handler = SIG_DFL;
530        force_sig(SIGSEGV, current);
531 }
```

Figure 19.7   Set up an extended stack frame for signal handling

458–459   the parameters are as described at lines 388–389 of Section 19.3.1, with the addition of a pointer to a struct siginfo.

461   although having the same name, frame is used this time as a pointer to the larger struct rt_sigframe, as described in Section 19.2.1.

464   given these parameters, this function makes space for a larger struct rt_sigframe on the stack (see Section 19.3.3).

466–474   see description of lines 396–404 in Section 19.3.1.

475   this points the pinfo field of the rt_sigframe to the struct siginfo, which is also part of the stack frame.

476   this points the puc field of the rt_sigframe to the struct ucontext, which is also part of the stack frame.

477   this copies the information from the struct siginfo in the kernel to the struct siginfo on the user stack. The function is described in Section 19.4.1.

478–479   if any of the last four writes to user space failed, then we force a SIGSEGV on the process.

482–492 this creates the `ucontext` on the stack.

482 this sets the flags to 0. This field is currently unused.

483 this sets the link to 0 (`NULL`). This field is currently unused.

484 this copies in the address of the alternate stack, whether it is in use or not. Of course, if no alternate stack has been set up, this field will be `NULL`.

485–486 the `sas_ss_flags()` function returns information about the status of the alternate stack (see Section 17.6.3). We make this available to the handler.

487 this copies in the size of the alternate stack.

488–489 this is the function that sets up the context information in the stack frame (see Section 19.4). The parameters are pointers to a `struct sigcontext` and a `struct _fpstate` (both fields of the `struct sigframe`), and to the saved registers on the stack as well as the contents of the first `long` of the `blocked` bitmap.

490 this copies in the whole of the `blocked` bitmap, pointed to by `set`, an input parameter to the present function.

491–492 if any of the writes involved in setting up the `ucontext` failed, we force a `SIGSEGV` on the process.

496–507 this block of code set things up to return from user space to the kernel when the handler has finished. It is almost identical to lines 421–432 of Section 19.3.1.

501 this copies `0xb8` into the first byte of `retcode[]`; `0xB8` is moved immediately into EAX. The immediate value will be in the next four bytes.

502 the immediate value is `__NR_rt_sigreturn`, the number of the `rt_sigreturn()` system service, described in Section 19.5.2.

510–530 see the description of lines 435–455 of Section 19.3.1 for comments on this block of code.

19.3.3 Getting a pointer to the stack frame in user space

Before setting up a stack frame in user space, the kernel must determine whether to do this on the standard user mode stack or on an alternate stack provided just for that purpose. The function that makes this decision is shown in Figure 19.8, from `arch/i386/kernel/signal.c`. It is called by the functions that set up a user stack frame (see Sections 19.3.1 and 19.3.2).

```
364  static inline void *
365  get_sigframe(struct k_sigaction *ka, struct pt_regs * regs, size_t
                                                            frame_size)
366  {
367      unsigned long esp;
370      esp = regs->esp;
373      if (ka->sa.sa_flags & SA_ONSTACK) {
```

```
374                    if (sas_ss_flags(esp) == 0)
375                        esp = current->sas_ss_sp + current->sas_ss_size;
376        }

379        else if ((regs->xss & 0xffff) != __USER_DS &&
380                !(ka->sa.sa_flags & SA_RESTORER) &&
381                ka->sa.sa_restorer) {
382                esp = (unsigned long) ka->sa.sa_restorer;
383        }
384
385        return (void *)((esp - frame_size) & -8ul);
386    }
```

Figure 19.8   Determining which stack to use

365   the parameters are a pointer to the `struct k_sigaction` for this signal, a pointer to the saved user-mode registers, and the size of the stack frame to be built.

370   we default to using the stack in use before entry to the kernel. This may be the alternate stack (e.g. if it was in use and the handler called a system service).

373–376 this is the X/Open sanctioned signal stack switching. If the SA_ONSTACK bit is set in the `sa_flags` field for this signal, an alternate stack should be used if one is set up.

374   the function is in Section 17.6.3. A return value of 0 means that the alternative stack is set up but not in use. If it were actually in use, the value would be SS_ONSTACK.

375   so, we set `esp` to point to the top of the alternate stack.

379–383 the foregoing is the X/Open signal stack switching. However, legacy systems may not be using the SA_ONSTACK flag but may still want to switch stacks, and a further test is necessary to cover all possibilities.

379–381 if all of these three conditions are TRUE, then we switch stacks:

- The saved value of the selector for the stack segment shows that a user-defined alternate stack (which would be in the user data segment) was not in use at the time of entry to the kernel;

- The SA_RESTORER bit is not set, so the user is not supplying a stub function to return to kernel mode;

- But the `sa_restorer` field is valid; as this cannot be pointing to a stub function, it must be pointing to the top of an alternate stack.

382   in that case the stack pointer is set to the value of `sa_restorer`, which points to the top of the alternate stack.

385   in all cases, we pull the stack pointer down to make room for the new stack frame. ANDing that value with `unsigned long −8` clears the low-order 3 bits, effectively rounding it down to be on an 8-byte boundary.

19.4 Setting up signal context on the user stack

As part of the process of setting up a user stack frame, a significant amount of information is copied there from the kernel. This includes the struct siginfo supplied with the signal, some information relevant to signals from the thread structure, and the information in the struct pt_regs on the kernel stack. This information is going to be removed from the kernel stack when the process returns to user mode to handle the signal, but it will be required again when the process returns to kernel mode after handling the signal, so it is saved on the user mode stack in the meantime. There are two main functions supplied for copying this information, with a number of subsidiary functions for use if FPU information has to be copied as well.

19.4.1 Copying extra signal information to user space

When a struct siginfo is being used to supply extra information about a signal, the contents of this structure have to be copied from within the kernel to user space, where the signal handler can access the data. The function to do this copying is shown in Figure 19.9, from arch/i386/kernel/signal.c.

```
33   int copy_siginfo_to_user(siginfo_t *to, siginfo_t *from)
34   {
35       if (!access_ok (VERIFY_WRITE, to, sizeof(siginfo_t)))
36           return -EFAULT;
37       if (from->si_code < 0)
38           return __copy_to_user(to, from, sizeof(siginfo_t));
39       else {
40           int err;

47           err = __put_user(from->si_signo, &to->si_signo);
48           err |= __put_user(from->si_errno, &to->si_errno);
49           err |= __put_user((short)from->si_code, &to->si_code);
50
51           err |= __put_user(from->si_pid, &to->si_pid);
52           switch (from->si_code >> 16) {
53           case __SI_FAULT >> 16:
54               break;
55           case __SI_CHLD >> 16:
56               err |= __put_user(from->si_utime, &to->si_utime);
57               err |= __put_user(from->si_stime, &to->si_stime);
58               err |= __put_user(from->si_status, &to->si_status);
59           default:
60               err |= __put_user(from->si_uid, &to->si_uid);
61               break;
62
63           }
64           return err;
```

```
65        }
66    }
```

Figure 19.9   Copying extra signal information to user space

33   the parameters are pointers to the source and destination structures. Both are of type `siginfo_t` (see Section 17.1.5.1).

35–36   the memory manager checks that it is possible to write to the whole `struct siginfo` to user space. If not, the function returns an error value `EFAULT`.

37–38   an `si_code` value less than 0 means that the signal was sent by a trusted kernel subsystem, and the full structure can be copied, including the pad field. The function `__copy_to_user()` copies a block of arbitrary size.

39–65   otherwise, the signal was sent by a user process. This code is making sure that no padding at the end of the structure is copied to user space. This would be a potential security leak.

47–49   these three `int` fields are always present (see the description of `struct siginfo` in Section 17.1.5.1), so they are always copied. The function `__put_user()` is more efficient for copying integers.

51   the first 32 bits of the `union` are always present, so can be copied. Note that from here on, the shorthand names for the fields, as defined in Section 17.1.5.2, are being used.

52–63   this `switch` statement is making sure that only valid data are transferred to user space by treating each element of the `union` separately. It switches on the high-order 16 bits of `si_code`, which indicate the particular member of the `union` that is valid in each case (see Section 17.1.5.3).

53–54   in the `__SI_FAULT` case, the `_sigfault` member of the `union` is valid. This merely contains a 32-bit pointer, which has already been copied at line 51, so no further copying is done.

55–58   in the `__SI_CHLD` case, the `_sigchld` member of the `union` is valid. The first 32 bits of this (`si_pid`) have already been copied at line 51, so these other three fields are now copied. Note that there is no `break` – execution falls into the `default` case.

59–61   in all other cases (`__SI_KILL`, `__SI_TIMER`, `__SI_POLL`), the `si_pid` field has already been copied, so we copy the `si_uid` field now.

64   if any of the attempts to copy to user space returned an error, the return value will not be 0.

19.4.2   Copying the register state to user stack

The function that copies the register context to the user stack is shown in Figure 19.10, from `arch/i386/kernel/signal.c`.

```
318  static int
319  setup_sigcontext(struct sigcontext *sc, struct _fpstate
320       *fpstate, struct pt_regs *regs, unsigned long mask)
321  {
```

```
322        int tmp, err = 0;
323
324        tmp = 0;
325        __asm__("movl %%gs,%0" : "=r"(tmp): ""(tmp));
326        err |= __put_user(tmp, (unsigned int *)&sc->gs);
327        __asm__("movl %%fs,%0" : "=r"(tmp): ""(tmp));
328        err |= __put_user(tmp, (unsigned int *)&sc->fs);
329
330        err |= __put_user(regs->xes, (unsigned int *)&sc->es);
331        err |= __put_user(regs->xds, (unsigned int *)&sc->ds);
332        err |= __put_user(regs->edi, &sc->edi);
333        err |= __put_user(regs->esi, &sc->esi);
334        err |= __put_user(regs->ebp, &sc->ebp);
335        err |= __put_user(regs->esp, &sc->esp);
336        err |= __put_user(regs->ebx, &sc->ebx);
337        err |= __put_user(regs->edx, &sc->edx);
338        err |= __put_user(regs->ecx, &sc->ecx);
339        err |= __put_user(regs->eax, &sc->eax);
340        err |= __put_user(current->thread.trap_no, &sc->trapno);
341        err |= __put_user(current->thread.error_code, &sc->err);
342        err |= __put_user(regs->eip, &sc->eip);
343        err |= __put_user(regs->xcs, (unsigned int *)&sc->cs);
344        err |= __put_user(regs->eflags, &sc->eflags);
345        err |= __put_user(regs->esp, &sc->esp_at_signal);
346        err |= __put_user(regs->xss, (unsigned int *)&sc->ss);
347
348        tmp = save_i387(fpstate);
349        if (tmp < 0)
350                err = 1;
351        else
352                err |= __put_user(tmp ? fpstate : NULL, &sc->fpstate);
353
355        err |= __put_user(mask, &sc->oldmask);
356        err |= __put_user(current->thread.cr2, &sc->cr2);
357
358        return err;
359  }
```

Figure 19.10 Copy state to the user stack

319–320 the first two parameters are pointers to a struct sigcontext (Section 19.2.2) and a struct_fpstate (Section 19.2.4), both in the stack frame in user space. The third parameter is a pointer to the saved user mode registers on the kernel stack. The fourth is the first word of the blocked bitmap.

325 this saves the contents of the GS segment register to the local tmp variable.

326 now we copy tmp to the gs field of the struct sigcontext.

327–328 this repeats lines 325–326 for the FS register. These moves are necessary because the value of these registers is not saved in a `struct pt_regs`. Note that these are the values in the registers at this stage, not when the process entered the kernel, but as the kernel does not use these registers, that causes no problem.

330–339 other fields of the `struct sigcontext` are filled in, in order, from the saved values of hardware registers on the kernel stack. Note that this order is different from that of the `struct pt_regs`.

340–341 if the signal was sent by the kernel, information about the trap number and error code are available in the `thread` structure of the current process. These are copied to their own fields in the stack frame, thus making them available to the handler.

342–346 the values of the remaining registers are copied to their appropriate places in the stack frame.

348 if necessary, we save the floating point register values to the `_fpstate` field in the stack frame. The function to do this, as described in Section 19.4.3.1, first checks if it is necessary. It returns −1 if it is unable to copy, 0 if the FPU was never used, so we set up an error value to return.

352 otherwise, we copy either the pointer to the `struct _fpstate`, or NULL if the FPU was never used, to the `fpstate` field in the stack frame.

355 this copies the first 32 bits of the `blocked` bitmap to the `oldmask` field.

356 this copies the value of the hardware CR2 register from `thread`. The CPU writes error information here when a page exception is raised.

358 only if every one of the copy operations succeeded will the return value be 0; otherwise `err` will have some positive value.

19.4.3 Copying the floating point unit state to the user stack

As part of setting up to handle a signal, it may be necessary to make the FPU state available in user space. This is necessary only if the process has actually used the FPU, of course, so there is a function that does that checking and a number of others to do the actual copying.

19.4.3.1 Checking if the floating point unit state needs to be copied

The function that checks if the FPU state needs to be copied is shown in Figure 19.11, from `arch/i386/kernel/i387.c`.

```
321  int save_i387( struct _fpstate *buf )
322  {
323       if ( !current->used_math )
324            return 0;

329       current->used_math = 0;
330
331       if ( HAVE_HWFP ) {
332            if ( cpu_has_fxsr ) {
```

```
333                        return save_i387_fxsave( buf );
334                } else {
335                        return save_i387_fsave( buf );
336                }
337        } else {
338            return save_i387_soft(&current->thread.i387.soft, buf );
339        }
340  }
```

Figure 19.11 Checking if the floating point unit state needs to be copied

321   the parameter is a pointer to the area of the user stack reserved for FPU information, a `struct_fpstate`, as described in Section 19.2.4.

323–324   if this field in the `task_struct` is still clear, then the current process has not used the FPU. FPU state could not be relevant to the signal handler, so we return 0.

329   if the process has used the FPU before this, the state is now going to be saved and perhaps altered, so we mark it as invalid. This will cause the hardware registers to be reloaded on the next attempted FPU operation by the current process.

332–336   this block of code is executed if a hardware FPU has been detected at boot time.

332–333   if an extended FPU (with MMX instructions) was detected at boot time, we use this copy function (see Section 19.4.3.3). It returns 1 on success, -1 on failure.

335   otherwise, we use this copy function (see Section 19.4.3.2). It also returns 1 on success, -1 on failure.

338   if there is no hardware FPU (an original 386) then we use this copy function, the internals of which are heavily dependent on the emulator. As this is not really relevant to modern machines (is anybody actually running Linux on a 386?), it is not considered any further here.

19.4.3.2   *Saving standard floating point unit registers*

The function shown in Figure 19.12, from `arch/i386/kernel/i387.c`, saves the register state of a standard FPU to the signal-handling stack frame. It should be read with reference to Figures 2.17 (pages 33–34) and 19.5.

```
288  static inline int save_i387_fsave( struct _fpstate *buf )
289  {
290        struct task_struct *tsk = current;
291
292        unlazy_fpu( tsk );
293        tsk->thread.i387.fsave.status = tsk->thread.i387.fsave.swd;
294        if ( __copy_to_user( buf, &tsk->thread.i387.fsave,
295                                    sizeof(struct i387_fsave_struct) ) )
296            return -1;
```

```
297        return 1;
298   }
```

Figure 19.12 Saving standard floating point unit registers

288 the parameter is a pointer to the `struct _fpstate` in user space, to which the register state is to be written.

290 this takes a local pointer to the `task_struct` of the current process, where the register state will be saved by `unlazy_fpu()` in the next line.

292 this macro, described in Section 11.10.2.2, copies values from the hardware FPU registers to the `thread` structure, if necessary.

293 this makes a second copy of the status word in the `thread` structure.

294–295 this copies the state from `thread` to the user stack. This fills in the first nine fields of the `struct _fpstate`, up to and including `status`. One would have expected the `magic` field to have been expressly set to 0xFFFF at this stage. The remainder of the `struct _fpstate` is unused.

296 if unable to copy, we return failure (−1).

19.4.3.3   *Saving extended floating point unit registers*

When the FPU has XMM extensions there is some extra FPU state. The function to copy this is shown in Figure 19.13, from `arch/i386/kernel/i387.c`. It should be read with reference to Figures 2.18 (page ...) and 19.5.

```
300   static inline int save_i387_fxsave( struct _fpstate *buf )
301   {
302        struct task_struct *tsk = current;
303        int err = 0;
304
305        unlazy_fpu( tsk );
306
307        if (convert_fxsr_to_user(buf, &tsk->thread.i387.fxsave))
308             return -1;
309
310        err |= __put_user( tsk->thread.i387.fxsave.swd, &buf->status );
311        err |= __put_user( X86_FXSR_MAGIC, &buf->magic );
312        if ( err )
313             return -1;
314
315        if (__copy_to_user( &buf->_fxsr_env[0],
                                      &tsk->thread.i387.fxsave,
316                                    sizeof(struct i387_fxsave_struct)))
317             return -1;
```

```
318        return 1;
319 }
```

Figure 19.13 Saving extended floating point unit registers

300 the parameter is a pointer to the `struct _fpstate` in user space, to which the register state is to be written.

302 this takes a pointer to the `task_struct` of the current process, where the register state will be saved by `unlazy_fpu()` at line 305.

305 this macro, described in Section 11.10.2.2, copies values from the hardware FPU registers to the `thread` structure, if necessary.

307 this function, described in Section 19.4.3.4, fills the first eight fields of the `struct _fpstate` in user space, up to and including `_st`. It converts from the format used in `thread`.

308 as it returns 0 on success, any other value is an error, so an error indication of −1 is returned.

310 this copies the status word to user space.

311 this sets up the `magic` field in the `struct _fpstate`. This indicates that the extended information is valid. It is defined in `<asm-i386/sigcontext.h>` as

```
55    #define X86_FXSR_MAGIC   0x0000
```

312–313 if either of the foregoing writes failed, we return an error value of −1.

315–316 this copies the whole of the `fxsave` field of `thread` to the latter part of the `struct_fpstate`, beginning with the `_fxsr_env` field. We compare the `fxsave` field in `thread` (Figure 2.18) with the `_fxsr_env` and following fields (Section 19.2.4). Although different in the way they are declared, they are exactly the same in structure.

317 if unable to copy this, we return an error of −1.

19.4.3.4 *Converting and copy* FXSR *values*

The format in which the values in the FXSR registers are saved in `thread` is slightly different from that required on the user stack, so the function shown in Figure 19.14, from `arch/i386/kernel/i387.c`, converts between formats as well as copying from kernel to user space. It should be read with reference to Figures 2.18 (page 34) and 19.5.

```
227  static inline int convert_fxsr_to_user( struct _fpstate *buf,
228       struct i387_fxsave_struct *fxsave )
229  {
230       unsigned long env[7];
231       struct _fpreg *to;
232       struct _fpxreg *from;
233       int i;
234
```

```
235           env[0] = (unsigned long) fxsave->cwd | 0xffff0000 ;
236           env[1] = (unsigned long) fxsave->swd | 0xffff0000 ;
237           env[2] = twd_fxsr_to_i387(fxsave) ;
238           env[3] = fxsave->fip ;
239           env[4] = fxsave->fcs | ((unsigned long) fxsave->fop << 16) ;
240           env[5] = fxsave->foo ;
241           env[6] = fxsave->fos ;
242
243           if ( __copy_to_user( buf, env, 7 * sizeof(unsigned long)))
244                 return 1 ;
245
246           to = &buf->_st[0] ;
247           from = (struct _fpxreg *) &fxsave->st_space[0] ;
248           for ( i = 0 ; i < 8 ; i++, to++, from++ ) {
249                 if ( __copy_to_user( to, from, sizeof(*to) ) )
250                         return 1 ;
251                 }
252           return 0 ;
253  }
```

Figure 19.14   Converting and copying FXSR values

227–228   the parameters are a pointer to a `struct _fpstate` (Section 19.2.4) on the stack and a pointer to a `struct i387_fxsave_struct` (Figure 2.18) in `thread`.

235–241   on the user stack, the first seven items of floating point information are in the format used by a standard FPU, as seen in Section 19.4.3.2. In `thread`, all information is maintained in the format used by an extended FPU. These lines convert the data into the appropriate format, preparatory to copying it to user space.

235   the first value is the control word, with the high-order 16 bits set to all 1s.

236   the second value is the status word, with the high-order 16 bits set to all 1s.

237   the function, described in Section 19.4.3.5, calculates 2-bit tags for each of the eight registers, as saved in `thread`, and writes them here.

238–239   these two fields contain the floating instruction pointer. The 32-bit offset is in fip, with the 16-bit segment selector in `fcs`.

239   the high-order 16 bits contain the value from the last instruction opcode register (`fxsave->fop`); the low-order 16 bits contain the segment selector.

240–241   this is the 48-bit floating point operand. The 32-bit offset is in `foo`, whereas the 16-bit segment selector is in the low half of `fos`.

243   we copy this seven-element array to the first seven fields of the `struct _fpstate` on the user stack frame.

244   if it cannot be copied, we return an error value of 1.

246   the `to` field points to the beginning of the `_st[]` array on the user stack, immediately after the field just filled in. This is an array of `struct _fpreg`, each 10 bytes long (see Section 19.2.4).

247   the `from` field points to the beginning of the `st_space[]` array in `thread`, which contains values from the eight FPU registers. Each entry here is padded to be 16 bytes long.

248–251   this loop copies eight elements from `st_space[]` to `_st[]`. Each element is aligned on a 10-byte boundary on the stack.

250   if any of these copies fails, it returns an error value of 1.

252   otherwise, we return success.

19.4.3.5   *Calculating tag values*

Each of the low-order 8 bits in the `twd` field of the `struct i387_fxsave_struct` in `thread` represents the state of a corresponding FPU register, indicating whether it contains valid information or is empty. The function shown in Figure 19.15, from `arch/i386/kernel/i387.c`, converts each of these 1-bit tags to a 2-bit tag. The new tags distinguish four different states in a register:

- 0: ordinary valid information;

- 1: a value representing 0.0;

- 2: a special floating point number;

- 3: no valid information.

It returns a bitmap of these values.

```
104   static inline unsigned long twd_fxsr_to_i387
                              ( struct i387_fxsave_struct *fxsave )
105   {
106       struct _fpxreg *st = NULL;
107       unsigned long twd = (unsigned long) fxsave->twd;
108       unsigned long tag;
109       unsigned long ret = 0xffff0000;
110       int i;
111
112   #define FPREG_ADDR(f, n) ((char *)&(f)->st_space + (n) * 16)
113
114       for ( i = 0 ; i < 8 ; i++ ) {
115           if ( twd & 0x1 ) {
116               st = (struct _fpxreg *) FPREG_ADDR( fxsave, i );
117
118               switch ( st->exponent & 0x7fff ) {
119                   case 0x7fff:
120                       tag = 2;
```

```
121                            break;
122                        case 0x0000:
123                            if ( !st->significand[0] &&
124                                    !st->significand[1] &&
125                                    !st->significand[2] &&
126                                    !st->significand[3] ) {
127                                tag = 1;
128                            } else {
129                                tag = 2;
130                            }
131                            break;
132                        default:
133                            if ( st->significand[3] & 0x8000 ) {
134                                tag = 0;
135                            } else {
136                                tag = 2;
137                            }
138                            break;
139                        }
140                } else {
141                        tag = 3;
142                }
143            ret |= (tag << (2 * i));
144            twd = twd >> 1;
145        }
146        return ret;
147 }
```

Figure 19.15   Calculating tag values

104   the input parameter is a pointer to a struct i387_fxsave_struct in thread (see Figure 2.18, page 34).

107   this takes a local copy of the tag word from thread, cast to be unsigned long.

109   this default return value will be manipulated in the body of the function.

112   the parameters to this macro are a pointer to an i387_fxsave_struct and an integer indicating one of the eight registers. It evaluates to the address of the corresponding 16-byte register (specified by n) within the st_space[] array, cast as a pointer to char.

114–145   this goes through each of the eight registers in turn.

115–139   if the least significant bit of the tag word is set, then there is some information in this register. A tag of 0, 1, or 2 must be created, depending on the nature of this information.

116   this line sets st up as a pointer to the register currently being considered.

118–139   this switches on the low-order 15 bits of the exponent field of this register.

119–121   if all these bits are set, then the register contains a special floating point number, and the tag value is 2.

122–131	if these bits of `exponent` are 0, then the type of information in the register depends on the value in `significand[]`.
123–127	if all four elements of `significand[]` are 0, then the value is 0, so `tag` is 1.
129	if any element of `significand[]` is nonzero, then the register contains a special floating point number, and `tag` is 2.
132–138	this case is for all other values of `exponent`.
133–134	if the most significant bit of `significand` is set, then there is valid information in the register, so `tag` is 0.
136	otherwise, it is some special floating point number.
141	if the least significant bit of the tag word is clear, then there is no information in the corresponding register, so we have a `tag` value of 3.
143	as 2 bits are needed to represent the range of tag values, we shift the value left by the appropriate number of bits and add it to `ret`, for eventual return. Note that `ret` is an `unsigned long`, with the high-order 16 bits set at initialisation (line 109).
144	this makes the next bit of `twd` available for inspection at line 115.
145	we go around the loop again.
146	each pair of the low-order 16 bits in `ret` represent the tag value calculated for a specific register.

19.5 Returning to kernel mode after handling a signal

As described in Section 19.3, when a signal handler terminates it finds a return address on its stack that causes it to execute a stub routine. This stub routine in turn consists of an `INT 0x80` instruction, which calls a system service. Depending on the type of stack frame built for the handler, this system service is either `sigreturn()` or `rt_sigreturn()`. These two system services will now be considered.

19.5.1 Returning from a standard stack frame

The function shown in Figure 19.16, from `arch/i386/kernel/signal.c`, implements the `sigreturn()` system service. Remember that this is called from the entry code to a system service (see Section 10.4.3.2). At this stage a `struct pt_regs` has been built on the kernel stack for this system call.

```
249  asmlinkage int sys_sigreturn(unsigned long __unused)
250  {
251      struct pt_regs *regs = (struct pt_regs *) &__unused;
252      struct sigframe *frame = (struct sigframe *)(regs->esp - 8);
253      sigset_t set;
254      int eax;
255
```

```
256         if (verify_area(VERIFY_READ, frame, sizeof(*frame)))
257             goto badframe;
258         if (__get_user(set.sig[0], &frame->sc.oldmask)
259             || (_NSIG_WORDS > 1
260                 && __copy_from_user(&set.sig[1], &frame->extramask,
261                     sizeof(frame->extramask))))
262             goto badframe;
263
264         sigdelsetmask(&set, ~_BLOCKABLE);
265         spin_lock_irq(&current->sigmask_lock);
266         current->blocked = set;
267         recalc_sigpending(current);
268         spin_unlock_irq(&current->sigmask_lock);
269
270         if (restore_sigcontext(regs, &frame->sc, &eax))
271             goto badframe;
272         return eax;
273
274   badframe:
275         force_sig(SIGSEGV, current);
276         return 0;
277   }
```

Figure 19.16   Returning from a standard stack frame

249   there is one parameter on the stack, but its value is never used. Rather, its address is used, to find the bottom of the stack.

251   as the saved registers on the kernel stack begin with _unused (really EBX), this line sets up regs pointing to the struct pt_regs on the stack.

252   to understand what is going on here, it is necessary to recap a little. The stack frame set up on the user mode stack is shown in Figure 19.17. From the bottom up, this is a struct sigframe. When the signal handler terminates, it pops the return address (the pretcode field) to the EIP register. The stub then pops and discards the sig field, leaving ESP pointing to sc. Then the INT 80 instruction is executed and the kernel is entered. As part of the entry protocol, the value of ESP pointing to sc is saved on the kernel stack. This line subtracts 8 bytes from the saved value of ESP; that points frame back to the beginning of the struct sigframe.

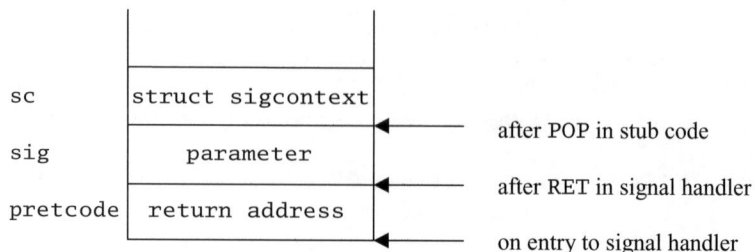

Figure 19.17   Stack frame on user mode stack

256–257   if it is not possible to read from the stack frame in user space, then we force a SIGSEGV on the process.

258–262   the handler may have changed its copy of the signal mask, so it has to be updated. If the signal mask cannot be copied from user space to the local set variable, we force a SIGSEGV on the process. Note that && has higher precedence than ||, so the _NSIG_WORDS > 1 is associated with the __copy_from_user(), not the __get_user(). In fact, the __copy_from_user() is called only if _NSIG_WORDS > 1 is TRUE.

258   this is for the first 32 bits of the signal mask.

259–261   for the case when there are more than 32 bits in the signal mask, we copy the remainder. This is i386-specific code so there will never be more than 64 bits.

264   this clears any bits not in _BLOCKABLE, just in case the handler tried to block an unblockable signal. The macro is defined in arch/i386/kernel/signal.c as

```
29   #define _BLOCKABLE (~(sigmask(SIGKILL) | sigmask(SIGSTOP)))
```

Remember that sigmask() sets the bit corresponding to its parameter, so _BLOCKABLE has all bits set, with the exception of SIGKILL and SIGSTOP. The sigdelsetmask() function was described in Section 17.2.3.1.

265–268   while manipulating the bitmap of the current process we ensure that signals cannot be posted to it by taking out the interrupt-safe spinlock, using the macros from Section 12.8.1.

266   the blocked bitmap is updated to the value just calculated in set.

267   here we reevaluate the signal state of the process (see Section 18.3.2).

270–271   this function copies the information back from the user stack frame (pointed to by frame) to the struct pt_regs on the kernel stack (see Section 19.6.1). If unable to do so, we force a SIGSEGV on the process.

272   this returns the value written to eax by the restore_sigcontext() function. This is the value from the eax field in the stack frame in user space. Control returns to the system call entry routine in Section 10.4.3.2, with this value in the EAX register.

274–276   this is the error exit, taken if we are unable to read from the stack frame in user space.

275   this function forces a signal on the current process, even if that signal is blocked (see Section 18.2.7).

276   a zero return value is a failure. Control returns to the system call entry routine in Section 10.4.3.2, with this 0 in the EAX register.

19.5.2   Returning from an extended stack frame

The function shown in Figure 19.18, from arch/i386/kernel/signal.c, implements the rt_sigreturn() system service. It is very similar to the function discussed in the previous section, and only the extra processing will be commented on.

```
279   asmlinkage int sys_rt_sigreturn(unsigned long __unused)
280   {
281         struct pt_regs *regs = (struct pt_regs *) &__unused;
282         struct rt_sigframe *frame = (struct rt_sigframe *)(regs->esp - 4);
283         sigset_t set;
284         stack_t st;
285         int eax;
286
287         if (verify_area(VERIFY_READ, frame, sizeof(*frame)))
288                 goto badframe;
289         if (__copy_from_user(&set, &frame->uc.uc_sigmask,
                                                        sizeof(set)))
290                 goto badframe;
291
292         sigdelsetmask(&set, ~_BLOCKABLE);
293         spin_lock_irq(&current->sigmask_lock);
294         current->blocked = set;
295         recalc_sigpending(current);
296         spin_unlock_irq(&current->sigmask_lock);
297
298         if (restore_sigcontext(regs, &frame->uc.uc_mcontext, &eax))
299                 goto badframe;
300
301         if (__copy_from_user(&st, &frame->uc.uc_stack, sizeof(st)))
302                 goto badframe;
305         do_sigaltstack(&st, NULL, regs->esp);
306
307         return eax;
308
309   badframe:
310         force_sig(SIGSEGV, current);
311         return 0;
312   }
```

Figure 19.18   Returning from an extended stack frame

279–288   see lines 249–257 of Section 19.5.1.

282   note that this time the stack pointer is pulled down only by 4 bytes. The stub did not pop the `sig` field in this case. Also, it is cast as a pointer to a `struct rt_sigframe`.

289–290   if it is not possible to copy the full mask of blocked signals from the user space stack frame to the `set` variable, we force a `SIGSEGV` signal on the process.

292–299   see lines 264–271 of Section 19.5.1.

301–302   the `uc_stack` field contains information about the stack in use. If it is not possible to copy this information from user space to the local `st` variable, we force a `SIGSEGV` signal on the process.

<table>
<tr><td>305</td><td>this function checks and, if necessary, restores the user mode stack as specified by <code>st</code>. It was described in Section 17.6.2.</td></tr>
</table>

305 this function checks and, if necessary, restores the user mode stack as specified by `st`. It was described in Section 17.6.2.

307–311 see lines 272–276 of Section 19.5.1.

19.6 Copying information back from user space

Before running the signal handler, a significant amount of information was copied from the kernel stack and the `struct thread` to the user stack. All of that information has to be copied back from user space to kernel space after the handler has run. There is one main function for that, and a number of subsidiary ones, all of which are considered in this section.

19.6.1 Restoring signal context from user space

The function that does the bulk of the work of restoring the context from user space is shown in Figure 19.19, from `arch/i386/kernel/signal.c`.

```
188  static int
189  restore_sigcontext(struct pt_regs *regs, struct sigcontext *sc,
                                                        int *peax)
190  {
191      unsigned int err = 0;
192
193  #define COPY(x)     err |= __get_user(regs->x, &sc->x)
194
195  #define COPY_SEG(seg)                               \
196      { unsigned short tmp;                           \
197          err |= __get_user(tmp, &sc->seg);           \
198          regs->x##seg = tmp;        }
199
200  #define COPY_SEG_STRICT(seg)                        \
201      { unsigned short tmp;                           \
202          err |= __get_user(tmp, &sc->seg);           \
203          regs->x##seg = tmp|3;      }
204
205  #define GET_SEG(seg)                                \
206      { unsigned short tmp;                           \
207          err |= __get_user(tmp, &sc->seg);           \
208          loadsegment(seg, tmp);     }
209
210      GET_SEG(gs);
211      GET_SEG(fs);
212      COPY_SEG(es);
213      COPY_SEG(ds);
214      COPY(edi);
215      COPY(esi);
216      COPY(ebp);
```

```
217         COPY(esp);
218         COPY(ebx);
219         COPY(edx);
220         COPY(ecx);
221         COPY(eip);
222         COPY_SEG_STRICT(cs);
223         COPY_SEG_STRICT(ss);
224
225         {
226             unsigned int tmpflags;
227             err |= __get_user(tmpflags, &sc->eflags);
228             regs->eflags = (regs->eflags & ~0x40DD5) | (tmpflags & 0x40DD5);
229             regs->orig_eax = -1;
230         }
231
232         {
233             struct _fpstate * buf;
234             err |= __get_user(buf, &sc->fpstate);
235             if (buf) {
236                 if (verify_area(VERIFY_READ, buf, sizeof(*buf)))
237                     goto badframe;
238                 err |= restore_i387(buf);
239             }
240         }
241
242         err |= __get_user(*peax, &sc->eax);
243         return err;
244
245  badframe:
246         return 1;
247  }
```

Figure 19.19   Restoring signal context from user space

189 the parameters are a pointer to the saved register values on the kernel stack, a pointer to the `struct sigcontext` on the user stack, and a pointer to an `int` into which a success or failure value will be written.

193–208 a number of macros are declared for use within this function.

193 this macro copies a specified field from the `struct sigcontext` in user space to the corresponding field on the kernel stack. If it cannot copy, the resulting error value is accumulated in `err`.

195–198 this macro copies a specified segment register value from the `struct sigcontext` in user space to the corresponding field on the kernel stack. If there is an error, the error value is accumulated in `err`.

197 the copying is done in two steps. First, we copy to `tmp` and check for errors.

198   now we copy from `tmp` to the appropriate place on the kernel stack. The use of a macro here allows an 'x' to be prepended to the segment identifier, as required by the naming convention in a `struct pt_regs`.

200–203   this macro also copies a segment register value, but it makes sure that the least-significant 2 bits are set. In case the user tried to change to kernel mode by clearing these bits, this sets them again.

205–208   this macro loads a particular hardware segment register with the corresponding value from the user stack. It is used for FS and GS. The `loadsegment()` function that it uses is described in Section 19.6.2.

210–211   this copies the `gs` and `fs` values from the user stack to the GS and FS hardware registers.

212–223   this copies the other segment registers and the general purpose registers from the user stack to the kernel stack, taking care that the user is not allowed access to kernel code or stack. This is overwriting the values pushed there by SAVE_ALL, on entry to the `sigreturn()` or `rt_sigreturn()` system services.

225–230   this copies and adjust the EFLAGS value.

227   this copies the `eflags` field from the user stack to the temporary `tmpflags`.

228   0x 40DD5 represents the flags that can be set by a user. First, all these are turned off in the copy on the kernel stack. Then, any subset of these requested by the signal handler are turned on. The end result is that any of these bits requested by the signal handler are turned on, as well an any other bits turned on beforehand.

229   the `orig_eax` field is used to identify the number of the system call that caused the process to enter the kernel. Putting −1 here means that it did not enter because of a system call but on the rebound after handling a signal.

232–240   this copies FPU state, if necessary.

234   this gets the pointer to the `struct _fpstate` on the user stack into the local `buf`.

235   if the pointer is valid, then there is state to be copied.

236–237   if it is not possible to read from the floating point area of the stack frame in user space, we return an error code of 1.

238   otherwise, we restore the state, using the function described in Section 19.6.3.1.

242   this copies the `eax` value from the user stack back to the `int` variable in the caller of this function, either `sys_sigreturn()` (Section 19.5.1) or `sys_rt_sigreturn()` (Section 19.5.2).

243   if all the calls to `__get_user()` (including those in the macros) were successful, this returns 0 (success). Otherwise, it returns a positive (error) value.

246   this is an error return value.

19.6.2 Loading a segment register

The macro shown in Figure 19.20, from <asm-i386/system.h>, loads a hardware segment register. It falls back on loading a 0 value if something goes wrong.

```
83    #define loadsegment(seg,value)                    \
84        asm volatile("\n"                             \
85            "1:\t"                                    \
86            "movl %0,%%" #seg "\n"                    \
87            "2:\n"                                    \
88            ".section .fixup,\"ax\"\n"                \
89            "3:\t"                                    \
90            "pushl $0\n\t"                            \
91            "popl %%" #seg "\n\t"                     \
92            "jmp 2b\n"                                \
93            ".previous\n"                             \
94            ".section __ex_table,\"a\"\n\t" \
95            ".align 4\n\t"                            \
96            ".long 1b,3b\n"                           \
97            ".previous"                               \
98            : : "m" (*(unsigned int *)&(value)))
99
```

Figure 19.20 Loading a segment register

86 parameter 0 is value. This is written to the specified segment register, seg.

88–92 because this code is in the .fixup section, normal execution passes directly from line 87 to the end of the macro. The "ax" signifies that this segment must be loaded into memory, and contains executable code. If it is executed, by a jump to label 3:, it pushes an immediate value of 0 onto the stack and then pops it from there to the specified segment register. This is because the i386 does not allow an immediate value to be written to a segment register.

94–96 this code is compiled into the __ex_table segment. It enters the two labels 1: and 3: into the exception table. The "a" attribute specifies that this section must always be loaded into memory along with the rest of the kernel. If the code at label 1: causes an exception, the code at label 3: will be tried instead.

98 the address of value is cast to be a pointer to unsigned long and then de-referenced. This guarantees that the value written is a full 32 bits.

19.6.3 Restoring the floating point unit state from the user stack

Restoring the FPU state is very similar to the process of copying the FPU state, described in Section 19.4.3. There is one main function that determines how much FPU state is to be copied and a number of subsidiary functions to do the actual copying.

19.6.3.1 Determining the state to be restored

If the `restore_sigcontext()` function finds that the FPU state needs to be restored from user space to the `thread` structure in kernel space, the function shown in Figure 19.21, from `arch/i386/kernel/i387.c`, is called. It determines the amount of FPU state that has to be copied back.

```
362  int restore_i387( struct _fpstate *buf )
363  {
364      int err;
365
366      if ( HAVE_HWFP ) {
367          if ( cpu_has_fxsr ) {
368              err = restore_i387_fxsave( buf );
369          } else {
370              err = restore_i387_fsave( buf );
371          }
372      } else {
373          err = restore_i387_soft(&current->thread.i387.soft, buf);
374      }
375      current->used_math = 1;
376      return err;
377  }
```

Figure 19.21 Determining the state to be restored

362   the parameter is a pointer to a `struct_fpstate` on the user stack.

366–372   this block of code is executed if a hardware FPU has been detected at boot time.

367–368   if an extended FPU (with MMX instructions) was detected at boot time, we use this restore function, from Section 19.6.3.3. It returns 0 on success.

370   otherwise we use this restore function, from Section 19.6.3.2. It also returns 0 on success.

373   if there is no hardware FPU (an original 386) then we use this restore function. The internals of this function are heavily dependent on the emulator. As this is not really relevant to modern machines it is not considered any further here.

375   the values in the hardware FPU registers have been invalidated by one or other of the restore functions just called. This setting of `used_math` notes that they require to be set up from the values in `thread` when the FPU is next used.

376   if the copy function used was successful, then 0 is returned; otherwise, we return the error value from the copy function.

19.6.3.2 Restoring normal floating point unit state

The function shown in Figure 19.22, from `arch/i386/kernel/i387.c`, copies standard FPU register values from the signal-handling stack to `thread`.

```
366  static inline int restore_i387_fsave( struct _fpstate *buf )
343  {
344       struct task_struct *tsk = current;
345       clear_fpu( tsk );
346       return __copy_from_user(&tsk->thread.i387.fsave, buf,
347                                sizeof(struct i387_fsave_struct) );
348  }
```

Figure 19.22   Restoring normal floating point unit state

342   the parameter is a pointer to the `struct _fpstate` in user space, from which the register state will be read.

344   this takes a pointer to the `task_struct` of the current process. The register state will be written to the `thread` field of this.

345   as the values in hardware registers may now be invalid, this macro, from Section 19.6.3.4, marks them as such.

346–347 this copies the state from the user stack to `thread`. The `struct _fpstate` was described in Section 19.2.4; the `struct i387_fsave_struct` in Section 2.7. It copies only that part of a `struct _fpstate` that exactly maps onto a `struct i387_fsave_struct`. If the copy succeeded, it returns 0 for success; otherwise, it returns the error value from `__copy_from_user()`.

19.6.3.3   Restoring extended floating point unit registers

When the FPU has XMM extensions there is some extra FPU state to be copied back. The function to handle this is shown in Figure 19.23, from `arch/i386/kernel/i387.c`.

```
350  static inline int restore_i387_fxsave( struct _fpstate *buf )
351  {
352       struct task_struct *tsk = current;
353       clear_fpu( tsk );
354       if ( __copy_from_user( &tsk->thread.i387.fxsave,
355       &buf->_fxsr_env[0], sizeof(struct i387_fxsave_struct)))
356            return 1;
357
358       tsk->thread.i387.fxsave.mxcsr &= 0xffbf;
359       return convert_fxsr_from_user(&tsk->thread.i387.fxsave, buf);
360  }
```

Figure 19.23   Restoring extended floating point unit registers

350–353 see lines 342–345 of Section 19.6.3.2.

354–355 this copies from the `struct _fpstate`, beginning at the `_fxsr_env` field, to the `fxsave` field of `thread`. This second part of the `struct _fpstate` maps exactly on to a `struct i387_fxsave_struct`.

356   if unable to copy, we return an error value of 1.

358   this zeroes bit 6 and bits 16–31 of the newly copied `mxcsr` in `thread`. These bits must be zero for security reasons.

359   this function, described in Section 19.6.3.5, fills the first part of the `fxsave` field of `thread` from the first part of the `struct _fpstate` in user space, so it overwrites some values written at lines 354–355. It returns 0 on success; any other value is an error.

19.6.3.4   Invalidating the hardware floating point unit registers

When FPU state is copied back from the signal-handling stack to the thread structure, there is no guarantee that it is consistent with the values in the hardware registers, so these have to be invalidated, using the macro shown in Figure 19.24, from `<asm-i386/i387.h>`.

```
35   #define clear_fpu( tsk ) do {                \
36        if ( tsk->flags & PF_USEDFPU ) {        \
37             asm volatile("fwait");             \
38             tsk->flags &= ~PF_USEDFPU;         \
39             stts();                            \
40        }                                       \
41   } while (0)
```

Figure 19.24   Invalidating the hardware floating point unit registers

35   the parameter is a pointer to the `task_struct` of the current process.

36   if the `PF_USEDFPU` bit in `flags` is clear, the process has not used the FPU, so the FPU registers are in an invalid state anyway. In this case the macro does nothing.

37   the `FWAIT` instruction checks for and handles pending unmasked FPU exceptions.

38   this clears the `PF_USEDFPU` bit.

39   this sets the TS (task-switched) bit in the CR0 register, to note that the FPU register values are now invalid (see Section 11.10.2.6 for the macro).

19.6.3.5   Converting and copying FXSR values

The format in which the values in the FXSR registers are saved on the user stack is slightly different from that required in `thread`. This has already been seen in Section 19.4.3.4, when copying values *to* the stack, so the function shown in Figure 19.25, from `arch/i386/kernel/i387.c`, converts between formats, as well as copying from user space to the kernel.

```
255  static inline int convert_fxsr_from_user( struct
256                         i387_fxsave_struct *fxsave, struct _fpstate *buf)
257  {
258       unsigned long env[7];
```

```
259        struct _fpxreg *to;
260        struct _fpreg *from;
261        int i;
262
263        if ( __copy_from_user( env, buf, 7 * sizeof(long) ) )
264             return 1;
265
266        fxsave->cwd = (unsigned short)(env[0] & 0xffff);
267        fxsave->swd = (unsigned short)(env[1] & 0xffff);
268        fxsave->twd = twd_i387_to_fxsr((unsigned short)(env[2]
                                                      & 0xffff));
269        fxsave->fip = env[3];
270        fxsave->fop = (unsigned short)((env[4] & 0xffff0000) >> 16);
271        fxsave->fcs = (env[4] & 0xffff);
272        fxsave->foo = env[5];
273        fxsave->fos = env[6];
274
275        to = (struct _fpxreg *) &fxsave->st_space[0];
276        from = &buf->_st[0];
277        for ( i = 0 ; i < 8 ; i++, to++, from++ ) {
278             if ( __copy_from_user( to, from, sizeof(*from) ) )
279                  return 1;
280        }
281        return 0;
282  }
```

Figure 19.25   Converting and copying FXSR values

255–256   the `i387_fxsave_struct` (in `thread`) was described in Figure 2.18 (page 34); the `_fpstate` structure (on the user stack) in Figure 19.5.

263–264   on the user stack, the first part of the FPU environment is saved as seven `unsigned long`. This information is copied into an array in the kernel. If unable to copy, we return an error value of 1.

266–273   these lines convert and copy the data from each element of the array into its own specific field in `thread`.

266   the first value is the command word, with the high-order 16 bits cleared to 0, then cast to be `unsigned short`, to match the `cwd` field to which it is being written.

267   the second value is the status word, with the high-order 16 bits cleared to 0, then cast to be `unsigned short`, to match the `swd` field to which it is being written.

268   this function (see Section 19.6.3.6) converts 2-bit tags from the `tag` field on the user stack to 1-bit tags for each of the eight registers. The result is then written to the `twd` field in `thread`.

269   the 32-bit offset of the 48-bit floating instruction pointer is stored in `fip`.

270   the first two bytes of the last noncontrol instruction executed are in the high-order 16 bits of `env[4]`; they are shifted down, and written to `fop`.

271   the 16-bit segment selector for the floating instruction pointer is in the low-order 16 bits of `env[4]`. The high-order bits are masked out and the resulting value written to `fcs`.

272–273   the floating operand is a 48-bit register. The 32-bit offset is stored in `foo`, and the 16-bit segment selector is in `fos`.

275   the `to` variable points to the beginning of the `st_space[32]` array (of `long`) in `thread`.

276   the `from` variable points to the beginning of the `_st[8]` array (of `struct _fpreg`) on the user stack. Each `struct _fpreg` is five `unsigned short`. These are the floating point registers.

277–278   this loop copies eight elements from `_st[]` to `st_space[]`. Each element is the size of a `struct _fpreg`, or 10 bytes.

279   if any of these copies fails, it returns an error value of 1.

281   otherwise, it returns success.

19.6.3.6   Converting floating point unit tag words

The tag bits for the eight registers were stored on the user stack as 16 bits, two per register. The function shown in Figure 19.26, from `arch/i386/kernel/i387.c`, converts them to the format expected in the `twd` field of `thread`. It is converting from 2 bits (four possibilities) per tag to 1 bit (two possibilities) per tag, and packing these into one byte.

```
90    static inline unsigned short twd_i387_to_fxsr(unsigned short twd )
91    {
92          unsigned int tmp;

95          tmp = ~twd;
96          tmp = (tmp | (tmp>>1)) & 0x5555;
97
98          tmp = (tmp | (tmp >> 1)) & 0x3333;
99          tmp = (tmp | (tmp >> 2)) & 0x0f0f;
100         tmp = (tmp | (tmp >> 4)) & 0x00ff;
101         return tmp;
102   }
```

Figure 19.26   Converting floating point unit tag words

90   the parameter is the bitfield as copied from the user stack.

95   start by inverting all the bits in the parameter, in the low-order 16 bits of the 32-bit `tmp`.

96   the first part of this, `tmp | (tmp >> 1)`, duplicates each of the valid bits. The second part, `& 0x5555`, clears the high-order bit of each pair. The transformation of each possible pair of bits is as follows.

		invert	duplicate	clear high-order bit
Valid	00	11	11	01
Zero	01	10	11	01
Special	10	01	x1	01
Empty	11	00	x0	00

So registers that contain data are now marked 01; empty registers are marked 00.

98–100 these lines now move one bit per register into the least-significant byte.

98 the first part of this again duplicates each bit, going from:

0 8 0 7 0 6 0 5 0 4 0 3 0 2 0 1,

where the number represents the register corresponding to the bit in that position, to

0 8 8 7 7 6 6 5 5 4 4 3 3 2 2 1.

ANDing with 0x 3333 distributes the valid bits as follows:

0 0 8 7 0 0 6 5 0 0 4 3 0 0 2 1.

99 the first part of this duplicates each *pair* of bits as follows.

0 0 8 7 8 7 6 5 6 5 4 3 4 3 2 1.

ANDing with 0x 0f0f gives

0 0 0 0 8 7 6 5 0 0 0 0 4 3 2 1.

100 the first part of this duplicates each group of *four* bits, as follows:

0 0 0 0 8 7 6 5 8 7 6 5 4 3 2 1.

ANDing with 0x 00ff gives

0 0 0 0 0 0 0 0 8 7 6 5 4 3 2 1.

The end result is that each of the low-order 8 bits is set or cleared, depending on the condition of the corresponding register.

20

Capabilities

Traditional protection domains in Unix were rather primitive. File access was governed by the identification (ID) number or the effective ID of the user or group. Access to the kernel was governed by superuser (or root) privilege. This was binary in effect. Either a process had all privileges, or it had none.

POSIX has developed this by partitioning the privileges of the superuser into a set of discrete capabilities. A process may have none, some, or all of these at any particular time. This allows a 'minimum necessary' policy to be implemented. A process can be granted just that subset of capabilities that it needs to carry out its current processing and for just as long as it needs them.

Linux has taken this capability mechanism on board. Many of the capabilities defined in Linux are POSIX ones, but Linux has extended the POSIX draft, and quite a number of the capabilities are specific to Linux.

Each process has three different sets of capabilities, which are encoded as 32-bit bitmaps in the `task_struct` (see Section 2.5). The effective set represents what the process is currently allowed to do. This is the set that is checked. The permitted set specifies those capabilities it may acquire. Capabilities can be acquired temporarily, if required. The inheritable set determines those capabilities a process will have after an `exec()`.

20.1 Data structures representing capabilities

As usual, we begin with data structures and then go on to consider the functions that manipulate these.

20.1.1 Defined capabilities

Somewhat like signals, each capability is identified by a mnemonic name, beginning with CAP_ and defined as a constant. These definitions are in <linux/capability.h>, lines 65–280. Most of that code is comment, which will not be reproduced here, but it is recommended to the reader, as it gives greater detail about each of the capabilities. Many of these capabilities are really the province of the input–output (IO) manager, or of file

The Linux Process Manager. The Internals of Scheduling, Interrupts and Signals   John O'Gorman
© 2003 John Wiley & Sons, Ltd   ISBN: 0 470 84771 9

systems, or the network manager. These are listed here for completeness but are not explained in any great detail.

20.1.1.1 File system capabilities

The first group are concerned with access to file systems.

0 CAP_CHOWN This capability overrides the restrictions on changing user and group ownership of a file.

1 CAP_DAC_OVERRIDE This overrides all access controls on files.

2 CAP_DAC_READ_SEARCH This overrides all restrictions regarding read and search on files and directories.

3 CAP_FOWNER This overrides all restrictions about allowed operations on files, based on owner ID.

4 CAP_FSETID This overrides restrictions on setting the S_ISUID and S_ISGID bits on a file. These bits allow a program to run with the rights of the owner or group owner of the executable file. There is a bit mask defined in <linux/capability.h> as:

```
104  #define CAP_FS_MASK      0x1f.
```

This contains the bits corresponding to all the capabilities in this group.

20.1.1.2 Process management capabilities

The second group of capabilities is more closely related to the areas discussed in this book.

5 CAP_KILL This overrides restrictions on sending a signal. A process with this capability can send signals to any other process (see Section 18.1.2.1).

6 CAP_SETGID This allows use of the setgid() and setgroups() system services. The setgid() system service sets the effective group ID of the current process. The setgroups() system service sets the supplementary groups for the process. Only the superuser, or a process with this capability, may use this function.

7 CAP_SETUID The setuid() system service sets the effective user ID (uid) of the current process. If the effective user ID (euid) of the caller is root, or the caller has this capability, the real and saved user IDs are also set.

8 CAP_SETPCAP   This allows a process to transfer any capability (in its permitted set) to any other process or remove it from any process.

20.1.1.3   Networking capabilities

The next group of capabilities are concerned mainly with networking and are merely listed here with the briefest of description.

9 CAP_LINUX_IMMUTABLE   This allows modification of files with the S_IMMUTABLE and S_APPEND attributes.

10 CAP_NET_BIND_SERVICE   This allows binding to TCP/UDP sockets numbered below 1024.

11 CAP_NET_BROADCAST   This allows network broadcasting, and listening to multicasts.

12 CAP_NET_ADMIN   This capability allows for general network administration.

13 CAP_NET_RAW   This allows the use of sockets of type SOCK_RAW.

20.1.1.4   Miscellaneous capabilities

These five are a mixed bag, not really relevant to the subject matter of this book.

14 CAP_IPC_LOCK   This allows the locking of shared memory segments (which might be used to implement IPC, hence the name).

15 CAP_IPC_OWNER   This capability overrides ownership checks in the internal implementation of System V IPC.

16 CAP_SYS_MODULE   This capability is needed in order to insert or remove kernel modules.

17 CAP_SYS_RAWIO   This allows access to IO ports by the use of ioperm() and iopl().

18 CAP_SYS_CHROOT   This allows the use of the chroot() system service, which changes the root directory. Only the superuser, or a process having this capability, may change the root directory.

20.1.1.5 Further process management capabilities

This is another group of capabilities closely related to the areas discussed in this book.

19 CAP_SYS_PTRACE   This allows the use of `ptrace()` on any process. Normally, the tracing process must be the parent of the one it wants to trace (see Chapter 22).

20 CAP_SYS_PACCT   This allows configuration of process accounting (see Chapter 23).

21 CAP_SYS_ADMIN   This allows general system administration.

22 CAP_SYS_BOOT   This allows the use of the reboot command.

23 CAP_SYS_NICE   Here, we ignore restrictions on the `nice()` system service, which decreases the priority of the calling process. Only the superuser, or a process with this capability, may specify a priority increase.

24 CAP_SYS_RESOURCE   This sets and overrides resource and quota limits.

25 CAP_SYS_TIME   This allows manipulation of the system clock and of the real-time clock.

20.1.1.6 Input–output capabilities

The final group of capabilities are concerned with input and output and are listed here merely for completeness.

26 CAP_SYS_TTY_CONFIG   This allows terminal devices to be configured.

27 CAP_MKNOD   This allows access to the privileged aspects of the `mknod()` system service.

28 CAP_LEASE   This allows the taking of leases on files. A lease is used with distributed file systems to ensure that a locally cached copy of a file is still valid.

20.1.2 Capability bitmaps

Each process has three different sets of capabilities, which are encoded as 32-bit bitmaps in the `task_struct` (see Section 2.5). They are defined as type `kernel_cap_t`; see Figure 20.1, from `<linux/capability.h>`.

```
47   #ifdef STRICT_CAP_T_TYPECHECKS
48
49   typedef struct kernel_cap_struct {
50       __u32 cap;
51   } kernel_cap_t;
52
53   #else
54
55   typedef __u32 kernel_cap_t;
56
57   #endif
```

Figure 20.1   Data structures representing capability bitmaps

49–51   formally, `kernel_cap_t` is defined as a `struct`, even if essentially it is only a 32-bit `unsigned` value (one bit per capability).

55   this is the simpler, but equivalent, definition.

20.2 Manipulating capability bitmaps

A number of macros and functions are supplied for manipulating the capability types defined in the previous section. These will now be examined, one by one.

20.2.1 Converting between capability types

As seen earlier in Section 20.1.2, when `STRICT_CAP_T_TYPECHECKS` is defined, the `kernel_cap_t` representing capabilities is a `struct`, not a scalar bitmap. Given these two different definitions, macros are required to convert between them; see Figure 20.2, from `<linux/capability.h>`.

```
290  #ifdef STRICT_CAP_T_TYPECHECKS
291
292  #define to_cap_t(x) { x }
293  #define cap_t(x) (x).cap
294
295  #else
296
297  #define to_cap_t(x) (x)
298  #define cap_t(x) (x)
299
300  #endif
```

Figure 20.2   Converting from an integer to a capability type, and vice versa

292   this macro converts an integer to a `struct` type.

293   this converts from a `struct` to a scalar.

297–298   the corresponding versions of these macros are needed when `STRICT_CAP_T_TYPECHECKS` is not defined. They are merely identity substitutions.

20.2.2   Creating capability bitmaps

A number of macros are provided for creating a capability bitmap as well as adding a capability to or removing it from a set; see Figure 20.3, from `<linux/capability.h>`.

```
302  #define CAP_EMPTY_SET        to_cap_t(0)
303  #define CAP_FULL_SET         to_cap_t(~0)
304  #define CAP_INIT_EFF_SET     to_cap_t(~0 & CAP_TO_MASK(CAP_SETPCAP))
305  #define CAP_INIT_INH_SET     to_cap_t(0)

307  #define CAP_TO_MASK(x)       (1 << (x))
308  #define cap_raise(c, flag)   (cap_t(c) |= CAP_TO_MASK(flag))
309  #define cap_lower(c, flag)   (cap_t(c) &= ~CAP_TO_MASK(flag))
310  #define cap_raised(c, flag)  (cap_t(c) & CAP_TO_MASK(flag))
```

Figure 20.3   Manipulating capability bitmaps

302   this macro evaluates to a capability structure with all bits cleared to 0.

303   this macro evaluates to a capability set with all bits set to 1.

304   this is the initial value for the set of effective capabilities. It is just the bit corresponding to `CAP_SETPCAP` (see Section 20.1.1.2). The `CAP_TO_MASK()` macro is on line 307.

305   the initial set of inheritable capabilities is `NULL` (all zeroes).

307   this macro converts a capability specified by number (or symbolic constant) to a bit map with the appropriate bit set. It does this by shifting 1 left x bits; bits to the right are zero-filled.

308   this adds the capability specified by flag to the set c. The result is a simple scalar.

309   this removes the capability specified by flag from the set c. The result is a scalar.

310   this tests if the capability specified by flag is set in the set c. It returns `TRUE` if it is, `FALSE` otherwise.

20.2.3   Combining two capability sets

In order to calculate the union of two capability sets, the function shown in Figure 20.4, from `<linux/capabiity.h>`, does a bitwise OR of the two capability bitmaps supplied as parameters, and returns the result.

```
312  static inline kernel_cap_t cap_combine(kernel_cap_t a,
                                            kernel_cap_t b)
313
314      kernel_cap_t dest;
315      cap_t(dest) = cap_t(a) | cap_t(b);
```

```
316        return dest;
317  }
```

Figure 20.4　Combining two capability sets

315　the two parameters are converted to scalars before being combined, using the `cap_t()` macro from Section 20.2.1; the result is a scalar.

20.2.4　Calculating the intersection of two capability sets

The function shown in Figure 20.5, from `<linux/capability.h>`, does a bitwise AND on the two capability bitmaps supplied as parameters and returns the result. So, only those bits that are set in both of the input capabilities will be set in the result, hence the title `cap_intersect()`.

```
319  static inline kernel_cap_t cap_intersect(kernel_cap_t a,
                                              kernel_cap_t b)
320  {
321       kernel_cap_t dest;
322       cap_t(dest) = cap_t(a) & cap_t(b);
323       return dest;
324  }
```

Figure 20.5　Calculating the intersection of two capability sets

322　the two parameters are converted to scalars before being combined, using the `cap_t()` macro from Section 20.2.1; the result is a scalar.

20.2.5　Removing specified bits from a capability bitmap

The function shown in Figure 20.6, from `<linux/capability.h>`, removes specified capabilities from the bitmap it is passed as a parameter.

```
326  static inline kernel_cap_t cap_drop(kernel_cap_t a,
                                         kernel_cap_t drop)
327  {
328       kernel_cap_t dest;
329       cap_t(dest) = cap_t(a) & ~cap_t(drop);
330       return dest;
331  }
```

Figure 20.6　Removing specified bits from a capability bitmap

326　the first parameter is the bitmap to be adjusted; the second specifies those bits to remove.

329　the inverse of the `drop` parameter will have a 0 for each capability to be dropped, a 1 for each of the others, so the AND of this inverse with the original bitmap will mean that none of the specified bits can be set in the result, and all other bits are left unchanged. The two parameters are converted to scalars before being combined, using the `cap_t()` macro from Section 20.2.1; the result is a scalar.

20.2.6 Inverting a capability set

The function shown in Figure 20.7, from `<linux/capability.h>`, inverts all bits in the supplied capability set.

```
333  static inline kernel_cap_t cap_invert(kernel_cap_t c)
334  {
335      kernel_cap_t dest;
336      cap_t(dest) = ~cap_t(c);
337      return dest;
338  }
```

Figure 20.7 Inverting a capability set

336 the two parameters are converted to scalars before being combined, using the `cap_t()` macro from Section 20.2.1; the result is a scalar.

20.2.7 Miscellaneous macros

The macros shown in Figure 20.8, from `<linux/capability.h>`, perform various manipulations on capability bitmaps. Note that all values are converted to scalars, using the `cap_t()` macro from Section 20.2.1, before any bitwise operations are performed on them.

```
340  #define cap_isclear(c)        (!cap_t(c))
341  #define cap_issubset(a,set)   (!(cap_t(a) & ~cap_t(set)))
342
343  #define cap_clear(c)          do { cap_t(c) = 0; } while(0)
344  #define cap_set_full(c)       do { cap_t(c) = ~0; } while(0)
345  #define cap_mask(c,mask)      do { cap_t(c) &= cap_t(mask); } while(0)
346
347  #define cap_is_fs_cap(c)      (CAP_TO_MASK(c) & CAP_FS_MASK)
```

Figure 20.8 Macros for manipulating capabilities

340 this checks if a particular capability set is NULL. If all the bits are cleared to 0, then `cap_t()` returns FALSE; negating this gives TRUE. Otherwise, if any bits are set, then `cap_t()` returns TRUE; negating it gives FALSE.

341 this macro checks if the first bitmap is a subset of, or is contained in, the second (i.e. whether or not there are any bits set in a that are not set in set). The (`cap_t(a) & cap_t(set)` gives any bits that are in a but not in set. If this is TRUE, (meaning a is not a subset of set), then we negate it, because it is not a subset. However, if there are no such bits (meaning a is a subset of set), then the result will be FALSE. Negating that means that `cap_issubset()` evaluates to TRUE.

343 this macro merely clears all the bits in the supplied capability mask to 0.

344   this sets all the bits to 1.

345   only those bits are still set in c that are also set in mask. Like the function in Section 20.2.4, this also calculates the intersection; but this macro actually changes c.

347   this macro checks if a particular capability is a file system capability. The parameter c is an integer. The call to CAP_TO_MASK() sets the bit corresponding to c, CAP_FS_MASK is defined as 0x1F or 0001 1111, or capability 0, 1, 2, 3, or 4, which are all capabilities associated with the file system. If the capability c matches any of these bits, the macro evaluates to TRUE.

20.3 Setting capability masks

Sometimes it is required to set the capability bitmaps in many, or all, processes at the same time. Two functions are provided to simplify this.

20.3.1 Setting capabilities for all processes

The function shown in Figure 20.9, from kernel/capability.c, sets capabilities for all processes other than process 1 and itself. The input parameters are pointers to the values to be set in the three capability lists.

```
100   static void cap_set_all(kernel_cap_t *effective,
101         kernel_cap_t *inheritable,
102         kernel_cap_t *permitted)
103   {
104         struct task_struct *target;

107         read_lock(&tasklist_lock);
108
109         for_each_task(target) {
110             if (target == current target->pid == 1)
111                 continue;
112             target->cap_effective      = *effective;
113             target->cap_inheritable    = *inheritable;
114             target->cap_permitted      = *permitted;
115         }
116         read_unlock(&tasklist_lock);
117   }
```

Figure 20.9   Setting capabilities for all processes other than 1 and self

107–116   all the manipulation of the process structure is done under the protection of a read lock [see Section 5.7.2.1 for the read_lock() function]. The comment in the source asks if a write lock is needed. It is certainly expecting to write to one or more task_struct.

109–115   we go through the whole process list, checking each one. The for_each_task() macro is from Section 3.1.3.

110–111   if the one being checked is the current process, or has a pid of 1 (init), we go around again.

112–114 otherwise, we copy the capabilities to be set into appropriate fields in the `task_struct` of that process. Note that it is the actual bitmaps that are copied; not the pointers.

116 see Section 5.7.2.4 for the `read_unlock()` macro.

20.3.2 Setting capabilities for all processes in a group

The function shown in Figure 20.10, from `kernel/capability.c`, sets capabilities for all processes in a given process group. The input parameters specify the process group and the values to be set in the three capability lists. It is almost identical to the function in Section 20.3.1, and only the differences will be noted.

```
79   static void cap_set_pg(int pgrp,
80        kernel_cap_t *effective,
81        kernel_cap_t *inheritable,
82        kernel_cap_t *permitted)
83   {
84        struct task_struct *target;

87        read_lock(&tasklist_lock);
88        for_each_task(target) {
89            if (target->pgrp != pgrp)
90                continue;
91            target->cap_effective    = *effective;
92            target->cap_inheritable  = *inheritable;
93            target->cap_permitted    = *permitted;
94        }
95        read_unlock(&tasklist_lock);
96   }
```

Figure 20.10   Setting capabilities for all processes in a given process group

89–90 if the one being checked is not in the specified group, we go around again.

20.4 Checking capabilities

Capabilities were introduced to control access to various functions within the kernel. So far, this chapter has dealt only with the recording of these capabilities. This section now goes on to examine the functions provided for checking such capabilities and deciding whether access should be allowed or not. As indicated earlier in the chapter, the whole area of capabilities is very much in evolution, so there are still old-style permissions in use and being checked as well as the new-style capabilities.

20.4.1 Checking for a particular capability

The function used within the kernel to check if a process has a particular capability or not is shown in Figure 20.11, from `<linux/sched.h>`. New privilege checks should use this interface, rather than `suser()` or `fsuser()`.

```
732        static inline int capable(int cap)
733        {
734  #if 1
735                if (cap_raised(current->cap_effective, cap))
736  #else
737                if (cap_is_fs_cap(cap) ? current->fsuid == 0 :
                                                    current->euid == 0)
738  #endif
739            {
740                    current->flags |= PF_SUPERPRIV;
741                    return 1;
742            }
743            return 0;
744      }
```

Figure 20.11   Checking for a particular capability

735   if the bit corresponding to the capability passed as parameter is not set in the `cap_effective` bitmap of the current process, then control passes to line 743 and the function returns FALSE. The `cap_raised()` macro was described in Section 20.2.2.

737   this line is now defunct; it looks like debugging code still left in.

740   this changes the `flags` field, to note that the process has indicated its intention of using superuser privileges. This shows that the implementation of capabilities is still unfinished business.

741   this returns TRUE; the process has the specified capability.

20.4.2   Checking for root privileges

The function in Figure 20.12 from `<linux/sched.h>`, is used to check if the current process has root privileges. It also sets a flag if it returns TRUE (to do BSD-style accounting where the process is flagged if it uses root privileges).

```
708  extern inline int suser(void)
709      {
710      if (!issecure(SECURE_NOROOT) && current->euid == 0) {
711          current->flags |= PF_SUPERPRIV;
712          return 1;
713      }
714      return 0;
715  }
```

Figure 20.12   Function to flag use of root privileges

710–713   when the SECURE_NOROOT flag is set, uid 0 has no special privilege. If the effective uid is 0 (superuser) and the SECURE_NOROOT flag is not set, then it returns success (1) and changes the `flags` field, to note that the process has used, or at least indicated its intention of using, superuser privileges. The `issecure()` macro is discussed in Section 20.4.4.

714   otherwise, it just returns FALSE.

20.4.3   Checking for root file system access

Figure 20.13, from <linux/sched.h>, shows a function very similar to that in Figure 20.12, except that it checks fsuid. This is the process credential that governs file system access.

```
717   extern inline int fsuser(void)
718   {
719       if (!issecure(SECURE_NOROOT) && current->fsuid == 0) {
720           current->flags |= PF_SUPERPRIV;
721           return 1;
722       }
723       return 0;
724   }
```

Figure 20.13   Checking use of fsuid privileges

20.4.4   Checking a security setting

Linux is moving towards a set of systemwide security settings, valid for all processes, which will allow any particular kernel to be configured to a security level suitable to the environment in which it is operating. Each secure setting is implemented using two bits. One bit specifies whether the setting is on or off. The other bit specifies whether the setting is fixed or not. A setting that is fixed cannot be changed from user level. Currently, only two secure settings are defined. The function shown in Figure 20.14, from <linux/securebits.h>, checks a secure setting.

```
14    #define SECURE_NOROOT (0)

19    #define SECURE_NO_SETUID_FIXUP (2)

26    #define issecure(X) ( (1 << (X+1)) & SECUREBITS_DEFAULT ?    \
27        (1 << (X)) & SECUREBITS_DEFAULT :                        \
28        (1 << (X)) & securebits )
```

Figure 20.14   Checking a security setting

14   when bit 0 is set, uid 0 has no special privileges. Bit 1 specifies whether this secure setting is fixed or not.

19   when bit 2 is set, setuid() to or from uid 0 has its traditional meaning. When clear, setuid() does not change privilege. Bit 3 indicates whether this secure setting is fixed or not.

26–27   if the fixed bit corresponding to this secure setting is set, then the macro evaluates to TRUE or FALSE depending on whether the on or off bit is set or not in SECUREBITS_DEFAULT.

28   otherwise, it evaluates to TRUE or FALSE, depending on whether the on or off bit is set or not in securebits. The default is for both of these secure settings to be off. The information about secure settings is maintained in a variable defined in linux/sched.c as

44   unsigned securebits = SECUREBITS_DEFAULT;

As can be seen, this is initialised to a default value, defined in <linux/securebits.h> as

4   #define SECUREBITS_DEFAULT 0x00000000.

But for those secure settings for which the fixed bit is clear, this can be changed. Currently, it is not changed anywhere in the kernel.

21

Personalities and execution domains

Linux can run executable files that were compiled for other operating systems, as long as they are compiled into i386 machine code. One aspect of this support is to emulate any system calls not provided by Linux. This would apply to an MS-DOS or Windows program. These emulators are user-level programs, not discussed any further here.

However, if the program was compiled for a POSIX-compliant operating system, then the kernel is able to handle it directly, with only minor differences to be ironed out (e.g. the way in which system calls are invoked, or the order in which signals are numbered).

Each of these different operating system environments is known as a personality. A Linux process always has some personality, even if only its own native one. It can change personality to run a foreign program and then change back to being a Linux process again.

It is not absolutely necessary to treat each personality completely differently. As different flavours of Unix have so much in common, groups of personalities can be gathered together into what are known as execution domains. Such a domain can handle one or more personalities.

21.1 Data structures supporting personalities

As usual, we will begin the chapter with an examination of the data structures used to implement all of this, beginning with personalities.

21.1.1 Personality types

The current personality of a process is determined by the value set in the `personality` field of the `task_struct` (see Section 2.3). The different personalities currently supported by Linux are defined in the enumeration in Figure 21.1, from `<linux/personality.h>`. The values defined here go in the low byte of the personality field. The other bits are in the high-order bytes and are defined in Section 21.1.2. They indicate particular peculiarities of different personalities that have to be catered for when implementing the appropriate execution domain.

The Linux Process Manager. The Internals of Scheduling, Interrupts and Signals   John O'Gorman
© 2003 John Wiley & Sons, Ltd   ISBN: 0 470 84771 9

```
45   enum {
46       PER_LINUX           = 0x0000,
47       PER_LINUX_32BIT     = 0x0000 | ADDR_LIMIT_32BIT,
48       PER_SVR4            = 0x0001 | STICKY_TIMEOUTS | MMAP_PAGE_ZERO,
49       PER_SVR3            = 0x0002 | STICKY_TIMEOUTS | SHORT_INODE,
50       PER_SCOSVR3         = 0x0003 | STICKY_TIMEOUTS |
51                                             WHOLE_SECONDS | SHORT_INODE,
52       PER_OSR5            = 0x0003 | STICKY_TIMEOUTS | WHOLE_SECONDS,
53       PER_WYSEV386        = 0x0004 | STICKY_TIMEOUTS | SHORT_INODE,
54       PER_ISCR4           = 0x0005 | STICKY_TIMEOUTS,
55       PER_BSD             = 0x0006,
56       PER_SUNOS           = 0x0006 | STICKY_TIMEOUTS,
57       PER_XENIX           = 0x0007 | STICKY_TIMEOUTS | SHORT_INODE,
58       PER_LINUX32         = 0x0008,
59       PER_IRIX32          = 0x0009 | STICKY_TIMEOUTS,
60       PER_IRIXN32         = 0x000a | STICKY_TIMEOUTS,
61       PER_IRIX64          = 0x000b | STICKY_TIMEOUTS,
62       PER_RISCOS          = 0x000c,
63       PER_SOLARIS         = 0x000d | STICKY_TIMEOUTS,
64       PER_UW7             = 0x000e | STICKY_TIMEOUTS | MMAP_PAGE_ZERO,
65       PER_MASK            = 0x00ff,
66   };
```

Figure 21.1   Personalities supported by Linux

46   this is the standard Linux environment

47   with a view to future expansion, this defines a backward-compatible version of Linux with a 32-bit address limit. Note that it is the same personality number as the previous one, with a 32-bit limit defined.

48   this is for SVR4 executables.

49   this is for SVR3 executables.

50–52   these are both for SCO versions of Unix.

53   this is for operating systems used on WYSE terminals.

55–56   these are for BSD and SunOs executables.

57   this is for XENIX executables.

58   this is another personality for 32-bit Linux executables.

59   this is for IRIX5 32-bit executables.

60   this is for IRIX6 32-bit executables.

61   this is for IRIX6 64-bit executables.

62 this is for RiscOs executables.

63 this is for Solaris executables.

64 this is for UnixWare 7.

65 this is not a personality, but rather a mask used for stripping out the low-order byte of the `personality` field.

21.1.2 Flags for bug emulation

The high-order byte of the value identifying a personality contains flags for bug emulation. These are defined in the enumeration shown in Figure 21.2, from `<linux/personality.h>`.

```
31    enum {
32        MMAP_PAGE_ZERO =    0x0100000,
33        ADDR_LIMIT_32BIT = 0x0800000,
34        SHORT_INODE =       0x1000000,
35        WHOLE_SECONDS =     0x2000000,
36        STICKY_TIMEOUTS =   0x4000000,
37    };
```

Figure 21.2   Flags for bug emulation

32 SVR4 and UW7 map page 0 as read only, so the protection on page 0 has to be changed when moving to one of these personalities.

33 versions of Linux running on architectures with larger address spaces (e.g. Alpha) will have to take some action when moving to a personality with this flag set.

34 some operating systems, based on SVR3, seem to have a shorter version of the `struct inode`, a fundamental data structure in the input–output (IO) subsystem. The IO manager would have to be aware of this when moving to a personality with this flag set.

35 this is not used.

36 this is relevant only to the IO manager. It is used in the implementation of the `select()` system service. If set, we do not modify the given timeout parameter to reflect the time remaining.

21.1.3 Manipulating personalities

A number of macros are provided for manipulating personality values, as shown in Figure 21.3, from `<linux/personality.h>`.

```
95   #define personality(pers)    (pers & PER_MASK)
100  #define get_personality      (current->personality)
```

Figure 21.3   Manipulating personalities

95   this returns the base personality without the flags. PER_MASK (see Section 21.1.1) strips of all but the lowest 8 bits.

100   this evaluates to the personality of the currently running process.

21.2   Data structures for tracking execution domains

An execution domain consists of data and code that specify how fundamental operations, such as system service handling or signal numbering, are to be carried out for a particular personality. Execution domains can be loaded and unloaded dynamically.

This section will consider the basic structure used to identify an execution domain as well as the systemwide structures used for tracking all known domains. This includes a default domain, which will also be examined.

21.2.1   The `exec_domain` structure

The information that identifies any particular execution domain to the process manager is stored in a `struct exec_domain`; see Figure 21.4, from `<linux/personality.h>`. The `task_struct` has an `exec_domain` field, which points to the descriptor representing the execution domain currently in use (see Section 2.1).

```
75   typedef void (*handler_t)(int, struct pt_regs *);
76
77   struct exec_domain {
78       const char            *name;
79       handler_t             handler;
80       unsigned char         pers_low;
81       unsigned char         pers_high;
82       unsigned long         *signal_map;
83       unsigned long         *signal_invmap;
84       struct map_segment    *err_map;
85       struct map_segment    *socktype_map;
86       struct map_segment    *sockopt_map;
87       struct map_segment    *af_map;
88       struct module         *module;
89       struct exec_domain    *next,
90   };
```

Figure 21.4   Description of an execution domain

75   this is a prototype of the function used to change domain and personality. It takes two parameters: the number of the interrupt used to call the system service, and a pointer to the saved registers on the kernel stack.

78–79	the first two members are referenced by offset from assembly source (in entry.S), so their relative positions here are important.
78	this is a pointer to an ASCII string giving the name of the domain.
79	this is a pointer to the handler used in this domain to change domain and personality.
80–81	each execution domain can handle a range of personalities (this may be as small as one). These two fields contain the bounds of that range.
82	this is a pointer to the signal mapping field.
83	this is a pointer to the reverse signal mapping field.
84–87	the next four fields are unused at present. They are intended for extending the sort of mapping presently implemented for signals to error codes and into the area of network communication. They are merely described here, not explained.
84	this is a pointer to a struct map_segment, which will map error codes.
85	this is a pointer to a struct map_segment, which will map socket types.
86	this is a pointer to a struct map_segment, which will map socket options.
87	this is a pointer to a struct map_segment, which will map address families.
88	this is a pointer to a struct module, representing the module that implements the particular execution domain.
89	all valid execution domains are kept on a linked list, threaded through this field.

21.2.2 The execution domain list

The kernel maintains a linked list of all registered execution domains. The various data structures involved in this are shown in Figure 21.5, from kernel/exec_domain.c.

```
23    static struct exec_domain *exec_domains = default_exec_domain;
24    static rwlock_t exec_domains_lock = RW_LOCK_UNLOCKED;
25
26
27    static u_long ident_map[32] = {
28         0,   1,   2,   3,   4,   5,   6,   7,
29         8,   9,  10,  11,  12,  13,  14,  15,
30        16,  17,  18,  19,  20,  21,  22,  23,
31        24,  25,  26,  27,  28,  29,  30,  31
32    };
33
34    struct exec_domain default_exec_domain = {
35         "Linux",
36         default_handler,
37         0, 0,
```

```
38         ident_map,
39         ident_map,
40     };
```

Figure 21.5   The execution domain list

23   this is the head of the linked list of `struct exec_domain`. It is initialised pointing to the default domain, which is always present (see lines 34–40).

24   this lock gives mutual exclusion on the list.

27–32   different execution domains may have numbered signals in different ways. One important aspect of the implementation of an execution domain is to be able to map between these different numberings – in both directions. Sometimes it needs to know: 'What is the Linux equivalent of signal x?' Other times, the question is: 'What is the equivalent, in this domain, of Linux signal x?' This mapping is implemented by using two 32-bit arrays. One is for mapping from standard Linux to a particular execution domain, the other from a particular domain to standard Linux, but standard Linux is itself an execution domain like any other so, for consistency, it is also necessary to supply an identity mapping, as given by the initialisation values of this array.

34–40   this is the `struct exec_domain` representing the default execution domain, or standard Linux. It is always present, the last entry on the list.

35   this domain's name is 'Linux'.

36   this field is a pointer to the handler for the domain. Here, the default handler is used (see Section 21.2.3).

37   these two fields represent the bounds of the range of personalities handled by this domain. In the present case, it handles only personality 0, Linux.

38–39   these two fields point to the signal conversion maps. In this case, both point to the identity map (see lines 27–32).

Note that the remaining fields are not initialised. In particular, the link field is not initialised to NULL.

21.2.3 The default system service handler

When the default execution domain is used, the handler is set to `default_handler()`, as shown in Figure 21.6, from `kernel/exec_domain.c`. This implements a change of handler and domain, when required by the `exec()` of a foreign binary image.

```
43    static void
44    default_handler(int segment, struct pt_regs *regp)
45    {
46         u_long    pers = 0;

58         switch (segment) {
59    #ifdef __i386__
```

```
60          case 0x07:
61                  pers = abi_defhandler_lcall7;
62                  break;
63          case 0x27:
64                  pers = PER_SOLARIS;
65                  break;
66   #endif
67          }
68          set_personality(pers);
69
70          if (current->exec_domain->handler != default_handler)
71                  current->exec_domain->handler(segment, regp);
72          else
73                  send_sig(SIGSEGV, current, 1);
74   }
```

Figure 21.6   The default system call handler

44   the parameters are the number of the interrupt used to call the system service, and a pointer to the `struct pt_regs` on the stack.

46   this sets a default personality of PER_LINUX.

58–67   there are only three possible interrupts used to enter the kernel in any Unix system on an i386. Note that this code is i386-specific, even though it is in an architecture-independent file.

60–62   if it used `lcall7`, this is a statically linked SVR4 binary, so we set the personality correctly. The appropriate personality is defined in `kernel/exec_domain.c` as:

```
251  u_long abi_defhandler_lcall7 = PER_SVR4;
```

63–65   if it used `lcall 27`, then it is a Solaris x86 binary. We set the personality to PER_SOLARIS.

68   if it used the only other possibility, INT 80, then it is a Linux binary, and `pers` still has its default value from line 46. In any case, we set the appropriate personality (including the execution domain, if necessary), using the function from Section 21.4.1.

70–71   if the execution domain just set for this personality specifies some handler other than (this) default, then we run that handler.

73   otherwise, if the handler registered for this new execution domain is `default_handler`, there is something wrong. We send a SIGSEGV to the current process, using the function from Section 18.2.7. The default handling for this signal is to terminate the process.

21.3   Registering and unregistering execution domains

It is not necessary that all execution domains be registered and loaded at boot time. Linux allows a domain to be loaded and registered dynamically, without rebooting the operating system. A domain can also be unloaded in the same way. Two functions are provided for this.

21.3.1 Registering a new execution domain

When a structure representing a new execution domain is to be added to the existing linked list of exec_domain structures, the function shown in Figure 21.7, from exec_domain.c, is used. This would typically be called by the initialisation code of the module implementing that domain.

```
109  int
110  register_exec_domain(struct exec_domain *ep)
111  {
112          struct exec_domain       *tmp;
113          int                      err = -EBUSY;
114
115          if (ep == NULL)
116                  return -EINVAL;
117
118          if (ep->next != NULL)
119                  return -EBUSY;
120
121          write_lock(&exec_domains_lock);
122          for (tmp = exec_domains; tmp; tmp = tmp->next) {
123                  if (tmp == ep)
124                          goto out;
125          }
126
127          ep->next = exec_domains;
128          exec_domains = ep;
129          err = 0;
130
131  out:
132          write_unlock(&exec_domains_lock);
133          return (err);
134  }
```

Figure 21.7   Registering a new execution domain

110   the parameter is a pointer to the struct exec_domain representing the new domain. This structure has been described in Section 21.2.1.

113   this sets up a default return value of EBUSY.

115–116   a valid pointer must be supplied; NULL is invalid.

118–119   if the link field is valid, that means the structure is already linked into the list and is in use. It cannot be registered a second time, so we return EBUSY.

121–132 as the linked list of domains is going to be manipulated, we take out a write lock on it, using the macro from Section 5.6.

122–125 this loop searches along the linked list of domains, beginning with the head pointer exec_domains, until it comes to the NULL pointer in the last one.

123–124 if an existing entry matches the one now being inserted (meaning it is already there) we break out of the loop and return EBUSY (from line 113).

127 this new domain is not in the list, so we insert it at the head of the list. This line sets its next pointer to the previous first entry.

128 now we set the header field to point to this new entry.

129 this sets up a success return value.

133 the return value is 0 for success; on failure, it is either EBUSY or EINVAL.

21.3.2 Unregistering an execution domain

When the structure representing an execution domain is to be removed from the linked list of handlers, the function shown in Figure 21.8, from kernel/exec_domain.c, is used. This would typically be called by the termination code of the module implementing that domain.

```
136  int
137  unregister_exec_domain(struct exec_domain *ep)
138  {
139      struct exec_domain        **epp;
140
141      epp = &exec_domains;
142      write_lock(&exec_domains_lock);
143      for (epp = &exec_domains; *epp; epp = &(*epp)->next) {
144          if (ep == *epp)
145              goto unregister;
146      }
147      write_unlock(&exec_domains_lock);
148      return -EINVAL;
149
150  unregister:
151      *epp = ep->next;
152      ep->next = NULL;
153      write_unlock(&exec_domains_lock);
154      return 0;
155  }
```

Figure 21.8   Unregistering an execution domain

137 the parameter is a pointer to the structure representing the domain to be removed.

141   the value in `epp` is the address of the header of the list, the pointer variable `exec_domains`, from Section 21.2.2. So `epp` is pointing to a pointer to a `struct exec_domain` (the first in the list). This line is redundant, as it is repeated at line 143.

142–147   as the linked list of domains is going to be manipulated, we take out a write lock on it, using the macro from Section 5.6.

143–146   this loop searches along the linked list of domains, until it comes to the `NULL` pointer in the last one.

144–145   `epp` is always the *address* of the pointer to the *next* element; `*epp` is the pointer to the next element. So this is checking if the next element is the one being sought. If it is, we jump out of the loop (holding the write lock).

147   if all entries in the list were checked, and no match was found, we give back the lock.

148   we return `EINVAL`, as the parameter supplied did not point to a valid `struct exec_domain` in the list.

150   control transfers here when a match has been found, with `epp` pointing to the `next` field in the predecessor of the one to be removed. The entry to be removed is identified by the supplied parameter `ep`.

151   the `next` field in the predecessor is set to point to the `next` field in the successor. This bridges over the one to be removed, which is now out of the list.

152   this marks the structure just removed as not in use.

153   we give back the lock on the linked list.

154   we return success.

21.3.3 Adjusting execution domain module usecounts

The macros shown in Figure 21.9, from `<linux/personality.h>`, are used when a process changes execution domain, to keep track of how many processes are using the module that implements a particular domain.

```
111  #define get_exec_domain(ep)                          \
112  do {                                                 \
113       if (ep != NULL && ep->module != NULL)           \
114            __MOD_INC_USE_COUNT(ep->module);           \
115  } while (0)
120  #define put_exec_domain(ep)                          \
121  do {                                                 \
122       if (ep != NULL && ep->module != NULL)           \
123            __MOD_DEC_USE_COUNT(ep->module);           \
124  } while (0)
```

Figure 21.10   Adjusting execution domain use counts

111–115   this macro increments the use count when a process enters an execution domain.

111   the parameter is a pointer to a `struct exec_domain`.

113–114   if the execution domain exists, and a module has been loaded to implement that domain, then we increment the use count field in that module

120–124   this macro decrements the use count when a process leaves an execution domain.

122–123   if the execution domain exists, and a module has been loaded to implement that domain, then we decrement the use count field in that module

21.4   Setting a new personality

Personality is changed only when a new executable file is run, and for that reason it is considered the domain of the file manager. A function called `search_binary_handler()` goes through a list of installed binary handlers until it finds one that recognises the format of the new executable file. It then calls the `load_binary()` method associated with this binary format. As part of its work, this function calls `set_personality()`, passing it the personality number corresponding to the new executable file.

Changing personality is handled in two stages; there is a macro that checks the parameter, to decide if the personality needs changing and a worker function that actually changes values.

21.4.1   Checking if personality needs to be changed

The macro shown in Figure 21.10, from `<linux/personality.h>`, checks that the personality requires changing and, if so, calls the `__set_personality()` function (see Section 21.4.2) and evaluates to whatever that function returns. Otherwise, it evaluates to 0: success.

```
105  #define set_personality(pers)                                    \
106  ((current->personality == pers) ? 0 : __set_personality(pers))
```

Figure 21.10   Macro to change personality

21.4.2   Changing personality

The function shown in Figure 21.11, from `kernel/exec_domain.c`, does the actual work of changing the personality and the execution domain if necessary.

```
159  int
160  __set_personality(u_long personality)
161  {
162      struct exec_domain      *ep, *oep;
163
```

```
164        ep = lookup_exec_domain(personality);
165        if (ep == current->exec_domain) {
166            current->personality = personality;
167            return 0;
168        }
169
170        if (atomic_read(&current->fs->count) != 1) {
171            struct fs_struct *fsp, *ofsp;
172
173            fsp = copy_fs_struct(current->fs);
174            if (fsp == NULL) {
175                put_exec_domain(ep);
176                return -ENOMEM; ;
177            }
178
179            task_lock(current);
180            ofsp = current->fs;
181            current->fs = fsp;
182            task_unlock(current);
183
184            put_fs_struct(ofsp);
185        }

192        current->personality = personality;
193        oep = current->exec_domain;
194        current->exec_domain = ep;
195        set_fs_altroot();
196
197        put_exec_domain(oep);
198
199        printk(KERN_DEBUG "[%s:%d]: set personality to %lx\n",
200        current->comm, current->pid, personality);
201        return 0;
202  }
```

Figure 21.11   Function to change personality

164   this gets a pointer to the `struct exec_domain` corresponding to the new personality. See Section 21.4.3 for the function, which also increments the use count in the module implementing this execution domain.

165–168   if this execution domain is the same as that of the current process, then we simply change the personality and return success. Remember, one execution domain can service more than one personality.

170–185   if the current process is sharing its file system structure with some other process, that cannot continue now that the current process is going to change execution domain, so this block of code changes the root file system type. This is largely the province of the file manager and will just be touched on here.

173 this function, which is part of the file manager, allocates a new `fs_struct` and copies values from the old one to it. It returns a pointer to the new structure in `fsp`.

174–177 this block of code is for the rare occasion when it is not possible to allocate memory for a new `fs_struct`.

175 the `lookup_exec_domain()` function at line 164 incremented the use count field in the module implementing the execution domain it found. Now that it is not possible to change root file systems, the personality is not going to be changed, this process will not be using the new execution domain, so the number of users needs to be adjusted back to where it was. This macro merely decrements the use count in the module implementing that execution domain (see Section 21.3.3).

176 as there is a problem with allocating memory, we return ENOMEM.

179–182 otherwise, a `struct fs_struct` has been allocated. While linking it into the current `task_struct`, we take out a lock on that structure, using the function from Section 7.2.5.

180–181 we remember the old one, but set up the new one.

184 this function, which is part of the file system manager, decrements the use count on the old `struct fs_struct`. If this makes it 0, then we return the space to the memory manager.

192 whether the file system had to be changed or not, we change the `personality` field in the `task_struct`.

193 this saves a copy of the pointer to the current execution domain.

194 this sets the execution domain of the current process to correspond to the new personality, as determined at line 164.

195 this function is part of the file system manager. It sets up a new root file system.

197 we decrement the use count in the module implementing the old execution domain (see Section 21.3.3 for the macro).

199–200 we print this message on the console, giving the name of the program, the `pid` of the process, and the number of the new personality.

21.4.3 Finding the execution domain corresponding to a personality

The function shown in Figure 21.12, from `kernel/exec_domain.c`, is passed the identifier for a particular personality and returns a pointer to the execution domain corresponding to it.

```
76    static struct exec_domain *
77    lookup_exec_domain(u_long personality)
78    {
79        struct exec_domain *    ep;
80        u_long                  pers = personality(personality);
81
```

```
82        read_lock(&exec_domains_lock);
83        for (ep = exec_domains; ep; ep = ep->next) {
84        if (pers >= ep->pers_low && pers <= ep->pers_high)
85              if (try_inc_mod_count(ep->module))
86                      goto out;
87        }
88
89   #ifdef CONFIG_KMOD
90        read_unlock(&exec_domains_lock);
91        {
92             char buffer[30[;
93             sprintf(buffer, "personality-%ld", pers);
94             request_module(buffer);
95        }
96        read_lock(&exec_domains_lock);
97
98        for (ep = exec_domains; ep; ep = ep->next) {
99             if (pers >= ep->pers_low && pers <= ep->pers_high)
100                 if (try_inc_mod_count(ep->module))
101                        goto out;
102       }
103  #endif
104
105       ep = &default_exec_domain;
106  out:
107       read_unlock(&exec_domains_lock);
108       return (ep);
109  }
```

Figure 21.12   Finding the execution domain corresponding to a particular personality

80   this macro from Section 21.1.3 guarantees that only the 8 low-order bits are set.

82–107   this lock guarantees mutual exclusion on the linked list of struct exec_domain [see Section 5.7.2.1 for the read_lock() function].

83–87   the exec_domains field is a pointer, heading the linked list of such domains. This loop searches through the list. It will terminate when it gets to the last one; the ep pointer will be NULL.

84   for each one, if the personality being checked is outside the bounds of the particular execution domain, we go around again.

85   this line is executed if it is within the range handled by this execution domain. The function try_inc_mod_count () is part of the implementation of kernel modules, which is not considered in this book; it returns TRUE if it succeeds. If the use count of the module implementing this domain cannot be incremented, we try another one.

86   otherwise a suitable one has been found and can be returned to the caller.

89–103   execution should only get here if all the registered execution domains have been tried and none fits. So we attempt to load a module that implements an appropriate execution domain. CONFIG_KMOD means that the kernel module loader is installed.

90–95   the read lock is not necessary for these lines, so it can be given back [see Section 5.7.2.4 for the read_unlock() macro].

93   this builds up a parameter (for the function called on the next line) in the buffer declared at line 92. The argument pers is a long and is converted to decimal format.

94   an attempt is made to load the module that implements this personality. Kernel modules are not covered in this book.

96–102   now that a new module may have been loaded at line 93, we try again. This code is a repeat of lines 82–87.

105   this line is executed only if, even after loading a new module, all registered execution domains have been tried and no appropriate one has been found. The next best one is the default. This is always first in the list.

108   this returns a pointer, either to the execution domain being sought or to the default one.

22

Tracing processes

Unix provides a facility by which one process can control, or trace, the execution of another. Although this can be implemented at different levels of granularity it generally means that the process can be stopped at predetermined points. When stopped in this way, its variables can be read (and changed) by the tracing process. This tracing mechanism is typically used when a process is not behaving in the expected way and the software developer needs more fine-grained information about just what is going on, line by line. Linux, as a good Unix clone, also provides this tracing ability.

22.1 Setting up a process to be traced

The first step in all this is to set up a particular process to be traced. This involves checking permissions, checking flags in the `task_struct`, and stopping the traced process. The function to do that is shown in Figure 22.1, from `kernel/ptrace.c`.

```
55   int ptrace_attach(struct task_struct *task)
56   {
57       task_lock(task);
58       if (task->pid <= 1)
59           goto bad;
60       if (task == current)
61           goto bad;
62       if (!task->mm)
63           goto bad;
64       if(((current->uid != task->euid) ||
65           (current->uid != task->suid) ||
66           (current->uid != task->uid) ||
67           (current->gid != task->egid) ||
68           (current->gid != task->sgid) ||
69           (!cap_issubset(task->cap_permitted,
                                    current->cap_permitted)) ||
70           (current->gid != task->gid)) &&
                                    !capable(CAP_SYS_PTRACE))
```

The Linux Process Manager. The Internals of Scheduling, Interrupts and Signals   John O'Gorman
© 2003 John Wiley & Sons, Ltd   ISBN: 0 470 84771 9

```
71              goto bad;
72          rmb();
73          if (!task->mm->dumpable && !capable(CAP_SYS_PTRACE))
74              goto bad;
75
76          if (task->ptrace & PT_PTRACED)
77              goto bad;

80          task->ptrace |= PT_PTRACED;
81          if (capable(CAP_SYS_PTRACE))
82              task->ptrace |= PT_PTRACE_CAP;
83          task_unlock(task);
84
85          write_lock_irq(&tasklist_lock);
86          if (task->p_pptr != current) {
87              REMOVE_LINKS(task);
88              task->p_pptr = current;
89              SET_LINKS(task);
90          }
91          write_unlock_irq(&tasklist_lock);
92
93          send_sig(SIGSTOP, task, 1);
94          return 0;
95
96  bad:
97          task_unlock(task);
98          return -EPERM;
99  }
```

Figure 22.1   Set up a process to be traced

55   the only parameter is a pointer to the `task_struct` of the process to be traced.

57–83   the `task_struct` is locked, using the function from Section 7.2.5, so that no other process (not even the traced one itself) can access it, until all the modifications have been made.

58–59   it is not possible to trace `init`, or groups of processes at the same time [0 or negative process identification (pid) numbers]. If the supplied parameter does not identify one specific process, return EPERM.

60–61   a process cannot trace itself, either.

62–63   a process without a memory context would be a zombie; tracing such a process does not make sense, and so it is not allowed.

64–71   only certain processes have the right to trace others. The parentheses in this `if` statement have to be paired up carefully. If even one of the first seven conditions is TRUE, and the tracing process does not have the CAP_SYS_PTRACE capability, then the request is invalid.

64–66 the user identification (uid) number of the caller must match the uid, saved uid, and effective uid of the process to be traced.

67–68 the gid of the caller must match both the effective and saved gid of the process to be traced.

69 the permitted capabilities of the target process cannot be greater than those of the caller. Tracing a process with greater capabilities would be a potential security leak (see Section 20.2.7 for the macro).

70 the gid of the caller must match the gid of the process to be traced.

The capable() function was discussed in Section 20.4.1. If the caller has this capability, then all the foregoing checks are irrelevant – it can trace any process.

72 this is a read memory barrier, which forces strict computer processing unit (CPU) ordering between the two processes.

73–74 by forcing a process to crash, and produce a core dump, one can get access to confidential data within the address space of a process. To prevent this, a security-sensitive process is not allowed to produce a core dump. This is indicated by setting the dumpable field in its mm_struct to 0. A process that is not allowed to produce a core dump cannot be traced, either, for the same reasons, unless, of course, the tracer has the CAP_SYS_PTRACE capability. The capable() function is described in Section 20.4.1.

76–77 if the PT_PTRACED flag is already set in the task_struct, we return EPERM. A process can have only one tracer at a time.

80 the checking is finished at this stage; the remainder of the code sets up tracing. We set the PT_PTRACED flag. This indicates to the system that the process in question is being traced.

81–82 if the tracer has this capability, we set the PT_PTRACE_CAP flag as well.

83 the lock on the task_struct of the process to be traced can be released at this stage.

85–91 the process list may be manipulated here, so the tasklist_lock on the whole list is needed now.

86–90 if the tracer is not the immediate parent of the process being traced, this block of code sets it up as the parent.

87 this macro was described in Section 3.1.1. It removes task from the family tree.

88 we redesignate task as a child of the tracing process (current).

89 this macro was described in Section 3.1.2. It relinks task back into the family tree, as the youngest child of the tracing process.

93 this sends a SIGSTOP signal to task. It is going to be traced, so we stop it right now. The send_sig() function was described in Section 18.2.7. The third parameter, 1, means that the signal is being sent from kernel mode.

94 we return success.

22.2 Discontinuing tracing a process

The tracer may decide to stop tracing at any time. Any changes made to the process structure must be undone and the traced process allowed to continue cleanly on its way, as if nothing had happened. This is implemented in two steps. First, there is an architecture-independent function, which does most of the work. It, in turn, calls an architecture-specific function, to turn off single stepping in the processor.

22.2.1 Architecture-independent disabling of tracing

The function used to disable tracing is shown in Figure 22.2, from `kernel/ptrace.c`.

```
101  nt ptrace_detach(struct task_struct *child, unsigned int data)
102  {
103        if ((unsigned long) data > _NSIG)
104              return -EIO;

107        ptrace_disable(child);

110        child->ptrace = 0;
111        child->exit_code = data;
112        write_lock_irq(&tasklist_lock);
113        REMOVE_LINKS(child);
114        child->p_pptr = child->p_opptr;
115        SET_LINKS(child);
116        write_unlock_irq(&tasklist_lock);

119        wake_up_process(child);
120        return 0;
121  }
```

Figure 22.2   Discontinuing the tracing of a process

101   the parameters are a pointer to the `task_struct` of the process being traced and the number of a signal to be delivered to the child.

103–104   if the value of the second parameter is greater than _NSIG (See Section 17.1.1) then we return `EIO`. It must be a valid signal number.

107   this architecture-specific function is discussed in Section 22.2.2. It turns off the single-stepping bit in the EFLAGS register of the traced process.

110–116   the child must be returned to the state it was in before tracing began. This includes its original place in the family tree, if this was changed by the function in Section 22.1.

110   the process is no longer being traced, so all bits in this field are cleared.

111   the `data` parameter is made available to the traced process in its `task_struct`.

112–116   the process list is being manipulated here, so the `tasklist_lock` on the whole list is needed.

113   this macro was described in Section 3.1.1. It removes `task` from the family tree.

114   the child's original parent was saved here when it was created.

115   this macro was described in Section 3.1.2. It relinks `task` back into the family tree, as the youngest child of its original parent. Note that this may have moved it down in relation to its siblings.

119   this function, described in Section 4.7.5, changes the state of the traced process to `TASK_RUNNING` and moves it to the runqueue.

22.2.2   Architecture-specific disabling of tracing

When tracing is turned off, and a previously traced process is going its own way, it is important to ensure that the single-step bit is cleared in the EFLAGS register. This is taken care of by the function shown in Figure 22.3, from `arch/i386/kernel/ptrace.c`.

```
142  void ptrace_disable(struct task_struct *child)
143  {
144       long tmp;
145
146       tmp = get_stack_long(child, EFL_OFFSET) & ~TRAP_FLAG;
147       put_stack_long(child, EFL_OFFSET, tmp);
148  }
```

Figure 22.3   Clearing the single-step bit

146   this reads the saved copy of the EFLAGS register on the kernel stack, using the function from Section 22.4.3.1. Then it clears the TRAP_FLAG (single-stepping) bit. EFL_OFFSET defines the position of the EFLAGS value on the stack (see Section 22.4.3.4).

147   that value is written back to the kernel stack of the traced process, using the function from Section 22.4.3.2. When the child next runs, this is the value that will be copied back to the hardware register.

22.3   Accessing the memory space of a traced process

The whole purpose of tracing a process is so that the tracer can access its memory space, as and when required. The functions provided for accessing the memory space of the traced process will be examined in this section. There are actually three memory spaces involved here. These functions are always executed by the tracer, so the user space of the current process is always involved. The memory management functions for accessing this have been seen many times before. The traced process is actually stopped, and it must be possible to access the user space of a stopped process. This is a new aspect of the memory manager. Then there is the kernel space of the current process, which is also involved in the transfer of data.

22.3.1   Reading data from a traced process

The function that reads from the memory space of a traced process is shown in Figure 22.4, from `kernel/ptrace.c`.

```
183  int ptrace_readdata(struct task_struct *tsk,
                                unsigned long src, char *dst, int len)
184  {
185       int copied = 0;
186
187       while (len > 0) {
188            char buf[128];
189            int this_len, retval;
190
191            this_len = (len > sizeof(buf)) ? sizeof(buf) : len;
192            retval = access_process_vm(tsk, src, buf,
                                                this_len, 0);
193            if (!retval) {
194                 if (copied)
195                      break;
196                 return -EIO;
197            }
198            if (copy_to_user(dst, buf, retval))
199                 return -EFAULT;
200            copied += retval;
201            src += retval;
202            dst += retval;
203            len -= retval;
204       }
205       return copied;
206  }
```

Figure 22.4   Reading from the memory space of a traced process

183   the parameters are a pointer to the `task_struct` of the process being traced, the address in the memory space of that process from which to read, a pointer to the location in the tracer to which the data are to be written, and the length of the data.

185   this variable is used to accumulate a count of bytes as they are transferred. Its final value is returned to the caller.

187–204   this loop is traversed repeatedly until all the information requested has been copied to the tracing process.

191   if the total remaining to be transferred (`len`) is greater than one buffer-full (128 bytes), then we transfer a buffer-full this time; otherwise we transfer the full amount.

192   this memory management function transfers `this_len` bytes from the area in the (stopped) traced process indicated by `src` to `buf[]` in the kernel. It returns the number of bytes actually read. It is a twoway function; it will copy to or from user space. The value of the final parameter indicates the direction of the transfer. 0 means copy *to* the kernel; 1 means copy *from* the kernel.

193–197 this block of code is executed if we were unable to read on this iteration of the loop.

194–195 if previous reads were successful, then we break out of the loop and return the number of bytes read so far.

196 if this was the first attempt to read, we return EIO.

198–199 now we attempt to copy retval bytes from buf[] in the kernel to dst in the calling process. If unable to do so, we return EFAULT.

200 we increment copied by the number of bytes read this time.

201–202 we advance the source and destination pointers by the number of bytes copied.

203 there are retval fewer bytes to be read next time around.

22.3.2 Writing data to a traced process

The function shown in Figure 22.5, from kernel/ptrace.c, writes data to the memory space of a traced process. It is very similar to the function described in Section 22.3.1, so only the differences will be noted.

```
208  int ptrace_writedata(struct task_struct *tsk, char * src,
                                    unsigned long dst, int len)
209  {
210      int copied = 0;
211
212      while (len > 0) {
213          char buf[128];
214          int this_len, retval;
215
216          this_len = (len > sizeof(buf)) ? sizeof(buf) : len;
217          if (copy_from_user(buf, src, this_len))
218              return -EFAULT;
219          retval = access_process_vm(tsk, dst, buf,
                                    this_len, 1);
220          if (!retval) {
221              if (copied)
222                  break;
223              return -EIO;
224          }
225          copied += retval;
226          src += retval;
227          dst += retval;
228          len -= retval;
```

```
229        }
230        return copied;
231  }
```

Figure 22.5 Writing to the memory space of a traced process

208–216 see lines 183–191 in Section 22.3.1.

217–218 now we attempt to copy `retval` bytes from `src` in the calling process to `buf[]` in the kernel. If unable to do so, we return EFAULT.

219 this memory management function transfers `this_len` bytes from `buf[]` in the kernel to the area in the traced process indicated by `dst`. It returns the number of bytes actually written. The final parameter means copy *from* the kernel.

220–224 see lines 193–197 in Section 22.3.1.

225–228 see lines 200–203 in Section 22.3.1.

22.4 Manipulating register values in the traced process

Two functions are provided to read and write the saved register values of the process being traced. As the tracer is currently running, the traced process must be in the TASK_STOPPED state, so its register values are currently saved on its kernel stack. It is these values that are manipulated, using a number of subsidiary functions for accessing the stack.

22.4.1 Writing to a register

The function shown in Figure 22.6, from `arch/i386/kernel/ptrace.c`, writes to the field in the `struct pt_regs` on the kernel stack of the traced process, corresponding to a specified hardware register.

```
73   static int putreg(struct task_struct *child,
74       unsigned long regno, unsigned long value)
75   {
76       switch (regno >> 2) {
77           case FS:
78               if (value && (value & 3) != 3)
79                   return -EIO;
80               child->thread.fs = value;
81               return 0;
82           case GS:
83               if (value && (value & 3) != 3)
84                   return -EIO;
85               child->thread.gs = value;
86               return 0;
87           case DS:
88           case ES:
89               if (value && (value & 3) != 3)
```

```
90                          return -EIO;
91                      value &= 0xffff;
92                      break;
93                  case SS:
94                  case CS:
95                      if ((value & 3) != 3)
96                          return -EIO;
97                      value &= 0xffff;
98                      break;
99                  case EFL:
100                     value &= FLAG_MASK;
101                     value |=
                            get_stack_long(child, EFL_OFFSET) & ~FLAG_MASK;
102                     break;
103             }
104             if (regno > GS*4)
105                 regno -- 2*4;
106             put_stack_long(child, regno - sizeof(struct pt_regs), value);
107             return 0;
108     }
```

Figure 22.6   Writing from a register

73–74   the parameters are a pointer to the `task_struct` of the traced process, a byte offset for the register from the bottom of the stack, and the value to be written.

76–103   as each register takes up four bytes on the stack, dividing the offset by 4 gives the ordinal number of the register on the stack. Registers are identified by symbolic constants, defined in Section 22.4.3.3. This `switch` statement does some preliminary processing appropriate to different register types.

77–81   this is used if dealing with the FS register.

78–79   a value other than 0 is being written, *and* both of the low-order bits are not set. Any attempt to clear the low-order 2 bits (to change to kernel space) is invalid, so we return EIO. A value of 0 is, however, valid.

80   the value of the FS register is not saved in the `struct pt_regs` on the stack, rather in the `thread` structure. This assignment changes the saved value.

81   we return success. No further code is executed in this function.

82–86   the comments on lines 77–81 apply also to the GS register.

87–92   these apply to the data or extra segment registers (DS and ES, respectively).

89–90   any attempt to clear the low-order 2 bits (to change to kernel space) is invalid, so we return EIO. A value of 0 is, however, valid.

91   we clear the high-order 16 bits of the `value` parameter, just in case they were set. A segment selector is only 16 bits. The high-order bits must be 0. Note that this does not change the saved value, yet.

93–98   this applies to the stack or code segment registers (SS and CS, respectively). Any attempt to clear the low-order 2 bits (to change to kernel space) is invalid, so we return EIO.

95   note the subtle difference here. We check only that both of the low-order bits are not set. A value of 0 would not be legitimate here.

97   we clear the high-order 16 bits of the value parameter, just in case they were set. A segment selector is only 16 bits. The high-order bits must be 0. Note that this does not change the saved value, yet.

99–102   this applies to the EFLAGS register (EFL). The user can change only a subset of the bits in this.

100   only those bits set in FLAG_MASK are still set now in value. This mask determines the bits to which the user has access (see Section 22.4.3.4).

101   this reads from EFLAGS on the stack of the traced process, removes any bits allowed by FLAG_MASK, and adds the remainder to value. The get_stack_long() function is described in Section 22.4.3.1. The EFL_OFFSET, which is a negative offset from the top of the stack frame, is defined in Section 22.4.3.4.

104–107   any other (e.g. general purpose) registers fall through the switch statement, so that all registers, except FS and GS, are dealt with here.

104–105   if the specified offset is greater than 40, we reduce it by 8. This is to overcome a discrepancy between the order of registers in a struct pt_regs and the order assumed by the enumeration used in regno (see Section 22.4.3.3), where FS and GS are interpolated between ES and ORIG_EAX.

106   we write value to the appropriate place on the stack of the traced process.

- regno is a byte offset from the bottom of the stack.

- regno − size(struct pt_regs) is a negative byte offset from the top of the stack frame, which is what the put_stack_long() function wants (see Section 22.4.3.2).

107   we return success. Note there is no error return from this function.

22.4.2 Reading from a register

The function shown in Figure 22.7, from arch/i386/kernel/ptrace.c, reads the saved value of a specified hardware register from the kernel stack of the traced process.

```
110  static unsigned long getreg(struct task_struct *child,
111         unsigned long regno)
112  {
113         unsigned long retval = ~0UL;
114
115         switch (regno >> 2) {
```

```
116        case FS:
117            retval = child->thread.fs;
118            break;
119        case GS:
120            retval = child->thread.gs;
121            break;
122        case DS:
123        case ES:
124        case SS:
125        case CS:
126            retval = 0xffff;
127
128        default:
129            if (regno > GS*4)
130                regno -= 2*4;
131            regno = regno - sizeof(struct pt_regs);
132            retval &= get_stack_long(child, regno);
133        }
134        return retval;
135  }
```

Figure 22.7 Reading from a register

110–111 the parameters are a pointer to the task_struct of the traced process, and a byte offset for the register from the bottom of the stack.

113 we set up a default return value of all 1s.

115–133 as each register has 4 bytes of space on the stack, dividing the offset by 4 gives the ordinal number of the register on the stack. The switch statement does some preliminary processing appropriate to different types of register.

116–121 if dealing with the FS or GS registers, we set up retval as the full 32 bits saved in the thread structure. These registers are not part of a struct pt_regs, so are not saved on the stack, rather they are saved in the thread structure.

122–126 for the four-segment registers, we clear the high-order 16 bits of retval. Note that there is no break; control falls through into the default case.

128–132 all registers except FS and GS are dealt with here, with retval set from line 113 or line 126.

129–130 if the specified offset is greater than the offset of GS (40), we reduce it by 8. This is to overcome a discrepancy between the order of registers in a struct pt_regs and the order assumed by the enumeration used in regno; see Section 22.4.3.3, where FS and GS are interpolated between ES and ORIG_EAX.

131 the previously calculated value of regno is an offset from the bottom of the stack frame. Subtracting the size of a stack frame from this converts it to a negative offset from the top of the stack frame.

132 this reads the value from the appropriate place on the stack of the traced process. The `get_stack_long()` function is described in Section 22.4.3.1. This value is bitwise ANDed with whatever was in `retval` beforehand, so the high-order 16 bits of a segment register are guaranteed to be 0. All 32 bits of any other register are valid, because `retval` was all 1s beforehand.

134   we return the appropriate value.

22.4.3   Manipulating the stack of the traced process

Two functions are provided to read and write 32-bit values on the kernel stack of the process being traced.

22.4.3.1   Reading from the stack

The function shown in Figure 22.8, from `arch/i386/kernel/ptrace.c`, will read an `int` from the kernel stack of the traced process. The offset specifies how far the field to be read is from the top of the stack frame, as stored in `thread.esp0`.

```
47    static inline int get_stack_long(struct task_struct *task, int offset)
48
49        unsigned char *stack;
50
51        stack = (unsigned char *)task->thread.esp0;
52        stack += offset;
53        return (*((int *)stack));
54    }
```

Figure 22.8   Reading from the stack of the traced process

47   the parameters are a pointer to the `task_struct` of the process being traced, and a negative byte offset indicating how far down from the top of the stack to read.

51   the `esp0` field of `thread` points to the top of the stack frame. It is cast to be a pointer to `char`, so that the stack can be read with a granularity of one byte.

52   the `stack` variable now points to the required part of the stack.

53   we cast `stack` to be a pointer to `int` and then de-reference it. This returns the four bytes beginning at `offset`.

22.4.3.2   Writing to the stack

The function shown in Figure 22.9, from `arch/i386/kernel/ptrace.c`, will put a `long` on the kernel stack of the process specified by `task`. The offset specifies how far this `long` is down from the top of the stack, as stored in `thread.esp0`. See the comments on Section 22.4.3.1.

```
62    static inline int put_stack_long(struct task_struct *task,
63          int offset, unsigned long data)
64    {
65          unsigned char * stack;
66
67          stack = (unsigned char *) task->thread.esp0;
68          stack += offset;
69          *(unsigned long *) stack = data;
70          return 0;
71    }
```

Figure 22.9   Writing to the stack of the traced process

22.4.3.3   Offsets for register fields on the stack

The functions that manipulate saved register values on the kernel stack of a traced process reference these fields by offsets from the base of the stack. The different offsets used are shown in Figure 22.10, from <asm-i386/ptrace.h>. These are in the same order as a struct pt_regs (see Section 10.3.1.1), except that the FS and GS registers are included (lines 13–14 in Figure 22.10).

```
4     #define EBX 0
5     #define ECX 1
6     #define EDX 2
7     #define ESI 3
8     #define EDI 4
9     #define EBP 5
10    #define EAX 6
11    #define DS 7
12    #define ES 8
13    #define FS 9
14    #define GS 10
15    #define ORIG_EAX 11
16    #define EIP 12
17    #define CS 13
18    #define EFL 14
19    #define UESP 15
20    #define SS 16
21    #define FRAME_SIZE 17
```

Figure 22.10   Offsets for register fields on the stack

4–12   these are the standard fields in a struct pt_regs.

13–14   these fields are not in a struct pt_regs. This is the logical place to have them, putting them in here makes the remaining offsets in this figure to be out by 2.

15–20   these are the standard fields in a struct pt_regs.

18–20   these three fields were saved by the hardware, on an INT 80.

21   this is not a register; rather, it is the number of long fields in a stack frame.

22.4.3.4   *Accessing the* EFLAGS *register*

Care has to be taken when accessing the saved value of the EFLAGS register of a traced process. A number of constants are defined to help with this, as shown in Figure 22.11, from `arch/i386/kernel/ptrace.c`

```
31    #define FLAG_MASK 0x00044dd5

34    #define TRAP_FLAG 0x100

39    #define EFL_OFFSET ((EFL-2)*4-sizeof(struct pt_regs))
```

Figure 22.11   Accessing the EFLAGS register

31   bits set in this mask determine the flags to which the user has access.

34   the trap or single-stepping flag is bit 8.

39   this is the position of EFLAGS on the child's kernel stack, as a negative byte offset from the top of the stack frame. EFL-2 converts from the numbering scheme used in Section 22.4.3.3 to the order used in a `struct pt_regs`. Multiplying that by 4 gives a byte offset from the bottom of the stack. Subtracting the size (in bytes) of a `struct pt_regs` from this will give a negative result, the number of bytes the EFLAGS field is down from the top of the stack frame.

22.5   Traced process handling a system call

All the foregoing functions are called by the tracing or debugging process. There is one other function, called by the traced process, immediately before and after it processes a system call (see Section 10.4.3.3). This is shown in Figure 22.12, from `arch/i386/kernel/ptrace.c`.

```
442   asmlinkage void syscall_trace(void)
443   {
444         if ((current->ptrace & (PT_PTRACED|PT_TRACESYS)) !=
445         (PT_PTRACED|PT_TRACESYS))
446               return;

449         current->exit_code = SIGTRAP |
450               ((current->ptrace & PT_TRACESYSGOOD) ? 0x80 : 0);
451         current->state = TASK_STOPPED;
452         notify_parent(current, SIGCHLD);
453         schedule();

459         if (current->exit_code) {
```

```
460                 send_sig(current->exit_code, current, 1);
461                 current->exit_code = 0;
462         }
463  }
```

Figure 22.12 Notifying the tracer of a system call

444–445 both the PT_TRACED and the PT_TRACESYS bits must be set in the ptrace field of the current (traced) process; otherwise the function returns without doing anything.

449–450 this sets up an exit code, which will be available to the tracing parent. The SIGTRAP bit is set. Then, if the PT_TRACESYSGOOD bit is set in the ptrace field of the current (traced) process, bit 7 is set as well. This distinguishes between the delivery of a SIGTRAP signal and a system call.

451 this marks the traced process as stopped.

452 this sends a SIGCHLD signal to the tracing process (see Section 18.2.6.3).

453 this calls the scheduler to give up the computer processing unit (CPU). The tracing process will be run (eventually).

459–462 when this process runs again, it checks if the tracer passed back information to it in its exit_code field. It interprets that code as a signal number, which it then sends to itself. Normally, if the tracer finds SIGTRAP in the exit_code field of the traced process, it clears it to 0, so these lines are not executed, but if some other signal is specified as the reason for stopping the tracer leaves that value in the exit_code field of the traced process. By sending that signal to itself at this stage, the traced process is effectively continuing with that signal.

460 see Section 18.2.7 for the function.

461 now we clear the exit_code field, as the information in it has been acted upon.

22.6 Displaying debugging information

Sometimes the kernel needs to display information about its internal state to the user or system manager. Linux provides a series of functions for this. They are typically called when some inconsistency is detected in kernel variables, and they display on the console such information as the values in registers and on the stack.

22.6.1 Displaying interrupt and bottom-half state

The show() function in Figure 22.13, from arch/i386/kernel/irq.c, displays debugging information about the state of interrupt handling, bottom halves, and values on the stack.

```
197  static void show(char * str)
198  {
199      int i;
```

```
200        int cpu = smp_processor_id();
201
202        printk("\n%s, CPU %d:\n", str, cpu);
203        printk("irq: %d [", irqs_running());
204        for(i=0; i < smp_num_cpus; i++)
205             printk(" %d", local_irq_count(i));
206        printk(" ]\nbh: %d [", spin_is_locked(&global_bh_lock) ? 1 : 0);
207        for(i=0; i < smp_num_cpus; i++)
208             printk(" %d", local_bh_count(i));
209
210        printk(" ]\nStack dumps:");
211        for(i = 0; i < smp_num_cpus; i++) {
212             unsigned long esp;
213             if (i == cpu)
214                 continue;
215             printk("\nCPU %d:", i);
216             esp = init_tss[i].esp0;
217             if (!esp) {

222                 printk(" <unknown> ");
223                 continue;
224             }
225             esp &= ~(THREAD_SIZE-1);
226             esp += sizeof(struct task_struct);
227             show_stack((void*)esp);
228        }
229        printk("\nCPU %d:", cpu);
230        show_stack(NULL);
231        printk("\n");
232  }
```

Figure 22.13   Displaying debugging information

197   the parameter is a pointer to an informational message, displayed at line 202.

200   this gets the identification (ID) number of the processor on which we are running (see Section 7.2.1.4).

202   this prints the message supplied as a parameter and the number of the CPU.

203   this prints the numeric value returned by `irqs_running()` (Section 14.5.1.5). A value of 1 means that the kernel is running in interrupt context; 0 means it is not.

204–205   for each CPU, we print the number of interrupts currently being handled, using the macro from Section 16.5.1.2.

206   this prints 1 or 0, depending on whether the global bottom-half lock is held or not. The `spin_is_locked()` macro is described in Sections 5.3 (for the uniprocessor case) and 5.4.3.4 (for the multiprocessor case).

207–208 for each CPU, we print the number of bottom halves currently being handled. Bottom halves were discussed in Section 16.3.

210–228 this prints stack dumps for all CPUs.

211–228 we go through each CPU in turn.

213–214 we skip the CPU we are running on and go around again. This one will be dealt with in greater detail at lines 229–231.

215 we print the CPU identifier.

216 this gets the address of the top of the stack for this CPU.

217–224 this caters for the possibility that a CPU is not yet fully initialised. The `esp0` field is set to NULL in `cpu_init()`; it is initialised when the CPU returns to user space.

222–223 in that case it just prints <unknown>, and goes on to the next CPU.

225 the literal constant `THREAD_SIZE` is defined in `<asm/processor.h>` as

```
450  #define THREAD_SIZE (2*PAGE_SIZE).
```

On the i386, `PAGE_SIZE` is 0x1000, so `THREAD_SIZE` is 0x2000 or, in binary, 0010 0000 0000 0000. Then `THREAD_SIZE-1` is 0001 1111 1111 1111. That makes `~(THREAD_SIZE-1)` 1110 0000 0000 0000. ANDing that with `esp` ensures that the least-significant 13 bits in `esp` are set to 0. This means it is pointing to the bottom of the space allocated to the `task_union` (see Section 3.3.1).

226 adding the size of a `task_struct` points `esp` to the bottom of the stack space.

227 the function is discussed in Section 22.6.2. It displays values from the stack.

229 when the information about the other CPUs has been printed, we then show the information about our own CPU.

230 calling `show_stack()` with a NULL parameter causes it to display the stack of the current process.

22.6.2 Displaying stack values

The function shown in Figure 22.14, from `arch/i386/kernel/traps.c`, prints the last 24 entries on the stack. It is passed a pointer to a stack area as a parameter.

```
166  void show_stack(unsigned long * esp)
167  {
168      unsigned long *stack;
169      int i;

174      if(esp==NULL)
175          esp=(unsigned long*)&esp;
```

```
176
177        stack = esp;
178        for(i=0; i < kstack_depth_to_print; i++) {
179            if (((long) stack & (THREAD_SIZE-1)) == 0)
180                break;
181            if (i && ((i % 8) == 0))
182                printk("\n      ");
183            printk("%08lx ", *stack++);
184        }
185        printk("\n");
186        show_trace(esp);
187    }
```

Figure 22.14 Printing the stack contents

174–175 this is a debugging aid: `show_stack(NULL)` prints the back trace for the current CPU. The (NULL) parameter `esp` is on the stack, so taking the address of `esp` points `esp` to the bottom of the stack of the current process.

178–184 this loop works its way through the stack area, printing each entry. The limiting variable is defined in `arch/i386/kernel/traps.c` as

```
88    int kstack_depth_to_print = 24.
```

So, it will print the last 24 32-bit entries on the stack.

179–180 ANDing the stack pointer and `THREAD_SIZE-1` effectively sets the 19 high-order bits of `stack` to zero. If the 13 low-order bits are also 0, we have come to the end of the stack area, so we break out of the loop; this prevents us overrunning the stack area if there are fewer than 24 `long` on the stack.

181–182 we are going to output eight values to the line; this outputs a new line after every eight and indents the next line.

183 this de-references `stack` and prints it as an 8-digit hex number, followed by a space; then it increments `stack`. Unary operators have equal priority, but group right to left.

186 this function is described in Section 22.6.3. It traces back through call frames on the stack and prints this information. Note that it is passed `esp` as a parameter, not `stack`, so it begins at the bottom of the stack again.

22.6.3 Displaying call frames on the stack

The function shown in Figure 22.15, from `arch/i386/kernel/traps.c`, traces back through the call frames on the stack. It prints only those entries on the stack that might be return addresses.

```
134  void show_trace(unsigned long * stack)
135  {
136       int i;
137       unsigned long addr;
```

```
138
139          if (!stack)
140                  stack = (unsigned long*)&stack;
141
142          printk("Call Trace: ");
143          i = 1;
144          while (((long) stack & (THREAD_SIZE-1)) != 0)    {
145                  addr = *stack++;
146                  if (kernel_text_address(addr)) {
147                          if (i && ((i % 6) == 0))
148                                  printk("\n      ");
149                          printk("[<%08lx>] ", addr);
150                          i++;
151                  }
152          }
153          printk("\n");
154 }
```

Figure 22.15   Printing return addresses from the stack

139–140   if the `stack` parameter is NULL, then we take its address as parameter. This means we are to work with the current stack.

144   this prevents us from running out of the stack area. ANDing the stack pointer and `THREAD_SIZE-1` effectively sets the 19 high-order bits of `stack` to zero. If the 13 low-order bits are also 0, we have come to the end of the stack area, so we terminate the loop.

145   we take the 32 bit contents of that stack location. We de-reference `stack` and then increment it. Unary operators have equal priority, but group right to left.

146–151   if the value is an address either in the text segment of the kernel or in the region allocated to loadable modules it *may* be the address of a calling routine; if so, we print it so that someone tracing down the cause of a crash will be able to figure out the call path that was taken.

146   the function is part of the memory manager.

147–148   we are going to print six values to the line. This outputs a newline after every six and indents the next line.

149   we output the value as an 8-digit hex number, followed by a space.

150   the variable `i` is used to count the number of data items per line.

22.6.4   Displaying register contents

When a process is terminated because an exception cannot be handled, the saved values of the registers on the stack are displayed as an aid to debugging. The function to do this is shown in Figure 22.16, from `arch/i386/kernel/traps.c`.

```
189  void show_registers(struct pt_regs *regs)
```

```
190  {
191       int i;
192       int in_kernel = 1;
193       unsigned long esp;
194       unsigned short ss;
195
196       esp = (unsigned long) (&regs->esp);
197       ss = __KERNEL_DS;
198       if (regs->xcs & 3) {
199            in_kernel = 0;
200            esp = regs->esp;
201            ss = regs->xss & 0xffff;
202       }
203       printk("CPU:  %d\nEIP: %04x:[<%08lx>]
                       %s\nEFLAGS: %08lx\n",
204                      smp_processor_id(), 0xffff & regs->xcs,
                       regs->eip, print_tainted(), regs->eflags);
205       printk("eax: %08lx ebx: %08lx ecx: %08lx edx:
206       %08lx\n", regs->eax, regs->ebx, regs->ecx, regs->edx);
207       printk("esi: %08lx edi: %08lx ebp: %08lx esp:
208       %08lx\n", regs->esi, regs->edi, regs->ebp, esp);
209       printk("ds: %04x es: %04x ss: %04x\n",
210       regs->xds & 0xffff, regs->xes & 0xffff, ss);
211       printk("Process %s (pid: %d, stackpage=%08lx)",
212            current->comm, current->pid, 4096+(unsigned long)current);
217       if (in_kernel) {
218
219            printk("\nStack: ");
220            show_stack((unsigned long*)esp);
221
222            printk("\nCode: ");
223            if(regs->eip < PAGE_OFFSET)
224                goto bad;
225
226            for(i=0;i<20;i++)
227            {
228                 unsigned char c;
229                 if(__get_user(c, &((unsigned char*)regs->eip)[i])) {
230  bad:
231                      printk(" Bad EIP value.");
232                      break;
233                 }
234                 printk("%02x ", c);
235            }
236       }
237       printk("\n");
238  }
```

Figure 22.16 Displaying register contents

192 this is a flag indicating whether the function was called from within the kernel (1) or not (0). Here it is given a default value.

196 this is the address of the saved stack pointer on the stack, so `esp` is set pointing into the kernel stack.

197 this is a default value, the selector for the kernel data segment.

198–202 if the saved value of the CS register shows that the process was running in user mode before the occurrence of the exception whose handler called this function, then we make some adjustments.

199 we change the assignment made at line 192, to note that the process was not in kernel mode when the exception occurred.

200 now `esp` contains the actual saved stack pointer, pointing into the user mode stack.

201 now `ss` contains the selector for the user stack segment (i.e. the low-order 16 bits of the saved SS register).

203 204 the message gives the number of the CPU; the address of the faulting instruction (from the kernel stack) in the format **selector:[offset]**, the string returned by `print_tainted()`, and the value of EFLAGS on the kernel stack. The `print_tainted()` function outputs information about whether loaded modules have a GPL licence or not.

205–206 this prints the saved values of the four general purpose registers from the kernel stack.

207–208 this prints the saved values of the index registers, and base pointer, from the kernel stack. The final value is a pointer to either the kernel stack or the user stack (see line 200).

209–210 this prints the saved values of DS and ES from the kernel stack, clearing the high-order 16 bits before doing so. The final value is the selector for either the kernel data segment or the user stack segment (see line 201).

211–212 this prints the name of the program being executed, the `pid` of the process, and the address of the bottom of its stack page. The `current` macro always points to the `task_struct` of the current process. Incrementing this by 4096 (one page) gives the address of its stack page (see Section 3.3.1).

217–236 this block of code is executed only if the process was running in kernel mode when the exception occurred (see line 198).

220 this function, from Section 22.6.2, prints out the values on the kernel stack at the time the exception occurred. Its parameter is `esp` which, from line 196, is the address of the `esp` field in the `struct pt_regs`. It will print the 24 entries above this on the stack.

223 PAGE_OFFSET marks the division between user memory (below) and kernel memory (above). If in kernel mode, and `eip` is pointing to user memory, there is something wrong.

226–235 this prints the next 20 bytes of code, for debugging purposes.

229–232 this reads one byte. If successful, this macro returns 0. Otherwise, it prints the error message and breaks out of the `for` loop.

234 this prints that byte in hexadecimal, followed by a space.

237 this finishes the whole output with a new line.

23

Process accounting

BSD Unix introduced a mechanism for process accounting into the kernel. Whenever any process exits, an accounting record of type `struct acct` is written to a special accounting file. Linux also implements this mechanism.

Accounting can be turned on or off, and the name of the accounting file be specified, by the `acct()` system call. The BSD mechanism does no more than write these records, providing the raw accounting information. It is up to user-level programs to do useful things with the accounting log.

Accounting records are relatively small, but they are permanent and they do accumulate. It is possible that an accounting file could grow until it actually used up all the free space in the disk on which it resides. To prevent that, the system automatically turns off the writing of accounting records when the free disk space falls below a predetermined level. Such writing is resumed only when the level of free space rises above another (usually higher) predetermined level.

The kernel checks the level of free space before writing each record. Because in some circumstances this could be a totally unnecessary overhead, the checking is short-circuited if space has been checked recently. This is driven by the timer interrupt.

23.1 Data structures

There are a number of global variables used by this accounting subsystem, as well as a data structure describing the format of the record written to disk.

23.1.1 Variables used by the accounting subsystem

The global variables used by the accounting subsystem are shown in Figure 23.1, from `kernel/acct.c`.

```
67    int acct_parm[3] = {4, 2, 30};
68    #define RESUME                 (acct_parm[0])
69    #define SUSPEND                (acct_parm[1])
```

The Linux Process Manager. The Internals of Scheduling, Interrupts and Signals John O'Gorman
© 2003 John Wiley & Sons, Ltd   ISBN: 0 470 84771 9

```
70   #define ACCT_TIMEOUT        (acct_parm[2])

76   static volatile int        acct_active;
77   static volatile int        acct_needcheck;
78   static struct file         *acct_file;
79   static struct timer_list   acct_timer;
```

Figure 23.1   Variables used by the accounting subsystem

67   these constants control the amount of free space on the disk that triggers the suspension and resumption of the process accounting system as well as the time delay between each check; see the description of the following three lines.

68   this is shorthand for the first element in the array. When free space goes above this percentage, accounting can be resumed.

69   this is shorthand for the second element in the array. When free space goes below this percentage, accounting must be suspended.

70   this is shorthand for the third element in the array. This is the time delay in seconds before free space is checked again.

76   this is a binary flag that records whether accounting is turned on or off.

77   this is a binary flag, set each time the timer expires. It determines whether free disk space needs to be checked before writing a record or not.

78   this is a pointer to a data structure within the file manager, a `struct file`. This represents the accounting file to the operating system.

79   this is the timer structure used to trigger periodic checking of free disk space (see Section 15.3.1.1 for this structure).

23.1.2   The format of an accounting record

The information that is saved to the accounting file each time a process exits is encapsulated in the `struct acct` shown in Figure 23.2, from `<linux/acct.h>`.

```
35   #define ACCT_COMM   16
36
37   struct acct
38   {
39       char ac_flag;

44       __u16        ac_uid;
45       __u16        ac_gid;
46       __u16        ac_tty;
47       __u32        ac_btime;
48       comp_t       ac_utime;
```

```
49        comp_t        ac_stime;
50        comp_t        ac_etime;
51        comp_t        ac_mem;
52        comp_t        ac_io;
53        comp_t        ac_rw;
54        comp_t        ac_minflt;
55        comp_t        ac_majflt;
56        comp_t        ac_swaps;
57        __u32         ac_exitcode;
58     char ac_comm[ACCT_COMM + 1];
59     char ac_pad[10];
60   };
```

Figure 23.2   The format of an accounting record

35   this is the maximum length allowed to store the name of the program running when the process exits.

39   a number of bits in this field are used to indicate the status of the process when it terminated (see Section 23.1.3 for the defined bits).

44–45   these give the real uid and gid of the process.

46   this is an identifier for the controlling terminal, if the process had one.

47   this is the time at which the process was created, in Unix format.

48–56   to save space in the file system, these fields are compressed into a comp_t, a format specific to the accounting file (see Section 23.4).

48–49   these give the time spent by the process in user (ac_utime) and kernel (ac_stime) mode.

50   this is the elapsed time (in ticks) from when the process was created until it terminated.

51–56   these statistics are related to the memory and input–output (IO) managers and will be dealt with very summarily here.

51   this is the memory usage at the time it terminated.

52   this is the count of bytes transferred using character IO.

53   this is the number of blocks read or written using block IO.

54   this is the number of minor page faults.

55   this is the number of major page faults.

56   this is the number of times the process was swapped out.

57   this is the exitcode passed to the exit() system service.

58 this is the command name that ran the program now exiting. There is room here for a 16-character name plus a terminating 0.

59 this is padding, for future expansion.

23.1.3 Process status flags

The `struct acct` discussed in the foregoing section has an `ac_flag` field. The possible bits that can be set in that field are shown in Figure 23.3, from `<linux/acct.h>`.

```
66   #define AFORK      0x01
67   #define ASU        0x02
68   #define ACOMPAT    0x04
69   #define ACORE      0x08
70   #define AXSIG      0x10
```

Figure 23.3 Accounting flags

66 this bit indicates that the process is still running the same program as its parent was before it forked.

67 this bit indicates that the process has used superuser privileges.

68 this bit is not relevant on an i386 system.

69 this bit indicates that the process has written a core dump to disk.

70 this bit indicates that the process was killed by a signal.

23.2 Freeing disk space

There are two functions involved in this. One is executed when the timer expires; it merely sets a flag indicating that the free space needs checking. Then there is the main checking function, called each time before writing an accounting record.

23.2.1 Marking that free space needs checking

The function shown in Figure 23.4, from `kernel/acct.c`, is executed by the timer whenever it expires. It merely sets the `acct_needcheck` flag. The address of this function is written to the `acct_timer` structure by the system service that sets up accounting, `acct()`.

```
85   static void acct_timeout(unsigned long unused)
86   {
87       acct_needcheck = 1;
88   }
```

Figure 23.4 Marking that free space needs checking

23.2.2 Checking free space

The function that actually checks the level of free space in the file system is shown in Figure 23.5, from `kernel/acct.c`. It checks the amount of free space and suspends or resumes accounting accordingly.

```
93    static int check_free_space(struct file *file)
94    {
95        struct statfs sbuf;
96        int res;
97        int act;
98
99        lock_kernel();
100       res = acct_active;
101       if (!file !acct_needcheck)
102           goto out;
103       unlock_kernel();

106       if (vfs_statfs(file->f_dentry->d_inode->i_sb, &sbuf))
107           return res;
108
109       if (sbuf.f_bavail <= SUSPEND * sbuf.f_blocks /100)
110           act = -1;
111       else if (sbuf.f_bavail >= RESUME * sbuf.f_blocks /100)
112           act = 1;
113       else
114           act = 0;

120       lock_kernel();
121       if (file != acct_file) {
122           if (act)
123               res = act>0;
124           goto out;
125       }
126
127       if (acct_active) {
128           if (act < 0) {
129               acct_active = 0;
130               printk(KERN_INFO "Process accounting paused\n");
131           }
132       } else {
133           if (act > 0) {
134               acct_active = 1;
135               printk(KERN_INFO "Process accounting resumed\n");
136           }
137       }
138
139       del_timer(&acct_timer);
140       acct_needcheck = 0;
```

```
141        acct_timer.expires = jiffies + ACCT_TIMEOUT*HZ;
142        add_timer(&acct_timer);
143        res = acct_active;
144  out:
145        unlock_kernel();
146        return res;
147  }
```

Figure 23.5   Checking free space

93   the parameter is a pointer to the `struct file` representing the accounting file.

99–103   this takes out the big kernel lock (see Section 5.5). This is needed because the accounting file could be closed by another process and even on a uniprocessor `acct_needcheck` could be set by a timer interrupt.

100   this prepares to return the value of `acct_active`.

101–102   if the file pointer is invalid (i.e. there is no accounting file open) or the `acct_needcheck` flag is not set (the time between checks has not expired), we return the value in `acct_active` (i.e. whether accounting is turned on of off). The kernel lock is given back on the way out.

103   now that the critical section is past, we give back the kernel lock.

106   this gets information about the file system to which the accounting file belongs into the `sbuf` structure. The function is part of the virtual file system manager, not considered in this book.

107   if unable to do so, we return the value in `acct_active`.

109–114   this checks the free space in that file system. The `f_bavail` field gives the number of free blocks. The `f_blocks` field gives the total number of blocks in the file system.

109–110   if free space is at or has fallen below SUSPEND % of the total, we set `act` to -1.

111–112   if free space is at or above RESUME % of the total, we set `act` to 1.

114   otherwise (free space is between SUSPEND and RESUME) we set `act` to 0.

120–144   the big kernel lock is needed again for this section of code.

121–125   this is probably paranoid; it is checking that the specified file actually is the accounting file. Because any process (with the requisite permission) can change the accounting file, it is just possible that it might have been changed in the meantime. This is why the kernel lock is needed.

122–124   if free space is above RESUME %, we return TRUE; if below SUSPEND %, we return FALSE. If in between, we return the value of `acct_active` (i.e. whether accounting is enabled or not).

127–137   this changes the value of `acct_active` (to enable or disable accounting), as necessary.

127–131   this block of code is executed if accounting is enabled.

128–131   this is for the case where free space is below SUSPEND.

129 marks accounting suspended.

130 this prints the message at KERN_INFO priority.

132–137 this block of code is executed if accounting is already suspended.

133–136 if free space is above RESUME, we mark accounting as active and print a message at KERN_INFO priority.

139–142 the timer must have expired in order to have got past line 101, so it is reset here.

139 this removes the timer from its place in the timer list (see Section 15.3.2.5).

140 this flag was set when the timer expired. Free space has just been checked, so this flag can be cleared.

141 this sets up the expires field in the timer for the next interval. ACCT_TIMEOUT is in seconds; multiplication by HZ converts it to ticks. It was defined in Section 23.1.1.

142 this function inserts the timer at its correct place in the timer list, as determined by its expiry time (see Section 15.3.2.2).

143 the return value is now the value in acct_active. This is either its previous value or may have been set at line 129 or line 134.

145–146 this gives back the big kernel lock and returns the value in res.

23.3 Writing to the accounting file

The actual process of writing to the accounting file is handled in two steps. First, there is a wrapper function, which checks that there *is* an accounting file and guarantees that no other process can remove it while this one writes to it. It then calls a second function, which does the actual work of writing the accounting record.

23.3.1 Checking that there is an accounting file

The function shown in Figure 23.6, from kernel/acct.c, is called from do_exit() (see Section 9.1). It checks that there is an accounting file and gets a pointer to the struct file representing it.

```
349  int acct_process(long exitcode)
350  {
351      struct file *file = NULL;
352      lock_kernel();
353      if (acct_file) {
354          file = acct_file;
355          get_file(file);
356          unlock_kernel();
357          do_acct_process(exitcode, acct_file);
358          fput(file);
```

```
359        } else
360            unlock_kernel();
361        return 0;
362    }
```

Figure 23.6 Checking that there is an accounting file

349 the parameter is the `exitcode` passed to the `exit()` system service.

352 the big kernel lock is taken out before even checking for the existence of the accounting file. This file can be removed by another process, so this lock guarantees that if it is found to exist it will remain in existence until it is marked as in use by this process. The function was explained in Section 5.5.

353–360 only if an accounting file is actually open is any work done.

355 we atomically increment the use count field in the `struct file` representing the accounting file. The function is part of the IO manager.

356 now that the use count is incremented, even if another process tries to delete the accounting file, only the use count will be decremented, it will not actually be deleted, so the big lock can be given back (see Section 5.5 for the function).

357 this is the function that actually writes an accounting record to the file (see Section 23.3.2).

358 this function decrements the use count field in the `struct file`, so indicating that this process is finished with it.

23.3.2 Writing an accounting record

The function shown in Figure 23.7, from `kernel/acct.c`, writes an accounting entry for an exiting process. The `struct acct` is built here and then written into the accounting file.

```
275  static void do_acct_process(long exitcode, struct file *file)
276  {
277        struct acct ac;
278        mm_segment_t fs;
279        unsigned long vsize;
280
285        if (!check_free_space(file))
286            return;
292        memset((caddr_t)&ac, 0, sizeof(struct acct));
293
294        strncpy(ac.ac_comm, current->comm, ACCT_COMM);
295        ac.ac_comm[ACCT_COMM - 1] = '\0';
296
297        ac.ac_btime = CT_TO_SECS(current->start_time) +
                                (xtime.tv_sec - (jiffies / HZ));
```

```
298        ac.ac_etime = encode_comp_t(jiffies -
                                          current->start_time);
299        ac.ac_utime = encode_comp_t(current->times.tms_utime);
300        ac.ac_stime = encode_comp_t(current->times.tms_stime);
301        ac.ac_uid = current->uid;
302        ac.ac_gid = current->gid;
303        ac.ac_tty = (current->tty) ?
                              kdev_t_to_nr(current->tty->device) : 0;
304
305        ac.ac_flag = 0;
306        if (current->flags & PF_FORKNOEXEC)
307            ac.ac_flag |= AFORK;
308        if (current->flags & PF_SUPERPRIV)
309            ac.ac_flag |= ASU;
310        if (current->flags & PF_DUMPCORE)
311            ac.ac_flag |= ACORE;
312        if (current->flags & PF_SIGNALED)
313            ac.ac_flag |= AXSIG;
314
315        vsize = 0;
316        if (current->mm) {
317            struct vm_area_struct *vma;
318            down_read(&current->mm->mmap_sem);
319            vma = current->mm->mmap;
320            while (vma) {
321                vsize += vma->vm_end - vma->vm_start;
322                vma = vma->vm_next;
323            }
324            up_read(&current->mm->mmap_sem);
325        }
326        vsize = vsize /1024;
327        ac.ac_mem = encode_comp_t(vsize);
328        ac.ac_io = encode_comp_t(0);
329        ac.ac_rw = encode_comp_t(ac.ac_io /1024);
330        ac.ac_minflt = encode_comp_t(current->min_flt);
331        ac.ac_majflt = encode_comp_t(current->maj_flt);
332        ac.ac_swaps = encode_comp_t(current->nswap);
333        ac.ac_exitcode = exitcode;
339        fs = get_fs();
340        set_fs(KERNEL_DS);
341        file->f_op->write(file, (char *)&ac,
342        sizeof(struct acct), &file->f_pos);
343        set_fs(fs);
344  }
```

Figure 23.7   Writing to the accounting file

275   the exitcode parameter comes from do_exit(). The second parameter is a pointer to the struct file representing the accounting file.

285–286   first we check to see if there is enough free disk space to continue with process accounting. If not, we just return. The function has been described in Section 23.2.2.

292–333   this fills the accounting `struct` with the needed information as recorded by the different kernel functions.

292   this zeroes all fields in the `acct` structure (declared at line 277). This structure is allocated on the stack and could contain random values.

294   the `ac_comm` field contains the name of the program running when the process terminated. This copies a fixed 16 characters.

295   this puts a terminating `\0` into the last element of `ac_comm[]`. Should this be `ac_comm[ACCT_COMM]` rather than `ac_comm[ACCT_COMM – 1]`? There are 17 bytes in `ac_comm[]` (see the definition in Section 23.1.2), and this line writes to byte 16.

297   process creation time is in the `start_time` field of the `task_struct` (in ticks). The macro (from Section 15.2.5.3) converts it to seconds. The current wall time in seconds is in `xtime.tv_sec`. Because `jiffies / HZ` is the number of seconds since the kernel booted, then `(xtime.tv_sec – (jiffies/HZ))` is the time in seconds at which the kernel booted. So, the `ac_btime` field contains the time is seconds at which the process began.

298–300   these three fields are encoded in 16 bits (see Section 23.4).

298   this is the length of time (in ticks) for which the process ran (current time minus start time).

299–300   these give the time the process spent in user and kernel modes (in ticks).

301–302   these give `uid` and `gid` of the process now terminating.

303   if the process has a terminal attached, this writes the ID number of that terminal; otherwise, it just writes 0.

305–313   this sets various bits in the `ac_flag` field, depending on the flags field in the `task_struct`. These bits are defined in Section 23.1.3.

305   this clears all bits in the `ac_flag` field.

306–307   if the process is still running its parent's program, we set the AFORK bit.

308–309   if the process has used superuser privileges, we set the ASU bit.

310–311   if the process wrote a core dump to disk, we set the ACORE bit.

312–313   if the process was terminated by a signal, we set AXSIG.

315–326   this block of code deals with memory usage statistics, which it accumulates in the `vsize` variable.

327–332   these fields are encoded into 16 bits (see Section 23.4).

327   at this stage `vsize` has the total memory usage (in Kb). We write this to the `ac_mem` field, in compressed format.

328   the `task_struct` does not contain information about IO usage, so a 0 is written here.

329   dividing a `comp_t` by 1024 would leave the six high-order bits of the mantissa. Is this a meaningful value? In any case, this is compressed again. This and the previous line seem to represent unfinished business.

330–332   these give further memory management information (see the description of these fields in `task_struct`, Section 2.4).

333   this `exitcode` value was passed in as a parameter. Basically, it gives the reason why the process terminated.

339–343   this block of code is writing the `struct acct` to the accounting file. It is really the preserve of the IO manager. Because it is using an internal file manager function, which expects to be dealing with the user data segment, it has temporarily to override that in favour of the kernel data segment, where the `struct acct` is. This technique is relevant to anyone using an internal kernel function.

23.4   Encoding an unsigned long

To conserve space in the accounting file, process times are stored as 16-bit floating point numbers. The encoding is a 13-bit fraction with a 3-bit exponent. The function shown in Figure 23.8, from `kernel/acct.c`, shows how an integer is compressed into this 16-bit format.

```
232  #define MANTSIZE     13
233  #define EXPSIZE      3
234  #define MAXFRACT     ((1 << MANTSIZE) - 1)
235
236  static comp_t encode_comp_t(unsigned long value)
237  {
238      int exp, rnd;
239
240      exp = rnd = 0;
241      while (value > MAXFRACT) {
242          rnd = value & (1 << (EXPSIZE - 1));
243          value >>= EXPSIZE;
244          exp++;
245      }

250      if (rnd && (++value > MAXFRACT)) {
251          value >>= EXPSIZE;
252          exp++;
253      }

258      exp <<= MANTSIZE;
259      exp += value;
260      return exp;
261  }
```

Figure 23.8   Encoding an `unsigned long`

232 the value is going to be expressed in the form A * 8^b. The mantissa A is a 13-bit integer.

233 the exponent b is expressed in 3 bits, so can have values from 0 to 7.

234 the mantissa is unsigned; so its maximum value is 13 1s. (1 << MANTSIZE) is 0010 0000 0000 0000, so ((1 << MANTSIZE) – 1) is 0001 1111 1111 1111.

236 the function returns comp_t, defined in <linux/acct.h> as

```
26 typedef __u16 comp_t;
```

240 the algorithm used is to increase the exponent repeatedly until the value will fit in the mantissa. This sets the initial value of exp to 0; so the first format tried is mantissa * 8^0.

241–245 this loop increments the exponent each time, until the value can be represented in the mantissa. If the supplied value is less than MAXFRACT, then the loop is never executed.

242 (1 << (EXPSIZE – 1)) is 100. rnd will be 1 or 0, depending on whether bit 2 in value is set or not. This is a marker for whether the result needs to be rounded up or not. If that bit is set, then a value of 4 or more will be lost in the shift on the next line.

243 value is divided by 8.

244 exp is now one power of 8 higher.

250–253 this is checking for both rounding and overflow.

250 if rnd is 0, then the second part of the expression is not executed, value is not incremented. But if rnd is 1, then value is rounded up by 1. If this would make it greater than MAXFRACT then one final adjustment must be made.

251–252 value is divided by a further 8, and exp is moved up by 1.

258–259 these lines shift the exponent into its place in the three high-order bits of the comp_t and add on the mantissa, which goes into the low-order 13 bits.

260 this returns exp, which contains the converted value.

24

Virtual 8086 mode

The i386 has a compatibility feature that enables it to execute programs written for earlier 16-bit processors. There are two processor modes available for running such programs: real mode, and virtual 8086 mode.

Real mode effectively turns the processor into a (very fast) 8086. All the memory management and protection facilities are disabled, so 16-bit programs, compiled for an 8086, find themselves at home in this environment. However, the machine can do nothing else but run that 16-bit program. The processor always begins in this mode when powered up. But Linux cannot run in this mode. So the process manager is not concerned with real mode.

Virtual 8086 mode allows 16-bit programs to run within the context of the memory management, protection, and process control mechanisms supported by the i386. The operating system creates a process, that runs a 16-bit program in virtual 8086 mode. This process can run alongside other 32-bit protected mode processes. The computer processing unit (CPU) converts 20-bit 8086 addresses into 32-bit virtual addresses and then uses the paging mechanism to map these to physical memory.

Although the virtual 8086 facility can be used by any program (it is entered by means of a system call), it is used mainly by the Linux DOS emulator, `dosemu`.

24.1 Data structures

As with so many other chapters in this book, we begin with a description of data structures, in this case the structures used to implement the virtual 8086 mode.

24.1.1 Information supplied by user

Before a process enters vm86 mode, the user encapsulates a certain amount of control information in a data structure, which is then passed to the appropriate system service.

There are actually two different system calls available to enter vm86 mode [see the manual pages for `vm86(2)` and `vm86old(2)`]. Each uses a different data structure to encapsulate the information that the user needs to provide to the operating system when it is emulating a virtual 8086. As will be seen in this section, one of these is a subset of the other.

The Linux Process Manager. The Internals of Scheduling, Interrupts and Signals   John O'Gorman
© 2003 John Wiley & Sons, Ltd   ISBN: 0 470 84771 9

24.1.1.1   Standard vm86 information

The standard data structure used to encapsulate vm86 information is shown in Figure 24.1, from `<asm-i386/vm86.h>`. This is used with the `vm86old()` system service.

```
98   struct revectored_struct {
99        unsigned long __map[8];
100  };
101
102  struct vm86_struct {
103       struct vm86_regs           regs;
104       unsigned long              flags;
105       unsigned long              screen_bitmap;
106       unsigned long              cpu_type;
107       struct revectored_struct   int_revectored;
108       struct revectored_struct   int21_revectored;
109  };

114  #define VM86_SCREEN_BITMAP   0x0001
```

Figure 24.1   Data structure encapsulating vm86 information

99   this is a 256-bit bitmap, used at lines 107 and 108.

103   this contains a copy of values in the hardware registers. The `vm86_regs` structure itself will be discussed in Section 24.1.1.2.

104   apparently, the only bit defined in this field is VM86_SCREEN_BITMAP (see line 114). If this bit is set, then the DOS screen memory area is to be treated as read only.

105   each bit in this field represents a page of the DOS screen memory area. The bit is set if the corresponding page is paged in.

106   this is the type of the real CPU on which the emulation is running. The enumeration is in Section 24.1.1.3.

107   see line 98 for the structure. A bit set in this indicates that the corresponding interrupt is not to be handled in 8086 mode but, rather, the processor is to switch back to protected mode to handle it.

108   a bit set in this indicates that the corresponding DOS function within INT 0x21 is not to be handled by the 8086 mode handler but that the processor is to switch back to protected mode to handle it.

24.1.1.2   Register save area as seen by user

When a user process requests the process manager to run in vm86 mode it supplies a set of initial values for the registers. The format for these is shown in Figure 24.2, from `<asm-i386/vm86.h>`.

```
68   struct vm86_regs {
72        long                   ebx;
```

```
73          long            ecx;
74          long            edx;
75          long            esi;
76          long            edi;
77          long            ebp;
78          long            eax;
79          long            __null_ds;
80          long            __null_es;
81          long            __null_fs;
82          long            __null_gs;
83          long            orig_eax;
84          long            eip;
85          unsigned short  cs, __csh;
86          long            eflags;
87          long            esp;
88          unsigned short  ss, __ssh;
92          unsigned short  es,   esh;
93          unsigned short  ds, __dsh;
94          unsigned short  fs, __fsh;
95          unsigned short  gs, __gsh;
96    };
```

Figure 24.2 Stack layout as seen by user program

72–78 these are the standard registers, in the same order as in the `struct pt_regs`.

79–82 this is the place in the stack frame where XDS and XES would normally be saved. As segment selectors are not part of 8086 mode, these have no meaning. They are kept here as fillers, along with space for XFS and XGS, but are never used.

83–88 these are standard positions in a stack frame.

84 even though IP is only a 16-bit register in 8086 mode, its value is saved in this 32-bit field to keep the stack frame compatible.

85 the `cs` field stores the 16-bit value from the CS register; the `__csh` is only an (unused) filler for the high-order 16 bits. Together, they correspond to the `xcs` field in `pt_regs`.

88 the `ss` field stores the 16-bit value from the SS register; the `__ssh` is only an (unused) filler for the high-order 16 bits. Together they correspond to the `xss` field in `pt_regs`.

92–95 these are 16-bit versions of the four data segment registers. In vm86 mode, they replace the four unused 32-bit values at lines 79–82. Each is padded out to 32-bits by the unused second variable (e.g. `__esh`).

24.1.1.3 Different types of computer processing unit

One of the items of information that the user must supply on entry to vm86 mode is the type of the CPU on which it is running. The definitions shown in Figure 24.3, from

<asm-i386/vm86.h>, cover the different types of CPU that can be encountered. The first three are redundant, as Linux runs only on 386 or higher.

```
27   #define CPU_086    0
28   #define CPU_186    1
29   #define CPU_286    2
30   #define CPU_386    3
31   #define CPU_486    4
32   #define CPU_586    5
```

Figure 24.3   Different types of computer processing unit

24.1.1.4   Extended vm86 information

There is also an extended version of the vm86_struct, as shown in Figure 24.4, from <asm-i386/vm86.h>. This is used with the vm86() system service.

```
116  struct vm86plus_info_struct {
117       unsigned long force_return_for_pic:1;
118       unsigned long vm86dbg_active:1;
119       unsigned long vm86dbg_TFpendig:1;
120       unsigned long unused:28;
121       unsigned long is_vm86pus:1;
122       unsigned char vm86dbg_intxxtab[32];
123  };
124
125  struct vm86plus_struct {
126       struct vm86_regs                regs;
127       unsigned long                   flags;
128       unsigned long                   screen_bitmap;
129       unsigned long                   cpu_type;
130       struct revectored_struct        int_revectored;
131       struct revectored_struct        int21_revectored;
132       struct vm86plus_info_struct     vm86plus;
133  };
```

Figure 24.4   Extended vm86_struct

116–122   this is the extra information included in the vm86plus_struct (see line 132). It consists of a long bitmap, followed by a 32-byte array.

117   when bit 0 is set then if interrupts are enabled after handling a fault the process manager should return immediately to 32-bit mode. The controlling program (e.g. dosemu) wants to handle all hardware interrupts itself (see Section 2.6.1).

118   this bit is used by the DOS debugger. If set, then the information in the vm86dbg_intxxtab[] field at line 122 is valid.

119   bit 2 is also used by the DOS debugger. It specifies that the 8086 program is to run in single-step mode.

120   bits 3–30 are unused.

121   although a user may provide information as a `vm86_struct` or a `vm86plus_struct`, internally the process manager always maintains the information in the latter, extended, format. So, although it is always there, sometimes the `vm86plus_info_struct` is valid, other times it is not. Bit 31 is used to distinguish this: when set, it indicates that the data in the `vm86plus_info_struct` are valid.

122   this array is a bitmap, with one entry for each of the 256 interrupts. The DOS debugger sets the bit corresponding to any interrupt that it wants to handle itself in 32-bit protected mode.

125–133   this is the extended structure. It is identical to the `vm86_struct` of Section 24.1.1.1, except that line 132 is added.

24.1.2   Stack layout

Whichever of the data structures described in the previous section is actually provided by the user, it always remains in the user address space. However, a slightly expanded version of it is built on the kernel stack.

The standard stack layout, as used in 32-bit protected mode, is the `struct pt_regs` (see Section 10.3.1.1). In vm86 mode, registers are only 16 bits wide. But the stack layout used for saving registers is made to be similar to a `struct pt_regs`, by the use of padding fields. In this way pointers can be cast from one type to another.

24.1.2.1   A vm86 stack frame

The format of the data structure built on the stack on entry to vm86 mode (Section 24.4.1) is shown in Figure 24.5, from `<asm-i386/vm86.h>`.

```
173  struct kernel_vm86_struct {
174       struct kernel_vm86_regs           regs;

183  #define VM86_TSS_ESP0 flags
184       unsigned long                     flags;
185       unsigned long                     screen_bitmap;
186       unsigned long                     cpu_type;
187       struct revectored_struct          int_revectored;
188       struct revectored_struct          int21_revectored;
189       struct vm86plus_info_struct       vm86plus;
190       struct pt_regs                    *regs32;

201  }
```

Figure 24.5   The kernel stack while in vm86 mode

174   the `kernel_vm86_regs` structure will be described in Section 24.1.2.2.

183 this defines an alias for the flags field of this structure (line 184). This is the top of the register save area.

184–189 these fields are identical to the remaining fields in a struct vm86plus_struct.

190 this is a pointer to the struct pt_regs built on the stack above this, by the standard system call entry routine of Section 10.4.3.2.

24.1.2.2 Register save area as seen by the kernel

Figure 24.6, from arch/i386/kernel/vm86.c, shows the order in which registers are saved on the stack in vm86 mode. The main change from a struct pt_regs is that the old segment descriptors are not useful any more and are forced to be zero by the kernel, and the real segment descriptors are at the end of the structure.

```
145  struct kernel_vm86_regs {

149        long              ebx;
150        long              ecx;
151        long              edx;
152        long              esi;
153        long              edi;
154        long              ebp;
155        long              eax;
156        long              __null_ds;
157        long              __null_es;
158        long              orig_eax;
159        long              eip;
160        unsigned short    cs, __csh;
161        long              eflags;
162        long              esp;
163        unsigned short    ss, __ssh;
167        unsigned short    es, __esh;
168        unsigned short    ds, __dsh;
169        unsigned short    fs, __fsh;
170        unsigned short    gs, __gsh;
171  };
```

Figure 24.6 Stack layout as seen by kernel

149–163 this part of the structure is identical in size and order to a struct pt_regs. Hence pointers to one can be cast to the other without any problem.

167–170 these fields are not present in a struct pt_regs. They are actually pushed onto the kernel stack by the interrupt hardware when in vm86 mode before anything else. They are also restored (last) by an IRET to vm86 mode.

24.1.2.3   Converting between structures

To make it easier when converting from one form of register save area to another, a number of macros are provided that measure off appropriate parts of the struct kernel_vm86_regs; see Figure 24.7, from arch/i386/kernel/vm86.c.

```
60    #define VM86_REGS_PART2 orig_eax
61    #define VM86_REGS_SIZE1 ((unsigned)                          \
62        (&(((struct kernel_vm86_regs *)0)->VM86_REGS_PART2 )))
63    #define VM86_REGS_SIZE2 (sizeof(struct kernel_vm86_regs)
                                             VM86_REGS_SIZE1)
```

Figure 24.7   Calculating the size of a struct kernel_vm86_regs

60   this is just setting a marker within the rather large struct kernel_vm86_regs, at orig_eax.

61   this and the following macro are used when copying from a struct vm86_regs to a struct kernel_vm86_regs, and vice versa. The VM86_REGS_SIZE1 macro actually evaluates to the size of a struct kernel_vm86_regs, up to (but not including) the orig_eax field.

63   this macro evaluates to the size of the remainder of the struct, from orig_eax (inclusive) to the end.

Figure 24.8 shows the relationship between the structure of the information supplied by the user and how it is stored internally by the process manager while executing in vm86 mode.

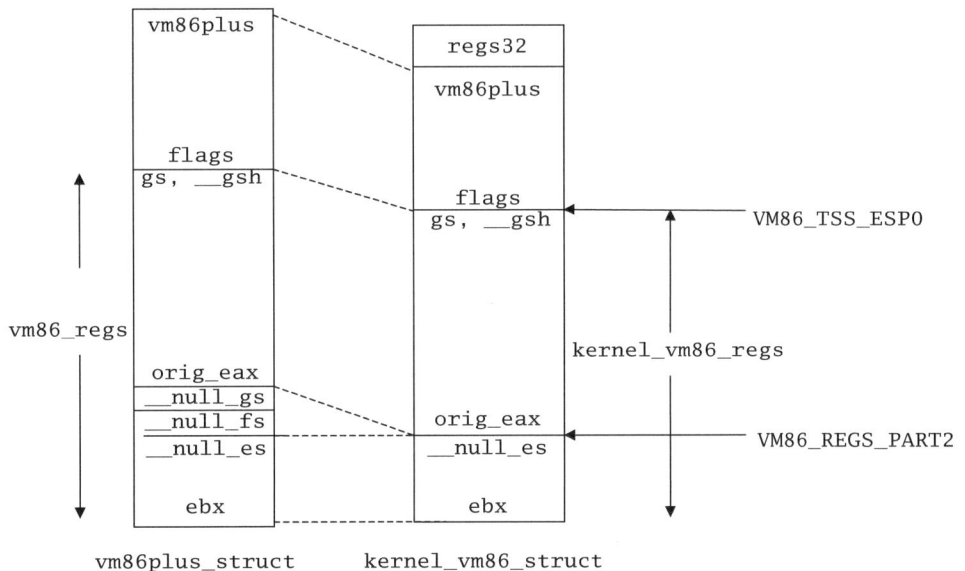

Figure 24.8   User-supplied information copied to the stack

24.1.2.4   *Converting from 32-bit to 16-bit and 8-bit values*

The macros shown in Figure 24.9, from `arch/i386/kernel/vm86.c`, facilitate the handling of data structures defined in previous sections.

```
36   #define KVM86        ((struct kernel_vm86_struct *)regs)
37   #define VMPI         KVM86->vm86plus

43   #define AL(regs)     (((unsigned char *)&((regs)->eax))[0])
44   #define AH(regs)     (((unsigned char *)&((regs)->eax))[1])
45   #define IP(regs)     (*(unsigned short *)&((regs)->eip))
46   #define SP(regs)     (*(unsigned short *)&((regs)->esp))
```

Figure 24.9   Macros for converting from 32-bit to 8-bit and 16-bit registers

36   KVM86 casts the `regs` pointer variable within scope to be a pointer to a `struct kernel_vm86_struct` (see Section 24.1.2.1).

37   VMPI is a shortcut for the `vm86plus` field of the `struct kernel_vm86_struct` pointed to by regs. This is in fact a `vm86plus_info_struct` (see Section 24.1.1.4).

43–46   the `regs` parameter of these four macros is a pointer to a `struct kernel_vm86_regs`, as defined in Section 24.1.2.2.

43   this macro converts the pointer `regs` to be a pointer to the saved AL on the kernel stack (byte 0 of `eax`).

44   this macro converts the pointer `regs` to be a pointer to the saved AH on the kernel stack (byte 1 of `eax`).

45   this macro converts the pointer `regs` into the value of the low-order 16 bits of the saved IP on the stack (bytes 0 and 1 of the `eip` field).

46   this macro converts the pointer `regs` into the value of the low-order 16 bits of the saved SP on the stack (bytes 0 and 1 of the `esp` field).

24.1.3   Information in the `thread` structure

While in vm86 mode, the process manager maintains some extra information in the `thread` structure of the process. The fields in question, from `<asm-i386/processor.h>`, are shown in Figure 24.10 These fields have been seen already, in Section 2.7; their relevance will be more obvious in this context. One of these, the virtual flags register, is of particular importance and will be dealt with in detail in Section 24.2.

```
366   unsigned long        esp0

378   struct vm86_struct   * vm86_info;
```

```
379   unsigned long            screen_bitmap;
380   unsigned long            v86flags, v86mask, v86mode, saved_esp0;
```

Figure 24.10   vm86 information in the `thread` structure

366   as described in Section 2.7, this field always contains the value in the ESP register *before* the current stack frame was built. It enables the process manager to roll back the stack. On entry to vm86, this value is copied to `saved_esp0` (line 380). After the `kernel_vm86_struct` has been built on the stack, the address of the `flags` field from that structure is stored here. In this way it points to the top of the saved 8086 style register values.

378   this points to the structure in user space. It will be used to copy information back there when leaving vm86 mode.

379   the value supplied by the user is written here. It represents those pages of the DOS screen memory that are actually paged in. It is the domain of the memory manager.

380   the `v86flags` field is the virtual flags register, maintained by Linux while in vm86 mode (see Section 24.2). The `v86_mask` field contains processor-specific bits that are valid in vm86 mode. This mask is built on entry to vm86 mode (see Section 24.4.2). These bits are: the nested task bit and the IOPL field, for 386 and later; the alignment check bit, for 486 and later; and the identification flag bit, for Pentium processors. `v86mode` does not seem to be used anywhere. While in vm86 mode, `saved_esp0` is used to save the original value from `esp0` (line 359), which will be restored when returning to protected mode.

24.2   The virtual flags register

The processor runs in vm86 mode when the VM bit is set in EFLAGS. This bit cannot be set directly by software, so, effectively, the processor enters vm86 mode when a saved copy of EFLAGS, in which the VM bit is set, is copied to the hardware register. This is typically done on return from interrupt handling (including a context switch).

Because changes to and from vm86 mode are controlled by the VM bit in EFLAGS, access to this register is carefully controlled by the operating system while running in vm86 mode. The mechanism used to implement this control is the input–output privilege level (IOPL). When running at an IOPL of 0, as vm86 does, a trap is generated any time the program attempts to access the EFLAGS register. The handler for this trap monitors a software version of EFLAGS known as the virtual flags register, in `thread.v86flags`. It emulates instructions that read or write EFLAGS by reading or writing the virtual flags register.

In this section I describe several macros and functions used to maintain that virtual register.

24.2.1   Bits in the EFLAGS register

The various bits in the EFLAGS register itself that are relevant to vm86 mode are shown in Figure 24.11, from `<asm-i386/vm86.h>`.

```
15   #define TF_MASK      0x00000100
16   #define IF_MASK      0x00000200
```

```
17    #define IOPL_MASK     0x00003000
18    #define NT_MASK       0x00004000
19    #define VM_MASK       0x00020000
20    #define AC_MASK       0x00040000
21    #define VIF_MASK      0x00080000
22    #define VIP_MASK      0x00100000
23    #define ID_MASK       0x00200000
24
25    #define BIOSSEG       0x0f000
```

Figure 24.11   Masks for the EFLAGS register

15–18   these form part of the original 8086 FLAGS register.

15   bit 8, the trap flag, is set to enable single-step mode (for debugging). When set, a single-step interrupt (debug exception) is generated after every instruction. It is cleared (by hardware) before entering the debug handler and when an interrupt or exception is taken by the CPU.

16   when bit 9, the interrupt enable flag, is set, the CPU responds to maskable interrupts.

17   bits 12–13 concern, the input–output (IO) privilege level field. This indicates the privilege level required to perform IO instructions. Such instructions can be executed only if the current privilege level (CPL) of the CPU is numerically less than or equal to IOPL. It can only be modified when working at a CPL of 0 (highest). In vm86, IOPL is used to protect the IF bit in EFLAGS and has nothing to do with IO.

18   bit 14, the nested task flag, is set if the current task was initiated by a CALL, an interrupt, or an exception. It controls the operation of the IRET instruction. When clear, a normal return takes values from the stack. This is the default in Linux. When set, the interrupt return is through a task switch.

19–23   these are part of the extended 32-bit EFLAGS register.

19   when bit 17, the virtual 8086 mode flag, is set, vm86 mode is enabled.

20   when bit 18, the alignment check flag, is set, it enables alignment checking of memory references, and the generation of the alignment check exception.

21   bit 19, the virtual interrupt flag, is a virtual image of the IF flag in bit 9. When CPL is 3 (lowest) and IOPL is less than 3, then the CLI or STI machine instructions operate on VIF, not IF. In such a case, if VIF is cleared, then an INTR interrupt (vectors 32–255) is not acted on, rather it sets VIP (see line 22). When eventually software attempts to set VIF, the processor checks VIP and, if set, it generates a general protection fault. Before finishing, the handler for this sets VIF and clears VIP.

22   when bit 20, the virtual interrupt pending flag, is set, it indicates that an interrupt is pending. When both VIF and VIP are set, a general protection fault is generated.

23   when bit 21, the identification flag, is set, it indicates that the processor supports the CPUID instruction.

25   this is the address of the basic input–output system (BIOS) segment.

24.2.2 Manipulating the virtual flags register

A number of macros are provided for manipulating the virtual flags register, `thread.v86flags`; see Figure 24.12, from `arch/i386/kernel/vm86.c`.

```
51    #define VFLAGS   (*(unsigned short *)&(current->thread.v86flags))
52    #define VEFLAGS      (current->thread.v86flags)
53
54    #define set_flags(X,new,mask)                              \
55                  ((X) = ((X) & ~(mask)) | ((new) & (mask)))
56
57    #define SAFE_MASK        (0xDD5)
58    #define RETURN_MASK      (0xDFF)
```

Figure 24.12 Macros for manipulating virtual flags

51   this macro takes the address of the `v86flags` field of the `thread` structure of the current process, casts it to be a pointer to `unsigned short`, and then de-references it. So VFLAGS is a shortcut for the low-order 16 bits of the virtual flags field of the current process.

52   VEFLAGS, in contrast, is a shortcut for the full 32-bit virtual flags field of the current process.

54–55   the operating system wants to keep fairly strict control over the bits that can be set in the virtual flags register. This macro implements such control. It turns off all the bits represented by `mask` and then turns on those bits of `new` that are also in `mask`. Other bits in `X` are not affected. Two typical masks are defined in lines 57–58.

57   these are the bits in EFLAGS that the user can legitimately specify on entry to vm86 mode. 0xDD5 is 0000 1101 1101 0101. Bits 0, 2, 4, 6, 7, and 11 are the ordinary arithmetic status flags. Bit 8 is the trap enable flag. Bit 10 is the direction flag. None of these has any special meaning for vm86 mode. Bits 12–13 must be 0, specifying an IOPL of 0. Bit 14 (nested task) must be turned off, by default.

58   RETURN_MASK is 0000 1101 1111 1111. This contains all the bits in SAFE_MASK as well as the three reserved bits, 1, 3, and 5. As these bits are not used by the processor, this is effectively equivalent to SAFE_MASK.

24.2.3 Getting the virtual flags

When a process running in vm86 mode executes an instruction to push the value of the FLAGS or EFLAGS register onto the stack, the processor generates a general protection interrupt and the operating system intervenes. The operation is carried out by software, not hardware. What is actually pushed on the stack is a combination of the hardware value and the virtual flags register.

The combination of bits is as follows. First, the interrupt enable and nested task bits of the hardware value are turned off, and the IOPL field is set to 0. Then, if the VIF bit is set in the virtual flags field, the interrupt enable bit is turned on. Finally, any bits of the `thread.vm86mask` that are set in the virtual flags field are also set.

The function that carries out the foregoing operations is shown in Figure 24.13, from `arch/i386/kernel/vm86.c`.

```
308  static inline unsigned long get_vflags(struct kernel_vm86_regs * regs)
309  {
310       unsigned long flags = regs->eflags & RETURN_MASK;
311
312       if (VEFLAGS & VIF_MASK)
313            flags |= IF_MASK;
314       return flags | (VEFLAGS & current->thread.v86mask);
315  }
```

Figure 24.13   Getting the virtual flags

310   RETURN_MASK is 0000 1101 1111 1111. So, this takes a copy of the saved EFLAGS from
           the kernel stack, with bits 9 (interrupt enable) and 14 (nested task) turned off, and an IOPL (bits
           12–13) of 0. This line is really just setting up default values.

312–313   if the virtual interrupt bit VIF_MASK in VEFLAGS (the full v86flags field of thread) is set,
           then we set the interrupt enable (IF_MASK) bit in the value about to be returned.

314   the return value is the local flags, plus any bits in VEFLAGS that are also set in v86mask (i.e.
           that are valid for this processor).

24.2.4   Setting values in the virtual flags register

Two functions are provided for setting values in the virtual flags register. One sets bits in the
32-bit VEFLAGS; the other in the 16-bit VFLAGS. Both are shown in Figure 24.14, from
`arch/i386/kernel/vm86.c`.

```
292  static inline void set_vflags_long(unsigned long eflags,
                                        struct kernel_vm86_regs * regs)
293  {
294       set_flags(VEFLAGS, eflags, current->thread.v86mask);
295       set_flags(regs->eflags, eflags, SAFE_MASK);
296       if (eflags & IF_MASK)
297            set_IF(regs);
298  }
299
300  static inline void set_vflags_short(unsigned short flags,
                                         struct kernel_vm86_regs * regs)
301  {
302       set_flags(VFLAGS, flags, current->thread.v86mask);
303       set_flags(regs->eflags, flags, SAFE_MASK);
```

```
304        if (flags & IF_MASK)
305             set_IF(regs);
306  }
```

Figure 24.14   Setting values in the virtual flags register

292   this function is used in the emulation of POPFD. It is passed a 32-bit value eflags (the value just popped from the user stack) and a pointer to the saved 8086 style registers on the kernel stack. It adjusts bits in the virtual flags register in thread, and also in the saved value of EFLAGS on the kernel stack. The eventual IRET will copy this value to the hardware register.

294   see the description of the set_flags() macro in Section 24.2.2. It operates on the v86mask bits. Only those bits of v86mask as specified by eflags are now set in VEFLAGS. Other bits in VEFLAGS are not affected.

295   this only operates on the SAFE_MASK bits. Only those bits of SAFE_MASK as specified by eflags are now set in the saved copy of EFLAGS on the kernel stack. This is the value that will be copied to the hardware register by the eventual IRET.

296–297   if the IF_MASK bit was set in the supplied eflags, then we set the VIF bit in VEFLAGS. If the VIP bit was also set in VEFLAGS, then it returns to 32-bit mode, to handle the pending interrupt. The set_IF() function is described in Section 24.2.5.

300–306   this function is used in the emulation of POPF. It is passed a 16-bit value flags, the value just popped from the user stack, and a pointer to the saved 8086 style registers on the kernel stack. It is almost identical to set_flags_long() (see lines 292–298).

24.2.5   Manipulating bits in the virtual flags register

A number of functions that manipulate bits in the virtual flags register are shown in Figure 24.15, from arch/i386/kernel/vm86.c.

```
275  static inline void set_IF(struct kernel_vm86_regs *regs)
276  {
277        VEFLAGS |= VIF_MASK;
278        if (VEFLAGS & VIP_MASK)
279             return_to_32bit(regs, VM86_STI);
280  }
281
282  static inline void clear_IF(struct kernel_vm86_regs *regs)
283  {
284        VEFLAGS &= ~VIF_MASK;
285  }
286
287  static inline void clear_TF(struct kernel_vm86_regs *regs)
288  {
289        regs->eflags &= ~TF_MASK;
290  }
```

Figure 24.15   Manipulating bits in the virtual flags register

275–280	this function sets the virtual interrupt enable bit in the virtual flags register and checks for a pending interrupt.
277	this sets the VIF bit in the virtual flags register in thread.
278–279	setting the interrupt enable bit in the previous line implies that interrupts were disabled before that. If an interrupt occurred while they were disabled, the virtual interrupt bit would have been set in VEFLAGS. Now that interrupts are enabled, this line checks that bit and, if set, it returns to 32-bit mode to handle the interrupt (see Section 24.8.1). The return value, indicating the reason for returning, is VM86_STI, as defined in Section 24.8.3.
282–285	as described in Section 24.2.2, VEFLAGS is the v86flags field of the thread of the current process. This function clears the VIF bit in this. The supplied parameter is never used
287–290	this function clears the TF (trap enable) bit in the saved value of EFLAGS on the kernel stack.

24.3 Macros to read and write memory

As will be seen later in this chapter, the software involved in implementing vm86 mode does a certain amount of emulation of CPU operations, specifically manipulating stacks and reading the instruction stream. Both of these operations involve accessing user space.

A whole series of macros (using inline assembler – apparently gcc does not get the necessary 16-bit arithmetic correct) are provided for reading and writing 8-bit, 16-bit, and 32-bit values, and adjusting pointers appropriately. The comment in the code admits that they are ugly, but we have seen worse.

24.3.1 Emulating PUSH instructions

Three macros are provided for writing 8-bit, 16-bit, and 32-bit values to memory and adjusting a pointer. Each is passed three parameters. The first parameter is base, the second is offset. This conforms to 8086 base:offset addressing mode. The third is the value to be written. These macros emulate the PUSH instruction.

24.3.1.1 Pushing a byte

The inline assembler code that pushes a byte onto the stack is shown in Figure 24.16, from arch/i386/kernel/vm86.c. The supplied value is written to the location *before* that specified by ptr. This is equivalent to pushing a byte onto a stack, hence the name pushb().

```
330   #define pushb(base, ptr, val)              \
331   __asm__ __volatile__(                      \
332       "decw %w0\n\t"                         \
333       "movb %2,0(%1,%0)"                     \
334       : "=r" (ptr)                           \
335       : "r" (base), "q" (val), "" (ptr))
```

Figure 24.16 Macro to write a byte to memory

332   this decrements the low-order 16 bits of parameter 0 (%w0), that is, `ptr`. It is now pointing one byte earlier on in memory.

333   the destination operand is an indirect memory reference. The 0 is displacement, parameter 1 is `base`, parameter 0 is `ptr`. The whole instruction moves the low-order byte of parameter 2 (`val`) to the memory location specified by the parameter-1:parameter-0 combination (i.e. `base:ptr`).

334   the output parameter `ptr` is write only for this instruction (`"="`), and can be in a register (`"r"`). The previous value is discarded and replaced by output data.

335   these are input parameters: a register can be used for parameter 1, `base`; parameter 2, `val`, is to be in one of the four general purpose registers; parameter 3, `ptr`, is to occupy the same storage as parameter 0 and is the original value given to that parameter.

24.3.1.2   Pushing a word

The inline assembler code that writes a word to memory, and decrements the pointer by 2 bytes, is shown in Figure 24.17, from `arch/i386/kernel/vm86.c`.

```
337  #define pushw(base, ptr, val)            \
338  __asm__ __volatile__(                    \
339      "decw %w0\n\t"                       \
340      "movb %h2,0(%1,%0)\n\t"              \
341      "decw %w0\n\t"                       \
342      "movb %b2,0(%1,%0)"                  \
343      : "=r" (ptr)                         \
344      : "r" (base), "q" (val), "" (ptr))
```

Figure 24.17   Macro to write a word to memory

339   this decrements the 16-bit parameter 0 (%w0); that is, `ptr`. It is now pointing one byte earlier on in memory.

340   this moves the high-order byte of parameter 2 (%h2), that is, `val`, to the memory location specified by the parameter-1:parameter-0 combination (i.e. `base:ptr`).

341–344   see the comments on lines 332–335 of Section 24.3.1.1.

24.3.1.3   Pushing a long

Finally, there is the third macro in the set, which writes a 32-bit `long` to memory and adjusts the pointer by 4 bytes. See Figure 24.18, from `arch/i386/kernel/vm86.c`, for the code; Figure 24.19 illustrates the procedure.

```
346  #define pushl(base, ptr, val)            \
347  __asm__ __volatile__(                    \
348      "decw %w0\n\t"                       \
349      "rorl $16,%2\n\t"                    \
350      "movb %h2,0(%1,%0)\n\t"             \
```

```
351        "decw %w0\n\t"                              \
352        "movb %b2,0(%1,%0)\n\t"                     \
353        "decw %w0\n\t"                              \
354        "rorl $16,%2\n\t"                           \
355        "movb %h2,0(%1,%0)\n\t"                     \
356        "decw %w0\n\t"                              \
357        "movb %b2,0(%1,%0)"                         \
358        : "=r" (ptr)                                \
359        : "r" (base), "q" (val), "" (ptr))
```

Figure 24.18   Macro to write a long to memory

348   this decrements ptr. It is now pointing one byte earlier on in memory.

349   parameter 2 is the 32-bit value to be written. Rotating it left 16 bits swaps the high-order word with the low-order word. Note that this is a rotate, not a shift, see the left hand-side of Figure 24.19.

350   this moves the high-order byte of parameter 2 (val) to the memory location specified by the parameter-1:parameter-0 combination (i.e. base:ptr).

351   this decrements the 16-bit ptr again.

352   this moves the low-order byte of parameter 2 (val) to the memory location specified by the parameter-1:parameter-0 combination (i.e. base:ptr).

353   this decrements ptr again.

354   rotation of val left 16 bits swaps the high-order and low-order words back again, as they were on entry.

355–357   this repeats the operation of lines 350–352.

Figure 24.19 attempts to illustrate what has been going on in the foregoing lines of code.

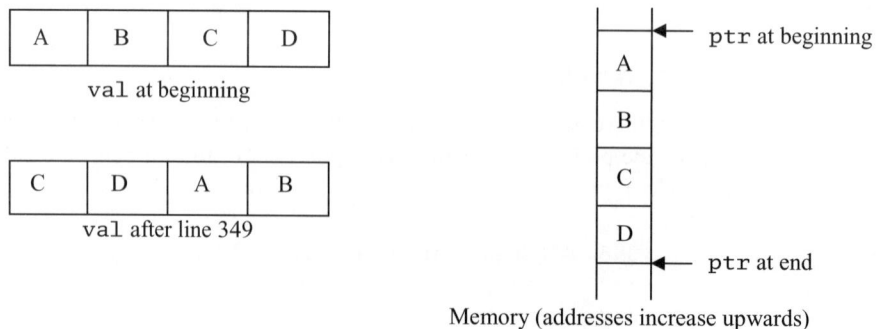

Figure 24.19   Writing a 32 bit value

24.3.2 Reading values from memory

There are three mirror macros to the foregoing, for reading values from memory and adjusting a pointer. Each is passed two parameters. The first is `base`; the second is `offset`. The macro then evaluates to the value read. These can be used to emulate the popping of a stack (hence their names) but they can also be used to emulate reading from an instruction stream and advancing an instruction pointer.

24.3.2.1 Reading a byte

The macro shown in Figure 24.20, from `arch/i386/kernel/vm86.c`, is passed an 8086 style segment address and offset pair. The macro evaluates to the value of the byte at that address and also increments the `ptr` variable.

```
361  #define popb(base,ptr)                          \
362  ({ unsigned long __res;                          \
363  __asm__ __volatile__(                            \
364      "movb 0(%1,%0),%b2\n\t"                      \
365      "incw %w0"                                   \
366      : "=r" (ptr), "=r" (base), "=q" (__res)      \
367      : "" (ptr), "1" (base), "2" (0));            \
368  __res; })
```

Figure 24.20   Reading a byte from 8086 memory

364   the source operand, `0(%1,%0)`, is an indirect memory reference. The 0 is displacement, parameter 1 is `base`, parameter 0 is `ptr`. Parameter 2 is the local `__res`. The "b" specifies the least-significant byte. The whole instruction moves a byte from the specified address to the least-significant byte of `__res`.

365   this increments the low-order 16 bits of parameter 0, which is the pointer `ptr`. By restricting it to 16 bits, the segment will not overflow; rather the pointer will wrap around, which is standard 8086 semantics.

366   there are output parameters. All are write only ("="); the previous value will be replaced. Parameters 0 and 1 may be in registers ("r"). Parameter 2, `__res`, must be in a general purpose register.

367   these are input parameters. Parameter 3 is to occupy the same storage as parameter 0; it is the initial value of `ptr`. Parameter 4 is to occupy the same storage as parameter 1, `base`. Parameter 5 is initialised to 0 and occupies the same storage as parameter 2, `__res`. Only the least-significant byte of this 4-byte parameter is written to, while the macro evaluates to the whole `long`; hence the need for this initialisation.

24.3.2.2 Reading a word

The corresponding macro to read a word from memory and adjust a pointer is shown in Figure 24.21, from `arch/i386/kernel/vm86.c`.

```
370  #define popw(base,ptr)                              \
371  ({ unsigned long __res;                             \
372  __asm__ __volatile__(                               \
373       "movb 0(%1,%0),%b2\n\t"                        \
374       "incw %w0\n\t"                                 \
375       "movb 0(%1,%0),%h2\n\t"                        \
376       "incw %w0"                                     \
377       : "=r" (ptr), "=r" (base), "=q" (__res)        \
378       : "" (ptr), "1" (base), "2" (0));              \
379  __res; })
```

Figure 24.21   Macro to read a word from memory

373–378   see the comments on lines 364–367 in Section 24.3.2.1.

375   this moves the next byte from memory to the high-order byte of __res.

24.3.2.3 *Reading a long*

Finally, there is the macro shown in Figure 24.22, from `arch/i386/kernel/vm86.c`, which reads a 32-bit value from memory and increments the pointer by 4 bytes.

```
381  #define popl(base,ptr)                              \
382  ({ unsigned long __res;                             \
383  __asm__ __volatile__(                               \
384       "movb 0(%1,%0),%b2\n\t"                        \
385       "incw %w0\n\t "                                \
386       "movb 0(%1,%0),%h2\n\t"                        \
387       "incw %w0\n\t"                                 \
388       "rorl $16,%2\n\t"                              \
389       "movb 0(%1,%0),%b2\n\t"                        \
390       "incw %w0\n\t"                                 \
391       "movb 0(%1,%0),%h2\n\t"                        \
392       "incw %w0\n\t"                                 \
393       "rorl $16,%2"                                  \
394       : "=r" (ptr), "=r" (base), "=q" (__res)        \
395       : "" (ptr), "1" (base));                       \
396  __res; })
```

Figure 24.22   Macro to read a `long` from memory

384–387   see the comments on lines 364–365 of Section 24.3.2.1.

386   this moves the next byte from memory to the high-order byte of __res.

388   parameter 2 is the 32-bit value that is being written to. Rotating it left 16 bits swaps the high-order word with the low-order word (see Figure 24.19 for an illustration of this).

389–392   this repeats lines 384–387, reading the remaining two bytes.

393   this swaps the high-order and low-order words of parameter 2, __res, back again, so that they are now in the correct order to return to the caller.

394–396   see the comments on lines 366–368 of Section 24.3.2.1, except that the __res parameter is not initialised to 0 in this case, as the macro actually writes to all four bytes of it.

24.4 Entering vm86 mode

Entry to vm86 mode is by means of a system call. As a discussion of system calls is outside the scope of this book, only a summary will be given here, in Section 24.4.1. The system call then goes on to call internal kernel functions, which will be described in full in Section 24.4.2.

24.4.1 The system call

A process can use one of two different kernel entry points to switch to vm86 mode. The only difference between them is that the vm86() system service passes a vm86plus_struct as a parameter, whereas the oldvm86() system call passes a vm86_struct (see Section 24.1.1 for the difference between these). The case when the extended information is passed will be described here; the other case is a subset of this.

When a process running in 32-bit protected mode wants to enter vm86 mode, it first creates a struct vm86plus_struct in its own address space. This is filled in with the values required in the hardware registers when the switch is made to 8086 mode, as well as other information such as the type of the real CPU on which it is running and any re-vectored interrupts or DOS functions. The fields of this vm86plus_struct have already been described in Section 24.1.1.4.

The entry to vm86 mode is made by a system call, passing a pointer to the vm86plus_struct just set up. As with all system calls, the values in the hardware registers are saved on the stack, in struct pt_regs format. This structure stays on the stack all the time the process is in vm86 mode. It is restored to the hardware registers and removed from the stack only when leaving vm86 mode.

The system call handler then builds a struct kernel_vm86_struct underneath that on the stack. That structure has been described in Section 24.1.2.1. It has room for all the data in a vm86plus_struct, and some more, particularly a pointer to the struct pt_regs above it.

Then the values in the vm86plus_struct are copied from user space into the appropriate parts of the kernel_vm86_struct just created on the stack (see Section 24.1.2.3 for an overview of this copying). The pointer field regs32 in this kernel_vm86_struct is set to point to the beginning of the struct pt_regs, above it on the stack. The address of the vm86plus_struct back in user space is recorded in the vm86_info field of thread.

At this point, the system service handler pushes two parameters onto the stack and calls the do_sys_vm86() function (see Section 24.4.2). The first of these parameters is a pointer to the kernel_vm86_struct it has just created on the stack; the second is a pointer to the task_struct of the current process.

The stack layout at this stage is shown in Figure 24.23.

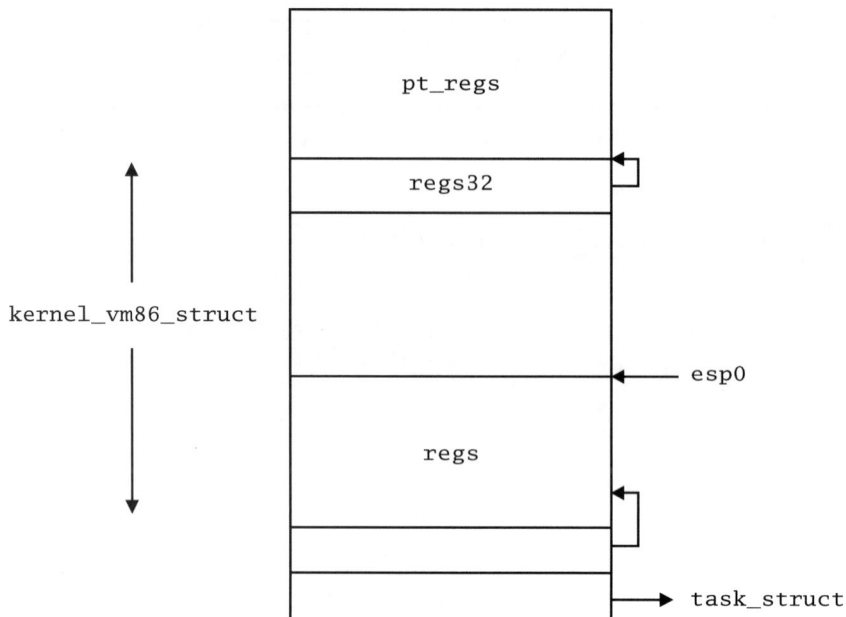

Figure 24.23   Stack layout on entry to vm86 mode

24.4.2   Internal processing

The main work in switching to vm86 mode is done by the internal function do_sys_vm86(); see Figure 24.24, from arch/i386/kernel/vm86.c.

```
206  static void do_sys_vm86(struct kernel_vm86_struct *info,
                                         struct task_struct *tsk)
207  {
208      struct tss_struct *tss;
212      info->regs.__null_ds = 0;
213      info->regs.__null_es = 0;
224      VEFLAGS = info->regs.eflags;
225      info->regs.eflags &= SAFE_MASK;
226      info->regs.eflags |= info->regs32->eflags & ~SAFE_MASK;
227      info->regs.eflags |= VM_MASK;
228
229      switch (info->cpu_type) {
230      case CPU_286:
231          tsk->thread.v86mask = 0;
232              break;
233      case CPU_386:
234          tsk->thread.v86mask = NT_MASK | IOPL_MASK;
235          break;
236      case CPU_486:
237              tsk->thread.v86mask = AC_MASK | NT_MASK | IOPL_MASK;
```

```
238             break;
239        default:
240             tsk->thread.v86mask = ID_MASK
                                      | AC_MASK | NT_MASK | IOPL_MASK;
241             break;
242        }

247        info->regs32->eax = 0;
248        tsk->thread.saved_esp0 = tsk->thread.esp0;
249        tss = init_tss + smp_processor_id();
250        tss->esp0 = tsk->thread.esp0 =
251                        (unsigned long) &info->VM86_TSS_ESP0;
252        tsk->thread.screen_bitmap = info->screen_bitmap;
253        if (info->flags & VM86_SCREEN_BITMAP)
254             mark_screen_rdonly(tsk);
255        __asm__ __volatile__(
256            "xorl %%eax,%%eax; movl %%eax,%%fs;
                                         movl %%eax,%%gs\n\t"
257            "movl %0,%%esp\n\t"
258            "jmp ret_from_sys_call"
259
260            :"r" (&info->regs), "b" (tsk) : "ax");
261
262 }
```

Figure 24.24   Function to switch into vm86 mode

206 as described in the previous section, `info` is a pointer to the `kernel_vm86_struct` just set up on the stack, and `tsk` is a pointer to the `task_struct` of the process.

212–227 various changes are made to the copy of the 8086 style registers that has just been built on the stack. These are values supplied by the caller, not saved values from hardware registers. This code is ensuring that the caller did not supply any illegal values.

212–213 these two fields are not valid, they are merely placeholders in the structure. They should have been cleared to 0 by the caller, but they will be restored to the hardware registers by RESTORE _ALL later on in the processing. So, just in case, they are cleared here.

224–227 the saved value of the EFLAGS register is also special: it cannot be assumed that the user has set it up safely, so this block of code makes sure that, where appropriate, flag bits are inherited from protected mode.

224 the value of the EFLAGS register passed in by the user is copied to VEFLAGS, which is a shortcut for `thread.v86flags`. This is the virtual flags register, maintained by Linux while in vm86 mode (see Section 24.2). Note that it is set up exactly as the user specified it.

225–227 now the value supplied by the user has been checked and, where appropriate, altered, all the extra bits, over and above the SAFE_MASK bits, are turned off. Then any of these extra bits that were set in 32-bit mode before the system call are turned on. Finally, the VM bit is turned on.

225   only those bits allowed by SAFE_MASK can be set in the value supplied by the user; any others are cleared. These bits have been described in Section 24.2.2.

226   this line is operating with the values of EFLAGS saved in the pt_regs structure at the top of the kernel stack (i.e. the values in the hardware EFLAGS register when running in 32-bit protected mode before the system call). Any bits set in this that are not part of SAFE_MASK are set in the 8086 version of EFLAGS. This ensures that a caller entering vm86 mode cannot set bits in EFLAGS that were not already set in its own register, cannot give itself extra privilege.

227   finally, we set the VM_MASK bit in EFLAGS. This is the mode-switch bit. When this copy of EFLAGS is moved into the hardware register, the machine will run in vm86 mode.

229–242   various bits are set in the thread.v86mask field, depending on the physical CPU installed. These are defined in Section 24.1.1.3.

230–232   if running on a 286, no extra bits are valid.

233–235   on a 386, both the nested task bit (NT_MASK) and the IOPL field (IOPL_MASK) bits are valid.

236–238   on a 486, the alignment check bit in the EFLAGS is valid; so the AC_MASK is set as well.

239–241   on all others (Pentium), the identification bit in the EFLAGS register is valid, so the ID_MASK is set as well.

247   the saved value of EAX in pt_regs would have contained the number of the system service. This is now cleared to 0, setting up a default (success) return value, for eventual return to 32-bit protected mode.

248   the value in the esp0 field of thread is saved while in vm86 mode. It will be restored when leaving (see Section 24.8.1). This esp0 field will have its own value while in vm86 mode (see lines 250–251).

249   the tss for this CPU is found. The TSS (task state segment) was described in Section 7.2.3. The smp_processor_id() macro is from Section 7.2.1.4.

250–251   the esp0 field in both the tss and thread is set to the address of the flags field in the kernel_vm86_struct on the stack. That means it is pointing to the second part of the structure, after the 16-bit register save area (see Figure 24.23). Remember that esp0 always points to the end of the register save area.

252   the value for screen_bitmap supplied by the user is copied into the appropriate field of thread. Bits set in this indicate pages of the DOS screen memory that are actually valid.

253–254   if the VM86_SCREEN_BITMAP bit was set in flags by the user, then we mark the screen as read-only. The function is part of the IO manager and is not considered here.

256   the XORL instruction effectively zeroes the EAX register. That value is then written to the hardware FS and GS registers.

257   parameter 0 (a pointer to the register save area of the kernel_vm86_struct on the stack) is copied to the hardware ESP register. This is setting up for the next line.

258   this is a direct jump to `ret_from_sys_call`, with the ESP register pointing to the beginning of the 8086 style register save area on the stack (see Section 10.6.1). Owing to the jump instruction used, control never returns here. The `ret_from_sys_call` routine pops `regs` from the stack to the hardware registers. These are not the values that were saved there by SAVE_ALL on entry to the system service, rather they are the 16-bit values that have just been built on the stack by the foregoing function. This includes especially the VFLAGS value, with the VM bit set (see lines 224–227). Once this is reloaded, the machine is in vm86 mode.

259   there are no output parameters.

260   there are input parameters. Parameter 0 is a pointer to the `regs` field of the kernel stack. This pointer may be in a register (`"r"`). Parameter 1 specifies that `tsk` is to be in the EBX register. The `"ax"` operand specifier indicates that the value in EAX will be altered, as indeed it is at line 256.

There is quite an amount of information left on the stack when this system service exits (there is a sense in which it exits only temporarily at this stage). At the top of the stack is a full `struct pt_regs`, built there on entry to the system service. Underneath that is the second part of the `kernel_vm86_struct`, from VM86_TSS_ESP0 (or flags) onwards. Only the first part of this, the `kernel_vm86_regs`, was popped by `ret_from_sys_call`.

24.5   Trap handling in vm86 mode

Once the CPU is set to run in vm86 mode it continues in that mode until it is interrupted. The value of `EFLAGS` loaded by the hardware interrupt mechanism has the VM bit cleared, so it switches back to handle the interrupt in protected mode. If the previously running process is restored after the interrupt handling then, by popping values that the interrupt mechanism saved on the kernel stack, it switches back to vm86 mode again.

The protected mode interrupt handling has been considered in detail in earlier chapters. There it was seen that first-level interrupt handlers check if the CPU was running in vm86 mode when the interrupt occurred. If so, special handlers are invoked, either `handle_vm86_trap()` or `handle_vm86_fault()`. The first of these functions is considered in this section; the second in Section 24.6.

Figure 24.25, from `arch/i386/kernel/vm86.c`, shows the function that is called to handle any trap that occurs when the CPU is running in virtual 8086 mode. It is called by the first-level trap handler (see Section 11.1.3).

```
427  int handle_vm86_trap(struct kernel_vm86_regs * regs,
                                            long error_code, int trapno)
428  {
429      if (VMPI.is_vm86pus) {
430          if ((trapno==3) || (trapno==1))
431              return_to_32bit(regs, VM86_TRAP + (trapno << 8));
432          do_int(regs, trapno,
                          (unsigned char *)(regs->ss << 4), SP(regs));
433          return 0;
434      }
```

```
435        if (trapno != 1)
436            return 1;
437        if (current->ptrace & PT_PTRACED) {
438            unsigned long flags;
439            spin_lock_irqsave(&current->sigmask_lock, flags);
440            sigdelset(&current->blocked, SIGTRAP);
441            recalc_sigpending(current);
442            spin_unlock_irqrestore(&current->sigmask_lock,flags);
443        }
444        send_sig(SIGTRAP, current, 1);
445        current->thread.trap_no = trapno;
446        current->thread.error_code = error_code;
447        return 0;
448    }
```

Figure 24.25   Trap handling in vm86 mode

427   it is necessary to be clear on the state of the kernel stack on entry to this function. On top of the stack is the `struct pt_regs` pushed there by the system call handler on entry to vm86 mode. Under that is the second half of the `kernel_vm86_struct` built by the system call handler, from the flags field onwards. The first part of that `kernel_vm86_struct` was popped into the hardware registers at the end of the vm86 entry code, but the second part stays on the stack until the process finally leaves vm86 mode. Under that again is the `pt_regs` pushed there when this current trap occurred, partly by the hardware, partly by the first-level trap handler. Together, these last two form a `kernel_vm86_struct`, even if the two halves of it came from different places at different times. The first parameter is a pointer to that `struct pt_regs` built on the kernel stack by SAVE_ALL, but cast to be a pointer to `kernel_vm86_regs` by the first-level handler, before calling this function. The second parameter is either an error code supplied by the hardware, or a 0 supplied by the first-level handler. The third parameter is the number of the trap that caused this interrupt.

429–434   the VMPI macro casts `regs` to be a pointer to a `kernel_vm86_struct` and then selects the `vm86plus_info_struct` from it; this is the extended information field on the stack. If the `is_vm86pus` bit is set in that, then the `vm86plus_struct` is valid [it was supplied by a call to `vm86()`]. Otherwise, a call to `vm86old()` did not supply this information.

430–431   for traps 1 (debug) or 3 (breakpoint), we return immediately to protected mode execution and handle the trap there. The controlling process that launched the 8086 program is debugging it, or has set breakpoints in it, and wants to get control back to itself. The function is described in Section 24.8.1. The return code will have the reason for the return, VM86_TRAP, in the least-significant byte, with `trapno` in the next byte.

432   otherwise, the generic vm86 interrupt handler (see Section 24.7) is called. It is passed a pointer to the saved registers at the point the trap occurred, the number of the trap that occurred, the 20-bit address of the base of the user stack segment, and the value of the user stack pointer, as saved on the kernel stack. The SP() macro was described in Section 24.1.2.4.

433   a return value of 0 means that the trap has been handled.

435–447   if vm86 mode was entered by calling `vm86old()`, then the extended information was not available, and this code is executed.

435–436   with any trap other than 1 (debug) it just returns. The return value of 1 means it was not handled here, and the calling routine [the first-level trap handler `do_trap()`] must handle it. So, the remainder of the code is handling the debug trap.

437–443   this block of code is executed only if the current process is being traced. If so, the `SIGTRAP` signal is unmasked for the current process. It is about to be sent a `SIGTRAP` a few lines further on, so it must be able to handle that signal.

439   the signal mask of the current process is going to be manipulated, so we take out a spinlock on it. This is to prevent an interrupt handler accessing it while it is being changed. The value of `EFLAGS` is saved in the local `flags` so that interrupt state can be restored at line 442.

440   this function, from Section 17.2.1.1, is called to clear `SIGTRAP` in the mask of blocked signals in the current process.

441   see Section 18.3.2. The signal state of the process has changed, so it must be reevaluated.

442   we give back the spinlock and restore `EFLAGS`.

444   in any case, whether the current process is being traced or not, we send it a `SIGTRAP` signal [see Section 18.2.7 for the `send_sig()` function]. If the process is not being traced, then the signal should be masked, but that is up to the process itself.

445   we update the `trap_no` field in the `thread` structure of the current process. Because of lines 435–436, `trapno` must be 1. This, and the following item of information, are now available to the signal handler.

446   we update the `error_code` field in the `thread` structure of the current process. This is the error code generated by the CPU, or supplied by the first-level handler function, and passed as a parameter to this function.

447   a return value of 0 means that the trap was handled (by sending a signal).

24.6   Handling faults in vm86 mode

Because changes to and from vm86 mode are controlled by the VM bit in `EFLAGS`, access to this register is carefully controlled by the operating system while running in vm86 mode. The mechanism used to implement this control is the IOPL. When running at an IOPL of 0, as vm86 does, then any attempt to use the `CLI`, `STI`, `PUSHF`, `PUSHFD`, `POPF`, `POPFD`, `INTx`, `IRET`, or `IRETD` instructions triggers the general protection exception. All these instructions read or write the `EFLAGS` register. The general protection exception handler (see Section 11.4) calls the function `handle_vm86_fault()`, which supplies its own emulation of these instructions. It actually reads or writes a software version of `EFLAGS` known as the virtual flags register, in `thread.vm86flags`. As this is a rather long function, the discussion will be broken down into three parts.

24.6.1   Macros and local variables

The first part of the `handle_vm86_fault()` function is shown in Figure 24.26, from `arch/i386/kernel/vm86.c`.

```
450   void handle_vm86_fault(struct kernel_vm86_regs * regs,
                                                      long error_code)
451   {
452       unsigned char *csp, *ssp;
453       unsigned long ip, sp;
454
455   #define CHECK_IF_IN_TRAP                                          \
456       if (VMPI.vm86dbg_active && VMPI.vm86dbg_TFpendig)            \
457           pushw(ssp, sp, popw(ssp, sp) | TF_MASK);
458   #define VM86_FAULT_RETURN
459       if (VMPI.force_return_for_pic && (VEFLAGS & IF_MASK))    \
460                   return_to_32bit(regs, VM86_PICRETURN);   \
461       return;
462
463       csp = (unsigned char *) (regs->cs << 4);
464       ssp = (unsigned char *) (regs->ss << 4);
465       sp = SP(regs);
466       ip = IP(regs);
```

Figure 24.26   Macros and local variables

450   see the discussion of the parameters at line 427 of Section 24.5.

455–457   this macro is used when emulating a POPF, POPFD, IRET, or IRETD, all of which move a value from the bottom of the user stack to the hardware EFLAGS register. The VMPI macro has been defined in Section 24.1.2.4 as the KVM86->vm86plus field of regs. This is the extra information. The present macro examines two fields in this. If the process is being debugged, and is running in single-step mode, then we pop the bottom 16 bits off the user stack, set the TF_MASK bit in it, and push it back on again. This resets the trap flag, which was cleared automatically by the hardware. So, single-step mode will be reenabled when this value is eventually restored from the stack to the hardware register.

458–461   this macro is a common exit path, used in this function at the end of each section of code that emulates a faulting instruction. The CPU checks for hardware interrupts after each instruction; an emulator has to take care of this as well.

459   this checks if the user has specified that hardware interrupts are to be handled in protected mode, and interrupts are enabled in the virtual flags register.

460   this breaks out of vm86 mode and returns to 32-bit protected mode, clearing down the whole stack frame (see Section 24.8.1). It gives VM86_PICRETURN as the reason for returning.

461   if the condition on line 459 was not TRUE, then we return to the general protection interrupt handler that called this function.

463–466   the two foregoing macros are not executed at this stage but only when they are actually inserted at later places in the code, so the main processing of the function begins here, by setting up some variables containing the saved values of the segment and offsets for instruction and stack pointers.

463   `regs->cs` is a 16-bit field, containing the address of the user code segment. But all 8086 segment addresses are aligned on 16-bit boundaries. This means that the least-significant 4 bits are always 0 and are not stored. So, shifting this address left 4 bits gives the 20-bit address of the beginning of the user code segment. Finally, it is cast as a pointer to `unsigned char`. In brief, `csp` is set up as a byte pointer to the beginning of the code segment in use before the interrupt.

464   likewise, `ssp` is a pointer to the beginning of the user stack segment.

465   the `SP()` macro (Section 24.1.2.4) takes the address of the `esp` field in `regs`, casts it as a pointer to `unsigned short`, and de-references that pointer. So `sp` is the 16-bit value in the stack pointer field in `regs`, pointing to the bottom of the user stack.

466   likewise `ip` is the 16-bit instruction pointer field in `regs`, pointing to the faulting instruction in the user code segment.

Between them, these last four lines set up segment:offset pointers to code and stack as at the moment when the general protection fault occurred. These pointers are used in the remainder of the function when it emulates its own versions of the trapped instructions.

24.6.2   Two-byte instructions

The main body of the function determines which machine instruction caused the fault and deals with each as appropriate. It first deals with two-byte instructions; see the code in Figure 24.27.

```
468         switch (popb(csp, ip)) {

471         case 0x66:
472         switch (popb(csp, ip)) {

475             case 0x9c:
476                 SP(regs) -= 4;
477                 IP(regs) += 2;
478                 pushl(ssp, sp, get_vflags(regs));
479                 VM86_FAULT_RETURN;

482             case 0x9d:
483                 SP(regs) += 4;
484                 IP(regs) += 2;
485                 CHECK_IF_IN_TRAP
486                 set_vflags_long(popl(ssp, sp), regs);
487                 VM86_FAULT_RETURN;
490             case 0xcf:
491                 SP(regs) += 12;
```

```
492                        IP(regs) = (unsigned short)popl(ssp, sp);
493                        regs->cs = (unsigned short)popl(ssp, sp);
494                        CHECK_IF_IN_TRAP
495                        set_vflags_long(popl(ssp, sp), regs);
496                        VM86_FAULT_RETURN;
497
498                default:
499                        return_to_32bit(regs, VM86_UNKNOWN);
500            }
```

Figure 24.27   Two-byte instructions

468   the macro popb() was described in Section 24.3.2.1. Here it is passed the address of the user
code segment and the value of the instruction pointer within that segment. It evaluates to the byte
at that location. This is the instruction that caused the exception. It also increments the value of
ip, so it is now pointing to the next byte in the code. It works as if the machine executed that
instruction. The remainder of the function deals in turn with each possible instruction that could
have caused the fault.

471–500   if the first byte of the instruction is 0x66, then it is a two-byte instruction, so we read again and
switch on the second byte.

475–479   the faulting instruction was PUSHFD (0x 66 9C). This instruction pushes the 32-bit hardware
EFLAGS register onto the stack.

476   we decrement the value of the user stack pointer saved on the kernel stack by 4. This makes room
on the user stack for the 4 bytes that should have been pushed.

477   we advance the value of IP saved on the kernel stack by 2, to skip over this 2-byte instruction.
The popb() advanced only the local ip variable.

478   the get_vflags() function is described in Section 24.2.3. It calculates a value for the flags
register which is then written into the 4-byte space on the stack, created at line 476. It starts with
the value from the hardware register, as saved on the kernel stack by SAVE_ALL. As default
settings the interrupt enable and nested task bits are turned off and the IOPL field is set to 0.
Then various bits are set, depending on specific conditions. If the VIF bit is set in the virtual flags
field, the interrupt enabled bit is set here. Any of the bits permitted by vm86mask that are set in
the virtual flags field are also set in the value being returned. So, a 32-bit flags value is pushed on
the stack; but not from the hardware register rather, from a combination of that and the virtual
flags register maintained by Linux.

479   the macro was defined in Section 24.6.1. It returns either to 32-bit protected mode or to the
general protection handler that called this function. Despite appearances, execution never falls
through into the next case.

482–487   the faulting instruction was POPFD (0x 66 9D). This instruction pops 32 bits from the stack to
the hardware EFLAGS register.

483   we increment the value of the user stack pointer saved on the kernel stack by 4. This completes
the pop.

484   we advance the value of the user IP saved on the kernel stack by 2. The popb() advanced only the local ip variable.

485   the macro was defined in Section 24.6.1. If the process is being debugged, and is being single stepped, we make sure that the single-step bit is set in the saved value of EFLAGS at the bottom of the user stack (the value that is about to be popped at the next line).

486   the first parameter reads the 32-bit value from the user stack. This is passed to the function (Section 24.2.4), which adjusts bits accordingly both in the virtual flags register VEFLAGS and in the saved copy of EFLAGS on the kernel stack. For VEFLAGS, it makes sure that, of the v86mask bits, only those bits set in the value just popped are set in VEFLAGS. For the saved copy on the stack, it makes sure that, of the SAFE_MASK bits, only those bits set in the value just popped are set in the copy saved on the kernel stack. This copy will be restored to the hardware registers when the interrupt handler exits.

487   the macro was defined in Section 24.6.1. It returns either to 32-bit protected mode or to the general protection handler that called this function.

490–496   the faulting instruction was IRETD (0x 66 CF), which among other things restores EFLAGS from a stack. This instruction is emulated by moving values from the user stack to the kernel stack, so that when the general protection handler does an IRET in protected mode, control will actually return to the user program in vm86 mode.

491   we complete the IRETD by incrementing the saved value of the user stack pointer, as saved on the kernel stack, by 12 bytes. This line logically should come after line 495. The values for EFLAGS, ECS, and EIP are still there, and will be used in later lines.

492   the saved value of the user IP on the kernel stack is replaced by the low-order 16 bits of the 32-bit value from the bottom of the user stack, the return address.

493   the saved value of the user CS on the kernel stack is replaced by the low-order 16 bits of the 32-bit value from the new bottom of the user stack, the code segment. Between them, this and the previous line have set up the segment:offset address to which control will return.

494–496   see lines 485–487.

498–499   if the second byte of the two-byte instruction is any value other than one of the three just seen, then it is an illegal instruction or one that this code cannot handle, so we return to 32-bit protected mode, with a parameter VM86_UNKNOWN.

24.6.3 Single-byte instructions

The remainder of the function, shown in Figure 24.28, deals with single-byte instructions.

```
503        case 0x9c:
504            SP(regs) -= 2;
505            IP(regs)++;
506            pushw(ssp, sp, get_vflags(regs));
```

```
507                         VM86_FAULT_RETURN;

510             case 0x9d:
511                         SP(regs) += 2;
512                         IP(regs)++;
513                         CHECK_IF_IN_TRAP
514                         set_vflags_short(popw(ssp, sp), regs);
515                         VM86_FAULT_RETURN;

518             case 0xcd: {
519                         int intno = popb(csp, ip);
520                         IP(regs) += 2;
521                         if (VMPI.vm86dbg_active) {
522                             if ((1 << (intno & 7)) &
                                        VMPI.vm86dbg_intxxtab[intno >> 3])
523                             return_to_32bit(regs, VM8_INTx + (intno << 8));
524                         }
525                         do_int(regs, intno, ssp, sp);
526                         return;
527             }

530             case 0xcf:
531                         SP(regs) += 6;
532                         IP(regs) = popw(ssp, sp);
533                         regs->cs = popw(ssp, sp);
534                         CHECK_IF_IN_TRAP
535                         set_vflags_short(popw(ssp, sp), regs);
536                         VM86_FAULT_RETURN;

539             case 0xfa:
540                         IP(regs)++;
541                         clear_IF(regs);
542                         VM86_FAULT_RETURN;

551             case 0xfb:
552                         IP(regs)++;
553                         set_IF(regs);
554                         VM86_FAULT_RETURN;
555
556             default:
557                         return_to_32bit(regs, VM86_UNKNOWN);
558             }
559  }
```

Figure 24.28 Single-byte instructions

503–507   the faulting instruction was PUSHF (0x 9C). In vm86 mode, this instruction pushes the 16-bit
hardware FLAGS register onto the stack. As it is emulated here, what is pushed is a combination
of the hardware value (as saved on the stack by the interrupt) and the virtual flags register.

504   we decrement the value of the user stack pointer saved on the kernel stack by 2, thus making room on the user stack for the 2 bytes that should have been pushed.

505   we increment the instruction pointer saved on the kernel stack by 1, as it is a single-byte instruction. The `popb()` back at line 468 advanced only the local `ip` variable.

506   we push the 16-bit flags value onto the user stack, incrementing the local pointer. The `get_vflags()` function (Section 24.2.3) starts with the copy of the hardware register pushed onto the kernel stack by `SAVE_ALL`. The interrupt enable and nested task bits are turned off and the `IOPL` field is set to 0. Then various bits are set, depending on specific conditions. If the `VIF` bit is set in the virtual flags field, the interrupt enabled bit is set here. Any of the `vm86mask` bits that are set in the virtual flags field are also set in the value being returned.

507   the macro was defined in Section 24.6.1. It may return to 32-bit protected mode or to the general protection handler that called this function.

510–515   the faulting instruction was `POPF` (0x 9D). In vm86 mode, it pops 16 bits from the stack into the hardware `FLAGS` register.

511   we increment the value of the user stack pointer saved on the kernel stack by 2, thus completing the pop.

512   we increment the user instruction pointer saved on the kernel stack by 1, as it is dealing with a single-byte instruction. The `popb()` back at line 468 incremented only the local `ip` variable.

513   the macro was defined in Section 24.6.1. If the process is being debugged, and is being single stepped, it sets the single-step bit in the saved value of `EFLAGS` at the bottom of the stack (the value that is about to be popped at the next line).

514   the first parameter pops the 16-bit value from the user stack. This is passed to the function (Section 24.2.4), which adjusts bits accordingly both in `VEFLAGS` and in the saved copy of `FLAGS` on the kernel stack. For `VEFLAGS`, it makes sure that, of the `v86mask` bits, only those bits set in the value just popped are set in `VEFLAGS`. For the saved copy on the stack, it makes sure that, of the `SAFE_MASK` bits, only those bits set in the value just popped are set in the copy saved on the kernel stack. This copy will be restored to the hardware registers when the interrupt handler exits.

515   the macro was defined in Section 24.6.1. It may return to 32-bit protected mode or to the general protection handler that called this function.

518–527   the faulting instruction was `INTx` (0xCD).

519   the number of the interrupt is the next byte in the instruction stream, so we get that into `intno`.

520   we advance the value of the user IP saved on the kernel stack by 2, for a two-byte instruction. The `popb()` advanced only the local `ip` variable.

521–524   this is the equivalent of `CHECK_IF_IN_TRAP`. It is executed only if the process is being debugged, irrespective of whether or not the single-step bit is set.

522–523   basically, this is checking if the bit corresponding to `intno` is set in the `vm86_intxxtab[]` bitmap. A bit set means that the corresponding interrupt is to be handled in 32-bit protected mode by the debugging process. This array is indexed on the high-order 5 bits of `intno`, so there is one 8-bit entry for each eight interrupts. When this entry is extracted, the bit corresponding to `intno` is calculated using the low-order 3 bits. `(intno & 7)` takes only the three least-significant bits of the interrupt number. `(1 << (intno & 7))` sets a bit corresponding to the interrupt number MOD 8. If the bit is set in the array, then it returns to 32-bit protected mode, with `VM86_INTx` in the low-order byte, and `intno` in the high-order byte of the return value. Otherwise, control goes on to line 525.

525   we handle that interrupt request. The function is described in Section 24.7.1.

526   afterwards, we return to the general protection exception handler that called this function.

530–536   the faulting instruction was `IRET` (0xCF). This instruction is emulated by moving values from the user stack to the kernel stack, so that, when the general protection handler does an `IRET`, control will actually return to the user program.

531   we complete the `IRET` by discarding 6 bytes off the value of the user stack pointer, as saved on the kernel stack. This is 2 bytes each for `FLAGS`, `CS`, and `IP`.

532   the saved value of the user `IP` on the kernel stack is replaced by a 16-bit value taken from the bottom of the user stack, the return address.

533   the saved value of the user `CS` on the kernel stack is replaced by a 16-bit value taken from the new bottom of the user stack, the code segment. Between them, this and the previous instruction have set up the segment:offset address to which control returns.

534–536   see lines 513–515.

539–542   the faulting instruction was `CLI` (0xFA), disable interrupts.

540   we increment the value of the user instruction pointer as saved on the kernel stack by 1, as it is dealing with a single-byte instruction.

541   the function was described in Section 24.2.5. It clears the virtual interrupt enable bit in the virtual flags register in `thread`. It does not disable interrupts in hardware.

542   the macro was defined in Section 24.6.1. It may return to 32-bit protected mode or to the general protection handler that called this function.

551–554   the faulting instruction was `STI` (0xF6), enable interrupts.

552   we increment the value of the user instruction pointer as saved on the kernel stack by 1, as it is dealing with a single-byte instruction.

553   the function was described in Section 24.2.5. It sets the interrupt enable bit in the virtual flags register in `thread`. The comment in the code points out that this emulation is incorrect: the `sti` instruction should actually enable interrupts after the *next* instruction.

554   the macro was defined in Section 24.6.1. It may return to 32-bit protected mode or to the general protection handler that called this function.

556–557   if any other instruction caused the fault, nothing can be done about it, so return immediately to 32-bit protected mode, with an error code of `VM86_UNKNOWN`.

24.7 Vectored interrupts in vm86 mode

Vectored interrupts that occur while running in vm86 mode can be handled in two different ways. They can be handled in vm86 mode, using an 8086 style interrupt table, located at 0x 0000:0000 in the user's memory space; they can also be handled in protected mode, using the interrupt descriptor table (IDT) as usual. Which method is used for any particular interrupt is determined by the software interrupt redirection map, the int_revectored field of the vm86_struct. This section examines the processing involved in all of this.

24.7.1 Handling a vectored interrupt in vm86 mode

Vectored interrupts, either traps or INTx, will be handled by indexing into the 16-bit interrupt table, or the 32-bit IDT. A special function is provided, to check for all sorts of conditions; see Figure 24.29, from arch/i386/kernel/vm86.c. This function is called from handle_vm86_trap() (vm86pus is set) and handle_vm86_fault() (if an INTx).

```
398   static void do_int(struct kernel_vm86_regs *regs, int i,
                                  unsigned char * ssp, unsigned long sp)
399   {
400       unsigned long *intr_ptr, segoffs;
401
402       if (regs->cs == BIOSSEG)
403           goto cannot_handle;
404       if (is_revectored(i, &KVM86->int_revectored))
405           goto cannot_handle;
406       if (i==0x21 && is_revectored(AH(regs),
                                  &KVM86->int21_revectored))
407           goto cannot_handle;
408       intr_ptr = (unsigned long *) (i << 2);
409       if (get_user(segoffs, intr_ptr))
410           goto cannot_handle;
411       if ((segoffs >> 16) == BIOSSEG)
412           goto cannot_handle;
413       pushw(ssp, sp, get_vflags(regs));
414       pushw(ssp, sp, regs->cs);
415       pushw(ssp, sp, IP(regs));
416       regs->cs = segoffs >> 16;
417       SP(regs) -= 6;
418       IP(regs) = segoffs & 0xffff;
419       clear_TF(regs);
420       clear_IF(regs);
421       return;
422
423   cannot_handle:
424       return_to_32bit(regs, VM86_INTx + (i << 8));
425   }
```

Figure 24.29 Handling an interrupt in vm86 mode

398 the parameters are: a pointer to the saved registers on the kernel stack, in vm86 format; the number of the interrupt; a pointer to the beginning of the user stack segment; and the offset of the stack pointer into this segment.

402–403 if the value of CS saved on the kernel stack indicates that the interrupt occurred while executing code in the BIOS segment, then it must be passed to a protected mode handler (see Section 24.2.1 for the definition of BIOSSEG).

404–405 if that interrupt is specifically marked as requiring protected mode handling, then we pass it on. The function is described in Section 24.7.2.

406–407 if the interrupt is 0x21 (DOS) and the particular DOS function requested has been marked as requiring protected mode handling, then we pass it on to the protected mode handler for INT21.

408 at this stage it has been determined that the interrupt is to be handled in vm86 mode. We calculate a pointer to the appropriate entry in the interrupt table. The 8086 program has its own interrupt table at 0x0000 in its own memory space. We multiply the interrupt number by 4 and cast it as a pointer to long.

409–410 the function attempts to read the value (long) in the interrupt table corresponding to this interrupt, into segoffs. A nonzero (error) return value means the interrupt table (in user space) cannot be accessed. In that case the interrupt cannot be handled in vm86 mode, so we go to handle it in protected mode.

411–412 at this stage segoffs contains the segment:offset address of the interrupt service routine. Shifting it right 16 bits converts it to be just the segment part of the address. If this shows that the handler is in the BIOS segment, we transfer control to the protected mode handler, because vm86 does not use BIOS routines. BIOSSEG is defined in Section 24.2.1 as 0x0F000.

413–421 the remainder of the function sets up to handle an interrupt in 8086 mode.

413–415 these three lines write values for FLAGS, CS, and IP onto the bottom of the user stack, as if pushed there. The interrupt handler is going to run in vm86 user mode; when it terminates, it will find these values on the stack and return to the user program.

413 the get_vflags() function, see Section 24.2.3, returns the 32-bit flags value. The low-order 16 bits of this is pushed on the user stack, using ssp as base, and sp as pointer [see Section 24.3.1.2 for the pushw() macro].

414 this pushes the 16-bit CS register value, as saved on the kernel stack, onto the user stack.

415 this pushes the 16-bit IP value. Note that IP(regs) is a macro from Section 24.1.2.4.

416 this replaces the CS value saved on the kernel stack with the segment part of the handler address.

417 this is the esp field of regs, treated as an unsigned short, so it decrements the stack pointer saved on the kernel stack by 6, to take account of the 6 bytes pushed at lines 413–415. It would be more logical if this came after line 415.

418 this line clears any high-order bits set in segoffs (i.e. it converts it to be just the offset part of the address of the handler). That value is then assigned to the low half of eip on the kernel stack.

419   interrupt handlers expect the trap-enable bit of EFLAGS to be cleared on entry. The CPU does this automatically, so the emulation clears them in the value of EFLAGS saved on the kernel stack (see Section 24.2.5 for the function).

420   interrupt handlers also expect the interrupt enable bit to be clear in EFLAGS. This function, from Section 24.2.5, clears that bit in the virtual flags register of thread.

421   this returns to the function that called it, either handle_vm86_trap() or handle_vm86_fault(). Ultimately, control will return to ret_from_intr, which calls RESTORE_ALL to restore values from the kernel stack to the hardware registers. The POPF in RESTORE_ALL will not be executed in hardware but will be emulated, so bringing in values from the virtual flags register in thread. Because CS and IP on the kernel stack have been changed at lines 416 and 418, ret_from_intr will not go back to the user program but will jump to the 8086 interrupt handler, which will then run in vm86 user mode. When that in turn executes its IRET, it will find values on the user stack put there at lines 413–415, so it will return to the user program at the point where the interrupt occurred in the first place. The short-circuiting of the return can be illustrated as follows.

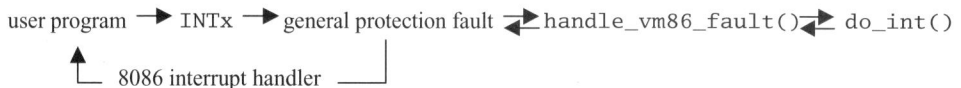

user program ➜ INTx ➜ general protection fault ⇄ handle_vm86_fault() ⇄ do_int()

⌐ 8086 interrupt handler ⌐

423–424   if the earlier processing determined that the interrupt was to be handled using the 32-bit IDT, then we return to 32-bit protected mode. The return code VM86_INTx is in the low-order byte of the return value, and the interrupt number in the high-order byte.

24.7.2   Checking the revectored bitmap

The worker function shown in Figure 24.30, from arch/i386/kernel/vm86.c, is given an integer value and a pointer to a bitmap. If the corresponding bit is set, it returns −1; otherwise, it returns 0.

```
317  static inline int is_revectored(int nr,
                                    struct revectored_struct * bitmap)
318  {
319      asm_____volatile__("btl %2,%1\n\tsbbl %0,%0"
320          :"=r" (nr)
321          :"m" (*bitmap),"r" (nr));
322      return nr;
323  }
```

Figure 24.30   Checking a bitmap

317   the struct revectored_struct was described in Section 24.1.1.1 as an array of eight longs.

319   we test the bit in parameter 1 (the long pointed to by bitmap) corresponding to parameter 2 (nr). The carry flag (CF) is set or cleared accordingly. The sbbl is the AT&T mnemonic for the SBB instruction, subtract with borrow. If the carry flag is clear, subtracting parameter 0 from itself will result in 0. If the carry flag is set, then the subtraction with borrow will result in parameter 0 (nr) + 1 being subtracted from parameter 0, with the result being −1.

320   this is the output parameter. It is write-only for this operation ("=") and may be in a register ("r").

321   parameter 1 is the de-referenced bitmap, a memory operand ("m"). Parameter 2 is the input value of nr; it may be in a register.

322   the return value is 0 if the bit was clear, −1 if set.

24.8 Leaving vm86 mode

Previous sections have illustrated how, in the course of handling an interrupt, a process may leave vm86 mode and return to 32-bit protected mode. A number of worker functions that implement that change of mode are considered in this section.

24.8.1 Returning to protected mode

The vm86 mode was originally entered by means of a system call. So, returning to 32-bit protected mode is always by means of the ret_from_sys_call routine. The code to do this is shown in Figure 24.31, from arch/i386/kernel/vm86.c.

```
264   static inline void
              return_to_32bit(struct kernel_vm86_regs * regs16, int retval)
265   {
266        struct pt_regs * regs32;
267
268        regs32 = save_v86_state(regs16);
269        regs32->eax = retval;
270        __asm__ __volatile__("movl %0,%%esp\n\t"
271           "jmp ret_from_sys_call"
272           : : "r" (regs32), "b" (current));
273   }
```

Figure 24.31   Returning to protected mode

264   the input parameters are a pointer to saved registers in vm86 format, and a return value, which is to be passed back to the original caller of the system service.

268   the state of the vm86 machine is copied from the area pointed to by regs16 back to the user space. The function to do this is described in Section 24.8.2. A pointer to the saved registers on top of the kernel stack (in pt_regs format) is returned in regs32.

269   the retval to be returned to the caller is placed in the EAX position on the stack.

270   the ESP register is adjusted so that it now points to the beginning of this struct pt_regs on the stack. This discards the 16-bit stack frame.

271   we exit through `ret_from_sys_call` (see Section 10.6.1). This restores the machine to the state it was in before the original system call to enter vm86 mode.

272   these are both input parameters. Parameter 0, which may be in a register ("`r`"), is the pointer `regs32` to the struct `pt_regs` on the stack. Parameter 1 specifies that the value of the global variable `current` (a pointer to the `task_struct` of the current process) is to be in the EBX register.

24.8.2   Writing vm86 state to user space

Before a process returns to protected mode, it saves the state of the virtual 8086 machine in user space. In this way it can return to vm86 mode at any time and take up execution of the 8086 program exactly where it left off [by calling `vm86()` again]. The function to do this is shown in Figure 24.32, from `arch/i386/kernel/vm86.c`.

```
65    struct pt_regs *
                FASTCALL(save_v86_state(struct kernel_vm86_regs * regs));
66    struct pt_regs * save_v86_state(struct kernel_vm86_regs * regs)
67    {
68            struct tss_struct *tss;
69            struct pt_regs *ret;
70            unsigned long tmp;
71
72            if (!current->thread.vm86_info) {
73            printk("no vm86_info: BAD\n");
74            do_exit(SIGSEGV);
75            }
76            set_flags(regs->eflags, VEFLAGS,
                                    VIF_MASK | current->thread.v86mask);
77            tmp = copy_to_user(&current->thread.vm86_info->regs,
                                            regs, VM86_REGS_SIZE1);
78            tmp += copy_to_user(&current->thread.vm86_info->
                                            regs.VM86_REGS_PART2,
79                    &regs->VM86_REGS_PART2, VM86_REGS_SIZE2);
80            tmp += put_user(current->thread.screen_bitmap,&current-
                                    >thread.vm86_info->screen_bitmap);
81            if (tmp) {
82            printk("vm86: could not access userspace vm86_info\n");
83            do_exit(SIGSEGV);
84            }
85            tss = init_tss + smp_processor_id();
86            tss->esp0 = current->thread.esp0 =
                                            current->thread.saved_esp0;
87            current->thread.saved_esp0 = 0;
88            ret = KVM86->regs32;
89            return ret;
90    }
```

Figure 24.32   Writing vm86 state to user space

65 the `save_v86_state()` function is expecting to be called with its single parameter in EAX, not on the stack.

66 the function is passed a pointer to a vm86 mode `struct kernel_vm86_regs`; this structure was created on the kernel stack by the interrupt or system call that is now requesting a return to 32-bit mode. The function returns a pointer to a `struct pt_regs`, which contains the state of the machine when it last left protected mode.

72–75 we check that there really is a valid address in user space to which the vm86 information is to be saved. If the `vm86_info` field in the `thread` structure of the current process does not contain a valid pointer, there is a serious inconsistency. It would appear to be attempting to leave vm86 mode without ever having entered it. We exit with a warning message.

74 this terminates the process (see Section 9.1).

76 the `set_flags()` macro has been described in Section 24.2.2. It copies the virtual flags register from `thread` to the EFLAGS position on the stack; but it takes special action for the `VIF_MASK` and `v86mask` bits. Only those set in VEFLAGS (the virtual flags register) are set in the result; any others that might have been set in the stack copy beforehand are turned off.

77–80 these lines copy information from the stack frame to the user space.

77 this copies the first VM86_REGS_SIZE1 bytes; the literal constant is defined in Section 24.1.2.3, and the diagram in Figure 24.8 may also be of help. It is the size of the structure, up as far as `orig_eax`. It copies it to user space, using the pointer stored in `thread.vm86_info`.

78–79 we copy the second part of the structure, starting at `orig_eax`, to user space. The literal constants used are from Section 24.1.2.3.

80 we copy the `screen_bitmap` field of `thread` to the `screen_bitmap` field back in user space.

81–84 if anything other than 0 is returned by any of the three foregoing functions, then there was some problem; typically, it was not possible to access user space. So, we print a warning message and terminate the process, using the function from Section 9.1.

85 this constructs a pointer to the `tss_struct` corresponding to the current processor. The `smp_processor_id()` macro is from Section 7.2.1.4.

86 this copies the `saved_esp0` field of `thread` into the `esp0` field of `thread` and also into the `esp0` field of the `tss_struct` corresponding to the current processor. This is setting both `esp0` fields as they were on entry to vm86 mode.

87 we clear the `saved_esp0` field of `thread`. This is no longer valid now that all the data on the stack are invalidated.

88 KVM86 casts the pointer `regs` to be a pointer to a `struct kernel_vm86_struct` above it on the stack (see Section 24.1.2.1 for the code, and Figure 24.23 for an illustration). Its `regs32` field is a pointer to a `struct pt_regs`, so this function returns a pointer to the protected mode save area that was built on the stack when the `vm86()` system service was called.

24.8.3 Returning values from vm86 mode

When a process returns from vm86 mode to 32-bit mode, a 16-bit return value is returned to the caller, in the EAX register. This is a faceted value. The low-order byte gives the type (i.e. the reason for the return). The high-order byte may contain an argument, giving further subreasons. For example, if the reason for the return was because it could not handle an INTx, then the type will be VM86_INTx, and the argument will be the number of the interrupt. Definitions for the various return values are given in Figure 24.33, from <asm-i386/vm86.h>.

```
37    #define VM86_TYPE(retval)    ((retval) & 0xff)
38    #define VM86_ARG(retval)     ((retval) >> 8)
39
40    #define VM86_SIGNAL       0
41    #define VM86_UNKNOWN      1
42    #define VM86_INTx         2
43    #define VM86_STI          3
48    #define VM86_PICRETURN    4
49    #define VM86_TRAP         6
```

Figure 24.33   Return values from vm86 system call

37   this macro masks off all but the low-order byte, thus giving the type of the return value.

38   this macro moves the high-order byte into the low-order position, thus giving the argument of the return value.

40   return was due to a signal. It does not seem ever to be used.

41   this means that a general protection fault was caused by an operand for which there is no handler in handle_vm86_fault(). It is used in Section 24.6.

42   this value is returned if it is specified that a particular vectored interrupt is to be handled in protected mode (Section 24.6.3) or the do_int() function cannot handle a particular vectored interrupt for whatever reason (Section 24.7.1). In that case, the high-order byte of the return value will contain the vector number.

43   this value is returned if the VIP_MASK bit is set in VEFLAGS (see Section 24.2.5). This means that virtual interrupts have been enabled by an STI or by a POPF or IRET, both of which pop from the stack to the flags register.

48   if the user has specified that hardware interrupts from the programmable interrupt controller (PIC) are to be handled in 32-bit mode, and the IF_MASK bit is set in VEFLAGS, then the return value is VM86_PICRETURN (see Section 24.6.1).

49   if trap 1 (debug) or 3 (breakpoint) has occurred, this is the value returned (see Section 24.5).

Index